THE DETERMINED SPY

ALSO BY DOUGLAS WALLER

Lincoln's Spies

Disciples

Wild Bill Donovan

A Question of Loyalty

Big Red

Air Warriors

The Commandos

THE DETERMINED SPY

The Turbulent Life and Times
of CIA Pioneer Frank Wisner

DOUGLAS WALLER

DUTTON

DUTTON

An imprint of Penguin Random House LLC
penguinrandomhouse.com

LIBRARY OF CONGRESS CATALOGING-IN-PUBLICATION DATA

Names: Waller, Douglas C., author.
Title: The determined spy : the turbulent life and times of CIA pioneer
Frank Wisner / Douglas Waller.
Description: New York : Dutton, 2025. | Includes bibliographical references and index.
Identifiers: LCCN 2024018096 | ISBN 9780593184424 (hardcover) |
ISBN 9780593184448 (ebook)
Subjects: LCSH: Wisner, Frank, 1909-1965. | Espionage,
   American—History—20th century. | United States. Central Intelligence
   Agency—History—20th century. | United States. Central Intelligence
   Agency—Officials and employees—Biography. | People with bipolar
   disorder—Biography.
Classification: LCC UB271.U52 W578 2025 | DDC 327.12730498092
   [B]—dc23/eng/20240529
LC record available at https://lccn.loc.gov/2024018096

Printed in the United States of America
1st Printing

BOOK DESIGN BY PATRICE SHERIDAN

TO JUDY

CONTENTS

PART FOUR: SIDELINED

THE DETERMINED SPY

PROLOGUE

IT WAS A SUNNY, warm Friday evening on September 12, 1958, when the Wisners' oldest son, Frank George Wisner II, walked out of the family's Locust Hill farmhouse near Galena, Maryland, on the Eastern Shore, just in time to see his father slip quietly into the backseat of a sedan. His father, Frank Gardiner Wisner, did not look back at his twenty-year-old son, who was confused, upset, and emotionally exhausted by the mental disease his father suffered. Aunt Elisabeth, his father's older sister, who had rushed to the farm to help the family deal with the crisis, sat next to Wisner in the backseat. Down-to-earth, deeply devout, simple in her habits, and focused on charitable works, such as the Red Cross, Elisabeth could always calm her brother when she was with him. Frank thought his sister was essential in his life and Elisabeth could clearly see now that her brother desperately needed medical help.

The psychiatrist behind the wheel started the engine. Another psychiatrist sat in the front seat, leaning around to talk to Wisner. The car sped down the dusty dirt lane that snaked away from the farm and headed to the Sheppard and Enoch Pratt Hospital a little more than eighty miles away near Baltimore. Wisner's wife, Polly, walked up to her son as the car drove away and told him that his father was being taken to a mental institution. Three close friends—business partner John Graham; White House national security adviser Gordon Gray; and Desmond FitzGerald, who ran Asia operations for Wisner at the CIA—had spent much of the morning with Polly and Elisabeth convincing Wisner that he needed to go with the psychiatrists to Sheppard Pratt. Henry Sears, who owned a nearby farm and had partnered with Wisner in land ventures, had stopped by earlier and made the same pitch. "Frank, you simply have to do this," Sears told him.

Frankie—that was the nickname that mother and father had given their oldest son—said nothing. He walked back into the farmhouse, where he collapsed into an upstairs bed and slept for most of the next forty-eight hours. Home that summer from college, he was wiped out from taking care of his dad, who for more than a month had been drinking heavily and roaming the farmhouse at night, unable to sleep. Frankie worshipped his father. It was agonizing for him to witness the alcohol abuse, the hyperactivity, the sleep deprivation—all flashing lights for the mood disorder tormenting Wisner.

Polly followed her son back into the farmhouse. Her husband's nervous breakdown had been torturous for her. When he was like this, Wisner could be rough with people, particularly with Polly, whom he thought too controlling when he was in his agitated state. Mental illness took a toll on marriages. Polly and Frank had been deeply in love and Polly had been totally devoted to her husband and his career in Washington. Yet what affection there had been between the couple was dissipating by fall 1958. Still, they stayed together. Though not a woman to complain openly, Polly was deeply embarrassed by her husband's aberrant behavior. She did not want his reputation—indeed, the entire family's reputation—indelibly stained by this. Hoping he somehow would just snap out of it, Polly told many friends only that Frank was going to the hospital for "a complete rest."

* * *

Frank Gardiner Wisner was one of Washington's most powerful men—though few in the city had the security clearance to know it. He led the Central Intelligence Agency's clandestine service, whose thousands of committed spies and saboteurs conducted covert operations all over the world. Wisner had pioneered the United States government's entry into secret political warfare, with a mission to fight the Soviets using the same covert tools—such as espionage, guerrilla attacks, and propaganda—that the Russians employed. He had organized infiltration and psychological operations against the Soviet Union and its satellite countries in East Europe, had overseen coups in Iran and Guatemala, and had been privy to America's deepest and darkest secrets. And now he was on his way to an insane asylum.

Memos that Wisner was entering a mental facility raced through Washington. James Angleton, the CIA's top counterintelligence officer, told the Federal Bureau of Investigation that Wisner had suffered a complete nervous breakdown. FitzGerald notified Gordon Gray. President Eisenhower's national security aide alerted others in the White House. The CIA prepared cover stories to keep other government agencies in the dark as much as possible about Wisner's condition. But harsh gossip spread quickly in Washington and abroad. "Frank Wisner has gone off his rocker," columnist Joseph Alsop wrote U.S. ambassador Charles "Chip" Bohlen, a seasoned American diplomat and a close Wisner friend who was at the time posted in the Philippines.

It had not always been apparent that Wisner was mentally ill. In the nine months before he checked into a mental hospital, he had often appeared normal at top-level intelligence meetings, he had testified before Congress on Communist penetration in Latin America, he had sent Vice President Richard Nixon speeches by East Bloc leaders, and he had talked a young CIA officer into not quitting the agency. Solidly built, a handsome man at forty-nine, he seemed the last person friends expected to become unhinged. And Wisner's illness was a roller coaster. At times Wisner in fact was sane. At other times he was falling apart but putting up a good facade.

But episodes of erratic behavior began to pile up. During a visit back to Washington in June, Bohlen found Wisner "very tense and wound up," he told Joe Alsop. Polly agreed. The drinking in the evening became a problem. Friends noticed he had a strange physical tic. He would flex his arm muscles, then his jaw muscles. Children who visited began asking their parents what the matter was with Mr. Wisner, who seemed frenzied. He became verbose, even sending Elisabeth a seven-hundred-word telegram describing a dove shoot he planned to have. He did not seem to friends to be using his tremendously large vocabulary with the facility and diversity he had once had. His words became imprecise. Yet in moments of anxiety or anger, which occurred more often now, Wisner's words flowed with machine-gun rapidity. He quarreled with Polly, who locked up the liquor cabinet at their Georgetown home; he told off-putting stories; and he had heated arguments at Washington dinner parties. Billie Morrone, his secretary at work, discovered stacked up on his desk his uncashed paychecks, which the CIA finance office always delivered to him in a sealed envelope with his name on the front. And there was the nervous breakdown he had suffered nearly two years earlier when Soviet tanks crushed a popular revolt in Hungary.

In March Wisner had flown to Singapore to be on scene for what he thought would be a successful CIA operation to oust Sukarno, the strongman of nearby Indonesia, which has more than seventeen thousand islands stretched over an archipelago longer than the distance between New York and Los Angeles. The CIA paid for Polly to accompany her husband on the five-week trip, which would take him to a half dozen Southeast Asian countries; the agency likely hoped that she would keep him in check if he had any flare-ups.

Sukarno had run afoul of the Eisenhower administration, which considered him too neutral and Communist leaning for America's Cold War with the Russians. Secretary of State John Foster Dulles and other top U.S. officials also did not like Sukarno, who by then had been married five times. "I think it's time we held Sukarno's feet to the fire," Wisner had declared, but the highly secret operation, code-named "Haike," failed. The rebellious colonels and the psychological warfare the CIA counted on to oust Sukarno sputtered. The Indonesian strongman proved to be more adept and tenacious at holding on to power than the CIA had anticipated. Director Allen Dulles shut down the operation, which had cost the agency $10 million.

As the coup attempt unraveled, Wisner did, too. At a stopover in Manila to see Bohlen, he was utterly depressed, convinced America was losing the Cold War. Greeting him at Washington's airport, FitzGerald found Wisner confrontational and disconnected from reality. Exhausted, the spymaster took five days off at his Locust Hill farm in Maryland. It wasn't enough. In the late summer, FitzGerald finally talked his boss into a longer respite at Locust Hill. But still Wisner did not improve.

Desperate but not knowing where to seek help in the medical community, Polly phoned Elliott Randolph, an eye doctor at Johns Hopkins University's ophthalmology institute. A longtime friend of the couple, he had been a weekend guest at Locust Hill in the past. Randolph told Polly her husband needed a psychiatrist. She talked Frank into visiting Dr. Eugene Meyer, a psychiatry professor at Johns Hopkins University who happened to be the brother of Polly's old friend Katharine Graham, the wife of *Washington Post* publisher Phil Graham.

Their sessions did not go well. Wisner had always had a disrespectful view of doctors and believed that since he was the paying customer, he could keep them waiting for appointments rather than the other way around. And he didn't like Meyer. Wisner thought he was smarter than that psychiatrist and tried to bully him. Meyer soon gave up and Polly booked Frank with another psychiatrist,

Dr. Zigmond Lebensohn at Sibley Memorial Hospital in Washington. Lebensohn was considered an innovative physician in the treatment of patients afflicted with mania and depression, which the doctors by this time suspected was what Wisner had. Wisner liked Lebensohn and thought of him as an intellectual equal. Lebensohn could see that outpatient treatment would not be enough for Wisner.

Polly reached out to her husband's CIA colleagues like FitzGerald. Word went up the agency's chain of command that their clandestine service chief was seriously ill and needed institutional care. Dulles alerted the CIA's medical staff that his top covert action deputy must be hospitalized.

The CIA took an enlightened attitude toward mental illness in its ranks, considering those who suffered from it to be Cold War battle casualties. Heavy drinking, which agency officials also believed was more prevalent in their organization than elsewhere, was looked upon as an occupational hazard. Field officers were encouraged to seek mental health treatment so they could return to work and, at least in the lower ranks, not have their careers negatively affected. Since its founding in 1947, the CIA had recognized that it needed a psychiatric service as increasingly complex agency operations exposed mental illness problems in its ranks. Psychiatrists were also needed for psychological screening of job applicants to "keep the fuzzy-heads out," as one CIA director put it. A psychiatric division was formed; by 1958 it had six psychiatrists and two clinical psychologists who kept close watch on the workforce and stayed in touch with the country's top clinics in the field for updates on new research.

If CIA doctors could not treat an officer, the patient was sent to a "cleared" psychiatrist or institution on the outside that the agency had vetted to make sure that what the spy divulged in therapy stayed in the room. Sheppard Pratt was one of those cleared facilities that had admitted CIA officers in the past. The agency told Polly that she should check her husband into that facility, which happened to be conveniently near enough to both their farm and their Washington home that she could visit him often.

The institute, which had begun taking patients at the end of the nineteenth century, was founded by Moses Sheppard, a wealthy Quaker merchant in Baltimore. Sheppard bequeathed enough of his estate to buy a three-hundred-forty-acre farm north of the city, where he wanted a mental institution to be built. Instead of warehousing patients in squalid conditions, which was then the standard of care in many state facilities, the institute would treat people experiencing mental illness with kindness and the latest medical advances. Later Enoch Pratt, another Baltimore philanthropist, donated $1.6 million of his fortune to the project. The Sheppard and Enoch Pratt Hospital became one of the nation's premier mental health hospitals, with brick Victorian buildings topped by tall towers and lush grounds landscaped to look like a beautiful park. A staff of psychiatrists, many of them leaders in their field, cared for the two-hundred-plus patients usually there.

Wisner at first wanted no part of Sheppard Pratt. He refused to believe he was that sick. He was angry and confused. He was proud of what he had achieved in life—a standout track star in college, a successful New York lawyer, a decorated World War II veteran, a powerful Washington national security official. He found being sent to a mental facility terribly humiliating. No longer was he king of his spy dominion, no longer king even of his own family. Yes, other CIA officers had returned to their old jobs after treatment, but Wisner worried deeply that checking into an insane asylum would finish his career. It was a legitimate fear. Senior officers in the agency were already whispering that when, or if, Wisner returned, it would certainly not be to the high-stakes and pressure-packed post of clandestine service chief.

There was likely another reason he wanted no part of Sheppard Pratt. It was a secret that Wisner knew he could not share with his family, with outsiders in the Congress or other parts of the U.S. government, or even with many in the CIA. Agency psychiatrists had been involved in more than just screening and caring for mentally ill officers. For a while, some had worked in what congressional investigators later concluded was one of the seamiest programs in the CIA's secret war against the Soviets.

MKUltra was the code name for a collection of projects, overseen by an eccentric chemist named Sidney Gottlieb, to create human robots behind enemy lines or identify moles in the CIA by injecting them with mind-altering drugs, putting them in trances with hypnosis, or perhaps jolting their brains with electric shocks. The CIA was convinced that the Russians had developed mind-control drugs to break men and that Russia had even purchased on the international market enough lysergic acid diethylamide, or LSD, for fifty million doses. The latter was a wild overestimate; the Russians had bought only enough of the hallucinogen for a few thousand tests. But no matter: the CIA believed it was in an arms race with Moscow to control human behavior.

The agency program housed 162 top secret projects, many contracted with universities and private medical centers; the projects researched everything from seeing how dogs and cats could be brainwashed to be guided bombs, to magician tricks that could distract an enemy agent's attention so he could be given a drug without his knowledge. Wisner's fingerprints were all over MKUltra, which required his approval for its most controversial aspects. The agency tested its drugs first on volunteers, then later on unwitting human subjects. Disastrous results occurred when mentally distraught Frank Olson, an Army civilian scientist, leaped to his death from a tenth-floor room at the Statler Hotel in New York City about a week after Gottlieb had slipped LSD into his drink without him knowing it. Wisner was one of the senior agency officers who had had to clean up after that mess.

MKUltra's projects to test the psychogenic properties of various plants ended up hitting home for Wisner, too. During his son Frankie's sophomore year at Princeton University, a researcher approached him to ask if he would be interested in joining an experiment testing the effect of peyote, a Mexican cactus containing psychoactive alkaloids, on humans. *Absolutely not!* Wisner ordered when his son asked permission to be a project guinea pig. He couldn't tell Frankie why.

In the end, the CIA never produced any mind-altering drugs or procedures that were actually useful in clandestine operations. MKUltra scientists created only mischief and major foul-ups for the agency. Wisner knew full well that some of the treatments civilian mental institutions employed—like shock therapy and hypnosis—were the same ones the CIA had been trying its best to weaponize for covert warfare. He did not want his brain fried by shrinks.

* * *

The two Sheppard Pratt psychiatrists arrived at twelve thirty p.m. that Friday to interview Wisner first at his Locust Hill farm and then during the car drive to the hospital. The doctors immediately found Wisner, described only as a "government official" on his patient card, to be a "strongly domineering, authoritative, high-energy level person," as they wrote in their psychological summary for case number 25835. It didn't take them long to guess that he was suffering from "manic depression," generally recognized since the time of Hippocrates as a debilitating disease that combined mania's intense frenzy with depression's relentless misery. The name was changed in 1980 to "bipolar disorder," which many doctors and their patients consider less stigmatizing—although some psychiatrists and patients today still prefer the term "manic-depressive illness," believing it more accurately conveys the seriousness of the disease.

More to the point, the Sheppard Pratt psychiatrists wrote that Wisner appeared to be "in an acute manic phase," which was a clinical way of saying he was in danger of dying because of exhaustion from the manic symptoms he was experiencing—hyperactivity, not sleeping or eating properly, drinking heavily. Wisner was experiencing a psychiatric emergency. Fifteen percent of bipolar disorder patients died because the acute mania literally wore out their bodies. Polly might have saved her husband's life by getting the Sheppard Pratt doctors to the farm that day.

The psychiatrists found Wisner's mind out of control. Showing no concern for the passage of time, he was intense, hyperalert, and extremely defensive. Noting the movements of everyone around him, he seemed almost like a hunted animal. He was perceptive at times, confused in other moments. He became selectively attentive, not wanting to hear what was going on about him at some points, then at others dominating the conversation like a lawyer in a courtroom.

Wisner, in short, was not a pleasant man to be around. To the psychiatrists, he acted like a megalomaniac, pounding a clenched fist on the table to make points and throwing out thinly veiled threats to the friends, relatives, and doctors who tried to help him. The psychiatrists worried he might be suicidal.

This was not anything like the Frank Wisner his friends and family knew when he was sane. A Mississippian, he hardly had a Southern drawl, and he spoke clearly, his choice of words flowing easily; he never stumbled over his grammar. Occasionally he would let slip a Southern expression. "I hope you don't think I'm trying to teach my grandmother how to suck eggs," he would say when telling an aide how to draft a letter. Barrel-chested, he had wide, piercing brown eyes and three small chicken pox pockmarks on his face. Richard Helms, his devoted deputy, noted how Wisner would prop a foot on his desk drawer, spread the first two fingers on both hands, and slide them down the sides of his mouth as he sorted out a difficult spy problem in his mind.

He was not a religious man. He had a deep understanding of history. He was modest and could be self-effacing. He took life and the role he played influencing American foreign policy seriously, bringing nearly a religious fervor, agency colleagues said, to his war with the Russians. Yet he enjoyed telling "Mark Twain–like stories," said Helms. He had favorite poems and limericks he liked to recite and didn't mind passing along a dirty joke he thought funny. He had an extraordinary range of activities and interests outside his CIA work, such as the working farm he kept up in Maryland and the substantial business interests he pursued in Mississippi. Even the Sheppard Pratt psychiatrists could see that their patient was "a person of superior intelligence with a remarkable memory and a wide range and store of knowledge," as they put it in their report.

Wisner had launched some of the most difficult and controversial operations of the CIA's early years and he inspired a cadre of covert warriors to carry out future missions. A large following of devoted friends in and out of government affectionately called him "Wiz." He was always an entertaining party companion. "He was a man of enormous charm, imagination, conviction that anything, *anything* could be achieved and he could achieve it," recalled *New York Times* reporter Harrison Salisbury. Wisner also had a kind and gentle side, particularly with children. Elizabeth Winthrop Alsop, the daughter of columnist Stewart Alsop, was touched when the spymaster took the time to write her a long letter praising a play she had put on as a ten-year-old.

As the sedan approached the white stone gatehouse at the Sheppard Pratt entrance on Charles Street, Elisabeth in the back seat with her brother patted his knee and whispered soothing words, hoping they would ease his anxiety and suspicion of the asylum he was about to enter. They did not. Wisner felt he had devoted his entire life to fighting the scourge of Communism by means fair and foul. He remained extremely upset at friends and family so intent on having him confined to a hospital. They were destroying his reputation as well as any future usefulness he might have in the Cold War, betraying him to the Communists. They were killing his soul, Wisner believed. His body, he fervently feared, would follow soon.

PART ONE

PRELUDE

Chapter 1

LAUREL

THROUGH THE EARLY 1800s, the millions of acres of virgin pine forest in southern Mississippi had been home to Native Americans, to trappers, and then to settlers who saw this vast resource of trees merely as obstacles to be chopped down and cleared for hardscrabble farming. But after the Civil War, with forests in the North becoming depleted and continental railroads finally reaching into southern Mississippi, Northern lumbermen began invading to harvest its rich Piney Woods. The region became a major industrial center feeding wood-hungry builders in other parts of the country.

Laurel was one of the Yankees' conquests in southern Mississippi. It was a nondescript, rough-edged mill town in the heart of the Piney Woods, eighty-five miles southeast of the capital of Jackson. The town had been named after a toxic underbrush that grew in the pine forest. Laurel was located in Jones County, or the "Free State of Jones" as it came to be called because the anti-secessionist sentiment among many of its farmers too poor to own slaves had made the county a magnet for deserters and Unionists during the Civil War.

One of the Northern lumbermen who came to Laurel in 1897

to harvest the towering trees was Frank Gardiner Wisner's father, Frank George Wisner, who could trace his American lineage back to 1714. Frank George Wisner's father was George E. D. Wisner, a tailor and Union corporal during the Civil War who had fought in General William Sherman's army during the battle for Atlanta. After the war, George Wisner settled in Clinton, Iowa, and married the daughter of a former Hessian infantryman who had immigrated there. In 1873, the couple had one son, Frank George Wisner.

Frank George's father died of tuberculosis when his son was not quite four years old, leaving the family impoverished. The boy was a fine student—he delivered his high school's valedictory—but there was no money for college after he graduated from high school, so Frank George signed on with the Chicago and Northwestern Railway Company, where he worked for the next seven years as a conductor.

In 1897, Frank George married into wealth. Petite Mary Jeannette Gardiner, who looked much younger than her twenty-two years, was the daughter of one of the most prominent families in Clinton. Her father, Silas W. Gardiner, who had lost both legs in a tram accident, owned a successful lumber mill and was known in Clinton as much for his love of literature and the arts as he was for his business acumen. Jeannette was the product of a Davenport finishing school that inspired in her a passion for reading, and her name occasionally appeared in newspaper society columns, sometimes for performing in amateur musicals. Her wedding in Grace Episcopal Church to Frank George Wisner was described in the local paper as "brilliant."

Clinton had been the leading lumber town between Minneapolis and St. Louis. But by the time Frank and Jeannette married, the Northern forests were becoming exhausted and the lumber business in Clinton had fallen off. After shopping around, Silas Gardiner went with relatives to Laurel to chop and mill the yellow pine and start anew. They were joined in the venture by the family of another lumber baron, Lauren Eastman. Frank George Wisner and his new bride moved to this isolated Mississippi settlement to work in what became the Eastman-Gardiner Lumber Company. Jeannette was so proud that her "precious Frank," as she called him in her love letters, soon became a top executive in the Mississippi business.

Within a decade, Eastman-Gardiner had a high-tech plant in Laurel with eleven hundred employees turning out a quarter million feet of lumber daily. The company, which eventually headquartered in an opulent mansionlike building, added to their Piney Woods land holdings for many miles around. Though tree cutting and mill work could be dangerous, it paid more than tenant farming. Bonuses were handed out and the company instituted a ten-hour workday even before it was mandated by the state. By 1905, Eastman-Gardiner had become one of Mississippi's largest companies. The town, whose population eventually grew to some twenty thousand persons, boasted more millionaires per capita than any city in the nation. To pamper buyers who visited, Eastman-Gardiner and four other lumber firms that resettled there arranged the building of the Hotel Pinehurst, one of the finest in the South.

The socialite wives and privileged children of the Eastman-Gardiner men also came to Laurel to stay. Along a wide, tree-lined street given the New York name "North Fifth Avenue," they constructed grand mansions in the Georgian and Classical Revival styles. The families also arrived with highly progressive values by Mississippi standards. For workers' children, they built schools that were considered the best in the state. The schools included one for Black children that needed to be separate in order to abide by the state's strict racial separation laws. Eastman-Gardiner's African American workers were paid the same wage as their white counterparts—considered then a radical move that helped spawn one of the first Black middle-class communities in the South.

A handsome man with dark eyes and a long forehead, his hair parted neatly on the side, Frank George Wisner was among Eastman-Gardiner's next generation of energetic leaders. He oversaw mill operations and became the company's treasurer as well as a founder and president of the First National Bank of Laurel, which Eastman-Gardiner set up. Wisner was elected a city alderman and served several terms on the school board. He also had a wide range of interests outside lumber, such as growing tung trees for tung oil, manufacturing starch from sweet potatoes, and standardizing syrup to make the cane that Mississippi farmers cultivated more marketable.

Wisner joined mansion row, building at 726 North Fifth Avenue a comfortable Midwestern-style stick-and-shingle home that he and Jeannette called the "Green Barn" because it was painted a dull military green. Its front door opened into a large foyer with high-quality pine beams Frank had carefully selected from the mill, and a fireplace. Off the foyer there were a music room with matching grand pianos, a wood-paneled library with hundreds of books, and a main dining room, also wood paneled, served from a kitchen and a butler's pantry. Separate staircases—one for family members, the other for the servants—went up to a second-floor foyer, with bedrooms and sleeping porches branching off it. Outside, ceiling fans hung from the wraparound porch to make Mississippi summers more tolerable. The backyard had a spacious two-story garage and a swimming pool on a little hill.

Jeannette became involved in a variety of civic activities, as was expected of the wife of a prominent town leader. She meticulously attended to a terraced garden, which the local newspaper complimented; served in her church's women's auxiliary; and became an officer in the National Society of the Colonial Dames of America in Mississippi. The activities could be a strain for her. Slight of build, she was frail, constantly sick, and in later years accident-prone. Shy and withdrawn, Jeannette always wore glasses with a sad look on her face in photos. Later, her grandchildren, who called her "Gammy," found her wonderful. She spent hours reading to them and taught them how to draw and play card games. But family members eventually suspected that Jeannette had suffered from depression.

She experienced heart-wrenching tragedy with the children she tried to bring into the world. George Brockway Wisner, her first child, born in 1899, died a year later after suffering one illness after another. The baby boy's death shocked friends and crushed Jeannette. Elisabeth Gardiner Wisner was born in 1903 and survived into adulthood. But Jeannette's third child, Louise Gardiner Wisner, died in 1907, three months after her birth, another crippling blow for Jeannette. She was understandably nervous when she became pregnant once more. Would this child survive?

* * *

Frank Gardiner Wisner was born on June 23, 1909, most likely at home in one of the bedrooms of the Green Barn. Mississippi had no bureau of vital statistics when Frank arrived, so there was no public record of his birth, except for a baptism memorandum from Laurel's St. John's Episcopal Church a year later.

Jeannette's depression could have been passed on to her new son. Doctors at the time knew little about the mental illness. They dismissed the very idea that a young child could even be afflicted with depression or mania. Psychiatrists today recognize that these diseases can occur in childhood—although detecting them can be difficult—and that genetics plays a big part in determining whether a person is stricken with depression or mania, although exactly how still baffles doctors. Depression affects about twice as many women as it does men, and little boys have a greater chance of inheriting depression from a mother with the disease.

Frank Gardiner was a rambunctious, intense, and bright child, always running instead of walking, relying on his wit to make up for his lack of size. By the time he was three years old he was giving orders to the Black servants in the house, which no one else would have dared to do. He was bossy with his older sister, Elisabeth, though she took it in stride. The two children were unusually close, spending hours together in the playroom their parents had set up in the Green Barn's attic. Frank Gardiner was considered too small for rough-contact sports but he played them nevertheless, looking fierce in his leather football helmet and pads. His father, who was a vestry-man at St. John's, had to drag his son to church and in the pew kept a hand clamped on his neck so he wouldn't act up. The boy might have displayed symptoms of bipolar disorder. Or it might have been attention deficit hyperactivity disorder (ADHD). Or Frank Gardiner might have just been a busy kid.

Frank George Wisner's career took off as his son was growing up. Developing a national reputation as both a lumberman and an advocate of forest conservation, Frank George made regular trips to Washington to testify before Congress on issues that affected his industry, like corporate taxes (Wisner wanted them lower). He became president of the National Lumber Manufacturers Association, whose members hailed him as the "little giant of Mississippi," and he became a regular at White House conferences on forestry. During World War I, he served on a lumber subcommittee of the War Industries Board, advising the Wilson administration on wood for barracks.

Wisner refused compensation for being president of the lumber association. He accepted only a dollar a year for his War Industries Board service, which became a grind and kept him away from home for months. Still, Frank George could afford to work in Washington for free. Back in Laurel he was a wealthy man. His tax return for 1919 showed he earned $30,104, which is more than $500,000 in today's dollars. He began giving sizable chunks of money to his children. Frank Gardiner received $4,920 in 1926, which is more than $80,000 in today's dollars. The lumber association also gave Frank Gardiner and his sister $10,000 each in association bonds (more than $170,000 in today's dollars) because of their father's free service to the group. In 1916, Frank George put down $18,523 (just over a half million in today's dollars) to join sixty-four other men in buying a 556-ton schooner docked at Gulfport, Mississippi.

Frank Gardiner respected his hard-driving father. But he was never close to him. Frank George was a dour, straitlaced man who extolled to no end the virtues of education and public service to his children. After lunch each day, Frank George would lie on the floor for a half hour power nap, and at night he would always drink a shot of Demerara rum to help him sleep. Frank Gardiner hated his father being away for long stretches on lumber business; he would act up and be especially disobedient toward his mother during these absences.

Young Frank's relationship with Jeannette was even more complicated. Mothers with depression can show more anxiety and less warmth or have few simple interactions with infants and toddlers, which can affect a young boy into his adulthood. It is difficult to accurately assess from afar and a century later the impact Jeannette had on her son. Frank loved his mother, but her child-rearing became odd at times. When her son was naughty, Jeannette would give him a switch and tell him to go into a closet and spank himself, which Frank did, crying and moaning. He would then come out and tell her the devil had taken flight. Jeannette had been afflicted with arthritis since early in her marriage. She leaned on Elisabeth and Elisabeth's future husband, Alexander Field Chisholm, for care and often was unable to travel because she did not feel well. Her son suspected she was just a hypochondriac and he came to resent her passive and dependent nature. After he left college, he had little to do with her. The Sheppard Pratt psychiatrists thirty years later suspected that Frank Wisner's relationship with his mother had something to do with his manic depression.

* * *

Elisabeth, who looked so much like her mother, excelled in school, making practically all A's on each report card. After Laurel High School, she attended the elite National Cathedral School in Washington, DC, and then went to Smith College in Massachusetts, where she graduated cum laude in 1924 with a major in music. Her brother's grades were good early on, too—A's and B's, for example, in fifth grade—and his "deportment" always got an A. He showed a flair for line drawings, penciling unusually accurate sketches of birds flying, gladiators fighting, and jazz musicians playing their instruments. Frank Gardiner became scrappier in his teenage years, enjoying hard-fought matches on the tennis court and qualifying as a "pro-marksman" in the Winchester Junior Rifle Corps. But in high school his grades grew uneven. He received mostly B's with an occasional A, and several times his report cards noted he had been given a lower grade for his deportment.

In Mississippi, Laurel High School had an excellent reputation. Its graduates with straight A's were automatically accepted into the prestigious University of Chicago without having to take an entrance exam. Frank Gardiner was far from having those kinds of grades when in 1925 he graduated early at the age of sixteen. His father, who was willing to spend anything on Frank Gardiner's education, decided the boy was too young for college and needed a year or two of seasoning in a college-prep school first. The elite of Frank Gardiner's generation attended the exclusive Groton School in Massachusetts to prepare for college. But Frank George instead chose for his son the finishing school wealthy Southern families sent their children to in the South—Woodberry Forest School in Orange, Virginia.

Set on twelve hundred acres of central Virginia land once owned by President James Madison's brother, Woodberry Forest boarding school had been educating boys since 1889, emphasizing "intellectual thoroughness and principled integrity," according to its current website. Among the more than one hundred sixty students enrolled there, Wisner showed promise in subjects like geometry and English. But the school's teachers soon found him seriously behind in physics, algebra, and Latin, the latter of which was taught by the demanding Rawleigh Taylor. Still, Taylor and the other instructors were confident that with enough time they could bring the boy up to speed. What young Frank and the school also discovered, to the delight of both, was that he excelled in athletics. He played junior varsity football and by his second year was setting school records in track and field for the broad jump. Awarded a varsity letter, Frank Gardiner Wisner was one of Woodberry Forest's "high-class performers," the school yearbook proclaimed.

When Frank Gardiner came home for his spring break in 1927, he announced to his parents that he wanted to go to the University of Virginia. They were delighted. Frank George immediately wrote John Carter Walker, Woodberry Forest's headmaster, and asked if his son was ready for the big move. The no-nonsense Walker was not afraid to be frank with the parents of students not measuring up to the private school's standards; he would tell them bluntly when a boy was wasting Woodberry Forest's time and his family's money. The headmaster sent back a letter with an emphatic *NO*. Young Frank had passed English, French, and history, but he was still deficient in algebra and Latin. Woodberry Forest was an important prep school feeder to the University of Virginia. Walker placed a high value on college entrance tests, which he believed determined the worth of the instruction his school provided. He was not about to sully Woodberry Forest's fine academic reputation by sending out a student like young Mr. Wisner, who he thought was unprepared for the rigors of college work.

The rejection shocked Frank and Jeannette. They did not intend to take no for an answer. The couple began firing off to Walker letters pleading with him to change his mind and arguing that their son's diploma from Laurel High School was all he really needed to be admitted to UVA. The courses he took at Woodberry Forest should have been considered as extras to make him even more qualified to enter the university. Jeannette enlisted Laurel High School officials to put pressure on Walker. The officials were proud of the education their school provided, and they agreed that Frank met UVA's entry requirements. Young Frank was counting on being able to enroll in the university in the fall, his father wrote Walker. The boy "will make good" if given a chance.

The Woodberry Forest headmaster had a low opinion of public

schools like Laurel High, which he thought dumbed down their academic standards. But he did not want to get into a spat with the Mississippi education system. He decided on a compromise. In a letter to the father, Walker agreed "to do everything we can, short of assuming full responsibility, to assist Frank to qualify for admission to the University of Virginia." Walker didn't think Frank Gardiner met the requirements for entrance. But the headmaster said he would send the boy's credits to UVA and he would write to the university's dean that if he admitted young Wisner based on the classes he had completed at Laurel High and Woodberry Forest, "we shall be very glad." "More than this we cannot do," Walker starchily wrote Frank's father.

It was hardly a full-throated endorsement of young Wisner's application to UVA. But Walker's convoluted compromise was enough to get him into the school in the fall of 1927.

Chapter 2

UNIVERSITY OF VIRGINIA

FOUNDED BY THOMAS JEFFERSON at the foothills of the Blue Ridge Mountains in Charlottesville, the University of Virginia by the time of the Civil War ranked second in size only to Harvard. The nation's third president had arranged the school like an academic village; he had designed its buildings, overseen the construction of its Rotunda, planned its curriculum, and picked its faculty. By the time Wisner entered, women had been admitted to study in some departments, and the school's first president, Edwin Anderson Alderman, had instituted progressive reforms like financial aid for needy students.

Frank Gardiner Wisner arrived as a future member of the "Greatest Generation," who would fight an economic depression with the New Deal, fascism and Nazism in a second world war, and Communism in a cold war. Of course, he knew none of this when he arrived on campus in the fall of 1927. Wisner considered himself a "standpatter" Republican, although the next year he wrote his parents that he had hated seeing the Democratic Party take such a "cruel beating" in the presidential race, which Herbert Hoover won handily. The only enemy the university's students seemed to be fighting at that point was Prohibition. There was heavy drinking on campus.

Wisner was an unusually dutiful letter writer—far more conscientious than most college students would have been. Every Sunday, almost without fail, he sat down and penned his parents a lengthy note with details about his schoolwork and social life. He confided to them as most college students wouldn't have. On a first-ever European tour with a friend during his summer of 1928 break, nineteen-year-old Wisner sent his parents travelogues of each country they visited, complete with maps and cartoons he drew at different stops. He mailed home one hundred thirty pages of what he saw during the two-month trip, showing an attention to detail that a spy would. In the southern French city of Nîmes, for example, he noted with a drawing on the side of his letter "the famous Pont du Gard, a huge bridge in three tiers, built by.the Romans as a part of the 26-mile-long aqueduct to Nimes." Wisner signed his letters as "Brother." He referred to Elisabeth in them always as "Sister." In many Southern families, equivalent names were given to the boy and girl as "Brother" and "Sister"—or they were nicknamed "Bubba" and "Sissie."

Wisner's freshman and sophomore grades were uneven. He scored C's in chemistry and French, A's in English, and B's in Italian. He began to show an aptitude for psychology, making A's in the subject during his sophomore year. Moreover, his grades improved each semester. And the athleticism he had shown at Woodberry Forest blossomed at UVA. Wisner became a world-class track star, regularly winning meets in the two-hundred-twenty-yard dash and broad jump during Southern Conference competitions. He set records for high hurdles and sprints, besting nationally known athletes like the University of Kentucky's John "Shipwreck" Kelly. Woodberry Forest, whose teachers had wagered that he would fail, now hailed their athletically distinguished alumnus in *The Woodberry Oracle* school newspaper.

Wisner built up his body from the sport, gaining seven pounds of muscle. He looked trim and fit—and on the track field, intense—standing up well mentally to the intensity of intercollegiate competition. "It is so much harder to lose when so much is expected of you," he confessed to his parents. "Once an athlete is recognized as superior, everyone redoubles his efforts to show him up." By his junior year, Wisner had been awarded the UVA *V* in track. By his senior year, he was captain of the track team, accumulating a stack of news clippings on his victories and becoming more of a university celebrity than the football players. His father could not have been prouder, arranging for a Birmingham paper to mail him the photo plate it had used for a picture of his son at a meet.

Wisner soon became a big man on campus. He was inducted into Delta Kappa Epsilon, living in the DKE house and eventually becoming president of the social fraternity. He was named to the Interfraternity Council and elected to the student senate. The university had clubs for practically everything and was filled with secret societies. Wisner was admitted to four of them: the 13 Society, for high-achieving students; the Eli Banana Society, for students from wealthy families (Wisner was elected "Grand Banana"); the IMP Society, whose members raised money for philanthropies and marched around campus wearing horned hoods; and the most secret, the Seven Society. A person's membership in that group was not disclosed until after he died.

Compact at five foot ten, with chiseled looks, Wisner acted the part of a campus leader. "Within the university world," said a friend, Wisner "was more of a man than the boy student. He had poise, balance, a detachment which when coupled with a good figure and rather handsome appearance set him above and apart from the more awkward and less developed" classmates. He started smoking a pipe, likely to make him appear older, and drove around campus in an old Ford. He was popular, with a wide circle of friends, many of whom he remained close to for life.

Wisner enjoyed chasing girls at UVA, and he was not shy about keeping his parents filled in on his love life. "I know more girls up here now than in the whole state of Mississippi," he bragged in one letter to them. "Am hoping I am not spoiled a little by it," he wrote in another note. For a long time, he dated Margaret Rogers, the daughter of an Asheville, North Carolina, parson. She was the "best I ever played around with," he wrote home. The affair seemed serious enough to Jeannette that she began acting like a future mother-in-law to the girl and her family. But soon the romance with Margaret cooled. Wisner went on to other women. At one point, he concluded that a serious love life was entirely too complicated, so he decided to swear off it. "I may give up girls (in a serious way) as entirely too distracting an influence," he wrote his parents.

For a college student, that attitude ran against the grain, but for young Wisner, it was typical. He was never intense in his personal relationships. He had an offbeat sense of humor and an interest in esoteric subjects. He liked being around old people. He would draw cartoons on a sheet of paper during boring classes. In his textbooks he underlined passages that interested him and scribbled comments in the margins when he questioned the accuracy of what he was reading.

Mood disorders that can often afflict students in their college years clearly did not affect Wisner during his. Just the opposite. The University of Virginia shaped Wisner's character, building up a huge self-confidence in him and setting him on an upward trajectory. He flourished at the school.

Wisner's grades improved his junior year. He still had academic hiccups. He flunked German one semester and quickly dropped the course. In most of his other subjects, he earned A's and B's. Wisner now found classes far more interesting. He enjoyed, in particular, his psychology, art history, and History of Morals courses. Their professors were "excellent," he wrote his parents. By his senior year, Wisner was putting in longer hours studying subjects he found markedly more difficult than in previous years, yet he was enjoying the pressure. He began to worry that his extracurricular activities—even the track and field competition he treasured—were impinging on his study time. Classmates nominated him to be president of their graduating class and he was glad when he lost the election because he had no time to devote to the office.

For his final senior exams, Wisner wrote his parents that he was "literally scared stiff" about all the work he had to do. Math and Italian were "getting meaner" and he was practically living in the psychology lab. His final exam in experimental psychology was the hardest he had ever taken. For philosophy he wrote a ten-thousand-word thesis on the "Psycho-biological Tradition of Athletics with Special Reference to the Theory of *Einfühlung* [empathy]."

Wisner succeeded under the pressure. He scored 95 percent on his difficult experimental psychology exam. Other professors congratulated him when he scored the highest on their tests. He ended up with A's and B's for his senior year and proudly finished his four years with a solid B average. Wisner had completed enough courses to give him a major in English, psychology, or philosophy. He graduated from UVA on June 12, 1931, with a Bachelor of Science degree.

An assistant dean at the university tried to talk him into taking an aide's job in the psychology department and beginning work on his PhD so he could teach that subject. Other professors offered him instructorships. Wisner, however, could not see himself as a college professor. He decided instead to enroll in UVA's law school. With his excellent undergraduate grades, he had no problem being accepted.

* * *

Wisner plunged into his first-year law school courses, finding them not as difficult as classmates had warned him they would be and far more interesting than he had expected. He coped easily with his first exam in criminal law and began scoring A's on other tests. He continued competing on the track team and worked three afternoons a week as an assistant track coach.

By his second year of law school, Wisner had made mostly A's with a few B's in his courses, which put him on the dean's list. He now found the second-year work in classes like contracts, legal bibliography, real property, and torts "very exacting," as he wrote his parents, underlining the word. His second-year tests were "the most harrowing set of exams that I have ever been through," he said. But he loved all the classes and found his instructors stimulating.

During his entire time in law school, Wisner showed little interest in criminal law. His second year, he attended a party where Clarence Darrow was the guest of honor. He found the famed criminal defense lawyer and the three hours he spent talking to him underwhelming. "I have never had such a disappointing experience," he wrote home, describing Darrow as "only an iconoclastic old fogey without a single positive contribution to make. No matter what you say, 'he's again' it.'" Wisner's first love became civil law.

He weaned himself off track and field by the end of his second year of law school. Wisner had gained a reputation nationwide as one of the country's top athletes in the sport. The Newark Athletic Club even offered to pay his way to compete in the tryouts for the 1932 Summer Olympics in Los Angeles during his summer break. Performing on a world stage certainly sounded attractive, but Wisner decided not to attempt it because his father was not keen on him taking a break from law school and a paying summer job to compete in the Olympics. Frank George was dealing with other issues. Jeannette remained in frail condition, with travel exhausting her, and Frank George was having painful dental problems. In addition, although he continued to be invited to White House conferences on home building and his annual net income remained at around $500,000 in today's dollars, business conditions in Laurel had deteriorated because of the Depression and depleting timber supplies.

To compensate, the family had begun diversifying, investing in the new Masonite Corporation, which had developed a revolutionary way to manufacture artificial particleboards from a mill's wood waste, and drilling for oil, which had been found in underground deposits around Laurel. Frank George even dabbled in foreign affairs, spending time in New Orleans working to keep the Soviet Union from dumping lumber and cotton into the U.S. market. He did not have a lot of spare cash to fund a summer stay in Los Angeles for his son.

Giving up track and field was sad yet somewhat liberating for Wisner. He wrote his parents that he was "glad not to have to worry about the strain of competition and sorry not to be able to contribute my share again." He took up other recreational pursuits, like learning to play bridge, which he discovered he enjoyed.

During his final year of law school, Wisner rented a room on Fry's Spring Road in Charlottesville. He was elected to the editorial board of the *Virginia Law Review*, an honor that came with a lot of hard work for the students producing the monthly periodical. (Wisner's father had a Senate Finance Committee clerk in Washington send his son a hearing transcript to help him write a paper for the *Law Review*.) Wisner earned straight A's during his final year—"a very fine record," the school's dean noted on his transcript. The son proudly wrote his parents each time he received a test score or final grade—many of them the highest for his class. Academic honors accumulated as 1933 stretched into 1934. Wisner was inducted into Phi Beta Kappa, the country's most prestigious honor society; the Raven Society, the school's honor society named after Edgar Allan Poe, who had attended UVA in 1826; the Phi Delta Phi legal fraternity, which made him its chapter president; and the Order of the Coif, another scholastic society for law students. The faculty also voted unanimously to award Wisner the $500 Samuel Baker Woods Jr. Memorial Award for being the school's top law student during the 1933–1934 session.

On June 12, 1934, Wisner received his law degree, graduating third in his class. John Carter Walker, Woodberry Forest's headmaster, who had doubted Wisner's chances of even surviving his freshman year, wrote Wisner that he was proud of what his former student had achieved at the university. It reflected well on Woodberry Forest. Wisner's father received congratulatory notes from friends. Wisner's picture even appeared on the front page of the *Washington Post*, which reported on his being inducted into Phi Beta Kappa.

Wisner left the university enormously proud of what he had accomplished. It had been his first time in a world much larger than little Laurel and he had succeeded beyond everyone's expectations. He had silenced his doubters, making top grades, excelling in sports, and holding himself to Mr. Jefferson's ideals. For the rest of his life, Wisner regularly referred to UVA as "the university." For him, there was no other college that counted.

Chapter 3

NEW YORK

AFTER GRADUATING FROM THE University of Virginia, Wisner took a vacation from June until August 1934 in the Caribbean and Central America, sunning himself on the beaches of Jamaica and Cuba, sipping tropical drinks in Costa Rica and Panama. He had no intention of ever returning to Laurel and using his law degree in the family business, which did not bother his father. Frank George and the other Mississippi lumber barons were in retreat. Years of uncontrolled cutting and milling had left vast swaths of the Piney Woods barren. Timber holdings were sold. Lumbermen moved to the West to harvest its virgin forests. It was also not yet clear whether oil drilling around Laurel would compensate for lost profits. The town's Yankee families sent their children north to be educated and to find lucrative jobs.

Wisner boarded the train for New York City. Easily passing the state's bar exam, he joined the venerable eighty-year-old law firm of Carter, Ledyard & Milburn at 2 Wall Street in September. Its founding partners, all dead by the time Wisner arrived, had handled a raft of high-profile cases—drafting wills for the wealthy, unsnarling complicated admiralty disputes, representing industry giants like the Standard Oil Company, and fighting Tammany Hall's Boss

Tweed to recover $6 million he had plundered. Franklin Roosevelt had spent four years as a young lawyer at the firm. The attorneys Wisner now joined were recognized around town as the top experts in their fields of law, many occupying high positions in the New York City Bar Association.

Wisner set himself up in a flat at 424 East Fifty-seventh Street, but he spent little time there. At the outset he practically lived at the Carter, Ledyard & Milburn office. New York firms like CL&M provided the foundation for American governance, offering bright young men like Wisner entrée into the nation's leadership elite if they were willing to work grueling hours in the beginning. The joke eventually making the rounds of the practice was that Wisner had set an in-house record working for firm curmudgeon Edwin De-Turck Bechtel and not getting fired; it required "as much of skillful diplomacy as legal skill," according to a CL&M history. Wisner started out in the drudgery of estate, corporation, and tax work, but after a year and a half graduated to working with the firm's big-name clients like the American Express and Pepsi-Cola companies. He became seasoned as well in civil trial work, breach-of-contract disputes, libel and fraud suits, immigration and naturalization cases, and even speech writing for the firm's political causes.

Wisner could not help but feel that he was in some ways a second-class lawyer in the firm, being a Southerner with a state university degree, not an Ivy League graduate or from a moneyed East Coast family. But he impressed his bosses at Carter, Ledyard & Milburn with his hard work. He began his law career at the top salary of $2,100 a year that the firm gave new hires and by 1939 was earning more than $9,000 a year (more than $200,000 in today's dollars). Wisner's law colleagues also liked and admired the Mississippian, who looked like "a fledgling Marlon Brando," according to one book describing him. He dreamed up athletic competitions with the other attorneys, he could become playful in the middle of dreary legal proceedings, and at office parties he had coworkers in stitches with his impersonations poking fun at the senior partners.

Years later, Wisner said the time he spent at Carter, Ledyard & Milburn prepared him well to be able to think, to draft documents, to express himself, and to argue a point. Law work also embedded in him a verbose style of writing. In New York, Wisner also began to inch his way into America's foreign policy establishment. He joined the prestigious Council on Foreign Relations. He was admitted into the University Club and the Lunch Club, important for circulating in the world of high finance and law. Occasionally he ran into William J. "Wild Bill" Donovan, a senior partner of the Donovan, Leisure law firm, which happened to be located three floors below CL&M at 2 Wall Street. (Donovan was being talked up as a future candidate for national office and would later be a key player in Wisner's intelligence career.) Sunday evenings Wisner often found himself at the White Horse Tavern on Hudson Street, where he gathered with fellow lawyers and debated the threats of fascism and Nazism in Europe.

* * *

In a 1932 letter to his parents during his second year of law school, Wisner had mentioned a girl down from Richmond whom he had taken to a buffet dinner his DKE fraternity had hosted in the fall. Her name was Polly Knowles. It was hardly love at first sight. Still in his no-romantic-entanglements frame of mind, Wisner had quickly moved on to other girls as dates for the midwinter dances. About three years later, Wisner ran into Polly a second time at a theater party in New York City. Polly was escaping her parents' home in Rye, New York, to sneak cigarettes and cruise cocktail parties with her girlfriends in the Big Apple. At the theater party, this sophisticated and elegant daughter of a shipping magnate was not shy about speaking her mind. It intrigued Wisner.

Mary Ellis "Polly" Knowles was three years younger than Frank, born on June 28, 1912, in Pensacola, Florida, where her father, John Ellis Knowles, and mother, Marian Burbank Knowles, lived in a large house they called "Harbourview" on the coast of Pensacola Bay. Knowles's grandfather had moved to Pensacola from Virginia and had fought for the Confederacy during the Civil War. A Yale graduate, Knowles, who went by Ellis, worked for a bank in Pensacola that had fallen on hard times after employees signed off on bad loans during a Florida land boom, and it had eventually gone bankrupt. He moved the family north when Polly was six years old, first to Port Chester and later to nearby Rye, New York, where he went into the shipping business. The family's early financial troubles had a profound effect on Polly, who later in life abhorred any kind of debt, refusing to buy stocks on margin and avoiding taking out mortgages when she could.

A gregarious man, Ellis Knowles did well in the shipping business and contributed heavily to charities in Port Chester and Rye. He was an excellent golfer, winning amateur tournaments and known on the course by the nickname "Old Panther Piss" because of his aggressive play. His popularity was interrupted by one dark episode. When he applied to join a country club in Rye, members tried unsuccessfully to blackball him because of the Pensacola bankruptcy and rumors there were Jews in his ancestry.

As was the case with many Southern white girls, Polly had been raised by a Black nanny whom she loved. She was never close to her mother, who in later years spent her time sitting on a couch smoking and watching professional wrestling on television. Her father was old-school when it came to his daughter, believing girls needed to be trained only to be good wives. He gave Polly and her two brothers lucrative stock buys over the years. But he did not give her the college education he provided to his two sons, a decision he later came to regret. Polly loved to argue with her father, particularly over politics. Knowles enjoyed their debates as well. He admired her spunk.

Instead of college, Polly in 1928 was sent as a teenager to St. Timothy's in Catonsville, Maryland, which was begun in 1882 by two sisters who wanted their boarding institution to be more than just a finishing school for girls hunting husbands. Developing a

European-style curriculum that emphasized hard work, imagination, and learning outside the classroom (students took the train to Washington to tour art museums), St. Timothy's was determined to prepare young women academically and emotionally for the outside world.

Polly loved her two years there. She plunged into school clubs, joined the hockey team, and played a ferocious game in tennis tournaments. She developed a reputation for being an engrossing storyteller, the center of attention when groups gathered. Other girls were envious of her glamorous figure, her widow's peak, and her haunting wide blue eyes. St. Timothy's 1930 yearbook hailed her as a master networker, only half jokingly noting that her occupation was "knowing someone that you know" and predicting that she would grow up one day to be "a social register."

In Polly, Wisner found an energetic, fierce, and determined personality—slightly tense at times, said friends. She did not have his academic background, but she was unusually bright, although it did not always show through. At times when she spoke, the cross of a light Southern accent and what sounded like a British accent crept into her voice. Only occasionally did she lose her temper. More often, she could be extremely thoughtful with people. Her consideration gave her deeply loyal friends for life.

Frank began dating her steadily. They made a good-looking couple: he was handsome; she was elegantly beautiful. They enjoyed the company of each other and the company of mutual friends. They were both natives of the South, both Episcopalians, both from old, established, and well-off families. They held the same views on politics and shared similar opinions of other acquaintances. The romance was exciting for both. They came to love each other deeply.

Polly and Frank got married in Christ's Church in Rye on September 19, 1936. The reception afterward at the Apawamis Club was festive, with champagne flowing. Frank was dashing in his morning coat and top hat. Polly looked like she had stepped out of a fashion magazine, wearing a sleek white silk wedding gown.

The newlyweds set up house just six doors down from Frank's old flat on East Fifty-seventh Street. Polly was proud of her husband's legal career, Frank just as proud of her outgoing and engaging nature. He made the money; she had the good taste. They formed a close partnership, enjoying doing things together, neither wanting to venture out and be away from the other. Polly called him "Wiz." When he later gained a little weight, she teasingly called him "Fatso." In playful moments, Frank called her "Squirrel Eye."

* * *

Wisner's father died on April 24, 1938, at the fairly young age of sixty-five, while on a business trip to New Orleans. He had been taken to a New Orleans hospital several days before, suffering from pneumonia. "A loss such as this is hard to bear at a time when Mississippi needs men of brains, energy and vision for development of the commonwealth," editorialized the *Jackson Daily News.* "Frank Wisner is a man among men." Local, state, and national figures attended his funeral at St. John's Episcopal Church. Mississippi's governor ordered the state flag to be at half-mast.

Jeannette disappeared for a while after her husband's death. A distant relative finally found her in Clinton, Iowa, and arranged for her to be taken back to Laurel, where Elisabeth and her husband kept a close watch on her. Polly always addressed Jeannette as "Mother Wisner" in letters to her. She occasionally consulted her mother-in-law on decorations for her New York apartment. But Polly was never particularly close to Jeannette. Frank even less so. He gravitated toward Polly's father, giving Ellis Knowles legal advice over the years. The care of Wisner's mother in Laurel was left largely to his sister, Elisabeth, and her husband, Alexander, who also advised Wisner on Mississippi investments. Frank, meanwhile, turned to the spy world.

PART TWO

WORLD WAR II

Chapter 4

THE OSS

IN SEPTEMBER 1938, WISNER traveled to Europe, making stops in Belgium, Holland, and Nazi Germany. He could feel firsthand the threat Adolf Hitler posed not only to the continent but also to the rest of the world. After Germany invaded Poland a year later, Wisner became convinced it was only a matter of time before America would be at war in Europe. How that would come about, he did not know, but he wanted to be in uniform when it happened. He had also become bored with Wall Street law work. Some friends joined the British or Canadian armed forces after Great Britain declared war on Germany, but that did not interest Wisner. He wanted to be in the U.S. Navy.

Wisner had always been fascinated by boats. He talked about them a lot and he enjoyed watching regattas, but he was no yachtsman, and he knew nothing about sailing a vessel. He considered the Navy more elite than the U.S. Army. Many of his friends ended up in the sea service for the same reason. On October 16, 1940, five months after the German invasion of France, Belgium, Luxembourg, and the Netherlands, Wisner sent in his application for a commission in the U.S. Naval Reserve.

He asked to skip the entry rank of ensign and to come into service one step above as a lieutenant junior grade, which was often done by doctors and lawyers. He included in his application letters of recommendation from four of his colleagues at Carter, Ledyard & Milburn. He needed them. The qualifications Wisner claimed for being a Navy man were weak. Asked about his proficiency in foreign languages, he listed English as "excellent," his French as "fair," and Italian as "indifferent." He admitted that he had no seagoing experience save for traveling on a cruise line and sitting in a small boat as a boy.

Six months after submitting his application, Wisner was finally commissioned in the Naval Reserve as a lieutenant junior grade. Polly and the two boys they now had—Frank George II, named after Wisner's father, and John Ellis Knowles Wisner, named after Polly's father—had moved from their East Fifty-seventh Street apartment to the Quarry Close farm in Greenwich, Connecticut, which was near where her parents lived. Jeannette proudly sent Laurel's papers the news that her son had joined the Navy.

After passing a physical on July 21, 1941, Wisner was ordered to report for duty four days later to take four weeks of quick training on how to wear the uniform, salute, and follow orders, along with classes on foreign intelligence, the censoring of cable and radio traffic, and rudimentary spying techniques. Wisner had no idea what he would be doing with this instruction. He was told only that he would be assigned to something called Volunteer Special Service to perform unnamed intelligence duties that the commandant of the Third Naval District on Church Street in New York City would assign him.

What Wisner got assigned to was paper pushing, cutting, and shredding that could not have been more boring. Working in a dingy former post office building, he vetted the records that applicants for Naval commissions submitted, clipped out of newspapers stories that might interest his commanders, and arranged for information collected by the Navy's cable and radio censorship units to be shared with other intelligence outfits that might find it useful. Soon he was promoted to lieutenant, but it didn't make the work any less dull. The peacetime shore Navy had little equipment and few opportunities for officers. While working his day job with the Navy, Wisner had plenty of time to play the stock market, looking to invest in companies he thought would expand if the U.S. joined the war. His investments, along with the money the couple received from both families, enabled them to live comfortably at the Quarry Close farm, with Polly draped in mink and other fur coats. Later Wisner joked with his sons that during his New York duty, he "commanded a cutter"—that is, the scissors he used for newspapers.

The day after Japan bombed Pearl Harbor on December 7, 1941, Wisner boarded the subway to the old post office on crutches with his leg in a cast. He had torn ligaments in a touch football game that weekend. Thinking he was a war casualty, men and women packing the subway car separated so he could take a seat. A man came out of the packed crowd and somberly asked him: "Sir, how did that happen to you?" Wisner didn't dare tell him it was a football injury. "It's secret," he answered. "Oh," the man said, and whispered what the Navy lieutenant had told him to the other subway riders.

Wisner soon began carving out time to actually be an intelligence officer, and he passed along to other agencies shipping information he picked up, which they found helpful. The Office of Economic Warfare in Washington, DC, appreciated the tips he and the men under him provided on export companies they uncovered trying to evade sanctions and trade with the Axis powers. Wisner also began feeding intelligence on German arms factories that might be targeted by bomber planes to a shadowy group called the Office of Strategic Services, which few knew about. Among operatives in the OSS's New York office, Wisner became known as "our friend" in the Office of Naval Intelligence.

Since the American Revolution, makeshift spy outfits had been cobbled together for each conflict only to be largely disbanded in peacetime. The idea of a permanent U.S. intelligence service was alien. As he made major decisions in 1940 and 1941 to prepare the country for war, Franklin Roosevelt was practically blind to what lay ahead for him overseas. It made him feel physically ill at times. The Army and Navy had tiny foreign intelligence units that were largely dumping grounds for poorly performing officers. The State Department provided little foreign intelligence as well.

Four months before the Pearl Harbor attack, Roosevelt signed a vaguely worded one-page order creating the Coordinator of Information and naming as its head "Wild Bill" Donovan, who had urged FDR to set up this overseas intelligence operation. About a year later, the organization was renamed the Office of Strategic Services.

Born in 1883 in Buffalo's poor Irish First Ward, Donovan got his Wild Bill nickname for heroics during World War I, after which he was awarded the Medal of Honor. His appointment as spymaster left FDR's aides in the White House scratching their heads. Donovan was a prominent New York Republican who had campaigned unsuccessfully to succeed Roosevelt as the state's governor in 1932. Though the two men had traded insults during that race, eight years later these political enemies found common cause. A part of the Republican Party's internationalist wing, Donovan believed as Roosevelt did that the United States must prepare for war and that it desperately needed a foreign intelligence service.

Donovan, whose code number on OSS documents was always "109" (which happened to be his room number at OSS headquarters on Navy Hill next to today's State Department), eventually built up a spy organization of more than ten thousand espionage agents, commandos, and intelligence analysts, with overseas stations in every part of the world. But in the days after Pearl Harbor, he was still scrambling to put together secret operations with whatever men and women he could find available. Frank Wisner, whom he had mingled with occasionally at Lower Manhattan's Down Town Association, became one of those recruits.

Navy lieutenant commander Turner McBaine, an OSS officer in New York, had occasionally dropped by Wisner's office in the past to pick up intelligence that McBaine always found useful. This young Naval officer impressed him, so McBaine began lobbying his superiors to bring Wisner into the spy organization. The lieutenant commander would soon be tasked with spying in the Middle East; he envisioned Wisner joining him as his deputy. On one of his many trips to New York, Donovan chatted informally with Wisner and asked if he would like to be a part of the OSS. Wisner did not need much courting. He had made good friends with his fellow Naval officers, but he was eager to escape his dreary desk job, and even if he had been transferred to sea duty, spy work seemed to Wisner more interesting than floating on a ship.

In April 1942 David K. E. Bruce, the OSS's Secret Intelligence Branch chief, who also knew Wisner and his former CL&M partners, sent a note to the Navy stating that if the sea service could see its way clear to transferring its lieutenant to Donovan's spy organization, "it would be most helpful to us and greatly appreciated." Meanwhile, the OSS did a quick security check on Wisner, not expecting to find any problems since he had already been vetted by Naval intelligence, and had him visit the agency's Washington headquarters for formal interviews with four senior OSS officers and then with Donovan himself. The spymaster insisted on meeting and clearing all intelligence officers for his organization.

Wisner told Donovan and the other top OSS officials that his legal training plus the skills he had picked up in Naval intelligence would make him valuable to the OSS. Donovan, in fact, was always on the lookout for operatives like Wisner. He checked all the right boxes for Wild Bill—a lawyer and military man, fit and trim as he neared his mid-thirties (five feet, ten inches tall; a hundred sixty pounds, still mostly muscle from his track days). Though not an Ivy Leaguer (Donovan gravitated toward them), Wisner came from Wall Street, the spy chief's old home. In early October 1943, the Navy finally approved the transfer of seven of its intelligence officers to the OSS. Wisner was one of them. Donovan "is very much pleased to know that you are joining us," an OSS aide wrote him.

* * *

Wisner arrived in Washington's Union Station midmorning on October 25, 1943. The directions from the OSS that he had received in New York nine days earlier were sparse but explicit. He carried one suitcase. The OSS told him it had to be a bag that did not have his initials engraved on the outside. He was instructed to pack enough civilian clothes for two weeks and he should include one suit (not his Sunday best), a pair of slacks, shoes that could be used for tromping around in a forest, and perhaps an old jacket plus a sweater. No one at the spy school he was scheduled to attend must know who he was, his letter of instruction said, so the clothes he brought should have nothing that might identify where they had come from like labels and laundry marks. Polly cut them all out. He was also ordered to leave behind his watch or any other jewelry that had his name engraved on it.

Wisner was ordered to tell no one—not even Polly—where he was going and what he would be doing. If pressed by friends or family, he should just tell them "you are likely to be in and out of Washington for a few weeks," the instruction for recruits said. Polly was given a post office box number in the capital in case she wanted to send a letter to her husband. Invariably, some recruits did not take the silence order seriously and arrived at OSS training with their cover already blown because they had bragged to family or friends about why they were going to Washington. OSS recruiters realized they had to do a better job of warning applicants to keep their mouths shut.

Wisner flagged a cab and told the driver to take him to 2430 E Street Northwest. That was the address for OSS headquarters on Navy Hill, a three-story granite building with long stone columns in front that used to house the Public Health Service. An armed soldier with a ferocious-looking guard dog stood at the front gate and checked Wisner's identification against a list he had been given. The soldier waved him through. Inside, the headquarters building's long corridors were filled with men and women scurrying about with serious looks on their faces. Many of them wore American uniforms. Some were British or Free French officers assigned to the OSS as liaisons.

Wisner found the room he had been told to go to. An OSS officer there handed him a four-page "Desk Indoctrination Memo for O.S.S. Basic Course" and told him to read it while the officer watched. One passage from the memo lectured Wisner on how he should be secretive during training:

> Remember this: If you use the words "I" and "My," some fact about yourself will follow it. (Example: A man who says, "MY daughter told me. . . . ." has already told you several facts about himself—whether he realizes it or not.) Don't be conspicuous by not talking; be friendly, even "communicative." Always think first before speaking. It is an art that requires practice to live self-consciously, to be inconspicuous, and to be discreet. It is, however, perfectly possible to be friendly with others without telling anything thoughtlessly about yourself or your personal history. This is an Important Part of your training for further work in the OSS.

After Wisner finished, the officer asked if he had any questions. Wisner did not, so the officer told him to have a cab take him back to Union Station, where he should buy a train ticket to Towson, Maryland, which is about eleven miles from Baltimore. Wisner did as he was told.

He arrived at the Towson train station in the late afternoon of October 25. A nondescript OSS truck with the back flaps down took Wisner and other recruits waiting at the station through the rolling Maryland countryside to what had once been the Oldfields School, which the OSS was leasing from Major Watts Hill. The old school, now designated E-2, was part of a series of secret schools the OSS intentionally set up within a sixty-mile radius of Washington, DC, so the OSS brass could keep watch over them. Donovan had drawn much of the training of his spies and commandos from the British secret services, sending many of his instructors to schools in England and Canada to learn how to teach the dark arts, and borrowing a few British officers to come to the United States to teach special courses. One aspect of the United Kingdom's instruction Donovan did not adopt was the sumptuous estates the British used for training their men. Donovan wanted his spies toughened up at spartan camps.

The secret E-2 complex consisted of a main building with thirty rooms and five bathrooms, a caretaker's quarters with more rooms and a section partitioned off as an infirmary, and a big garage. Six large tents had also been pitched next to the main building to house the overflow of students who had been arriving lately so E-2 could train up to seventy-seven at a time. The grounds around the complex, which the OSS also leased, offered ample room for a firing range, demolitions instruction, and field exercises.

From a clerk at the front desk in the main building, Wisner received another set of instructions: there would be no time off since each day and night would be filled with classes; meals would cost officers like Wisner sixty cents a day; the garage had a tiny store where he could buy cigarettes; a bar would be open in the evening but Wisner probably would not have a free moment to buy a drink. The clerk also dumped into his arms several two-inch-thick manuals on spy tradecraft, the German army, and the makeup of the OSS. He was told to have them read by the next morning. The manuals took Wisner almost all night to digest. The instructors did not have a minute to spare. To handle the influx of students, the basic secret intelligence course had been shortened the previous year from three weeks to two. A lot of material had to be crammed into that shortened time.

Wisner emptied his pockets of forbidden items—like his driver's license, Navy identification card, and keys—and turned them over to the clerk, who put the items into a bag without looking at them.

He received a set of Army fatigues with only his "school name" printed on them. Each student was given a school name, which he would go by during his stay at E-2. In some cases, it was just the student's first name, or a person's nickname, or, in other instances, a fictitious name. Wisner's school name was simply "Frank." No one knew his last name. The importance of cover was relentlessly drilled into the students' heads over the next two weeks. Cover—that is, keeping absolutely secret a spy's identity and the intelligence organization to which he or she belonged—was essential to practically all activities of an OSS officer. Maintaining cover kept a secret agent and his operation alive.

Wisner found an air of mystery and deception permeating E-2 and its training. The instructors tried to maintain an informal civilian atmosphere in the school, but that was only to catch Wisner and the other students off guard. The trainees were not only forbidden from disclosing their real identities; they were also ordered to lie about who they were under their assumed names. At the same time, they were instructed to try to pierce the cover of their fellow students. The school thus tried to create, behind a relaxed facade, an atmosphere of tension like what a trainee would experience as a spy in the field. Wisner and the others were encouraged not to strike up friendships with classmates. The other person might be infiltrated behind enemy lines and the OSS did not want to risk the chance of a pal back home disclosing his real name. Even the instructors did not inquire about a student's identity unless it was absolutely necessary. Wisner and the other students were being prepared psychologically for the lonely life of a spy—who was in a never-ending gamble with detection.

The next morning, instead of reveille from a blaring bugle, a company clerk blasted a popular show tune over loudspeakers to wake up the students. After an hour of physical exercises and then breakfast, Wisner and his classmates began a series of daily courses, one after the other lasting well into the night, with no breaks except for lunch and dinner. They learned about the operations of Axis intelligence services and the basics of subversive warfare, such as security for undercover operations, counterespionage measures to use against enemy spies, and interrogation techniques, in addition to how to shadow suspects, raid houses, plant listening devices, print propaganda leaflets, and read and sketch maps.

Most OSS officers like Wisner operated in the field primarily as organizers, setting up secret groups of foreign-born agents who actually stole the secrets, sabotaged the enemy's military equipment, or passed out propaganda flyers. Wisner was taught the basics of putting together these agent networks—or "chains," as the OSS called them. He learned the use of "cutouts," who were intermediaries who handled all the dealings with a subagent for him. That way, if an operation was blown, the cutout would escape and Wisner could still operate in the field to reactivate what was left of his chain with a new cutout. He learned the cell system for organizing his spy network. The agents in his network would be divided into small units of subagents called "cells." One member of each cell would know one member of the group above him, and another member of the same cell would be the only one who knew the identity of the unit below him. That way, a blown operation would usually result in the loss of only one group—at most three groups—before further enemy detection could be blocked off.

The students learned how to set up safe houses in enemy territory where a spy could hide out with a friendly family. They were given quick classes in how to communicate their intelligence to higher headquarters and in how to set up letter drops, in which an officer left written material with an intermediary, such as a newsstand dealer, or inside an object, like a hole in a tree, for a headquarters courier to pick up later. They also familiarized themselves with the various cipher and code systems the OSS used to transmit information over the radio.

Wisner, who was already an expert shot with rifles from the time he had spent since his teenage years hunting birds, was given eight hours of weapons training and shown some of the exotic "gadgets" Donovan's technicians had concocted to wreak havoc in the field, such as pistols with silencers, explosives shaped like lumps of coal the agents called "Black Joe," and explosive powder made to look like baking flour nicknamed "Aunt Jemima." They were introduced to the K-pill, which could be slipped into an enemy agent's drink to knock him out, and the L-tablet, a poison spies could swallow if captured to kill them instantly. British major William Fairbairn, an expert in unarmed combat, dropped by for a three-hour class in gutter fighting's foul moves, like gouging eyes, driving the heel of a hand up under the jaw, or karate-chopping just below the Adam's apple for a quick kill.

Wisner and the others spent one night roaming the fields around E-2 on simulated sabotage missions, navigation exercises using a compass, and observation and reporting skills tests. Toward the end of the two weeks, Wisner was also sent out with a false identity on what was called a "scheme," in which he tried to talk his way into a nearby Baltimore defense plant and walk out with company documents. The schemes had become highly controversial for the OSS. They were a headache for local police, who often caught the students trying to slip into the facilities. FBI director J. Edgar Hoover threatened to prosecute any trainee posing as one of his agents to gain admittance into an arms plant. Donovan would not be intimidated into abandoning the schemes, but he soon put rules in place for how far the students could go in their infiltrations. Wisner was told he could not try to impersonate a White House aide to gain entry.

On the last night of training, the instructors treated Wisner and the other students to a farewell party. Plenty of liquor was served. It was a final test, though the students did not realize it. The instructors wanted to see how their charges acted with their guard down. A thorough evaluation was then prepared on each of them and sent to Washington, where headquarters officers decided what the best fit was in the OSS for each graduate—or if some were not suited for any kind of spy work. A significant number of students were ruled unfit during training and washed out. Some who made it through training proved to be psychologically or emotionally unsuited for dangerous field operations. As the Allies ramped up their offensives in 1943, demand for OSS officers overseas swelled, which led to a massive recruiting effort back home. By mid-1943, OSS headquarters began receiving worrisome complaints of incompetence in the field—officers unable to handle the stress or deemed too loquacious for a secret organization. Fifty-two OSS officers had emotional breakdowns during the war. Several months after Wisner completed his basic course, Donovan began an assessment program to screen out the recruits who were obviously unfit for clandestine work—some 20 percent.

The E-2 evaluators had high hopes for Wisner. They rated him "an intelligent, conscientious, thoroughly reliable person" who was "well poised" and took a "practical approach" to problem-solving. The trainers found him to be "very cautious and painstaking, sometimes overly so," but it did not "impede him in taking action." Wisner was a good judge of men—an important attribute for an agent handler—and he "inspired a great deal of confidence in his ability" in those around him, another important attribute. He would do well in the field.

"He has a very pleasing personality, is a good mixer and can keep his own counsel," the evaluators concluded. Their only caveat: "He must, however, guard against his tendency to over-cautiousness."

After finishing at E-2, Wisner was given six dollars to cover a meal and a train ticket for the trip back to OSS headquarters in Washington. His two weeks of schooling had not been intended to produce a polished operative. The complete training of a secret agent took at least sixteen weeks. Spy school could never teach him what to do in every situation. This was not rote learning, with students memorizing the proper tactics according to habit or from repetition. Wisner was being taught to think on his feet, to be flexible in operations, to be creative and willing to experiment with new approaches. The precise situation an OSS officer and his team might encounter in the field could not be foreseen. If officers kept repeating a pattern in their method of operation, they stood a good chance of being detected by the enemy. A successful spy must constantly be able to "adapt old methods and develop new ones," according to one agency report. Wisner would also have to make it up as he went along because the young OSS was making it up as it went along. Some spies—particularly those with military backgrounds—did not do well in this kind of environment. But Wisner would thrive.

Back at headquarters on December 8, Wisner checked out twenty items he would need for his clandestine work overseas. They included a Hermes portable typewriter, a medical kit for jungle operations, a Kodak Bantam camera with six rolls of film, a .38-caliber Colt automatic pistol with fifty rounds of ammunition and a shoulder holster, a compass, a special wristwatch OSS officers wore, and a sun-signaling mirror. Eight days later he signed up for a $10,000 U.S. Government Life Insurance policy. He was going to Cairo.

Chapter 5

CAIRO

THE YANKEE CLIPPER FLEW a roundabout route. The plane, with Wisner aboard, took off from Washington on December 15, 1943, and headed south to Miami, where it refueled for the next leg to Puerto Rico, and then to British Guiana and Brazil by December 20. After making an overnight stop on Ascension Island in the middle of the South Atlantic Ocean, the Clipper flew to the Gold Coast region of West Africa, and then headed northeast, stopping in Nigeria and the Sudan. The plane finally reached Cairo, Egypt, on the afternoon of Christmas Eve. Wisner found the nine-day flight so exciting and interesting that he slept little when he had the opportunity to do so aboard the aircraft. The many American bases and fortifications he saw along the way impressed him. After the war, Wisner could clearly see the United States becoming "an international power of the first magnitude," he later wrote Polly.

Wisner climbed down the Clipper's ladder, lugging his musette bag with the .38-caliber pistol stuffed inside. He spotted Turner McBaine, the Naval officer who had recruited him in New York and still had visions of Wisner being his deputy in the OSS intelligence division he had been running in Cairo for more than a year. The two men piled into a jeep and sped off to a Christmas party that Lieutenant Colonel Valerian Lada-Mocarski was hosting at his quarters. Wisner was to report to Lada-Mocarski, the highly respected commander of the Cairo OSS detachment's Secret Intelligence Branch.

Before his Cairo trip, Wisner had been inoculated for smallpox, yellow fever, tetanus, cholera, and typhoid. He was now thankful for the shots. His senses were attacked by the combination of vehicle exhaust fumes, incense, and the stench of sweating and defecating pack animals as he rode in the jeep with its top down along streets jammed with well-stocked bazaars, fruit vendors, cafés, and weary-looking prostitutes lounging on balconies. At stops, the jeep was surrounded by begging children, peddlers, porn dealers, and pimps. Cairo's weather that winter had been harsh, with heavy rainstorms giving rise to waves of typhoid fever, malaria, dysentery, and mumps. Among the troops, venereal disease also was rampant. The Europeans found refuge in upper-class neighborhoods, with their smart department stores, pricey hotels, ministry and parliamentary buildings, and compounds for royal family members like King Farouk's immense Abdeen Palace. One of the palaces of Prince Abbas Halim housed the American legation at 6 Sharia Rustum.

For more than four hundred years, Egypt had known nothing but occupation. In 1517, the land came under Ottoman rule, which French conquerors under Napoleon interrupted briefly during the late eighteenth century. Following the French rule, European merchants and professionals arrived to control the country's commerce and build the Suez Canal with local forced labor. In 1882, the country fell under England's rule, which Egyptians came to hate. Though London relaxed its grip by the early twentieth century, granting Egypt protectorate status, British functionaries still called the shots behind Egyptian ministers, preserving political and financial stability along with the canal that gave the British Empire its shortest route to resource-rich India. After riots in 1919, Egyptians were given more independence, control of their diplomatic affairs, and a constitution that later increased the power of young King Farouk. But British troops remained, and a British high commissioner still wielded considerable clout.

King Farouk and his prime minister had wanted their country to remain friends with Germany after Britain declared war. But with its deepwater ports, important railways, and cheap labor, Egypt was too valuable a military base for the Allies ever to allow any encroachment by the Nazis. British defenses in the west were caught unprepared for General Erwin Rommel's attack east from Tripoli in March 1941. By June 1942, Rommel's tanks had reached El Alamein on the Mediterranean coast just west of Alexandria; the British embassy and general headquarters in Cairo began burning files. But a month later, the British line at El Alamein was still holding. Royal Air Force bombing ruptured Rommel's thousand-mile-long supply line. By August aggressive general Bernard Law Montgomery had taken over the British Army in Egypt and forced Rommel to retreat west. After November and the Anglo-American Torch landing at Morocco and Algeria, Rommel was trapped. The Axis army eventually surrendered in May 1943.

Cairo was safe. British and American commanders prepared for the landing at Sicily two months later. By the time Wisner arrived, the Egyptian capital remained a major supply and coordinating point for operations in the Middle East, the Mediterranean, and North Africa. But anti-British sentiment again was rising in Cairo. King Farouk, who had an impressive intelligence service for a monarch, was becoming a headache for London, which never got over his flirtation with the Axis.

More than a thousand American service members poured into Cairo after the Torch invasion. It was a small number compared to the 126,000 British and Dominion soldiers garrisoned in the vast Citadel of Muhammad Ali, but the U.S. presence was enough to cause friction between the two contingents. The British were stiff and reserved, the Americans casual and breezy. American officers, who were paid more, began outbidding British officers for apartments and servants. The Americans' post-exchange stores were better stocked. The British grumbled that the GIs earned medals too easily and had the edge in attracting women. The Americans thought the British were snobbish, unfriendly, hidebound, and protocol obsessed. As far as the Americans were concerned, their headquarters—now full of officers with inflated ranks, huge egos, and not enough to do—was no longer an important or exciting place to be. The U.S. contingent also cared nothing about Britain's preoccupation with preserving its colonial empire.

Donovan's men, however, worked assiduously to cultivate their cousins. The OSS, which operated out of a villa at 8 Rustum Pasha Street, moved quickly to establish an information-exchange program with the British intelligence and special operations detachments that were scattered in offices all over Cairo.

* * *

Wisner and the other OSS officers awoke early Christmas morning, bleary-eyed from the previous night's drinking, and put in a full day's work. Their walled-in villa headquarters had a broad veranda surrounded by a manicured lawn and looked like a "bastard version of the Taj Mahal," according to one operative's description. In deference to the holiday, the men quit work early at four thirty p.m. Wisner then joined a party of officers who "had tea in the shadow of some of the ancient and venerable monuments of the far past," he wrote Polly.

Wisner quickly discovered that the Cairo station worked hard and played hard. For New Year's Eve, McBaine and Lada-Mocarski took him to an elaborate party hosted by a wealthy Egyptian at a swanky club. "I was amazed by the display of beauty, expensive clothes and jewelry," he wrote Polly. Since few spoke English, Wisner made a clumsy attempt to converse with the guests in French, which they spoke fluently. Wisner mangled his pronunciation and Lada-Mocarski had to rescue him from embarrassing himself. The party was still going strong when the three Americans left at two

fifteen a.m. Soon Wisner, McBaine, and Lada-Mocarski were inseparable on the Cairo social circuit. "I believe I shall find the work
assigned me here very intriguing," Wisner wrote Polly, "and I most
earnestly hope that I may measure up to the responsibilities that
have fallen upon me."

He was in the thick of espionage operations. Cairo had become
the OSS's base station for wide-ranging spying in the Middle East,
Central Asia, and the Balkans. Using powerful radio transmitting
equipment with a three-thousand-foot-long antenna to communicate with far-flung agent networks, the OSS's Cairo staff hoped to
be running—or was running with mixed success—agent operations
in Egypt, Lebanon, Syria, Palestine, Jordan, Iraq, Saudi Arabia,
Iran, Afghanistan, Turkey, Greece, Albania, Romania, Bulgaria,
Hungary, and Yugoslavia.

Wisner was assigned as the chief intelligence reports officer for
the station. He had the big job of overseeing, processing, evaluating,
and disseminating the hundreds of intelligence reports pouring into
the base station from all the operations in the region. He also had
to maintain a working relationship with other foreign intelligence
agencies, which in Cairo meant staying on the good side of the British. Wisner didn't have time to clean the pistol issued to him, and
even if he did, he had no use for it. He was an analyst who worked
in an office, not a spy in the field. Even so, he roamed Cairo with
experienced agents every chance he could to get a feel for the city
and what it was like to plumb its secrets.

After a short stay in McBaine's quarters, Wisner joined five
other OSS officers in renting a modern and spacious white villa that
was a jeep ride from the station and had three large balconies, two
of which overlooked the Nile. They nicknamed it "Navy House."
The rental came with a houseboy and an inventive cook who made
decent meals from the bland canned food the OSS bought from a
military commissary. His five roommates, Wisner wrote Polly, were
"an attractive and amusing crowd." A former newspaper reporter,
bright and well-read, Percy St. Clair Wood was the guerrilla opera-

tions chief in Cairo and one of the most likable Navy officers in the station. Amariah Atwater, a salesman in civilian life, ran the station's maritime unit, which outfitted small boats that operatives used to infiltrate along coastlines. Stephen Bailey, a Rhodes scholar who had taught government and economics in college, now worked under Wisner processing intelligence reports, as did Walter Lowrie Campbell, who had left a wife and two children in Greenwich, Connecticut, to join the Navy. Yale graduate Rolfe Kingsley, an energetic young Marine Corps lieutenant, became one of Wisner's most loyal intelligence officers, accompanying him when he moved to other duty stations during the war. As the senior officer in the group, Wisner sat at the head of the dining room table.

Wisner put in long hours at the Cairo station. He worked six full days a week and two-thirds of the day on Sunday. The OSS officers kept to the same daily routine as their British cousins. Wisner began at eight a.m. and worked until one p.m. He was off until four thirty p.m., when he returned to the office and pored over reports until seven thirty p.m., then usually collapsed into bed after he had dinner. The odd schedule was dictated by Egyptian culture and Cairo's insufferably hot afternoons. During the siesta period, Wisner took a leisurely lunch, wrote letters home, got in some exercise (he had Polly mail him a half dozen tennis balls), and went shopping or sightseeing. He enjoyed wandering about the bazaars. Never had he seen "such a colossal collection of junk gathered together in any one place, all of it for sale," he wrote Polly. And with so much American money floating around, Wisner found everything in Cairo expensive. Just living costs ate up half his salary. He did snare a few bargains: a pair of red leather slippers with turned-up toes and a couple small brass ashtrays.

* * *

The times Wisner tried to collect intelligence walking about Cairo by himself or cruising the social circuit rarely proved fruitful. He was still unsure about who in the city was worth cultivating for useful information. To make himself understood by the locals, who spoke little English, he was forced to rely on his crude French, so it seemed to him a waste of time and money to buy information with such poor communication skills. Besides, his desk job cleaning up the reporting procedures the professionals in the field practiced became challenging enough for him.

The Cairo station had experienced considerable turmoil since the first OSS officers arrived in April 1942 to gather intelligence for the Torch invasion. It was not a well-run outpost. Setting up diplomatic or business covers to hide the real reason Donovan's operatives were in the Egyptian capital had been difficult. Establishing communication channels to feed the information that field agents discovered to military commanders in the region or back to Washington had been a headache. Three months before Wisner arrived, OSS inspectors had issued a scathing report on the station. Inspired and imaginative leadership there was "wanting," the report complained. No "organized planning" was being done for espionage operations. The station was plagued with manpower shortages. Hardly any secret agents were being infiltrated into enemy-occupied countries. Some OSS missions, like the one in Turkey, were operating under the Cairo station's supervision, and Washington was clueless about what they were doing. Security was sloppy. British intelligence dominated the region and they tried to bully the OSS station into being little more than an adjunct of His Majesty's secret services.

Donovan swooped into Cairo the next month and shook up the organization. He made Lada-Mocarski the head of the station's secret intelligence gathering. Lieutenant Colonel John Toulmin, a former Boston banker, was brought in as executive officer to clean out the deadwood. Cairo also desperately needed fresh blood with management ability to improve the reporting and evaluating of intelligence coming into the station. That was why Wisner was sent there.

It was surprising that he was able to find, in such short order, a number of problems that needed to be corrected in how intelligence

was reported to the Cairo station and in how it was evaluated once
it got there. After all, Wisner had had only two weeks of training to
do this job. But he had good common sense and that guided him in
the changes he made. He found that the OSS officers sent to Cairo
were poorly trained in how to observe and report intelligence. They
were well instructed in how to steal secrets but not in what to do
with what they had stolen. He could see that far too much time was
being wasted in the reports office on administrative housekeeping
chores, at the expense of actually producing good intelligence. Too
many people were bumping into one another in the office. Wisner
had learned enough in a Wall Street law firm to know that at some
point an operation's efficiency begins to decrease as the number of
people involved in it increases.

He streamlined procedures. He set up a uniform numbering
system to manage the large volume of OSS reports coming in and
untangled duplicate code names often in them. He improved the
quality and timeliness of those reports, consulting British Secret
Intelligence Service officers in Cairo for tips on how they assembled
and disseminated their information. He organized classes for new
OSS officers who arrived at the station poorly trained in how to report what they collected in the field. He cautioned agents against coloring their information with their own biases and improved the
editing of their reports at the station. More importantly, Wisner interviewed officers in military commands that received the OSS reports for feedback on the intelligence they found useful and what was
not worth reading. Within six months, Wisner had turned the reports
office into an important unit shaping the Cairo station's intelligence
output. He found the work "interesting and varied, but it is very exacting," he wrote Polly. As a Wall Street lawyer, Wisner had had considerable experience with detail work. He thrived in it in Cairo.

* * *

It was a city of guilty pleasures. Temptation lurked everywhere for
soldiers wanting to be tempted. British officers and civilians tended

to shed inhibitions in the Egyptian capital, which offered alcohol and sex in abundance. The Continental Hotel had a dance floor taken up by a cabaret, belly dancers, and acrobats. British officers were drawn to Madame Badia's nightclub with its anti-Nazi comedy acts and sexy chorus girls, who would later change into evening gowns to dance with men in the audience. The summer before Wisner arrived, the luxurious Auberge des Pyramides opened on Mena Road and soon became one of King Farouk's favorite stops. And then there was the Kit Kat Club, often frequented by spies who knew to keep their conversations to a whisper so they could not be overheard by snoops at neighboring tables.

A stuffed-shirt admiral whom Donovan sent on an overseas inspection tour had been terrorizing OSS stations in Europe and North Africa. When the Navy man reached Cairo, Wisner and Kingsley, who had been alerted to expect trouble, convinced him to join them at Madame Badia's nightclub, where they filled him with cheap gin martinis and put him in the loving arms of a belly dancer. She escorted him back to their quarters. The admiral awoke the next morning stretched out on the dining room table with a throbbing headache. He had no memory of what had happened the night before with the belly dancer, but he worried that it wasn't good. To keep Kingsley and Wisner quiet, the admiral sent Donovan a glowing report on the Cairo station.

The OSS station had its share of pretty women sent from Washington to handle clerical chores. In his letters to Polly, Wisner openly confided about the pernicious effect Cairo's nightlife had "on good Americans and Britishers far from home and wife." Polly already knew. Other wives back in New York had told her about husbands who had strayed in Cairo. Polly picked up no gossip that Frank was one of them.

* * *

Wisner soon developed a reputation in Cairo as a problem solver. The intelligence-reporting operation was now considered first-rate.

Compliments arrived from OSS headquarters in Washington. Wisner's cooperative attitude earned him high praise from the British, who made him an Honorary Officer of the Military Division of the Most Excellent Order of the British Empire. As a reward, Wisner was promoted to lieutenant commander on March 1, 1944.

Two months later, however, he was transferred to a job that he did not want and that he took only under protest. The OSS's clandestine operations in the Balkans were extremely important to Donovan—a way to weaken the underbelly of Hitler's empire with sabotage and subversion, the spymaster thought. He gave the Balkans a lot of attention and made periodic visits to Cairo, which he wanted to be command central for the OSS's secret war to peel off nations like Hungary, Bulgaria, and Romania from Nazi control.

But there were problems in Turkey, which Donovan had envisioned as a key launching pad for OSS missions into the Balkans. Secret operations there had been blown. Nazi spy services had rolled up OSS networks. The Cairo station was feuding with the OSS men in Turkey. McBaine and other Cairo officers had a low opinion of the OSS intelligence coming out of Turkey. To Washington, the Istanbul mission seemed to be adrift. Wisner was sent to clean up the mess.

Chapter 6

ISTANBUL

WHEN WISNER ARRIVED IN June 1944, Istanbul was experiencing one of its prettiest springs, with wisteria, jacaranda, and Judas trees all in full bloom under bright sunshine. Americans who preceded him found this city of 740,000 people one of the most beautiful in the world, with its majestic mosques and their towering minarets, its grand old palaces, and its tranquil gardens. At one of the city's best hotels, the Park, foreign businessmen, military officers, reporters, diplomats, and spies observed an unspoken truce, and wartime antagonisms were set aside for the sake of fine dining and drinks from a well-stocked bar. Across a broad boulevard from the Park Hotel stood the German consulate, whose ambassador, Franz von Papen, had an excellent view of the Bosporus Strait. By World War II, the official American presence at the Istanbul consulate and the U.S. embassy in Ankara had bulked up to eleven diplomats, twenty-one clerks, and scores of representatives from the military services and civilian wartime agencies.

In AD 330, Roman emperor Constantine the Great made the city his imperial capital and named it Constantinople. After the empire split, Constantinople was rebuilt, expanded, and renamed Byzantium by Emperor Theodosius III; it became the capital of the Byzantine Empire. The city was again renamed after the Ottoman Turks, who invaded in 1453, made it the capital of their empire, and decided to call it Istanbul. Following the Ottoman Empire's collapse after World War I—during which the empire had sided with defeated Germany— Turkey was finally established as a republic in 1923 after General Mustafa Kemal Atatürk led a revolt to drive out occupying forces. Over the next fifteen years, Atatürk imposed sweeping reforms to modernize the nation. The capital was moved to Ankara, but for Turks and Westerners, Istanbul remained the country's heart.

Wanting to stay neutral at World War II's outset, Turkey, whose army had only obsolete military equipment, tried to please all sides. For both the Allied and Axis powers the country was a strategic prize. The British and the Americans wanted Turkey as a launching point for driving the Germans out of the Balkans. The Russians, whom the Turks hated, eyed Istanbul and the Bosporus for control of the Black Sea and access to the Mediterranean. The Germans sought a foothold to defeat the Russians and import Turkish raw materials. From the west and north, warring belligerents soon reached perilously close. OSS officers who had arrived after the United States entered the war set up an evacuation site to enable a quick flight out of Turkey if the Germans invaded.

Istanbul became a spy haven. Hundreds of thousands of foreign businessmen, government officials, and refugees from the Nazi regime traveled through Turkey, making it fertile territory for the gathering of intelligence on Central and Eastern Europe. Some seventeen foreign intelligence services were active in Istanbul, which teemed with international informants who were professionals at the business of peddling secrets. The British had more than two thousand diplomats, military officers, and intelligence agents in the city. The Axis countries had some fifteen hundred clandestine operatives there. In the Park's ornate lobby, hotel employees could be hired to snitch on foreign guests checking in or out by any intelligence officer with cash in his pocket. As long as a foreign spy service did not target the Turkish government or meddle in local politics, Turkey's security services looked the other way. Sometimes they even helped an Axis or Allied officer, slipping him useful information, such as border registration lists. How cooperative the Turkish security men were usually depended on how well a side was doing in the war.

Donovan jumped into Turkey's spy game in April 1943, sending Lanning "Packy" Macfarland, an Illinois savings and loan executive he had known from Republican Party work, to Istanbul to set up an OSS mission. Operating under the cover of working as a Lend-Lease officer, Macfarland was given a wildly ambitious assignment: to mount espionage and subversion operations in Bulgaria, Romania, and Hungary, with the goal of getting those countries to break away from Germany.

Macfarland enjoyed dressing like a spy with a trench coat and slouch hat, but he had no espionage experience to speak of and he was laughingly casual about security. The Midwest banker, however, was a big talker and he energetically set out to build a secret operation he thought would rival that of his Axis competitors. He gave his agents plant code names. Macfarland's was "Juniper." Archibald Coleman, a former Treasury Department agent and a bit of a braggart like Macfarland, was assigned to run the most important agent networks, which was code-named "Cereus" after a cactus in America's West that bloomed at night. The agent in charge of the day-to-day management of the Cereus chain was a Czech engineer in Istanbul and a source the British spy service, MI6, had handed off to Macfarland. The Czech said his name was Alfred Schwarz—although the OSS later suspected that he had made up that name. Schwarz, whose code name became "Dogwood," recruited twenty-nine disgruntled German expats or well-connected foreigners whom he knew in Istanbul. He told Coleman and Macfarland that these agents—who were given plant names like Begonia (for an Austrian arms buyer) and Hibiscus (for a Greek technician)—could establish important contacts not only in the Balkan countries but also in Austria and Germany.

Seven months after setting foot in Istanbul, Macfarland sent Donovan a "Dear Bill" letter boasting that his Cereus chain had achieved spectacular results. Schwarz's operatives had made inroads into the Hungarian army's general staff, which planned to send an officer to Istanbul to discuss Hungary's breaking away from the Axis. Dogwood's agents would soon be infiltrated into Romania and Bulgaria to spark revolts. Macfarland reported that he had even succeeded in developing an elaborate espionage operation inside Germany. It all sounded too good to be true, which it was.

Only later did Donovan and his aides learn that the Istanbul mission, which Macfarland ran like an absentee landlord, had glaring weaknesses. Basic rules of tradecraft had been violated. "Packy was a disaster," concluded Rolfe Kingsley, who accompanied Wisner to Istanbul. Schwarz turned out to be a temperamental, egotistical, and domineering employee. Macfarland and Coleman had no control over him. Dogwood refused to identify the subagents who worked for him, claiming their names had to be kept secret to protect them. Macfarland and Coleman never demanded to know who these people were, so there was no way of vetting the information they provided (much of it vague hearsay) to verify its accuracy. Dogwood also turned out to be oblivious to the fact that many of his sources were double agents pretending to be loyal to him but actually working for the Germans.

A U.S. Naval attaché in Istanbul had alerted the OSS early on that an informant had told him that local Axis services would try to have their agents hired by Donovan's expanding mission in the city, which was exactly what happened. Slow to realize how effectively the enemy had penetrated his operation, Macfarland ignored pleas to tighten things up. He was sleeping with two women—one of whom was feeding his pillow talk to the Germans, the other tipping off the Russians. Meanwhile, much of his mission's intelligence that reached Cairo wasn't distributed by the OSS because it was deemed worthless.

The careless handling of agents also resulted in the arrests of

many of the contacts the Dogwood chain had made in Europe—
although neither Macfarland nor Donovan realized it at the time.
Helmuth Graf von Moltke, from one of Germany's most revered
military families, had traveled to Istanbul and met with Schwarz's
agents to discuss the network of anti-Nazi military officers, left-
wing civil servants, and professional people he had organized in
Kreisau, Silesia, who were plotting how they could help the Allies
bring down Hitler's regime. The Gestapo arrested Moltke shortly
after he returned to Berlin and executed him. A three-man OSS
team, code-named "Sparrow," parachuted into Hungary. They were
there to follow up on contacts Dogwood's agents had made with
representatives of the nation's military command who were allegedly plotting to have Hungary switch sides and join the Allies. The
trio was arrested in short order by the Gestapo and packed off to a
prisoner of war facility.

British intelligence officers in Washington were the first to tip
off Donovan in early 1944 that he had a problem. Macfarland had
gone rogue in Istanbul, officers with Britain's Special Operations
Executive complained. He was hiring foreigners the SOE had rejected because of their Axis ties and poaching legitimate agents who
were on London's payroll. British services were ordered to keep
their distance from Macfarland's gang.

Donovan quickly realized he had to clean house in Istanbul.
More than bad luck had blown the Moltke and Sparrow missions, he
suspected. The congenial Macfarland was "loved by everyone" but
respected by few, noted one memo to Donovan. The British weren't
the only ones blackballing Macfarland: the U.S. ambassador and his
Naval attaché refused to work with him. For an OSS mission chief,
another memo concluded, Macfarland was far too "casual."

* * *

Late morning on June 13, a week after the Allies landed at Normandy for Operation Overlord, Wisner and three of his aides from

Cairo stepped off the train at Istanbul's busy Haydarpaşa Station. The four officers had flown by plane from Cairo to Adana in south-central Turkey three days earlier and from there taken the train to Istanbul. Donovan's advisers had assured him that Wisner, Kingsley, and the two other men with them were the best Cairo had to take over Macfarland's failed intelligence operation. The British respected Wisner, Donovan was told, and he had already begun to repair frayed relations with Turkish officials before he left Egypt.

To preserve a semblance of civilian cover, Wisner wore one of two dark suits he had bought in Cairo, along with a sports jacket, two pairs of gray flannel slacks, five neckties, and seven shirts. He purchased them all with OSS money for $112, which Wisner thought was a bargain. Civilian suits in Cairo were expensive and their quality was usually poor. He had the coats made roomy enough so he could wear a shoulder holster with a .45-caliber pistol. He thought he would need a handgun more in Istanbul than in Cairo.

Wisner hoped to slip into Istanbul unnoticed. But Macfarland made that impossible. Wisner looked out the train window and, to his horror, saw the OSS mission chief dressed in full Army uniform and surrounded by a group of Turkish officers with a small brass band to greet him. Wisner and his three aides sneaked through several cars, hopped off the train so Macfarland wouldn't see them, and took a cab to the Pera Palace Hotel, where they had reservations. Later a bellhop knocked on the door to Wisner's room and handed him a note from Macfarland, who said he was sorry he had missed Wisner at the station and gave him the address where he wanted to meet the Naval officer for drinks that evening.

At that address, Wisner walked down steps to a dimly lit club where he could see only a few businessmen (one of them Japanese) sipping drinks. A good place for two clandestine operators to meet, Wisner thought, so he sat down at a table and waited for Macfarland. A few minutes later, lights illuminated a stage, a curtain parted, and, to Wisner's shock, a line of high-stepping Turkish chorus girls danced out like the Rockettes, with Macfarland in the middle dressed in a female costume and kicking as high as he could. They all sang "Boo Boo Baby I'm a Spy."

Macfarland was hardly alone in flouting cover. One of his subordinates who was a heavy drinker would routinely shout, "Hello, spies!" when he greeted colleagues in a bar. A piano player at the Park Hotel struck up "Boo Boo Baby" when MI6 and Soviet intelligence officers entered its ballroom. Sylvia Press, a seasoned OSS counterintelligence officer, was appalled when another embassy officer once loudly greeted her and other OSS analysts in a crowded restaurant as "the boys and girls of Omega Sigma Sigma!"

Wisner, who found that Macfarland could be disarming, for the moment had to bite his lip over the antics. Macfarland still headed up the mission. Wisner and the men he had brought with him were only taking over the secret intelligence branch of the OSS mission. But Wisner thought that Macfarland was a dangerous buffoon who was there only because he was an old pal of Donovan's. Operating in an environment as complicated as Istanbul—with hostile spies everywhere—was difficult enough for a seasoned intelligence professional. For amateurs like Macfarland and his subordinates, it could be disastrous.

Wisner had one of his men and an inspector flown in from Washington do autopsies of the Cereus chain. They concluded there wasn't much to salvage in the failed network. Harry Harper, the reports officer Wisner had brought with him, investigated Dogwood's organization for four weeks and delivered to his boss a grim eight-page secret report. With the arrest of the Sparrow team and other European sources, Schwarz's network had collapsed by June 1, Harper concluded. Of the twenty-eight agents Schwarz finally identified, Harper considered only five of them useful and he questioned how much value those five really had. A thorny problem now, as Harper saw it, was what should be done with Schwarz. He was too dishonest to be of further value. The crafty egotist was well-known among Axis spy agencies. He couldn't be retained, but he had to be let go in a way that wouldn't cause him to do more damage to the OSS out of anger.

Irving Sherman, the outside investigator Wisner brought in, took a huge swipe at Donovan in his report. "The organization we set up to handle Central European intelligence was unwisely conceived, badly staffed, and directed in the first instance by mediocrities," Sherman wrote, leaving unsaid that Donovan was the one who had organized the mission. "It was doomed to failure from the start, and it finds us today with nothing of our own available for secret intelligence from Central Europe."

Wisner agreed with the conclusions of both reports, and although he never made it explicit in his after-action memos, he also thought Donovan bore a healthy share of the blame for the mess in Istanbul. Even Macfarland knew enough to declare to Wisner on July 31 that he was completely shutting down the Cereus chain. But the move was not enough to save his career. Ten days later he was sent home. On August 10, Wisner assumed overall command as chief of the OSS mission in Istanbul. It was now his job to revive OSS operations in Central Europe.

* * *

From the balcony of his quarters, Wisner had a spectacular view of the Bosporus. He sketched the scene in a charcoal drawing. Like in Cairo, the Istanbul mission had pretty women, and Wisner and the other male officers often sailed with them down the strait on lazy weekends. On one voyage a Russian woman joined the Americans and drank everyone under the table, chugging red wine from a bottle. As he had in Egypt, Wisner became deeply interested in local history and customs in Turkey. He enjoyed learning about the country, and for the rest of his life, he came to love all things Turkish. He brought home a red fez that he wore around the house and he had a bagful of Turkish trinkets for his children.

The OSS mission he now led had thirty-four members under numerous covers, such as low-level diplomats, military attachés, businessmen, and even newspaper reporters. Two days after his taking over the mission, $75,000 was transferred to him under State

Department cover to pay for covert operations. Wisner realized that
there was not much he could do immediately with the money, but he
set about to move quickly on a number of small steps. He scrapped
useless operating procedures Macfarland had set up in the mission,
encouraged the energetic officers to do sound work, and got rid of
the deadwood, who were sent back to Washington with Macfarland.
Relations with the British and Turkish security services were improved. Wisner also managed to distribute large quantities of propaganda leaflets in neighboring countries the Nazis occupied.

There was one bold move that Wisner did propose. Emissaries
from Bucharest, the capital of Romania, had approached his intelligence team in Istanbul and told the OSS officers that the nation's
strongman, Marshal Ion Antonescu, wanted to break his alliance
with Germany and negotiate peace terms with the United States,
Great Britain, and the Soviet Union. Romania had been a loyal and
hard-fighting member of the Axis, granting Germany access to its
rich petroleum reserves and sending thirty of its army divisions to
join in Hitler's invasion of Russia. In return for becoming practically a satellite of Germany, Romania was allowed to annex valuable
regions to its north and northeast. But after the Wehrmacht offensive stalled at Stalingrad in early 1943 and the Romanians suffered
more than a half million casualties on the Eastern Front, a shaken
Antonescu began sending signals to the Allies that his country was
interested in switching sides in return for postwar protection guarantees.

When he first arrived in Istanbul, Wisner had been leery of
Macfarland's troubled mission launching any kind of big new operation. But now he believed a golden opportunity had fallen into his
lap. Both Romania and Bulgaria (Germany's ally to the south) appeared to him to be within weeks of quitting the Axis. Wisner asked
both the Cairo station and OSS headquarters in Washington to give
him permission to prepare to infiltrate an exploratory mission into
those two countries. If his bosses approved, Wisner thought he
could have a team in Bucharest within a matter of days. Donovan,

who had long been eager to penetrate the Balkans, gave him the green light. The spymaster alerted his Russian counterparts, whom he had been trying to cultivate in the war on Germany, that he intended to send an OSS team into Romania "for intelligence purposes only."

The evening of August 23, Wisner heard the startling news on BBC Radio. The dictatorial and anti-Semitic Antonescu had been ousted in a coup organized by Romania's King Michael. After installing a coalition government to replace the authoritarian regime, the monarch ordered the nation's army not to resist the advancing Russian troops and instead to train its weapons on the Germans. By then Wisner had all his plans in place to take advantage of the opportunity. The Romanians had already offered visas for an OSS team to enter the country. All Wisner needed to work out was a way to fly in his detachment.

Bulgaria remained a German ally for two more weeks. Wisner considered Romania the bigger prize of the two. An outpost in Bucharest might "develop into one of the most important single OSS bases on the continent," he wrote one of his superiors. Wisner might have been engaging in hyperbole, but he didn't think so. He convinced Washington to allow him to lead the OSS mission into Bucharest.

Chapter 7

BUCHAREST

A STOLEN LUFTWAFFE TRANSPORT plane with Wisner and an assistant on board landed at the Popeşti grass airfield northwest of Bucharest on September 1, 1944. For the mission, now code-named Hammerhead, Wisner had time to bring with him only a radio in a suitcase and a signal plan with frequencies for transmitting coded messages back to Istanbul. Rolfe Kingsley had stayed behind to run the Istanbul mission. Lieutenant Harper, Wisner's reports officer, would take a four-man team into Sofia, Bulgaria, several days later.

Wisner had climbed aboard the transport plane only after several days of heated negotiations with Romanian representatives in Istanbul. A Romanian air force officer had hijacked the German Junkers the night of the Antonescu coup and flown it to Istanbul. For the trip back, the transport took off before dawn and flew east and then north over the Black Sea, staying low to the water to keep under the German radar still functioning in Bulgaria. The pilot then flew westward, hedgehopping over the melee of Russian soldiers advancing, Germans retreating, and Romanian troops milling about in the Constanța area. The pilot could not be sure that a Russian or German soldier would not fire a shot to bring the plane down. Before taking off, he had been able to at least confirm that the Popeşti airfield and the area around it were free of Germans.

Romania had launched its military operations against Germany and Hungary a week earlier. The Soviets' 2nd Ukrainian Army now had the services of 141,916 Romanian enlisted soldiers with their 6,899 officers. Chaos reigned. Though in disarray, Wehrmacht troops still fought street to street in parts of Bucharest and battled to hold the Ploieşti oil fields north of the capital. A Russian tank column moved south through Bucharest to the Danube River, where Soviet units concentrated. Meanwhile, some seventy German warplanes remained near the capital. As his plane circled the airfield, Wisner was astounded to see two American B-17 Flying Fortresses parked near the runway. All communications between Bucharest and Istanbul had been cut, so Wisner knew next to nothing about conditions in the country when he arrived. He made a mental note to check out why on earth the U.S. warplanes were there.

Wisner had had no time to pack any clothes in his rush to get aboard the transport plane. He had brought none of his uniforms. Until they arrived more than a month later, he had to improvise. He found a Bucharest tailor who fashioned for him an Eisenhower-like combat tunic with an American flag sewn on one shoulder and a sealskin cap with a U.S. Navy insignia stitched to it. A shoemaker sold him boots that looked like they had come from the Romanian cavalry. He looked like he was going out on Halloween in a costume his mother had made for him to be a British commando with American Navy patches. He would have been court-martialed if he had worn that outfit back home, he knew, but there was nobody there to charge him.

Wisner was thrilled to finally be at the front. "I have caught up with the war and I do not intend to get behind it again," he later wrote Polly, who did not know what front he was at. Numbering all his letters so his wife could keep track of the ones that reached her at the Quarry Close farm and the ones that didn't, Wisner always wrote that he was in the fictional country of "Ruritania."

From the Popeşti airfield Wisner found a car and driver to take him to the newly formed Romanian government, which had moved to the Romanian National Bank building, a solid structure chosen because it had been safe from the German aerial and artillery bombing of the preceding week. He marched right in and found the government in session. A Romanian official took him to Prime Minister Constantin Sănătescu, who was meeting with government ministers. They included Valeriu C. "Rică" Georgescu, the undersecretary of state for the national economy, who had been alerted by Romanian representatives in Istanbul that Wisner was coming and who later became valuable in opening doors for him in the government. Wisner found the foreign minister in the group and talked him into sending the plane back to Istanbul to bring the rest of his team of nine intelligence officers and enlisted men along with their equipment. Three of the OSS officers Wisner wanted flown in spoke passable Russian. A number of others, whose parents had come from Romania, were fluent in that language.

Wisner also discovered why the two American B-17s were parked at Popeşti. Unknown to him, a team of nine officers and three enlisted men from the U.S. 15th Air Force and the OSS had flown in the two bombers with fighter escorts to the airport to begin evacuating thirteen hundred fifty Allied airmen shot down on bombing runs over Romania. The new government was releasing them from prison camps. Among the OSS men were research analysts and field photographers sent to assess the damage Allied bombers had done to the Ploieşti oil fields.

* * *

The OSS contingent in Bucharest quickly grew to fourteen officers and seven enlisted men. Wisner became the top U.S. spy in Romania with the communications, housekeeping, and intelligence-collection sections under him. For a young Navy lieutenant commander, the responsibilities and power he had quickly accumulated were heady. And it was happening in a city known as the

"Little Paris" of Eastern Europe for its bohemian airs, café-lined city streets, erotic vaudeville shows, beautiful women, and cultured men (some with varnished fingernails).

Bucharest had also become an espionage haven like Istanbul. Germany's Abwehr and Gestapo used the Romanian capital as a base for collecting intelligence in Southeastern Europe and the Middle East. Britain's MI6 soon found the city valuable for launching operations into Germany. Soviet agencies recruited snitches among the local Communists. Journalists from the belligerent nations roamed the city collecting tidbits that they passed along to intelligence officers (Wisner soon became one of their recipients). A favorite nest for the spies was the fashionable Athénée Palace Hotel, which was close to the Royal Palace.

As the Red Army moved in to take over the capital, Wisner's OSS team found vehicles to rent and established a radio link with the OSS headquarters in Bari, Italy, to help the Air Force contingent arrange for B-17 bombers to shuttle former POWs out of the Popeşti airfield. His men also photographed the procession of Russian combat forces that now rumbled through the streets of Bucharest. Wisner was surprised at how few vehicles there were in their columns. Most of the soldiers marched on foot or crowded atop some of the tanks or they rode on horse-drawn carts of all shapes and sizes. He learned later that many of the ragged troops had broken into stores of liquor and engaged in widespread looting, rape, and murder as they made their way through the countryside toward Bucharest. It took Russian officers ten days to bring a halt to the pillaging, Wisner reported to his superiors. Donovan and Lieutenant General Pavel Fitin, who headed the foreign intelligence department of the People's Commissariat for State Security, or NKGB, had reached an agreement that Soviet troops would not bother Wisner's team.

Wisner and his aides set up their headquarters and residence in the grandiose thirty-room mansion at 5 Alea Modrigan, which was bathed in floodlights and known as the Colossus. Mitu Bragadiru, who ran the largest beer brewery in the country, owned the estate.

He and other wealthy Bucharest residents were eager to let the Americans move into their homes to head off the Russians seizing their property. Still, Bragadiru did not hide his Nazi sympathies, trying at one point to convince one of Wisner's officers that the Germans were actually "gentlemen."

The mansion, with Romanian guards posted outside, was quickly bustling inside with Wisner's team and members of the 15th Air Force contingent installing offices there. Rooms were cleared for a communications center. Bragadiru's cooks and servants served meals in the mansion's large dining room. A garden outside was converted into a crowded parking lot for the Americans' motor pool. Neighbors were happy to loan Wisner their Fords, Cadillacs, and Mercedes limousines to keep them from being confiscated by the Russians.

The "Beer Baron of Bucharest," as Bragadiru was informally known, moved to the servants' quarters next to the mansion with his twenty-four-year-old wife, the beautiful Alexandra "Tanda" Caradja, who was a Romanian princess. Reportedly a descendant of Vlad the Impaler (also known as Vlad Dracula), Tanda had red hair and flashing green eyes. She was one of Bucharest's most skilled and gregarious hostesses, and she opened doors for Wisner among the royal family. The princess looked remarkably like Polly. But she was also a "psychopathic liar," as a longtime acquaintance who was no friend of Tanda described her to a U.S. intelligence official many years later.

Wisner wrote Polly about the "magnificent house" that he now occupied, adding that "my every want is cared for by a beautiful princess in whose eyes I can do no wrong." But he was quick to assure his wife that Tanda was "safely married." He labored nonstop every day until he collapsed into bed at night exhausted; he told Polly he believed he was "doing a fairly unique piece of work."

Much of the evacuation of airmen had been completed in the two days before Wisner arrived. His intelligence officers helped gather the remaining stragglers found in camps and hospitals. For the most part, the airmen had been treated well by their Romanian captors, who had refused to turn them over to the Germans. For those who needed medical help, American doctors, along with drugs and blood plasma, were flown in to treat them before they boarded aircraft. The Russians cooperated in the evacuation. Donovan cabled Pavel Fitin that he appreciated the help. For the U.S. airmen still flying combat missions, the return of their comrades provided a tremendous morale boost. Ground crews at a U.S. base in Caserta, Italy, cheered when planes carrying the former POWs landed.

Another important assignment Wisner's team took over was determining how much damage Allied air sorties had done to the Ploieşti oil facilities, which had helped fuel the Wehrmacht's war machinery. For more than a year, Ploieşti had been an important OSS intelligence target. It took some haggling, but Wisner managed to obtain clearance from the Russians to truck OSS analysts and experts from the 15th Air Force north to the fields so they could photograph damage and screen documents in order to assess the bombing's impact on German oil resources. From their inspection and review of facility records, Wisner's men concluded that the air raids had reduced Ploieşti's output to a small fraction of what it had been before the attacks.

Wisner's team also uncovered more targets that the 15th Air Force could strike, which the Russians could see was helpful for their offensive. His men were able to give intelligence officers at the Allied force headquarters in Caserta an idea of the composition of Hungarian and German divisions north of Bucharest in Transylvania and provided intelligence on the German submarine fleet in the Black Sea. Wisner quickly started receiving rave reviews from higher headquarters. A regular courier plane service was set up to rush several large bags of his intelligence reports to Caserta, where they were forwarded to American military headquarters in Cairo and London and to OSS headquarters in Washington, where Donovan passed them around to the Joint Chiefs of Staff, the State Department, and the White House. (The courier planes returned

to Popeşti with code pads, radio parts, American cigarettes, chocolate, and the chewing gum that Wisner always needed.) Caserta's
intelligence section began sending him daily questionnaires on information it urgently needed. Soon Wisner could see overhead
American Flying Fortresses on their way to attack targets his team
had identified.

Donovan fed to the NKGB's Fitin regular reports containing the
intelligence Wisner's team had produced on German deployments
and their oil reserves, along with updates on the Wehrmacht targets
Allied planes had attacked. The OSS chief had an ulterior motive in
this information sharing with the Soviet Union. The evacuation of
U.S. airmen and the targeting help Wisner's team provided the Russians became valuable cover for other spying Wisner and his officers
did, which Donovan knew Moscow would not appreciate.

The OSS director realized that he and Wisner had to tread cautiously with the Soviets, who never shed their paranoia that their
American and British allies were out to screw them. But so far, Wisner told Donovan, the Russians had bought his cover story that the
OSS team was strictly an American military unit evacuating downed
pilots and exchanging tactical information with their Red Army
partners. If the Soviets suspected the OSS team was spying on them,
Wisner believed they would shut down his radio communications
with the outside, which they hadn't done, he cabled Donovan. The
OSS chief was glad to hear that news. If the Soviets did try to interfere with the team's communications, Donovan wanted Wisner to
notify him quickly so he could get it stopped.

* * *

To build the espionage operation Donovan secretly wanted in Romania, Wisner had to start from scratch. He threw all his energy
into it, working late into the evening each day cultivating sources in
Bucharest, then spending each night radioing reports to Bari or preparing documents for the bags the courier plane picked up in the

morning. Fortunately for Wisner the Romanian government and Bucharest's high society welcomed him with open arms. He found it remarkable that so much intelligence was there for the picking. He developed a wide range of sources among top Romanian military officers, intelligence officials, the capital's political class, wealthy businessmen, government ministers, and political party leaders (even the Communists), all eager to help with insights and documents.

Wisner became lifelong friends with many of Romania's elite, like economics undersecretary Rică Georgescu and his glamorous wife, Lygea. The Georgescus and other prominent Romanians had self-serving reasons for cooperating. As autumn leaves began to fall, Romanians, some of whom had grown wealthy collaborating with the Nazis, fervently hoped American and British troops would replace the brutal Soviet occupiers they feared were intent on taking over the country and their businesses. Wisner could make no promises of Allied aid. Still, he was swamped with offers of help. He had daily interviews with top officials who received him without an appointment. He often brought along ground coffee and American cigarettes as icebreakers. Romanians offered jewelry, expensive cars, and medals to pin on his makeshift uniform. And soon he had walk-in access to top courtiers in the Royal Palace.

In his cables back to Washington, Wisner gave his Romanian sources disease code names like "Tonsillitis" for Teodore Manicatide (a general staff employee who delivered military intelligence on Germany, Hungary, and his own country) and "Appendicitis" for Dinu Alimanestealu (a former Romanian naval officer with lines into his country's sea service). Wisner's code name became "Typhoid."

* * *

Four years earlier, in September 1940, King Carol, dubbed "Carol the Cad" because of his kleptocratic reign, had abdicated with his mistress, leaving his eighteen-year-old son, Michael I, to rule as a figurehead under Antonescu. The fascist marshal had continued the

Romanian government's tradition of incompetence and corruption, taking in 200,000 German soldiers by 1941 as part of his Axis alliance. Though Michael, a great-great-grandson of Queen Victoria and a committed Anglophile, had succeeded with pro-Allied politicians and senior army officers in ousting Antonescu in August 1944, the twenty-two-year-old king and his "kindergarten" court (called that because of the youth of his advisers) were becoming hopelessly isolated by the fall of 1944 as the Red Army began to rule over his country. "An oversized playboy," as one of Wisner's officers described him, he roamed from palace to palace. Beloved as an outdoor sportsman, he spent many of his days socializing with Western diplomats.

Wisner thought it was important that he be among the Westerners in whom Michael confided. The king could give him a window into Romanian political disputes the palace had to referee. Wisner, however, first had to earn the confidence of the monarch, who kept things to himself and was slow to establish close relations with others. But the two men bonded quickly. Wisner presented Michael with a Dodge sedan and a U.S. Army jeep, the latter of which caused the monarch to lose his customary reserve and give the lieutenant commander a bear hug. Michael had Wisner as a guest at Peleş Castle, a royal retreat in the Carpathian Mountains where Wisner had a grand time bagging a gaggle of ducks on a hunt and showing off his weapons skills by using a mirror as he fired a rifle backward over his shoulder at a target. He also won over Queen Anne, who looked out for the Naval officer as he tiptoed around palace intrigues.

Soon Wisner was meeting regularly with Michael at the sprawling and well-guarded Royal Palace in Bucharest or with his senior advisers at posh hotels like the Ambassador or the Athénée Palace. He filed regular reports to Donovan on the infighting in the royal court, the squabbling among Romanian political factions, and the pressuring by Russian generals who wanted Michael to put in place a future Romanian government that was pro-Moscow. "[Rivals] in the government are bickering while the country is falling apart," Wisner worried in one memo that Donovan forwarded to the secretary of state. Michael might have to intervene. But as things stood, Wisner warned in another memo, "if the king is left too much alone, he will not be able to stand out against the increasing demands of the Communists and the Russians."

Tanda became a key ambassador for Wisner's acceptance by Romania's high society. The princess had the charm and dazzling good looks to escort Wisner around the capital and offer him entrée into virtually any social circle. Skilled at entertaining lavishly, she hosted gaudy balls and elaborate dinners at the Bragadiru mansion, where Wisner (who loved her cook's moussaka the best) could mingle with Soviet generals, senior Romanian civilian and military leaders, and influential young counselors from the palace. With flowing champagne, trays of cigarettes, and gay music from a small orchestra, dances at the Colossus, which sometimes stretched to dawn the next day, became the talk of the city—with the American Naval officer the sought-after celebrity at them. Wisner, though, was careful to keep his name out of the society columns of Bucharest newspapers. His men and he kept a light touch at the almost nightly parties in the Bragadiru mansion and other venues, letting the cocktail conversation flow where it might. Rarely were they disappointed with their intelligence take.

Wisner began sleeping with the princess. It was a wartime fling, though, and he never considered leaving Polly to be with his mistress. The affair was not a well-kept secret. Fellow OSS officers were soon aware that the two were lovers, and it was likely that the Romanians and the Russians knew as well.

After a month, Wisner's team vacated the Bragadiru mansion. "Eating, working, sleeping, drinking, and loving other men's wives, all under one roof while husbands and enlisted men were around, was just a bit too much for some of us," Robert Bishop, a counterintelligence officer on Wisner's team, wrote later. The Americans also needed more room. The team's new residence of marble and inlaid wood, almost as elegant as the Colossus, was a block and a half away at 33 Batiste Street. This mansion had been owned by Professor Mihai Antonescu (not closely related to Marshal Antonescu), Romania's dapper deputy prime minister and foreign minister during the war who would be executed for war crimes in 1946. Wisner never explained to Polly why his team had switched quarters, writing her only that the new mansion was "splendid." And there was a big surprise just before they moved in. Moreno Klarsfeld, a wealthy Jew and friendly local who had found the villa for Wisner (and who OSS counterintelligence officers later learned had been working for the Germans), discovered $12 million worth of gold that Mihai had stashed in the attic. It was hidden in sandbags along with Swiss banknotes, much of the loot stolen from Jews.

Wisner faced an extremely complicated situation in Bucharest, which he and the other OSS officers had little training or experience to navigate. It worried some of his staff. The Romanian elite who wined and dined them did not necessarily have America's best interests at heart. "These people were also the ones who quite brazenly referred to 'the next war,' meaning a war between Russia and the Anglo-Americans, which they would give their eye-teeth to help bring about," reported Sylvia Press, one of Wisner's counterintelligence operatives. She feared that some of her American colleagues "have forgotten that Romania was until recently an Axis satellite. Many Romanians speak very good English and are on the most intimate terms with American officers and men—who sometimes drink a little more than would appear wise in the circumstances." Press never fingered Wisner as one of the OSS officers becoming too cozy with the Romanians, but it was clear she had him in mind.

Wisner, however, was not naive to the fact that there were Romanians trying to play him. He knew he was walking a tightrope. He could see that all Romanians, except for the country's Communists, hated and feared the Russians. And the Russians hated and distrusted the Romanians. Wisner and his team were "subjected to strong conflicting pressure and it was necessary to exercise a constant caution and restraint in order to avoid the appearance of 'taking sides,'" he wrote in one memo to Washington. Wisner found that any slip of the tongue made by him or his officers—no matter how minor—was immediately seized upon "and magnified" by one faction or the other. He said he then had to scramble to correct "misapprehensions and misunderstandings."

Even with Romanian cooperation, Wisner found the spy work to be a grind. He had countless jobs to attend to. For more than a month, his headquarters was the center of U.S. operations in Romania. Wisner's spies and analysts produced the only military, political, and economic intelligence the Allies were receiving from the country. His communications shop provided the only radio channel to the outside world. His unit became the only link between American and British forces in the Mediterranean and the Russians. Woefully behind, the British had just one intelligence officer in Bucharest during that time. Wisner helped him transmit his messages to London. When more Allied officers began arriving in early October, the first briefing they had in-country was with this Navy lieutenant commander or one of his aides. Wisner loved being his own boss there. For the rest of his life, he considered Romania his best posting—more of a lifelong love in terms of the work he did than Cairo or Istanbul.

Donovan panicked when a rumor reached him at the end of September that the Russians had ordered Wisner to leave the country in forty-eight hours. The rumor proved to be false. But Donovan's reaction demonstrated how important Wisner had become to him. The spymaster was routinely forwarding Typhoid's reports to Roosevelt and other senior administration officials. Imperfect as it was, Wisner's networking during those first few weeks resulted in quite a haul of documents the Germans had left behind in their hasty retreat. His men scooped up armfuls of material on Romanian oil exports during their tours of the Ploieşti fields. Petroleum shipments and their destination ports in Germany were tracked from manifests at the international shipper Schenker and Company. The team found German military manuals and reports on Nazi intelligence operations that contained the identities of four thousand Axis officials and espionage agents. Gestapo, Abwehr, and consulate documents from the German embassy were turned over to Wisner by the Romanian general staff. Luftwaffe and Messerschmitt Aircraft Company offices in Bucharest were raided. Even Hitler Youth members in Romania were identified. In all, more than a ton of documents was discovered. Eight OSS analysts spent three months sorting, indexing, and flying the material back to Washington.

* * *

Donovan sent fifteen hundred pages of Nazi documents to the Russians. Wisner dutifully tried to cultivate good relations with the Red Army commanders who arrived in Bucharest. The Russians at first appeared to him to be friendly and polite, although a bit aloof, but willing to fraternize, at least for the moment. In the beginning, the Soviets did nothing to interfere with Wisner's extensive, and fairly obvious, dealings with the Romanian army's general staff. He found the Russians at first "not unduly inquisitive," he wrote in one after-action memo. Soviet officers even gave him occasional intelligence briefings. Donovan ordered him not to arouse Russian suspicions, which Wisner tried not to do.

At the Bragadiru and Antonescu estates, he hosted numerous dinners for senior Soviet officers, which could become drawn-out affairs with lots of vodka, whiskey, and singing. In photos of them mingling, the Soviet and American officers occasionally had relaxed looks on their faces. Wisner managed to pry smiles out of a half dozen Red Army officers when he showed an American movie after their dinner. At another dinner party, his team passed out cigarettes and ground coffee to staff aides and presented a matched pen and pencil set to Major General Ivan Burenin, the military commandant for the area, who liked the gift. Burenin, in turn, let Wisner's officers interrogate German prisoners. After lengthy negotiations Wisner was able to set up an arrangement for sharing intelligence with the NKVD counterespionage service (the People's Commissariat for Internal Affairs), although the two sides never completely opened up to each other. But Wisner persevered. His men even hired two local Communists to give them advice on how to schmooze with the Russians.

In Washington Donovan also hoped to portray himself as above-board, so he provided Fitin with the names of everyone in Wisner's Bucharest team. Surely the NKVD had already sniffed them out, the OSS chief reasoned. What Donovan did not tell Fitin was that Wisner was now under secret orders to devote more attention to targeting the Soviets with his spying. His network began to monitor closely the activities of the Red Army in Romania. Among the documents that Wisner's men found but did not share with the Russians were five thick books full of German intelligence reports on the Soviet armed forces. The Romanian navy slipped Wisner information on the Russian navy. Romanian agents on the OSS payroll were able to penetrate the Russian intelligence service and the local Communist party. To the delight of OSS counterintelligence officers, the heavily guarded villa that one top general, Vladislav Vinogradov, occupied at the corner of Dumbrava Roșie and Dimitrie Orbescu streets could be easily spied on by OSS officers in neighboring homes.

For a while, the Russian military command in Romania was confident that Wisner's operation was working only against the Germans. In early November 1944, Foreign Minister Vyacheslav Molotov phoned Bucharest from Moscow, curious about what Wisner was up to in the Romanian capital. The commander of the Soviets' 2nd Ukrainian Army cabled back that the OSS mission had been cooperating closely with his headquarters and had been a big help. For the moment, Molotov was satisfied.

* * *

At first, the Romanians were also appeased. The Russian presence might not be as bad as they feared, many thought. As soon as the

Red Army's high command had established its headquarters in Bucharest, discipline began to be enforced and orders went out to halt the looting. Tensions with the Soviets were easing daily, Wisner's men reported to Washington. The occupiers were correct in their interactions with the Romanians, though never particularly friendly. The same could be said for the other side. "When Russian soldiers pass, Romanians curse them and declare that the Germans were much better," an OSS report noted.

Still, restaurants now remained open until nine o'clock at night. Russian military police began patrolling Bucharest streets and making arrests among its soldiers, although thefts and rapes continued to be problems. Wisner's officers initially suspected that some of the incidents involving Russian troops were minor but the Romanian general staff had inflated them "for our 'benefit,'" as one put it.

The Russians laid down harsh armistice terms, demanding $300 million in reparations that appeared to be beyond the Bucharest government's ability to pay. But the Romanians intended "to carry out their obligations," Donovan told FDR. Roosevelt did not challenge dictator Joseph Stalin's demands. Because of the damage the Romanian army had inflicted on the Red Army, British prime minister Winston Churchill thought Stalin's terms were generous. To demonstrate that it wanted to cooperate, the Romanian government had also begun arresting its pro-Nazi army officers and senior cabinet officials who were guilty of war crimes, although the detentions did not come as fast as the Russians, Donovan, or Wisner wanted. The Soviets eventually gave the Bucharest government a list of forty-seven war criminals they wanted in jail immediately.

Romanian Communists who had been living in Russia began returning home. Stalin and his military commanders in Bucharest, however, did not think much of these exiles and at first had no intention of granting them special privileges or positions of power in their country. So far, senior U.S. diplomats did not believe that Moscow had any definite plans for Romania beyond making it pay dearly for collaborating with the Nazis. Wisner's sources alerted him to Romanians who had already sold out to the Russians, but Wisner thought these opportunists might be getting ahead of themselves. Top Romanian officials told him they did not believe that Stalin intended to "Sovietize the country," Donovan wrote Roosevelt.

On October 13, Wisner wrote an upbeat note to Polly. He was delighted that three of her letters had arrived two days earlier. He enclosed photos of some of the people who worked for him. Wisner was proud of how well Polly had kept home and family together at Quarry Close. His work in "Ruritania," he told her, kept him so busy, he had not had time to collect or spend his back pay as a lieutenant commander for nearly two months.

* * *

But as the fall days grew colder after September, Russian behavior changed. The Soviets' goal in Romania, which had been difficult for Wisner to decipher at first, became much clearer during the next six months. Step by step, the OSS team members could see Moscow's plan to openly harass and politically pressure Romania into becoming a Communist nation loyal to the Union of Soviet Socialist Republics unfold.

The reparations Stalin demanded, which turned out to be far more substantial than the Romanians had initially realized, were destroying their economy. For its occupation army, which would grow to 100,000 troops over the next four years, Moscow demanded 2.5 million tons of grain, vegetables, and tobacco; more than fifteen thousand horses; and nearly 1.75 million head of cattle—far more than the Romanian economy could deliver and still remain afloat. Russian troops resumed their looting, particularly of the country houses and agricultural equipment the wealthy owned. Some $2 billion worth of "legitimate war booty," as the Russians called it, was taken from businesses and individuals. Telephone and telegraph lines across the country were torn down. Red Army troops even ransacked the German legation building in Bucharest and carted off furniture.

It appeared to Wisner (and to British officers in the country) that the Soviets were intentionally trying to sabotage the Romanian economy with their heavy-handed pressure. Industrialists told him the winter wheat crop would be lost if the planting was not accomplished in the next few weeks. But the Russians had confiscated farm trucks and tractors, making the sowing impossible. On November 2 Wisner sent to Washington a memo alerting Donovan that the Soviets had begun removing hundreds of tons of drilling and refining equipment from the Astra Româna and Româna Americana refineries for shipment to the Soviet Union. The Russians, he warned, were "wrecking the Romanian petroleum industry."

Stalin also pivoted and began building up the Communist party in Romania. Moscow-trained activists arrived to help it organize. The Soviets gave the Romanian Communists arms that other political groups had to surrender and, for party muscle, salted their ranks with a number of thugs from the old Iron Guard fascist paramilitary organization. Communists were sent into factories to organize unions. They cleverly portrayed themselves in ways they knew would be popular among Romanian workers and peasants—all to reinforce the message that the country would be better off with a Moscow-friendly government. Land reform was overpromised. Russians confiscated medical supplies and equipment from the local Red Cross and turned them over to the Communists to distribute so they would get the credit.

Romania's free press was suppressed. The Russians also decided to banish American and British reporters from the country. Soviet troops confiscated private radios so Bucharest residents could not receive information from the outside. To compensate, Romanians clamored for American newsreels. Wisner did what he could, secretly distributing phonograph records, magazines, and films from the U.S. Office of War Information, which he had sneaked in from Istanbul.

Communists who wormed their way into the Romanian government blocked or made ineffective most of its programs. A reliable source told Wisner the Russians were also trying to undermine King Michael. In the successive coalition governments that were formed, the Communists focused on gaining control of key ministries, such as justice, public information, education, and interior. Romanian military assets were gradually siphoned off. The Russians ordered two Romanian warships along with their crews to sail to a Soviet harbor. Political opposition leaders were soon put under surveillance and then restricted from moving around the country at all. Pro-Communist demonstrations were organized, with the people ordered to attend the parades showing "little enthusiasm," according to a memo from Wisner's team. Also, incidents, many of them bloody, were staged and then blown out of proportion by the Communist media, which blamed them on "Fascist police methods" and "Hitlerite butchery."

Donovan relayed to Roosevelt ever-grimmer cables from Wisner. One sickening report from an OSS team member detailed Russian soldiers and a Red Army colonel systematically raping and beating German women who had worked as clerks in Bucharest and who had been interned at St. Catherine's Hospital in the capital after the Soviet takeover.

* * *

As they took control of Romania, the Russians became more hostile to the OSS team. After a month, the Soviets no longer bought Wisner's cover story that his officers were there to evacuate airmen (they had all been evacuated) or that his men were still assessing damage Allied bombers had inflicted and collecting intelligence on more German targets (most of that work had been completed as well). The Russians began to grumble openly about how long they would have to put up with these American spies in their midst. Wisner heard more and more that his officers were referred to as "imperialists" and "fascists" by their Russian counterparts. One December morning, he found his motor pool surrounded by Soviet soldiers who claimed his vehicles were fascist property the Red Army must confiscate. Romanians who worked with the team as clerks began to be harassed. Requests and complaints Wisner filed with the Russians went unanswered. It became too dangerous for OSS officers to observe demonstrations by opposition parties. On several occasions Wisner's men were threatened, and even arrested, by Soviet troops when they took photos of public anti-Communist demonstrations. Senior Russian officers never apologized when that happened.

Soon the Soviet combat soldiers following Wisner's operatives were replaced by better-dressed and clean-shaven security men. American intelligence officers estimated that twelve hundred NKVD operatives were now in Bucharest. Wisner's small team was no match for this battalion-sized force of seasoned security agents.

* * *

Romanians at first believed that Washington and London would protect them from the Russians taking over their country. To Donovan, Wisner sympathetically relayed their feelings of betrayal when it became clear that neither Roosevelt nor Churchill would come to the rescue. Challenging Russian control of Romania was never contemplated by the United States or Great Britain. In fact, unknown to Wisner, Churchill in October 1944 had struck a secret deal with Stalin and ceded to him control of Romania in exchange for British dominance in Greece. The United States never considered going to war with Russia to halt its takeover of Eastern Europe. The American public's opposition to a Soviet sphere of influence there was quixotic. Stalin knew it was. His intelligence agencies reported to him that the American people did not really care about the fate of Romania, Hungary, and Bulgaria, which had been German allies. Romania offered the United States its first window into the Cold War. But it was a window for observation only, not for intervention.

* * *

By mid-November, Wisner had forty-nine people working for him. He was a tough manager who did not put up with officers he considered unproductive, sending them home and letting Washington deal with the ruffled feathers. But Wisner had his own weaknesses, according to critics. At times he was lax with the team's finances, not keeping a close eye on the expense accounts of his officers.

There were also security lapses in his fast-moving operation. Romanian secretaries working for Wisner were found taking secret reports home to correct typographical errors, and safes containing classified material were left open in rooms where Romanian clerks roamed about. The OSS's work in Bucharest was "a fairly open secret," concluded counterintelligence officer Sylvia Press, who blamed, among others, chatty members of the Air Force delegation for leaks about Wisner's work. "Romanian girls and women frequently showed a surprising knowledge of OSS personalities," she said.

A cable from Donovan arrived in Bucharest on October 2 and it stung. In blunt language the OSS director warned Wisner about saying or doing anything in Romania that could be conceived as anti-Russian. Indirectly accusing Wisner of coloring the intelligence he cabled back to Washington, Donovan lectured that the Navy lieutenant commander and the officers under him should "report truthfully on the facts" and not show an anti-Soviet bias in their reporting.

Why the bolt out of the blue? Since 1943, Roosevelt and the Joint Chiefs had wanted to avoid ratcheting up tensions with the Russians. They did not want the Soviets to be targets of surveillance, and they especially did not want to take sides against them. Donovan had initially hoped for peaceful postwar coexistence with the Soviets. He had repeatedly sent instructions to his Bucharest station to maintain strict impartiality—particularly since no one in Washington appeared unduly alarmed by any of the Soviet moves in Romania. But Wisner had increasingly been sending up the chain of command reports that were critical of Russia's actions and that warned that Romania's situation was growing more dire.

Colonel John Toulmin, the OSS Cairo station chief who had seen Donovan's rocket, cabled Wisner not to take it "at all seriously." Wisner's reports were receiving a "favorable reaction" in the region and in Washington. They were considered "one of the big scoops of the war," Toulmin assured him. The old man "pops" a cable like that once in a while, "which doesn't make a great deal of sense." Toulmin did not find Wisner's reports slanted. Ignore Donovan's broadside, he told Wisner.

But Wisner, who was sensitive to criticism, could not ignore it. Up until then, Donovan had had nothing but praise for his reporting, which he deeply appreciated. Three days after the director's missive, Wisner fired back an equally blunt rebuttal. He told Donovan he couldn't understand why he was receiving this warning, insisting that his team had always been careful not to give "any impression whatever that we sympathize or take the part of Romanians as against Russians." His relations with Soviet commanders in Bucharest were "most cordial," he insisted—although clearly there were strains in those relations. Wisner did not respond directly to Donovan's critiques, but he did write that "we will continue to give broad coverage to all phases" of the "intelligence situation here." To demonstrate that he was not tilting toward the Romanians, Wisner cabled his superiors that he would not respond to King Michael's request for seven thousand rounds of ammunition for his Royal Guard. Wisner also accepted an invitation from the 2nd Ukrainian Army to have OSS officers join its headquarters as the Russian soldiers marched toward Budapest, Hungary. As for his reports on Soviet moves to take over Romania, Wisner continued filing unvarnished appraisals as he had before—alerting Donovan, for example, to pro-Russian propaganda in Bucharest and Communist mischief making in the government. Donovan continued forwarding these reports to Roosevelt.

Donovan, however, was not the only one critical of bias in

Wisner's reports. Some officers on his team worried that Wisner had too aggressive an attitude toward the Soviets. Bureaucratic warfare erupted between Army major Robert Bishop, Wisner's counterintelligence chief, who insisted his sources echoed Wisner's dark view of Soviet intentions, and two intelligence officers, Army lieutenant Louis Madison and Navy lieutenant junior grade Henry Roberts, who complained that Bishop's exaggerated reports conveyed a false impression that the Russians were behaving too heavy-handedly. Charges flew back and forth among the officers. Bishop accused Madison and Roberts of being Russian dupes and anti-Romanian. Bishop was eventually charged with falsifying alarming reports about the Russians, drinking too heavily, and living openly with a Romanian woman accused of having been a German agent. Wisner realized he had a problem with his counterintelligence operation. He tended, however, to side with Bishop, although there was strong evidence the major had trafficked in fictitious reports. Bishop reciprocated by spreading nasty rumors about Wisner's security breaches.

* * *

New Year's Eve 1944, Wisner sat down to write a long-overdue letter to his mother as he gazed out the window of a room in King Michael's Peleş Castle that had a spectacular view of the snow-covered Carpathians. The Neo-Renaissance palace made him feel like he was living in a fairy tale. Wisner signed his note "Brother," as he had with his college letters. Oddly, though, he wrote to his mother in the third person.

The Romanian king and queen treated him as if he were fellow royalty. At lunch that day, Anne had presented him with a beautiful silver-and-gold cigarette case. On Christmas Eve, Wisner and another officer had hosted a lavish party for all the Americans in Bucharest. They sang carols from sheet music he had mimeographed for them. The king and queen were now giving him refuge in the castle for two days of much-needed rest. Wisner was worn-out from the whirlwind of entertainment, from spying in Romania and reporting to Washington, from the constant jousting with the Russians, and, just recently, from coping with an expanded American presence in Bucharest.

By late November, Wisner's short tenure as America's top military man, intelligence officer, and diplomat in Romania had come to an end. Army brigadier general Cortlandt Van Rensselaer Schuyler arrived with a retinue of staff officers to lead the American Military Mission for Romania and to be the U.S. representative to the Allied Control Commission, which was a joint American, British, and Soviet organization set up to oversee Romania's armistice terms. A descendant of three of New York's oldest families and a West Point graduate, Schuyler was a no-nonsense career officer and a stickler for observing the chain of command. He would brook no freelancing by Wisner's spies. The general had been preceded by Burton Y. Berry from the State Department, who became the senior U.S. diplomat in Romania. A Balkan expert and a private person, Berry disdained the party circuit Wisner enjoyed cruising to rake up information.

Wisner had known his days of being America's sole minister in Romania would not last long. It was now important for him to stay on good terms with Schuyler and Berry. In other countries, relations between an OSS station chief and the American plenipotentiary were often strained. Diplomats sought to stay in a host nation's good graces, while spies stole secrets and broke local laws that disrupted those ties. Wisner did not want that kind of tension repeated in Romania. He went out of his way to help Schuyler's large team of some fifty aides settle in, familiarizing them with local customs and providing them with cars, a security detail, and contacts in the Romanian government and intelligence. He also ceded the Antonescu mansion to Schuyler's retinue. Wisner's unit moved to a building a block away on Strada Oțetari. The gracious lieutenant commander impressed the Army general, who said the Romanian contacts Wisner sent his way "have proven invaluable."

But Schuyler made it clear from the beginning that this Navy man now worked for him. The general was impressed with the job Wisner had done developing sources and collecting intelligence. But Schuyler, who had brought several military intelligence officers with him, ordered that he be kept fully informed of the clandestine operations Wisner mounted and the intelligence reports he produced. Schuyler also told Wisner firmly that the OSS unit must maintain "cordial relations" with the Russians. He wanted nothing to disrupt his work on the Allied Control Commission. No surprises. No incidents. The general did not want to be embarrassed. To calm the Soviets, Schuyler ordered that the OSS staff be reduced to seven officers and eight enlisted men.

Wisner was dumbfounded by that directive. The NKVD vastly outnumbered his tiny force. But he carried out the cutbacks. Wisner agreed that Schuyler and Berry must now be the arbiters of who collected what from whom in the country. The general and his top diplomat should be able to cultivate King Michael and his court for intelligence. (The Russian command soon got wind of Schuyler consolidating his hold on American operations in Romania and assigned the NKVD to begin tailing the general.) But Wisner balked when Berry told him he wanted to take over all the intelligence duties from Wisner's unit. So did Donovan when he learned of Berry's power play. The good relations Wisner had wanted to maintain with the diplomat became strained.

As he was writing his New Year's Eve letter to his mother from Peleş Castle, Wisner was still dickering with Berry to keep the OSS team spying in Romania. Berry had a right to collect intelligence, Wisner agreed, but so did he. The spy and the diplomat finally reached an uneasy truce on sources. Two days after Thanksgiving in 1944, Wisner had cabled Caserta that three new Russian infantry divisions would be arriving in Romania by December 1, not to pass through but instead to expand the occupation army. Two days later, after consulting with Berry, Wisner cabled Caserta again that the Russians had stripped more than one thousand tons of casting and tubing from the Româna Americana Oil Company and put it on a train to Moscow. With Berry's okay, Wisner protested to General Vinogradov, who insisted the American-owned equipment was legitimate war booty and refused to halt its removal.

As 1944 ended, Wisner decided that his mission in Romania had shrunk to the point that there was no reason for him to remain in the country any longer. It was inevitable, he knew, that he would be supplanted by Schuyler and Berry, but it felt humiliating nonetheless. He had developed close friends in Bucharest's government and aristocracy, but he had to give them up as sources to the U.S. officials over him. Besides, there was the practical problem that he was "too well marked" by the NKVD at this point "to be able to function on a clandestine basis," he admitted in one memo.

Wisner confided to his mother in his New Year's Eve letter that the OSS would let him leave Romania in a couple weeks. He planned to fly to Italy first for briefings with his superiors and then make his way back to the United States by February, hopefully to enjoy a few weeks' leave with Polly and the children before taking a new assignment.

Wisner had had his fill of Russian *and* American commanders handcuffing his actions in a foreign country. He cabled Donovan that he wanted a "more active area" for his next assignment. The OSS director, who said he remained "deeply impressed" with how his young Navy officer had handled himself in Bucharest, promised he would talk with Wisner about a next assignment—possibly in Central Europe or the Far East.

Wisner wrote his mother, but did not tell Donovan at this point, that he was not as eager as he once was to set up a new OSS station. During the past seven months in Istanbul and Bucharest, Wisner wrote Jeannette, he had had two "extremely exacting assignments and have just about had my share of the work of setting up new bases." But Wisner's superiors recognized that he had a talent for jumping into difficult situations and creating intelligence operations from nothing. Wisner did not know it then, but this would become his life's work. He had developed a talent for being a pioneer.

* * *

Until the end of his mission, Frank Wisner continued to send Donovan's headquarters cables that Moscow was intent on establishing pro-Soviet regimes in all of Eastern Europe. He was presaging the Cold War. Wisner, however, was losing heart. Washington was not listening to his warnings.

The final personal blow for him came in January 1945, shortly before he left for Washington. Under direct orders from Stalin, Soviet soldiers quickly began rounding up what would be more than eighty thousand ethnic Germans in Romania (men and women aged sixteen to forty) and loading them in the dead of winter into railcars bound for labor camps at Russian mines. Berry also reported this human tragedy to the White House. No distinction was made between Romanians of German origin who had supported Hitler and those who had not. Bodies were just needed to fill slave labor quotas at the mines. OSS officers watched helplessly as roads were blocked off, houses were searched, and civilians were marched out and piled into the backs of military trucks for the drive to a rail yard. On January 12, Wisner rushed to the crowded Mogoşoaia train station to witness the deportation. At tremendous risk to himself, he managed to convince indifferent Russian soldiers to remove a few acquaintances from the deportation list. But he could do nothing for the other poor souls being packed thirty to a boxcar.

In his final intelligence report from Bucharest, Wisner struggled to remain balanced in his estimate of Soviet intentions in Romania. He settled for leaving it as an open question. The U.S.S.R. had been "careful to avoid giving the appearance of taking over the country," Wisner wrote. It was still too early to conclude this was "the Russian ultimate objective." But Wisner was privately sure that it was. The Romanian deportations convinced him of the utter ruthlessness of Soviet intentions toward Eastern Europe. They shook him to the core. For the rest of his life, he held a personal grudge against the Russians. In Romania he began his long cold war against the Soviet Union. "Frank was always frightened to death by what he had seen in Romania," Polly later recalled. Witnessing "the Russians putting collars on German prisoners," shoving them "into boxcars and sending them off into the wild. . . . He really felt more strongly about it than anything I can remember."

* * *

Before heading back to the United States, Wisner turned in the .45-caliber pistol he had never had occasion to use and checked out an olive drab canvas field bag in which to pack what few clothes he possessed. He had to obtain Soviet clearance to fly out of Bucharest, which the Americans always found galling because sometimes it could take weeks to be approved.

Wisner left the Romanian capital in late January, stopping in Athens before he arrived in Caserta for several weeks of debriefings at its OSS station. In Caserta he met with top generals and sat down with W. Averell Harriman. The U.S. ambassador to the Soviet Union was on his way from Moscow to Yalta, the resort city on the Crimean Peninsula's southern coast, for Roosevelt's meeting with Churchill and Stalin to discuss postwar reorganization of Germany and Europe. For three hours one evening, Wisner briefed Harriman on what he believed was the Kremlin's plan to control Romania and other Balkans nations. Wisner was convinced Stalin would do as much as he thought he could get away with. Harriman gave him "a full hearing," Wisner recalled. "However, since this was on the eve of the Yalta Conference . . . there was still room for hope that the situation might not be as serious as I feared."

In early February, Wisner flew to Casablanca and from there boarded a plane to Washington. Back in the United States, he was awarded the prestigious Legion of Merit medal for his work in Romania. (He had Polly's father frame a copy of its citation.) His superiors lavished praise on him. "One is impressed with the varied and important accomplishments of the Bucharest City Team," a senior OSS officer wrote. Notwithstanding the one sour note that Donovan had cabled, the fact that none of the customers who received his intelligence complained about the product "is an indication of the efficiency of OSS, Bucharest," the senior officer's memo continued. "It was an independent, largely self-sustaining unit—able to get on with a minimum of housekeeping from above." In other words, Wisner did not require a lot of babysitting in the field.

Bishop notwithstanding, Wisner also developed a devoted following of officers who worked under him. "I have never seen a fellow my own age handle himself with such ability, firmness, and yet finesse, as Wisner has done," Marine captain William Cary, Wisner's executive officer in Bucharest, wrote to Donovan. Cary claimed several State Department diplomats told him privately that they found "Wisner's political reporting as frequently more thorough than Berry's." Even Berry acknowledged that the Navy lieutenant commander was a skilled intelligence operative. Yes, Wisner's Bucharest team made "slight mistakes," wrote Colonel Edward Glavin, whom Donovan had made head of the OSS's Italian operations. But Bucharest was "an excellent 'dry run' for what we will go through [with the Soviets] in Sofia, Belgrade, Budapest, and Vienna."

In the canvas bag he lugged back to Washington, Wisner brought a book of Romanian stamps that Donovan presented to a grateful Roosevelt, who was an avid collector. He also had in his bag a letter King Michael asked to be delivered to FDR; it gave the monarch's assessment of the peril Romania faced. Wisner's view of recent developments in the Balkan nation was different from what the White House was seeing in the newspapers, Donovan told Roosevelt. It would be worthwhile for White House aides to discuss this with Wisner, who had just arrived in Washington, the OSS director advised. However, there was no evidence Wisner ever briefed FDR's senior aides.

In frail health, Roosevelt had just returned from Yalta, where he had not pressed the Romanian issue with Stalin. Roosevelt had had other priorities, such as securing Russian cooperation in the Pacific War and deciding the fate of Germany after the war ended. He had not intended to confront Stalin over the Red Army's moves in Eastern Europe. Roosevelt's concern about Stalin's intentions for that region was growing, but the American president's focus there was directed toward Poland, where he felt the United States had a greater chance of exerting its influence. FDR did not consider Romania, with its seamy history of alignment with Nazi Germany, a good test case.

Over the ensuing months, Communist tactics in Romania and other East European nations became so aggressive and relentless that they weakened the will in the region to resist and sapped the energy of opposition leaders. Donovan watched as the Communists also increasingly made life difficult for the OSS city teams in the Russian-controlled countries. Moscow refused to allow OSS contingents to enter Budapest and Warsaw. Donovan's officers were forced out of Bulgaria by December 1944 and out of Romania and Albania by September 1945. American spying in those East European countries would now have to be done by agents operating covertly.

* * *

Wisner landed in Washington on February 8, 1945, and after several days of meetings at OSS headquarters on Navy Hill, he took the train to New York to reunite with Polly and the two boys at the Park Avenue apartment to which his wife had relocated the family. He came with an assortment of souvenirs from Romania—Wehrmacht medals; a shard of the church next to the Royal Palace, which the Germans had bombed; and a Romanian icon. He had had a German pistol, but the children never saw it because customs agents at his arrival airport had confiscated it. He also came with a wealth of war stories that for years captured the rapt attention of his children.

Wisner was devastated to learn that many Romanian employees at the U.S. mission in Bucharest had eventually been jailed on trumped-up espionage charges. Romanian security services tortured many to sign confessions. A Romanian secretary who had served as Wisner's translator killed herself so Soviet agents couldn't force her to incriminate her American friends in the mission. Wisner pressed State Department officials to help Romanians flee the country. He remained forever loyal to friends he had made in Bucharest, such as Rică Georgescu, whose children Wisner helped reach the United States after they had been held hostage in Romania by its security service. In droves, Romanian exiles became regular guests at his home. The country remained always his first love—the tragic victim, he thought, of Soviet evil and American indifference. He considered it one of the great failures of his intelligence career that he had not been able to change that reality. After he left Bucharest, a Romanian comrade wrote Wisner mournfully: "We have been separated from a true friend who understood us so well."

Chapter 8

BERLIN

POLLY WAS OVERJOYED TO have her husband home, even if it would be only briefly. "Brother has arrived safely," she telegraphed Wisner's mother in Laurel. "All is well."

Wisner could not say a lot about his overseas assignments, but he did tell Polly and friends that his work in Cairo, Istanbul, and Bucharest had been the most interesting and exciting he had ever done. He marveled that he had made friends with extremely interesting people. He was deeply grateful to the OSS for giving him the opportunity. Practically overnight, the agency had propelled him into the upper tier of America's national security community. Wisner was deeply proud of the note from Roosevelt thanking him for the stamps. He received it shortly before FDR's death on April 12.

Wisner was anxious to return to Europe, perhaps for more duty in the Balkans. A posting in the Far East did not sound attractive to him. While in Washington for six weeks, he had a physical exam, which declared him, at age thirty-five, to be fit to head back overseas. His blood pressure was low, his heart rate was normal, and he had twenty-twenty vision in both eyes and no allergies.

Two days later another doctor gave him a quick psychological exam, which was required of all OSS officers returning from overseas. The doctor could immediately see that the Navy lieutenant commander was "a superior officer," he wrote in his interview report. "He has forcefulness, tact and high intelligence." An energetic and confident young lawyer, Wisner was "proud of his past work in the Balkans" and well he should have been, the doctor noted. Wisner was a "diligent, self-critical individual who has sufficient energy to organize and lead a complex and stressful mission." The doctor, though, had a curious sentence at the end of his report observing that Wisner had "no significant signs of emotional instability." The fact that the physician used the adjective "significant" might have indicated that he had seen some slight symptom of mental instability, but it was not enough to disqualify Wisner from further duty.

For a while, headquarters considered posting Wisner to Czechoslovakia to be the senior OSS adviser to the U.S. ambassador in Prague—a position for which he was overqualified. Instead, Wisner was given a top secret security clearance and ordered to be in Germany when the Nazis surrendered. The orders came with a spot promotion to commander.

Within months after the June 6 landing at Normandy, the Allies had believed it would be only a matter of time before the Third Reich surrendered. The OSS had begun planning for a large intelligence operation inside Germany nine months before the Nazi capitulation on May 7, 1945. General George C. Marshall (the Army's chief of staff) and General Dwight Eisenhower's Supreme Headquarters Allied Expeditionary Force (SHAEF) favored having the OSS lead the intelligence mission in occupied Germany. Donovan had the trained experts the Allied forces would need, they felt. Wisner considered occupied Germany a dreary sequel to exotic Bucharest. It would be a complicated environment, he thought, not one that he would find pleasant. But his would be a far larger job than the one he had had in Bucharest. Donovan envisioned the OSS's German mission having two hundred intelligence and research officers along with 285 enlisted and clerical personnel to support them. Wisner would be their immediate supervisor.

On Victory in Europe Day, May 8, Eisenhower had more than 1.5 million men in sixty-one divisions in Germany. Allen Dulles, one of Donovan's stars, was picked to lead the OSS mission for Germany. The son of a liberal Presbyterian minister, Dulles had had his initial taste of spying as a first secretary with the American legation in Bern, Switzerland, during World War I. During the interwar years, he became wealthy as an attorney for the powerful Sullivan & Cromwell law firm in New York. Shortly after the Allies' Torch invasion of North Africa in November 1942, Dulles slipped back into Bern and set up a major OSS station for Donovan, running highly successful espionage operations against the Germans. Wisner would be Dulles's number two man, running the mission's day-to-day spying operation as its chief of secret intelligence.

On VE Day, Wisner inched his way down Paris's Champs-Élysée. He took out a camera and photographed the joyous throng of hundreds of thousands packing the wide avenue, and became swept up in the celebration himself. Wisner had been in Paris since April 26, picking officers for his staff and preparing plans for a postwar secret intelligence operation not only in Germany but also in four other countries his mission would oversee—Poland, Austria, Switzerland, and Czechoslovakia.   •

Richard Helms joined Wisner in Paris for three weeks to help him assemble the German team. Born into a wealthy family and educated in Europe, Helms had joined United Press as a Berlin correspondent after earning a Phi Beta Kappa key at Williams College. Covering the 1936 Nazi Party Congress in Nuremberg, Helms joined a half dozen other reporters for a lunch with Adolf Hitler, who impressed him as intent on going to war. After Pearl Harbor, Helms had been happy plotting merchant ship movements as a Navy officer until the OSS arranged for him to be transferred to its headquarters in August 1943. Donovan's agency had sent a request to the Navy for an officer who spoke French and German, had lived overseas, and had worked as a journalist. An IBM computer in the Navy's personnel office spit out Helms's name and he was now in the intelligence business. Helms had come to Paris from Luxembourg, where he had worked undercover on a project, pretending to be part of an Economic Analysis Unit. Back in Washington he had culled the names of thirty-five OSS officers who spoke German and would be suitable for the German mission.

On May 30, Wisner boarded a cargo plane for the little more than two-hour flight to Wiesbaden, Germany. Once more not knowing what to expect when the aircraft landed, he wore a steel helmet and a shoulder holster with a .45-caliber pistol. In his duffel bag, he had packed a change of uniform, wool blankets, a sleeping bag, and a can of insecticide powder.

General Omar Bradley had set up his 12th Army Group headquarters at Wiesbaden, a spa city on the Rhine west of Frankfurt where the Reich's wealthy had once rejuvenated themselves in the hot sulfur baths. Though some buildings had been flattened, Allied bombers had left intact a number of downtown structures, such as the casino and the main theater, as well as many plush villas in the Biebrich suburbs. Helms had established the OSS mission's headquarters in Biebrich at the cellars that produced Henkell Trocken, a favorite of Foreign Minister Joachim von Ribbentrop; the building had been bombed but sparkling wines were still made and stored there. Helms commandeered eight homes and an apartment building near the Henkell Trocken cellars to house the OSS staff and set up the mission's offices in the company's administrative building with its sweet sparkling wine smell. An officers' club called the "Battle Could" was soon organized to serve the bubbly for a dime a glass.

Wisner found Wiesbaden, even with its surviving amenities, to be "quite dreary," not a place in which to relax, he wrote his mother. Germany was "a beaten sullen country," he told her. Except for insolent teenagers, Wisner's men found Germans "disgustingly servile," as one OSS memo put it. Overwhelmed by the day and night bombing, the survivors had had their spirits deadened to apathy.

More than 4 million German soldiers had died in the conflict, nearly 2 million German civilians had perished, and more than 16 million had been driven from their homes. So few men were left in the country after the war, bigamy became widespread. The problems facing the German people and their occupiers "are so numerous and great as to stagger the imagination," Wisner wrote his mother.

Europe descended into anarchy immediately after VE Day. Many governments had been demolished or forced into exile, borders had been erased, towns and cities had been destroyed (seventeen hundred of them in the Soviet Union), forests had been lost, a millennium of precious architecture had been wiped out, and vast swaths of land were now devoid of humans. Up to 40 million people lay dead; another 40 million were displaced and on the move. The violence continued. Civil wars and ethnic cleansing erupted. Across the continent, vengeful victors beat, murdered, and enslaved the vanquished. Red Army savagery toward German civilians became so intense, Stalin ordered it scaled back, fearing a backlash. Germany became a land of wanderers and refugees. Millions of liberated slaves emerged from farms, factories, and mines. Some fifty thousand Jews surfaced, most in dreadful physical condition. Orphans by the hundreds of thousands roamed across the country, many in packs like wild animals. Among the millions of displaced persons, Nazi war criminals and collaborators moved surreptitiously with new identities and forged papers.

Hunger, malnutrition, and disease literally crippled Germans so that many of them could not work a full day. The economic life of the country was paralyzed. When Wisner arrived in Wiesbaden, Germany's industrial production stood at not more than 2 percent of existing capacity. "The normal food ration was only about 900 calories per day," according to one U.S. Army report.

Shortly after Wisner showed up at Wiesbaden, so did Dulles, on July 7. Wisner found morale at the sparkling wine cellars buoyed immediately when the famed Bern station chief got there to assume his duties. Less than two weeks later, however, Dulles was off to

Potsdam, on the southern outskirts of Berlin, where Harry Truman (who had become president after FDR's death), Stalin, Churchill, and Clement Attlee (who became prime minister after Churchill's defeat in Britain's general election) were meeting in the mock-Tudor Cecilienhof Palace of Crown Prince "Little Willie." Their conference to plan the postwar peace ratified the division of Germany into four occupation zones for American, British, French, and Russian forces and the capital of Berlin into four sectors for the powers. Intent on establishing a Soviet sphere of influence in Eastern Europe, Stalin insisted on pro-Moscow governments in the region as buffers against future invasions across his western border. As Roosevelt had, Truman insisted on the right of self-government for the war-ravaged East European nations, but, like FDR, he did not intend to press that demand to the point of starting another war, this one with Russia.

Dulles was in Potsdam to brief Henry Stimson, Roosevelt's war secretary who remained at that post under Truman, on the Japanese peace feelers he had received while still chief of the Bern OSS station. Stimson did not tell Dulles of the news Truman learned on the way to Potsdam: scientists in New Mexico had just succeeded in testing a nuclear device.

After returning from Potsdam, Dulles in August moved with Helms to the American sector in Berlin to set up his office while Wisner remained at the Wiesbaden headquarters to run intelligence collection for Germany and the four other countries under the mission's jurisdiction. Donovan asked that Dulles be given a civilian rank equivalent to that of a general and Berlin quarters fit for a military flag officer. The Pentagon balked. Dulles, instead, was assigned quarters at a comfortable but small villa on Im Dol Strasse in the upper-class Dahlem neighborhood of the Zehlendorf district, which Allied bombers had not destroyed. Helms and an espionage team of thirty took over a three-story brick office building at 19 Föhrenweg Strasse; inside it were an air raid shelter, an escape tunnel, and massive steel doors at each level. The building had once served as headquarters for a German general involved in the July 20, 1944, Valkyrie plot to assassinate Hitler.

Dulles at first wanted the mission's units in Wiesbaden and Berlin to hide their OSS affiliation—no names or phone numbers to appear on any published list—suggesting that they operate under the cover of an economic and political reconstruction organization for Germany. He believed Germans would be more friendly toward that kind of organization than toward what they might regard as a "secret police institution with which they will try to avoid contact," he wrote Donovan. He soon settled for a lighter cover, realizing that he would never be able to keep his mission secret from the Russians, and allowed his officers to mingle freely with German professional people and businessmen to develop sources.

Working for the Berlin mission chief took some adjusting on Wisner's part. Dulles looked like the headmaster of an upper-class English boarding school, usually dressed in a bow tie and tweed sport coat, his wiry gray hair slightly mussed, his mustache carefully trimmed, and a pipe almost always clenched between his teeth. He had sparkling gray-blue eyes and a soft voice that invited people to pour their hearts out to him. But Dulles's secretive nature could be maddening. One of his agents once joked that if you asked him "if it was raining outside, he'd laugh at you" and not tell. Occasionally it was a hearty laugh, when he was genuinely amused, but more often it was a mirthless "ho-ho" that he turned on when he was trying to ingratiate himself with a stranger or to deflect a question he did not want to answer. The country gentleman routine also masked a fierce competitor not willing to give up a single point on the tennis court—"a back alley fighter," as one of his agents put it—and a devious man who sized up people based on whether they could be useful to him.

Wisner and Dulles developed a distant relationship. Dulles presided over the German mission more than he ran it. The latter was Wisner's job. He was an efficient administrator. Dulles was not. Dulles enjoyed the limelight while Wisner shunned it. Demanding in his own way, Dulles was also a busybody, often meddling in his subordinates' operations when they interested him. For tasks he did not want to bother with, Dulles peppered Wisner and Helms with take-care-of-this orders in the morning while he ate his breakfast.

As had been the case in Istanbul and Bucharest, Wisner faced extremely complicated terrain in Wiesbaden, where he had to organize a spy network that served multiple customers: the intelligence section at SHAEF as well as the War and State Departments in Washington. And he did so with only meager information on the postwar condition of Germany and the countries to the east. The OSS, in fact, compiled a secret study of German occupation techniques in France, looking for lessons on how the agency should conduct its intelligence operations in occupied Germany.

Men and women with a variety of backgrounds and talents joined Wisner's team in Wiesbaden. He was delighted to have Rolfe Kingsley, his loyal and highly efficient aide from Istanbul, come to Germany to serve as his assistant. Liberal historian Arthur M. Schlesinger Jr., who had been serving as a research analyst in the OSS's London station, arrived to evaluate and pass along to higher headquarters the intelligence Wisner's operatives found in the field. Lieutenant Colonel Ides van der Gracht, an Austrian American who before joining the OSS had been the chief design architect for the Pentagon, was put in charge of Wisner's espionage section, which set up spy outposts throughout Germany. Virginia Rogers Murphy, a Barnard College graduate fluent in German, worked as both a secretary and an agent handler managing spies.

Dulles also brought with him to Berlin Germans who had been prized sources when he was posted in Bern, such as Gero von Schulze Gaevernitz, a wealthy international financier who had introduced him to valuable intelligence assets and resistance contacts in Germany; Fritz Kolbe, a short, bald German Foreign Office diplomat who had delivered to him some sixteen hundred classified Nazi political, military, and intelligence cables; and Hans Bernd Gisevius, a stern Abwehr major who had informed Dulles on dissidents remaining in Germany. Wisner, however, was skeptical of their value—and the worth of many of the other "good" Germans Dulles knew—now that the fighting had ended. Wanting to be influential in shaping postwar Germany, Dulles had compiled what became known as the "Crown Jewels" list of Germans he hoped would lead their nation's future governments, but Wisner and Helms did not think much of his initiative. The quality of the intelligence the good Germans provided was uneven and Dulles never became a kingmaker. The West Germans were soon deciding their affairs on their own.

Wisner quickly discovered that he commanded "a large staff of war weary people," he wrote his mother. Many of the some two hundred officers were willing to work but not enthusiastically. "I have my hands full trying to pull them together and set them off on the right course," he wrote. OSS officers who had collected fine-grain tactical intelligence on German troop strength and movements now had to be reoriented to gather broader political and military information on the Soviets. It was a task made more difficult for Wisner by the fact that many of his young officers, still new to the spy business, just wanted to go home and get on with their civilian lives.

Schlesinger thought that everyone at Wiesbaden was just more relaxed now that the European war was over—everyone, that is, except Wisner, "who was very high strung and deeply concerned about the communist menace," he said. Once more, Wisner could be brutal with underperforming officers. "You did what you were told," recalled Gerhard Van Arkel, an attorney assigned to Wiesbaden. "It was a very different arrangement from what had existed during the war. It was no longer free-wheeling. . . . Frank was the guy who put some discipline into the place. That much I know because I felt it myself." But as had been the case in his other postings, Wisner developed a loyal following among the hardworking officers at Wiesbaden.

Wisner soon had up and running ten spy stations operating throughout Germany and in Czechoslovakia. They were called production units, or "P-units," and they collected intelligence in such cities as Berlin, Munich, and Nuremberg. For months, Wisner shuttled day and night among his P-units to supervise their output. Meanwhile, at Wiesbaden he created a new intelligence tool called the Steering Division, which initially had thirty-eight staffers who directed his often inexperienced officers in the field on the high-priority targets for their intelligence gathering.

To assist Wisner, Donovan had aides scour prisoner of war camps in the United States and overseas for German soldiers willing to work for the Americans as spies. Exiles, such as a Bavarian parliamentarian who had fled to London, also offered to infiltrate into the regions they once represented to collect intelligence for P-units. To begin the difficult task of producing false identity papers for his new spies, Wisner had printing equipment and the craftsmen to operate the machinery secretly airlifted to Wiesbaden. He ordered twenty cars with no markings on them for his officers to roam the German countryside. By the first week of August, the P-units' fifty-eight officers with their fifteen drivers had produced 278 intelligence reports on military, political, social, and economic topics in Germany, Poland, and Czechoslovakia.

Wisner's operatives began by mopping up Germany's refuse—hunting for war criminals, weeding Nazis out of government agencies, and gathering art objects leaders like Hermann Göring had stolen. They were helped by the truckloads of enemy records they tracked down, such as 1.5 million negatives of official Wehrmacht photographs.

But the target soon became the Soviets, whose German zone was given the cryptonym "HBRebel" in secret OSS documents. Though the Joint Chiefs in Washington and Eisenhower's command in Europe never spelled it out on paper, spying on the Russians had been an unspoken priority for Donovan in the months before Germany surrendered. By August 1944, Donovan, who the year before had received a memo warning that Soviet propaganda was boasting that Communists would dominate all of Europe after the war, had assigned forty-four OSS researchers in Washington to track and analyze Red Army capabilities. Since December 1944, all of the OSS's overseas stations had been brainstorming ways to collect intelligence on the U.S.S.R. It only made sense, Donovan wrote in a memo to Marshall, since the United States and the Soviet Union after the war "will long remain, by far, the strongest nations in the world."

Realizing the highly sensitive nature of what he was doing, Wisner had his Steering Division compile a top secret list of information he wanted his agents to dig up from the territory the Russians controlled in Germany. It was a long list: details on the Russian military organization in their occupation zone, activities of the NKVD, dossiers on Soviet officials, political arrests carried out, economic regulations imposed, conscription of Germans for slave labor, agricultural conditions, and available fuel stocks. P-unit agents sneaked into East Germany to plant listening devices in the Soviet zone. Wisner's men also reached out to the British and French intelligence services in their zone for help in spying on the Russians.

Schlesinger considered himself an anti-Communist, but he thought Wisner became too preoccupied with the Soviets. Aides said the Mississippian brought a religious fervor to his job, sometimes seeming to brace himself when he talked about the Russians. Playing the armchair psychiatrist, Helms later in life believed Wisner's anti-Communist fervor and an extremely high fever Helms said Wisner once had in Berlin were what caused his mental health problems later. Helms did not know what he was talking about. Though the average age for the onset of bipolar disorder is about twenty-two years old, and Wisner was in his mid-thirties then, he showed no troubling signs while in Berlin. When one considers how brutal Stalin and his Red Army were in Germany and the other occupied countries, Wisner's personal hatred of all things Russian was understandable.

Wisner made no apologies for his obsession. He could be rude with other, more open-minded officers he thought were wasting his time on the subject. Schlesinger never challenged him and the two remained good friends for years after the war. It was clear to the historian that the wounds of Romania still festered inside his Wiesbaden boss. Germany was becoming the early battlefield for America's cold war with the Soviet Union. Wisner plunged ardently into this new conflict.

* * *

Carrying special passes that allowed him to enter the city, Wisner wandered about Berlin shortly after he arrived in Germany. The shattered capital was still in a chaotic state and the Soviets had not yet clamped down on travel, so Wisner and his other officers found they could roam quite freely among the city's four sectors. Occasionally, OSS officers even socialized with their Russian counterparts. At one drinking session, a Russian colonel who had consumed too much bragged that he was a proud member of a Soviet intelligence service and to prove it ripped open his shirt to show an eagle tattooed on his chest, which he claimed was the insignia of his spy unit.

One of the first places Wisner picked to visit was the Reich Chancellery on Voss Strasse, which Allied bombers and Russian artillery had heavily damaged. Just outside in the chancellery garden Wisner found the entrance to the Führerbunker, where Hitler had spent the last three months of his life. He climbed down into the deep and commodious air raid shelter. Although the Russians had been there first by a few days and had done some ransacking, Wisner was surprised to find much of the furniture and equipment in the bunker undisturbed. Even the electrical system still functioned, albeit feebly, with the lights flickering. He located the room where Hitler and Eva Braun took their lives. On the couch were large splotches of blood, still moist, he could see.

Back outside, Wisner spotted a shallow trench near the bunker's entrance where other aides had told him the bodies of Hitler and

Braun had been cremated. He did not see any ashes in the trench, but he noticed that its sides and bottom were charred and empty gasoline cans were scattered around the hole. Wisner assumed the Russians had carted the remains back to Moscow for coroners to examine.

Wisner had grabbed a wall hanging when he was inside the bunker. He returned to the shattered rooms and hallways of the chancellery to look for more souvenirs. (Dulles and Helms had also scavenged the building.) He found and pocketed several fistfuls of German Iron Cross medals and bits of broken furniture and fixtures. On top of a pile of debris in one corner, he found a sketchbook. He also grabbed a small bust of Göring and a book signed by Reichsführer-SS Heinrich Himmler.

Within weeks of setting up the German mission, Wisner was visiting Berlin regularly to confer with Dulles at his Föhrenweg Strasse office. Soviet artillery and seventy-five thousand tons of Allied aerial bombs had left eleven square miles of the city's center a pile of rubble, and had damaged or destroyed more than one-fifth of the 1.5 million surrounding homes. Berlin was eerily silent except for the tinkling sounds of *Trümmerfrauen* ("rubble women") tapping bricks to clear debris and the buzzing noises of billions of flies swarming over some 100,000 rotting corpses strewn among the rocks or floating in sewage-clogged canals. Wisner covered his nose because of the stench.

The lack of food, medicine, and shelter for civilians quickly overwhelmed the arriving American forces. A vibrant city of 4.5 million people before the war, Berlin now had 2.3 million— mostly dazed, homeless, and hungry women, children, and old men, many of them refugees from the East who had fled west to escape the Russians. Ravaged by dysentery, typhoid fever, and diphtheria, city residents were dying at a rate of about a thousand per day.

Crime was rampant. Gangs of displaced persons ran wild, killing innocents and looting what little there was to steal. Children covered in sores because of malnutrition banded together to rule over city blocks. The arriving Russians made matters worse. The frontline Red Army troops who came first behaved well, but the second-echelon soldiers who moved in next raped and pillaged, with their officers grabbing the more expensive goods like wines from Göring's cellar. Alcohol abuse became a serious problem. Soviet military police gunned down one group of drunken soldiers discharging their weapons.

As he had in Romania, Stalin slowly set about installing a Communist regime in East Germany. Careful at first not to antagonize Germans, he gave lip service to democracy and the emergence of political parties, though under tight Soviet oversight. Berlin clocks were set to Russian time. To win hearts and minds, propaganda posters extolling the Red Army's victory went up in the Russian zone. Soviet military commander Marshal Georgy Zhukov advertised himself as a friend of Germans. Communist newspapers and Moscow-approved films flooded the Russian zone, artists were given guidelines to follow, and an education department was established to indoctrinate students. Russians screened the nominees whom four approved political parties submitted for government positions. The NKVD and the NKGB became ruthless in ferreting out political opponents who did not cooperate, sending many of them to the old concentration camps the Nazis had run. Meanwhile, hundreds of thousands of Wehrmacht soldiers joined millions of war prisoners and German civilians already toiling away in Russian labor camps.

As they had done in Romania, Russian troops also began dismantling what was left of German factories and sending their machines and supplies back to the Soviet Union. Wisner's men reported that Red Army soldiers were looting what little there was of the German agricultural harvest in their zone. German railroad tracks were replaced with the broader Russian gauge to haul equipment and food stocks to the Soviet Union. Donovan early on alerted Truman to the plundering.

The Russians were not the only ones confiscating war booty. The British sent German factory equipment in their zone to the government in Greece. The French moved food, fuel, and industrial machinery from their zone to France. The Americans packed off to the United States technical documents, research equipment, and German scientists from their zone for the U.S. missile program.

* * *

For two months, from May to July 1945, Stalin deftly held up the American and British occupation forces from entering their sectors in Berlin. The delay gave Russian soldiers time to plunder the U.S. sector—the OSS could count only one in twenty homes still standing there with furniture the Soviets had not taken—and it enabled Moscow to install a Communist power structure in West Berlin's government that became almost impossible for American occupiers to dislodge.

The delay also gave the Soviets time to insert an espionage and counterespionage network into West Berlin, which put Wisner's intelligence team at an immediate disadvantage when it entered the sector. The Russians operated on what American intelligence officers soon called the "total espionage principle," in which practically every government or nongovernment activity served some type of spy function. So, for example, the NKVD, which was responsible for internal order, planted trusted Communists in the Berlin police department both to fight crime and to keep watch on the OSS. Wisner's counterintelligence officers scrambled to collect information on the NKVD, the NKGB (the domestic and foreign intelligence service), and the GRU (the Soviet military's intelligence service). They quickly realized that the Soviet spy services knew a lot more about U.S. intelligence than U.S. organizations knew about Russian intelligence.

* * *

The light cover Dulles accepted for the Berlin operating base made it an easy target for Communists and ex-Nazis to penetrate. Wisner's security officers stepped up their vetting of Germans who had been hastily hired for menial duties when the Föhrenweg Strasse office was started. They tried to turn the Communists they discovered into double agents to spy on their Russian employer. The former Nazis they uncovered were fired.

By late summer 1945, the Soviets began cutting off American access to the Russian zone, which put a serious crimp in OSS intelligence gathering in East Berlin. Tensions rose between the Americans and Russians. The Soviets began to quibble more about U.S. transport planes flying over the Russian zone to supply the American sector in Berlin. Army military police clashed with Russian thugs sent to West Berlin to kidnap German dissidents considered a threat. Soviet propaganda organs began distributing screeds against FDR, accusing him of having been a "dictator of democracy," and against Allen Dulles, whom they accused of conniving with German and American financiers when he headed the OSS station in Bern. Marshal Georgy Zhukov, the first commander of the Soviet occupation zone, ordered that Russian soldiers be accompanied by a senior officer when they met with Americans. And at those meetings, which were never to be in a Red Army office, they were to keep quiet.

Wisner's job was not made any easier by General Lucius Clay, a politically savvy Southerner who led the entire American mission in Berlin and kept the OSS there on a tight leash for fear of alienating the Soviets. It frustrated Wisner and his operatives, who saw no value in keeping the Russians happy. The OSS had to go underground to operate clandestinely in the Soviet sector, and that was not easy. With Berlin deep inside the Soviet zone, everything needed for the basics of spying had to be flown or trucked in. Bicycles and automobiles (with spare tires) were a must for agents riding around Berlin, which was four times the size of Washington, DC. Barter items—such as liquor, wristwatches, and women's stockings—had to be imported for bribing local officials. C rations and medicines were required for the care of German snitches. Safe houses where foreign agents could live and meet their OSS handlers were needed, but homes or apartments were scarce anywhere in bombed-out Berlin.

The printing equipment Wisner brought to Wiesbaden was only the start of an ambitious initiative his officers had to mount to create false identity papers for spies. Fortunately, his counterespionage agents were able to exploit the formidable document fabrication operation the Germans had once had. OSS officers found two SS trucks packed with phony Soviet IDs, rubber stamps bearing the signatures of senior Red Army officers, counterfeit banknotes, and phone books for Russian towns that listed hundreds of thousands of names spies could use. From a German police office, Wisner's operatives learned where to find a Russian typewriter, reams of blank German paper, and travel passes. Helms had Russian clothing for operatives to wear flown in, plus suitcases and briefcases with secret compartments for hiding stolen documents. Cover experts pored over hundreds of newspapers for personal stories secret agents could adopt in the Soviet zone if Russian security agents started grilling them on their backgrounds.

The cover and deception unit had to produce a staggering array of phony papers a spy might need to show to make it past Russian checkpoints: identity documents, such as passports and birth certificates; labor documents, such as factory passes and union cards; military documents, such as service records and discharge papers; ration cards for food and clothing; travel papers, such as driver's licenses and rail passes; and political documents, such as party membership cards and trade association certificates. For a long time, Wisner did not have the fully capable document operation he needed to infiltrate agents safely into the Russian zone. Machinery for fabricating material, along with the nine cover and deception experts needed for the unit, was slow to arrive in Berlin. Russian guards also soon became more expert at spotting phony papers. Spies were supposed to enter the enemy zone with fresh sets of identity papers for each visit so as to reduce the risk of being captured, but most of the time, they did not possess that new paperwork because Wisner did not have the personnel or equipment to continually produce it. So infiltrations became extremely dangerous for the secret agents attempting them.

* * *

Wisner's officers kept a close lookout for signs that subversive Nazi agents were hiding in villages, riding trains, or stowed aboard ships—and waiting to strike at the Americans. They found just the opposite among the docile Germans. Veterans of the Wehrmacht, Abwehr, SS, and the SS's intelligence service, the Sicherheitsdienst (or SD), were eager to help the OSS team spy on the Russians.

Schlesinger said he felt "queasy" about enlisting former German intelligence officers. Wisner was not. His Berlin base began using ex–Wehrmacht officers, eager to ingratiate themselves with the West, to run agent chains in the Soviet zone. An informant told Wisner's spies that as many as a thousand Red Army deserters were hiding out in Berlin wearing civilian clothes; OSS officers began looking for the Soviet soldiers in that group who might actually know something, and found ex-NKVD agents among the defectors. A German counterespionage agent whom the OSS gave the code name "Zigzag" had the names of scores of Abwehr colleagues he thought might be useful. A former Abwehr naval intelligence analyst, identified in classified documents as Barbara Güttler, fed Helms's unit intelligence she had gathered working as a newspaper reporter in the Russian zone.

Wisner and Dulles were impressed with Major General Reinhard Gehlen, a senior Abwehr officer U.S. Army intelligence agents had recruited who had fallen out of favor with Hitler for his pessimistic reports from the Eastern Front. Gehlen was now eager to reassemble his old spy network for the Americans to use. The Kremlin also enthusiastically used Germans for its spying on the West, even drafting former Wehrmacht officers, Hitler Youth leaders, and Nazi agents to spend several years in the Soviet Union training Russians for police work in East Germany and the Balkans.

Wisner and his officers found snitches in other unusual places. In a highly sensitive operation, he did favors for Germany's papal nuncio, Cardinal Cesar Vincenzo Orsenigo, such as transmitting his enciphered messages to Rome in exchange for information Orsenigo gathered for the P-unit in Nuremberg. A Catholic envoy code-named "Beechnut" was also recruited to provide the OSS team information that he picked up in Berlin's Russian sector. Nothing ever came of the Beechnut operation, but the OSS officers thought it was worth a try.

Soon Wisner had what amounted to an espionage assembly line. The German mission by July had compiled code names for nearly fifteen hundred operations and their operatives. The spy games the two sides played on each other became complicated. For example, when Helms's "bird dog" Zigzag was sent to East Berlin to hunt for useful Abwehr or Gestapo officers, he met an old friend who worked as an NKVD bird dog looking for prey in West Berlin. The NKVD bird dog was talked into becoming a double agent and working for the OSS. To keep his NKVD handlers happy, the OSS officers occasionally gave him Gestapo small fry he could offer to the Russian spy service.

The games became dangerous as well. NKVD kidnapping teams sneaked into West Germany to hunt for defectors. General Clay eventually allowed Wisner's officers to wear civilian clothes and carry concealed weapons in Berlin's American sector, "which helped the security of our operations," according to a top secret OSS memo.

In the month of August, Wisner's P-units filed more than seven hundred reports to higher authorities in Europe and Washington, many of them gleaned in the open by just interviewing sources on economic and political subjects, such as the food situation in the Russian zone, the black marketeering the Red Army tolerated, and the economic reorganization the Soviets were imposing. A German agriculture expert, for example, provided them with the state of grain, potato, and meat production in the Russian zone, along with

estimates of shortfalls and the commodities the Red Army was rak-
ing off for its troops.

Headquarters became insatiable for more. How large was the
Soviet diplomatic mission in Berlin? What were the ranks of its military and civilian personnel? How ingrained was the Russian Communist Party in the military? How much control did Moscow
impose on local commanders? What types of planes were parked on
Russian airfields? The questions never stopped coming.

Wisner had one other espionage assignment—a highly sensitive
one. In addition to the Russians, he was ordered to spy on the British
and the French in their zones. Donovan had discussed this delicate
mission with Dulles as early as January 1945. The OSS director assumed the British would spy on the Americans. Wisner's officers
thus had informants reporting to them on political conditions and
police activity in the British zone. A secret directive ordered OSS
operatives in Austria, as they were spying on the Russians, to report
any "incidental" intelligence on MI6 that they picked up along the
way. Anticipating that British and French authorities would impose
"increasingly severe restrictions on American travel," another secret
memo revealed, Wisner and his men were setting up a clandestine
courier service into their zones to bring out intelligence. OSS
sources in the French zone disclosed that the French were hoarding
goods the U.S. and the British zones needed, that three Abwehr officers had agreed to spy for Paris, and that a German major general
had been approached about working for the French intelligence service. In a project code-named "Marietta," Wisner's men planted a
Czech woman to work as a secretary in the office that the U.S. allowed the French spy service to have in Austria; her orders were to
warn the Americans if French spies were up to any mischief.

* * *

American fraternization with German women grew out of hand.
Venereal disease among GIs soared. Clay and his senior officers

tried to ban fraternization but quickly realized they would never succeed. A generation of German women found it normal to trade sex with an American soldier for a chocolate bar. Ultimately, GIs brought home about fourteen thousand German brides. The officers and enlisted men who worked for Wisner played just as hard in their off-duty hours as the regular GIs did. Liquor flooded parties that stretched into the early-morning hours. Drunken OSS officers raced their jeeps through Berlin's empty streets. Many took on German mistresses and there were rumors, never confirmed, that Wisner had one-night stands as well.

* * *

By late summer, Berlin was becoming as lawless as the Wild West. GI pilfering from supply depots was common and the MPs who joined in the thievery were called the "Lootwaffe." Robberies and murders of Germans by gangs of U.S. soldiers were up, prompting a line repeated often by the civilian population: "An American is just like a Russian, with his trousers pressed." Some of the GI crime stories were planted by the Russians to stir up trouble for General Clay, but enough of them were true that Eisenhower realized he had a serious problem.

Black marketeering was out of control. Berlin became the center for it. From the Reichstag building to the Brandenburg Gate, black-market vendors could be found peddling cigarettes, food rations, cameras, women's silk stockings, jewelry, bicycles, and cars. Even more disturbing was the shady selling by many U.S. officers (one of them was a general) who were supposed to be cracking down on the problem among enlisted subordinates.

Wisner had a strong moralistic streak, though he realized that spying could involve dirty work. Donovan had approved his station chiefs overseas stockpiling items like cameras, wristwatches, and even nonmilitary pistols to use as bribes for information. To conduct any effective operation in the territory the Russians occupied,

Wisner's officers needed those goods plus razors with blades, fountain pens, flashlights, a dozen different types of food, cigars, U.S. dollars, and sterling currency. Wisner himself had also flown to Switzerland to buy ladies' jewelry for bribes in operations. He soon discovered, however, that he had a black-market problem among his officers.

Major Andrew Haensel, one of his Berlin officers, had gone too far. Haensel and Captain Gustav Mueller, a pal who ran the 3rd Army's OSS detachment in Munich, were nabbed by Army criminal investigators at the city's airport trying to sneak in 138 Swiss watches from Switzerland to sell on the back market in violation of military regulations and Swiss export laws. The pair claimed the watches were for spy operations, but Wisner knew immediately that the two Army officers had no spy duties that would bring them together and that he had not approved sneaking in 138 watches. Haensel and Mueller had duped him, his intelligence production chief Ides van der Gracht, and Helms. But not eager to air that dirty laundry in an open court-martial, the Army eventually allowed Haensel and Mueller to quietly resign from the service.

Dulles dismissed the entire affair as a "minor" irregularity, but it was not. The Haensel-Mueller case became a major embarrassment for Wisner and him, who both had to undergo lengthy interrogations by an investigative board trying to unravel how the watch scheme had unfolded under their noses. The board concluded that the Berlin mission needed to tighten its financial controls, which Wisner agreed was necessary. But in doing so, Wisner discovered that Haensel and Mueller were not the only miscreants. Many other P-unit officers were building nest eggs by bartering on the side some of the goods and cash they were supposed to be using for their spy trade.

*　*　*

September was another productive month for Wisner's intelligence officers. They churned out more than eight hundred reports.

Sixty-four of his counterespionage spies battled Russian operatives in Berlin and a half dozen other German cities. The Soviets were trying to recruit American GIs or to spy on them. Wisner's men continued to try risky endeavors, such as the OSS agent who succeeded in passing himself off as an Austrian Communist in the British zone of Vienna in order to socialize with Russian officers in their zone.

But at the end of September, the future operations of the German mission stood frozen, as did the activities of more than ten thousand OSS employees in Washington and around the world. Harry Truman, who had never particularly liked Donovan and was intent on downsizing America's mammoth national security machine now that the wars in Europe and Asia had ended, ordered the OSS closed and its functions parceled out to the Pentagon and the State Department. Donovan, who was out of a job by the end of September, sent to all his overseas stations a cable informing them that on October 1, his meticulous deputy, Brigadier General John Magruder, would take over the OSS's secret intelligence and sabotage units, which had been moved to the War Department. Magruder's operation would now be called the Strategic Services Unit and the OSS contingents in Germany and Austria would remain on duty under the SSU.

Wisner felt blindsided. Toward the end of October, he flew to Washington to scope out what had happened, and cabled back to his senior aides in Berlin that from the rounds he had made among top administration officials he was confident a future intelligence organization would be coming. Key military officials favored it, Wisner said.

But that new organization would not be coming soon. Dulles, Wisner, and the other officers in Germany for now were stuck with the SSU and Magruder, whose orders were to shrink the American spy presence in Germany. Dulles moved to consolidate operations and cut his budget, ending up with sixty intelligence officers and analysts. His orders from Magruder, a thin and nervous man whose hands trembled, were to preserve operations deemed of value for a permanent espionage service and to liquidate the other projects not considered necessary.

Remarkably, the number of intelligence reports from Berlin and the other P-units dipped only slightly in the month of October, although their quality did suffer and many agent cables considered worthless or unreliable were never disseminated. Dulles's efforts to keep operations going weren't helped by Magruder's lame promise to officers in the field that if they hung on for at least three months, the Truman administration, he hoped, would come up with a permanent intelligence organization by then and the hangers-on would be given preferential treatment when it came to future hiring.

Productivity plummeted by early November. While the NKVD and the NKGB remained aggressive, Wisner's counterespionage operations against them all but halted. It became impossible for him to plan new operations because he could not be sure that he would have anyone to carry them out. Suspecting that the SSU was on life support, some officers began filling out their paperwork to go home. Army intelligence units in Germany, like vultures, began dangling job offers with much higher pay to other men and women still on Wisner's payroll. The biggest resignation, which embittered Wisner and Helms the most, came on October 10, 1945, when Allen Dulles left the mission to return home.

Magruder cabled Wisner and Helms, pleading with them to stay in Germany. They agreed to sit tight. The SSU projects left in the country now operated under the cover of education, research, or refugee control outfits. Helms took over all the spying from Berlin. A good organizer, he moved to hold the pieces together and produce useful intelligence. Armed with a list of top-notch officers he wanted to keep, Wisner, meanwhile, raced doggedly all over Germany, encouraging those left in his P-units to keep snooping. On the morning of November 17, he visited the Berlin operating base for a pep talk. Because of the cutbacks it had experienced, he was surprised at the high morale he found there. Helms had twenty-six agents and informants; eleven of them were salted among the Russian, British, and French zones while five were posted in Poland. "Berlin continues to be a mine of intelligence, which can never be fully exploited," Wisner wrote in a follow-up memo to Magruder's Washington headquarters. "It is very much the center of activity" for the emerging cold war with Russia.

* * *

Wisner's own morale, however, finally cracked the next month. The tipping point was bicycles. He was infuriated when penny-pinching Pentagon bureaucrats refused to pay for two hundred bikes he urgently needed for his operatives to ride during their infiltrations into the Soviet zone to record troop movements. Wisner resigned from his post. Helms, who was anxious to return to his family and was becoming bored with the Berlin job, did so as well.

As bitter cold weather arrived, making the hunger and desperation tormenting Germany only worse, Wisner and Helms boarded a Navy cargo plane in Frankfurt on December 11. The flight back to Washington, DC, took eighteen hours over six days with stops in Paris, the Azores, and Newfoundland. It gave the two officers plenty of time to talk about the future of U.S. intelligence and the need for a postwar spy service. When Roosevelt was still alive, Donovan had drafted a plan for such an agency, which he wanted to lead after World War II. But a political foe, most likely J. Edgar Hoover, leaked a copy of his proposal to the press, which accused FDR of wanting to set up an "American Gestapo." Roosevelt shelved the idea.

For his work in Germany, Wisner was awarded the Army Commendation Ribbon. London made him an Honorary Officer of the Most Excellent Order of the British Empire. Polly said she was "bursting with pride" over her husband's World War II service. She and the boys hoped he would be home by New Year's Day 1946. In the months that followed his arrival in New York, he told Polly where he had been the past two years but revealed little about what he had done.

World War II had a profound effect on Frank Wisner. It was an exciting part of his life that he thought he would never experience again. He had made important friends, like Allen Dulles, who would play critical roles in his future. Wisner left the battlefield a seasoned intelligence expert schooled in the stark realities of a future superpower competition. Up close in Romania and Germany, he had witnessed the Russians at work. He saw, as not many did at the time, the Soviet threat to U.S. national security and he was convinced that it had to be met head-on with all the tools in America's military and diplomatic arsenal, including intelligence gathering and covert operations. The contest would be long and dangerous, Wisner believed. He did not realize until later how much he wanted to be a part of it.

PART THREE

THE COLD WAR

Chapter 9

HOME

WISNER RETURNED TO A country that was in a fearful mood at first. Consumer goods and houses were in short supply. Demand, so long suppressed because of wartime rationing, was ready to explode. Worries from a depression-scared generation spread that another depression was inevitable. But economic doom did not come. Veterans had no trouble finding jobs. Unemployment sank to a record low. Men who had spent their young years fighting overseas were now eager to resume their civilian lives, find good jobs, and raise families. (Their children would become known as the baby boomers.) The G.I. Bill of Rights provided money for veterans to attend college. Home construction surged, fueled by the G.I. Bill's affordable mortgages, which in turn stimulated sales in appliances for the homes. Factories retooled to produce goods for consumers. Automobile sales soon soared. The middle class swelled. The United States became the world's richest nation.

Wisner found it difficult to relax when he returned home—keyed up, Polly said, from his "extraordinary experience" in Europe during the war. On his first night back in New York, Frank and Polly attended a dinner with old friends John and Elizabeth

Graham, and Wisner talked nonstop into the early-morning hours. He made no time for recuperating. The Navy granted him three weeks leave, which he and Polly spent in Montego Bay, Jamaica, with the Grahams, but Wisner still could not unwind.

Before he separated from the OSS and the Navy by early January 1946, Wisner turned in the special passport the State Department had issued to him when he was stationed overseas. He toyed with the idea of joining the department's Foreign Service, but instead returned to the job that no longer held much interest for him—at Carter, Ledyard & Milburn.

The full partnership the law firm bestowed on Wisner did come with its rewards. The *Martindale-Hubbell Law Directory* gave him a top rating as a lawyer on his way up. Stock dividends from investments in Laurel, to which his mother contributed regularly, reached about $300,000 annually in today's dollars. One wealthy client gave him box seats to New York Yankees baseball games. But the mountains of corporate and estate cases he returned to, interspersed with legal chores he did for his father-in-law, soon bored him. At home, Wisner was not deeply involved in the lives of his two sons, Frank II and Ellis, or of his daughter, Elizabeth Gardiner, who was born on June 5, 1947, and whom the family called Wendy. Polly was only a little more attentive. The children were left largely to the care of a live-in nanny who took the boys to school and tended to little Wendy.

Wisner and the other OSS veterans were under strict orders from Donovan never to disclose to outsiders details about their World War II spy work. With his family and law colleagues, Wisner shared only tidbits, such as recollections of the Russians taking everything not nailed down in Eastern Europe and Germany. The men with whom he did confide when he returned to New York were OSS veterans like himself. Wisner frequently lunched or dined with Allen Dulles, who had returned to his law firm, Sullivan & Cromwell. The two traded wartime gossip as well as legal favors. Both also talked about returning to intelligence work. Occasionally Wisner and other OSS vets gathered at Donovan's elegant Sutton Place town house in New York to reminisce. Helms, who had decided to remain with the SSU instead of returning to journalism, passed along news to Dulles and Wisner about Cold War spying or asked for their recollections about World War II agents he was considering hiring.

Dulles, who was elected president of the Council on Foreign Relations, sponsored Wisner for membership in the prestigious New York group. Wisner relished attending the council's lectures and mingling with foreign policy heavyweights. After becoming a member, he had Polly's father invited to join the group.

The lunch, dinner, and cocktail conversations of Wisner and the other OSS veterans invariably dwelled on politics in Washington, the Cold War abroad, or the dismal state of American intelligence collection. Wisner liked Harry Truman, though he thought Roosevelt's successor had made a strategic error in closing the OSS. But Wisner, oddly, did not blame Truman for the intelligence deficit that resulted.

* * *

The cognoscenti of Roosevelt's national security community were shocked and depressed over Harry Truman becoming the seventh man to assume the presidency after the death of a president. The failed Missouri haberdasher had never earned a college degree. But Truman was a complex man, extremely well-read, who kept a Tennyson poem on the virtues of common sense folded in his wallet. Soon he convinced many of his skeptics that the country remained in good hands. Yet without a doubt, he was ill prepared to assume the national security burdens left by Roosevelt, who had kept his vice president largely in the dark about challenges overseas. Only on Truman's twelfth day in office did he receive for the first time a full briefing on the Manhattan Project to build a nuclear weapon.

Truman found Washington overpopulated with prima donnas and began referring to the White House as "the great white jail." In

his first three months in office, he was confronted with more difficult and far-reaching decisions than any president before him:
among them, launching the United Nations, dealing with the menacing Red Army in Eastern Europe, rebuilding devastated Berlin,
and dropping atomic bombs on Hiroshima and Nagasaki. He made
those decisions with a notably weak national security team. Secretary of State James Byrnes knew his way around domestic politics
but had little diplomatic experience. Secretary of War Robert Patterson was a lawyer skilled mainly in military logistics. Only Navy
Secretary James Forrestal had a vision for how foreign policy should
be conducted.

Truman at first believed that the Russians had always been
America's friends and that they wanted to be friends. He could not
see why that would not remain the case. Misunderstandings among
nations, like those between two fellows in Missouri, could be worked
out, and Truman believed he had a gift for dealing with other men.
Stalin had made a good first impression with the new president—
though the murderous Russian dictator was skilled in making good
first impressions.

By the beginning of 1946, however, U.S.-Soviet relations were
deteriorating. Stalin was becoming more verbally belligerent. Truman began snapping back in private meetings with Soviet envoys in
ways FDR never would have. By 1946, Truman saw clearly that the
United States was transforming into a world power, but she was a
strategic giant lumbering into uncharted territory, facing the prospect of the threat of war becoming the new normal. A tidy deskman
who disdained the freewheeling, informal foreign policymaking
that Roosevelt had practiced, Truman in January 1946 ordered an
interagency appraisal of U.S. national security in the face of the
Russian threat.

At this point, Joseph Stalin turned out to be even less sure about
how his government should wage the Cold War. The steely-eyed
dictator, who had ended up playing his cards skillfully during World
War II, was not certain how to proceed in peacetime. He knew only
that he had to move cautiously. The Americans, after all, had the

atomic bomb. He did not and would not for another three years. Russia wasn't the all-powerful enemy many in Washington thought it was. Though the Red Army dominated Eastern Europe and Communist ideology found fertile ground in Western Europe, the Soviet Union had been crippled by the war. Its economy was shattered and its military worn-out. The illusion in Washington of a potent U.S.S.R. was due partly to the fact that Truman had no intelligence service in early 1946 to tell him differently.

What the Soviets did have was a formidable peacetime espionage apparatus with an international reach, which at the moment was three decades ahead of the United States. What Truman had was a mess. General Magruder tried valiantly to hold together in the SSU a secret intelligence-gathering unit until Washington could decide what it wanted in the way of a permanent peacetime spy agency. But the SSU's best intelligence officers were leaving in droves. The special operations and propaganda capabilities that had existed in the OSS had been quickly liquidated. And Secretary of State Byrnes, whom Truman had picked to manage a new intelligence-collection and -analysis effort, did not do so.

When Truman took office, he discovered that he had no one source to inform him on the threats he faced overseas. Each government department or agency concerned with national security had its own intelligence service that was walled off from the other services, so when Truman needed information, he had to go to two or three organizations to get it. He would also have to have someone do a little digging for the material. Truman found he had to become his own intelligence officer, regularly reading a tall stack of documents to find what he wanted—an impossible burden for a president.

White House counsel Clark Clifford bluntly warned his boss that the U.S.-Soviet rivalry was "the gravest problem" he faced as president. In a highly classified memo, the Joint Chiefs warned Truman that in the atomic age the lack of an efficient intelligence service "might bring national disaster." Truman agreed and became increasingly annoyed that he did not have such a service.

He was modest in what he wanted: some kind of compact digest of information that would be laid on his desk each day. Beyond that, he was not sure about what else he needed in the way of a secret service. Truman agreed with a basic tenet of Donovan's thinking—that a president must have a permanent peacetime foreign-intelligence-gathering capability—but he had no clue as to what that capability should look like. His budget director warned him that getting the military and the State Department to agree on the formation of a new intelligence organization would be one of the most difficult undertakings of his presidency. It would be messy.

It was. For four long months, a fierce bureaucratic battle raged in Washington among officials in the War and State Departments, neither wanting to cede their intelligence capabilities to a new spy service.

* * *

On January 24, Truman had Rear Admiral Sidney Souers in for lunch. A wealthy St. Louis business executive and Truman crony, Souers had spent the war as a Naval Reserve intelligence officer. When the plates were cleared, the president presented the Navy man with a black cloak, a black hat, and a wooden dagger—a playful way, Truman thought, to celebrate his making Souers the director of the new Central Intelligence Group. Souers did not particularly want this job and he did not know what to do with his new position. He took the posting with the understanding that he would be in it for only six months in order to begin some kind of basic intelligence organization.

Donovan ridiculed the new CIG as little more than "a good debating society," which was not far from the truth. Truman, who did not want a large spy agency, had managed to hammer out an arrangement that allowed the military and the State Department to keep control of their intelligence services. Souers, whose budget would be drawn from the Pentagon and State accounts, would be responsible for coordinating, planning, evaluating, and disseminating intelligence. (No covert operations capability was planned and the special paramilitary units that had been the pride of the OSS had been done away with.) A National Intelligence Authority—composed of the secretaries of state, war, and the Navy, plus a representative from Truman's White House—would supervise Souers's organization.

The CIG began in three office rooms next to the White House with only about eighty employees—tiny by federal government standards—and an intelligence capability that existed mainly on paper. The Central Intelligence Group did deliver to Truman the daily intelligence summary he so wanted. It came in the afternoon and Truman took it to the family quarters to read each evening. One top secret CIG report warned him that the Soviet Union believed conflict with the capitalist world was inevitable, but Moscow needed to avoid that conflict for the moment while it rebuilt its country.

But the CIG was no more than an appendage of the State, War and Navy Departments. By controlling Souers's budget and the people who served under him, the diplomats, generals, and admirals could be sure they would rule over the CIG and also maintain their special roles advising the president. They were stingy with the money and manpower they provided Souers. The Army's intelligence section hoarded its best officers and dumped its poor performers on the CIG. Souers was allowed to send his daily summary to Truman. But Byrnes asserted State Department privilege and delivered a daily foreign intelligence report from his diplomats. The admiral, not wanting to make waves, did not fight to gain more independence for the CIG. Truman could soon see that the pile of intelligence reports on his desk had not shrunk much—and that the CIG was not working.

Anxious to shed his detestable job and return to his business in Missouri, Souers, after less than six months as director, recommended to Truman that Lieutenant General Hoyt Vandenberg be made his replacement. Truman agreed and Vandenberg became the CIG's second director on June 10. An air commander during World War II, Vandenberg was an ambitious, high-ranking career man well connected on Capitol Hill. His uncle was Senator Arthur Vandenberg, the senior Republican on the Senate Foreign Relations Committee. The general wanted to be chief of staff of a future Air Force, with a fourth star pinned to his uniform. He saw the CIG directorship, which he took over for a little less than a year, as a stepping stone to the Air Force job he coveted.

Vandenberg moved aggressively, badgering the Army, Navy, and State Department to give the CIG more power. He beefed up the agency's capability to put out intelligence reports, he took over spying in Latin America from J. Edgar Hoover (who was not happy with the FBI giving up that territory), and he created a domestic contact service that interviewed American businessmen for any useful information they might have picked up during overseas travels. The general also gathered in remnants of Magruder's Strategic Services Unit in the War Department to form the Office of Special Operations (OSO), which enabled him to have spies and saboteurs overseas. By December, he commanded 1,816 intelligence officers, analysts, and support personnel, one-third of whom were posted overseas under the new Office of Special Operations.

Vandenberg held the CIG directorship about twice as long as Souers had, but the general left the agency in May 1947 as frustrated as the admiral had been over its lack of power and independence. Vandenberg had been constantly embroiled in bureaucratic battles with hidebound Pentagon intelligence officers. He ended up gaining only watered-down authority and he still had to beg for money from three departments, which treated him like a teenager coming to his dad for an allowance. The departments also kept shorting him on his allowance. The $12 million the CIG received for fiscal year 1947 was $10 million less than what it needed.

* * *

After a year and half in New York, Polly said she could see that her husband was becoming "extremely bored with [the] law." Carter,

Ledyard & Milburn was not the place Frank Wisner envisioned spending the rest of his life. Even the more interesting aspects of his legal work could not match the excitement he had experienced leading espionage operations. Though Wisner said little to them about the war, law colleagues could see that the frustration he felt dealing with the Soviets in Bucharest and Berlin still burned inside him. Wisner had joined Dulles, who was similarly bored with Sullivan & Cromwell, in trying to keep a hand in the business of stealing secrets. The two, for example, lobbied in Washington for a new intelligence agency.

In the summer of 1946, Stephen Penrose, who had served with Wisner in Cairo and now worked as an intelligence officer for the CIG, had a long talk in New York with his old friend, trying to persuade him to sign up with the new intelligence agency. Penrose admired Wisner and the former Navy commander was still recognized by others in intelligence circles as an espionage mastermind from his World War II days. CIG's leaders thought an extraordinarily able person like Wisner would be ideal for heading future operations in Latin America.

Wisner was interested, but he told Penrose that he had to be "sufficiently persuaded" that the CIG was there to stay. Wisner also had to be convinced that he would have some freedom to operate in the intelligence organization and that the position would be a career change for him and not just temporary duty. Wisner already suspected that the CIG could not offer anyone permanent employment. From the lines he still kept open to Washington, he was well aware of the agency's weaknesses and the rigid Pentagon bureaucracy that controlled it from the outside. He thought Souers was an ineffective leader. He never divulged what he thought of Vandenberg. Wisner also claimed he did not have "Potomac fever" and the urge to stay in Washington forever.

It turned out that Wisner did not have to turn down an offer from the CIG because an offer never ended up being made. Senior Army officers in the organization (Wisner called them the "whiskey colonels") worried that he would be a maverick like Wild Bill Donovan. The idea of him being formally offered a job was dropped.

But important military and diplomatic friends from Wisner's World War II years urged him to move to Washington. Dulles, who had become something of a career adviser, had an unusual suggestion. He told his Mississippi protégé that he should work his way into an inconspicuous federal job and then use that position to quietly assemble a cadre of secret agents who would wage political warfare against the Soviets, which was exactly what Wisner ended up doing.

Chapter 10

WASHINGTON

THE PHONE CALL FROM Charlie Saltzman came at the end of September 1947. A West Point graduate and former New York Stock Exchange executive, Saltzman had been a brigadier general during the war, serving as Mark Clark's deputy chief of staff. Wisner had known him for about ten years, mainly by reputation, and thought highly of the man, which was why he listened closely to what Saltzman was proposing over the phone. The former Army officer was now assistant secretary of state for occupied areas. It was an enormously important job, Wisner believed. Saltzman's office was taking over from the U.S. Army the American administration of its occupied territories, such as Germany. Saltzman would oversee the $400 million worth of U.S. economic and military aid flowing into troubled Greece and Turkey as part of the Truman Doctrine to contain Soviet expansion that the president had announced in March. The office also would have some responsibility for implementing $17 billion in economic aid to the wrecked economies of Western Europe under the Marshall Plan (named after its sponsor, Secretary of State George Marshall).

Saltzman needed a deputy and he needed him quickly. He

offered Wisner the job at a starting salary of $9,975—not as much as
what he was pulling in at the law firm, but it was the highest the
State Department could pay a nonpolitical appointee. Wisner would
be the diplomat's "alter ego" with full powers and decision-making
authority in Saltzman's absence. Wisner consulted friends he
trusted, but he had to do it fast. Saltzman wanted him in Washington and ready to work by October 10. Dulles, who checked out the
job, strongly urged Wisner to take it, as did the others he called.
Wisner's law partners agreed—reluctantly this time—to give him a
year's leave of absence. (These high-profile positions could be risky,
Wisner knew, so he wanted something to fall back on.) He phoned
Saltzman and told him he would be at his desk as a deputy assistant
secretary of state on October 10.

Everything happened so quickly, Frank and Polly did not have a
moment to sit down and ponder what effect the move would have on
their lives. But they sensed it would be profound. Wisner believed
that in this job, "he could do something to save the world," Polly
recalled. They decided that she and the children would remain in
New York for now, since the boys were still in school, and they still
had to find a place to live in DC.

* * *

Polly did not join Frank in Washington until January 1948, when
the boys had finished their school term in New York. She did not
know anyone well in the city except for Katharine Graham, whom
she had met in New York during the war. Kay was the daughter of
Eugene Meyer, a millionaire financier who had bought the *Washington Post* in 1933. He was allegedly a distant father. Her mother was
the perpetually unhappy Agnes Ernst Meyer, who Kay said had no
parenting skills. Kay was painfully shy, she lacked self-confidence,
and she was deathly afraid of being perceived by others as boring.
Over coffees and gossiping sessions and games of tennis, she became
close friends with fun-spirited Polly, whom she always found laughing

and hatching ideas for things they could do. Polly was deeply grateful for Kay taking her under her wing and introducing her to Washington society.

Their husbands got along as well. Phil Graham was an irreverent, breezy Floridian who had clerked for a Supreme Court justice and during the war served in the Pacific as an Army intelligence officer. Kay found him captivating; they had married in 1940. By 1946, Eugene Meyer was grooming his son-in-law to take over the *Washington Post* in two years. Graham impressed Wisner, who had always enjoyed palling around with men who succeeded because of their intelligence and personal drive, not because of the money they had inherited. Wisner could see that Graham was becoming a top-flight newspaper publisher, moving decisively to improve the long-moribund *Post*. Both men were from the South and enjoyed duck hunting together. Both shared a sense of revulsion about the horror they saw the Soviets perpetrating. They also shared, although they did not know it then, a disease that would one day profoundly affect their worlds.

* * *

One of Washington's oldest sections, founded in 1751, Georgetown had been a vibrant port village for slave and tobacco ships sailing up the Potomac River. Freed Blacks settled there after the Civil War. In the 1930s, New Dealers populated its relatively affordable houses northwest of the Capitol. After World War II, Georgetown was one of the few surrounding areas where returning veterans, destined to be the District's future leaders, could settle with their families. The mass production of suburban housing around Washington in northern Virginia and southern Maryland was just beginning. Frank and Polly began by renting a multistory brick house built in the early nineteenth century at Thirty-fourth Street NW between O and P Streets in Georgetown; the house had a garden terrace they used for entertaining. The family lived there until summer 1948, when they moved to a second rental house at 1308 Twenty-ninth Street NW, across from the residence of syndicated columnist Drew Pearson. They stayed there the next three years.

* * *

Wisner was given a spacious fourth-floor office with a high ceiling in the new State Department building erected just after World War II at Twenty-first Street NW and Virginia Avenue in Foggy Bottom. Impressing others at State with his energy, he plunged into the work, attending meeting after meeting with Saltzman or acting in his boss's absence at Washington and international conferences that were deciding important political, cultural, and economic matters for the occupied territories. Wisner also soon found, as Dulles thought he would, an avenue into clandestine operations. An obscure State Department and Pentagon committee organized three years earlier had recently been exploring ways the United States might fight the underground psychological warfare that the panel could see the Soviet Union waging worldwide against U.S. interests and on behalf of Communism. This interagency panel—now given the bland name State–Army–Navy–Air Force Coordinating Committee, or SANACC—had decided that the United States must fight fire with fire and begin its own covert psychological operations to counter what the Russians were doing in their global shadow war. The only question remaining—and it was a big question—was who should direct and control this covert action.

Wisner became a big player in these highly secret deliberations. Saltzman chaired the SANACC, but when he could not be there to preside over this important committee, Wisner took his place to steer its deliberations. The former Navy commander, who had taken on World War II clandestine projects far beyond the authority of such a young officer, was now doing the same as a rookie State Department official in the new cold war.

Wisner quickly found he was a junior member in an elite club of foreign policy heavyweights grappling with how the United States should respond to the Soviet threat. These were men he came to admire deeply, such as Undersecretary of State Dean Acheson, the key architect of the Truman Doctrine and an intellectual force behind the Marshall Plan who would soon be secretary of state; Averell Harriman, a wartime envoy to Stalin and Churchill who now as commerce secretary and Marshall Plan coordinator advocated a tough, businesslike approach to the Soviet Union; and State Department philosopher George Kennan, whose "Long Telegram" from Moscow in 1946 and anonymous "X" article in the journal *Foreign Affairs* the next year introduced the containment approach to Soviet expansionism. With access to these top minds, Wisner quickly became a State Department insider to whom Dulles now went for favors.

* * *

Incomes were rising. Consumer goods now filled store shelves. Automobiles were becoming plentiful on sales lots. *The Jack Benny Show* was a favorite on the radio but competing with more "television machines" bringing grainy black-and-white moving pictures into living rooms.

No one had an exact date for when the parties of what became known as the "Georgetown set" began. The Wisners were among their early hosts at the houses they rented on Q Street and then Twenty-ninth Street. In the mid-1930s, Georgetown had become known for its formal dinner parties. Not now. A younger generation, tested by war, fearful of the Soviets, yet confident in American superiority, began buying homes in Georgetown and having far more informal dinner parties for the leaders of Washington's emerging political, media, and government classes. A new camaraderie emerged. This generation enjoyed one another's company.

Along narrow cobblestone streets, their redbrick houses, many of them mansions, congregated in the five to six blocks south and east of the Wisner home, stretching down to M Street NW, which parallels the Potomac. The early members of the Georgetown set included Kay and Phil Graham, Avis and State Department counselor Charles "Chip" Bohlen, Adele and Undersecretary of State Robert Lovett, Evangeline and former OSS station chief David Bruce, Jane and Robert Joyce (who had returned to the State Department after serving in the OSS), columnists Stewart and Joseph Alsop, and the Wisners. The food at the Wisner house, served on elegant china, was always good. For large parties, Polly, who became important in building up Georgetown's social structure, had a team of Black cooks and servants help her.

The children were hustled up to their rooms before the guests arrived. Everyone smoked. Polly placed a silver chalice stuffed with cigarettes on the dining room table. (Frank smoked Camels and later Winstons.) Everyone drank—many of them heavily, some becoming embarrassingly drunk. The Wisners' son Ellis would come down the morning after and see rooms filled with empty old-fashioned and martini glasses. During his early days in Georgetown, Frank was not a heavy drinker, tending to nurse a glass of bourbon through much of the night. Polly enjoyed vodka on the rocks.

Wisner could be counted on to be a life of the party, often the last to leave. But he wasn't the only one. Bohlen, Joyce, Phil Graham, or Joe Alsop claimed the title on some nights. Some attendees liked to dance, play charades and backgammon, or hold friendly bets, but these weren't the reasons most came. Debating the issues of the day was the principal pastime of the Georgetown set's parties. Almost always they were foreign policy issues. No one much cared about domestic subjects. And as the crowd size grew, there were affairs on the side—most not too discreet, since everyone in the set gossiped about them the day after.

Stewart and Joseph Alsop became unofficial leaders of the Georgetown set. Invitations to the parties they threw at their houses were highly sought—and sometimes unnerving for government officials being shaken down for news. By the summer of 1946, their three-times-a-week "Matter of Fact" column was running in more than fifty newspapers. A Yale graduate and former OSS commando whose British wife, Tish, had worked for the MI5 counterintelligence service, Stewart Alsop was the cerebral, low-key, and casual brother. Wisner was closer to him (a trusted OSS comrade) than to his older brother, Joe, a fastidious and flamboyant Harvard man with a snobby manner and an acid tongue.

Joe was a master cultivator of confidential sources. His "zoo parties," as he soon called them, were held in an ugly modernistic house he built on Dumbarton Street NW; its cinder block exterior was painted yellow. He was also a homosexual, although not openly. Frank and Polly were both tolerant toward gays, not minding that their boys regularly visited Joe's house, where he loved spoiling them and other Georgetown set children with ice cream. Frankie called him "Uncle Joe." Enraged by columns the Alsop brothers wrote critical of the FBI, Hoover—who griped that "both of the Alsops are foul balls"—had agents monitor them loosely and report to him anything they turned up on the pair.

* * *

Georgetown was not the only important venue for Frank and Polly Wisner. The couple also planted roots in Maryland's countryside. When Frank II and Ellis woke up Christmas morning 1946, they almost immediately spotted on the fireplace mantel of the New York apartment a drawing of a pony that their father had sketched. Frank and Polly had bought the animal for the boys. It was stabled at the farm they now owned. The year before, the couple had purchased the Locust Hill farm near Galena on Maryland's Eastern Shore. It was within convenient distance for weekend visits—a four-hour drive south from their Manhattan apartment, a little more than three hours north from their rental home in Washington. Locust Hill consisted of 369 acres, 208 of which were tillable on flat Eastern

Shore land between the Sassafras and Chester Rivers, with a couple of small streams that joined up through the property. Wisner paid about $40,000 for Locust Hill, which was a lot of money back then, but still a bargain with the Eastern Shore area being economically depressed at the time.

The boys speculated that their father and mother had multiple reasons for buying Locust Hill. Wisner truly believed in the Jefferson ideal of the noble farmer, which he wanted to emulate. He was also a conservationist. Frank and Polly wanted their children to have a healthy country life. For Wisner, the farm would bring him some measure of solace. For Polly, it was a weekend and holiday refuge from hectic city life. An old friend, investor Henry Sears, who had taken Wisner duck hunting on the farm he owned nearby, also assured them they would be snaring a great deal with the Locust Hill property and urged them to buy it—before the couple fully knew the deal they were getting into. Locust Hill was a working dairy farm, most of whose land was good only as pasture, and it had always had a manager to run day-to-day operations with at least four farmhands. It turned out that the previous owner had shorted them on the number of cows that were supposed to come with the property and the herd that was left never turned a profit for Wisner. He always had to dip into his pocket to cover shortfalls. But Frank and Polly didn't care. Locust Hill brought them immeasurable pleasure.

Its main large farmhouse was an eighteenth-century Georgian structure divided into three sections. The first floor had several big fireplaces, a living room, a study Wisner loved to read in, a kitchen in the back with a bedroom above it, and a dining room with a porch running off it in the back and a couple of bedrooms above it. Winding steps also led up to the second floor, where a couple more bedrooms were located. Interior designer Margaret Weller, an old friend from Frank's UVA days, helped Polly furnish the farmhouse with simple but high-quality antique pieces.

Close by were several tall grain silos dating back to the 1930s, a hay barn with a milking barn attached to it, plus stalls for some seventy-five dairy cows and a shed in the back for cattle. There were also a couple of chicken houses, one of which was converted into a calf pen. Dozens of different types of vegetables were grown in a garden that Wisner enjoyed tending. He took great pride in the looks of the place, investing heavily to rebuild and upgrade it. Perry Wheeler, Polly's Georgetown gardener, helped her lay out the gardens and planted trees and boxwoods. Next to the farmhouse, Wisner also added a small pool and pool house, which the kids loved, and he had a contractor with a backhoe come in to dig a wide hole in nearby swampland for a duck pond. Polly, not impressed, called it "Lake Eyesore."

The farm never became a place where Wisner could truly unwind from the DC rat race, though. He hardly ever relaxed, working as hard on his short weekends at Locust Hill as he did the rest of the week in Washington. The farm became only a huge release for his nervous energy. Practically all his daylight hours there were spent doing chores—cutting thistles, clearing trees, shoveling manure from cow stalls, climbing onto a tractor to mow pastures, and picking okra, squash, beets, and tomatoes from his garden. When he was not digging earth outside, he was in the kitchen cooking, which he was good at. He made hearty breakfasts and for dinners served Southern dishes like seafood gumbo. The one piece of recreation Wisner enjoyed was hunting the plentiful ducks on Sears's property with his children or with friends he invited to the farm.

Frankie and Ellis loved Locust Hill because it finally offered them the opportunity to be with their father more, working with him in the fields or sitting with him in a duck blind. They called him "Daddy"; sometimes more affectionately he was "Dee Daw." It was a different type of upbringing for them. The boys grew up learning how to tend cows with their father rather than how to play golf or tennis. They cherished those precious times doing chores with him.

Wisner still left Polly with most of the child-rearing duties, though by her children's account, she was not a warm mom. Frank II never remembered his mother giving him a hug. The children called her "Ma" or "Mother." She was almost always formal with them. If a child wasn't filling his time constructively, Polly would fill it for him. She continually asked the boys what they were reading.

* * *

On July 26, 1947, Truman, who had become convinced his military was wasting money, signed the National Security Act into law. It merged the Army, the Navy, and a new Air Force into a Department of Defense, headed by a defense secretary, with the military's most senior officers in a Joint Chiefs of Staff advising him and the president. It had been such a knock-down, drag-out battle badgering the military services to agree on a new Defense Department—the Navy adamantly opposed the measure—that little attention was paid to a provision in the act, whose wording Donovan helped draft, setting up a Central Intelligence Agency. At hearings before Congress, some witnesses worried that this new CIA would become an "incipient Gestapo."

That would not be the case. But the CIA would become an independent government agency, responsible directly to Truman and overseen for him by a National Security Council. Instead of depending on handouts from the Army, Navy, and State Department, the new CIA would have its own budget and be able to hire its own people.

Everything about that budget and what the CIA did with the money became one of the most closely held secrets in the U.S. government. Only a few officials with the right clearances at the White House's Bureau of the Budget reviewed the CIA's spending request that was submitted to Congress. Once there, the CIA, which was referred to in documents and cables by more than twenty different cryptonyms, had its budget buried in different sections of the Defense Department money bill, which were reviewed by a small group of the members from the House and Senate appropriations committees. A tacit agreement was reached with congressional leaders that no one in the legislative branch would ask a lot of questions about how the CIA money was spent. The new National Security Council would broadly oversee the operations the agency carried out "with the utmost secrecy," Truman and the other NSC members ordered.

Bureaucratic wars die hard in Washington. An act of Congress did not guarantee a strong Central Intelligence Agency. The military services and the State Department could not kill this new spy organization. But that didn't mean they had to cooperate with it. The National Security Act Truman signed gave the CIA a firm foundation in law, which it previously lacked. But very little else changed. The CIA's creation in no way diminished the intelligence activities of the Pentagon and the State Department. The CIA's director was supposed to coordinate all these activities, but it was a toothless authority. The new agency could not tell the other departments what to do with their intelligence operations.

Moreover, Truman and the Congress conceived of the CIA as an organization that would simply collate information other agencies produced on the Soviet Bloc and coordinate American intelligence-collection operations overseas. The CIA would be a protective unit that would warn the U.S. government of foreign troubles ahead, so there would be no more surprises like Pearl Harbor. It was not envisioned as a covert operations outfit that would secretly intervene in the affairs of nations overseas with clandestine political, psychological warfare, and paramilitary operations to prevent trouble from happening in the first place.

Whatever its mission would be, Wild Bill Donovan wanted to lead the new CIA. He had surrogates lobby Truman to make him director of central intelligence. Truman never considered offering him the job, particularly not after Donovan called Truman a "tragic figure" on the campaign trail. Some thought it was the State Department's turn to have its representative lead the CIA, since two military officers—Souers and Vandenberg—had already held the top intelligence job. But a civilian director of central intelligence was too much for the military community to bear. Allen Dulles, the State Department's candidate for CIA director, was passed over for another admiral from the Navy, Roscoe Hillenkoetter, who had replaced Vandenberg on May 1, nearly three months before Truman created the agency. Hillenkoetter had played only a marginal role in the debate over the National Security Act. Vandenberg had testified on it before Congress. Hillenkoetter also got knocked down a peg with the first agency paycheck he drew. Because it had been assumed that the CIA director would be a military officer, the annual salary for the position was trimmed to $14,000 from $15,000. The reason: it was considered unseemly for a CIA director's salary to be higher than that of the Army chief of staff or the chief of Naval operations.

Hillenkoetter—friends called him "Hilly"—had seen intense combat in World War II. Wounded when the Japanese attacked the USS *West Virginia* battleship at Pearl Harbor, he became the senior officer of the surviving crew. Hillenkoetter also had diplomatic and intelligence experience. He had served before America's entry into the war as an assistant Naval attaché in France and after Pearl Harbor as an intelligence officer on Admiral Chester Nimitz's Pacific Fleet staff. Though he was smarter than many gave him credit for, Hilly had a "nattering nature," as one author described it, and could be slow to make up his mind. One thing he quickly decided, however, was that he did not want to be CIA director. He probably never should have been given the job in the first place. Newly promoted to admiral, Hillenkoetter did not have Vandenberg's rank or aggressiveness. Though congressmen thought he was a nice enough fellow, Hilly was unaccustomed to dealing with them and his testimonies before their hearings often became strained affairs. The rear admiral took personal offense at hostile questions. Hillenkoetter soon longed to be back at sea, which was where Wisner thought he belonged instead of in Washington.

* * *

The world careened from one crisis to another as Wisner settled into his new State Department job during the fall of 1947. The Russians had Bulgarian agrarian leader Nikola Petkov executed—his body stashed in an unmarked grave. A Soviet veto in the Security Council stifled United Nations action in Greece. Russian troops grew menacing along Iran's border. India and Pakistan convulsed in violence as their British rule ended. The Philippines was racked by Hukbalahap guerrilla attacks. Communist-inspired strikes rocked Italy and France. Britain's economy tanked. To counter the Marshall Plan's propaganda gains, Moscow organized the Communist Information Bureau (Cominform) among its satellites and party faithful in Western countries.

Quickly recognized as a problem solver at international conferences, Wisner had flown to Germany to inspect its camps for hundreds of thousands of displaced East European refugees who had fled the Red Army. He saw more than the fact that these were wretched and desperate souls trapped in a humanitarian crisis. The camps were full of die-hard anti-Communists, Wisner believed. They had the potential to be valuable agents the United States could recruit, train, and infiltrate back into Soviet-occupied Eastern Europe for espionage, sabotage, and propaganda missions. He hatched the idea for a secret $5 million program, code-named "Bloodstone," to do just that.

Wisner's only problem: there was no one to carry out his plan. Hillenkoetter opposed the CIA enlisting émigré groups. Wisner decided that a separate agency was needed to mount the operation.

Chapter 11

WIZ'S SECRET WAR

THE NATIONAL SECURITY COUNCIL convened a meeting on August 19, 1948, in the Cabinet Room of the White House. The NSC members sat around the long black table that stretched over most of the length of the room. A portrait of Woodrow Wilson hung over the fireplace mantel at one end. Tall arched windows along a side of the room let in plenty of sunlight. Truman, who had been sworn in as president in this room after Roosevelt died, had not attended many NSC meetings, but he made a point of being at this one because an important decision would be made. James Forrestal (now secretary of defense) and Secretary of State George Marshall sat to his right. Other top national security officials in the administration, including CIA director Roscoe Hillenkoetter, arranged themselves in the remaining chairs around the table. They had gathered that summer day in the Cabinet Room to pick the leader of a highly classified covert operations organization that the NSC had okayed two months earlier.

The directive setting up this clandestine outfit was so secret, cabinet officers who served on the National Security Council were asked to read a copy of it at the White House and then return it to a security officer who locked the document back up in a safe. Responding to what it believed was a "vicious" psychological warfare campaign the Soviet Union was waging against the United States, the NSC on June 18 had approved a directive, designated NSC 10/2, that set up an Office of Special Projects—later renamed just as vaguely the Office of Policy Coordination—to launch a wide range of covert operations against the Soviet Union. The subversive warfare the Kremlin had perfected would be thrown back at it. The Office of Policy Coordination—or OPC, as it quickly came to be called—would secretly conduct economic and political warfare against the U.S.S.R., wage anti-Soviet propaganda campaigns, carry out guerrilla attacks, and aid anti-Communist resistance groups inside the East European satellite nations.

Psychological warfare traced back to the days of the Romans. George Washington had dabbled in it as president, and during World War II, Wild Bill Donovan had launched a broad covert warfare campaign against the Axis powers. But after the Japanese surrender, covert operations, always considered by Americans to be un-American, were largely liquidated. By 1948, however, a covert warfare capability had wide support in the White House, the State Department, and the Pentagon, although the policymakers believed that it should be carried out on a limited basis. The National Security Council knew it was taking a big step. Covert operations, many of them violating the laws of foreign countries, had to be carefully controlled and orchestrated. Truman assumed Forrestal and Marshall would closely supervise them, which ended up not being the case. They were busy men.

George Kennan, whom Marshall picked to direct the State Department's policy planning staff, had been the intellectual driver in setting up the Office of Policy Coordination. An emotional and somewhat neurotic man who suffered bouts of melancholy, Kennan had as pessimistic an attitude as Wisner toward the Soviets. He argued forcefully that the U.S. government needed a covert political warfare capability and prodded cabinet members to set up such a unit.

But where to put this secret outfit? Though he wanted to control what OPC did in peacetime, Marshall did not want this operation housed inside his State Department, fearing its sinister activities could jeopardize his diplomatic programs if exposed. Likewise, Forrestal didn't want the unit in the Defense Department, though he wanted to be able to control it during a war. The NSC had lost confidence in Hillenkoetter being able to handle the mission. The CIA director, who did not want his agency mixed up in these subversive operations, had been first given the covert warfare assignment (much to his displeasure) and had organized it in his Office of Special Operations, but it had been a half-hearted effort that performed poorly.

The solution everyone came up with was a bureaucratic anomaly. OPC's budget would come from money Congress had appropriated for the CIA. Hillenkoetter would provide the new organization with office space and the funds to run its operations. But the admiral had no control over those operations; OPC's activities would be directed by the State and Defense Departments, bypassing the CIA. Large parts of Hillenkoetter's agency would be kept in the dark about exactly what that secretive outfit was doing. And the State Department, not Hillenkoetter, would pick the leader of this unit, although it had to be someone acceptable to the admiral.

Understandably, Hillenkoetter adamantly objected to this clumsy arrangement. It was a slap in the face, a vote of no-confidence, as he saw it, and a prescription for bureaucratic war without end. Allen Dulles, who had been advising the White House on how the CIA should operate, agreed that the arrangement made no sense. But Communist-inspired events overseas fueled the National Security Council's drive to quickly launch a covert war it did not see Hilly capable of waging. In addition to organizing strikes in France and Italy, Communists had staged a violent February coup replacing Czechoslovakia's government with a pro-Kremlin regime. General

Lucius Clay, the U.S. European commander, cabled the Pentagon the next month with a chilling prediction that war with the Soviet Union "may come with dramatic suddenness"—although the CIA had no evidence that would happen. A week after the National Security Council approved the directive to set up the Office of Policy Coordination, the Soviets blockaded rail, highway, and water traffic into Berlin, whose American sector had to be relieved by a U.S. airlift. Wisner, who visited Berlin during the blockade, favored U.S. tanks fighting their way to the German capital (the Soviets would not test a nuclear device for another year). Truman rejected that idea.

Kennan first asked Allen Dulles if he would head the new covert action unit. Dulles begged off. David Bruce's name was floated. The former OSS London station chief was not interested. Kennan finally forwarded to his bosses six candidates, with Wisner's name at the top. Kennan claimed that he did not know Wisner that well, "but his qualifications seem reasonably good." William Harding Jackson, a former Carter, Ledyard & Milburn law partner and an OSS veteran, told a colleague he hoped Wisner would turn down the job. That kind of pressure cooker "will kill him," Wisner's friend said.

Wisner ignored those warnings. He believed he was ideally suited to lead the future Office of Policy Coordination—and he was. Wisner had the background, training, temperament, and drive for this job. He fervently believed in OPC's mission. No one had to persuade him to take it on. Wisner had a passion for action. This would be a long cold war and he believed he could play an important part in America's winning it. Marshall, for one, admired the energy his deputy assistant secretary displayed.

In National Security Council meetings, slips of paper were always passed out to its voting members, who marked them indicating their department's approval—or disapproval—of an issue that was being decided. At the NSC's August 19 conference, the vote slips approved a recommendation from the State Department, which Hillenkoetter reluctantly went along with, that Frank Wisner be selected to head up what became the Office of Policy Coordination. Truman then agreed that Wisner would be their man.

While the approval process for his appointment crept along, Wisner worked deftly behind the scenes to shape the job he would take and to begin doing it. He brainstormed with colleagues on how European émigrés could be used in anti-Soviet operations. At a crucial August 6 White House meeting with Hillenkoetter, Kennan, and Defense Department officials—it had occurred nearly two weeks before Truman formally approved his leading the new outfit—Wisner ran circles around Hillenkoetter, maneuvering the hapless admiral into agreeing to give him the independence he wanted with the job. The young deputy assistant secretary, who had become a skilled bureaucratic tactician, insisted on dealing directly with the State Department and the Pentagon in launching covert projects—and not having to wade through the CIA's bureaucracy in each case. Fine, Hillenkoetter said, but he wanted to be "kept informed in regard to all important projects and decisions," even if he didn't have the power to veto them. Wisner agreed and had this arrangement put down on paper in a "memorandum of conversation," which Hillenkoetter and the others in the room signed. The crucial adjective in this memo was "important." Wisner would run only important projects by the admiral; the gap between them and all the other clandestine projects that Wisner did not consider important could be huge. Hillenkoetter had been outfoxed. Wisner had gotten him to agree to an Office of Policy Coordination pretty much independent of the admiral's CIA.

Wisner started work on September 5 at an annual salary of $10,305—not high by Wall Street standards but respectable in Washington. Hillenkoetter gave him a security clearance to see the CIA's most sensitive intelligence. Wisner became obsessed with secrecy, requiring aides who needed to read one of the several copies of the directive setting up his organization (NSC 10/2) to sign a special access document and then return the directive to the boss's safe when they were through. Wisner hated testifying before outside review boards and submitting justifications for the equipment he needed to low-level supply officers. It only increased the number of people who knew something about the Office of Policy Coordination, which soon was listed on documents under almost as many cryptonyms as the CIA.

It didn't take Communist agents long to sniff out Wisner's organization, although they were not quite sure what it did. A Czech intelligence report noted that the Americans had launched a covert action program with an inscrutable name, so they simply called it "Organization X."

The men in the State and Defense Departments who were assigned to work with Wisner's secret organization were longtime acquaintances he trusted. Kennan assigned Robert Joyce (an old Wisner friend from their OSS days together) and Asia expert John Paton Davies Jr. to be his policy planning staff representatives working with the OPC. The Defense Department's liaison to Wisner's unit became General Magruder, the Strategic Services Unit leader and another old friend. The guidance these representatives gave Wisner in their weekly meetings was broad, allowing him wide latitude to craft secret operations as he saw fit. The Office of Policy Coordination was a novelty for senior government officials little experienced in covert operations. John McCloy, soon to become American high commissioner for Germany, wanted only to be kept "generally informed" of OPC activities in that country.

Three days after assuming his duties, Wisner met with a handful of assistants he had borrowed from the CIA in the dilapidated J Building, which had been built at the beginning of World War II along the Mall's Reflecting Pool between the Washington Monument and Lincoln Memorial. Wisner eventually installed a secret recording system under his desk, on a phone, and under the conference table in his room that he could flip on for important conversations he was having. The CIA had allotted his OPC space in its run-down J and I Buildings, which were boxlike two-story wooden structures painted white, with creaking steps and tin roofs. Armed guards patrolled around the structures. Wisner nicknamed his office the "Rat Palace" because he had to share it with the rodents. The CIA's nearby K Building had a cafeteria that, with its warped floor and deteriorating walls, looked more like a prisoners' dining hall. Sometimes Wisner took a car to the director's dining room in the agency's headquarters on Navy Hill, where he could buy lunch for $1.20.

By November, Wisner had no more than fifteen people on his payroll plotting operations for Germany, Austria, and the Soviet-occupied Balkan nations. Over the next six months, he managed to place staffers on a French desk and have others begin projects in the Near East. "The rest of the world was still pretty uncovered," according to a secret OPC report. Like Donovan in World War II, Wisner in peacetime looked for the country's best and brightest. He favored energetic, bold, and imaginative men and women, even if they had no cloak-and-dagger experience, over former Army intelligence officers and FBI agents past their prime. The CIA was already a popular organization and Wisner's OPC became one as well, soon attracting a wide array of patriotic young operatives with political, business, military, and legal skills.

Wisner first tried to recruit Stewart Alsop to be his deputy. The columnist, who had parachuted into Nazi-occupied France for the OSS, turned him down. Wisner then cabled a message to Frank Lindsay, another OSS veteran who had infiltrated into Yugoslavia during the war and was now working in Paris with the Marshall Plan. Would Lindsay drop by his office the next time he was in Washington? Wisner asked in his telegram. Wisner had a job that might interest him. The next time he was in DC, Lindsay met with Wisner, who asked him to be his deputy. Lindsay, a Stanford University graduate who had been an atomic energy negotiator for the United Nations and a legislative aide in Congress, was hesitant at first and consulted his boss, Averell Harriman, back in Paris. Harriman told him to take the position. The Cold War was coming. Wisner's unit would be on the front lines of it. "Other people can do your job in the Marshall Plan," Harriman said. Lindsay did take the job and was soon one of Wisner's good friends.

Wisner's secretary, Billie Morrone, became his most loyal and devoted employee. A Christian Scientist who lived quietly in Silver Spring, Maryland, Morrone was a stocky, plain-faced woman in her middle-aged years when she came to OPC. Wisner, who was intent on hiring more women for his outfit, could be a demanding boss over them. He would get snappish on the rare occasions Morrone misspelled a word in a letter he had dictated. But Billie was unflappable. Well-mannered and dependable, she soon was handling not only Wisner's secretarial chores at the office but also his private financial affairs at home, such as paying household bills and managing savings accounts for the children. Other top Wisner staffers soon found out that if they wanted the boss's attention on a memo, it was best to route it through Billie.

The aides who joined Wisner's unconventional group early on came from a wide range of backgrounds. They included Joseph Bryan, a prominent Virginia journalist who dreamed up propaganda stunts OPC could play on the Soviets. James McCargar, who was the son of a prominent San Francisco banker and who had been a military intelligence officer during the war, was recruited to oversee operations in Southeastern Europe. Army colonel Boris T. Pash, a White Russian émigré, supervised a hodgepodge of special operations duties that included kidnapping and assassinations if needed. The flamboyant Michael Burke, a former University of Pennsylvania football star, was hired to put the infiltration skills he had learned in the OSS to use slipping operatives into the Soviet Union and its satellites. On a trip to Paris in the spring, Wisner talked E. Howard Hunt—a part-time novelist, flashy dresser, and former OSS agent who was in Europe working for the Marshall Plan—into joining OPC to be on its political and psychological warfare staff. Wisner also hired African American Richard Hines to chauffeur him around town in a government car. Hines later taught Wisner's son Ellis how to parallel park when he applied for his driver's license.

Carmel Offie was one of Wisner's most controversial recruits. An open homosexual described by people who knew him as a physically ugly man, Offie had been a highly skilled State Department fixer, collecting a loyal following of senior diplomats who greatly appreciated the favors he did for them (many ethically questionable). Offie abruptly resigned from the State Department under a cloud for cutting too many corners. Wisner put him in charge of finding refugees (some of them former German military and diplomatic officers with seamy backgrounds) to conspire against the Russians. The multilingual, workaholic, and opportunistic fixer also found Polly a top-flight cook for her household and had the Wisner children over to his house frequently to watch cartoon movies that he showed on a projector in his large basement. Files soon began growing in the FBI and the DC Metropolitan Police Department on Offie's arrests for homosexual activities.

The OPC staff soon began calling Wisner "Wiz," as Polly did. An aide posted at a desk outside his office as a sort of gatekeeper was known as the "Ozzard of Wiz." The work became intense, but the men and women around Wiz remained a fun-loving bunch. Free spirits in the psychological warfare section liked to fire BB guns at balloons in one office. Many of his aides drove MGs and Jaguars to work. Wisner was content with a beat-up old Willys-Overland car that looked like a jeep.

Recruiting became a constant struggle. Wisner needed thousands of operatives. He had CIA men and former OSS officers serve as spotters to find talented students on elite campuses like Yale's and Princeton's. He brought in OSS veterans and, like Donovan had done when he began his agency, found prospects among longtime associates. They were referred to as "FOW"—friends of Wisner. The Army at first resisted transferring its officers to OPC but soon relented. Like Donovan, Wisner preferred recruiting men and women based on how suitable they seemed to be as unconventional operators rather than for any specific skills they might have—"bold Easterners," Stewart Alsop once called them.

For the hundreds of recruits pouring in, their spy training was cursory and makeshift, much of it a holdover of the OSS instruction. Students were first sent to an auditorium in an Agriculture

Department building, where they received a three-day orientation on intelligence collection and the CIA. Tradecraft classes in handling agents and secret communications were held at Building T-30 and Alcott Hall, with their low ceilings and poorly ventilated rooms. Future guerrilla fighters were sent to the Fort Benning, Georgia, Army post for parachute and paramilitary training.

The number of operatives in Wisner's force did not so much grow as it exploded. Within a year his OPC had a $4.7 million budget with 302 agents and five overseas stations. By the beginning of 1952, Wisner had an $82 million budget that grew to $200 million by the end of the year, with 2,812 staffers plus 3,142 contract personnel and forty-seven foreign stations, making his organization larger than the rest of the CIA. Hillenkoetter's security officers fretted that Wisner's force was expanding too rapidly with too little regard for proper vetting of all these new hires. Wisner complained that obtaining CIA security clearances was a cumbersome process that bogged down his putting talented officers into the field. The agency, for example, checked a prospect's name seven different ways. Wisner began putting spies in the field while this time-consuming vetting dragged on.

At first the CIA diverted funds from its other programs to pay for the Office of Policy Coordination. But as his operation grew, Wisner found another important money source. At the end of 1948, he paid a visit to Richard Bissell, a lanky former Yale economist working as a senior officer for the Marshall Plan in Washington. Wisner, whom Bissell had met socially at Georgetown parties but otherwise had not had any contact with on official business, told Bissell he needed money to finance covert operations the OPC was carrying out, many of them in Europe. Wisner could not divulge what these secret operations were, but he told Bissell he had flown to Paris and received Harriman's approval to have money skimmed off for OPC from a special $200 million–a-year Marshall Plan fund that paid for administrative and other miscellaneous expenses, and there was not to be much accounting for how the money was spent.

Bissell was baffled by the request—Wisner would say nothing about how the money would be used—but he ultimately released the funds to the OPC.

* * *

Within the close confines of Washington's top secret world, Frank Wisner quickly became a star. Even Hillenkoetter had to admit that his rival was a highflier, and gave him superlative efficiency reports. Wisner's salary was soon increased to $10,330 a year—more than an Army brigadier general made—and it kept on increasing. One CIA report antiseptically described him as "a man of intense application . . . a singular choice to create a covert organization from scratch"— which was true. He showed up for work always well tailored and manicured, his shoes bought from John Lobb in London.

Wisner's working style was simple—complete immersion in whatever interested him. His day began at about eight thirty in the morning, each hour consumed by attending meetings, dictating to Billie Morrone, reviewing the reports of aides, and crafting his own recommendations to others in the government. He met weekly with his division chiefs, with Kennan, and with the OPC representatives from the State Department and the Pentagon. He would look at the clock when he thought too much time was being taken in a meeting on a particular subject. Lunch (if he didn't eat it in the director's dining room) was usually at his desk. Rarely did he finish before seven thirty in the evening and rarely did he not have a social obligation for the night.

Wisner could not have cared less about the minutiae of administrative details and regulations. He hated bureaucracies and admin chores and openly acknowledged that he wasn't good at them. Colleagues said he was more of an idea man. But he could be skilled at playing one organization off another and coldly ruthless in bureaucratic squabbles, which earned him devoted enemies in the CIA and other parts of the government. He was overwhelmingly preoccupied with the here and now—particularly when it had to do with his operations. Sitting around theorizing about, say, a future hot war with the Soviet Union bored him. Wisner didn't hate organizational structure, but he was intent on using it to further his own agenda.

His subordinates considered him a charismatic leader. They liked working for him, admired him and his strong sense of right and wrong, although they at times found his intensity tiresome and chafed at his micromanaging. Wisner had strong likes and dislikes. He appeared impatient and urgent about everything he undertook. He wore out a number of personal assistants and overloaded Billie with work. He detested presumptuous employees who lobbied him for promotions. He dressed down operatives in the field who did not follow his orders to the letter. Sloppy note-taking of what he had said at a meeting particularly irritated him. At different times he could be dour, irascible, acidulous, droll, and earthy with his humor. He would look startled when told an officer had already gone home at the end of the day. That reaction usually reached the officer, who never again left before the boss.

Wisner at that point displayed many of the symptoms of what psychiatrists call hypomania: when a person shows boundless energy and enthusiasm, an effusion of ideas, an expansive mood, increased perceptiveness, and overpowering charm. Hypomania can be intoxicating. Some artists feel their creative and productive best when in a hypomanic state. Lord Byron, George Frideric Handel, Vincent van Gogh, and Winston Churchill experienced hypomania. Its qualities, such as high physical and intellectual drive, are revered in political Washington. Wisner was admired for his work appetite. He rarely showed fatigue. He did not need much sleep. He was extremely bright and could think quickly on his feet. He was capable of juggling multiple tasks at the office, on the farm, and with the family's business interests in Laurel, but almost incapable of just relaxing and enjoying a baseball game on television. He could be verbose (another possible symptom of hypomania), but his family believed that might have been a product of his training as a lawyer (they're always wordy in briefs). He could become extremely angry when he thought someone had crossed him, but everyone gets that way now and then, and in Wisner's case, he tended to bottle up his anger. No one, least of all Wisner, suspected that he was hypomanic.

* * *

Wisner's socializing with the Georgetown set quickly became an extension of work. The people who came to his house, to the Graham house, to the Alsop houses, and to the Georgetown set's other homes did so for more than just having fun. They attended the parties to get business done after hours. Government officials not invited to these soirees were contemptuous of them. Foreign Service officer Thomas L. Hughes dismissed Wisner and his ilk as "big-time elitists, congratulating themselves at night for what they had achieved during the day." But Wisner, who belonged to Washington's Metropolitan Club and F Street Club, made no apologies for being a master networker. His endless presence in the Georgetown salons clearly gave him a definite advantage over other government officials who weren't invited. Through being at the same parties so many times, Wisner and Kennan—and their wives, Polly and Annelise—became close friends who discovered they had a lot in common. At the parties, Wisner got to charm Acheson and Harriman, and grew closer to Helms (who was becoming an officer on his way up in Hillenkoetter's CIA).

Polly became a key player in Frank's networking. An avid and gregarious hostess, she came off to others as elegant and well-read, a wife who was more than just a backup for her husband. Polly openly advocated progressive causes popular in Georgetown, such as civil rights. A skilled retailer of gossip, she wanted to know everything being murmured on the side—and she usually did, passing along the morsels to Frank. Friends often found her talking to them in a whisper and appearing spellbound over what they had to say, like they imagined a good CIA wife would do.

Some of the hardest work at the parties was done by the journalists hunting for scoops and the government officials hoping to manipulate them. The Alsop brothers, whose column appeared in more than a hundred newspapers by the end of 1948, were the most energetic harvesters. The one thing Harry Truman and the Kremlin could agree on was that they both hated Stewart and Joseph Alsop. Truman called them the "Sop Sisters." *Pravda* accused the duo of being "warmongers and militarists." The Wisners' relationship with the Alsops grew complicated. While Frank enjoyed more the company of Stewart and Tish Alsop, who also owned a rural Maryland farm, Polly grew closer to Joe, who taught her how to buy fine art and quality antiques.

The brothers had two rules for their column. First, never express an opinion that could not be supported by the facts they had gathered, and, second, always include one exclusive piece of information in each column. They claimed they did not push too hard for scoops at the Georgetown set parties, but that was not always the case. Chip Bohlen eventually became fed up with Joe's constant probing. So did Wisner. And the brothers, especially Stewart, could be thin-skinned when the barbs were directed at them. To further whatever cause he happened to be pursuing, Wisner routinely planted stories with Joe, who was always eager for the tips and made no apologies for being used by the spymaster. The two men were like-minded on many foreign policy issues. Joe thought war with the Soviet Union increasingly likely and he agreed with Wisner that long-term U.S. strategy to defeat the Russians must include covert warfare that should be kept secret from Americans.

* * *

On the weekends they could get away, Wisner drove with Polly and the kids in a station wagon to the farm early Saturday morning and left Sunday evening. Frank was not a churchgoer. Polly attended the early-morning communion at the Shrewsbury Parish Episcopal Church near the farm.

Polly handled most of Locust Hill's business chores. Frank was as much a chaotic manager on the farm as he was at OPC. Deputy Frank Lindsay remembers walking into Wisner's office one day to find him stuck on the phone with Polly, who was giving him detailed instructions on the disposal of cow manure at the farm. Wisner had hired Billy Sigman, a local herdsman, to be the farm manager. (At the job interview, Frank, when he heard Sigman's name, blurted out, "Goddamn, that's a German Jew!" Sigman said he had no idea that was the case.) But Polly handled the farm business with Sigman. Wisner tried a number of schemes at Locust Hill that did not work, like feeding broccoli stalks to cows (the cows didn't like them). He bought sixty head of Jersey cattle for milking but soon discovered the venture was not profitable, and he invested more than $2,000 with Henry Sears and others in a failing business to reprocess alfalfa for poultry and cattle feed.

Locust Hill, however, became far more valuable as a venue to entertain people in Wisner's spy business. Country homes in rural Virginia and Maryland were a way for Washington's elite to escape and relax. Locust Hill became a way for Wisner to escape and network. He invited diplomats, CIA officials, administration bigwigs, Romanian expats, and journalists to the farm for weekends of duck hunting, seafood gumbo, shots of bourbon, and confidential conversations in a secluded setting.

A Saturday and Sunday were also reserved each year for when Frank and Polly's longtime Southern friends, who were not part of the Washington circle, came to Locust Hill for what was called the "mud weekend." They played bridge, charades, and a game they called Racing Pyramids, where after several drinks two teams formed human pyramids that competed for who could move forward the fastest without collapsing to the floor.

The children of the influential people invited to Locust Hill also found its host fun to be around. At the farm, Wisner enjoyed mingling with the children, playing backgammon and Parcheesi with them and making a point of speaking to them on their level. He showed them a humorous side many never forgot. He called little Wendy, who was absolutely devoted to her father, "my black-eyed tyrant." "Wisner had this grin," recalled Elizabeth Winthrop Alsop, Stewart Alsop's daughter. "When he looked at me, it always came with a wink—kind of [a] conspiratorial 'you and I are in this together' type of a wink. This was heady for an eleven-year-old."

Chapter 12

ALBANIA

WISNER'S OPC HIT THE floor running. Al Cox, a China hand from the OSS, was sent to Taiwan to advise Chiang Kai-shek's Nationalist government, which had evacuated to the island to escape Mao Zedong's Communist army on the mainland. Merritt Ruddock, a free spirit who wore riding boots to the office, was dispatched to London to work with British special operations experts.

Wisner divided his organization into five functional groups: psychological warfare (using newspapers and radio for propaganda), political warfare (to bribe foreign officials, among other things), economic warfare (to manipulate overseas economies and currencies), preventive direct action (a euphemistic way of saying "sabotage and subversion"), and a miscellaneous function that took on jobs that didn't fit in the other groups. He was forced to accept a grab bag of projects cast off by the CIA and other agencies: for example, to float balloons over Iron Curtain countries to drop propaganda leaflets and to deliver cash under the table to anti-Communist labor unions in Western Europe. Wisner got so many phone calls from Donovan about how he should run OPC that he stopped taking the calls, which irritated Donovan, who could be thin-skinned.

Warned by CIA reports that the Soviets were tightening their grip over their satellites behind the Iron Curtain, Wisner focused first on placing officers in Europe. As his force grew, he branched out to Middle Eastern, South Asian, and Far Eastern countries with stations. South America and sub-Saharan Africa remained low on his priority list for the first two years.

But even in high-priority Europe, Wisner's stations had only skeletal staffs that could not do much more than signal to local intelligence services and anti-Communist groups that American help was on the way. Marshall Plan officials wanted Wisner's operatives to move quickly in France, where the Communists were making headway sapping French morale and subverting the American aid program, they feared. Wisner promised to do what he could, including secretly paying for the distribution in France of the just released movie *Joan of Arc* starring Ingrid Bergman. Marshall Plan officials thought the film might have an "electrifying effect upon French psychology."

Wisner moved just as quickly to establish Germany as his main base for anti-Soviet operations. By the end of 1948, he had some thirty agents at three bases in Germany (their number would swell to 253 in two years). Hillenkoetter's CIA station in Karlsruhe proved to be surprisingly cooperative in helping Wisner's field representative begin his anti-Soviet propaganda work. It took more prodding from Wisner to get the U.S. Army's senior officers in other parts of Germany on board with his project to recruit and train political refugees and deserters from the Soviet zone to be OPC agents.

The U.S. government "should stop thinking of the Soviet Union as a monolithic nation and investigate the internal strains," Wisner lectured. To help OPC discern the strains that it could exploit, he hired two German consultants considered experts on the Soviet Union: Gustav Hilger, a Russian-born German who had served in the Reich's embassy in Moscow, and Nicholas Poppe, a Russian social scientist well-versed in the Soviet Union's various ethnic groups.

Wisner paid no attention to the prominent roles both Hilger and Poppe had played in the Nazi regime. His was an unconventional war that required unconventional norms of behavior. The CIA and the KGB observed an unspoken rule that neither agency killed the other's officers but that the foreign agents both sides hired could be picked off. Wisner ordered that defectors receive special handling to drain them of the intelligence they might bring. Foreign spies might need to lie completely dormant for years before they could gain the confidence of their government bosses and steal secrets for the Americans, Wisner realized. In moments of crisis, if there was any doubt about the legality of an operation overseas, the default should be to press ahead with the mission because that would be what the other side would do. It was dirty work, but Wisner, who had a moralistic streak, was never bothered by it. He was spying, he believed, for a greater good.

* * *

Germany notwithstanding, it was only a matter of time before relations grew toxic between the Office of Policy Coordination and the CIA's clandestine branch that fielded its spies, the Office of Special Operations. Wisner and Hillenkoetter clashed as well over the OPC fiefdom. Though he promised to be a close collaborator, Wisner rarely attended Hillenkoetter's staff meetings and ferociously fought CIA officers who tried to tread on OPC turf. Wisner pushed to control his own budget, while Hillenkoetter shoved just as hard to supervise how Wisner spent his money. Hillenkoetter's officers also resented that Wisner's force was showered with more funds to spend, soon outbidding OSO for the services of the same foreign sources and groups in the field. "OPC was born rich while OSO remained relatively poor," according to one CIA history.

There was a clash of cultures as well. Like Donovan, Wisner and his OPC were mission oriented and action oriented, hatching covert operations that would have an immediate impact on world events.

The intelligence officers in OSO, who had largely bowed out of the covert operations business, were more circumspect, more committed to attracting little attention, and more attuned to the long term and the unspectacular task of gathering secrets. OSO officers considered themselves the professional clandestine officers. They regarded OPC men as reckless amateurs. Wisner dismissed OSO officers as "a bunch of old washerwomen gossiping over their laundry." The rift also became personal. OPC officers were often paid more than their OSO counterparts.

Wisner tried to hammer out an intelligence-sharing agreement with OSO, but little came of it. Hillenkoetter's espionage officers treated their OPC counterparts as outsiders, and Wisner's men were just as reluctant to share secrets with OSO officers. In stations overseas, the U.S. government had operating what amounted to two spy organizations—one reporting to the State and Defense departments, the other answering to the CIA; both often competing for the same sources, and neither talking much to the other. The feuding became even worse in Washington, where the two operations were crowded next to each other in temporary buildings along the Reflecting Pool. OSO officers often found a job applicant they had rejected walking over to a neighboring building and being hired by the OPC for more money.

FBI agents gleefully monitored the bureaucratic battle for Hoover. One internal bureau memo quoted Hillenkoetter as declaring that Wisner "had to go." If the admiral actually said that, he was being naive. Frank Wisner was becoming one of the most powerful men in Washington. The secret organization he led was unprecedented in American history. A master at playing departments against one another, Wisner amassed a great deal of political clout, far outpacing Hillenkoetter, whom he regarded as a weakling. Within six months of taking over OPC, Wisner had elevated himself in the ranks of Washington's influential people to a position even higher than the directorship of central intelligence. He had become an unofficial adviser to the U.S. government on foreign and intelligence policy in general. And his advice was listened to in the halls of power.

* * *

Wisner, who was registered on voting rolls as an independent, wanted Truman to win the 1948 election. Confounding pollsters who counted him out, Truman did just that, defeating heavily favored Republican governor Thomas Dewey, while Democrats captured the House and the Senate. The trauma of the Depression and World War II was in the rearview mirror. Americans were eager to join the good life of the middle class with guaranteed employment, a house, a car, and a TV set. Though a pocket of resistance to internationalism could be found in the center of the country, the American Century that *Time* magazine publisher Henry Luce had articulated in 1941 was believed to be at hand. The nation's economic power overseas was unrivaled—"the rest of the world lies in the shadow of American industry," wrote British historian Robert Payne—and the United States had assumed international duties as a world superpower. Truman's inauguration speech was devoted exclusively to foreign affairs. And in their "expanding affluence, few Americans doubted the essential goodness of their society," writes American historian David Halberstam.

For secretary of state in Truman's new term, Marshall was succeeded by Dean Acheson, who had bought a redbrick house on P Street NW in Georgetown and occasionally attended the set's parties—although he never took well to pesky Joe Alsop's presence at the affairs. Acheson, who became a better target than Truman for angry conservatives, did little to hide his contempt for fuzzy-headed critics and had a talent for boiling down complex problems to their essences so he could decide them. Fortunately for Acheson, his decision-making method was not tested immediately. The first eight months of Truman's new term were fairly quiet for him. The Berlin Airlift succeeded and the Russians backed down, ending the block-

ade. The North Atlantic Treaty Organization, a defense pact as con-
sequential as the Marshall Plan, was created. (The one cloud was the
suicide in May of Defense Secretary James Forrestal, who suffered
from mental illness.)

The first six months weren't a breather for Wisner, though. He
had proceeded cautiously at first, initiating few operations, focusing
his attention instead on building his organization. Like Donovan
during World War II, Wisner was eager to work with and learn
from the British, who had been running intelligence operations
against the Russian Communists since World War I and whose MI6
officers now thought Wisner and his operatives naively did not appreciate what tough adversaries the Soviets were. Wisner did and
believed he needed at least a year to plan and organize his outfit
before it could plunge into operations. But he was not given that
kind of time.

Kennan prodded Wisner to move faster. Wisner had barely
settled behind his OPC desk when the policy planning chief urged
him to find ways to aid non-Communist labor unions in Western
Europe. Kennan feared the Marshall Plan would not succeed if
Communist-dominated unions blocked the distribution of goods
and services to rebuild the continent. He also wanted OPC to be the
organization that dealt with émigrés and coordinated their activities
against Russia. Kennan was impatient. He reviewed what Wisner
planned to do in 1949 and 1950 and considered it only the bare minimum. Kennan had a raft of operations he wanted to add to the list.
Wisner marveled at the not-so-subtle way his State Department colleague applied his pressure. His memos never explicitly directed
Wisner to launch an operation. Instead, Kennan's notes gave OPC
the "policy clearance" to launch a covert operation. Wisner got the
message—stop planning, start doing.

The U.S. military's sense of urgency was as unrelenting as the
State Department's. No one at the Pentagon was concerned about
putting the brakes on OPC. The military's foot was on the acceler-
ator. The generals and admirals viewed Wisner's covert operations

as preliminaries for the eventual hot war that they believed they would have to fight with the Soviets. While the State Department wanted Wisner to quickly launch such nonwar pursuits as spreading rumors and organizing non-Communist front groups, the Defense Department wanted to implement programs important for its future war, such as organizing guerrilla forces in East Europe, preparing for sabotage and assassination operations, forming stay-behind networks to slow a Red Army advance, and helping NATO pilots who had been shot down escape back to friendly lines. The Pentagon was willing to stockpile in European warehouses enemy equipment captured during World War II that OPC could use.

They were ambitious plans—and totally unrealistic. An Air Force official wanted Wisner's men to deliver him a Soviet Tu-4 strategic bomber with a Russian pilot in its cockpit. At one heated session with an OPC representative, an Army colonel slammed his fist on the table and shouted: "I want an agent with a radio on every goddamn airfield between Berlin and the Urals!" Recalls Wisner's deputy Lindsay: "We didn't have the sense to say, 'no.'"

There were a few times when the Truman administration realized it was asking too much of Wisner's unit too soon. On September 2, three days before he started his OPC job, the National Security Council, worried about the vulnerability of Venezuelan petroleum installations, ordered Wisner to draw up a plan for securing the facilities. The NCS quickly realized the assignment placed an excessive burden on the new organization and looked for another agency to take it. But in most cases, Wisner saluted and scrambled to launch operations on a piecemeal basis before his team was ready to begin them. There was no time for long-term planning and preparation.

Many of the projects Wisner's brain trust hatched in the beginning were off-the-wall—like the plan to replace toilet paper on the Vienna-to-Budapest train with tissue that had the face of Hungary's Communist leader printed on it; or a plot to assassinate Stalin, which was quickly abandoned; or a program to air-drop over the Soviet Union high-grade consumer goods to make Russians realize the shoddiness of their products. A joke often played on a newcomer to the psywar team had a staffer rush up to him with a memo detailing a plan to dump out of planes over the Soviet Union millions of four-foot-long condoms that were stamped "MADE IN USA. MEDIUM SIZE." The document was titled "Operation Penis Envy."

Wisner had a weakness for self-styled wheeler-dealers who had no business being anywhere near an intelligence operation. He handed $400,000 over to a former Polish airman who promised to bring him back a Russian MiG jet fighter from the black market. The Pole spent the money on a wild weekend of girls and booze in Munich. Wisner recognized that his control over OPC was too loose and struggled to bring order. Much of the chaos, however, was due to the fact that he ran his organization like a law firm, rewarding managers who churned out the most covert action projects. It resulted in the launching of a number of half-baked initiatives that had not been carefully vetted. As their numbers swelled overseas, OPC officers in the field also began developing their own operations, over which Washington headquarters had only lax control. With all this project proliferation, Wisner, not realizing it, sometimes even assigned the same operation to two different units, which only added to the confusion.

* * *

Harry Truman's breather ended on August 29, 1949, when the Soviets exploded an atomic bomb. America's nuclear weapons monopoly of the previous four years was over. In multiple memos to the White House, the CIA warned that the Soviet threat to U.S. security would now increase dramatically, Moscow would become even more intransigent in East-West negotiations, and Russian subversive warfare would accelerate worldwide. "The survival of the free world is at stake," an NSC report concluded. Wisner, who had a security clearance that gave him access to the U.S. government's most sensitive nuclear secrets, agreed.

Less than a month after the Soviet detonation of a nuclear

device, Wisner's officers in Washington put the finishing touches on a secret plan to set up a front group called the National Committee for a Free Europe (NCFE). The committee's broad goals would be to work to restore social, political, and religious liberties in East Europe, using media like radio broadcasts to spread propaganda messages among the region's captive citizens. To outsiders, the NCFE would appear to be autonomous, with its own fundraising staff and board of directors, but Wisner's organization would secretly subsidize the organization's projects and call the shots behind the scenes.

Wisner's covert support of NCFE and a number of other anti-Communist front groups—he called it the "Mighty Wurlitzer," with him at the seat of a secret government organ playing propaganda and political chords around the world—was up to that point unprecedented in American history. Never before had a U.S. agency secretly created private organizations or penetrated private entities that already existed on the scale that Wisner now did. He was breaking new ground with what became some of the most successful operations he ever launched.

But he was playing catch-up with the Soviets. In the one to two years after World War II, the United States had had little capability or interest in matching the Soviet Union's propaganda effort. Donovan's psychological warfare force in the OSS had largely been liquidated. The feeling among leaders in Washington was that if the world was just given the facts about U.S. objectives overseas, that would be enough to bring people around to the American way of thinking. The United States would simply set a good example and that would suffice.

But by 1947, Russia's black propaganda (or "disinformation") tactics had become far more aggressive with the Communist Information Bureau, which Moscow had organized. In March 1949, Cominform staged one of its biggest publicity stunts of the Cold War, hosting a U.S.-bashing conference of Soviet and American intellectuals at the elegant Waldorf Astoria Hotel in New York's Midtown Manhattan. The Manhattan conference ended up being a publicity disaster for Moscow: the State Department refused to grant visas for European participants and anti-Soviet activists staged protests in the hotel and along Park Avenue. But the Communists' preemptive propaganda strike—in this case into the heart of America's financial sector—forced U.S. policymakers to reconsider their idealistic approach immediately after the war. Wisner's OPC was given the mission of battling Cominform with American psychological warfare. Impressed with how the Waldorf conference had been disrupted, Wisner dispatched his devious fixer, Carmel Offie, to Europe to organize anti-Communist counterdemonstrations at the events Cominform staged there.

Wisner and Kennan also concluded that other sectors of Western society were in danger of Soviet subversion and that OPC had to fight the threat with front organizations like the ones the Communists were fielding. Millions of dollars were poured into this battle for hearts and minds. To counter Moscow's extensive cultivation of young people through groups such as the World Federation of Democratic Youth, Wisner secretly arranged for OPC money to go via "pass-throughs" (intermediaries obscuring the source of the funds) to the U.S. National Student Association, which forwarded the cash on to foreign student organizations opposed to Communism. He sent OPC funds, laundered through New York and European banks, to the American Federation of Labor's semiautonomous Free Trade Union Committee, which funneled the payments to anti-Communist labor organizations all over Europe. To organize anti-Communist intellectuals, writers, and artists, he secretly delivered money to a wealthy Naples, Florida, friend, Julius "Junkie" Fleischmann, who became the pass-through for sending cash to the Congress for Cultural Freedom.

The Free Trade Union Committee's representatives sometimes clashed with Wisner over how the OPC money was spent, and he found the leaders of the Congress for Cultural Freedom often woolly-headed and difficult to control. The National Committee for a Free Europe, on the other hand, became the longest-running and most successful covert action project that Wisner ran. It had been the brainchild of George Kennan. Allen Dulles, who served as the committee's lawyer, introduced Wisner to Dwight Eisenhower (then Columbia University's president) and to other prominent people from the business, legal, and philanthropic worlds who agreed to be sponsors, thus giving the committee the veneer of an organization spontaneously formed by concerned private Americans. Every week, a check from the Wall Street financial firm of Wisner's old friend and Locust Hill neighbor Henry Sears, who served as another of his pass-throughs for OPC cash, arrived at the committee's well-appointed suite of offices on the third floor of New York's Empire State Building. Wisner was also careful not to upset J. Edgar Hoover, paying the FBI director a visit to fill him in on the committee's activities, since OPC officers would be working with the group on the bureau's turf in New York City. His ego properly stroked, Hoover agreed to cooperate.

The committee soon gave rise to Radio Free Europe. The Bolsheviks had pioneered the use of radio for propaganda. Donovan's OSS had had stations broadcasting music and propaganda into Nazi Germany during the war. Wisner got clearance from the Pentagon for Radio Free Europe to establish its programing headquarters and set up part of its broadcasting equipment in Munich. RFE broadcasts into Eastern European countries began in July 1950. Four 340-foot-tall towers, called "Truth Beacons," transmitted from a new station in a Bavarian forest near Munich. Its 135,000 watts of power made it one of the most powerful stations in Europe, almost three times stronger than the largest U.S. station. In addition to RFE, 250 million newspapers and other printed materials were dropped over the next two years by balloons that floated across countries behind the Iron Curtain.

* * *

Wisner's early political action operations to promote foreign governments friendly to the United States—such as channeling funds to political organizations and politicians in Europe to strengthen them against the Communists—were mostly benign and relatively easy to carry out. To Greece, a country Wisner often vacationed in and was deeply in love with because of its rich history, he sent Al Ulmer, who set himself up in a hilltop mansion to pass out cash to Greek military and intelligence officers eager to fight Communist guerrillas destabilizing the country.

The more difficult political operation would be to infiltrate agents into the Soviet Bloc to stir up trouble. As Wisner had seen during his tour of postwar Europe as a deputy assistant secretary of state, a huge pool of potential spies and saboteurs lay before him. More than two million displaced persons were in the American-occupied zone of Germany (many not wanting to return home to land the Russians now controlled) and more than 850,000 refugees huddled in camps across Europe—quite a large reservoir, he thought, and ripe for recruitment. What was more, thousands of displaced Eastern European "notables"—politicians, military officers, royalty, businessmen—were scattered throughout the West or exiled in the United States. They could provide leadership. The CIA and military intelligence agencies had already been extracting information on dissent within the U.S.S.R from these displaced persons and refugees. Wisner wanted the recruitment expanded to field shadow warriors for covert operations.

Kennan agreed and, with the National Security Council's backing, gave Wisner the okay to quickly begin organizing a Russian refugee organization headquartered in West Germany, with branches in Paris and New York City, all of which OPC would guide. This group should be small, with high-quality leaders who represented the important anti-Communist parties and factions, Kennan advised. At the outset, the group should focus on caring for the welfare of Russian refugees in Germany and Austria and then graduate into political work. *We'll discuss operations into the Soviet Union later,* Kennan told Wisner in a top secret memo on September 13. That same day, Wisner fired off to his subordinates a memo announcing that he had a green light from the State Department to form this "Russian welfare committee" for Germany and Austria. "We should move rapidly into the first phase of organizing this group," Wisner told his aides, pointing out that Kennan's marching orders were vaguely worded, which Wisner believed gave OPC wide latitude in carrying out the operation.

Kennan further proposed setting up a political warfare school to train the refugees and displaced persons in guerrilla tactics to use behind the Iron Curtain. It was given the code name "CACinnabar." Though he allowed Wisner considerable freedom in launching this initiative, Kennan knew the dangers of undertaking overly ambitious and poorly planned operations. He intended to keep a close eye on how Wisner carried this one out. The NSC wanted him to as well.

Recruiting and training refugees to parachute into enemy territory, use firearms, organize resistance units, and operate radios became a priority for OPC. The Pentagon helped, allowing Wisner's refugees to attend Army, Navy, and Air Force schools. Some CIA and OPC officers feared that air-dropping émigré agents behind the Iron Curtain would be a futile gesture. The Russians had far more experience in waging political warfare than the Americans, so they would surely recognize more readily when an operation was being run against them. From his experience with Soviet security controls in Romania, Wisner realized the dangers as well.

What was not clear to Wisner and his men was how much of a newcomer OPC was to this game and how transparent Wisner's secret operations were to every country he wanted to protect from Communism. It seemed that whatever plot the Americans hatched, the Communists' superior spy networks detected it. The Czech and Polish intelligence services were particularly adept at infiltrating OPC's refugee groups. Soviet Bloc secret services soon became busy rolling up anti-Communist cells, which practiced poor security. "Soviet and satellite intelligence services have the same easy access to the bulk of the émigré 'intelligence' product as we do," admitted one CIA report. Kennan believed that the Baltic states of Latvia, Estonia, and Lithuania were ripe for liberation from the Soviets, but one of the two refugee agents infiltrated into Lithuania (considered the best target for freeing) was killed by Soviet security forces and the other reported back that the Soviets had succeeded in wiping out Lithuania's small resistance movement. Operations to infiltrate agents into Ukraine (many of them turning out to be unreliable) fared little better. Soviet agents easily rounded them up.

Wisner's first major test of whether OPC could roll back a repressive Communist regime in Eastern Europe came in the tiny country of Albania, which was ruled by the dictator Enver Hoxha. It would become one of Wisner's largest, most ambitious, most audacious covert operations—OPC's "first major undertaking," he told his staff in a June 10 pep talk, to prove to Washington that putting America's shadow warfare capability in the hands of OPC had been a wise decision. Its code name was "BGFiend."

Albania was the smallest and poorest country in Europe. Only about a tenth of its population could read and write, and some three-quarters had suffered from diseases such as tuberculosis, malaria, and syphilis. By the time Wisner set his sights on the nation, a number of economic and educational reforms had begun to bring Albania out of its plight. The first roads and rail tracks had been laid, construction of factories and power plants had begun, and a large number of schools had been established. Geography made the nation inviting for Wisner's operation. It bordered just two other countries—Greece and Yugoslavia—that were both hostile to Stalin, so Albania was politically isolated to a degree within the Soviet Bloc. Moreover, Wisner's agents had easy physical access to their target. Covert forces staging at bases on the island of Malta or in Italy could sail across the Adriatic Sea to reach Albania's shore. But though the nation was primitive, its secret service was not. Albanian Communists had honed their security skills during World War II by fighting Italian and German occupiers, and after the war by battling armed fascist and Nazi collaborators who still roamed the country. Albania's government now had a professional counterintelligence service that had set up a network of informants throughout the nation to tip agents off to suspicious activity.

Enver Halil Hoxha, a former grammar school teacher who had been part of the Communist resistance during the war, rose to power postwar after King Zog's monarchy was abolished. Hoxha became a heavy-handed authoritarian devoted to Stalin. Along with economic reforms, Hoxha outlawed religion and private property ownership, jailing, killing, or exiling thousands of landowners, clerics, and politicians opposed to his collectivization.

On June 22, Carmel Offie and a team of assistants delivered to Wisner a top secret memo outlining BGFiend's ambitious operation to ultimately overthrow the Hoxha regime in Albania and replace it with a democratically elected government friendly to the United States. Wisner's aides ignored a CIA analyst's report dismissing the idea of an internal revolt ever succeeding against the strongman. Offie's team plotted out on paper a detailed, step-by-step plan for an operation that would end up with Hoxha gone and Albania a freedom-loving American ally.

BGFiend's "preliminary objective," Wisner's aides told him, would be to set up an Albanian National Committee, which, secretly supervised by OPC, would organize and train Albanian refugees in guerrilla tactics at a base outside the country. Then the Albanian National Committee would have its trained guerrillas organize and instruct friendly natives inside Albania. After the coup, the committee would create a provisional government that would function until elections could be held.

These were wildly optimistic preliminary goals, but no one in Wisner's organization raised any questions about them. BGFiend's preliminary objective would have three "corollary objectives"— again just as wildly optimistic. First, the conditions forcing Washington to spend a lot of its money fighting Communist guerrillas in Greece would be eliminated. Albania at the time was serving as a base for the guerrilla war against Greece, and the project hoped to eliminate the Greek Communists' sanctuary there. The second corollary objective was to eliminate an important Soviet outpost on the Adriatic. And corollary objective number three was to alter the strategic balance in the Balkans. The OPC staff hoped the revolt in Albania would encourage resistance groups in other Balkan nations, rattling their regimes and disrupting Soviet control—a sort of democratic domino theory.

America's involvement in this coup would be kept hidden, Wisner's men assured him, although they never explained how a plan with so many moving parts could be made leakproof. The devil in all those details would be worked out, everyone believed. Although they could provide only a general outline of how BGFiend would be conducted because it was such a complex operation, Wisner's officers were confident that the operation's four principal phases would succeed. Phase one was the political phase when the Albanian National Committee would be formed. The propaganda barrage against the Hoxha regime, both covert and overt, would come next in phase two. Then there would be the guerrilla organizing and training phase. And finally, phase four: the coup d'état. As simple as that.

Earlier in June, a delegation of OPC officers, with copies of BG-Fiend's complicated plan in their locked briefcases, flew to London for a two-week conference with their counterparts in Britain's secret service to hammer out the final details of the operation. It would be a joint United States–United Kingdom initiative. The British code-named their part in the project "Valuable." In fact, it had been the British who had first hatched the coup plot and who had talked the Americans into joining them. Since late 1948, London had been mulling an operation to overthrow the Hoxha government, which had clashed with the Royal Navy's warships and provided a haven for Greek Communists. Eager for American money to fund the project, Britain's Secret Intelligence Service had enlisted an enthusiastic Wisner, who over a lunch at London's Buck's Club had agreed with a handshake in March to have OPC join the covert operation to detach Albania from the Soviet Bloc.

Offie and his team were eager to move ahead by June 22. They told Wisner they expected the Albanian National Committee to be operating by July 1. (That was an aggressive timeline for completing phase one.) How long it would take to accomplish the second, third, and fourth phases of BGFiend "will depend to a great degree on the intensity and effectiveness of the propaganda phase," which was phase two, Offie's team wrote in their top secret Project Outline on June 22. BGFiend would need about twenty OPC agents to train the guerrilla force and fifty Albanians for support duties such as driving vehicles, manning vessels, and delivering messages. For its air assets, Offie's team wanted three C-47 transport and communications planes, a B-26 medium bomber, and one helicopter. On the ground in Albania, the agents would need thirty cameras, twenty-five radio sets, a propaganda transmitter, five thousand gold sovereigns, and five thousand gold napoleons. All told, for the first six months of the operation, BGFiend would cost $900,000, Wisner's men estimated. They recommended that he give the project they outlined his final approval.

Wisner was nervous. Immediately after reading Offie's memo on June 22, he fired back a note to his aide. Wisner was under tremendous pressure from the White House to get this project moving. But he was a detail man. Wisner wanted Offie and the team planning BGFiend to give him more exact times for "the various phases of the operation"—no vague dates. He wanted his aides to spell out more clearly in the plan that at the end of each phase, the Office of Policy Coordination would consult with the State Department before proceeding with the next step. And "it should be clearly provided," Wisner wrote, that OPC would consult with the Joint Chiefs of Staff when his agency was ready to embark on any phase that would result in "shooting." Wisner clearly did not want OPC leaping ahead of the U.S. government at any point. He did not want Offie or others in his organization freelancing or going rogue on this project. He wanted them on a short leash.

The $900,000 Offie's team requested for the first six months of BGFiend also worried Wisner. He did not think that such a large amount could be spent wisely that quickly. He demanded more details on the expenditure and ordered his men "to try to scrape up arms and ammunition" from the stockpiles of captured foreign weapons the services held, which would not cost OPC money. His agency would soon be inundated with cash, but Wisner did not know that at that point. "Our funds are not unlimited," he lectured Offie. "Although the Albanian operation is a most important one at this time, there will be many other operations upon which we will have to spend substantial quantities of money." This was one of Wisner's first major covert missions and he was clearly on edge about its launching. He wanted every "i" dotted, every "t" crossed.

Offie's team scrambled to provide more facts and change the wording of their Project Outline. They rushed a revised draft back to Wisner later that day. He read it once more and formally approved BGFiend late on June 22.

Offie set about organizing training camps in Germany and Italy for the Albanian émigrés who would be his guerrilla fighters. Michael Burke, Wisner's tall and handsome football star, was dispatched to find recruits among the Albanian exiles and begin their instruction, although neither Burke nor any of the other Americans sent overseas knew much about Albania or its people. London's officers called the Albania recruits "pixies," because they seemed to the snobbish Brits to be short and messy looking. Office of Policy Coordination documents began referring to Albania as "Pixieland." The British offered Malta, their island colony in the middle of the Mediterranean Sea, as a base for launching operations into Albania— prompting Wisner to quip at one point that whenever Washington wanted to subvert a nation, it could always count on Great Britain owning a piece of property "within easy reach."

In August—a month later than what Offie had projected—a Committee for a Free Albania was formed in Paris. BGFiend's organizers began spending about $6,000 a month. But less than two months after he had signed off on the Albanian operation, Wisner received an alarming memo from a member of the BGFiend team who was having second thoughts about the project. The memo writer, whose name remains a secret, acted as a sort of whistleblower, imploring Wisner to pause, take a deep breath, and "assess the true status of the operation and evolve remedial measures for its control and development if we are to assure its reasonable success."

Everyone in Wisner's organization recognized that the stakes for the United States government, and for OPC, were high with BGFiend. The project would have a profound effect on U.S. foreign policy and its failure could threaten "the development and perhaps even existence of OPC," the memo warned. The future of Wisner and his outfit could ride on this project. When they embarked on BGFiend, Wisner's men realized "that we were not, in fact, actually prepared organizationally and logistically to implement it." But OPC decided to rush into the venture because international events, like Albanian-supported Communists fighting in Greece, compelled Washington to move quickly and because Wisner and his men believed—naively, it turned out—that by actually undertaking a project like BGFiend, they were speeding up the development of the OPC organization in a way that could not otherwise be done "except under the pressure of actual operations." Wisner, Offie, and the others saw the Albania gambit as a "pioneer" undertaking that "would provide OPC with invaluable lessons for future operations." But learning by doing could be dangerous in a complex undertaking like BGFiend. The memo writer worried that the lessons Wisner's staff should have been learning in the development of that project were "being neglected in favor of rapidly growing vested interests. . . . As a result we stand a very good chance of being faced with a failure the nature and causes of which will be confused in an exchange of recriminations." In other words, lessons would be lost in the backbiting that was sure to follow the operation's collapse.

In a section that must have stung for Wisner, the whistleblower claimed that the operation's problems started at the top. Not only did the project suffer from a dearth of high-quality officers at the ground level, but there was "no central locus of authority for dealing

with this project" in Washington, no chain of command "by which
the appropriate instructions can be issued and carried out; nor
is there one central office where everything about Fiend is known,"
the memo stated. In other words, Wisner's chaotic management
style was making a mess of the undertaking.

Furthermore, security for the project was weak. The British did
not appear as worried about that problem as their American partners, who concluded it was impossible now to prevent other friendly
or unfriendly intelligence services from finding out about Fiend-
Valuable. By November, OPC assumed that the Soviet, Albanian,
and Yugoslav services knew what the British and Americans were
up to. The whistleblower by August had already considered BG-
Fiend "endangered" because of the security breaches. The entire
operation needed to be reorganized and streamlined, his memo
recommended.

More bad news landed on Wisner's desk less than a month later.
A secret September 7 memo, titled "Revaluation of the Project BG-
Fiend," concluded without a doubt that OPC's intentions "are no
longer secret and that Soviet intelligence is undoubtedly aware of
[the] contemplated U.S.-British intervention in Albania." That
meant Albanian security forces were sure to counter with more controls, such as restricting travel by the nation's citizens and issuing
new identity cards. "As a result, the successful accomplishment of all
phases of project BGFiend will become increasingly difficult," the
memo predicted. MI6 was now pessimistic about the operation and
Britain's role in it. It was obvious to British intelligence that "the
Albanians will not carry on a sustained fight for their own liberation," the memo concluded. Unless the Americans intervened with
a large "shock force," London did not see how the Hoxha regime
could be overthrown.

Intervening with a large force was out of the question, as far as
Washington was concerned. But the September 7 memo insisted
that "it would be premature to even consider abandoning Fiend"
until OPC tried to infiltrate agents into the country to scout out

resistance sentiment and to see if those agents could succeed in operating clandestinely there. What Wisner's men were proposing was a deadly trial-and-error approach with a cold-blooded rationalization. Even if the pixies who were infiltrated into Albania "accomplish nothing and are arrested, the Soviet security services will be forced to focus on Albania, which will, in itself, be of advantage to us, particularly if we take action elsewhere." What was more, "OPC is gaining valuable experience by this operation at a relatively small cost," the memo argued, crassly writing off the lives of any Albanian agents killed in the operation as small potatoes. Wisner should have been more worried about bureaucratic repercussions, the memo continued. "If OPC abandons this project at the present low-ebb stage, we will have a difficult time convincing the Department of State that we were capable of mounting similar larger operations in other Soviet satellite areas." The memo urged Wisner to continue BGFiend, which he did.

But soon the news from London was bad. The British and the Americans planned for eighty Albanians to be sent back into their homeland to determine the resistance potential there and assess the strength of the government's security forces. From their base in Malta, a British yacht in October landed thirty pixies, divided into five-man units, on the southern Adriatic coast of Albania. They discovered Hoxha's formidable security forces waiting to ambush them. The project ended in disaster. Fifteen of the men fled to Greece to escape Albanian secret police hot on their trail. Ten were presumed to be dead or missing. That left just one five-man team that managed to send out radio transmissions with the disconcerting news that the locals were not enthusiastic about joining their cause and that government informants seemed to be everywhere, tipping off the police to the pixies' movements.

Wisner's officers concluded that the Albanian agents the British infiltrated were "low-quality" with poor leaders, as one memo put it. They were no match for the Albanian police. But the U.S. infiltration effort did not fare much better. Wisner had wanted to sneak fifty OPC-trained pixies into Albania by September, but all the agents could not be recruited and trained in time, so the operation was suspended. Midmorning on November 15, Wisner convened a meeting in the Pentagon with MI6 officers from the British embassy in Washington. The time had come, he told his British colleagues, for them to reexamine the Albanian operation and decide how much of the old plan they could continue in light of the fact that the pixies they were recruiting were poor quality, only one five-man team was reporting regularly by radio from inside Albania, and the entire operation was riddled with "serious security leaks."

The British were also now worried about poor security for the operation. It was clear that the French, Italian, Greek, and Soviet intelligence services knew practically everything about Fiend-Valuable. The outside services were collecting a considerable amount of operational details from "the conversations and correspondence between the Albanians themselves," the MI6 officers concluded, and it was "impossible" to get the pixies being trained to stay quiet about what they were doing. The American and British agents agreed that they would have to limit the amount of information they supplied to Albanian opposition leaders and to the paramilitary teams. Wisner was not opposed "in principle" to continuing their reconnaissance of the country, but "we cannot continue on the basis of our present pattern of operation," he concluded.

Two weeks later, a "revaluation" report arrived with more bad news for Wisner. It was envisioned that while the reconnaissance teams were being infiltrated, a psywar blitz would be launched with a radio transmitter on a ship parked off the Adriatic coast beaming in messages and planes dropping propaganda leaflets on the country. But as of November 29, no broadcasting attack had begun because OPC had run into problems procuring the ship and transmitting equipment. Not until the beginning of March 1950 were a British vessel and crew finally hired for $56,000 to begin the broadcasting operation off the coast. The leaflet drops faced a problem OPC could not solve: even with more schools, 45 percent of the some one million Albanians were still illiterate, so they couldn't read the leaf-lets' messages.

By the beginning of December 1949, it was clear to Wisner's men and to their British colleagues that the Hoxha regime would not be overthrown in the near future without a huge infusion of guns, supplies, sound leadership, and propaganda from the West. The Albanian people could not be counted on to battle for their libera-tion without this aid, Wisner's team decided. The Americans and the British would have to wade into this mission with far more resources than had been envisioned back in June. But it was an open question whether Washington and London were prepared to go that far.

For now, OPC managers, still refusing to concede failure, de-cided, with Wisner's okay, that BGFiend should be continued, but with a new plan that took into account the past failures. They looked for a new base, perhaps in Germany, to train two hundred fifty Al-banians. The British were closing down their training and holding facility in Malta. More heavily armed reconnaissance teams that stood a better chance of fending off Albanian security forces would be sent in. Pie-in-the-sky notions of toppling Hoxha quickly would be shelved for the moment. Instead, BGFiend would try to reduce the value of Albania to the Soviets by undermining Communist au-thority and harassing Hoxha. The Albanian people would be en-couraged to resist and to keep hope alive for their eventual liberation. The Albanian agents infiltrated into the country would think smaller and try to organize a skeletal resistance organization that could be expanded into a larger guerrilla movement if that was possible.

Wisner's team and a delegation of MI6 officers from the British embassy held a weeklong conference in early December to work out the details of the toned-down Albanian operation. Everyone as-sumed the pixies could not be counted on to keep quiet about Fiend-Valuable. The American and British officers decided to set up a holding area in Germany's U.S. zone that could accommodate as many as three hundred Albanians who might be potential infiltra-tors. This would be an open compound. They assumed the Albanian security service would penetrate it, which Hoxha's agents eventually did. For their actual training, the Albanian recruits would be trucked to a secret site and kept isolated there, away from the prying eyes of Hoxha's spies.

One of the Brits busily drafting Annex A of the new plan, which covered details for infiltrating the pixie agents, was Kim Philby, the charming chief of the MI6 detachment at the U.K.'s Washington embassy who was responsible for coordinating Great Britain's end of the Albanian operation with his American cousins. Highly regarded by both his British and U.S. colleagues, Philby was hardworking, relaxed in his dealings with others, and unflappable. Always stylishly dressed, he was a clear thinker and a doer, not prone to theorize much, which impressed the Americans. Since he was four years old, he had had a slight stutter, which gave him an innocent-like quality that endeared him to others. Philby was also a world-class drinker who liked nothing better than to knock back a pitcher of martinis during raucous parties at his house on Nebraska Avenue NW.

Philby made a point of being unfailingly polite toward Wisner. Privately he dismissed the OPC chief as "balding and running self-importantly to fat." Wisner was slightly suspicious of Philby—although it was no more or no less than the suspicions he had of all foreign colleagues. Though he had always been an unabashed Anglophile, Wisner had the smallest of qualms about becoming too close to the British Secret Intelligence Service in this operation. He did not want to have his OPC penetrated by the Brits. As such, he decided to limit the access Philby and the other MI6 agents had to the OPC offices along the Reflecting Pool.

Chapter 13

ASIA AND EASTERN EUROPE

AS WISNER WALKED UP the steps of the Dai-ichi Life Insurance Building, helmeted military guards with spit-shined boots and white gloves swung open the massive doors. Douglas MacArthur had picked out this impressive multistory building for his general headquarters in downtown Tokyo because it was air-conditioned and across the street from the entrance to the grounds of the Imperial Palace. Inside, Wisner walked up another flight of stairs to another set of doors that guards swung open and then another flight of stairs and another set of doors swinging open until he stood, a bit winded, as aides quietly opened the final set of doors to MacArthur's expansive office complex. The smell of incense was overpowering. Wisner was ushered into a room where the general sat at a desk raised on a dais. A large plate glass window was behind him. Bright sunlight shone in, nearly blinding Wisner, who, squinting, stared up at the dais, where MacArthur appeared to him as a sort of black silhouette. The spymaster felt like he was appearing before God.

That was how MacArthur wanted him to feel. Joe Alsop had received the same lighting treatment when he visited the Far East commander, and he had likely tipped off Wisner on what to expect.

The Dai-ichi Building headquarters was bloated with sycophants, political cronies, and hangers-on from the last war, all orbiting around one vainglorious satrap who at age seventy was now the senior officer in the United States Army. Visitors did not so much meet with MacArthur as they sat as if in a theater to witness a carefully rehearsed performance from the general. He was the only one who spoke. No one questioned or challenged the grandiose statements of this self-proclaimed prophet.

Wisner had flown to Tokyo in April 1950 to try to talk MacArthur into allowing the CIA to collect intelligence and mount covert operations in his theater, which the general had resisted as strongly as he had Donovan's attempts to intrude with the OSS during World War II. Wisner had planted only a small flag in Asia. His OPC had bought Civil Air Transport for $950,000; it became the agency's highly valued air arm in the region. He had sent cash to a Chinese Nationalist warlord on the island of Hainan off mainland China's southern coast. The CIA had managed to place in South Korea a few officers who were not sending much in the way of reports back to Washington. The State Department did not want to touch a larger plan Wisner backed to destabilize the Chinese Communists, the CIA had been thwarted in an operation to penetrate the Japanese cabinet in Tokyo, and MacArthur had largely blocked the agency from moving into the Far East Theater in a big way with anything else.

Reinforcing MacArthur's disdain for outsiders was his chief intelligence officer, General Charles Willoughby, a pompous German American who, like MacArthur, sported a custom-tailored uniform, along with a monocle, and who was one of the top bootlickers on MacArthur's staff. Historians have judged Willoughby to be one of the dumbest intelligence chiefs in World War II, and now in the postwar command, "Sir Charles," as other staffers called him behind his back, continued to downplay the Communist threat in the Far East. Wisner believed Willoughby was a fool, but he tried his best to butter up the officer.

Wisner thought he had secured MacArthur's grudging acceptance of the CIA in his theater, but it would take many more pilgrimages to Dai-ichi by senior CIA officers over the next year before the general completely opened up his territory to the agency. MacArthur's monologue during their meeting included a long lecture on the threat the Communist Huks posed in the Philippines, which lay outside his area of command. Wisner sat and listened during the entire meeting, as he was expected to do. He joined many others in the Truman administration who came to despise the general.

The night before he flew back to Washington, Wisner attended a dinner party hosted by members of MacArthur's staff. He sat next to a mysterious woman who at one point leaned over and whispered to him: "I know what you have heard about what is going on here in Japan and this Far Eastern zone. But don't believe it. Please be sure when you get back to tell people in authority that things are very bad, very bleak, and there's likely to be considerable trouble."

"How do you know that?" Wisner asked.

"I can't tell you," the woman answered.

"If you can't tell me, I can't really bring it back," Wisner said.

"Well, it was my son who told me," she finally said, explaining that her son had appeared to her in a dream. There was the color red signifying blood in her dream.

"I will report that I have heard this story," Wisner assured her.

As the dinner party broke up, Wisner cornered a MacArthur aide and asked him about the lady seated next to him. "She's a really nice woman," the aide said, "but she's never recovered from the death of her son who was killed in the D-Day landings."

Back in Washington, Wisner relayed the conversation he had had with the woman to Helms, who oversaw intelligence-collection projects in Europe for the CIA's Office of Special Operations and within a year would lead OSO's espionage worldwide. Wisner at one point had tried to talk Helms into joining OPC, but his World War II comrade had begged off. Helms had always been skeptical of the covert operations Wisner mounted, though they remained close friends. The two men often shared rides in staff car trips from the CIA shacks on the Reflecting Pool to the headquarters building on Navy Hill. Helms was as baffled as Wisner was about the woman's dream. They thought nothing more of it until two months later.

Right now Wisner had no time to pay attention to vague premonitions. His trip to Tokyo notwithstanding, he had little interest in the Far East at that point. He was focused mostly on Europe and the refugee programs, labor activities, propaganda campaigns, and clandestine political action operations his OPC had underway there. Europe was the area deemed most vulnerable to Communist encroachment. Wisner had no sense of potential danger lurking in Asia, largely because MacArthur had excluded the CIA from uncovering any threat there.

Wisner in the 1950s saw his nation's generation of younger Americans begin to define themselves by a different set of social and economic norms. Research for a birth control pill, which would give women control of their bodies, was accelerating. An urban counterculture that came to be called the "Beat Generation" began dabbling in drugs and rejecting old measures of success. Rebel stars Marlon Brando and James Dean captured the movie screen. Teenagers with easy access to cheap transistor radios fell in love with a swivel-hipped Mississippi rock and roller named Elvis Presley. Fifteen-cent hamburgers at a fast-serve San Bernadino restaurant called McDonald's had begun to catch on. Television was becoming a political, journalistic, and economic power, the TV admen of Madison Avenue the new titans of commerce with their one-minute spots.

Wisner was not tech savvy. He watched little television, save for a news show once in a while or an occasional sporting event, and he rarely went to the movies. He had no favorite style of music nor the aptitude to play an instrument. Certainly, Elvis did not interest him.

* * *

Wisner returned from his Asia trip assuming that the U.S. government would "make a major effort in the field of covert operations," as he put it in a top secret May 8 memo. Washington was terrified of the Soviet threat, so money was no object. Wisner knew he would get everything he needed from the Truman administration. The next four years would be crucial for America's subversive war against the U.S.S.R., Wisner believed. In the May 8 memo, he wrote that a lot of money would have to be spent "establishing, stockpiling and operating overseas supply bases," setting up and strengthening "effective organizations to direct and execute covert operations" overseas, putting in place a "worldwide communications system," and training professional spies and saboteurs in "adequate facilities of all types."

The mission ahead was clearly monumental, and Wisner was nagged by private worries over how all this would come about. Because what he was doing was unprecedented in peacetime United States history, there was not a large pool of men and women in the country willing to abandon their present jobs and jump into this unconventional activity. Recruiting would always be a problem, Wisner feared. He was finding it increasingly difficult to hide these covert projects—particularly the big ones in which millions of dollars were being spent—so they could not be traced back to the U.S. government. Truman needed plausible deniability. Wisner was also discovering that his covert operations were more difficult to run because a vast ocean separated America from its targets in Europe. The Soviets had a shorter commute to work.

Wisner had an even more immediate headache. He could not be sure that he would even have an organization to carry out these grand plans. For a year and a half, his Office of Policy Coordination had operated outside the U.S. government's usual bureaucratic controls. Wisner had what amounted to his own secret and powerful fiefdom accountable to no one. No agency—not the National Security Council, nor the Budget Bureau, nor the office of the president, nor any congressional committee—examined the CIA's budget, or Wisner's budget within it, with any kind of thoroughness. Likewise, there was no separate organization to evaluate the results of Wisner's covert operations. That could not last, Wisner knew—at least not the operating-independently part.

Since October 1949, Hillenkoetter had been lobbying the National Security Council to merge his Office of Special Operations with Wisner's OPC, a proposal that Dulles had favored. Relations between the two units had begun to thaw by mid-1950. OPC and OSO would soon begin integrating their operations in a few parts of the world where it made sense for the two rivals to work together. Wisner was now willing to provide OSO with intelligence that his officers collected in their operations. He also had no problem with OSO and OPC being folded together as long as the new clandestine service enjoyed the same autonomy that his Office of Policy Coordination had within the CIA. But the fight—and it was a big fight—came over who would lead this combined group. Hillenkoetter pushed for his OSO chief, Robert Schow, to take over a merged OSO-OPC. Predictably, Wisner would not agree to that. Neither would the State Department, which considered Schow unacceptable and demanded that Wisner have the top clandestine service job.

While this bureaucratic tug-of-war dragged on behind closed doors, Wisner continued with his secret war to undermine the Soviet Union. He did so, however, without the partner with whom he had worked so closely in the formation of the Office of Policy Coordination. Beset with stomach ulcers and frozen out of Acheson's inner circle because of clashes he had had with the secretary of state over foreign and defense policy, George Kennan resigned as policy planning director and as the senior State Department overseer of Wisner's covert operations. Kennan stayed on in the department as a counselor for six months, but when it became clear that Acheson had no more use for him, Kennan exiled himself to Princeton University, feeling like an outcast.

Out of government, Kennan went through a curious conversion. He claimed later that he regretted how Wisner's organization had turned out, telling friends he originally envisioned the Office of Policy Coordination being a small operation that would be used

intermittently when needed. Kennan insisted that he had not foreseen and never wanted OPC to be such a vast enterprise with thousands of employees and hundreds of secret projects around the world
over which the State Department now had little oversight. (Tension,
in fact, had grown between OPC's psywar program and the State
Department's propaganda effort in its public affairs bureau.) Kennan
later pronounced the directive setting up the Office of Policy Coordination, NSC 10/2, "the worst mistake I ever made." If he could
have, Kennan said, he would have killed OPC. Before he left State,
he recommended to his superiors that the department wash its hands
of Wisner's organization and not appoint anyone to take his place as
the top liaison with OPC.

Kennan's remorse rang somewhat hypocritical. Wisner loyalists
pointed out that Kennan's and Wisner's names had been on a lot of
OPC program documents. For a man who claimed to be so repulsed
by those covert operations, he had sure been in the thick of them at
the time. Also, it had been Kennan who had egged on Wisner to
pursue more secret projects, which required Wisner to expand his
organization to carry them out. Oddly enough, Kennan was careful
to trash OPC but not its director. Kennan, Wisner, and their wives
remained close social friends.

Acheson ignored Kennan's advice not to appoint a replacement
to give policy guidance to Wisner's outfit. On January 1, 1950, the
secretary made Kennan's workaholic deputy, Paul Nitze, director of
the policy planning staff. A distinguished Harvard student and successful Wall Street investment banker, Nitze during World War II
had worked for the Board of Economic Warfare and immediately
afterward had been vice-chairman of the U.S. Strategic Bombing
Survey, assessing the effectiveness of the Allied air campaign. Always stylishly dressed, patrician mannered, and more hard-line than
Kennan, Nitze was eager to expand Wisner's shadow war against
the Soviets. The two men and their families became good friends.
Like Wisner, Nitze also owned a Maryland farm—his in La Plata—
which the Wisners visited often. During one Fourth of July weekend

there, Ellis Wisner remembers Nitze singeing himself while trying
to set off fireworks.

*   *   *

Wisner's inbox was beginning to be filled with reports carrying dire
warnings about the Russian threat. The State Department estimated for him that the U.S.S.R. was spending about $2 billion a year
on propaganda activities. How the department came up with that
fantastic number (more than $24 billion in today's dollars) was never
clear. But the squishy figure squared with what others told him.
General Albert Wedemeyer, a pal from their World War II days and
now commander of the 6th Army at the Presidio of San Francisco,
delivered a shotgun to Wisner along with his estimate that the Russians had a "50 to 1" advantage over the United States in psychological warfare. A worried Averell Harriman, who had recently left the
Truman administration as its commerce secretary, cornered Wisner
and lectured about how essential it was now for Washington to "re-
capture the peace mantle from the Russians." The press and Congress were clamoring as well for an American response to Soviet
subversion. Wisner, who was just as alarmed over what he declared
were "notable triumphs" of Communist propaganda, thought there
should have been a way to tell the public and Congress that the administration was aware of the value of psychological warfare and was
pursuing it—but just not to mention that Wisner's OPC was the
agency doing it.

The Kremlin's spy agencies tried to carefully track the psychological warfare initiatives Wisner rolled out. What Soviet intelligence did not uncover—or could not realize—was the trouble the
Americans were having with their secret war. Often the simple truth
that Marshall Plan diplomats put out in Europe did more to counter
Soviet subversion than the secret schemes of Wisner's propagandists. Moreover, as a practical matter, just because Wisner secretly
funded an anti-Soviet front group did not mean that he had total

control of what that organization did. Many of these groups had boards of directors with independent streaks to them. Though they were engaged in anti-Communist activities approved by the U.S. government, some of these groups became virtually autonomous. All Wisner could do to control them was cut off their funding if he thought they strayed too far. In their day-to-day activities, the front groups did not always do the bidding of their secret bankrollers. Money was wasted on activities that had little relevance to the war Washington was fighting against Moscow. Exiled political leaders tasked with organizing anti-Communist émigrés sometimes fought among themselves more than against the Russians. As the 1950s began, Wisner was quickly discovering that playing the Mighty Wurlitzer had its headaches.

The Office of Policy Coordination provided the bulk of the funding for the National Student Association, which grew to about $200,000 annually. More than two hundred fifty students had their expenses paid to attend youth festivals in Moscow, Vienna, and Helsinki. During the summer of 1951, OPC grants increased as well for projects in Latin America and Southeast Asia. Among the additional missions assigned to some students were reporting on Soviet and Third World personalities and observing Communist security practices. The secret funding of NSA later became highly controversial when its details were leaked to the press. It turned out that Allard Lowenstein, NSA's charismatic president, was kept in the dark about the CIA's payments to the organization and about the agency's secretly arranging a draft deferment for Lowenstein so he could continue his anti-Communist crusade during the Korean War.

Wisner's under-the-table cash for the American Federation of Labor's Free Trade Union Committee, which peaked in 1950, met with mixed success. Wisner's men, with their Ivy League, military, or corporate law backgrounds, never mixed well with the blue-collar émigrés of the free trade committee, whose leader, Jay Lovestone, was a notorious schemer. Lovestone wanted OPC's money, but with no strings attached to how his more seasoned labor operatives would spend it. He called Wisner's novices the "Fizz kids." Wisner was willing to be generous, but not with a blank check. The spy chief demanded a full accounting from Lovestone, who fought him. The bickering between the two men festered throughout 1950 and finally became white-hot when Lovestone suspected Wisner was wooing the AFL's rival, the Congress of Industrial Organizations.

* * *

By the early 1950s, more than twenty-five major news agencies were cooperating with Wisner's covert war, their owners, editors, and journalists sharing his fear of Communist subversion. Moviemakers willingly promoted the Army, the Navy, and the Air Force in their films. The Office of Policy Coordination secretly put $300,000 into the production of an animated movie version of George Orwell's *Animal Farm*, a satire about the evils of Stalinism. Wisner, however, was intent on a wider role for his clandestine operatives in the cultural world. The Congress for Cultural Freedom became one of Wisner's most effective and innovative operations. Showcasing American high culture, the congress grew into one of the world's major patrons of the arts, sponsoring an unprecedented range of cultural activities with literary prizes, art exhibits, and music festivals, all the while trying to undermine Communism's appeal among artists and intellectuals.

Sidney Hook, a New York University philosophy professor, was the guiding American hand on the CCF's executive committee as well as the founding chairman of the Congress's U.S. affiliate, the American Committee for Cultural Freedom. These organizations were liberal dominated, which did not bother Wisner's officers, who found non-Communist leftists in Europe more reliable in fighting Communism than the rightists. His officers tended to have highbrow tastes in what they subsidized, tilting toward modernist literature and abstract expressionist paintings, which they believed would have more impact on foreign opinion. They were reluctant, on the other hand, to back avant-garde or experimental music, instead favoring European works that the Soviets had banned or U.S.-centric pieces that highlighted, for example, African American performers (which also put a positive gloss on U.S. race relations, they believed).

After the Congress for Cultural Freedom was formally established at the end of November 1950 (with OPC providing the bulk of its operating budget), Wisner more or less sat back and watched his creation play itself out. A Pentagon memo pronounced the congress's activities "unconventional warfare at its best." That proved to be the case, but the operation came with assorted hiccups. The psywarriors could not always control what the artists did with the OPC's money. A poet touring South America on OPC's dime threw away his antidepression pills and climbed an equestrian statue in a Buenos Aires square naked, declaring he was "Caesar of Argentina." Wisner could not dictate how foreign audiences would react to his culture output; Paris reviewers tended to be brutal with American symphony orchestra concerts. He also had to accept the reality that most foreigners got their impression of the United States not from literary journals or art exhibits but rather from the movies Hollywood produced, over which Wisner had no control. Fortunately for him, the studio executives tended to be as intensely anti-Communist as he was.

* * *

The National Committee for a Free Europe by its second year was spending $18 million annually. The cover story for the source of that money was that fundraisers had brought in the cash. Actor Rock Hudson exhorted contributors during one radio appeal, promising that the committee was "supported entirely by contributions by American citizens"—which was not the case. Private fundraisers paid for only about 17 percent of the committee's budget. Wisner's OPC kicked in the rest.

The Free Europe Committee spent its early months engaged in modest activities, such as aiding East Bloc refugees arriving in the United States, providing research grants to émigrés studying aspects of the Communist system, and establishing its own publishing house called Free Europe Press. By 1950, Wisner became more aggressive and had the committee start sending across the satellite nations' borders balloons that would explode when they rose above an altitude of thirty thousand feet and shower the populace with propaganda leaflets. Helms was skeptical. A stiff wind could blow a balloon off course so leaflets written in Czech might be dumped on Hungary, he pointed out. But Wisner would not be dissuaded. The balloons began ferrying millions of leaflets.

Wisner and the State Department ordered the Free Europe Committee to take a nuanced approach with the propaganda messages being sent into Eastern Europe. The material the committee published or broadcasted "should not promise imminent liberation or encourage active revolt," a secret OPC memo to NCFE's leaders instructed. Yes, Washington's "ultimate objective" was to weaken the Soviet grip on the satellite nations. The United States was not abandoning East Europe to the Soviets. But the reality was that the West, at the moment, was virtually impotent in the region. The committee could not promise what the United States could not deliver.

But the National Committee for a Free Europe was having problems organizing behind any single message, let alone a nuanced one. The committee had set up a number of exile national councils representing different ethnic or political factions in Eastern Europe and their leaders continued to be embroiled in "petty intrigues, partisan differences and self-jockeying for precedence and influence," State Department liaison Robert Joyce lamented in a memo to Wisner. Someone was going to have to force those exile leaders "to come to their senses." Security was becoming a problem, as it had been with practically every émigré group Wisner had organized. Soviet agents had no difficulty infiltrating refugee populations. Exile leaders openly bragged about the help they were receiving from the U.S. government, and a number of them guessed correctly that NCFE's funds came from some kind of spy organization. Wisner's men tried to clamp controls on the exile leaders, but the leaders often resisted with hardball tactics he found even more worrisome. They began making end runs, taking their complaints to congressmen whose districts had heavy ethnic populations.

Expanding the reach of Radio Free Europe, the committee's most successful offshoot, proved challenging. Its transmitters could not be built just anywhere. Eastern Europe's Communist regimes became relentless in jamming RFE's medium-wave and shortwave transmitters in West Germany. The Soviets also waged an intensive diplomatic campaign to dissuade countries from accepting the antennas and the KGB tried to penetrate radio staffs to disrupt them. Wisner was relentless as well. He was finally able to negotiate an agreement with the Portuguese government to place an array of high-powered transmitters north of Lisbon, which offered the best propagation conditions for shortwave broadcasts into the East Bloc. By 1953, RFE had 252 American and 1,526 foreign employees working in eight news bureaus and operating twenty-six transmitters, including Portugal's advanced facility. They saturated the satellite countries with broadcasts in a half dozen languages.

Wisner early on realized he could not just build RFE transmitting towers and hand the microphones to the exiles to say what they wished—not with the exile leaders so divided among themselves and the political factions squabbling as they did. The U.S. government would end up with a "tower of Babel," said the CIA's Cord Meyer. American editorial controls were imposed to allow the exile broadcasters some autonomy but at the same time to ensure that the messages they put out on the airwaves were coherent and credible.

After five months on the air, Wisner thought RFE's broadcasts had done a decent job of keeping liberation hopes alive in the satellite nations and telling their populations "that they are not forgotten by the free world," he wrote in a November 22 memo. Seven and a half hours of programs were being broadcast each day to Bulgaria, Czechoslovakia, Hungary, Poland, and Romania. One-third of the programs was devoted to news and the remaining two-thirds were taken up with "features," Wisner said, "ranging from political satires to controlled speeches by exiles." Scripts were written by the exiles but edited by the American staff. Wisner's propagandists wanted four themes stressed in these broadcasts: those opposed to the Communist regimes would ultimately prevail; they would be armed against Soviet propaganda; they should not be provoked into taking hasty or unwise actions; and they should "look about you and remember those who cruelly serve the Soviet tyranny." Wisner's operatives scoured their State Department sources for both negative and positive information coming out of the East Bloc. The negative information would predictably be used to ridicule the Communist leaders, but the psywar specialists wanted positive information on these leaders as well to "give them a build-up before delivering the knockout punch," one Machiavellian OPC memo explained.

It was too early to judge how effective RFE was, Wisner realized. Sixty-nine million persons lived in RFE's target area and his staff estimated that only 3.1 million of them had radio sets to receive its medium-wave or shortwave signals. Wisner believed a "grape vine" in each country also spread Radio Free Europe's message. But the biggest indicator that RFE was having some kind of effect, Wisner calculated, was the fact that the state-run radio in those nations had begun to denounce the RFE broadcasts. To encourage defections, a half hour show in Russian was soon directed toward Soviet troops stationed in the satellite nations.

For all the nuanced messaging it wanted, Radio Free Europe's early output had a shrill and hectoring tone to it, which its station managers eventually moderated to make the broadcasts appear more like straight news shows. But their programs still had an edge that made other media outlets nervous. State Department officials worried RFE was tarnishing the U.S. government's Voice of America,

which prided itself on beaming regular news into Europe and the
East Bloc. British Broadcasting Corporation managers wanted to
keep their distance from RFE, which they felt mixed too much
opinion into its newscasts. Wisner dismissed the sniping as professional jealousy. Radio Free Europe, he fervently believed, now gave
the United States a psychological advantage in the Cold War. He
wanted to broadcast into the heart of the Soviet empire as well.

* * *

In the hallways of Wisner's Washington headquarters, they became
known as the two "radios." The first was Radio Free Europe, which
broadcast into East Europe. The second was Radio Liberty, which
Wisner organized in 1951 to broadcast into the Soviet Union itself.
The second radio would prove to be a more difficult undertaking
than the first.

Wisner took a different approach in setting up the American
Committee for the Liberation of the Peoples of the U.S.S.R. (given
the unwieldly acronym "AMCOMLIB"). His deputy, Frank Lindsay, registered the organization in Delaware, a favorite state for
headquartering these front groups because of its lenient corporation
laws. Unlike the National Committee for a Free Europe, the American Committee for the Liberation of the Peoples of the U.S.S.R.
began with little fanfare. The group was staffed with quiet academ-
ics and journalists who had covered Soviet affairs; its public money
came not from showy fundraisers but instead from friends of the
committee's members. AMCOMLIB was intended to be more secretive and, Wisner hoped, more manageable. It had an objective
similar to the Free Europe Committee's: to organize Russian émigrés into an effective political warfare force and to give them Radio
Liberty, which was capable of reaching listeners inside the Soviet
Union. Wisner's officers consulted Kennan before he left the State
Department on the organization of AMCOMLIB, whose cryptonym became "Cinderella," and on Radio Liberty, whose target,

Kennan advised, should be the Soviet Union's Bolshevik party, not its people. The Russians listening to the radio broadcasts should be portrayed as oppressed friends.

The Russian exile groups ended up being no less conflict-ridden than the satellite groups of the Free Europe Committee. Wisner managed to cajole five Russian exile factions into forming a Council for the Liberation of the Peoples of Russia with AMCOMLIB used as its American front group. The council would publish a newspaper, set up a research institute in West Germany, and broadcast radio programs into the Soviet Union. But the alliance of assorted anti-Soviet Mensheviks, monarchists, military fascists, and minority nationalities like the Ukrainians proved to be shaky, and the bickering continued.

Wisner's officers wanted Radio Liberty to be the voice of Russia's "political center," whose goal was destroying the Soviet government's monopoly on information. It would be "Russians speaking to Russians," a Wisner aide explained. But in the station's early stages, Russians could not hear Russians. Radio Liberty's transmitter in Munich lacked the power to break through the Soviets' heavy and continuous jamming.

* * *

Wisner spent a good deal of time flying around Europe on listening tours, soliciting the views of America's top generals there on the unconventional war he must plan. He often carried a diplomatic bag with a State Department document instructing that the secret papers inside the bag could be viewed only by him. Flag officers continued to describe for him a frightening world as they saw it. Pentagon planners had even picked out a day the Soviets would invade Western Europe: July 1, 1952. It was uncertain whether Wisner, at that point, actually believed those scary forecasts. His men in Europe took them seriously. Michael Burke, who trained Albanian fighters in Germany, had a route mapped out to flee west with a backpack full of emergency supplies and gold sovereigns if the Russians attacked.

Army and Air Force commanders thought Wisner could be doing far more to create a guerrilla force in Eastern Europe that would massively retard a Soviet advance. The Joint Chiefs acknowledged that establishing guerrilla networks behind the Iron Curtain was difficult, but they believed that Wisner had the only organization capable of carrying out the mission. Wisner thought the generals were engaging in massive wishful thinking. But he went along with the orders.

By mid-1951, he was up to his ears in covert operations in Europe. Cash from the tens of millions of dollars available to him was being passed out to European politicians, newspaper editors, and labor leaders. He had projects to split Italy's left-wing socialists from their alliance with the Communists, to foment unrest in Czechoslovakia, to target Bulgarian officers for recruitment, to set up stay-behind guerrilla networks in France and Scandinavia to harass the Red Army if it invaded, and to smuggle anti-Communist leaflets into Soviet barracks in East Germany.

For other missions, the challenges confronting Wisner often proved to be beyond formidable. Red Army targets tended to be inaccessible for guerrillas. Communications with inside groups could be fragmentary, many times conducted by outside émigré leaders of dubious reliability. And the Communist security services were always oppressive. Wisner parachuted four Romanian refugees, whom his men had spent months training, into the country he so loved; the refugees were to contact resistance groups and supply them with money and weapons. Romanian police captured and executed the four, so Wisner canceled a more complex infiltration mission. In mid-1950, he launched an ambitious project, code-named "ZRElope," to train two thousand East Europeans at a secret base on Grand Bahama Island, near Florida; they would later infiltrate the Soviet Union for political warfare and resistance operations. But there were practical hang-ups. The project's managers could not recruit and vet enough high-quality candidates to meet the goal of two thousand. Training costs proved too high ($30,000 per student). ZRElope died slowly over the next two years. Another operation, code-named "Red Cap / Red Sox," attempted to recruit KGB officers who were serving overseas to defect and to infiltrate Wisner's agents into the Soviet Union to foment armed resistance. But approaching KGB agents in foreign posts proved immensely difficult and some three-fourths of the eighty-five OPC agents infiltrated into the U.S.S.R. "disappeared from sight and failed their missions," according to one CIA history. Red Cap / Red Sox became a sore subject inside the Office of Policy Coordination.

"Blowback" is spy jargon for an operation that ends up with uncomfortably bad results that are unanticipated and unintended. Nowhere was the blowback more embarrassing for Wisner than in Poland. In the summer of 1950, Polish émigrés who claimed they were from a Warsaw resistance group called WIN (the Polish initials for the Freedom and Independence movement) approached Wisner's officers in London claiming they had five hundred underground operatives, twenty thousand sympathizers, and 100,000 potential recruits in Poland eager and ready to battle their Soviet occupiers. Wisner took the bait and gave the representatives more than $1 million in gold sovereigns for the revolt. WIN turned out to be a Communist-controlled group that became $1 million richer with Washington's money. For months, Wisner's agency was the butt of jokes on Warsaw government radio broadcasts. "The affair represents an appalling setback," Bob Joyce wrote in one postmortem.

* * *

In a February 8, 1950, memo, Wisner and his men calculated that Albania now fell below Bulgaria, Hungary, Romania, Czechoslovakia, and Poland "in terms of relative importance." But they were still invested in Project BGFiend even though its scaled-back version only attempted to make life miserable for Hoxha and the Kremlin.

Wisner wanted to ramp up economic warfare initiatives to cripple Albania's economy—although it was hard to see how an economy already suffering greatly from Communist misrule could have been crippled even more. A psywar campaign to stir up dissatisfaction and anxiety among the Albanian population fared better. In autumn the national committee began publishing and distributing five thousand copies of an Albanian language newspaper titled *Shqiperia*. News bulletins also appeared in English, French, and Italian. During the next two years, more than six million cartoon and propaganda leaflets were dropped over the country. Voice of Free Albania was broadcast three times a day from a secret location near Athens. Wisner's psywarriors also tried dirty tricks, such as mailing letters and parcels from Europe to Communist officials in Tirana with black-market items designed to embarrass them.

Wisner's pixies fared as badly in their infiltration operations as the MI6 guerrillas had. The first year of "body drops," as they came to be called, was a dismal failure. With a communications plane flying off the Adriatic coast to keep in radio contact with the pixies, thirty-nine agents were sent overland or by airdrop from October 1950 to October 1951. Only two agents succeeded in that mission to distribute propaganda, collect intelligence, and organize resistance groups. Among the others, two agents were reported killed by Albanian police, who always seemed to be waiting for the infiltrators; four were captured and put on trial; four were unaccounted for; and seventeen fled to Greece with Albanian security troops chasing them. At the end of the first year of OPC infiltrations, a U.S. intelligence estimate concluded that resistance inside Albania represented only a "nuisance" for the regime, certainly "not an immediate threat."

In August 1950, Kim Philby flew with Wisner and Joyce to London for a meeting on the subversive warfare projects the British and Americans ran jointly, such as BGFiend. Instead of giving him space in their OPC offices, Wisner's men set up a command center with Philby in the Pentagon where both intelligence services could oversee the Albanian operation. At one point, when news of a failed pixie infiltration arrived at the center, Wisner turned to Philby and said: "We'll get it right next time."

Philby knew that would not be the case. He was working for the other side. Philby had been recruited by Soviet agents shortly after he graduated from Trinity College, Cambridge, in 1933. During World War II, Philby rose through the ranks of MI6. His position made him an important Russian intelligence asset, a double agent who could tell Moscow not only what Britain's spymasters were doing but also what they intended to do. He was unimpressed with what he considered amateur officers in Donovan's OSS, but he nevertheless managed to cultivate key sources in the American agency. Near the end of the war, Philby was overseeing an MI6 unit collecting intelligence on Soviet espionage around the world—in effect, he was spying on his two employers.

As the Cold War set in, Philby continued to dazzle his superiors, winning awards for what was considered superb work. (He was also being awarded medals in secret from Moscow.) His name was soon being mentioned as a future chief of MI6. From his perch as head of Britain's intelligence service in its Washington embassy, Philby cultivated powerful friends in the CIA, who shared more secrets with him than they should have. He developed a talent for sabotaging his own work—crafting detailed plans to fight the Soviets, then betraying those plans to the Soviets—with nobody in MI6 the wiser. Philby put on a good show of determination to defeat the Russians, though few of his operations seemed to succeed.

Wisner was mystified. Why were so many of OPC's projects to penetrate the East Bloc failing so miserably? he asked himself over and over. He continued to persevere, and so did the British, but among old intelligence hands in Washington and London, suspicions grew that there was a leak somewhere. Fingers began to be pointed both ways. Philby no doubt tipped off the Russians to the Fiend-Valuable project, but recently released KGB archives indicate that he might have only sent the Russians a short and vague description of the operation, and it remains an open question how much of what Moscow got from Philby was shared with Albanian intelligence. The Russian and Albanian services were not particularly close at this time. Frank Lindsay, Wisner's deputy, later questioned whether the KGB would have risked a prime asset like Philby by passing along too much of his intelligence to the Albanians. Russian and Albanian agents were collecting a huge amount of information from the pixies while they were being trained in Germany or after the secret police scooped up and tortured many who had been infiltrated into Albania. The Albanian exile community in Italy was also a rich vein for Hoxha's spies. Without Philby's help, the Communists clearly had enough intelligence to subvert Wisner's operation in Albania.

But as he moved into the next phase of BGFiend in 1951, Wisner became convinced that talkative guerrillas were not solely to blame for failures in Albania. He had shared many drinks with Philby, but Wisner was a shrewd man. He joined a growing number of national security officials in Washington who suspected that Philby was the leaker. Though James Jesus Angleton, who soon would be promoted to chief of the CIA's counterintelligence staff, still believed that Philby was no traitor, Bill Harvey, also with CIA counterintelligence, became convinced that he was an enemy spy. Hoover believed that as well and was enraged over Britain's failure to arrest the man.

With the CIA demanding that he be fired, Philby in June 1951 was summoned to London to discuss the disappearance of British diplomats Guy Burgess and Donald Maclean, fellow turncoats who had fled to Russia. His paranoia growing, Philby buried his spy camera and accessories near the Potomac River and left for England, never to return to DC. Convinced he was innocent, MI6's leadership allowed Philby to leave the service with a generous severance package. But Britain's counterintelligence service, MI5, remained suspicious like the CIA and continued investigating the traitor. For years, the Anglo-American intelligence relationship—and Wisner's relationship with his cousins—would be poisoned by Philby's betrayal.

Wisner knew that 1951 was a critical juncture for the Albania operation. Yet despite BGFiend's horrible results, the tragic loss of lives, and the fact that no insurrection materialized, Wisner and his Albania team remained undeterred—still enthusiastic about continuing infiltrations. More than $1 million was being spent on BGFiend annually, and its budget kept growing from year to year. But Wisner and his aides failed to realize that even weak regimes could be difficult to overthrow with just covert paramilitary forces. Albania had fewer than seventy thousand men under arms. Its regular police force totaled seven thousand, no more than half of them reliable. But Hoxha's secret police, the Sigurimi, numbered just under ten thousand agents, most of whom the CIA judged to be "firm communists." They were enough to make his control of Albania difficult for a guerrilla movement to crack.

The Office of Policy Coordination decided that the 1952 agent operations would emphasize quality over quantity. "A small number of high-grade teams," trained on a group of tiny islands Wisner rented in the Gulf of Corinth near Greece, would be infiltrated into Albania "to carry out narrowly defined and limited missions," according to a secret report. But the results continued to be poor. By the end of 1952, only about 15 percent of the agents succeeded in staying undercover and radioing back intelligence.

For 1953, Wisner and his BGFiend officers were determined to pour more pixies into Albania (the latter ones better trained than the first batch), hoping against hope that they might succeed in weakening the Hoxha regime and in strengthening the opposition. Weapons were stockpiled at a secret warehouse in Athens to arm four thousand men for the eventual revolution. But the only thing growing was the bureaucracy for the operation. For 1953, OPC had twenty-six staffers and contractors employed overseas on BGFiend, along with ten officers working on the project in the Washington headquarters.

The British gradually realized the futility of the Albanian operation and quietly began withdrawing from it. MI6 considered the Americans who hung on terribly naive.

Ironically, the Soviets never publicized their victory in Albania. They did not want the fact that the United States was willing to go to such great lengths to support nationalists and anti-Communists emboldening those same elements in other nations behind the Iron Curtain. The British and the Americans (particularly Wisner) were also not interested in publicizing their failure. It was a rare case where East and West shared the same goal.

Chapter 14

KOREA AND THE PHILIPPINES

THE HOME PHONES OF more than a half dozen top U.S. officials began ringing the evening of June 24, 1950. Wisner received his call at Locust Hill, where he had been spending the weekend. Quickly he packed the car and rushed back to Washington. The officials had been ordered to return immediately to their desks.

When he arrived at the I Building, Wisner found the flood of cables, which computers were only just beginning to organize, turning into an even bigger deluge, particularly those from Asia. He grabbed a fistful of paper and rushed to read them in his office, a largely bare room he hadn't dressed up much. On June 25, Far East time, some seven divisions of elite, battle-tested troops from North Korea's Korean People's Army had poured across the South Korean border, intending to quickly conquer the nation below in a well-planned multipronged attack. In a National Press Club speech on January 12, Acheson had mistakenly not included South Korea in America's "defensive perimeter" for the Pacific, delivering an oblique signal that the East Asian nation was available for conquering. Eighteen days after Acheson's speech, Stalin gave dictator Kim Il Sung the okay to invade. A Russian toady who had undergone military training in the U.S.S.R., Kim had received from Moscow heavy arms and Soviet generals who wrote his war plans. The tiny U.S. force that advised South Korea's poorly trained, equipped, and led army was no match.

Blindsided by the attack, Truman feared it would be the start of World War III. He was furious with Hillenkoetter for not warning him. The admiral was already being scapegoated for the agency's failure to predict, among other things, the Communist coup in Czechoslovakia, Yugoslav strongman Josip Broz Tito's defection from Moscow, and the 1948 riot in Bogotá, Colombia, while George Marshall was attending a conference there. The South Korean invasion was now being ranked as another Pearl Harbor–like intelligence failure.

As has often been the case in CIA history, agency officials were able to dig up somewhat exculpatory evidence—for the Korean Peninsula, intelligence reports it had issued before the invasion with warnings, albeit a little vague, of an impending crisis that could result in the North invading the South. The CIA reports did not predict a time or place for when or where the actual attack would occur. And in Korea, the CIA wasn't the only agency surprised. General Willoughby, MacArthur's incompetent intelligence chief, had been caught napping as well. MacArthur, who had sought to downsize the U.S. commitment to South Korea and whose command was responsible for the coordination of intelligence collection in the region, at first dismissed the June 25 invasion as "probably only a reconnaissance in-force," which he could handle "with one arm behind my back."

Truman decided immediately to contest Kim's invasion—his opportunity to show that the United States had learned the lesson of Munich. General Omar Bradley, Joint Chiefs chairman, believed Russia was not ready for war with the United States and was only "testing us" with the North Korean attack. Truman believed a line must be drawn and asked for immediate intelligence on Soviet capability and Moscow's possible next move. The CIA agreed with

Bradley, reporting back that Moscow was likely probing Washington's commitment to its containment policy while looking for political advantage in Asia, but was not ready to commit its forces to a fight with the United States that might spark a global war.

After ordering U.S. troops to the peninsula, Truman fired his defense secretary, Louis Johnson, the worst cabinet pick the president thought he had ever made; Johnson had succeeded in angering practically every senior official in the administration. Truman shared Wisner's low opinion of MacArthur. The only orders Mac followed, so the saying went, were the ones he had issued. The general, who had visited South Korea only once and had not spent the night there, believed the rules other military commanders must follow did not apply to him. But Truman did not feel he had the political clout to sack MacArthur just yet.

Republic of Korea forces and the American troops that were rushed to the peninsula—both unprepared for war—spent the month of July losing battles against superior North Korean soldiers and retreating south. For the U.S. military it was one of the most nightmarish and humiliating months in its history. The ignominious fallback was finally halted in August at the Pusan Perimeter in the peninsula's southeast corner, where U.S., R.O.K., and arriving United Nations forces finally held the line. The tide began to turn. The American position grew stronger. The North Korean divisions, their supply lines stretched too far, were running out of fuel and ammunition. Wisner's son Ellis asked his father if the Korean War would last long. Wisner said he did not think so, but his answer was tentative.

* * *

As American soldiers and arms poured into the Pusan Perimeter, a new spymaster took over the CIA at the beginning of October. For a year, the State Department had been anxious to be rid of Roscoe Hillenkoetter. After three years as director of central intelligence,

Hillenkoetter was just as anxious to be rid of the job and return to sea duty. Under fire for intelligence failures, the admiral got his wish and shipped out to lead a cruiser division in the Korean War. A senior State Department official sounded out Wisner on whether he wanted his name put in the mix of possible Hilly successors. Wisner declined to seek the post. Instead, he was adamant that the next DCI should be a civilian. Rotating in and out military men to lead the CIA "has disastrous consequences," Wisner argued in one memo. The agency needed a continuity of leadership that could not be provided by a succession of Pentagon officers, each of whom had to be educated on how to do the specialized job, Wisner contended. Generals and admirals viewed the directorship as "an unwelcome stopgap to fill in between more desirable" Army, Navy, or Air Force jobs they might land. Moreover, the military man had "an ingrained sense of awe in the presence of superior rank," Wisner wrote, making him less likely to challenge the chain of command with uncomfortable truths. The National Security Council recommended to Truman that the next DCI should be a civilian, a military retiree, or an officer who would be taking the directorship as his last active-duty job.

Truman largely ignored the advice (along with the names that others had floated for the position) and picked General Walter Bedell "Beetle" Smith, who had been Eisenhower's chief of staff during the war and who had recently wrapped up a two-and-a-half-year tour as U.S. ambassador in Moscow. Deemed a stronger leader than Hillenkoetter, Smith on October 7 (two days after his fifty-fifth birthday) took over a troubled CIA, with a mandate from Truman to reform the agency after its multiple intelligence failures. Everyone, including the *Washington Post* and the *New York Times*, was happy with the choice.

Smith was hardly in the best of health for the spymaster's job. He had checked into Walter Reed Army hospital at the end of March 1950 with severe ulcers, a partial pyloric obstruction, and chronic gastritis. Doctors carved out half of his stomach, which left him

nearly forty pounds lighter, undernourished, and understandably irritable. Twice Truman had offered him the directorship while he
was recovering, and twice he refused. But after the North Korean
invasion and the CIA's failure to anticipate it, Smith accepted, telling a friend: "I expect the worst and I am sure I won't be disappointed."

Smith was not as ignorant about spying as he sometimes made
himself out to be. As Ike's hard-nosed chief of staff, he had overseen
intelligence functions and worked with Donovan's OSS. Churchill
called him the "American Bulldog" for his tenaciousness. Smith
liked better his nickname "Beetle" because it captured his hyperactivity. On his personal stationery, he had a small black beetle em-
bossed.

Smith was said to be even-tempered—that is, he was always angry. He told Wisner and other senior CIA officers that he "screamed
like a wounded buffalo" when he was disappointed about something,
but they shouldn't take it too hard because he really did appreciate
the devoted service of his subordinates.

Beetle came to the job with a number of advantages. He could
not be bullied by the military intelligence chiefs because he easily
outranked them. He was far more forceful than Hillenkoetter and
he had more political access than Hilly's predecessor, Vandenberg.
Smith had no problem getting an audience with Truman whenever
he wanted; he could work well with Marshall, who had just become
secretary of defense; and he was respected by members of Congress.
Curt, blunt, and given to salty language, Beetle Smith was a master
of bureaucratic warfare, knowing when to fight and when to give
ground. He was as highly thought of as his mentor, Dwight Eisenhower.

Simultaneously with Smith's appointment as director, the CIA
announced that William Jackson—who had been a partner with
Wisner at Carter, Ledyard & Milburn—would be the deputy director
of central intelligence. As a U.S. Army Air Forces colonel, Jackson
had served in a number of intelligence jobs during the war and

afterward had joined Allen Dulles in writing a lengthy report on needed CIA reforms. Wisner, delighted with the choice, hoped that Jackson could smooth Beetle Smith's rough edges. Smith, who had read Dulles's report on reorganizing the CIA's clandestine arm and liked it, persuaded Dulles to come to the CIA as a consultant and six months later to be his deputy director for operations overseeing the agency's intelligence collection and Wisner's covert action programs in the Office of Policy Coordination.

Smith's first reaction when he was briefed on Wisner's responsibilities was somewhere between being perplexed and dumbfounded. The portfolio was so wide-ranging and still growing. Several months before the general's appointment, the National Security Council had approved another expansion of OPC's political and psychological warfare duties. The Korean War became a game changer. On the defensive, MacArthur finally lifted his ban on major CIA activity in his theater. As they had been in Europe, Wisner's secret warriors were now accepted as one of America's counterthrusts in Asia, with money and people rushed in. The effect on his Office of Policy Coordination was profound. The State Department and the Joint Chiefs now recommended launching paramilitary activities in both Korea and China. The administration gave Wisner the okay to have the National Committee for a Free Europe launch a propaganda campaign blaming the Soviets for the Korean War. As Washington saw it, the Communist attack that everyone had feared would begin in Europe had taken place in Asia.

Following less than a year after the fall of China to the Communists, the Korean War marked a turning point for the CIA and for Frank Wisner. The requirements of that war, the eventual involvement of China in the conflict, and the concern that war in Europe might follow, all led to a fourfold expansion of the CIA and Wisner's mission. Korea helped transform Wisner's OPC from a unit capable of rolling out a limited number of ad hoc operations to an organization conducting an ongoing shadow war on a massive scale. "In concept, manpower, budget, and scope of activities, OPC simply skyrocketed," one CIA history reported. Wisner's manpower tripled from 584 in 1950 to 1,531 in 1953, with most of the growth taking place in Far East paramilitary activities. Wisner now commanded a true army.

He did not know where he would put the horde of staff officers, clerks, and secretaries soon to be descending on his Washington headquarters. He assumed the administration would give him more space. Wisner's covert operations quickly expanded from Korea and China to Taiwan, French Indochina, Thailand, and Japan. He planned to set up a secret reception and training center in the United States and possibly in Alaska and the Aleutian Islands off Alaska, where Russian infiltrators would be trained for his Far East operation into eastern and northern Siberia. Members of the National Security Council worried that Wisner's expanded army might spark a third world war—but they did not worry to the point that they wanted Wisner's operation not to expand.

He scrambled to send Korean and Nationalist Chinese infiltrators across the lines to attack targets in the North Korean army's rear area. For his Washington headquarters, he tried to find smart people, not necessarily versed in clandestine warfare, but people who knew something about Asian wars. Elitist Desmond FitzGerald was among his early hires. A wealthy Wall Street lawyer who had served as a liaison officer to a Chinese regiment during World War II, FitzGerald had roomed at Harvard with Nitze, who had introduced him to Wisner. Joe Alsop had recommended FitzGerald as well. After the North Korean invasion, Wisner asked "Desie," as friends called him, to be his executive officer in OPC's Far East Division responsible for anti-Communist operations in Korea and other Asian nations. FitzGerald accepted and with his second wife, Barbara, a British actress, soon joined Wisner's coterie of Georgetown set friends and Locust Hill overnight visitors.

Wisner and his Asia officers believed they were fighting a war in Korea much like the one the OSS had waged during World War II, which stressed stay-behind agents and guerrilla forces who could count on a captive populace that was cooperative. On paper, the OPC mission in Korea appeared to enjoy a number of advantages and opportunities. The country's rugged mountain terrain could hide a guerrilla base. There were factions in North Korea's relatively young Communist Party and anyone could join it with little vetting. The CIA believed that in such a fluid situation, a clandestine resistance movement could form against the Communists.

But the OSS formula "did not fit Asia," recalled James Lilley, who was recruited by the CIA while at Yale and sent to Taiwan because he had been born in China, the son of an American oil executive stationed there. Wisner's mission in Korea soon became confused and riven with "green and untried case officers" working in the field, according to one intelligence report. Wisner and FitzGerald failed to realize what the officers in the Albania operation had never realized—that even in a developing country, a well-functioning security service could enable a repressive regime to keep a tight grip. North Korea's security service was far more skilled than OPC's Far East Division had anticipated. The OPC men found no resistance movement there because the Communist nation had none.

Nevertheless, a massive clandestine effort was launched. Six bases were established in Japan for the one thousand OPC officers Wisner sent there to work on Korea. Three hundred officers were posted in Taiwan to train guerrillas, carry out reconnaissance missions, broadcast propaganda to mainland China, and send out balloons with leaflets. A secret base costing $28 million was set up on the island of Saipan to train guerrillas for Korea, China, Tibet, and Vietnam. Planes from the U.S. Far East Air Force were used to drop agents and supplies into North Korea; the pilots were issued small gold bars in their escape and evasion kits in case they were shot down and needed bribe money.

Most of the operations the charming and overeager FitzGerald oversaw flopped. Some teams parachuted into North Korea's northern border were able to radio back their observations of arms and supplies coming south over rail lines and roads. The others were on the run within days of being dropped. The 8,500 guerrillas trained in Taiwan were sent out on crudely conceived missions that produced little except casualties. The propaganda broadcasts and the seventy-five million leaflets dropped on mainland China had little impact. Hundreds of agents infiltrated into Communist-controlled territory were forced to send back fabricated intelligence reports after being captured—which early in his tenure Beetle Smith suspected was happening—or, even worse, unscrupulous CIA officers in the field sent Washington glowing reports on their infiltration projects, which had actually ended in disaster. "We didn't know what we were doing," recalled Donald Gregg, just graduated from Williams College and sent to the region after a quickie course in paramilitary operations. "It was swashbuckling of the worst kind."

The Korean War ended up being fought to a draw primarily by conventional armies. To break the stalemate, MacArthur, in the last great success of his military career, launched the daring amphibious landing of thirteen thousand men at the port of Incheon on Korea's western coast on September 15, trapping more than half the North Korean army in a giant pincer movement. CIA operatives had infiltrated the narrow entrance to the port and collected landing intelligence. Two weeks later, MacArthur's forces reached the 38th parallel, putting all of South Korea back under United Nations control.

At the beginning of October, MacArthur confidently pushed north across the 38th parallel, intent on destroying North Korea's armed forces and oblivious to the threat of up to 300,000 Chinese troops waiting on the other side of the Yalu River near the border. On October 15, MacArthur met Truman on Wake Island, a coral atoll in the West Pacific, and assured the president that he had won the war and there was very little chance China would intervene. Thirty-nine days later, twenty-seven Chinese divisions crossed into North Korea in a massive counterattack that Willoughby and the CIA had assured superiors would not happen.

The Chinese onslaught pushed U.N. forces back south in a second humiliating retreat, which was finally halted on January 25, 1951, by General Matthew Ridgway the new on-scene commander. Ridgway fought his way back north, retaking Seoul on March 15 and again reaching the 38th parallel. Fed up with MacArthur's public insubordination and his demands to expand the war into China (with nuclear weapons if needed), Truman, who wanted to end the conflict rather than escalate it, fired the popular general on April 11, replacing him with Ridgway. Wisner thought the firing was long overdue.

Armistice talks, first at Kaesong and then at neighboring Panmunjom, dragged on for two more years while savage fighting continued along with OPC's secret war for Ridgway. A cease-fire was declared on July 27, 1953. The fact that 70 percent of the U.S. war prisoners held in China during the Korean conflict made confessions or signed petitions calling for an end to American aggression led Dulles and Wisner to investigate whether Peking had some type of brainwashing capability with drugs or exotic devices. The CIA eventually concluded the Chinese had just used brutal interrogation and indoctrination techniques, not drugs, to break down American GIs.

* * *

During the summer of 1950, Wisner took a break from his frantic work to rush agents to Korea and sat down for a lunch in Washington that one of his aides, Edward Lansdale, had arranged to discuss a crisis in a different country, the Philippines. The Air Force officer had arranged the luncheon to introduce Wisner and several other senior administration officials he gathered that day to Ramon Magsaysay, a young Filipino congressman Lansdale thought might just be the answer to the Communist Huk insurgency in the Southeast Asian archipelago. Magsaysay, in Washington lobbying Congress for benefits for Philippine veterans of World War II, had been introduced to Lansdale, whom Wisner had tasked with preparing a psychological warfare operation against the Huks. Lansdale was impressed with the counterinsurgency ideas Magsaysay ticked off, which the Air Force man typed on a sheet of paper. They matched the game plan Lansdale had prepared. At almost six feet, Magsaysay towered over most Filipinos. An artisan's son, he had fought the Japanese during the war and afterward won a seat in the Philippine House of Representatives; he was chairing its Defense Committee when he visited Washington.

Wisner liked the Air Force officer and his gutsy operating style. Reserved in manner and with a pencil mustache, Lansdale had a talent for cultivating others but could be highly secretive about his own activities. Yet he thought and acted more like an advertising man (which in civilian life he had been in California) than a spy. Once he threatened OPC colleagues with a grenade for not backing him fully. Author Graham Greene used him as a character for his book *The Quiet American.* During the war he had worked initially as an Army first lieutenant with the Military Intelligence Service in San Francisco and then moved to Donovan's OSS, setting up a training program on the West Coast (though he had no OSS training himself). After Japan's surrender, Lansdale was posted to the Philippines to assume military intelligence duties. He fell in love with the country. In 1947, Lansdale transferred to the Air Force, which he considered more forward-thinking than the Army, and by 1949 he was working for Wisner's agency in Washington, assigned as an analyst on the U.S.S.R. plans desk. He soon arranged for a transfer to the Far East Division, believing that the Philippine Islands was an important Cold War battleground. The division had no political warfare plan to combat the Huks, so Lansdale set out to put one down on paper.

As he could often be with these kinds of approaches from foreign officials, Wisner was cautiously impressed by Magsaysay's presentation at lunch. The OPC director agreed to provide the Filipino with quiet OPC support, arranged in a way that Magsaysay would not be privy to the source. Wisner had OPC representatives pressure Philippine president Elpidio Quirino into making Magsaysay secretary of national defense. With North Korean forces reaching their farthest point south at Pusan, Lieutenant Colonel Lansdale flew back to the Philippine Islands in September 1950, armed with an ambitious mission—if not an unrealistic one at that point—to reverse the Communist advance in that country.

His operation was highly secret. Even the CIA's station chief in Manila was kept in the dark about it. Lansdale's cover story was that he had been assigned as President Quirino's intelligence adviser, with orders sent to the U.S. ambassador to cooperate and a separate communications channel linking him directly to OPC in Washington set up. The Philippines had been a de facto colony since the United States had seized it from imperial Spain in the 1898 Spanish-American War. Its path to freedom had been interrupted by Japan's three-year occupation in World War II. Lansdale believed that the vicious cycle in which an independent Philippines was now trapped— a corrupt Manila government, an exploitive landowning class, and an abusive fifty-thousand-man military, all driving the poor to the some fifteen thousand Huk guerrillas—could be broken only by Magsaysay.

Lansdale began with an initiative Wisner's men did not always undertake in other foreign countries. He toured the Philippines to learn more about the nation and its culture, even venturing into the jungle to interview and cultivate Huk leaders and to observe how their guerrillas operated. Magsaysay and the Air Force lieutenant colonel became close friends, driving and flying around the Philippines to reorganize and reform its army and constabulary force so the government security forces operated less as enemies of the people. In addition to launching effective civic action programs, the two men focused on cleaning up off-year elections in November 1951 to put reform-minded candidates in office. Lansdale could also play rough in psychological operations, sometimes having two holes punched into a captured Huk's throat to drain his blood and make it look to frightened comrades as if he had been attacked by a vampire.

Lansdale made Magsaysay a national hero. Behind the scenes the Air Force officer developed a reputation as an authority on combating Communist guerrillas. His orders for a three-month stay in the Philippines were extended to a full year. The collapse of the Communist insurgency there became the most dramatic in U.S. military history. By the end of 1951, the Huk force had been nearly halved. Unlike with their covert operations elsewhere, Dulles and Wisner left the Philippine Islands effort largely in Lansdale's hands, demonstrating that giving an OPC officer autonomy in the field could work if the officer was as exceptional as that lieutenant colonel. Lansdale gave Wisner his greatest victory in Asia. He became famous in secret OPC circles as a man who could get things done— not only as a skilled counterinsurgent but also as a political kingmaker. In November 1953, Lansdale managed, with effective advertising and OPC cash under the table, Magsaysay's hugely successful political campaign to become president of the Philippines. Wisner talked Joe Alsop into writing a couple pro-Magsaysay columns during the race, never revealing to the columnist the part OPC had played in the story.

* * *

Wisner's success in the Philippines came with failures that cost men's lives elsewhere in Asia. The Korean War's outbreak put overwhelming pressure on Wisner to destabilize Communist China. A feudal and fragmented country of 500 million impoverished souls after the war, China had been badly governed—if you could even call it that—by Nationalist generalissimo Chiang Kai-shek, who fell to the better-led Communists under Mao Zedong in 1949 and fled with his poorly equipped army of 450,000 to the offshore island of Taiwan. Beetle Smith thought Chiang's army would only deteriorate over time and that U.S. aid to the Nationalist forces in Taiwan was largely wasted by Chiang's corrupt government. The generalissimo claimed he had 1.5 million sympathetic guerrillas in mainland China—a wildly inflated number, according to the CIA, which estimated only 165,000 anti-Communist insurgents were there and that number was getting smaller.

But once Mao's forces crossed the Yalu into North Korea, the need for intelligence on the precise number of Nationalist guerrillas in the People's Republic of China and their locations became an urgent matter for the CIA and for Truman (who regularly read Wisner's reports on his operations in the mainland). Once those guerrillas were located, unlimited U.S. support would immediately flow to them. Though Wisner had so far failed to organize resistance movements inside Europe's East Bloc, parachuting agents into China to organize a guerrilla force became the priority. His officers soon discovered, however, that the PRC was even tougher to crack than the U.S.S.R. Their access to potential intelligence sources and guerrillas in China was even more limited than in the Soviet Union.

Wisner tried the same propaganda plays in the Far East that he had used for Europe. He talked old friend Turner McBaine, with whom he had served in the OSS Cairo station during the war, into setting up the Asia Foundation, which Wisner bankrolled in an operation code-named DTPillar, to subsidize non-Communist scholars and academic programs in the region. As he had with the National Committee for a Free Europe and RFE, Wisner organized the Committee for a Free Asia and Radio Free Asia with mixed results. The only mainland Chinese who had radios to receive the propaganda broadcasts from a station on Taiwan were mostly Communist Party officials.

Wisner knew that Chiang Kai-shek's Nationalist Chinese government was weak, corrupt, and unlikely to take back the mainland. He hoped instead to create in China what came to be called a "Third Force" movement, which would be a democratic alternative to Mao's Communists and Chiang's Nationalists. The Third Force idea was the brainchild of Richard Stilwell, a take-charge infantry commander during World War II who was now detached from the Army to head Wisner's Far East Division, where FitzGerald served as his deputy. Stilwell, Wisner, and Beetle Smith were convinced that more than a half million potential Third Force guerrillas were scattered around mainland China, waiting to be organized for attacks on Mao's regime. There was only one problem with the Third Force plan: the 500,000 number was based on false reports entrepreneurial Asian sources had made up and peddled to the CIA for a fee. The effort to field guerrillas was going poorly as well. Of the 212 Chinese agents Stilwell and FitzGerald had parachuted into the mainland from 1951 to 1953 to organize a Third Force army, 101 had been killed and 111 had been captured (many by angry peasants). The casualties included two energetic yet poorly trained OPC officers, John Downey and Richard Fecteau. Out on their first clandestine foray, their plane was shot down over the mainland. The young pair was imprisoned in China for the next two decades. "After a lot of money was spent on this effort," said Lilley, Third Force "turned out to be a bust."

The difficulties Wisner encountered in mounting operations in Asia mirrored in many ways the problems he faced in Europe. There were Far East factions that ended up embarrassing Washington, such as that of Chinese warlord Li Mi. His fifteen hundred brigands holed up in Burma were being paid by FitzGerald to attack targets inside China, but they ended up pocketing much of the money to cultivate poppy fields for lucrative opium exports. As they had in Europe, intelligence-fabrication mills churning out reports like the Third Force count flourished in Asia, conning gullible CIA officers with plenty of money to throw around. "Our operations in the Far East are far from what we would like," Wisner euphemistically acknowledged in one meeting.

Chapter 15

BEETLE'S BARK

LIFE MOVED ON FOR Wisner at home despite his workplace woes. The family's fourth child arrived on July 15, 1950. Polly and Frank named him Graham Gardiner Wisner. Graham would later in life regret how little time he spent with his father as he grew up.

Late in 1951, Frank and Polly moved from their rental house to a permanent four-story federal-style home they bought at 3327 P Street NW in Georgetown with money Polly had inherited from her father. Polly decided not to obtain a historic designation for the yellow-painted structure, which had been built in 1835, because all the paperwork required made it too much of a hassle. The couple never considered themselves wealthy, but they were certainly well-off, with enough money to own now two expensive homes, decorate each with pricey furniture, hire servants, and send four children to private schools and later elite colleges.

The first floor, which served as the basement at the P Street level, had two bedrooms, a bath, a living room, and a small kitchen for the couple Polly hired to cook and take care of the house. A curving brown stone stairway led up to the front door on the second floor, which opened onto a long hallway. To the left were a formal sitting room and a library with high ceilings, chintz-covered furniture, and matching fireplaces. The library had the treasures of Wisner's life, such as a couple of Greek statues, a beautiful Italian Renaissance bull, his favorite books (many on the life of Jefferson), and an alcove niche with a small sofa and desk, where he liked to sit and read.

Farther down the hallway—before opening in the back into the multilevel showcase garden, which landscaper Perry Wheeler had helped Polly design—were the large square dining room and then the kitchen with a dumbwaiter running from the basement. On the third and fourth floors were Frank and Polly's master bedroom, a guest room, another sitting room, and bedrooms for the children and a nanny. (The couple eventually slept in separate rooms so Polly would not be disturbed by all the late-night phone calls Frank received from the agency.) Polly hired interior designer Margaret Weller to help her decorate the P Street home with expensive antiques, which were added to the pieces the couple had bought overseas or inherited from family.

After they moved into the P Street house, Frank and Polly began what the Georgetown set called the "Sunday night supper." It was born somewhat of necessity. Washington had few decent restaurants—serving food fast or slowly—and Sunday was a day off for most cooks and maids in Georgetown homes. (Polly had a variety of house staff over the years. Her father, for example, had arranged for a Scottish couple and their daughter to emigrate to the U.S. to wait on the family, with the wife cooking and the husband serving as butler and houseman.) So a tradition began: at least one Sunday a month, the Georgetown set would gather at a member's home for potluck. To impress the crowd with their meals, Polly and several other wives attended a Monday cooking class that Julia Child held. Wisner at one point was banned from food the class cooked after he griped that a juniper-berry-stuffed chicken was dry. The potlucks did have their calamities. A delicious-looking soufflé one wife brought to the Wisner home was allowed to rise for too long and exploded, causing a stir.

The Sunday night suppers started out small, but to Polly's

dismay, they soon grew into large affairs with dozens of senior government officials, diplomats, journalists, spies, and their wives attending. Clover Dulles convinced Allen, who had bought a Georgetown house on nearby Q Street NW, to ditch the dreary diplomatic receptions and instead drop in on the Sunday suppers. Dulles did so, bringing Clover to the gatherings or occasionally one of his mistresses.

As with previous parties, the Sunday suppers were washed down with rivers of alcohol. Joe Alsop called them the "Sunday night drunk." Many times, Joe commandeered the suppers for his house, with rules he enforced, such as regrets having to be delivered personally, the suppers ending at eleven p.m. on the dot, and him moderating subjects at the dinner table. The free-flowing alcohol, however, prompted unanticipated behavior, such as a Soviet expert standing on a kitchen chair with a mop over his head, bellowing out the "Internationale" anthem. Joe Alsop and Phil Graham sometimes had shouting matches over politics, usually followed the next day by letters of apology from both. Several times, Wisner stormed out of Joe's house after arguing with him. Mossad officers stationed in Israel's Washington embassy always accepted an invitation to attend the Alsop suppers.

The journalists who were regulars at Wisner's Sunday suppers soon caught the attention of Sheffield Edwards, the CIA's security director, who questioned whether agency secrets were leaking from these meals. Wisner assured Edwards that classified information did not escape when he was talking to reporters, but Wisner was conscious of the appearance of impropriety and told Edwards he had tried to limit his interactions with the press. But that was "most difficult to do," he wrote the security director. Joe Alsop called him frequently at the office. They discussed innocuous subjects, Wisner insisted, but the phone calls, which he knew the FBI could easily monitor if the agency told the bureau to do so, embarrassed him. Since frequent leaks appeared in Alsop columns, Wisner decided to keep a record of his contacts with the brothers, which he would supply to Edwards.

That satisfied the security director. And the evidence suggests that Wisner did keep a tight lip during the Sunday suppers. James "Scotty" Reston, the *New York Times*'s star investigative reporter, once complained that Wisner was "useless" as a source during the many hours he spent talking to him. As a result, Reston kept his distance from the Georgetown circuit, judging—quite correctly— that it was more a venue for Washington officials to try to manipulate journalists for favorable coverage of whatever agenda they were peddling. The unstated rule at the Sunday suppers was that Wisner and his agency colleagues did not talk about the work of the "pickle factory," their nickname for the CIA. Reporters could obviously benefit from morsels that might slip from the mouths of Wisner and the other officials, but the newsmen knew they would be banned from future suppers if they quoted the government attendees directly.

Wisner was a disciple, as Reston suspected, of news management rather than news leaking. He kept a wire service ticker in a room across the hall from his office so he could monitor the media in real time. He believed that saying "no comment" to a reporter was a ridiculous response, only inviting the journalist to assume that the nonresponse was an admission. Wisner preferred to tell a reporter he thought his story was erroneous. Wisner liked working with reporters and feeding his favorites tidbits he thought would serve the CIA's interests. That was why he kept his distance from Drew Pearson, whom he did not like and never invited to Sunday suppers because he thought the Washington columnist did not play by the rules and wrote unfavorable stories.

Wisner couldn't control Polly, however. His wife was very active socially, he told Sheffield, and he felt she had every right to continue her friendship with journalists like the Alsop brothers, whom she saw "quite frequently." Indeed, in Washington's political world, Mrs. Wisner was becoming a potent information player. Nearly every morning Polly, Kay Graham, and Evangeline Bruce held a three-way call to exchange Washington gossip. Phil Graham called it the "nine o'clock network." Chip Bohlen chauvinistically dubbed it the "petticoat circuit." Wisner was delighted with the conference calls because Polly always passed along items from it that she thought her husband might find useful in his work.

Kay Graham considered Polly her best friend in Washington. Polly didn't feel the same. She had other close friends in the Georgetown circuit and she was particularly adept at making each woman feel that she was her *best* friend. But the fact that the wife of one of the most powerful news figures in Washington regarded her as her closest confidante conferred on Polly enormous clout in the capital's perception game. It inevitably sparked gossip that Polly was angling for bigger things for her husband and herself. Rolfe Kingsley, Wisner's wartime OSS deputy (who with his wife remained close friends with the Wisners), insisted that Polly's ultimate goal was to make Frank secretary of state or president of the United States. She had the money and the drive to push her husband beyond what he thought he could achieve.

There was no hard evidence that Polly had such a goal or that Frank ever considered the possibility.

* * *

Within a month after assuming the CIA director's job, Beetle Smith, looking for security breaches, had an aide tour the Georgetown party circuit, where he knew Wisner and people who worked under him hung out. The general was aware of an irreverent element in the CIA and he was determined to clean house of it. (An employee who made derogatory remarks about Harry Truman was immediately fired.) Smith was miffed at the unfavorable publicity he thought his spy organization was receiving because of loose-talking CIA officers complaining about the agency at those parties. Allen Dulles, who also regularly talked to reporters, worried about the damaging leaks as well, while Wisner blamed some of them on chatty officials in other parts of the government, such as the Marshall Fund.

Joe Alsop's flattery had worked on Hillenkoeter, but Smith gave the columnist the cold shoulder and he ordered CIA people to have no dealings with the brothers. Despite Wisner's assurances that he was careful around reporters, Smith was uncomfortable with his OPC director's coziness with them. The general did not want any of his subordinates (Wisner included) to be talking to the press, even off the record. He regularly ordered Wisner to badger editors to spike stories he didn't like. Wisner did so and many times succeeded in getting the stories killed. Smith was also willing to adopt Wisner's news management ideas. To counter media speculation that the U.S. government was doing too little to aim propaganda at Russia and its satellites, the CIA director and his covert warfare director decided to bring in a select group of reporters and editors to brief them generally on the effort the agency was making if they pledged to keep its details secret.

Smith's press policy was all part of a new administration of the CIA that the general put in place, jolting Wisner—and blowing hot and cold over his operational machine. Under the very ineffective Hillenkoetter, Wisner had amassed considerable power. That all changed suddenly when the very effective Beetle Smith took over. The general was well aware that it fell on him to accomplish what Truman and Congress intended the CIA to be and he was more than willing to break crockery to accomplish that.

Smith and Wisner were bound to butt horns. The general thought his covert warfare chief surrounded himself with amateurs. A man of deep enmities, Smith was suspicious of privilege, observing that the OPC officers drove to work in fancy sports cars, while the workmanlike intelligence collectors of the Office of Special Operations had old station wagons. He distrusted, and hated, anyone who had worked for Democrat Dean Acheson.

Smith was intent on reforming what he considered an administrative nightmare at the Central Intelligence Agency. At first, he considered Wisner an obstacle to reform and treated him harshly. He saw his covert action deputy as a target to be cut down to size, as he would have done to a fatheaded private. Polly thought the general was by nature a mean man, given to fits of rage—although she had little on which to base that opinion, since her husband kept the rough time Smith gave him mostly bottled up.

Though he thought the drill sergeant act was juvenile, Dulles laughed off the wrath Smith targeted at him, not letting the general's tirades and bullying get him down. In fact, Dulles became skilled at handling the man, whose operating style and personality were totally opposite of his. Others at the CIA learned how to deal with Smith as well. The key was "you had to talk back to him," said Kermit Roosevelt, an OSS Middle East veteran whom Wisner had recruited. Wisner, who had always been sensitive to criticism, could never do that. He took the general's barbs personally.

In the face of the torment Smith inflicted on both Dulles and Wisner, it was inevitable that the two subordinates became comrades in arms. They joined in hosting private dinners for administration VIPs at the F Street Club, to which Smith was not invited. Wisner and Polly were also regulars among the select few attending parties at Dulles's home.

Smith, who had little experience in actually running spy operations, was inundated early on with memos suggesting how he should do his job. The State Department slipped him a note on the issues U.S. diplomats needed the CIA to address. A month before taking over, Smith received from Larry Houston, the CIA's general counsel, a top secret memo alerting him to problems he would inherit at the agency. Donovan—who had become a regular on radio broadcasts about the Soviet threat and who was pessimistic that Smith would be a good DCI—peppered the general with letters, memos, and reports from OSS pals advising him on people he should hire and programs he should pursue. Smith largely ignored the OSS spymaster's notes, giving him only boilerplate replies that he would keep his suggestions in mind.

The one piece of advice that Smith did pay attention to was the reform report that Dulles wrote with Bill Jackson and New York lawyer Mathias Correa; it recommended that the general take control of Wisner's Office of Policy Coordination. Smith agreed it was a ridiculous setup that no military commander would tolerate. In one of his first moves upon taking control of the CIA, Smith summoned Wisner to his office and curtly told him that from then on he and his OPC worked for Smith. *Don't bother laboring over a new lawyerly directive spelling out the change*, Smith told Wisner. (Smith had a low regard for lawyers.) *Just notify the State Department and Pentagon that your freelancing days of receiving vague marching orders from them are over*, he instructed Wisner.

Rather than plow through the bureaucratic undergrowth, Smith dealt directly with the highest administration officials—such as Bradley at the Joint Chiefs, Hoover at FBI, and Acheson at State—to get the green light for his initiatives. Immediately upon taking office, Smith acted in a way Hillenkoetter never could have—as an administration VIP. He devoted more time and attention to the president and his cabinet officers than he did to the intelligence officials under them. He regularly attended National Security Council conferences and had private weekly meetings with Truman. He ordered subordinates like Wisner to no longer accept a summons to the State Department or Pentagon to brief their peers. If other department aides wanted Wisner's help, they would have to come to his office.

As a measure of his integrity, Wisner loyally carried out Smith's order to come under the general's wing, realizing that operating a clandestine service on his own was unsustainable. He became—or tried to become—a team player. Wisner could see that Smith knew little about how covert operations worked, but he could also see that the general knew how to organize and how to run an organization. For his part, Smith continued to be an ass chewer, but he grew to respect Wisner's ability. Beetle's bark became worse than his bite and he never considered firing his able aide. After their initial rough patch, Smith and Wisner worked together closely, though there would always be bumps and bruises along the way.

The Dulles-Jackson-Correa report also recommended that the Office of Policy Coordination's covert warriors, the intelligence collectors in the Office of Special Operations, and the Contact Branch (which openly gathered information) be merged into a single clandestine unit. Smith saw the value in a merger, but he delayed imposing such a bureaucratically wrenching move for the moment, deciding instead to make the change gradually. Over the next year, Wisner, who now thought the merger made sense, began, with Dulles's consent, to integrate the OSO and OPC departments more quickly than Smith envisioned.

Smith and Dulles were appalled at the squalid conditions under which the CIA operated in Washington, both at the E Street headquarters and the shacks off the Reflecting Pool. The I, J, K, and L Buildings the CIA occupied along what became known as "cockroach alley" stank from the bugs and sewage everywhere. The stairs appeared to be the only things stable in the buildings. Dulles took to calling the structures "a damned pigsty" and along with Smith made it a personal priority to get money from Congress for a new headquarters building. Both men never fully appreciated, as Wisner did, that the pigsty was ideally located near Washington's power centers.

Meanwhile, Smith went about setting up a new structure for his inner circle. He created two deputy directorships: one for administration and the other for what was eventually called "plans" (again a bland-sounding name for the clandestine service). At the beginning of 1951, he made Dulles the deputy director for plans, with oversight of the Office of Policy Coordination and the Office of Special Operations. Wisner unhappily saw that move as a demotion for him. When Hillenkoetter had been director of central intelligence, Wisner had reported (more or less) to the admiral. Now he had two men between him and Smith: Jackson (the deputy director of central intelligence) and Dulles (the deputy director for plans).

Other bureaucratic moves rankled Wisner. Smith made the abrasive Stuart Hedden his inspector general; Wisner resented Hedden prying into his operations. Lyman Kirkpatrick, an OSS veteran who had worked in the Office of Special Operations, succeeded

Hedden as IG. Kirkpatrick came to hate both Wisner and Dulles, sending Smith scathing reports about the clandestine service.

Dulles also made moves that Wisner did not like. Dulles was enthusiastic about many of the OPC operations, such as the secret funding of the National Committee for a Free Europe and of Radio Free Europe. Like Wisner, Dulles was interested in projects that penetrated the Soviet Union, but also like Wisner, he knew well the difficulties in launching them. When the Pentagon forced Wisner to have wartime guerrillas retard a Soviet military advance on Western Europe, Dulles thought the mission was unrealistic and planning for it was a waste of time. But it was Dulles's dabbling in the CIA's support of international labor groups that began to irritate Wisner. When Dulles joined the agency, he brought with him Tom Braden, who had fought with the British in Africa before moving to the OSS. Braden, who with Stewart Alsop wrote a book on their OSS adventures, convinced his new boss to have him lead an International Organizations Division, which would create a network of civic groups and trade unions to fight Communism. Wisner adamantly objected, realizing that Braden was carving a chunk of OPC's operation from him. A rebellious sort, Braden won the bureaucratic battle. Dulles ordered Wisner to stop blocking the move and to allow Braden to form his division.

Beetle Smith came to be regarded by CIA officers as one of the best directors they ever had. Truman was delighted with Eisenhower's former chief of staff. "I think you've hit the jackpot with this one," the president gushed over the Current Intelligence Bulletin that Smith now prepared for him each day; it had what Truman had wanted from the beginning: a concise summary of information on what was happening around the world.

Though a close working relationship evolved between Smith and Wisner, it came with two conditions Smith considered ironclad: there would be no secrets kept from him and no surprises sprung on him. Wisner complied—well, sort of complied. He promised to keep the director fully informed on all matters "worthy" of his attention.

Since Wisner decided what was "worthy," he gave himself a loophole big enough to drive a truck through. Smith saw only the cables from the field that Wisner chose to bring to his attention. Smith, not completely confident that Wisner was keeping him adequately informed, hated the arrangement. He feared blunders were being or would be covered up. It was a legitimate worry. Wisner, at times, did try to bypass Smith when he thought a communication between OPC headquarters and the field might unduly upset the director.

Suspecting that both Wisner and Dulles were trying to hide things from him, Smith had a trusted aide begin screening all the plans directorate cables for him and deciding independently which ones the general should see. Wisner and Dulles strongly resented allowing any outsider to read their messages. They particularly resisted revealing the identities of people concealed by the pseudonyms they used. (If Smith's aide didn't have those identities, the cables he reviewed were practically unintelligible.) The weekly deputies' meetings that Smith convened also became cross-examination sessions for Dulles and Wisner. Smith would become furious when he learned of blown operations or serious errors from sources outside the CIA, such as a press report. He would not put up with any whitewash of bad news. Soon practically all the time at the general's deputies' committee meetings was taken up by Wisner's covert operations.

Even with the information filtering that went on, Smith quickly developed a harsh opinion about Wisner's operatives, and he delivered that opinion unvarnished to Wisner. As the general saw it, the CIA's problems in various parts of the world were due to poor security and the "use of improperly trained or inferior personnel," he told Wisner. The number and the quality of defectors from the Soviet Union "have been disappointing," Smith complained. Until Wisner built up a reserve of well-trained agents, the general told him he should limit his OPC activities to the ones he performed well rather than try to do everything. Smith pointedly reminded Wisner and the other deputies that the CIA's primary mission was intelligence gathering; he did not want any of Wisner's operational snafus to impinge on that mission. In a meeting with senior officials from other agencies, Smith was surprisingly candid, grumbling that many of the suggestions for initiatives that the agency should take in the field of psychological warfare were "a lot of God-damned dribble." He didn't name names, but his top aide sending him those initiatives would have been Wisner.

Smith started sticking his nose into one of Wisner's most cherished programs—BGFiend. Briefed by Wisner on a planned leaflet drop into Albania, the general immediately started tweaking the plan. He did not want any leaflets accidentally dropped on Yugoslavia, which would anger Tito, he told Wisner, and he wanted the plane to fly in and out as quickly as possible. Wisner changed the flight path so it would be a more direct route. At a morning meeting in mid-October 1951, Smith went further and "questioned seriously" the entire Albanian operation. A large amount of money and CIA sweat was being poured into BGFiend and Smith didn't see "what we are accomplishing, or, more important, what we are trying to accomplish."

The general had in front of him a memo alerting him to what it concluded was the "appalling lack of security on the part of Albanians" working in the operation and to the fact that the Albanian population "is much more reluctant to cooperate" with the guerrillas Wisner sent in. Even Dulles was becoming skeptical. Smith told Wisner he wanted a full status report on BGFiend, and he wanted to hear what the State Department thought of the program. Wisner responded the next month with a lengthy memo defending the project. Despite its obvious problems, Wisner's staff recommended that the CIA continue BGFiend. Smith went along but with misgivings.

Radio Liberty became another Smith target. At an August meeting with Wisner, Dulles, and a State Department official, the general complained that setting up a new Radio Liberty facility to broadcast propaganda into the Soviet Union was too expensive.

Smith suspected that programs beamed into Russia "would have little practical effect in the Soviet heartland" (which proved to be the case). The State Department official at the meeting chimed in that he doubted the five Russian émigré groups that formed the Council for the Liberation of the Peoples of Russia would stay unified behind the organization. Smith ordered Wisner to scale back. A newspaper could be published, and the research institute Wisner planned in Germany could be established, but he should first try broadcasting an experimental program into the Soviet Union using the transmission facilities Radio Free Europe already had in place. Smith did not like plunging into operations with only skimpy information on their chances of success.

For a secret intelligence agency, the CIA in its first two years had endured an unusual number of outside reviews of its affairs. It seemed as if practically everyone in the administration—nearly a half dozen panels and departments by one count—was poking into its business. Smith piled on as well with reviews he commissioned. He sent General Lucian Truscott, an Army pal from World War II, to inspect Wisner's work. "I'm going to go out there and find out what those weirdos are up to," Truscott vowed. He claimed he was flabbergasted to discover so many Ivy League dilettantes in the Office of Policy Coordination playing at being spies, their cloak-and-dagger delusions encouraged by Wisner. Smith had Truscott oversee CIA operations in critically important Germany. Wisner quickly learned how to manipulate the crusty general so Truscott wouldn't give him any more trouble.

Wisner got a more favorable review from Bill Jackson. OPC's mission was expanding and becoming more important, the deputy director reported to Smith, and Wisner had done an "outstanding" job in the face of "almost insurmountable obstacles." His outfit was "acutely undermanned" in terms of quantity and quality. The East European Division's Soviet branch was "very thin," the Far East Division was understrength, the psychological warfare and paramilitary divisions had not yet been organized, and just one junior officer looked after its spy training, over which OPC had little oversight.

Smith, however, felt that things were getting out of control with Wisner's outfit. More and more, the general began worrying out loud in meetings that the agency's covert operations had become so large compared to its intelligence-collection function "that we have almost arrived at the stage where it is necessary to decide whether CIA will remain an intelligence agency or becomes a 'cold war department.'" Smith didn't want the latter to happen.

The general did not doubt that he could get the money from Congress to expand covert operations. They rang "the cash register," he knew. But the CIA's budget was becoming so large that congressional appropriators were having trouble hiding it. Bob Joyce, the State Department's liaison to OPC, worried that the expansion of agency operations would inevitably lead to their exposure.

Smith decided to make changes. He wanted Wisner to distinguish between covert action operations (such as secretly bribing foreign officials and waging psychological warfare) and guerrilla warfare operations, which were large and practically impossible to be kept covert. Smith told the National Security Council he would like to dump the entire guerrilla warfare mission into the Pentagon's lap. Wisner and Dulles would not go that far, and they quietly frustrated Smith's attempts to radically shrink OPC's guerrilla operations. The Joint Chiefs also preferred that the agency do that kind of dirty work.

Too many of Wisner's officers were jumping into operations that would not withstand the test of close scrutiny, Smith was convinced. The OPC had undertaken numerous projects of doubtful value—often at the casual suggestion of a State Department or Pentagon officer, or simply because of a CIA man's own enthusiasm for covert warfare. By 1952, one Central European nation had forty different CIA covert operations going on in it—it was impossible for any one person to keep track of them all.

Smith wanted everything slowed down and Wisner's budget more closely scrubbed. He expanded the auditing staff to examine Wisner's spending in more detail. The general also appointed a special "Murder Board" to review closely every OPC project and eliminate the ones judged not necessary to carry out a formal commitment the unit had made to the State Department, the Pentagon, or the National Security Council. The Murder Board recommended eliminating about one-third of Wisner's projects. Smith approved.

The general commanded a lot of respect within the Truman administration. Other departments did not worry too much about the lack of oversight of the CIA budget, or at least not more than Smith did. But to cover himself, the general also set up a Psychological Strategy Board made up of State Department, Pentagon, and CIA officials who would review Wisner's programs and projects to determine if they were desirable and feasible. Gordon Gray, who had known Wisner from their days together at Woodberry Forest and who had risen to Army secretary and president of the University of North Carolina at Chapel Hill since then, became the staff director for the Psychological Strategy Board. But the PSB fell short of its purpose. Smith determined what operations to share with the panel and Wisner, who never liked the strategy board idea, found it easy to circumvent. The board members, busy with their regular jobs, did not review the operations in any kind of detail. The PSB ended up being a short-lived experience, and an unhappy one, Gray concluded—although he, Wisner, and their families remained close friends over the years.

The four leaders of America's clandestine war—Beetle Smith, William Jackson, Allen Dulles, and Frank Wisner—decided they should draft a memo on the future direction their conflict should take. The memo became known as the "Magnitude Paper." On the afternoon of Thursday, March 29, the four men gathered in Smith's headquarters office on Navy Hill to discuss the ultimatum they should deliver to the National Security Council on "where we go from here, and how far," as Smith put it in opening the meeting. Smith now said he was reluctantly willing to run the expanded covert operations the Murder Board had trimmed the agency down to, but he insisted on having the authority to do so, and the support he would need from the administration had to be made crystal clear.

He wasn't worried about the large amount of money that would be required; it was a drop in bucket compared to the total defense budget. But he was concerned that the authority for waging this wider war should be clear and the support for it (particularly in terms of qualified people to fight it) should be there. Smith wasn't so sure the people part would be forthcoming. The CIA had to recruit the right kind of officers, Smith worried, but he knew the military would not send him its best. The Pentagon was already notorious for short-changing him on the large numbers he needed.

Wisner spoke up. The missions the State Department and the Pentagon had already laid on for his outfit and the ones he expected to receive in the future "will be far beyond our present capacity to implement without greatly expanded machinery," he said. In other words, "we have reached the limits of the capabilities of the CIA as presently constituted," Smith said.

Smith put Wisner in charge of writing the Magnitude Paper for him. The general envisioned that a program that large would require a lot of deliberating by the National Security Council. He wanted to make sure the NSC knew what it was getting into. On May 8, Smith delivered to the council the important memo Wisner had written for him. The general hoped it would hit them like a bucket of cold water and wake the Truman administration up to the huge covert initiative it wanted to undertake.

Since 1948, the CIA had expanded its covert operations far beyond what the National Security Council envisioned, the Smith-Wisner memo began. But for future operations the administration wanted, OPC would need a major increase in its budget. High-level decisions would have to be made on the nature of those operations. If the Joint Chiefs wanted the CIA to take on the monumental job of retarding a Soviet advance into Europe during a war, priorities had to be set. Wisner's operations had already been stepped up considerably to carry out NSC directives in place to roll back Soviet power and frustrate the Kremlin, Wisner wrote. Those peacetime missions were huge, the Smith-Wisner memo stated. The CIA's "covert operations are outstripping its present administrative capabilities." The Truman administration had been engaging in a lot of wishful thinking, Wisner felt, although he put the thought more diplomatically in his memo. The covert operations the NSC now wanted for wartime would require a CIA staff "comparable to a major [military] command" with an extensive training and support capability. The China guerrilla force alone could number as many as 300,000 men. Without a sizable budget increase, the agency would have to divert to covert operations a larger amount of its resources for intelligence collection and analysis. The National Security Council needed to decide all those issues quickly, the memo insisted. Clandestine work wasn't whipped up like instant coffee. Long lead times were needed. "It requires approximately 18 months to build the base from which all-out covert operations can be launched."

The Magnitude Paper should have given Harry Truman and his NSC pause. After he retired, Truman would claim—somewhat disingenuously—that he had envisioned a small CIA organization just collecting and analyzing intelligence, the implication being that Wisner and other CIA cowboys had gone rogue with far more than what he had wanted. But as president, Truman went along enthusiastically with an expanded agency knee-deep in covert warfare.

The National Security Council's response to the Smith-Wisner Magnitude Paper "was not exactly the one that Smith had sought," an agency history noted. Instead of a red stoplight, or at least a yellow caution light, the NSC in October gave the general a bright green light. The council instructed him to expand OPC's operations immediately. All caution had ended after North Korea invaded. Everybody now wanted something from the CIA. The National Security Council wanted operations expanded in China, and Smith could not fob off guerrilla warfare there or in Europe on the Pentagon, which along with the State Department wanted his agency to go on a wartime footing. When the Soviets attacked, the Joint Chiefs envisioned the agency becoming a "Fourth Force" whose unconventional warfare capability the theater military commander could employ.

Wisner prepared a lengthy—and scary—war plan. He assumed hostilities would not begin before June 3, 1952 (a month before when Pentagon planners predicted the attack would start). War would commence with little warning, he forecast. West European countries belonging to NATO would be overrun. Both sides would use atomic weapons. Middle East oil would be vital for the West's response. The Soviets would use subversion and unconventional warfare on a global scale. Wisner would set up his own secret army to retard the Soviet advance. His plan was wildly ambitious—and unrealistic. He envisioned major operations to be staged not only in Europe and the Far East but also in the Near East, Africa, and the Western Hemisphere. Even with the planned buildup, he would have nowhere near the capability to carry all of this out in the foreseeable future. The Joint Chiefs, however, responded enthusiastically to Wisner's strategic plan.

In fall 1951, Wisner, who made a point of making two to three foreign trips annually, hopped on a plane to visit once more the various U.S. military commands in Europe to discuss his unconventional war plans. Smith wanted Wisner to spend more time abroad touring his stations. Interestingly, Wisner trusted Smith more than his subordinates in OPC to run his organization in his absence.

In Paris, Wisner stayed with old friends David and Evangeline Bruce. David was now the U.S. ambassador to France. In London Wisner paid a visit to Stewart Menzies, MI6's director. He also made stops in Turkey, Greece, Italy, West Germany, Holland, and Belgium, vacuuming up intelligence on political conditions in each country. He made it home in time for Polly and him to join Gordon and Jane Gray at the University of North Carolina–Notre Dame football game in Chapel Hill the third weekend of November; Notre Dame won 12–7.

During his European journey, Wisner marveled that he had the distinct "impression that CIA was gaining in maturity and stature. There is greater acceptance of CIA by American officials abroad and the Agency contribution is recognized. This presents an increased responsibility to live up to this recognition." Wisner correctly read the CIA's elevated prestige. Considered a premier organization for fighting the evil Soviet Union, with stockpiles of weapons around the globe and four Air Force air wings now available to transport its men and equipment anywhere, the CIA attracted the nation's best young minds for that noble crusade.

Not only was the CIA's reputation elevated. Wisner also toured Europe with more personal stature. Smith soon realized that Bill Jackson was not suited for the deputy director's job. On August 23, 1951, the general replaced him with Allen Dulles, although he did so with some trepidation. He knew Dulles was not a total team player. The same day, Smith moved Wisner up to take Dulles's old job as deputy director for plans. Wisner now oversaw both the Office of Policy Coordination and the Office of Special Operations, which were merged. He was now paid $14,000 a year (more than $168,000 in today's dollars), but the money little reflected his power. Running the entire clandestine service—intelligence collection, counterespionage, and covert action operations—Wisner was at the top of his game.

But there were slight signs that the crushing responsibilities he now assumed were coming with a price. Beginning in December 1950, the CIA had gone to a six-day workweek because of the national emergency the U.S. government felt it was in. However, Wisner did not work every Saturday, and the two weekends he usually took off each month were spent doing chores at the farm. When he became deputy director for plans, Wisner wanted eight personal assistants, exclusive of Billie Morrone and the other secretaries who worked for him. He began to complain to subordinates about too many assignments being thrown at him from different directions and about operations growing too big and unwieldy. Yet he continued to micromanage, becoming emotionally invested in operations, many of which he followed intently from the OPC war room. Staff meetings with him could become testy and occasionally unpredictable. One time he surprised everyone in the room by grilling a visiting State Department representative about Africa, still a low-priority continent for OPC. Obscure items—like keeping bauxite deposits on Palau in the West Pacific out of Soviet hands—would consume him at times.

Wisner paid close attention to CIA officers who behaved erratically or in a vacant manner, as one officer did in the field. Beetle Smith ordered that any officer who came back from the field after a mental crack-up should be interviewed by him personally or by one of his deputies, and that everything should be done to help the officer. He felt that one of the weakest links in the CIA security chain was continuing to employ psychologically unfit people. Something had to be done about it. Dulles was concerned as well. When Wisner reported that one of his men, who battled alcoholism, had killed himself with an overdose of sleeping pills, Dulles ordered a full investigation into how the officer had been hired in the first place, looking for lessons learned to better screen applicants with mental health issues. Wisner wondered if the CIA had a higher rate of officers attempting suicide than other government agencies. CIA shrinks promised to check it out.

If Wisner showed signs of fatigue and moroseness—they often surfaced among CIA men and women—his colleagues passed them off to the fact that he carried, after all, a global battle on his shoulders. He was leading a war against an implacable enemy believed to be an existential threat to America. The pressure on Frank Wisner was only going to increase.

Chapter 16

THE RED SCARE AND THE BLACK BOOK

BY THE FALL OF 1952, social ferment was beginning to bubble below the surface of a prosperous country. The number of middle-class families started to grow by more than a million a year. Consumerism became ravenous. Buyers drowned out savers, scooping up the wondrous new kitchen aids Betty Furness advertised on TV for Westinghouse and the bigger cars General Motors produced with their garish fins, automatic transmissions, and high-compression engines. To accommodate the increase in Americans traveling the roads who wanted a room for the night, the hugely successful Holiday Inn chain began. Financial experts emerged; their only concern was to maximize profits. In another year Hugh Hefner began publishing *Playboy* magazine, which would become a key part of the future sexual revolution. With Black Americans migrating to Northern cities, the Supreme Court was poised to move away from the segregation holding back those who remained in the South.

Americans were adjusting to a difficult and expensive new peace, in which old allies like Russia and China were now enemies and old enemies like Germany and Japan were now allies. Alarmists in the press added to public uncertainty, warning that the nation's defenses were unprepared for superior Soviet arms and soldiers. The Korean War and Russia's detonation of an atomic device left people fearful of a cataclysmic global conflict with no winners.

Then came the "Red Scare"—the fear that committed Communists and their sympathizers were infesting and eating away at the federal government and the private sector like termites. The worry had been building since 1946. Republican-leaning *Time* magazine became a voice of paranoia over Commies. Mystery novelist Mickey Spillane switched from gangsters to Bolsheviks as his book's antagonists. Truman worried about Reds and "parlor pinks" in America and went along with government surveillance of the suspicious ones. After his 1948 reelection, Republicans bitter over the prospect of four more years of Democratic rule took the low road and began accusing the Truman administration of being soft on domestic Communists.

A bachelor obsessed with cleanliness and a stylish dresser who lived with his mother, John Edgar Hoover had gone to night school to earn his law degree and had received a World War II draft exemption from the Army to serve as a Justice Department clerk. Demonstrating a talent for hunting down suspects, J. Edgar Hoover had shot up the ranks at Justice to become director of the Federal Bureau of Investigation and one of the most powerful men in the country. Politicians, fearful of damaging information Hoover had on them in the meticulous files he kept, dared not cross him. During World War II, Hoover and Donovan had had bitter turf battles, both men even planting moles in the other's organization to spy on the bureaucratic enemy. After the war, the FBI director was convinced that 100,000 Communists were on the loose in the country. If there was a World War III–like attack, Hoover had a frightening plan to round up twelve thousand Americans the bureau had identified as potentially dangerous to U.S. security and throw them into federal detention facilities the FBI had selected around the country.

Truman had little use for Hoover, fearful that his FBI was becoming an American Gestapo. But the hugely popular director was

politically untouchable. When Hillenkoetter's retirement was announced, the White House received mail urging that Hoover be
named CIA director and that the spy agency be folded into the FBI
so J. Edgar could clean out the Russia lovers in the CIA and protect
the nation's secrets. Hoover, for his part, had an equally low opinion
of Truman. During the 1948 presidential campaign, he fed information to Dewey and hoped that it would help the New York governor
win so he could make Hoover his attorney general. Post-OSS,
Hoover had envisioned running a worldwide intelligence operation like the one the bureau had had in Latin America during World
War II. Truman, along with other senior administration officials,
nixed that idea. But Wisner and Dulles continued to worry that the
FBI agents placed in U.S. embassies overseas as legal attachés were
in reality operating as intelligence officers.

It took months of delicate negotiations with Hoover, who had
long been paranoid that other agencies would run roughshod on his
turf if he didn't fight them, but Wisner finally hammered out an
operating agreement with the FBI director in late November 1950.
He agreed that his Office of Policy Coordination would not spy in
the United States nor engage in any type of law enforcement work,
such as making arrests. But Hoover agreed that Wisner's outfit
could engage in some domestic activities, such as recruiting people
to work in OPC, buying supplies for its operations, and hiring
American businesses to conduct research and special training for
covert operations Wisner mounted overseas.

Hoover never trusted Wisner to live up to his end of the bargain, and the FBI director had leverage over the OPC director to
make life miserable for him. The CIA depended on FBI investigations of its officers for security clearances, which Wisner wanted
done quickly but which the bureau could drag out. Hoover
complained—with some justification—that CIA security was lax.
The CIA, however, routinely hooked its officers up to lie detector
machines, which served as a deterrent to their betraying secrets.
Agency officers called the polygraphing being "fluttered" after its
code name, "LCFlutter."

Hoover assigned Sam Papich, who had been working as an intelligence operative in the bureau since 1941, to serve as the FBI's liaison with the CIA. An action-oriented sort of guy, Papich at first hated the job—he found both the CIA and the FBI often equally at fault in their bureaucratic clashes—but eventually he mellowed and Wisner grew to like him. Wisner quickly learned, however, that if he wanted any decision out of the bureau, he had to go directly to Hoover, who tended to micromanage as much as he did.

As was the case with most every intelligence officer who did not work for him, Hoover came to loathe Wisner. He ordered his agents to keep an eye on the clandestine service chief and those whom bureau men called "Wisner's weirdos." A rumor spread that Hoover had planted agents as cooks and butlers in some of the homes of the Georgetown set to keep watch on their partying. If they thought that had been the case, Frank and Polly kept quiet about it, but there was clear evidence that the agents probed. Occasionally FBI men dropped by the office of the Alsop brothers, whom Hoover was convinced held a grudge against him, and to ask who their sources were for columns that upset the director. Joe and Stewart always showed the agents the door, which earned the brothers a fattening dossier on their writings at bureau headquarters.

Hoover had reason to be angry that Wisner was bigfooting him. In a clear trespass on FBI turf, FBI agents caught CIA officers following German scientists brought to the United States to work on the American rocket program. After one of Wisner's men was spotted recruiting a foreigner in the U.S. to be part of an overseas operation, an FBI agent sat down with the CIA officer and politely explained that he could not do that. In 1952, Wisner's officers set up a secret mail-opening operation in New York for letters sent between the U.S. and the U.S.S.R. The operation, code-named HT-Lingual, produced intelligence of "marginal value," according to a CIA report, but Wisner did not inform Hoover about it for the project's first six years.

The CIA had its own growing list of complaints about FBI operations intruding on agency affairs. Dulles became angry when FBI agents took in and interrogated one of the CIA's sources, which "had pretty thoroughly blown our operation." Dulles also learned that FBI agents had gotten their hands on documents dealing with his personal life and with his wife, Clover, that the State Department had kept from the time he worked there. He demanded that the bureau expunge those papers, which Hoover refused to do. The FBI file on Dulles, particularly its memos on his extramarital affairs, never stopped growing.

A key congressional source with whom Hoover often traded tips was Joseph McCarthy, an alcoholic Republican senator from Wisconsin who had spent his first four years on Capitol Hill in obscurity until he announced in 1950 that he had a list of Communist Party and spy ring members in the State Department. To his own surprise, McCarthy had tapped a rich vein of millions of Americans afraid that sinister forces were subverting the nation. A skilled demagogue whose tactics came to be known as "McCarthyism," the senator never uncovered an actual spy ring, but he became a master at trafficking in innuendo and hurling charges that Communists had infiltrated the Truman administration and the U.S. Army. In the summer of 1951, McCarthy accused Secretary of Defense Marshall and Secretary of State Acheson of being part of a Communist conspiracy. By 1952, the Wisconsin senator was at the height of his power, with other Republican reactionaries in Congress rushing to join him in his baseless attacks. Acheson called McCarthy and his allies "the primitives." Truman called them "the animals."

Wisner thought McCarthy was focused on the wrong target. The Communist threat America faced was from the Russians on the outside, he argued, not from Communists inside the United States. The American Communist Party was a pathetically weak group, CIA officers believed. Wisner did his best to keep his clandestine service out of the senator's crosshairs. Walter Pforzheimer, who worked as the CIA's legislative liaison with Congress, managed in May 1950 to elicit a private promise from McCarthy that he would not bring charges of Communists being in the agency without at least giving the CIA a heads-up. Wisner tried to keep his operations from antagonizing the senator. He was furious when he learned that the American Committee for Cultural Freedom, which the agency bankrolled, was embroiled in a feud between pro- and anti-McCarthyites in its ranks. It would only bring them trouble, Wisner lectured, and he ordered a halt to the infighting. Wisner tried to cooperate with McCarthy when he could, arranging for the senator and his top aides to be briefed by his station chiefs when they traveled overseas. He also used the State Department as a secret funnel to McCarthy's staff to feed it exculpatory material on the CIA.

For three years, the charm offensive worked. While McCarthy continued his attacks on other federal agencies, he kept his hands off the CIA. But the senator played fair for only so long. He developed an underground of disgruntled former agency officers willing to trash the CIA.

Polly, Frank, and the rest of the Georgetown set despised McCarthy. Hardly a dinner passed when his name was not raised in disgust. Joe and Stewart Alsop nursed a deep-seated hatred of the senator. It amused the brothers when McCarthy accused them of being Reds. *Washington Post* reporters wrote stories critical of McCarthyism, but Phil Graham tried to walk a fine line between condemnation and acquiescence. Graham was a liberal turned conservative anti-Communist fighting for the financial life of the *Post*, whom McCarthy branded a Communist sympathizer.

Polly was terrified the Wisconsin senator would go after her husband. Wisner professed not to be concerned. "I have no doubt that McCarthy and his like within his staff have it in for me personally since my views about his entire performance are rather well known," he wrote his mother. "However, I want to assure you that this matter does not cause me to lose very much sleep."

Spies were lurking everywhere in the U.S., it seemed. Soviet espionage operations to steal secrets in the U.S. rattled not only the public but also official Washington and its security mavens like Wisner. Whittaker Chambers, a former *Time* magazine editor who had worked in the Soviet underground, testified before the House Un-American Activities Committee in 1948 that State Department official Alger Hiss was a Communist spy. (Truman called the hearings a "red herring.") A British court convicted Klaus Fuchs in 1950 of feeding the Soviets intelligence from his research as a theoretical physicist at the Los Alamos National Laboratory in New Mexico. Julius and Ethel Rosenberg were convicted the next year of providing American nuclear weapons design secrets to the Soviets. As the Rosenbergs waited in New York's Sing Sing prison for their June 19, 1953, date with the electric chair, Wisner and Beetle Smith brainstormed a propaganda barrage to counter Moscow's condemnation of their death sentences.

Other cases divided the Wisner family. Debate raged in fashionable Washington over whether the patrician Alger Hiss, who was eventually sent to prison on a perjury conviction, was a spy or a casualty of the Red Scare. Many Georgetown women, Polly included, rushed to his defense. In November 1953, a year before Hiss's release from incarceration, his wife, Priscilla, was accepted into the Georgetown Garden Club, of which Polly was a prominent member. Polly could have blackballed the other woman if she had wanted to. Considerable evidence accumulated in later years that Hiss had spied for the Russians. Frank, at the time, thought Hiss was guilty of espionage. Physicist J. Robert Oppenheimer, credited as the "father of the atomic bomb" developed by the Manhattan Project, was hounded by Hoover's agents and stripped of his security clearance for being too dovish and opposing the U.S. building the far more powerful hydrogen bomb. Polly thought "Oppie" was another innocent victim of the Red Scare. Frank was noncommittal.

But in other cases, it was crystal clear to Wisner that government officials were being victimized by Hoover and McCarthy. He was deeply upset over McCarthy targeting his old friend Charles Thayer, an OSS veteran who had directed the Voice of America, over rumors of Communist sympathies and homosexuality. Wisner found himself powerless as well to intervene in the case of State

Department China hand John Paton Davies—unfairly accused of being disloyal—other than to refuse to testify before the McCarran Committee on the role Davies had played in the work of Wisner's Office of Policy Coordination when Davies was in the State Department's policy planning office. But Wisner's officers did manage to spirit away CIA analyst William Bundy so McCarthy's staff couldn't sink its claws into him with a subpoena. Bundy's sin was contributing $400 to Hiss's legal defense fund.

Wisner could not hide Carmel Offie, however. The FBI's file on the OPC operative eventually numbered 425 pages and included a detailed biography of Offie, a record of his influential jobs in Europe before and during the war as a fixer for top diplomats, and praise for his OPC work by such senior State Department officials as Chip Bohlen, Robert Joyce, and George Kennan. Hoover's men also dug up a District of Columbia police report on Offie's 1943 arrest in Lafayette Square across from the White House for soliciting sex from young men. The FBI suspected he was using other venues and bathrooms—"Offie is a 'stinker' in his own right," read a handwritten note on one bureau memo—and having trysts with Joe Alsop, whom the bureau knew was a homosexual.

By the spring of 1950, the FBI was closing in on Carmel Offie. When the bureau learned that in addition to his DC house Offie owned two apartments in Paris plus a farm in Fauquier County, Virginia, it began secretly scouring his bank accounts and tax returns to discover how he paid for all these properties. The agents could find nothing incriminating. But the FBI did learn that the Bureau of Internal Revenue was investigating him for income tax evasion.

The FBI debated bugging Offie's DC home but decided not to. Instead, Hoover leaked the incriminating evidence he had collected on Offie to Senator McCarthy, who took up the chase and eventually demanded that the OPC officer be fired because he was gay. Wisner stubbornly fought to keep Offie on his staff. Even Dulles was inclined to retain him. Beyond not being bothered by Offie's sexual orientation, Wisner considered it a matter of honor: you did not betray a friend.

But Carmel Offie was swept up in what came to be called the "lavender scare" over homosexuals in government. The FBI concluded that he was not only a security risk—subject to blackmail by Soviet agents if they discovered his homosexuality—but that he also was, in fact, a Communist agent. Although it had no hard evidence to back them up, the bureau passed its suspicions on to Bill Harvey, a CIA counterintelligence officer who agreed that Offie was likely a Soviet mole. Paul Nitze, who led the State Department's policy planning office, also thought Offie might have been a hostile agent.

Peter Sichel, an OSS comrade of Wisner's who was now a manager at the CIA's headquarters in Washington, quietly went around to agency employees he suspected might be gay and, with Wisner's approval, warned them that they probably had no future in the CIA. The employees who were gay did not have to look far to see that was the case.

Offie's security clearance was revoked. Wisner had no choice but to move his aide outside of OPC to a job with the AFL's Free Trade Union Committee, where Offie helped funnel OPC money to the committee. After Offie's contract with the Free Trade Committee expired in 1952, Wisner moved him to a prestigious K Street law firm in Washington. But Offie remained bitter toward his old boss. He later stormed over to Wisner's house when Wisner was away and dragged off the cook he had found for Polly. Offie was convinced that Polly was to blame for Frank's break with him.

Hoover never gave up what became a vendetta toward Carmel Offie. The FBI director remained forever curious about what Offie had done for the Office of Policy Coordination. Hoover had his agents keep track of the man for the next twenty-two years, collecting rumors on his sex life, interviewing anyone who had anything mean to say about him, even recording in the Offie file each time he received a traffic ticket. It soon became clear, however, that Hoover's and McCarthy's pursuit of Offie and other Wisner comrades were warm-ups for a more important target: Frank Wisner himself.

* * *

Princess Tanda Caradja lived a mysterious life after Wisner left Romania in early 1945. In her travels around Europe, she used four different pseudonyms by a later count that the FBI made. In 1945, Tanda was able to book a flight to Italy and Switzerland, which was unusual because practically no Romanians could leave the country at that time. She was supposedly going on Romanian Red Cross business. But that was her cover story. The Red Cross did not recognize her as its representative, according to a U.S. intelligence report on her many movements. The real purpose of Tanda's trip was to transfer money that her beer magnate husband had made dealing with the Germans to a more secure Swiss bank account because it was in danger of being frozen. That same year, she met U.S. Army Air Forces pilot Robert Moevs, who was stationed in Romania, and the two began having an affair. In 1947, Tanda divorced her husband, Mitu, and married Lieutenant Moevs.

Moevs was transferred out of Bucharest in September 1947—Tanda did not join him—and ended up in Paris, where he later studied music. By then the couple was going their separate ways. Back in Bucharest, newspapers reported that Tanda was being sued for defrauding future tenants in an apartment project she planned to build. The U.S. intelligence report compiled on the princess stated that in November 1949, American security agents at the U.S. embassy in Vienna picked up Tanda, who was with another lover, Paul Laptev, and was posing as a refugee. The American agents arrested her as she was about to enter a Russian intelligence office. After being fingered by a Romanian agent the U.S. Army's Counter Intelligence Corps had caught, Tanda admitted that she was on a mission for Romania's Communist intelligence service. She told her interrogators that she had been ordered to contact Romanian friends in

Austria before traveling to Paris to spy. The Americans turned her over to French authorities, who took her to Paris, where Moevs eventually secured her release. The princess insisted the Romanian spy service had coerced her into gathering intelligence.

More Tanda reports followed. In early spring 1950, she again came to the attention of U.S. authorities when Lieutenant Moevs told authorities that he learned that his wife had been arrested by the Swiss—perhaps for overstaying her visa in the country. Tanda was again released to her husband, who took her out of the country. A June 9, 1952, U.S. intelligence report alleged that Tanda had been a member of the Iron Guard fascist paramilitary organization during the war and afterward had worked for Romanian intelligence. She was referred to in the report as a "dangerous Soviet agent." An intelligence report two months later claimed that Tanda, now divorced from Moevs, resided in Salzburg, Austria, living inconspicuously and selling off valuable personal belongings to sustain herself. In the spring of 1953, Tanda was reported to be seriously ill with a "tubercular condition" and allowed to visit France for treatment. A later September 1953 intelligence report, still referring to her as a "suspected communist agent," noted that she was now married to an employee of the French consulate in Innsbruck, Austria.

Tanda's postwar story would have just collected dust overseas had her dossier not been sent back to Washington, where it ended up in the hands of J. Edgar Hoover, who saw Frank Wisner's name on documents for the World War II years. The FBI director immediately recognized the value of what appeared to be a dalliance between a suspected Communist agent and one of Hoover's hated rivals.

FBI gumshoes began an intensive investigation of the Wisner–Tanda Caradja affair. By May 1952, they had collected enough evidence for an agent in the bureau's Washington field office to phone Wisner and say he wanted to discuss with him the "Bucharest incident." It had not taken the FBI long to piece together the extramarital affair. The beautiful princess had introduced Wisner "to the best Romanian and foreign social circles in Bucharest," according to a bureau memo. "This acquaintance ripened into more than a friendship and soon they were living together." Had Wisner at the time of the affair known about the spy connections of his love interest? The bureau had hints that he had. Hoover's agents picked up a rumor that an intelligence officer with the British mission in Bucharest had warned his American colleague that Tanda was a Russian operative, but Wisner ignored the warning. And through her affair with Wisner, an FBI memo alleged, Tanda was able to leave and reenter Romania as she pleased—at a time when only Romanian government officials could do so—which enabled her to visit France and Switzerland for "black market currency operations."

An FBI investigative memo on May 9 concluded that "it would appear that if the allegations regarding Wisner are true, it is conceivably possible that a loyalty investigation should be opened." Hoover had his agents present their findings to Beetle Smith and Allen Dulles, who began their own intensive probe.

Six months later, Smith fired back to Hoover a memo, marked "Top Secret Eyes Only," with the results of the CIA's investigation—which cleared his clandestine service chief. It was true that Wisner and his team had been billeted in Tanda Caradja's home. (Smith made no mention of the affair Wisner had had with Tanda.) And much later after the war, Tanda had confessed to Army counterintelligence that she had been a Communist informer and had worked for Russian intelligence. But Wisner, who had been filled in on all the allegations the bureau had collected on him, had had no association with Tanda since he left Bucharest in 1945, Smith insisted, and he knew nothing about her espionage activities. (It wasn't entirely true that since 1945 Wisner had severed all dealings with the princess. Sometime in late 1946 or the beginning of 1947, Tanda had contacted Wisner from Paris, and Wisner knew she had been divorcing Mitu to marry Moevs.)

Wisner had found that Romania's postwar exile community was a wasp's nest of political factions and petty rivalries, which made collaboration with them practically impossible for the CIA. He now found himself the victim of those squabbles. Beetle Smith's investigators discovered that it was a questionable source in Romanian gossip circles who had been responsible for the salacious charges that had been leveled against Wisner. The source was Nicolae Malaxa, a disreputable Romanian industrialist and financier of the fascist Iron Guard. Malaxa was a bitter enemy of Max Ausnit, an equally disreputable Romanian steel magnate accused of collaborating with the Germans. The two men made it a practice of spreading derogatory rumors about each other. Wisner came in Malaxa's sights because immediately after the war, when he had been with Carter, Ledyard & Milburn, Wisner had represented Ausnit in a legal dispute with Malaxa—who, it turned out, had hired Dulles's law firm, Sullivan & Cromwell, to represent him. The CIA's investigators concluded that the venal Malaxa had peddled rumors that Wisner was having an affair with a woman he knew was a Communist agent as payback for Wisner representing Ausnit.

On December 22, Smith wrote Hoover that the CIA had closed the Wisner case. Smith's clandestine service chief was exonerated of the charge that he had consorted with a woman he knew was a Communist agent. Smith warned Hoover that Malaxa and his cronies would likely try to smear other CIA officers who had served in Bucharest during the war. But the Caradja case was settled as far as the agency was concerned.

Wisner, however, could never be sure that Hoover would not bring the case up again or leak it to McCarthy, who by now was convinced the CIA was also riddled with Communists. Frank could not relax. Neither could Polly, who knew about the wartime fling yet didn't want it to derail her husband's career. The Tanda Caradja affair was never discussed in the Wisner family; the children heard only whispers about it much later in life. Wisner had a reputation for being a swashbuckler and in Laurel he engaged in business activities that probably would not survive today's conflict-of-interest rules, but he was a stickler for following the ethics regulations that did exist at work. At home he and Polly were scrupulous in their finances, taking only the deductions they were legally entitled to on their taxes. The fact that J. Edgar Hoover knew, or was convinced, that his rival had cheated on his wife was deeply humiliating for Wisner. The Princess Tanda Caradja affair left a scar. It added to the pressure mounting on him running covert operations all over the world. Wisner began sleeping less at night.

He had good reason to worry that he had not heard the last of this investigation. Hoover was not about to let go of the case.

* * *

Hoover and McCarthy had also long suspected that salted among the nearly 600,000 European refugees and displaced persons the United States had admitted by June 1953 were Nazi war criminals Wisner had sneaked in to work for the CIA. Eisenhower's headquarters had estimated at the end of the war that the number of Nazi security officers who worked for repugnant organizations like the SS, SD, and Gestapo numbered more than 200,000. SHAEF had a published list of 70,000 war criminals, whom the Army's Counter Intelligence Corps was charged with hunting down and arresting.

Three decades later, in the 1980s, critics would accuse Wisner of running a vast illegal smuggling operation to sneak thousands of Nazi intelligence agents and their collaborators into the United States to train for CIA missions or as rewards for jobs fighting Communists that they had performed for the agency overseas. The truth was not so spectacular. It was far more nuanced. Throughout his life, Wisner loathed the Nazis, but after World War II, he saw that they could be used in America's existential struggle with the Soviet Union. He studied closely, for example, how the Nazis had exploited weaknesses in their Soviet enemies during the war and he wanted to emulate those tactics now. Wisner and the officers who worked under him knew full well that some of the foreign agents they recruited had been Nazi collaborators. He understood clearly from his own surveys of Soviet defectors to the American side that a large majority of them had fled to escape retribution for their wartime collaboration with the Germans.

Moreover, the Allied commitment to prosecute war criminals and to root out Nazis and their collaborators waned as the years passed. Adept at hiding, Nazis collaborators became more difficult to identify among the hundreds of thousands of displaced persons. Extensive personnel records on them did not exist. Postwar Army counterintelligence officers tasked with finding them were inexperienced, they often did not speak East European languages, and they were overwhelmed by the large number of cases. By the mid-1950s investigating Nazi war crime allegations among those applying for entry into the United States was not a high priority for the Immigration and Naturalization Service.

Army counterintelligence officers continued to hunt for Nazis, but some became protected prey. Wisner's CIA wasn't the only agency doing the protecting. Under several military operations, one of which was code-named "Paperclip," more than seven hundred German scientists, engineers, and technicians—many of them committed Nazis, some tied to war crimes—were brought to the United States by the Pentagon to work on missile and chemical warfare programs. As for Wisner, the National Security Council gave him considerable leeway in choosing foreign recruits for his shadow war against the Soviets. The State Department and the Pentagon were not too picky about their backgrounds. Only results mattered. Information was needed quickly. There were no established CIA espionage networks in the East European nations, so Wisner's men made do with the foreign defectors who were at hand. The CIA downplayed accounts of the Nazi collaboration and frequent brutality of many East European émigré groups. "In its quest for information on the U.S.S.R.," one agency study concluded, "the United States became indelibly linked to the Third Reich."

Save for a few cases (like Prussian Otto von Bolschwing, whom the CIA helped hide his SS past when he was applying for a visa), Wisner did not smuggle cooperative Nazis into the United States. Instead, he established legal channels to resettle foreign agents and defectors from the Soviet bloc, which became a maddening exercise for him due to complex U.S. immigration laws. At Wisner's urging, Congress eventually passed a special law permitting the CIA to bring a hundred foreigners into the United States for national security reasons, with no questions asked about their pasts. A 1985 General Accounting Office investigation found, however, that the number of Nazis or collaborators Wisner brought into the United States under legal channels was actually small. Of the 114 cases the GAO reviewed, the congressional watchdog agency found only five instances in which the foreigners who helped the CIA had seamy pasts. But the immigration assistance Wisner gave to even those few ex-Nazis or collaborators was inexcusable considering the little good most of those people did for the CIA.

Wisner's men worked, unwittingly and wittingly, with a far larger number of questionable characters who remained abroad. Hoping to penetrate the Iron Curtain, his officers enlisted Ukrainian nationalists who had records of brutal collaboration with the Nazis during World War II. Salted in the Radio Free Europe and Radio Liberty staffs overseas was a sprinkling of Nazi collaborators, quislings, war criminals, and ex-fascists who had kept their pasts hidden. There was also the former Abwehr spy network commanded by Major General Reinhard Gehlen—his headquarters and extensive Russian files were set up in an OSS compound near Munich. Given the code name "Operation Rusty" with a mission to collect intelligence on East Germany and the rest of Eastern Europe, the Gehlen Organization, more than any single project, paired up the CIA with veterans of Nazi Germany's intelligence service. After much internal debate over whether it was a good idea to be collaborating with a group of military spies for a former enemy, the CIA took full control of the Gehlen Organization from the U.S. Army on July 1, 1949. Wisner, who had made early contact with General

Gehlen, was one of those in the agency backing the CIA's takeover of the organization. He made no apologies for doing so. Gehlen's spy network was a prize the Soviets would have dearly loved to get their hands on, Wisner rationalized. He urged Dulles to cultivate the Abwehr general, who went by the pseudonym "Robert Graber" and was an incredibly able man by Wisner's estimation. Dulles, who had sat in on several early debriefings of Gehlen in Washington, needed no encouragement. Gehlen had the only working intelligence network behind Soviet lines. "I don't know if he is a rascal," Dulles said of the Abwehr spymaster, who sent him and Wisner Christmas cards. "There are few archbishops in espionage. He's on our side and that's all that matters. Besides, one needn't ask him to one's club."

At the outset, Gehlen provided the Americans with intelligence they could not glean elsewhere, such as details on the makeup of Soviet military units, the field equipment they used, and the uranium they were extracting from Siberian mines. But as time passed, relations between the CIA and the German general became strained. The agency paid more than the Army, but the extra money came with more CIA controls, which Gehlen resented. Helms found the Abwehr spymaster and his multimillion-dollar organization hard to handle. The CIA later estimated that seventy-six of the six hundred operatives Gehlen had on his payroll were former SS, SD, SA, or Nazi Party members, some of whom were outright war criminals.

Wisner and Helms realized full well the optics problem they had working with a spy group that sheltered disreputable Nazis, but they made little effort to force Gehlen to clean house. Wisner and Helms turned out to be bothered less by *who* was producing the intelligence than they were by *what* the Gehlen Organization was producing. Helms soon found he was wasting money on intelligence purveyors in Gehlen's ranks who were fabricating reports. It also became obvious to Wisner, Helms, and others in the CIA that the Gehlen Organization had been penetrated by the East German and Soviet intelligence services. Not trusting Gehlen, the CIA began to spy on his organization in the early 1950s, in one case recruiting one of the general's top operatives to be an agency mole. Concluded one

CIA cynic in Germany's field operation: "American intelligence is a rich blind man, using the Abwehr as a seeing eye dog. The only trouble is—the leash is much too long."

* * *

By the early 1950s, the CIA's headquarters in Washington was in a condition best described as urban sprawl. By Smith's count, the agency was scattered among twenty-eight buildings in the capital area. Supplies for Wisner's clandestine service were further spread out early on in warehouses around the city. Smith worried about security for the sprawl.

The buildings along the Reflecting Pool had become so dilapidated that "the repairs needed repairing," Helms complained. Just to maintain the properties and shuttle employees among them cost the CIA $3 million a year.

When he was promoted to deputy director for plans, Wisner moved his office to the nondescript room 1050 in the L Building. The CIA's situation room, which as many as fifty officers could crowd into in order to monitor crises and important operations abroad, was located in the Q Building near Smith's headquarters on Navy Hill. Smith and Wisner also had around Washington an assortment of safe houses that they could use for private lunches and dinners with visiting foreign intelligence officials. Air-conditioning was a continuous headache. In Washington's muggy summer months, Smith, Dulles, Wisner, and other top officers sweltered in their offices and meeting rooms. But wangling money from the Budget Bureau and Congress for air-conditioning units was always a hassle. It left the CIA brass, figuratively and literally, steaming.

* * *

General John Magruder, the Defense Department's liaison to Wisner's clandestine service, typed out a dark memo on May 5, 1952: "We are in the midst of a world-wide campaign of psychological operations. The Cold War is a fact and the men in the Kremlin are at present the arbiters of its tempo and intensity." The CIA had only skimpy intelligence to validate that grim picture, but the agency was convinced it was the case.

The United States was competing against an overseas intelligence force that numbered some ten thousand men and women, the CIA estimated. Wisner's men believed their counterparts in Russia's foreign intelligence service were "some of the most brilliant, patient and careful officers in the world," as one CIA officer put it, adding that the KGB "has recruited more American citizens to work for Moscow than the CIA has recruited Soviet citizens to work for Washington." The Communist Party selected only loyalists to travel overseas, where Russian security men watched them closely, while any American could roam abroad with no restraints and be a target for Moscow's agents. CIA officers made cold calls to KGB officers, offering them money to spy for the United States. The Americans called them "nickel pitches." They rarely succeeded.

But there were glimmers of daylight here. Scores of Russian and East European diplomats and intelligence officers decided on their own to seek asylum in the West. CIA stations around the world also noticed by the fall of 1952 that Soviet embassy officers had begun to emerge from their diplomatic compounds more and "mingle with the crowd," Dulles told Beetle Smith. The CIA director ordered station chiefs around the world to keep on the lookout for potential recruits.

* * *

The KGB's 13th Department carried out its assassinations, called "wet affairs." Top CIA officers debated among themselves whether their agency should catch up with what Wisner considered a Russian lead in that capability. They had no moral qualms about targeted killings of hated Communists—neither did anyone else in the Truman administration, nor in Congress and the press, for that matter.

Assassination had been considered a legitimate weapon during World War II. Donovan had always been interested in exotic drugs that his OSS might use to bump off Hitler and other top Nazis. After the war, CIA leaders were divided only on the question of how feasible such targeted killings were and what kind of blowback the agency might face if it carried them out. Helms, who had had some experience with assassination attempts during the war, saw all kinds of practical problems with murders in peacetime—the CIA could have been subjected to blackmail by the hired assassin, he worried; such plots inevitably got exposed; and the enemy could have retaliated by killing U.S. leaders. Dulles thought those hits were simpler to carry out than doubters like Helms believed.

Wisner set up what could be loosely described as an "assassination capability" in a small office in his directorate. Called Program Branch 7, it was to be used mainly against double agents and low-ranking Communist officials. It was run by Boris Pash, a U.S. Army colonel assigned to the CIA who always shooed off nosy officers who approached him and asked about what exactly PB/7 was doing. Ultimately, Pash's office never carried out any assassinations or even made any concrete plans for a hit. Several times, however, Wisner and his men seriously suggested that a killing be considered. Officers in Asia floated with Washington the idea of poisoning Zhou Enlai, Communist China's number two man, when he visited a conference in Bandung, Indonesia. Dulles quickly killed the idea and ordered the paperwork on it burned. Wisner considered a plan to detonate a bomb planted in Stalin's limousine if he attended a four-power conference in Paris that the French had suggested. The summit never took place, and Beetle Smith nixed the plan to kill Stalin if it convened.

* * *

Wisner compiled what became known as the "black book," which described for the Psychological Strategy Board the major covert operations the CIA was undertaking. By summer 1952, he worried that too many people in the administration had access to its contents and that the black book was becoming too fat. Inside it, some one hundred projects were detailed. A year had passed since Smith and he had delivered their Magnitude Paper to the National Security Council, and the NSC's order for them to ramp up anti-Soviet programs had left the CIA with "too many balls in the air," Wisner now warned Smith. Though his spending amounted to only 1 percent of the federal budget, Wisner's clandestine operations had tripled in number the past three years, and he projected that by the beginning of 1953, he would need a budget three times larger than what the CIA spent on traditional intelligence collection. Asia was getting out of hand with so many operations. The CIA's Far East Division in Washington now dispatched an average of forty-five cables to its stations in the Pacific Theater each day. From the White House, the order was always the same: *give us more*. Smith was ordered to investigate reports of flying saucers. His officers found that one UFO sighting was actually the planet Jupiter.

Before it could be launched, a new major operation now had to be cleared by Wisner, Smith, the Murder Board, and the Psychological Strategy Board. Even so, Smith worried that this was not enough vetting, that his officers in the field could still get away with freelancing, and that the CIA was still assuming "too much responsibility and authority for its own good" on covert operations, as the CIA director wrote in one memo. To ease Beetle's mind, Truman at one point scribbled on White House stationery a note giving his spy chief a blanket presidential pardon in case a covert operation landed him in legal trouble.

At the beginning of August 1952, Wisner compiled a realistic, and somewhat pessimistic, box score for the CIA's covert operations. Radio Free Europe he judged a success with about two dozen studios in its Munich headquarters and more than sixteen hundred employees. His propaganda operation in Asia was equally aggressive: to counter Chinese and North Korean claims that the U.S. was waging bacteriological warfare, Wisner and Dulles hatched a plan to spread a rumor that invading Chinese troops had brought diseases into North Korea. Soviet influence was being contained in France and Italy. But the all-powerful Communist government in the U.S.S.R. had not been weakened one iota by the covert operations Wisner's officers had mounted inside the country. In Eastern Europe, Wisner saw no chance of loosening the Russian hold on Poland, East Germany, and Czechoslovakia. With Albania, which the CIA had devoted a huge effort to destabilize, Wisner was growing more disenchanted, now agreeing with Smith that BGFiend was becoming too costly and leaving less money available for other, more useful projects on the continent. The agency's analysts had already declared the operation a lost cause. Perhaps Washington would have been better off leaving the Russians saddled with that rotting satellite to drain resources from their treasury, Wisner thought.

* * *

Though the general had been their boss for more than a year and a half, Wisner and other senior CIA officers were still trying to figure out Beetle Smith. And Smith was still explaining his management style to his subordinates, admitting that the CIA staff and he were still getting used to one another—which meant he was not an easy man to get used to or to understand. Though he recognized that he was surrounded in Washington by a talented group of intelligence professionals, Smith constantly pestered Wisner and other managers with niggling complaints. He became easily irritated when the sponsors of clandestine projects stood before him poorly prepared to defend their ideas. Wisner promised to coach them better. Smith wanted reports sent to him kept short and to the point. If errors had been made in operations, he demanded succinct explanations about what would be done to fix them. Wisner tried to comply, one time telling Smith that a CIA officer had left a classified document in a State Department bathroom and CIA security officers were investigating the incident. Smith regularly snapped at Wisner and others for not sending him material he thought he should be reviewing or for being late with memos. Wisner dutifully forwarded to him minutiae like a report on fine-gauge nickel wire being moved illegally from the British zone to the Soviet zone in Germany. Smith howled when he caught officers in the field giving important orders he had not personally cleared. "Too many Indians were issuing instructions," he griped. He complained about "ludicrous" pseudonyms given to people in cables—some of them insulting—and wanted them cleaned up. Wisner wearily promised to investigate the ridiculous request. Wisner, however, was outraged when Smith told him at one point that he recognized "only two command channels" in the CIA—himself and the station chiefs overseas. Wisner and the other members of his staff were just hollow logs conveying his orders to the field. Wisner bitterly fought attempts by Smith, or anyone else, to weaken his power.

Occasionally the general did show flashes of humanity. Wisner talked him into giving his covert operations staff a fifteen-minute pep talk to boost flagging morale. As springtime came in 1952, the general allowed subordinates to organize an agency softball league—as long as they didn't publicize it. Otherwise, Wisner and fellow senior officers found it best to tiptoe around their crusty director. Wisner never hosted at his home dinner parties for VIPs visiting the CIA without first clearing it with Smith. Every other Thursday, Wisner and the other deputies convened for a dinner among themselves to discuss subjects they considered not ready to be brought before Smith.

The bottom line, though, was that Beetle Smith never really liked the CIA job. He decided to make his exit with the outgoing Truman administration and submitted his resignation on November 1, just three days before the 1952 presidential election.

* * *

Wisner spent hours at night glued to the television set, fascinated by TV's coverage for the first time of the Democratic and Republican conventions in Chicago. He was pleased with the two nominees the parties had selected—General Dwight Eisenhower, the war hero who headed the GOP ticket, and Illinois governor Adlai Stevenson for the Democrats—although he tilted toward Ike. Wisner had briefed Eisenhower's running mate, California senator Richard Nixon, on CIA activities in the past and considered him a man of some intelligence and talent but certainly no intellectual.

"This country is giving signs of beginning to come to maturity," Wisner wrote his mother, and Eisenhower seemed readier than most men to lead the nation through its mature phase. The last president to be born in the nineteenth century, Eisenhower had been shaped by his small-town Kansas values. He had been a shrewd and highly political general, keeping the Allies unified in war, yet in peacetime he could be naive and disdainful of politicking by others. He also had an ego and a volcanic temper, which he fought successfully to control. From World War II, Eisenhower had firsthand knowledge of clandestine operations and how to control them. Ike had thought highly of the performance of Donovan's OSS during the war, and afterward, as Army chief of staff, he had kept up-to-date on the current state of intelligence gathering. In fact, Eisenhower enjoyed significant experience in both intelligence and foreign policy matters, which Truman had lacked when he became president.

Frank and Polly hosted an election night party at their P Street house on November 4. Each of the guests bet a dollar on the states Stevenson and Eisenhower would carry. Wisner had a side bet with Donovan's daughter-in-law, Mary, on who would win. Mary picked Stevenson while Wisner predicted it would be Eisenhower.

Eisenhower won by a landslide, garnering more than 55 percent of the popular vote and trouncing Stevenson in the electoral college, 442 to 89. It gave him the mandate he wanted in order to lead the nation for the next four years. Wisner waited anxiously to see how Eisenhower and his Republican administration would view an intelligence agency created by a Democratic president. He hoped that the CIA "will someday come to be regarded as non-political," he told his Far East Division chief Richard Stilwell, "but we have no way of knowing whether it is so regarded at the present time." To cultivate the new administration, the CIA immediately set up a briefing room in New York City's Commodore Hotel, where the Eisenhower transition team was located. Most of the Georgetown set wanted Stevenson to win, although Phil Graham had backed Ike and had the *Post* endorse him. Washington's social circle had to re-orient to Republicans and no one did so more diligently than Polly and Frank. They made a point of having Sherman Adams, Eisenhower's new chief of staff, and Adams's wife, Rachel, over to the P Street house for a cozy dinner party with the Georgetown set. The networking became important for Wisner. Dwight Eisenhower would have a profound effect on him and the secret work he did.

Chapter 17

EISENHOWER

AS PRESIDENT-ELECT, DWIGHT EISENHOWER had little interest in sitting through hours of briefings from CIA analysts on foreign policy subjects, about which he knew quite a bit already. He led a Republican Party full of contradictions—on the one hand, its members were tired of Democratic foreign policy initiatives like the Marshall Plan sending American tax dollars overseas, but at the same time, the party did not want to find itself being accused of losing any country to Communism. Democrats branded Eisenhower bellicose, but he pursued a foreign policy toward the East Bloc no more aggressive than Truman's. Gordon Gray, a Wisner friend who would soon be a key Eisenhower adviser, found the general to be as "security conscious as any president we've had in history." Unlike Truman, Ike regularly attended National Security Council meetings.

With the country soon entering a mild post–Korean War recession, Eisenhower's major goals of peace abroad, lower taxes at home, a balanced federal budget, and no inflation all depended on cutting defense spending, which he thought was too high at $44 billion annually when he took office. Lowering tensions overseas was the obvious way to reduce military outlays, he knew. He favored targeting Third World countries with foreign aid to promote economic development and make them stable democracies. He found nuclear weapons more cost-efficient than conventional arms—when he took office, the United States had about 1,100 nukes; by the end of his presidency, the U.S. stockpile totaled nearly 22,000—yet he realized that any nuclear exchange with the U.S.S.R. would be unwinnable, so he preached disarmament. As for the CIA, Ike viewed that agency's covert action capability as a cost-effective alternative to the use of military power overseas.

During the transition, the guessing game and maneuvering began for who would succeed Beetle Smith as Eisenhower's director of central intelligence. Smith pushed Gordon Gray for the position. He also floated the name of Lyman Kirkpatrick, his inspector general at the agency. Donovan, who had continued to do odd jobs for the CIA, again had surrogates lobby for his being appointed its director. The former OSS chief was critical of Wisner, whose name was also mentioned as a Smith successor. But the person who always had the inside track was Smith's deputy, Allen Dulles, whose brother, John Foster Dulles, had been picked by Eisenhower to be his secretary of state. The press had speculated as early as 1950 that he would succeed Smith. Ike thought highly of Allen and likely would have made him his CIA director even if he had not picked Foster to be his secretary of state, but as a foreign policy spokesman for the Eisenhower campaign and now a cabinet nominee, Foster certainly was in a prime position to put in a good word for his younger brother with Ike.

Allen had always looked up to John Foster, who was the eldest of the five siblings in the Dulles family and always called Foster. He had been a fast-rising attorney at Sullivan & Cromwell and had recruited Allen to join the prestigious New York law firm after World War I. When Allen joined the OSS during the Second World War, Foster remained at Sullivan & Cromwell, dabbling in Republican politics. He became a foreign policy adviser to Dewey when he ran for president and then to Eisenhower in 1952. Allen slipped Foster CIA material for the foreign policy speeches he made on Ike's behalf during the campaign. Eisenhower had first met Foster in the late 1940s when the general was president of Columbia University and the two men discovered they shared the same views on foreign policy—although they never had a close personal relationship over the years. A dour man, Foster was obsessed with the economical use of his time, insisting on short, precise answers to his questions and disdaining rambling conversations. He was totally the opposite of Allen, who gaily enjoyed wide-ranging chats.

Foster saw his secretary of state job as primarily advising the president. He left the running of the State Department to others. He had walk-in privileges to the Oval Office, and he kept a white phone by his desk to speak to Eisenhower whenever he was available. But Ike considered himself as worldly as Foster, if not more so, and he kept a tight rein on his secretary of state. He talked a reluctant Smith into moving from CIA to the State Department to be its undersecretary so Beetle could keep an eye on Foster for him. Beetle hated Foster from the start.

The Georgetown set had an equally contemptuous view of the new secretary of state and his overmoralizing about Communism's dangers. Chip Bohlen circulated several ditties on Foster: "dull, duller, Dulles" and "Dooles, Dooles, do you take us for fools?" Wisner also never liked Foster, who received daily intelligence reports from the CIA and seemed to Wisner to be reflexively militaristic. Word of Wisner's disdain reached Foster's sister, Eleanor, who worked as an economics officer in the State Department and who complained about the "quiet cabal in Georgetown" denigrating her brother.

Donovan, jealous of Allen Dulles and bitter that he had been made CIA director, predicted that his OSS comrade would foul up the agency. As a consolation prize, Eisenhower made Donovan his ambassador to Thailand. Beetle Smith also did not want Dulles to succeed him, fearful, like Donovan was, that his deputy lacked self-restraint and that his enthusiasm for covert operations would get the CIA in trouble one day. But Dulles's appointment was cheered by the agency's rank and file, who considered him at heart a working spy like them.

For deputy CIA director, Dulles picked Lieutenant General Charles Cabell—"a stocky, aggressive Texan who did not seem to bring a huge amount of creativity to his job," Howard Hunt said dismissively. Cabell, however, had once served as director of Air Force intelligence and he had been one of the few senior officers in the military who believed in the concept of a centralized intelligence service and had tried to make it work. Wisner grew close to Cabell, whom friends addressed by his middle name, Pearre.

On secret documents, Dulles was identified by the pseudonym "Robert A. Ascham." His nickname among CIA officers was "Papa." For all their differences, Papa and Beetle shared some of the same management quirks. Dulles, like Smith, had trouble "intelligently reading" CIA cables filled with cryptonyms. A speed reader, Dulles also adopted the Smith rule that no memo laid before him could be longer than one page. A CIA security officer moved into Dulles's house to guard him, vet visitors, help him with the scrambler on his phone he always had trouble operating, and mix cocktails for parties. The guards also made sure he didn't leave classified documents behind on the desks of offices he visited. Dulles hated the security detail surrounding him when he moved around Washington.

Dulles ordered agency telephone operators to answer incoming calls with a number rather than with "CIA." But he disdained what appeared to him to be mindless security measures. He had the CIA building on Navy Hill identified as such, since every cabdriver knew where it was, and throughout his tenure as CIA director, he kept his home phone number and address listed in the public directory. He also left the front door to his Georgetown house unlocked.

Operatives who walked into his headquarters office on Navy Hill almost always found him chewing on his pipe, with a little smile on his face, and eager to hear stories from spies returned from the field. As he had in Bern, for his Navy Hill office, Dulles had carpenters build multiple access doors that led to separate waiting rooms so callers could be kept secret from one another. He worked in a small room that had a desk, a couch for visitors, a vibrating chair he sat in when his gout flared, a bookcase stuffed with volumes, a safe, and a television set (which he used as much for watching baseball games during boring briefings as he did for monitoring news events). Helms said Dulles was the first person he had heard use the term "tradecraft" to describe the mechanics of the agency's spying. He "liked the homespun sound of it," Helms wrote. Dulles also gave the CIA a sense of permanence by beginning to plan as soon as he assumed the directorship for the building of a new and modern agency headquarters to replace the ramshackle structures CIA officials occupied.

Wisner had a mixed relationship with his boss. They were World War II colleagues who worked together closely now concocting covert operations. Wisner kept a framed photo of Dulles hung in his farmhouse. When Dulles was traveling and Cabell was not available, Wisner was designated the acting CIA director. But Dulles and Wisner were never personally close. Polly called it a "love-hate relationship." Wisner thought Dulles was too public about the CIA's work and would have done better to be more secretive, as British spymasters were. Wisner, as well as other CIA managers, also found maddening Dulles's propensity for bypassing them and talking directly to officers in the field. The practice, though, created tremendous esprit de corps among his spies.

Dulles's World War II service as the OSS station chief in Bern had a profound effect on the way he now ran the CIA. As he had in Switzerland, Dulles in Washington showed the same charm, daring, and breadth of vision. He believed that intelligence was an important part of foreign and national security policy, he could pick up the phone and tap a vast worldwide network of associates and admirers to call on for favors, and he had recognized early on the dangers of Stalinism. But as in Bern, he could be careless with details and security; he tended not to run a tight ship; he was a risk-taker, reckless at times; and he could become preoccupied with spectacular espionage coups and covert operations to the detriment of traditional intelligence collection. Dulles believed the key to influencing other nations lay in knowing the right people and pulling the proper levers, largely overlooking the complex nature of modern society.

He organized the CIA so every function was covered by someone else, so he had the freedom to swoop in and meddle in any program that piqued his interest. Scheduled appointments could be delayed for hours as he huddled with an employee running one of his favorite projects. He often interrupted meetings to take phone calls from Wisner on a covert operation. He showed little interest in intelligence analysis. He never really understood the technical side of the CIA, which, for example, developed exotic surveillance gadgets, but he lavished money on scientific initiatives. As one of his top advisers put it, Dulles remained at heart the "great case officer," obsessed with the nitty-gritty of individual operations.

Dulles could have had direct access to Eisenhower whenever he wanted, but, unlike his brother, Foster, he chose to go through Sherman Adams first. At weekly National Security Council meetings, held every Friday at ten a.m., Allen took a seat at the end of the long table in the Cabinet Room and was usually the first person Ike called on for a report on the world. The CIA director kept his briefings short, to the point, and sprinkled with colorful anecdotes he knew would hold the president's interest. Allen was careful not to cross the line into Foster's territory and recommend policy. But Allen often acted as if he wanted Foster's job. He was practically treated as a secretary of state when he made high-profile trips abroad, and many diplomats in Washington thought he would have been a better secretary than his stern brother.

* * *

Hoover, who had kept close watch over the maneuvering in Washington to replace Beetle Smith as CIA director, had his agents continue loose surveillance of Dulles when he took the job so they could feed the FBI director any tidbits they picked up about Allen's and Clover's personal lives. Agents filed one report from a confidential informant who said Dulles was spotted in a Washington restaurant drinking heavily and talking loudly with a beautiful woman who was not his wife. Dulles constantly told FBI agents that he held their director in high regard, knowing that what he said would get back to the boss. A senior bureau official sent Hoover a memo assuring him that the new CIA spymaster posed no threat to the FBI. Hoover didn't believe it. On his desk, he had another memo suspecting that in the past Dulles had leaked to the *New York Times* a story that criticized the bureau.

During his first year as president, Eisenhower tried to ignore Joe McCarthy, which appalled Wisner and top Pentagon officials like Omar Bradley when the senator smeared distinguished Americans such as Marshall, Ralph Bunche, and even Beetle Smith. Ike wanted others in his administration to appease McCarthy as well. Foster did so, but Allen stood up to the demagogue, denying the charges he hurled against the CIA and openly refusing to allow his officers to be dragged before McCarthy's investigating panel. Dulles told six hundred assembled employees he would fire anyone caught cooperating with McCarthy and he appointed Helms to monitor and counter McCarthyite attempts to penetrate the agency with informers. Dulles's defiance sent morale soaring at the CIA.

Three months into the Eisenhower administration, Wisner clashed with McCarthy once more, this time over another of Wisner's close friends, Chip Bohlen. Ike had nominated Bohlen, a golfing buddy when the diplomat was posted in Paris, to be ambassador to Moscow. A realist when it came to the U.S.S.R., Bohlen believed little could be accomplished in the way of weakening Moscow's power behind the Iron Curtain. The best the U.S. could do was contain Soviet expansion. Wisner had to agree. McCarthy tried to derail the nomination, accusing Bohlen of selling out to the Russians during the Yalta Conference in 1945 and of being a closeted homosexual. (Bohlen had served as a translator at Yalta and had a well-deserved reputation for being a ladies' man before he married his wife, Avis.)

The Bohlen and Wisner families had become close friends. Frank publicly defended Chip and, when Bohlen was fighting the charges, let him stay in his P Street house while Avis was away. The Georgetown set also circled the wagons around the diplomat. Polly was as outspoken as Frank on Chip's behalf. Eventually the Senate confirmed Bohlen by a wide margin, 74–13, and he flew to Moscow a battered survivor of the nomination fight. After Bohlen's confirmation victory, Wisner hoped Washington would turn the corner on McCarthyism and the danger the senator posed.

But the McCarthy threat remained for Wisner. Another memo was slipped into his FBI file; it noted that he was a close friend of Bohlen and that both of them were part of the "Georgetown crowd" Hoover so despised. Bureau agents had also dug up more dirt on Wisner, which Hoover passed on to Dulles on November 23, 1953, in a letter stamped "TOP SECRET." An FBI informant claimed that Wisner had been seen in Paris six months earlier meeting Tanda Caradja. Another bureau informant claimed Wisner was being "blackmailed by two Romanians who had knowledge of Wisner's affair with this woman," according to the November 23 letter. More worrisome for Wisner and Dulles, by spring 1953 it appeared to them that the Wisner reports Hoover had collected had been passed on to McCarthy. The senator's investigators turned up even more damaging rumors that immediately after the war Wisner might have been involved in some kind of questionable sale of U.S. ships, which supposedly netted him a huge profit.

The FBI turned up another informant they identified as Don Surine, who claimed that in 1945 Wisner had requisitioned an Army plane to pick up medical supplies in Switzerland, and he flew there with Caradja on the plane. When they returned with the medical supplies, half were allegedly turned over to the Red Cross and the other half were sold to the Russians by Wisner and Tanda, who split the profits. Surine also claimed he was told that when Wisner lived in Caradja's home, he had set up a shortwave radio that he used "to put out pro-Russian material." In addition, Surine said that Caradja's brother now operated a hotel in Switzerland as a safe house for Soviet agents.

Even Hoover's own agents were suspicious of the Don Surine rumors. But Hoover ordered the allegations be sent to Dulles, whose security officers once more investigated them and found that what the FBI had turned up was old news that Beetle Smith had earlier checked out and found groundless. It turned out that Surine had gotten his information from none other than Romanian industrialist Nicolae Malaxa, Wisner's old nemesis who was targeting him once more with a smear campaign.

Neither Hoover nor McCarthy ever went public with their Wisner files. Even by the senator's loose standards, the charges against the clandestine service chief were flimsy. Wisner was a powerful man in the United States government who through the Dulles brothers had a direct channel to the Oval Office. Allen Dulles and Frank Wisner had excellent relations with the media. Hoover and McCarthy knew the CIA duo commanded direct access to the nation's television networks, newsmagazines, and newspapers, which they could utilize to plant or kill stories and to settle scores with political enemies. Wisner and Dulles could also place agency officers in media organizations for covert operations, they could have select journalists do odd jobs for them, and they could convince editors to keep some things secret. Furthermore, Dulles, whom the Senate had unanimously confirmed to be CIA director, had excellent relations with Congress, which exercised little oversight over his agency. Wisner was also expert at cultivating lawmakers. So was Polly. Hoover and McCarthy knew that any move to air the allegations against the CIA man would bring them trouble. So they chose to remain silent.

But Wisner still lived under the threat of exposure. He was now fighting on two fronts, abroad against the Soviets and at home against the FBI. The strain began to show. At office meetings, he

sometimes became brutal with assistants he felt had botched assignments, lashing out at them in front of others. Subordinates noticed
that the boss seemed to go on tirades over little things more often
than in the past.

* * *

By 1953, Wisner had major covert operations up and running in
forty-eight countries around the world. He also had hundreds more
small operations, such as hunting for a MiG jet the Pentagon wanted
badly to get its hands on to analyze the plane's capabilities. The CIA
message center was now processing more than nineteen thousand
cables to and from its overseas stations monthly, each one given a
special code to indicate its sensitivity. As deputy director for plans,
Wisner was immersed in countless management details, such as
wordsmithing directives the National Security Council issued on
CIA oversight, obtaining a chauffeur with a top secret security
clearance so Wisner could discuss sensitive items in the backseat
with other car passengers, and dealing with female officers who
complained about discriminatory pay and promotion policies.

Wisner would spend $100 million in 1953 for operations to
break up the East Bloc. Radio Free Europe and Radio Liberty,
which the Communist regimes still tried their best to jam, remained
his only means of reaching East Europeans and the Soviet people
with propaganda from the West. Dulles took a particular interest in
the labor, culture, trade, and student front groups Wisner secretly
bankrolled. He was pessimistic, however, about resistance agents
Wisner infiltrated into Eastern European nations being able to
spark revolts and he began to close down many of those operations.
"You don't have civil uprisings in a modern totalitarian state," Dulles
concluded. Wisner and Helms (who by then had been promoted to
Wisner's deputy in the plans directorate) agreed, though Wisner
kept alive his pet project in Albania, putting $402,000 into BGFiend
for 1953. It resulted only in the needless deaths of more pixies.

Wisner and Helms quickly discovered that Dulles did not want to dial back covert operations but rather to change their thrust. Several months after Dulles replaced Smith as CIA director, Helms was in his office to have an outgoing cable read and signed. As Helms was about to rise from his seat to leave after the spymaster put his name to the message, Dulles motioned him to stay. It was a busy morning, but Helms was used to Dulles interrupting the flow for impromptu brainstorming. "A word about the future," Dulles began as Helms settled back into his chair, and then the director added after a pause for effect, "The *agency's* future." As Dulles saw it, the CIA had two missions: first, to collect intelligence so another Pearl Harbor surprise attack didn't happen, and second, to launch covert operations to affect the course of events overseas. The agency's intelligence-collection programs were proceeding nicely, Dulles told Helms, so the CIA and he would focus on covert operations. Eisenhower and his top national security advisers had "an *intense interest* in every aspect of *covert action*," Dulles said, emphasizing the two points. Dulles was reading the mood of the White House correctly and he wanted his clandestine service—especially Helms, who he knew was a covert action skeptic—on board.

Helms left the meeting a bit rattled but convinced that Wisner and he could keep Dulles from going off on a harebrained operation. Helms believed that Wisner would not be "stampeded" by Dulles or the White House into "unwise" covert action projects.

* * *

Joseph Stalin had been in frail condition since August 1952. On the night of March 1, 1953, CIA analysts sent Wisner, Dulles, and Cabell a confidential memo alerting them that the Soviet dictator had suffered a stroke. The three men immediately began brainstorming who would assume power. The agency had recently detected signs of a slight softening in Soviet foreign policy toward the West. Shortly after two a.m. on March 4, the CIA phone at Dulles's home rang and a watch officer monitoring reports from the agency's station in Moscow informed him that Stalin lay unconscious and dying. Dulles phoned Wisner and other top aides, who rushed to his home. Wisner urged that for the moment Foster and Ike issue no provocative statements, which the president and the secretary of state agreed was the best course. The next morning, after Stalin's death was confirmed, Dulles huddled at the White House with top officials to speculate on how the Soviet Union might change with the dictator's passing and what the U.S. response should be.

John Foster Dulles was convinced the Kremlin was about to have a bloody power struggle that would lead to its downfall. Chip Bohlen in Moscow disagreed and argued that Stalin's death offered the U.S. a chance for a diplomatic breakthrough with the U.S.S.R. At the Locust Hill farm, Wisner had two mixed-breed puppies he had named "Joe Stalin" and "Ana Pauker" (after a Romanian Communist leader). He was glad the namesake for one of the dogs was no longer alive. Wisner organized a conference at CIA headquarters for representatives of all the national security agencies to mull over the ramifications of Stalin's death. He did not think it opened the possibility for diplomacy to wind down the Cold War. The Soviets would continue to be an implacable enemy, he believed. Wisner assumed the new Soviet regime would "initiate a series of provocative military, diplomatic, psychological and economic warfare matters, short of general war," he told Dulles, all designed to test the West and keep it from trying to make the regime's consolidation of power difficult. At the same time, Moscow would make "tactical peace overtures to the West," Wisner predicted, in order to "exploit neutralist sentiment in many countries." Washington should be ready to unmask phony Russian peace initiatives and to "react resolutely to any new aggression," he said.

A triumvirate consisting of Soviet politician Georgy Malenkov, security chief Lavrentiy Beria, and Stalin adviser Nikita Khrushchev emerged, with Khrushchev eventually outmaneuvering his two rivals to seize power as Communist Party first secretary and then premier. The CIA scrambled to quickly put together a twenty-page personality profile of the fifty-eight-year-old party boss, who was described as a crude peasant at heart with "beady blue" eyes, "a round animated face and lively humorous features"; he could be funny and charming at times, bombastic and bullying at other times, and he was "a heavy drinker." "He'll be ruthless when he has to," Wisner predicted to one of his officers. "So, we will be in the business of covert action for a long time."

Moscow demonstrated that ruthlessness three months after Stalin's death when Soviet and East German troops and tanks brutally crushed a revolt by several hundred thousand East German construction workers who had staged a wildcat strike. All Wisner could do was order his German stations to offer sympathy and asylum. Arming the strikers was out of the question. The Soviets had twenty-two divisions in East Germany.

Several days after the East German revolt, Wisner and Tracy Barnes boarded a Pan American plane in New York for a flight to Europe to visit CIA stations there over the next three weeks. A left-wing New Dealer who had evolved into a hard-line anti-Communist, the tall, handsome, and personable Barnes had first been noticed by Wisner after Harvard Law School when he worked for Carter, Ledyard & Milburn. Bored with legal affairs as Wisner had been, Barnes made his way in World War II to the OSS, where he parachuted behind the lines into France as a Jedburgh commando (earning a Silver Star for heroism). He eventually ended up in Bern working for Dulles. After the war, Wisner talked Barnes into joining his covert operations staff at the CIA. By the time the two men flew to Europe that summer of 1953, Barnes headed up Wisner's psychological and paramilitary warfare office and, with his wife, Janet, had become one of the weekenders at the Locust Hill farm.

For this trip, Wisner had left a raft of personal business at home. He had been finding a CIA job for a talented University of Virginia professor and had helped an agency retiree land a UVA teaching post. Frank had joined Barnes in investing in Historic Georgetown,

Inc., which was remodeling stores at Thirtieth and M Streets. Meanwhile, his brother-in-law, Alexander Chisholm, continued to manage lucrative stock purchases and sales in Laurel businesses for him and keep him updated on the attacks of lumbago Wisner's mother claimed to be suffering. Chis also suspected Jeannette was being a hypochondriac.

During their European trip, Wisner and Barnes visited the CIA stations in London, Bonn, Berlin, Frankfurt, Rome, and Paris. From the men in the field, the latest news was not good. Paramilitary activities, which had been so popular a year ago, were losing their appeal, Wisner and Barnes could see. The operational difficulties involved in establishing long-range paramilitary assets in the U.S.S.R. were practically insurmountable. Projects that infiltrated trained agents into Czechoslovakia, Bulgaria, and Poland were badly compromised by Communist penetration of the sponsoring political groups. A number of valued operatives had been rounded up and executed. The only bright note came from the Berlin station chief, who reported that a paramilitary project that infiltrated agents into East Germany held some promise of fruitful results.

On their London stop, Wisner carved out time for a train ride northwest to All Souls College, Oxford, to visit Isaiah Berlin, a Latvian political theorist, philosopher, and historian. Wisner liked to trade a bottle of bourbon and a carton of American cigarettes for Berlin's insights on maneuvering behind the Kremlin walls.

About a week after Wisner and Barnes returned to Washington, Eisenhower received word that a truce had been signed at Panmunjom, bringing to an end the cruel and debilitating war on the Korean Peninsula. The president, who had campaigned on the promise to extricate America from the quagmire, considered the armistice a major foreign policy achievement. Korea had taught him, moreover, that he faced domestic restraints if he wanted to commit U.S. military forces overseas. Eisenhower quickly found an alternative to sending in American troops to roll back Communism in the Third World. It was the CIA.

Chapter 18

IRAN

JOHN FOSTER DULLES FERVENTLY believed that Democrats had held the reins of power too long. They had grown lethargic in combating Soviet adventurism. He set American foreign policy on a new tack. Foster was no longer content to just contain Communism in Eastern Europe and to keep Kim Il Sung above the 38th parallel. With NATO in place to guard Europe and an armistice holding in Korea, Foster moved the battleground for the Cold War to the Third World. Eisenhower agreed with the shift, convinced that Wisner's covert action projects in Eastern Europe stood little chance of being successful and that the military option there was a nonstarter. The two men believed that the free world was being challenged in areas like Latin America, Egypt, Iran, and Vietnam, places in the developing world where Communism should not have been just contained—it should have been rolled back.

A confidential CIA analysis had warned as early as 1948 of rising nationalism in former colonies that could threaten U.S. political, economic, and military interests. Allen Dulles and Frank Wisner now quickly picked up on the shifting wind sock. In the director's morning meetings, Dulles and Wisner began putting Third World countries they had previously ignored on the agenda. Out of the blue at one session—or so it appeared to others in the room—the two men raised for discussion "the adequacy of our actions to combat Communism in darkest Africa," according to the meeting notes.

Another pillar of Foster's and Ike's war on Communism was what they considered to be the sin of neutralism. It would not be tolerated in the Third World. Leaders there were either for or against the United States. Those who stood neutral in the global competition between the free world and the Communist world—who found fault with the West and the Soviet Bloc and asserted independence from both sides—those leaders were considered Communist sympathizers or, even worse, outright Communists. "John Foster Dulles had taken the view that anything we can do to bring down these neutralists, anti-imperialists, anti-colonialists, extreme nationalist regimes should be done," said Harrison M. Symmes, one of the State Department's Middle East diplomats. With that kind of thinking, it was inevitable that Iran became a target.

*   *   *

By the time Eisenhower took office, Iran had become a strategic prize in Washington's geopolitical and ideological struggle with Moscow. It had not always been the case. For nearly 175 years, American policymakers had ignored Persia "because they had no reason to do otherwise," as one CIA report pointed out.

One of the world's oldest nations, its people intensely proud of their heritage, Iran, with its important trading routes and rich oil reserves, had nevertheless been a perennial target of foreign invaders and had spent most of its history struggling to find a way to live with other, more powerful nations. The British and Russian Empires had dominated its weak leadership by the nineteenth century, with London gobbling up lucrative concessions to run key sectors of Iranian commerce. In 1901, Iran's Shah sold access to the nation's oil reserve to a British financier, prompting growing public outrage that the monarchy was giving away the country by selling its oil rights for a pittance. Six years later, Britain and Russia, without consulting the Tehran leadership, signed a treaty giving London control of Iran's southern provinces while Moscow took over the north. The next year, the Anglo-Persian Oil Company was formed to take over oil exploration and development in Iran. In 1913, the British government bought controlling interest in the company, whose name was later changed to the Anglo-Iranian Oil Company. Many wells were drilled, more than a hundred miles of pipeline were laid, and a huge oil refinery was built on the desert island of Abadan in the Persian Gulf.

After the Bolsheviks seized power in 1917, Russia relinquished its interests in Iran and Britain rushed to fill the void left behind. In 1926, Reza Shah, a charismatic yet ruthless strongman from the Pahlavi dynasty, took power with Britain's blessing. Most Iranians were eventually glad to see the corrupt autocrat go fifteen years later. The day after his September 16, 1941, abdication, Reza Shah's eldest son, twenty-one-year-old Mohammad Reza, was sworn in as his successor. Insecure, considered by his father to be too soft to govern, and yet a mystic who believed God had chosen him to rule, Mohammad Reza Shah was physically brave and reckless behind the wheel of a car, yet in times of crises he often retreated from his duties as monarch. Surviving multiple assassination attempts, he would refuse to accept a cigarette offered by another man for fear it was laced with poison. The British found him maddening to deal with, but they allowed him to assume and stay on the Peacock Throne.

During World War II, the nation was divided into three sectors, with the Russians controlling the north, the British the south with its oil fields, and the Iranians the country's midsection, which included Tehran. Iran was used as a base for launching military operations in the Middle East and North Africa; its fuel output was kept out of German hands and in the tanks of British warships. After the war, Iran was in a vulnerable state, its people poor and its institutions weak. "One percent of the population ruled—and they were all grafters," Franklin Roosevelt observed sadly, "while the other ninety-nine percent live under the worst kind of feudalism." Iranian liberals and social reformers organized the nation's first political party, which was called the Tudeh (for the "Party of the Masses"). Its pro-Soviet faction, however, had seized control of the progressive group by 1944 and turned it toward Marxism, recruiting followers among the cities' poor. The young Shah understandably feared the fervently anti-monarchist Tudeh and cracked down on the party in 1949. With Britain's backing and advice, he consolidated his power over the Majlis (Iran's national parliament) and secured the right to choose the nation's prime minister. Pressured diplomatically by Washington and Tehran, Moscow, meanwhile, had pulled its occupation forces out of northern Iran after the war. A top secret U.S. intelligence report still suspected, however, that the Soviets might try to "stir up trouble" in the country, short of sending Red Army troops back in.

Tehran at the end of the 1940s teemed with camels roaming through parts of the city along with motorized taxis and horse-drawn droshkies. The city's northern flank rising up to the Elburz Mountains was open ground dotted by summer estates, while the southern part of the city was a swarming slum. Housed after the war in the vacated German embassy, the American diplomatic staff of seven (including a CIA station chief) recognized the British as the primary Western power in the country after the war.

The British, for their part, treated Iranian oil as property of His Majesty's government and were contemptuous of Iranian demands for more equity in the relationship—which only fed growing Iranian nationalism. Of its 41 million pounds in profits for 1947, the Anglo-Iranian Oil Company doled out only 7 million pounds to Iran and shorted the nation on higher salaries and better working conditions for its workers, as well as promised subsidies for schools, hospitals, roads, and telephone system projects. Anglo-Iranian Oil paid more in taxes to the British government than royalties to the Iranian government. The inequity of the agreement was made even more obvious to the Iranian public by the fact that Venezuela and Mexico split profits fifty-fifty with the American companies that extracted their oil. The British believed the Iranians were a bunch of ingrates whose oil would still be stuck in the ground if not for London's benevolence.

In 1949, the Majlis demanded that the Anglo-Iranian Oil Company come forward with a better deal for Iran. The oil company offered a "Supplemental Agreement" with minor concessions that Mohammad Reza Shah agreed to and tried to force the Majlis to accept. But militant deputies denounced the Supplemental Agreement as a collection of accounting tricks and demanded a true fifty-fifty split in the profits, one of them threatening that Iran would "nationalize the oil industry and extract the crude itself."

The Truman administration became more worried about Iran and the leadership of its thirty-year-old monarch. Mohammad Reza Shah, who had received royal treatment during a November 1949 visit to Washington, was pressed by Truman to focus on economic reforms to improve the lives of his people and keep the Communists at bay. The Shah was focused only on obtaining more arms from the U.S., but Truman refused to supply them.

Back in Iran, a new coalition of political parties, trade unions, and civic groups called the National Front was being formed. Its leader was sixty-seven-year-old Mohammad Mossadegh, an up-and-coming Majlis deputy intent on challenging the political order, the Shah's power, and the Anglo-Iranian Supplemental Agreement. With his droopy eyes and high forehead, Mossadegh had a talent for confounding practically everyone who worked with him. A charismatic speaker, he exaggerated some of his physical ailments and played well the role of a fragile old man, even pretending to faint at times. Fearing assassination, he conducted practically all of his official business at his home, often meeting government officials and foreign dignitaries in his gray pajamas. Mossadegh, however, quickly became an international celebrity. He believed ardently in the rule of law, which made him an enemy of the autocratic Shah, and he was dedicated to Iranians, not foreigners, running his country, which made him an enemy of the British.

London's Foreign Office dismissed Mossadegh as the leader of a "small band of extremists" fixated on the Anglo-Iranian Oil

Company. The U.S. embassy in Tehran cabled the State Department that Mossadegh was a "dramatic demagogue who appears without particular wisdom or background for government." The British believed that by strong-arming cooler heads in the Iranian government, they could contain Mossadegh. The American embassy, which recognized that Mossadegh's brand of rhetoric appealed to Persian ears, recommended that the United States, for now, try to cooperate with him.

Beginning in 1950, the Shah went through three prime ministers. Finally, the third one—General Ali Razmara, a ruthless and ambitious army chief of staff—promised to do London's and the Shah's bidding and push the Majlis to accept the Anglo-Iranian Supplemental Agreement with its cosmetic concessions. Mossadegh denounced Razmara as a flunky of the foreigners. By refusing to budge an inch, the British had united a broad range of Iranian political factions, including its Islamic clergy, against them and behind Mossadegh. Wisner was now keeping a close watch on Iran, worried that from all the political turmoil, the Communists might emerge to take power there. To combat a Tudeh coup, he wanted to have stockpiled near Iran enough small arms, ammunition, and demolitions to equip an anti-Communist guerrilla force of ten thousand for six months.

* * *

In January 1951, Iranian nationalists staged a mass rally to launch a movement to nationalize the oil company. Razmara tried mightily to defuse the crisis, but neither the British Foreign Office nor Anglo-Iranian Oil offered any help beyond telling him to keep a stiff upper lip. Truman administration officials were worried about what the Tudeh Communists were up to during this crisis, but the CIA could tell them little because the agency's knowledge of the Tudeh was thin at that point. On the other hand, on February 23, the U.S. embassy in Tehran, which had expanded as Washington had become more concerned about Iran, sent to the State Department a lengthy cable that should have been more reassuring. Iranians were actually frightened by the Communist show of strength in Korea and by what Tehran thought was the global weakness of the West, the cable noted. As a result, Iran had concluded that its hopes for survival lay in becoming more neutral, less pro-West, and more tolerant of the Tudeh Party. But the embassy believed that only a very limited number of Iranians supported Communism. The Tudeh Party was relatively small. It had many sympathizers, but they were attracted to the Tudeh's promise to get rid of hated regimes, not to Communist ideology.

But events drowned out the embassy's cooler heads. On March 7, a gunman (it was never determined if the man was a religious fanatic or an army soldier) assassinated Prime Minister Razmara. The next day, a parliamentary oil committee that Mossadegh led voted to recommend that the Majlis nationalize the Anglo-Iranian Oil Company, which it did on March 15, followed five days later by the less powerful Iranian Senate. Mossadegh was now the hero of Iran.

The assassination alarmed Wisner. He had his Middle East staffers fire off to deputy CIA director William Jackson a foreboding memo warning that U.S.-Iranian relations were deteriorating and that Iran was tilting more to the Soviet Union. With Razmara's assassination, the Tudeh might be in resurgence, Wisner feared. The Iranian government was weak. The Shah could be the next to be killed. The U.S. could also not discount the possibility that the Soviets might invade Iran, Wisner added.

Wisner's staff proposed a major covert operation in Iran. It would include a propaganda campaign aimed at supporting the Shah, chastising the Soviets, and splitting the Tudeh Party. Strings would be pulled behind the scenes to move Mossadegh in the direction Washington wanted him to go. Iranian clerics with delusions of grandeur, like Ayatollah Abolqasem Kashani, an anti-imperialist firebrand, would be bought off or discredited. Ties the Pentagon had with the Iranian military would be exploited.

The State Department opposed jumping into a big covert operation just then. The Shah and Iran's newly named prime minister, Hussein Ala, could handle things, the American diplomats believed. A grand covert plan like what Wisner envisioned involved "great dangers," a State Department memo worried. But Truman's National Security Council was adamant about not wanting Iran falling under Communist intervention, either by Soviet invasion or by internal subversion. That outcome could seriously threaten Iran's neighbors.

Allen Dulles lobbied Beetle Smith, who was still the CIA director at that point, to back the covert operation Wisner proposed. As things now stood, "Iran may be lost to the West in the coming 12 months," Dulles predicted. The CIA already had a few small propaganda projects underway in Iran. The full covert plan Wisner wanted could save the country, Dulles argued.

Dulles and Wisner were being alarmists. A national intelligence estimate produced on April 5 had a far more optimistic tone, concluding that the U.S.S.R. was "unlikely" to undertake military action in Iran. Largely confused by the infighting among the Shah, Mossadegh, and British oil interests, Moscow seemed content to be hands-off. The Kremlin, moreover, considered Mossadegh no friend and Mossadegh likewise distrusted the Soviets. Internal subversion also did not appear likely to succeed. The Tudeh Party was divided and not as powerful as Dulles and Wisner made it out to be.

Among the CIA hawks, though, was Kermit "Kim" Roosevelt, the chief of Wisner's Near East Division, who believed Iran was in a precarious position and the United States should do everything in its power to prevent the nation from falling under Communist control. With his oval face and tortoiseshell glasses, Roosevelt had a patrician pedigree for a spy. A grandson of President Theodore Roosevelt, he had graduated from Harvard and written his PhD dissertation on "Propaganda Techniques in the English Civil War." Joining the OSS early on, Kim Roosevelt was dispatched to the Middle East, where he served as chief of the agency's secret intelligence branch in the region. After the war, Donovan put Roosevelt's scholarly background to work compiling a secret history of the OSS.

Postwar, Roosevelt developed a reputation as a skilled Arabist, returning to the Middle East at times as a writer for the *Saturday Evening Post* and to research a book on Arabs and oil. On one visit to the region, he met Mohammad Reza Shah, who, at twenty-seven years old, impressed him as an intense young man "with a deep store of barely hidden energy," he later wrote. In Egypt, Roosevelt backed a group of reformist officers led by Gamal Abdel Nasser in their coup to oust King Farouk, who was commonly referred to in the agency as the "Fat Fucker." During one tour in the region, the CIA officer tried smoking opium but decided it didn't give him a noticeable high. British MI6 agent Christopher Montague Woodhouse wrote in his memoirs that Roosevelt "had a natural inclination for bold and imaginative action, and also a friendly sympathy with the British." Some accounts claim that Roosevelt was never overly impressed with Wisner's judgment and that he got along better with Tracy Barnes and developed his own back channel to Allen Dulles. Wisner's sons dispute that, pointing out that the Wisner and Roosevelt families became close friends. But Polly later told an interviewer that Roosevelt did keep an open line to Dulles, clearly something her husband must have told her.

Britain moved in April 1951 to crack down with a show of force, dispatching three frigates and two cruisers to the waters off Abadan Island and its refinery. The British confrontation came at a time when Americans were in a desperate fight to slow the North Korean army's advance on South Korea. Feeling challenged by a seemingly relentless Communist advance everywhere, Truman joined many in his administration who believed the Soviets now wanted to draw Iran into their orbit.

Britain insisted that the Shah nominate as prime minister the aging Sayyed Zia, whom London considered pliant. The Shah did so on April 28, but the Majlis that same day rebelled and voted by a large margin to make Mossadegh the premier. Mossadegh agreed to serve, but only if the Majlis approved an act he had drafted to nationalize of the Anglo-Iranian Oil Company. The Majlis did so by a unanimous vote that afternoon.

Events now moved rapidly. On May 1, Mohammad Reza Shah signed the historic law revoking the Anglo-Iranian Oil Company's concession and replacing it with the National Iranian Oil Company. (The next day the Majlis ignored a British demand that the new law be suspended.) On May 6, Mossadegh took office as prime minister, submitting his cabinet to the Majlis, which immediately approved it. The British, so long used to Iran's prime minister being their puppet, were stunned that there was now one who despised them.

Alarm bells now tinkled in CIA's headquarters. Mossadegh's elevation to the premiership "constitutes a radical departure in Iran's political development," an agency analytical memo concluded. His personal following in the Majlis was actually "small," CIA analysts noted, "and he is disliked and distrusted by the Shah." But among Iranians on the street, Mossadegh had a large following, which included peasants, laborers, tradesmen, religious fanatics, and the Tudeh Party. The agency feared the Tudeh in particular, warning that it might try to exploit Mossadegh's leniency toward the party and "foment violence and disturbances throughout the country." Again, officers in the field were more optimistic. The CIA station in Tehran cabled Washington that Mossadegh enjoyed far more widespread support than his predecessors because he had successfully tapped into the "spirit of nationalism" that presently dominated Iran. Instead of now trying to replace his government, which the station believed was not feasible, Washington should try to reach out to the new leader. "We believe Mossadegh would probably be receptive to direct approach," the station cabled. Dulles would not hear of it. "Only one thing could save the situation in Iran," minutes record him telling Beetle Smith on May 9. With U.S. backing, the Shah must "throw out" Mossadegh, dissolve the Majlis, and "temporarily rule by decree."

With Mossadegh messaging Washington that Tehran and London were on a collision course, Truman at the end of June convened his National Security Council, whose Middle East experts warned that the United Kingdom was considering an invasion of Iran. Such a risky move could cause Mossadegh's government to turn to the Russians for help. Henry Grady, the U.S. ambassador in Tehran, next weighed in with a cable alerting Washington that London was now looking for a way to topple Mossadegh, which the envoy considered "utter folly. . . . Mossadegh has the backing of 95 to 98 percent of the country." Truman now was truly alarmed—and frustrated, he said, with "the blockheaded British" who refused to give the Iranians a fair deal on their oil.

Fearing a major rupture of U.S.-U.K. relations because of Iran, Truman sent Averell Harriman, who knew the Shah and who had some expertise in Persian Gulf affairs, to Tehran on July 15 to try to mediate the dispute between Mossadegh and Great Britain. But bloody riots erupted in the streets before Harriman even began his meetings, both sides remained intransigent during the negotiations, and the talks collapsed by August 22. Before leaving Tehran, Harriman confided to the Shah that in order for the crisis to be resolved, Mossadegh might have to be removed from office.

With Truman refusing to back a British invasion, London began plotting the alternative—a coup to oust Mossadegh. Robin Zaehner, a seasoned MI6 operative in Britain's Tehran embassy, began meeting with Iranian opposition figures to suggest ways they could undermine Mossadegh. London also took military steps, such as dispatching three army battalions to neighboring Iraq, to try to intimidate the Iranian government, along with imposing punishing economic measures, such as making it impossible for the National Iranian Oil Company to function by sabotaging the Abadan refinery. The nation was plunged into political turmoil. Mossadegh, who soon discovered the coup plotting, threatened to retaliate by expelling British diplomats.

Wisner, meanwhile, remained focused on the Russian threat. He finally secured State Department approval in the summer of 1951 to launch covert projects to counter a Soviet invasion of

Iran—though Moscow had no intention of invading. Wisner began his pet project to recruit anti-Communist guerrillas in southwestern Iran's tribal areas and to set up airfields, drop zones, safe houses, and supply routes to and from the Persian Gulf. In August, he approved another political operation to undercut the Tudeh by infiltrating spies into the party, exposing Communist agents among labor groups, organizing anti-Tudeh demonstrations, and circulating a "black propaganda book" purporting to be a Soviet attack on Islam.

To placate the British, Secretary of State Acheson in the fall put a more hawkish ambassador in the Tehran embassy. He replaced Grady, whose Iranian nationalism sympathies had irritated the British, with Loy Henderson, a Cold War hard-liner who had served as U.S. ambassador in Iraq and India. Now as the top American diplomat in Tehran, Henderson quickly came to the conclusion that Mossadegh was "a madman who would ally himself with the Russians."

Mossadegh, meanwhile, was becoming hugely popular in the United States. *Time* magazine made him its Man of the Year for 1951. Speaking in eloquent French before the Security Council in October, he was received warmly at the United Nations, to which Britain had taken its case against Iran. The council voted to punt on the dispute, not even calling on both sides to negotiate in good faith, which represented a humiliating diplomatic defeat for London. Making a last stab at compromise, Truman invited the Iranian prime minister to the White House but the positions of Mossadegh and the British on Iran's oil remained far apart. From Tehran, Grady's upbeat cables were replaced with darker assessments by Henderson. "Corruption and nepotism are as prevalent under the Mossadegh government as under previous governments," the embassy messaged Washington the day after Thanksgiving, claiming that Iranians had little respect for the current regime. (It was not true; Mossadegh was still popular among the masses.) More ominous, the embassy now warned, was the Tudeh Party, which was "effectively organized as a force in politics and industry with an estimated full membership in Tehran of 8,000."

*　*　*

By 1952, Iran's economy was in shambles. Mossadegh could not overcome a crushing British embargo that prevented him from selling Iran's oil on the world market. Washington provided modest aid, but not enough to bail out Iran, which over the next six months began spiraling into bankruptcy with huge job losses. A CIA analysis forecast that unless Mossadegh introduced authoritarian rule, the Tudeh's chances of taking over the country "will substantially increase." The agency was focused on making sure that didn't happen. Wisner's Middle East team believed its covert operation against the Tudeh had prevented the Communists from gaining any Majlis seats in the recent elections. British intelligence was working covertly in the country as well, but against a different enemy: Mohammad Mossadegh. Through the spring, MI6 agents passing out generous bribes worked to fill the Majlis with deputies who would vote to depose the prime minister. It would be a legislative coup.

Beset with every political and economic headache imaginable, Mossadegh staged a bold gambit in July. He demanded that the Shah relinquish control of Iran's military and turn it over to him. When the monarch refused, Mossadegh resigned. The British pressured the Shah into making seventy-year-old Ahmad Qavam the prime minister. Qavam, who was eager to work with London, denounced Mossadegh, which sparked widespread street protests that the police refused to suppress. Shocked by the rebellion, which was paralyzing the country, Qavam and the Shah called out the military. Dozens of protesters were killed when soldiers opened fire. Young military officers shaken by the deaths began murmuring threats of mutiny. Realizing that he was losing control, Mohammad Reza Shah sacked Qavam and with the Majlis's overwhelming approval reinstated Mossadegh as prime minister, giving him control of the

War Ministry and a tremendous political victory. But coup rumors gained more traction after Mossadegh's slick out-then-in maneuver.

On July 29, Beetle Smith huddled with Wisner and Dulles in the director's conference room at CIA headquarters. They were trying to assess the repercussions of Mossadegh's grand Qavam maneuver. Smith had in his hands a memo from Kermit Roosevelt, who admitted that his officers' planning for a clandestine guerrilla force in southern Iran's Qashqai region was proceeding slower than anticipated. Loy Henderson had also cabled Smith that after a recent talk with Mossadegh, who seemed to him to be in a "disturbed mental condition," it was clear to the American ambassador that the Communist threat had been considerably enhanced by the Qavam episode. Smith agreed and worried that if Mossadegh did not receive financial relief from the United States, he would turn to the Soviet Union for help. Washington and London simply had to start working together on this problem, the CIA director felt. Acheson concurred and quickly gained Truman's approval to make $10 million in grant money available to the Iranian government.

The next day, Smith convened another meeting on Iran with Wisner and Dulles. He was in an expansive frame of mind. The CIA's top Middle East analysts had concluded that rather than being mentally unhinged as Henderson claimed, Mossadegh was "crazy like a fox," as one of the analysts put it. Smith decided that ousting Mossadegh at that point was not a wise move. The CIA chief believed that the prime minister and his National Front party were the "only anti-communist forces left in Iran." Given the lack of a strong military figure around whom a coup might have been engineered, Smith wondered if the only real chance of forestalling Communist moves lay in a change in Iran's monarchy, which might be brought about by letting stronger tribal leaders "have a whack at the royal power." In other words, a coup might have been a workable option, but it would have to be one against the Shah rather than against Mossadegh, Smith speculated.

The State Department agreed that Mossadegh's government should be maintained as long as he had the authority to govern or until it appeared certain that the Communists would take over. The department now approved Wisner's stockpiling of arms near the Iranian border; the weapons were to be used by friendly elements if Mossadegh's government collapsed. His men should also have gold sovereigns handy for tribes willing to work with the CIA, a State Department official advised.

Washington gave Wisner the green light to approach his cousins in MI6 about the American and British intelligence services working together on a plan for unconventional activities in the event that Mossadegh's government collapsed. But Wisner got what he thought was a curious response when he had his station in London broach the subject with the British. MI6 starchily told the CIA officers that Britain's Foreign Office felt it was "premature to enter into discussions on this subject at this time." Wisner and Roosevelt could guess why they were getting the cold shoulder from London. Since Mossadegh had assumed power, Britain, unlike the United States, cared little about having contingency plans in place to react to the Iranian government falling and the Communists moving in. British foreign policy all along had been intent on engineering the failure of Mossadegh's government and driving him from office. The Americans wanted to keep Iran from falling under Soviet control. Britain wanted to get the oil back.

The Foreign Office in London and the British embassy in Tehran had learned two important lessons from what they considered the Mossadegh-Qavam fiasco. First, the British plan to replace Mossadegh with Qavam had failed because protesters supporting Mossadegh took to the streets. The next time, Britain must have the mob on its side. Second, a fair number of officers in the Iranian army—which was poorly equipped, trained, and led—were less than loyal to Mossadegh. They might join a future rebellion. But the officers would have to be rallied by a senior commander they admired and trusted. British diplomats in Tehran thought they had found that man: retired major general Fazlollah Zahedi, a fearless, ambitious, and skillful military leader who had risen quickly through the ranks but whom the British had arrested during the war for being a Nazi sympathizer. Zahedi had been plotting on his own to oust Mossadegh as revenge for the prime minister firing him as interior minister. The CIA thought the general's pluses outweighed his minuses. In addition to being highly responsive to British overtures, Zahedi was considered pro-America. His son, Ardeshir, had studied in the United States for six years.

But by the time of the U.S. elections in November 1952, Britain's coup plans were at a standstill. Before planning could begin, Britain had to win U.S. cooperation. Then prime minister Churchill, who had returned to power in 1951, had spent the second half of 1952 trying to enlist Harry Truman. But the American president, who sympathized with nationalist movements like the one Mossadegh led and was contemptuous of the greedy imperialists who ran the Anglo-Iranian Oil Company, wanted no part of a covert operation to overthrow the leadership in Tehran. Then Mossadegh learned of Zahedi's meetings with British agents to plot a coup. He broke off diplomatic relations with the United Kingdom and tried to arrest Zahedi, who went into hiding. By the end of October all British diplomats and intelligence officers had been expelled from Iran. Great Britain's hopes for a coup were dead in the water. The Iranian general to lead it was missing, no British agents were in the country to organize it, and the Americans refused to back it up.

But the November elections brought London a glimmer of hope. Dwight Eisenhower had promised to inject more vigor into the battle against Communism, which encouraged Churchill and his foreign secretary, Anthony Eden. They now turned their attention to the new Republican team entering the White House and discovered a different attitude toward a possible coup in Iran. C. M. Woodhouse, the senior MI6 officer, flew to Washington within days after the elections to meet with State Department and CIA officials. Instead of arguing that Mossadegh must go because he had nationalized British property—the Americans couldn't have cared less about that, he knew—Woodhouse emphasized the threat the Communists posed and the need to oust Mossadegh if the West did not want the Soviets to take over Iran. Over the course of his Washington meetings, Woodhouse wrote later, he detected "steadily increasing interest" in his proposal for what the British now called "Operation Boot." Wisner and his plans directorate were now enthusiastic about regime change in Iran. Woodhouse's pitch was also music to the ears of the Dulles brothers, who were growing convinced that the United States had to overthrow Mossadegh. Woodhouse flew back to London with what he believed was an informal agreement from incoming administration officials that Zahedi would lead the coup and Kermit Roosevelt would be on the ground in Iran to help the general win that prize.

The CIA's top Middle East analysts had a more nuanced view of the situation. A little more than a week after the elections, an agency intelligence estimate forecasting what might happen in Iran through the year 1953 concluded that the Russians considered developments in the Persian Gulf moving in their direction and that they were certainly capable of stirring up trouble there, but Moscow would not take "drastic action in Iran during 1953," the estimate believed, unless the country became far more unstable than the CIA envisioned it would become. The intelligence estimate also threw cold water on British hopes for Mossadegh's quick removal. He would continue to benefit from the opposition's inability to unite against him, the agency's analysts predicted. Mossadegh was skillful at isolating his opponents, and the Majlis had granted him wide powers. Other analysts at the CIA also cautioned Dulles not to wish too hard for a change of regime in Iran. He might not like what he would get in the place of Mossadegh.

The CIA ended 1952 in limbo, waiting for marching orders from a new administration taking power after Eisenhower's inauguration on January 20, 1953. In December Roosevelt and his Middle East team met in Washington with British intelligence officers to hammer out what he hoped would be a joint U.S.-U.K. plan to have guerrillas stay behind in Iran to fight if the Soviets invaded. But the only joint initiative MI6 was interested in discussing was the covert operation to oust Mossadegh. With the country still under the Truman administration, Roosevelt at that point could only say that the CIA would study that idea.

*   *   *

But behind closed doors at the CIA, Beetle Smith, who was still the agency's director, ordered Roosevelt to fly to Tehran before Eisenhower's inauguration and quietly scout out the coup potential there. Smith, who would soon move to the State Department as its undersecretary, was sure Ike would approve the operation. In one meeting on Mossadegh, Smith clutched his stomach, which continued to give him trouble, and groaned: "Dump him."

What Roosevelt found on his scouting mission was a prime minister whose popularity was slipping because of economic instability in his country. Mossadegh's National Front coalition had begun to fracture. He had botched relations with the Ayatollah Kashani, who had begun organizing the mosques against him, and he had angered the Shah to the point that the monarch decided it would be best to leave the country. Mossadegh welcomed his exit, but Kashani organized street demonstrations calling for the still popular Shah to remain in Iran. The monarch canceled his travel plans. Mossadegh, so long a champion of the rule of law, now behaved more like a despot fanning the flames of xenophobia. The U.S. embassy in Tehran continued to cable Washington that it suspected the man was becoming mentally unstable.

Iranian politicians had a rich history of secretly approaching the Tehran embassies of foreign powers for assistance in whatever power plays they were hatching. Into Henderson's office at the U.S. embassy poured feelers from Iranian parliamentarians, generals, and representatives of the Shah who circulated Zahedi's name as a good replacement for Mossadegh.

Jeannette Wisner, with baby Frank Gardiner Wisner (*right*) and his older sister Elisabeth (*left*), had two other children die within a year after they were born. Jeannette was deeply anxious about Frank and Elisabeth surviving, and perhaps suffered from depression. Chisholm Foundation Archive

Frank Junior was small but scrappy as a little boy. He strikes a fierce pose here in his football uniform. Chisholm Foundation Archive

ABOVE: Frank Gardiner, at about age fourteen, with his mother and father, at the train station in Laurel, Mississippi. Frank George Wisner was a prominent lumberman, banker, and civic leader in Laurel. Wisner Family Collection

LEFT: At the University of Virginia, Wisner became a world-class track star, captaining the school's track team, regularly winning meets in the 220-yard dash, broad jump, and high hurdles, and at one point toying with the idea of trying out for the US team that went to the 1932 Summer Olympics. Chisholm Foundation Archive

Wisner excelled academically at the University of Virginia and its law school. He joined many of UVA's clubs and secret societies, among them the IMP Society, whose members raised money for philanthropies and marched around campus wearing horned hoods. Wisner is pictured here in the center, wearing a long white robe as a leader of the IMP. Wisner Family Collection

The elegant daughter of a shipping magnate, Polly Knowles was not shy about speaking her mind, which intrigued Wisner when they started dating in New York City in the mid-1930s. Chisholm Foundation Archive

After UVA law school, Wisner joined the venerable Wall Street law firm of Carter Ledyard & Milburn. Although he did not have the Ivy League credentials of his young colleagues, Wisner impressed the firm's partners with his hard work. He also began inching his way into America's foreign policy establishment, joining the prestigious Council on Foreign Relations. Wisner Family Collection

In Polly, Wisner found an energetic, fierce, and determined personality. She did not have his academic background, but she was unusually bright. The couple married in 1936—Frank dashing in his morning coat and top hat, Polly looking like she stepped out of a fashion magazine in her white silk wedding gown.
Wisner Family Collection

Four months before the 1941 Pearl Harbor attack, prominent New York Republican lawyer William "Wild Bill" Donovan was picked by President Franklin Roosevelt to head an overseas intelligence organization, eventually designated the Office of Strategic Services. Frank Wisner became one of the more than ten thousand operatives recruited for the OSS.
National Archives

Pictured here as a navy lieutenant commander, Wisner soon developed a reputation in the OSS as a skilled organizer of intelligence operations during World War II. Wisner Family Collection

Donovan envisioned Turkey as a key launching pad for OSS missions in the Balkans, but his secret operations there had been blown and Nazi spy services had rolled up OSS networks. Wisner, pictured here relaxing in his Istanbul apartment, was sent to Turkey to clean up the mess. Wisner Family Collection

In September 1944, Wisner was sent to Bucharest to organize an OSS intelligence outpost in Romania, which had broken from the Axis and wanted to join the Allies. Seen here on a pheasant hunt, Wisner became the top US spy in Romania. Wisner Family Collection

In a playful moment in Christmas 1944, Wisner shoots at a target behind him with a Romanian holding up a mirror. To build the espionage operation Donovan wanted in Romania, Wisner had to start from scratch. Chisholm Foundation Archive

Wisner and his aides set up their headquarters in the Bucharest mansion of a Romanian beer magnate. The brewer's beautiful wife, Alexandra "Tanda" Caradja, was a skilled hostess who introduced Wisner to Romanian high society. Soon Wisner and Princess Caradja were having an affair, which the FBI's J. Edgar Hoover later investigated. Wisner Family Collection

After the Third Reich surrendered in May 1945, Wisner worked for Allen Dulles in organizing a postwar OSS intelligence mission in Allied-occupied Germany. Wisner was tasked with running Dulles's spy network there, which soon focused on the Russians occupying the eastern half of the country. Chisholm Foundation Archive

In addition to Germany, the OSS mission also oversaw intelligence collection in postwar Poland, Austria, Switzerland, and Czechoslovakia. Above are the passes Wisner carried granting him permission to travel throughout Czechoslovakia. Wisner Family Collection

By then a Navy commander and a seasoned intelligence expert, Wisner flew back to the US at the end of 1945 to reunite with Polly and their two boys (Frank II and Ellis). He returned to his New York law firm but found the work boring. Wisner Family Collection

Seeing it as a way to move back into the intelligence business, Wisner in 1947 became the State Department's Deputy Assistant Secretary for Occupied Territories. His office had some responsibility for implementing the $17 billion in economic aid to Europe under the Marshall Plan (named after Secretary of State George Marshall). Wisner Family Collection

Wisner (*second from right*) joined an American delegation in Europe during the Berlin airlift in 1948. He found that his State Department job gave him an avenue into clandestine operations. Wisner Family Collection

Inundated with intelligence reports from different agencies and desperate to find a workable way to coordinate spying operations overseas, President Harry Truman in 1947 launched the Central Intelligence Agency. Truman also agreed to form a separate, highly secret outfit Wisner organized, called the Office of Policy Coordination, which would launch covert political action and psychological warfare operations overseas against the Soviet Union. Frank Gatteri, U.S. Army Signal Corps, Harry S. Truman Library

Well-versed in intelligence operations from World War II, Dwight Eisenhower as president wanted to inject more vigor into the battle against communism and was intensely interested in every aspect of CIA covert action.
Dwight D. Eisenhower Library

Wisner's Office of Policy Coordination and the CIA's first headquarters were located in a group of dilapidated wooden structures built at the beginning of World War II along the National Mall's Reflecting Pool between the Washington and Lincoln monuments. Wisner called it the "Rat Palace" because he had to share the space with rodents.
CIA History Office

Considering Iran a strategic prize in Washington's geopolitical and ideological struggle with Moscow, Eisenhower in 1953 approved a covert CIA operation, code-named Ajax, to oust its prime minister, Mohammad Mossadegh, whom the White House believed was too pro-Soviet.
Bettmann/Getty Images

Jacobo Arbenz, pictured here with his glamorous wife, María Cristina Vilanova, pursued industrial and agricultural reform with a passion as Guatemala's president, and was willing to work with Communists and defy the US. Wisner feared Guatemala was becoming a Soviet beachhead in the Western Hemisphere. The White House gave the CIA the green light to back a coup ousting Arbenz in 1954.
Rolls Press/Popperfoto/Getty Images

Wisner tours a civic action project in Laos in 1958. After North Korea invaded the South in 1950, Wisner was ordered to quickly expand CIA operations to battle Communists in Asia. Believing the covert war in the region would be much like the one OSS waged during World War II, Wisner rushed in hundreds of green and untried CIA officers. Most of their operations failed. Wisner Family Collection

One CIA initiative that did succeed in Asia was Edward Lansdale's counter-insurgency operation in the Philippines, which defeated the Communist Huk guerrillas and helped reformer Ramon Magsaysay assume the presidency in 1953. Wisner (*right*) poses proudly with Magsaysay (*center*) and Lansdale's deputy, Charles "Bo" Bohannon. Wisner Family Collection

In 1945, Frank and Polly bought the Locust Hill farm near Galena on Maryland's Eastern Shore. For Frank, who wanted to emulate the Jefferson ideal of the noble farmer, the farm became a refuge from Washington's hectic city life. Polly hired an interior designer to help decorate the inside of the main house, which was built in the eighteenth century. Wisner Family Collection

Wisner and his son, Ellis, tackle chores in front of the farm's old granary. Locust Hill was a working dairy farm with a manager and four hired hands to run operations. Wisner hardly ever relaxed there. Practically all his waking hours during weekend visits were spent clearing land, cleaning cow stalls, mowing pastures with his tractor, and tending to the garden. Wisner Family Collection

Wisner, pictured here reading in the library of Locust Hill's main house, regularly brought old friends and key Washington officials he was cultivating to the farm for weekends of duck hunting. Wisner Family Collection

Wisner socialized in Washington's power circles. Here he shares drinks with top US diplomats Charles "Chip" Bohlen (*far left*) and Llewellyn "Tommy" Thompson (*third from left*), and *Washington Post* publisher Philip Graham. Wisner Family Collection

Polly also cultivated influential people important for Frank's job, in what became known as the "Georgetown Set." Here she shares a lighter moment with the *Washington Post*'s Phil Graham and newspaper columnist Joseph Alsop (*center*). Wisner Family Collection

Elisabeth Wisner Chisholm, Frank's older sister who could calm her brother when he suffered from manic depression, was one of the people who talked him into checking into a mental health facility for treatment. Wisner Family Collection

In September 1958, Wisner checked into the Sheppard and Enoch Pratt Hospital, an innovative facility near Baltimore, where for 172 days doctors treated his manic depression with psychoanalysis and electric shock therapy. Photograph courtesy of Sheppard Pratt

After Wisner's release from Sheppard Pratt, returning to his pressure-packed job of leading the CIA's clandestine service was out of the question. Instead, agency director Allen Dulles appointed him to the less demanding post of chief of the CIA's London station. Frank and Polly, pictured here in London, thoroughly enjoyed their time in England, which ended in early 1962 when Frank began suffering manic-depressive episodes once more and was ordered home. Chisholm Foundation Archive

After London, Wisner served as an aide to John McCone, who succeeded Allen Dulles as CIA director. But when it became clear to him that he would have no meaningful role in the CIA's clandestine operations, Wisner resigned from the agency on August 31, 1962. That year, McCone presented him with an intelligence medal. Chisholm Foundation Archive

Five years after Wisner's suicide, a glass display case was put up in one of the clandestine service's hallways, which contained wartime photos of him, medals he had been awarded, framed commendation letters, and a brass bust of him made by American sculptor Heinz Warneke. Chisholm Foundation Archive

In 1997, on the CIA's fiftieth anniversary, Director George Tenet, seen here presenting the award to Polly, named Wisner one of the agency's fifty "Trailblazers" for establishing "the doctrine for the use of covert action" and inspiring a cadre of future secret warriors. Wisner Family Collection

Polly and Kay Graham became the closest of friends, sharing the tragic bond of seeing their husbands take their lives because of the same disease. Tormented by manic depression, Phil Graham put a shotgun to his head and killed himself in 1963. Wisner did the same in 1965. Wisner Family Collection

Polly, who married news columnist Clayton Fritchey in 1975, remained a top Washington hostess, whose party invitations were rarely turned down by the Capitol's government and media elite. She's photographed here socializing with Hillary Clinton and Ronald Reagan. Wisner Family Collection

A British intelligence delegation arrived in Washington on February 3 for a second round of meetings with Wisner, Roosevelt, and other Near East Division staffers to brainstorm a Mossadegh coup. The MI6 officers announced that they wanted Roosevelt to be the operation's "field commander." The Dulles brothers signed off but only if Roosevelt worked clandestinely. He was known in Tehran to have the Shah's ear and he had a prominent last name.

On March 1, Allen Dulles sent Eisenhower an alarming secret memo. A Communist takeover of Iran was becoming "more and more of a possibility," he predicted. (Dulles's claim was not backed up by events on the ground or by his Mideast analysts in Washington.) Through its contacts in the parties, the press, and the clergy, the CIA could spread rumors, smear politicians, and turn out anti-Tudeh demonstrators, a memo by Wisner's directorate reported, but those clandestine assets were "far from sufficient in themselves to prevent a Tudeh assumption of power."

The memos reaching Eisenhower's desk about Iran spiraling out of control began to have an effect on the president. At a March 4 meeting of the National Security Council, Allen Dulles warned Ike that a Soviet move into Iran, which the Joint Chiefs of Staff said they could not prevent militarily without starting World War III, would likely cause Arab nations, collectively with nearly two-thirds of the world's oil reserves, to fall like dominos "into Communist control." Diplomatically, the United States could recall its ambassador from Tehran, "disassociate itself" from the British to make itself more popular with Iranians, and buy the country's oil to prop up its economy, Foster Dulles said. None of those options appealed to Ike, who was gravitating more toward some type of covert operation in Iran. "If I had $500 million of money to spend in secret," Eisenhower blurted out at one point, "I would get $100 million of it to Iran right now."

The hand-wringing ignored the uncertainty emanating from the Soviet Union at that moment. Stalin died the day after Eisenhower's National Security Council meeting and Moscow's collective leadership in the months that followed showed little interest in a

Persian Gulf adventure. No matter: the CIA believed Washington still could not discount the danger of a Soviet thrust into Iran. Contradictory CIA reports filled Wisner's inbox. One on March 11 claimed Mossadegh had now "consolidated his grip on the reins of government," the opposition had "lost ground and energy," and the Shah was "in a state of nervous indecision." On March 31, however, Wisner's Tehran station cabled what turned out to be a false report that Majlis deputies opposed to Mossadegh planned to join retired Army officers in a coup that would take place "two or three weeks hence." Roosevelt, who thought Moscow's manipulation of Mossadegh "ever more blatant," chimed in with a back-of-napkin estimate that a CIA operation to oust him could cost as little as $200,000.

There were voices of dissent, but they were quickly silenced. Chip Bohlen, the new ambassador to the Soviet Union, opposed the idea of a coup. Foster ignored him. Roger Goiran, the energetic chief of the CIA's Tehran station, adamantly objected to the plan as well, arguing that it would forever join America with the British colonialism that Third World nations so hated. With Wisner's approval, Allen Dulles had Goiran transferred out of the station along with other skeptics there so only coup enthusiasts remained to guide the CIA.

Prodded by the Dulles brothers, Britain's Anthony Eden, and even Texas oilmen who believed Mossadegh was a Communist, Eisenhower in the third week of March approved a covert operation to oust the Iranian leader. Wisner cabled a message to MI6 in London: the CIA was now ready to discuss the details of a coup plot. On April 4, Allen Dulles approved a budget of $1 million that the Tehran station could use in any way it saw fit to bring about the fall of Mohammad Mossadegh. The station immediately established secret contact with Zahedi using the Naval attaché in the U.S. embassy and Zahedi's son, Ardeshir, as conduits for communications passed between the two groups. The CIA station quickly discovered that Zahedi had already organized a sizable network of officers in the Iranian military who had been making plans for a coup.

Zahedi and other sources painted for the CIA officers a complex and ever-changing picture of Iran, which the station relayed in a series of cables back to Washington over the month of April. The general told the CIA men the political situation had "completely changed" and he had to abandon for now a "direct attempt" to replace Mossadegh. The embattled prime minister had launched a surprise attack to crush opposition factions, ordered Army tanks to guard his house and the Radio Tehran station, closed schools, and now had the homes of the Shah's and Zahedi's families under surveillance. Zahedi insisted he could not proceed with a coup attempt until the Shah came out in support of the opposition, but at that point, the monarch was totally passive and indecisive, the CIA station cabled headquarters. "The Shah will do nothing, he will not fight for his privileges." The monarch was sympathetic to Zahedi becoming prime minister, but he preferred that the Majlis vote to remove Mossadegh rather than having the deed done by military force. The monarch also was inclined to postpone ousting Mossadegh until his popularity had further ebbed. On April 28, the station alerted Wisner that the Shah had gone completely weak-kneed. The monarch now was trying to placate Mossadegh to keep him from making public incriminating documents on the royal family. A source told the station that the Shah would no longer support Zahedi as prime minister.

While Iran was racked by political turmoil, Wisner set his Iran branch chief, John Waller,* to work putting together a highly detailed concept for a coup operation. On April 16, Waller turned in an eleven-page game plan titled "Factors Involved in the Overthrow of Mossadegh." With the best underground organization and the "widest local support," Fazlollah Zahedi had the "biggest chance" of

---

* John Waller and I may be distantly related. When I worked as a *Newsweek* correspondent covering the CIA, I approached Waller after he had retired as the agency's inspector general, and trotted out the possible family connection, hoping it would make him more willing to share sensitive information with me. It didn't. He remained tight-lipped.

mounting a successful coup, concluded Waller, an OSS veteran who had served as a vice-consul in the Tehran embassy. Zahedi was considered "competent, energetic, aggressive and patriotic," and the agency was willing to overlook his collaboration with the Nazis. The general was staunchly anti-Soviet, he had been preparing for a takeover of the government since summer 1952, and he was "anxious to settle the oil issue." The assets the agency controlled in Iran could not by themselves overthrow Mossadegh's government, but if those assets, along with unlimited CIA money, were combined with Zahedi's organization, "his chances of success would be greatly enhanced," Waller concluded.

The CIA assumed that Zahedi would not be able to establish a government or remain long in power without the Shah's backing, so it was "essential," Waller wrote, that Roosevelt convince the Shah to side with the general. Despite their recent ups and downs, Zahedi had good relations with the Shah, who ultimately favored the general's assuming power. Royal backing was critical. Without the Shah's support, the CIA should reconsider its plan to launch a coup with Zahedi. The agency would have a diplomatic and security disaster on its hands if a CIA-backed operation to replace Mossadegh with Zahedi failed, Waller warned.

There were political land mines out there, but Waller believed they could be avoided. The "Soviet reaction to a forced change in government would be limited in nature," he forecast. The Tudeh Party, which in the past had attacked Mossadegh, has now rushed to his defense because he challenged the Shah. The Tudeh might be able to turn out ten thousand demonstrators to Tehran's streets, but Waller noted that on April 15, the party produced only a tenth of that number for a pro-Mossadegh rally. Ayatollah Kashani wanted to be the power behind the scenes in a Zahedi government. The general didn't trust the cleric and neither did the CIA, so "Kashani's influence with the Zahedi government must be restricted or neutralized."

Waller ticked off other factions that would play parts in the coup. The bulk of Iran's security forces was loyal to the Shah, but soldiers in the rank and file would follow the orders of superiors, who had been appointed to their positions by Mossadegh. The prime minister had appointed the chief of Iran's police force, but the cops had not been able to maintain order in the face of mob violence, Waller noted. The Majlis would not be a factor in a coup. Thirty of its seventy-nine deputies were loyal to Mossadegh and the legislative body had backed his handling of the oil dispute and his retention of special powers. But the rest of the deputies were considered Mossadegh opponents and his National Front "has tended to break up" during the past year, Waller reported. A majority of the landowners were opposed to Mossadegh. The press was also anti-Mossadegh and could be manipulated to back Zahedi, Waller believed.

Waller could see that the mobs were important in Iranian politics and the coup the CIA was planning. Iranian politicians had a rich tradition of buying demonstrators and street thugs to press their causes and intimidate their rivals. Up until then, Mossadegh had been able to draw the largest street crowds to support him. Waller had little intelligence on how those mobs had been summoned and directed. But if a Shah-Zahedi alliance was able to put "the largest mobs in the streets" and if the army's garrison in Tehran refused to carry out orders to suppress them, "the overthrow of Mossadegh would be certain," Waller wrote.

But first, the Shah had to be brought on board. The CIA-Zahedi operation could not proceed without him, Waller concluded. Roosevelt must buttonhole the monarch and promise him generous U.S. aid if he ousted Mossadegh. The alternative, Roosevelt should stress, was "the continued disintegration and eventual collapse of Iran," the branch chief wrote. The CIA remained high on the Shah but found him "vacillating, hesitating and indecisive." He often failed to follow through with his decisions. If Roosevelt found that the monarch could not overcome his handicaps, if he would "not rise to the occasion," the CIA should scrap the operation, Waller recommended.

Waller was a key CIA strategist behind the coup plot. Roosevelt grabbed all the attention with a book he wrote after the coup. But Waller clearly was the brains of the operation and Roosevelt was carrying out his plans. (Wisner always knew that. It was likely the reason that he later considered presenting Waller with a commendation for his work on Iran and mentioned nothing about Roosevelt.)

But would Waller's plan even have a chance of being implemented? Signals out of Tehran continued to be mixed. Almost three weeks after drafting his game plan for toppling Mossadegh, Waller wrote a discouraging memo to Wisner and other members of the plans directorate. "The opposition to Premier Mossadegh appears discouraged and has shelved its immediate plans for the overthrow of the present government in favor of biding its time and conserving its assets," the Iran branch chief reported. The problem continued to be the ineffectual Shah "and his unwillingness to resist Mossadegh's demands." But the U.S. embassy cabled Washington two days later that although the royal court appeared to be weakening in its struggle with its prime minister, and the opposition deputies in the Majlis were unable to mobilize effectively against him, Mossadegh was not as strong as he had been five months earlier. Wisner authorized the Tehran station to spend one million Iranian rials (which equaled a little more than $11,000) a week to buy the cooperation of Majlis deputies. The CIA men, like their MI6 cousins, however, showed themselves to be unschooled in the culture of the deputies they were bribing, dismissing them as "rather long-winded and often illogical Persians" who had little appreciation for operational security, according to one CIA history.

Dulles was alerted on May 20 that an Iranian court ruling had made the Tudeh Party legal. It could now engage in overt activities, and some Tudeh members had been released from prison. The CIA station could not determine if Mossadegh was behind those moves. John Waller summarized for Wisner and the other clandestine service managers where things stood at the end of May. It was a complex situation as usual. The prime minister's "base of support in the Majlis is narrowing," Waller reported, "but the opposition still lacks the unity of leadership and design to challenge Mossadegh's authority effectively. While the Tudeh's popular strength remains about the same," it had grown politically stronger by its "continuing penetration of government agencies" and its disruption of Mossadegh's struggle with the opposition.

At the end of May, from his new post as undersecretary of state, Beetle Smith passed along to Eisenhower excerpts of a cable Loy Henderson in Tehran had sent the State Department; the cable described "the national state of mind in Iran," as the ambassador saw it. Beetle hoped it would cement the president's resolve for a coup. Politically conscious Iranians expected the United States to interfere in their country's affairs, Henderson claimed, and Iranian politicians friendly to the West would welcome secret U.S. intervention to support their political aims. It was the rank-and-file Iranians who distrusted foreigners, he said, and they would take notice if a lot of Americans were in their country. They were highly xenophobic. Only Iranians "sympathetic to the Soviet Union and to international communism have reason to be pleased with what is taking place in Iran," the ambassador maintained.

On May 13, Donald Wilber, a professor secretly consulting with Wisner's Near East Division, sat down in a safe house in Nicosia, Cyprus, with MI6 agent Norman Matthew Darbyshire, who had worked in Iran for several years and was fluent in the Persian language. The two men labored over a joint draft plan for the overthrow of Mossadegh, which they cabled back to their intelligence services eighteen days later. It was code-named "TPAjax."

Nicosia would be the rear headquarters, where the American and British officers would coordinate the operation. The CIA flew in radio equipment to set up a rapid three-way communications channel linking together Tehran, Cyprus, and Washington. The cables transmitted over it were code-named "Kubark."

Wilber and Darbyshire agreed with Waller that Zahedi was the only one who could rally opposition forces. The CIA decided it would pay the general $35,000 at the outset for his expenses. MI6 would chip in $25,000. Zahedi would persuade or bribe other officers to stand ready to carry out the coup, with $135,000 eventually budgeted for that task. Wisner's officers saw little value in bribing Iranian officers, however, suspecting that anyone who accepted cash would probably betray the operation if tortured.

To turn public opinion against Mossadegh, $150,000 was allocated for propaganda activities. Thugs would be paid to attack religious leaders and make it seem that Mossadegh had ordered them to do so. The CIA wanted Ajax "to appear legal or quasi-legal instead of an outright coup," according to one agency history. To give the operation that legislative sheen, the CIA considered it important that the Majlis vote to dismiss the premier. With the $11,000-plus it planned to spend weekly to suborn the Majlis, Wilber estimated they needed to buy fifty-three of its deputies. Darbyshire identified twenty deputies not then controlled who must be purchased, and he agreed that MI6 agents would approach them with bribe offers.

On the day of the coup, Wilber and Darbyshire envisioned thousands of paid demonstrators staging a massive anti-government rally, with army units Zahedi controlled arresting Mossadegh and seizing key government buildings. The CIA's Tehran station had made few inroads into the Iranian military, so Wisner sent George Carroll, an agency paramilitary expert with war experience in Korea, to the city to scope out the armed forces. Darbyshire estimated that at least a hundred leaders in the Tudeh Party, along with their front group organizers and sympathetic journalists, would have to be arrested. British agents, the CIA station, and Zahedi would compile that list.

Britain's Secret Intelligence Service was more than willing to follow the CIA's lead in Ajax. The Brits were delighted to have the American agency's cooperation and were envious of the money, men, and equipment the CIA could bring to the project. Wilber and Darbyshire rated their chances for success in a condescending manner toward the Iranians. The two intelligence officers realized they were imposing Western-style planning on the locals. The Iranians, they believed, were incapable of acting rationally. But Wilber and

Darbyshire believed their plan was comprehensive enough that it had "a reasonable chance of success even if not carried out 100 percent."

Loy Henderson was summoned back to Washington, and for an hour and a half on the morning of June 6, Wisner, Waller, and Roosevelt briefed him on the Ajax details the CIA and MI6 agents had hammered out in Nicosia. The ambassador was pessimistic, rattling off a long list of problems he worried the operation might encounter. Mossadegh, meanwhile, lurched from one political crisis to another, unaware that the United States had turned against him. He sent Eisenhower a letter pleading for American help in securing a $25 million loan from the Export-Import Bank. It took a month for Ike to send back a no-reply reply. The U.S. embassy in Tehran cabled Washington at the beginning of July that it had been receiving reports that Mossadegh "has lost much of the popular support which he previously enjoyed"—although the embassy admitted that it had no scientific polling to verify that this was true.

Eisenhower had given his tacit approval of the coup, but Allen Dulles did not consider that sufficient, so on June 14, he went to the White House to brief the president on Ajax and secure his formal sign-off. Ike showed no interest in the operation's details. He wanted only a broad-brush outline in order to give his blessing. He had participated in none of the meetings to set up Ajax. He had received only oral reports on the plan, and he had not discussed it with his cabinet or the National Security Council. That was the way he would operate with covert projects throughout his presidency, keeping a degree of distance from foreign policy's seamy side. Nothing would be on paper. The circle of advisers who knew of his decisions would be kept small. Over drinks in the evening with just Foster, Ike would be kept informed of CIA activities and maintain tight control. Kim Roosevelt worried that the cocktail briefings Eisenhower received were not as thorough as what the enthusiastic and hands-on Churchill was receiving from his staff. But Allen Dulles was fine with the arrangement. He no longer felt compelled to talk about Ajax at NSC meetings now that he had directly cleared the operation with Eisenhower.

Once Ike okayed Ajax, Wisner's propaganda experts began aggressively churning out anti-Mossadegh messages through newspapers, handbills, and sermons from the mosques. The State Department helped the CIA plant in American newspapers and magazines hostile stories that were then reproduced in Tehran. A favorite CIA line in many messages: "Mossadegh says he is the savior of Iran, but he does strange things for a savior." Agency artists drew cartoons poking fun at the prime minister. Posters plastered on walls showed Zahedi being presented to the Iranian people by the Shah.

How effective was the CIA propaganda campaign? Many voices were already denouncing Mossadegh, so it was hard to see how the messages the agency wedged into the chorus made much of a difference. What was more, the country's media consumers were highly segmented, so the CIA-generated stories reached mostly those who were already opposed to Mossadegh, not his backers or the undecided. Mossadegh also controlled the national radio broadcasts through which most Iranians got their news. The country's population was 90 percent illiterate.

Washington ended up being on the receiving end of a barb in the propaganda war. A July 1953 demonstration was staged in Tehran to commemorate the one-year anniversary of Mossadegh's return to power after the Qavam gambit. The premier's National Front managed to turn out only a measly couple thousand for its listless parade. The Tudeh, however, used the occasion to show off its street strength, fielding a disciplined and enthusiastic throng of at least 100,000. The Communists were seriously threatening, Washington feared. The CIA decided it had to move quickly. Ajax was scheduled to begin in mid-August.

Chapter 19

OPERATION AJAX

KIM ROOSEVELT HAD SLIPPED into Tehran unnoticed on July 19. He had taken a roundabout flight and car trip to Iran, made all the more uncomfortable by a painful kidney stone inside him that refused to pass. (Not wanting the coup to start without him, he ignored a doctor's advice to wait in Washington until the kidney stone had been surgically removed.) Planes took him to Paris, Rome, and then Beirut. From the Lebanese capital, Roosevelt traveled over a bumpy mountain road to Damascus, a trip he had made many times before. In Damascus he picked up Francis Granger, a CIA companion, and the two left in the cool of evening on the pipeline road to Baghdad. After an overnight in the Iraqi capital, the pair drove by car to the Iraq-Iran border, where a not-too-curious nor -bright customs officer waved them through at the crossing at Khanaqin. Hot and dusty, Roosevelt and Granger reached the U.S. embassy before it closed on July 19—Kim hoping to keep his arrival in the Iranian capital as secret as possible. If that proved impossible, he planned to pose as an American on a boondoggle in the city, going by the name "Jim Lockridge," moving among the homes of friends, and then spending a few days on a shooting expedition before being laid up with an ailment (the last part not too far from the truth with his stubborn kidney stone).

Roosevelt spoke no Persian but he could see with his own eyes that the country was in turmoil. Mossadegh's supporters wanted Ayatollah Kashani removed as Majlis speaker, and the prime minister eventually staged a rigged referendum to oust the entire legislative body. Newspapers for different political factions were relentlessly attacking one another. Mossadegh's National Front was crumbling. The value of the rial was plunging.

Roosevelt avoided the U.S. embassy compound and instead parked himself in the isolated mountain home of one of the senior embassy officers; in one room he kept a large safe packed with stacks of rial notes, and he enjoyed sunning himself in the backyard pool with a glass of whiskey between his forays into the city to attend meetings and pass out the cash. In addition to the CIA station officers recruiting sources and writing reports, he quickly assembled a motley crew of agents who included embassy military attachés who schmoozed with Iranian officers sympathetic to Zahedi; three Americans—with the code names "Jake," "Red," and "Uncle Ami"— who roamed bars and cabarets vacuuming gossip; and two Iranian organizers (dubbed "Boscoe One" and "Boscoe Two") who led a team of Iranian operatives tracking Mossadegh's allies, distributing pamphlets, and assembling street mobs.

Zahedi told the CIA station officers he had five senior Iranian military and security officers lined up for his operation and he was putting together several plans he could choose from to depose Mossadegh, to arrest the prime minister and his allies the night of the coup, and to take over the government. The CIA officers in Tehran were not impressed. Neither was Roosevelt when he arrived. Zahedi seemed to them to lack the drive, the energy, and, most important of all, the concrete plan to topple the government. He was going to need a lot of guidance, the CIA men concluded, and they would have to put together the necessary coup plans for him.

As part of the war of nerves to demonstrate that the United

States had lost confidence in Mossadegh, the State Department moved to cut back the contacts senior U.S. officials had with his government. Loy Henderson remained in Washington for the moment. The chief of the U.S. military mission in Tehran was told to act less friendly toward senior Iranian officers who supported Mossadegh. But there were limits to the quarantining they could impose, Wisner believed. Roosevelt wanted William Warne, who directed the Technical Cooperation Administration in Tehran and had numerous dealings with senior Iranian officials, moved out of the country as well. *Send him on a long vacation in Europe,* Roosevelt suggested. Obsessed with not having the U.S. role behind a coup leak out, Wisner nixed that move. Warne had not been cleared to know anything about Ajax. Wisner feared that if the State Department hustled out the technical administrator without telling him why, he might start asking questions and inadvertently blow the operation.

The CIA continued to be suspicious about Soviet maneuvers around that time to gain the advantage. Moscow had just appointed a top-level diplomat to be ambassador to Iran. The Kremlin also signaled that it was open to settling Iran's claim for $21 million worth of gold Tehran insisted the Russian government owed it from a 1942 financial agreement. The Soviet moves "may be designed to show Prime Minister Mossadegh that an alternative exists to economic and political ties with the West," an agency memo warned.

Roosevelt spent much of his first two weeks in Tehran organizing propaganda attacks on Mossadegh, whom the CIA station reported was "extremely nervous and unable to take food" since the weak National Front turnout for the July demonstration. Washington joined in the psychological warfare as well. The Shah's spirits were boosted when Eisenhower sent him a friendly letter, which made the monarch feel he had American backing. Waller planted a question that a reporter asked at a July 28 press conference Foster Dulles held; it enabled the secretary of state to declare his concern about growing Communist activity in Iran that Mossadegh was tolerating.

The psywar was having an effect, Waller told Wisner. Mossa-degh had received the message loud and clear: the U.S. government would not bail out Iran economically as long he cozied up to the Communists and refused to settle the oil dispute with the British. Moreover, Waller reported, the premier's "increasingly open es-pousal of Communist support has alarmed" two important groups that had been closely allied with him: the Qashqai tribe in southern Iran and the politically powerful Amini family. The CIA now had an opportunity to neutralize the Qashqai and the Aminis so they would not get in the way of Ajax. It had to be done discreetly, Waller advised. The two groups would never go along with Ajax if they thought the British were involved, so that connection had to be downplayed. It also might cost the CIA $5.25 million in economic aid and bribes to get the Qashqai and the Aminis on board with Mossadegh's removal, Waller estimated. Wisner was more than willing to pay for that kind of influence.

* * *

By the beginning of August, bribes were being passed out like candy around Tehran. Press attacks against Mossadegh reached a new vir-ulence with stories, planted by the CIA, accusing him of being a Communist, a Shah hater, and even a closet Jew. Roosevelt and the CIA station joined in Iran's rent-a-mob tradition, buying demon-strators who denounced Mossadegh and carried portraits of the Shah through the street. Tehran was soon filled with rumors that a coup was on the way. But as the days passed, Roosevelt found that he had a prime minister who still retained a following (although he seemed to be making every mistake a politician could make) and a monarch who was still indecisive and timid. Roosevelt needed de-crees dismissing Mossadegh from the Shah, but the Shah refused to take that momentous step.

To try to stiffen the Shah's spine, Roosevelt recruited two emis-saries. The first was the Shah's twin sister, Princess Ashraf, who despised Mossadegh. CIA and MI6 officers flew to the French Riviera and, with a mink coat and cash as sweeteners, convinced the princess to return to Iran (flying under her married name, Madam Chafik) to lobby her brother to cooperate with the coup plotters. The sister was unsuccessful.

The second emissary was an American general the Shah had long admired: H. Norman Schwarzkopf Sr., a colorful former New Jersey State Police superintendent who as a senior Army officer had trained Iranian police and security forces during World War II— and whose son, of the same name, led American forces that evicted the Iraqi army from Kuwait nearly forty years later in Operation Desert Storm. Given the code name "Roach" and the cover story that he was traveling through the region on private business, with Iran just being a brief stopover to visit old friends, Schwarzkopf landed in Tehran in late July. (He reportedly had several million dollars packed in his suitcases to pass along to Roosevelt's team).

On August 1, Schwarzkopf held an odd meeting with the Shah at Saad Abad Palace. The nervous monarch at first refused to speak out loud to his old friend, convinced that political enemies had bugged his palace. He ushered Schwarzkopf into a large ballroom, empty except for a table in the center; the two men sat on top of it and talked in whispers. The general pressed the Shah to immediately sign paperwork that would result in Mossadegh being forced out of office and Zahedi replacing him, but the monarch whispered that he still had not decided his next move. He was unsure the army would follow his orders and still paranoid about being defeated in a confrontation with Mossadegh. The Shah slept with a pistol by his bed, fearing an assassin would enter his room at night. His wife worried that he might have a nervous breakdown.

Schwarzkopf left the palace with the impression that the Shah could still be talked into backing the coup, but Roosevelt, not intermediaries, needed to talk to him to close the deal. That was a risky move. If the CIA man was spotted entering Saad Abad Palace, the news could spread like wildfire throughout Tehran and the operation might be blown. Roosevelt decided he had to take the chance and had an intermediary arrange the meeting.

A nondescript black sedan pulled up to Roosevelt's villa the next night around midnight. Roosevelt—wearing a dark turtleneck shirt, gray slacks, and rope-soled, cloth-covered Persian shoes called *givehs*—climbed into the backseat, where a blanket was folded in a corner. As the car neared Saad Abad Palace, Roosevelt huddled down on the floor and pulled the blanket over him. A sentry at the palace entrance silently waved the sedan through. Halfway between the gate and the steps leading up to the palace, the driver brought the sedan to the stop, turned off the engine, and left the vehicle. Roosevelt saw a slim figure walk down the steps, along the driveway, and to the car, where he opened the back door.

There was enough moonlight for them to see each other. The Shah remembered Roosevelt from their occasional meetings over the past six years. Roosevelt now informed the Shah that he was there representing Eisenhower and Churchill, which the American president would confirm by a phrase inserted in a speech he would deliver during the next twenty-four hours; the British prime minister would have a line inserted in a BBC broadcast. The Shah, appearing calm and collected, said the confirmation was unnecessary. "Your name and presence is all the guarantee I need," he told Roosevelt.

The CIA man made his pitch. Leaving Mossadegh in power "could lead only to a Communist Iran or to a second Korea," Roosevelt argued, stretching the truth with the Korean War analogy. The Shah was still hesitant about joining the plot, so Roosevelt delivered a polite ultimatum. The British and American governments had approved the overthrow of Mossadegh, which would make the Shah more powerful. If the Shah did not join them in a few days, Roosevelt said he would leave the country and put together "some other plan" to be rid of Mossadegh. The Shah said nothing and showed no reaction. He simply said that he would meet Roosevelt at the same time the next night after a car brought him to the palace.

At that palace meeting the next night, Roosevelt boasted to the Shah that he had $1 million for a coup and a team of "extremely competent" operatives to carry it out. He described for the monarch how Ajax would play out: the mosques, the press, and the street crowds mobilizing against Mossadegh; military officers delivering the decrees dismissing him; mobs taking over Tehran; and Zahedi emerging as the Shah's nominee for prime minister. But the Shah continued to agonize over his decision. Finally, he agreed to sign the two royal decrees, called firmans, that dismissed Mossadegh as prime minister and replaced him with Zahedi, but only if he and his wife were allowed to leave Iran for a safer spot immediately afterward. Roosevelt agreed that the Shah and Queen Soraya would fly to a hunting lodge on the Caspian Sea coast north of Tehran. If things went wrong, the couple would be prepared to take their plane to Baghdad.

The Shah knew that things could go wrong. Mossadegh was a ruthless politician, he feared. On August 3, the prime minister staged an obviously fraudulent referendum to decide the fate of the Majlis. With ballot stuffing rampant, the government claimed that about 99.5 percent of the vote was in favor of dissolving the legislative body.

Roosevelt next scoped out what Zahedi had to offer in the coup. A car and driver took him to the general's mountain hideout northeast of Tehran near the Tajrish neighborhood. Communications with the officer were difficult because Zahedi spoke only Persian and some German. Roosevelt could still not be sure that the army would follow Zahedi's and the Shah's orders. The Iranian military, as near as he could tell, was divided into pro-Shah, pro-Mossadegh, and fence-sitting factions, yet all shared a long tradition of waiting to see who controlled the streets before they acted. The CIA and the Pentagon knew little about the Iranian armed forces, their facilities, and their capabilities, but what was known left the American agencies uncomfortable. Iranian officers, the CIA believed, were as a rule indecisive and they covered up their failings with a lot of bombast and chest-beating. Concluded one U.S. embassy cable: "The Iranian is much more at home in the field of intrigue than he is on the field of battle."

Roosevelt and the Shah met for the last time the night and early morning of August 8 and 9. Roosevelt handed him a note he said was from Eisenhower with good wishes (which the CIA officer had actually written). They agreed that a courier would bring the two decrees to the palace on the morning of August 10. The Shah would sign them and then with the queen board a plane for the Caspian coast.

But a glitch that was almost comedic followed. The courier assigned to take the two firmans to the Shah for his signature arrived at the palace late on the morning of August 10 and found that the royal couple had already left for the Caspian coast. Roosevelt never knew if this was simply a missed connection or if the Shah had skipped out intentionally. Whatever it was, the CIA officer quickly arranged for Colonel Nematollah Nasiri, the commander of the Shah's Imperial Guard, to fly with the two decrees to the Caspian coast. Nasiri obtained the Shah's signature on the two firmans, but because fog and low clouds rolled in, making flying impossible, he had to have the documents taken back to Tehran by car.

The packet containing the two signed decrees finally reached Roosevelt's villa around midnight. But the Muslim weekend, which the Iranians observed on Thursday and Friday, was drawing near. Because everything would shut down, a government overthrow would not be practical. Roosevelt was forced to postpone the coup until Saturday, August 15. He moved his command post to the basement of the U.S. embassy compound.

But doubts swirled among the Americans. Back in Washington, CIA analysts questioned the rush to launch the final move in the operation. Iran had become increasingly unstable, but Mossadegh would likely survive through 1953, a draft national intelligence estimate concluded, and there was little danger of Communist domination in the next few months. Officers in the CIA's Tehran station also thought Zahedi was living in a dreamworld, proposing all kinds of pie-in-the-sky social and economic reforms that he would implement when he became prime minister. It was clear, the station cabled headquarters, that the general would need "firm realistic guidance" from Washington if he assumed power.

As dusk fell over Tehran on August 15, Roosevelt moved with a group of agents to a safe house near the embassy that was stocked with liquor to await news of victory to celebrate. Shortly after eleven p.m., Colonel Nasiri, who hated Mossadegh and whose Imperial Guard numbered seven hundred men loyal to the Shah, arrived at the home of General Taqi Riahi, a Mossadegh ally Roosevelt needed out of the picture, to arrest the army chief of staff. But Riahi was not there. Nasiri climbed back into his armored car and took his small column of tanks to the residence of Mohammad Mossadegh, the next person on his arrest list. But what Nasiri did not know was that another military column under Riahi's command was headed to Mossadegh's home to foil Nasiri's plan and arrest *him*. It turned out that the Roosevelt-Zahedi coup plan was not much of a secret in Tehran. Riahi bragged later that he had known about the coup plot six hours beforehand. Tudeh Party leaders had also been tipped off to the plot. A CIA postmortem concluded that an indiscreet Iranian army officer had betrayed the plan.

Shortly before one a.m. on August 16, Nasiri, with the two firmans in hand and a military contingent, arrived at Mossadegh's residence on Takht-e Jamshid near the U.S. embassy. He was met by the larger force Riahi had cobbled together, which arrested the colonel and threw him into jail. Throughout the night Roosevelt received snippets that indicated something "had gone very sour," he later said: a radio jeep did not arrive at the designated time, the telephone system was not put out of operation, and tanks (he couldn't tell to whom they belonged) were moving in unexpected directions.

The unraveling of the plot did not become clear to him until the sun rose and Mossadegh had Radio Tehran announce that a coup attempt by the Shah's bodyguard had been defeated. The Shah listened to the same broadcast at his Caspian Sea lodge and quickly fled with Queen Soraya in a Beechcraft plane that the Shah personally piloted to Baghdad. Troops loyal to Mossadegh fanned out through the Iranian capital and began arresting suspected conspirators. Rewards were offered for the capture of Zahedi. Jubilant crowds marched in the streets, chanting: "Mossadegh has won!" To the CIA station's relief, the Radio Tehran broadcast made no mention of any American involvement, Mossadegh saying on the air only that "foreign elements" had been working with the Shah. Nevertheless, CIA operatives raced to the security of the embassy compound or safe houses. Bleary-eyed from no sleep and in despair, Roosevelt cabled Washington that the operation had collapsed.

Allowing for the more than seven-hour time difference, it was one thirty a.m. on August 16 when the jangling phone woke Wisner up at his Georgetown home and the CIA watch officer on the line passed along the bad news from Tehran. Wisner could not go back to sleep. He began scrambling to contain what he thought would be huge damage for the United States government and for the CIA. Later that day, Wisner, as depressed as Dulles was over the debacle, sent Roosevelt a cable ordering him to pull out. The clandestine service chief had propaganda guidance sent out to the CIA stations in Karachi, New Delhi, Cairo, Damascus, Istanbul, and Beirut, pushing the line that with the Shah's firmans a Zahedi government was the only legal one in Iran. Wisner also wanted to know where the Shah was and whether contact could be made with him. If so, it had to be done extremely quietly. Wisner was now frantic to keep a lid on Ajax.

Roosevelt prepared an escape plan but then shelved it. He thought there still might be a slight chance for success. The MI6 agents in Nicosia had not given up hope either. The CIA station in Tehran cabled Wisner a postmortem of what had gone wrong with the coup attempt and then proposed steps the agency could take to rescue the operation, such as bringing to the attention of Iranians the decrees making Zahedi the prime minister that the Shah had legally signed, and putting pressure on General Riahi to arrest Mossadegh. But Wisner, who feared blowback from the coup attempt, was not buying a second round. He wanted his station chief in Baghdad, where the Shah was holed up, and Roosevelt in Tehran to keep their distance from any action the monarch might now take. On August 18, Wisner ordered Roosevelt to close down Ajax. We "tried and failed," a message to the Near East chief read. The operation was "not quite dead," Wisner agreed, but close to expiring, so it should not be continued. He ordered Roosevelt to begin Ajax's "liquidation." Beetle Smith at the State Department said the United States would now need to cultivate good relations with Mossadegh. Whatever the prime minister's faults, Smith rationalized, he had no love for the Russians.

Roosevelt in the past had intentionally reported little on what he was doing in Ajax to CIA headquarters. He was now ignoring Wisner's order as if he had never received it, which was not too difficult to do because Nicosia was a bottleneck in their three-way communications that caused delays in passing messages between Washington and the Tehran station. CIA headquarters was panicked, but the Iranians risking their lives in the field to overthrow Mossadegh were not. For them the struggle continued.

Even with extra police patrolling Tehran's streets, Roosevelt found a villa near the embassy where Zahedi could hide. Then he met secretly with the general the day after the first failed coup attempt and asked if he wanted to make a second try. Zahedi said yes. Roosevelt thought he still had many arrows in his quiver: Zahedi and a cabal of senior Iranian officers who wanted to be rid of Mossadegh, a network of agents and subagents, and the all-important decrees dismissing Mossadegh and replacing him with Zahedi that the Shah had signed. Roosevelt's team began making copies of the firmans and arranged for reporters from the Associated Press and *New York Times* to publish stories on them. Iranian newspapers, as Roosevelt expected, picked up the foreign reports and ran them in the country, spreading among the army and the people the message that what had happened on August 15 was not a coup but a legitimate change of government that the Shah had approved and that Mossadegh had foiled with his own coup.

Ignoring Wisner's order to come home, Roosevelt on Sunday afternoon, August 16, began hatching a new plan to oust Mossadegh. Monday and Tuesday, he would have his agents bribe politicians, mullahs, and others who could turn out crowds at a moment's notice. Street mobs on those two days would riot, claiming it was on behalf of Mossadegh, and then on Wednesday the demonstrations would recede and the military and the police would storm government buildings and arrest Mossadegh. For the second attempt, Roosevelt had seasoned Iranian street agents like the three Rashidian brothers—Assadollah, Qodratollah, and Seyfollah—and sabotage and propaganda organizers Ali Jalili and Farouk Keyvani. Desperately afraid of his team being captured by Mossadegh agents and the entire operation collapsing, Roosevelt hid those key people in the U.S. embassy compound and in homes that Americans owned around the city.

On Monday evening, August 17, Roosevelt had Zahedi; his son, Ardeshir; the Rashidian brothers; and other key members of his team who were not already in the U.S. embassy compound smuggled in by cars and closed jeeps for a four-hour planning meeting. The CIA officer had never had a backup plan in case the first coup attempt failed, so he was quickly improvising now. Because he was under a time crunch and communications with the outside were slow, he was not keeping Wisner in Washington informed about what he was doing.

Roosevelt began by having his Iranian agents spread false rumors that it was Mossadegh who had tried to oust the Shah, but loyal officers had stopped him. Hundreds of photographs of the two firmans were distributed throughout the capital. The CIA station had wanted to put the Shah on the radio to announce that he had signed the decrees and to defiantly condemn Mossadegh, but the frazzled monarch, who had not slept in three days, remained silent.

Mossadegh paid little attention to Roosevelt's latest propaganda blitz. With the Shah having fled, he never imagined that those who had attempted the Saturday coup would try a second time so soon. The prime minister and his cabinet members let their guard down, withdrawing loyal troops from the streets. Roosevelt, meanwhile, organized his armed force for the second try. He had a military attaché from the embassy bribe officers from several infantry regiments and a tank battalion to join the plot and be ready to crush street revolts. His next task was to arrange the disorder. Jalili and Keyvani, with $50,000 in their pockets, hired a crowd that would rampage on command. The fate of Mossadegh's government lay in the streets, Roosevelt realized, so he had to be able to produce crowds. He devised a plan to create both pro- and anti-government riots, but in the end, what a mob demanded mattered little. An anti-Mossadegh demonstration would be great, but a pro-Mossadegh crowd was just as good because it would harden both sides and perhaps provoke loyalist soldiers to crack down. The ultimate goal was to create chaos in Tehran.

By midmorning on Monday, August 17, gratifying reports trickled into the embassy compound, where Roosevelt had spent a second sleepless night. A gang of thugs his agents had hired to be Mossadegh supporters was marching from the slums of south Tehran to the city center. They were joined by true nationalists and Communists. The crowd, numbering in the tens of thousands, collected in Parliament Square, where a handful knocked down an equestrian statue of the Shah. Roosevelt was delighted. An anti-Shah demonstration would anger pro-Shah elements among the army and the public, he was sure. Mossadegh naively ordered the police not to intervene, which let the mob keep rampaging—more good news for Roosevelt because the chaos bolstered the message he wanted conveyed to Iranians: their country was spiraling out of control and needed a savior.

On Tuesday, August 18, with the police still under orders not to interfere, the rioting intensified, which Roosevelt hoped would reinforce the impression among Iranians that their country had descended into anarchy. That afternoon, Loy Henderson, who had returned to Iran on Monday, joined in the psywar campaign, marching into Mossadegh's office to complain that Americans were being harassed, and to threaten that the U.S. government would recall all of them if it did not stop. That shook the prime minister, who ordered his police chief to put an end to the demonstrations. The law enforcement authorities did so violently, which proved to be a serious mistake on Mossadegh's part. Many of the demonstrators police attacked with clubs, rifles, and tear gas were the prime minister's own supporters. The Tudeh also blundered at this point. Its leaders ordered their cadres to take to the streets and demand a "democratic republic," which stirred public fears of a Communist power grab like those that the nations in Eastern Europe had experienced.

Wisner had a terrible shock in the early-morning hours of August 18. The Shah, who had no idea that the tide was turning back to his favor in his home country, decided to board a British Overseas Airways Corporation jet in Baghdad that day and fly with Queen Soraya to Rome for what he thought would be a long exile. Shortly after two a.m. August 18 in Washington, John Waller's home phone rang. Wisner was on the other end of the line, as agitated as the Iran branch chief had ever heard him. The Shah had flown to Rome with the queen, Wisner anxiously told Waller, and "a terrible, terrible coincidence occurred. Can you guess what it is?"

Waller could not.

After the couple landed in Rome, they rode to the Excelsior Hotel to book a room. The Shah was crossing the street to the Excelsior and "can you imagine what may have happened?" continued Wisner, who didn't want to reveal the answer on an open line. Wisner told Waller to "think of the worst thing" that could have happened at that point.

"He was hit by a cab and killed," Waller answered.

"No, no, no, no!" Wisner practically shouted into the phone. He explained to Waller that Allen Dulles had decided to extend a European vacation he was taking and make a visit to Rome. "Now can you imagine what happened?"

"Dulles hit him with his car and killed him," Waller answered.

Wisner did not think that was funny. "They both showed up at the reception desk at the Excelsior at the very same moment," he barked into the phone, now irritated. "And Dulles had to say, 'After you, Your Majesty.'"

Waller now understood the gravity of what had happened. If word leaked to the media that the director of America's CIA had met the Shah of Iran in Rome, it could be blown up into an international incident that would be terribly embarrassing for the U.S. government. Wisner was relieved that the press never learned of that chance encounter.

On Wednesday morning, August 19, Roosevelt could only watch and wait in the embassy compound as events unfolded, but the news coming to him was encouraging. He had a fine mob assembled, which included not only the usual street thugs but also popular weight lifters, wrestlers, and acrobats from Tehran's athletic clubs. To beef them up, one of the Rashidian brothers, Assadollah, had convinced him to pay Ayatollah Kashani $10,000 to turn out demonstrators from the mosques. That day Roosevelt's agents also planted in Tehran newspapers a fabricated interview with Zahedi in which the general claimed his government was the only legitimate one in the country.

Throughout the morning, encouraging reports poured into Roosevelt's command post at the embassy. Crowds chanting "Death to Mossadegh!" and "Long live the Shah!" had surged out of Tehran's southern slums, with tribesmen from outside the city and soldiers in trucks and tanks joining them. Rioters attacked government buildings and pro-government newspapers, trading gunfire with Mossadegh's forces. A western garrison commander was marching his men toward the capital to join the insurgents. The military police headquarters had been captured and plotters from the first coup attempt were freed. And then the Radio Tehran station fell to the insurgents. Mossadegh, who had sustained his rule by street demonstrations, was now being overcome by them.

As Roosevelt munched on his lunch at around two p.m., there came from the radio that he had turned on an announcement by an

Iranian army officer, who declared excitedly: "The government of Mossadegh has been defeated! The new prime minister, Fazlollah Zahedi, is now in office. And His Imperial Majesty is on his way home!" Roosevelt and his agents in the command post danced a jig for joy. A communications technician handed him a cable from Washington that had been delayed in channels. It was from Beetle Smith, who ordered him to flee Tehran immediately. Roosevelt chuckled and cabled back that the coup was succeeding, Zahedi was safely installed, and the Shah was returning to Tehran triumphantly. Roosevelt was getting ahead of himself, but he was confident this was how events would play out from what he had heard and seen so far.

What Roosevelt wasn't aware of was that throughout the day, Zahedi had been moving from one hiding place to another, alerting sleeper cells throughout the military and directing army units into action. His soldiers arrested pro-Mossadegh politicians and military officers, seized general staff offices, and began taking control of Tehran. By afternoon a pitched tank-and-artillery battle was being waged at Mossadegh's house between units under Zahedi's control and loyalist soldiers manning barricades around the home. The heavy-weapons duel left bodies strewn around the sidewalks. With his guards' ammunition running out after two hours, Mossadegh and a few aides escaped over a back garden wall. Rioters rushed into the house, ransacked it, set fires, and dragged out furniture, which they sold to passersby. Roosevelt, meanwhile, fetched Zahedi from his safe house and arranged for a tank to take him to the Radio Tehran station, where the general declared in a broadcast that he was "the lawful prime minister by the Shah's order." When reporters found the Shah in the Rome hotel dining room and gave him the account of the successful coup, the young monarch cried out: "I knew it! I knew it! They love me!"

* * *

Back in Washington—where, for the past two days, Wisner and his aides had just been receiving snippets of Radio Tehran broadcasts that left them "wondering whether we were in, out, up, or down," said Helms—the plans directorate finally received definitive word around nine a.m. on August 19 that Mossadegh was on the way out. A staffer who had just been in the communications room rushed into Wisner's suite of offices and excitedly blurted out the news. With depression still lingering from what had happened the day before, everyone at first thought he was making a bad joke. Wisner soon realized he was not. Throughout the morning and the afternoon and late into the night, CIA officers hurried up and down the corridors of the clandestine service, clutching fresh slips of ticker tape, most of them with updates from news agencies in the Middle East. (During the entire day, Wisner's office received only two cables from the Tehran station.) Never had a day carried so much excitement, satisfaction, and jubilation for Wisner and his men. They did not want it to end.

An elated Allen Dulles cabled Roosevelt and the Tehran station his hearty congratulations the next day. Ajax was now Dulles's favorite project. But it was an operation that became one of the agency's most closely held secrets. The White House secretly awarded Roosevelt the National Security Medal, but Wisner decided not to pass out commendations to Waller and other CIA officers in Tehran and Nicosia who had worked on the operation, fearing word might get around about the honors and result in a security breach. On August 20, Ambassador Henderson sent a lengthy report to the State Department with a list of reasons the coup had succeeded. He made no mention of the role Roosevelt and the CIA had played—either because it was so secret that he did not want State Department officials not cleared to learn of it, or because he believed Roosevelt and the agency had played a minor role. Though in his private diary he expressed his admiration for what Roosevelt had accomplished, Eisenhower never publicly acknowledged the U.S. role in the Iran coup. At a National Security Council meeting the week after the overthrow, Foster Dulles also remained coy about the CIA's role. There is no documentary evidence that any congressional panel was briefed on the operation before or immediately after it occurred, although Allen Dulles might have later whispered the story of Ajax to congressmen he trusted. The agency's Near East Division wished that he wouldn't share details with so many. By its count, eighty-nine people in the U.S. and British governments were aware of Ajax, and the division considered that number excessive.

Outside official channels, the Alsop brothers and a handful of other reporters in Washington had known about the CIA plot ahead of time but printed nothing on it. If the president and his senior advisers believed they needed to launch a risky covert operation "to further the interests of the United States," Joe Alsop later rationalized, "it is not the business of individual newspapermen to put professional gain over that of the country."

The Shah believed Roosevelt was a major reason he had regained his power. Late on Saturday morning, August 22, the triumphant monarch stepped off a Dutch airliner that had been escorted by Iraqi jet fighters to Tehran's airport, and he was greeted by Zahedi, a royal honor guard, and an admiring throng. The next day, Roosevelt paid a visit to Saad Abad Palace. He later claimed in his memoir that over caviar and vodka toasts, the Shah told him: "I owe my throne to God, my people, my army—and to you!" A beaming Prime Minister Zahedi arrived a few minutes later, full of thanks. The Shah then presented Roosevelt with a golden cigarette case "as a souvenir of our recent adventure," he said.

The next morning, Roosevelt climbed aboard a plane, with tears in his eyes. At a stop in London, he regaled an appreciative Churchill for two hours with stories about the coup. "Young man," Roosevelt recalled the British prime minister telling him, "if I had been but a few years younger, I would have loved nothing better than to have served under your command in this great adventure."

After returning to Washington, Roosevelt was summoned to the White House to brief Eisenhower and his admiring senior staff on Ajax with maps and charts. Ike wrote in his diary that the CIA man's report "seemed more like a dime novel than an historical fact." Foster was enthusiastic about how the quick and inexpensive operation had accomplished a major foreign policy objective. In fact, he was too enthusiastic, Roosevelt worried. The agency officer cautioned that Ajax succeeded because the political stars had lined up perfectly in that case. If they had not, "we'd have fallen flat on our faces," Roosevelt said. Should the CIA ever "try something like this again, we must be absolutely sure that people and army want what we want. If not, you had better give the job to the Marines." But Foster, who sat back through the briefing practically purring like a cat, was not listening.

* * *

Zahedi moved quickly to consolidate his power, swearing in cabinet members, weeding out Mossadegh sympathizers in the government, releasing political prisoners, retaking control of the streets, and securing his predecessor's surrender the week after he was ousted. The CIA station cabled Wisner that the Tudeh Party appeared to be crippled, but it remained concerned that the Communists could bounce back. In case not all the political opponents had been neutralized, the Shah ordered Zahedi to wear a U.S.-made bulletproof vest when he ventured out in public. Feeling, he said, like "a new man," the monarch told CIA officers at the Tehran station that he planned to be more hands-on in the running of the country.

Wisner began working Washington's foreign aid apparatus to scrape together money to prop up the new Zahedi government. Within two days of his assuming power, the CIA secretly delivered to Zahedi $5 million so he could meet government payrolls at the end of August. Wisner worried that the general did not have a head for economics nor an adequate appreciation of the financial problems his new government faced. The British were even more suspicious of the new prime minister. Wisner believed Zahedi would need a lot of advice from the CIA. But the agency was now beginning to face resistance to its meddling in Iranian affairs. Wisner became irritated when the State Department shot down the approaches he wanted to make to Zahedi in the premier's negotiations with the Soviets. Wisner thought the diplomats were being too timid. But approaching Zahedi on negotiations with the Soviets was the State Department's job. Wisner had no business butting in. Yet he continued to dabble in other agencies' affairs, drawing up, at Dulles's request, a list of reasons for the U.S. government to increase its military aid to the Iranian government.

Mohammad Mossadegh was imprisoned for ten weeks, then put on trial for treason. The CIA did not want the military tribunal to make him a martyr. The Shah considered having him executed, but settled on a three-year prison sentence followed by house arrest for the remainder of his life. The Shah succeeded in making the former prime minister a nonentity. Mossadegh died in 1967 of jaw cancer at age eighty-four. No public mourning or funeral was permitted.

The British got back into the oil business in Iran, no longer controlling all of its petroleum assets but overseeing a sizable chunk nonetheless. A consortium of foreign oil companies signed a twenty-five-year agreement with Tehran for its oil. Britain received 40 percent of the lucrative concession, an American group of five companies received 40 percent of the shares, and the remaining 20 percent was divided between a Dutch company and a French company. Profits were shared with Iran on a fifty-fifty basis. Wisner, who received technical help from oil executive and old Romanian pal Ricǎ Georgescu, secretly advised Zahedi behind the scenes on the deal he should strike with the international consortium.

On August 28, Wisner sat down with Roosevelt and other top CIA officials to recap what happened from August 16 to 19 and for Roosevelt to explain why he had kept Wisner and headquarters largely in the dark about his coup activities on those four critical days. Roosevelt responded that he had had to choose between spending his time writing reports or "getting out and acting." He couldn't do both, so he chose getting out and acting. General Cabell, the agency's deputy director, accepted that explanation. Wisner remained silent on whether he did.

Postcoup, Wisner's plans directorate conducted a lengthy analysis of lessons learned in the agency's first great success overthrowing a foreign government. For example, there was the recommendation that at least two foreign assets should be assigned the same task in case one was unreliable and failed to perform. A careful accounting should be made of the cost benefit from paying foreign reporters to write favorable stories. The CIA station should have a printing-and-reproduction facility set up at the outset of a coup. And at least two empty and secure safe houses should be maintained for last-minute occupants during the final moments of the coup. But those were technical items. Broader, long-term lessons were ignored.

Yet the long-term lessons were more important. Agency lore over the years, fueled by a self-serving autobiography Roosevelt wrote and hyperbolic journalistic accounts, has portrayed the CIA as an all-powerful, omniscient secret unit triumphally organizing a coup to topple the Iranian government. The truth was less spectacular. The CIA's "role in these climactic events was not very significant," insisted Amos Perlmutter, a Middle East expert at American University. The Iranian operation, said Helms, "has been regarded as being far fancier or larger than it in fact was. There was really not an awful lot of money spent." In moments of candor, even Roosevelt admitted that the agency "did not have to do very much to topple Mossadegh, who was an eccentric and weak figure" to begin with. Iran did not prove that the CIA could overthrow governments anytime it wanted to. Iran was "a unique case," Roosevelt acknowledged. The CIA also benefited from good luck.

"Given the forces arrayed against Mossadegh, it is hard to see how he could have survived" in power, writes Ray Takeyh, a Middle East expert at the Council on Foreign Relations and a former State Department official. Iran's army, its militant clergy, and its wealthy class would not likely have just sat back and watched the country fall apart. Mossadegh's removal from office was probably inevitable regardless of what the West did. Roosevelt planted a lot of stories in newspapers, he hired many street demonstrators, he worked to stiffen the Shah's resolve, and he advised Zahedi on tactics. But the CIA man played more of a supporting role, his undercover work ultimately succeeding because the public, and particularly its political class, eventually became fed up with Mossadegh. The CIA was pushing Iranians to do what they were already inclined to do.

The second coup plot on August 19 was very much an Iranian affair, with many actors and a good bit of improvisation. Roosevelt did hire demonstrators for its street crowds. But many more with genuine hunger for change came out on their own. Although Roosevelt had had a hand in starting demonstrations, they swelled spontaneously and took on a life of their own that surprised even him. Instead of a master manipulator, he became more of a spectator, aiding where he could a revolt that had its own momentum.

Soon after the coup, Roosevelt was offered the command of another covert operation to oust a regime considered unfriendly to the United States—this one in Guatemala. Roosevelt begged off. He knew the Middle East well and he was confident he could play it by ear there, as he had in Iran, without much involvement from headquarters (and Wisner). He was not a Latin America expert. He could not take the same approach that he had taken in the Middle East. Wisner would keep him on a tighter leash, he was sure. Roosevelt also suspected that what had worked in Iran might not work in Guatemala.

* * *

The Iran coup, which Frank Wisner, Allen Dulles, and Dwight Eisenhower were so high on, ended up having unintended consequences. Though a national intelligence estimate in mid-November 1953 concluded that the Tudeh did not constitute "a serious present threat to the Iranian government," Wisner's clandestine service, engaging in overkill, kept up a covert propaganda operation against the party. The CIA's Tehran station distributed anti-Tudeh articles and cartoons to keep the Zahedi government aware of the Communist danger, and used a highly placed agent in Iran's Department of

Propaganda to churn out pro-U.S. messages. But political instability continued to mount, Wisner's officers reported. Less than a year after the coup, the CIA found corruption creeping into the Zahedi government, which troubled the Shah and was "strengthening the communist hand in Iran," an agency memo in June 1954 reported. A little less than three years after the coup, Dulles grew worried about reports coming out of the U.S. embassy in Tehran that the Shah's popularity was "rapidly decreasing," and he ordered Wisner to have the agency's station there check them out.

The reports were true. Over the next two and a half decades, the Shah modernized Iran's economy, raised living standards, and built schools, highways, and hospitals. He also deftly managed foreign affairs, increasing oil prices, turning Iran into a regional power, and maintaining close ties with the United States but at the same time developing good relations with the Soviet Union. The Shah also became increasingly dictatorial and isolated from his people. He refused to allow the middle class he built up to have a voice in national affairs, he used his repressive SAVAK secret police to crush dissent, he spent lavishly on arms, and he ignored a succession of U.S. presidents who urged reforms. The 1953 coup had bonded Washington to an autocrat it could not control.

The Shah's repressive rule finally turned Iranians against him. In 1979, their anger erupted with a revolution led by Islamic fundamentalists who sent him packing. Ayatollah Ruhollah Khomeini, who had been exiled for fourteen years, returned to Iran to take control of the country, with millions filling the streets to welcome him. After President Jimmy Carter allowed the Shah, who had been diagnosed with chronic lymphocytic leukemia, to enter the United States for treatment, enraged Iranians stormed the U.S. embassy in Tehran and held fifty-two Americans hostage for more than fourteen months. Khomeini, who formed the Revolutionary Guards, imposed a form of "religious fascism" at home and turned the county into a base camp for terrorism abroad.

In the late summer of 1953, however, no one in the White House fretted that what they had allowed the CIA to do in Iran was immoral and perhaps illegal or that it had set a dangerous precedent. The CIA, Eisenhower and his national security team believed, had offered a president a quick and relatively easy way to fix problems abroad, to change world politics, or to shape foreign societies to America's image—all without having to resort to open warfare or to go through the messy process of gaining the approval of Congress and the public. For the Eisenhower administration, Ajax became a powerful stimulant—one that would spark further ambitions for regime change in other parts of the world.

Chapter 20

GUATEMALA

POOR GUATEMALA.

About the size of Louisiana and lacking in precious resources such as gold, sugar, or spices, it had been an impoverished Spanish colony for three centuries. In 124 years of independence up until the end of World War II, the Central American nation had remained destitute, with a staggeringly high infant mortality rate among its 3.5 million people. Until 1944, it had been ruled by a succession of ruthless dictators governing on behalf of a tiny landed aristocracy. Three major U.S. companies had invested nearly $100 million in Guatemala: Empresa Eléctrica de Guatemala, a subsidiary of Electric Bond and Share, supplied 80 percent of the country's electricity; the International Railways of Central America laid 581 miles of single track; and the United Fruit Company harvested and exported the nation's bananas. It had also become a favorite vacation retreat for Allen and Clover Dulles.

Of the three companies, United Fruit became the colossus. By the turn of the century, the Boston-based company was the world's largest grower and exporter of bananas, owning more than 212,000 acres throughout Central America and the Caribbean. In

Guatemala, United Fruit became the country's largest landowner, controlling nearly forty thousand jobs; by 1950 the company had profits of more than $65 million, which was greater than the ordinary revenues the Guatemalan government took in. "It functioned as a state within a state," one history noted. Guatemalans on United Fruit plantations enjoyed better working conditions than most farmhands, but the company's meager wages still left them impoverished. A succession of dictators allowed the ruthlessly managed firm to operate as a private fiefdom, ignoring its accounting tricks to cheat the government out of revenue and never sticking up for the workers. Throughout Latin America, the company symbolized to revolutionary leaders the evils of Yankee imperialism. To Guatemalans, United Fruit became known as *"El Pulpo"* (the octopus).

United Fruit also had extraordinary access in Washington power circles. The Dulles brothers' law firm, Sullivan & Cromwell, had done legal work for the company. Officials in the White House and the State Department held substantial amounts of stock in United Fruit or had relatives who worked for the company. United Fruit also had two high-powered lobbyists working Congress on its behalf: Democrat Thomas "Tommy the Cork" Corcoran, a savvy former FDR adviser; and Robert La Follette Jr., a well-known Republican senator from Wisconsin whom McCarthy defeated in the 1946 primary.

Change—oh, so incremental—finally came to Guatemala on March 15, 1945. Juan José Arévalo, a large and imposing man who was the teachers' party candidate, was inaugurated as president that day. The charismatic Arévalo, who had no comprehensive socioeconomic program for his country beyond an airy call for "spiritual socialism," launched limited economic and democratic reforms. But they were enough to terrify Guatemala's upper class, which ended its honeymoon with the populist in a year. Arévalo, likewise, did not tamper with the privileges United Fruit enjoyed, but the company considered it a betrayal when he offered some legal protections for striking workers.

Washington, too, was shaken when Arévalo refused to show the customary deference of a docile neighbor toward the United States. Guatemala's unpardonable sins, in the eyes of the U.S. government, were the so-called persecution of benevolent American businesses and cozying up to Communism. Arévalo's lofty anti-Communist rhetoric did not impress U.S. officials like Wisner and his Latin American experts at the agency, who by August 1950 believed that the Communists had far more influence in Guatemalan affairs than its president admitted. But truth be told, Wisner and other senior CIA officials had only a "dim idea" of what was actually happening in Guatemala, according to one CIA history. "They saw events not in a Guatemala context, but as part of a global pattern of Communist activity."

During the six years of his presidency, Juan José Arévalo managed to survive more than twenty-five coup attempts plotted by Guatemala's wealthy landowners. On March 15, 1951, he turned over the reins of government to Jacobo Arbenz, a popular army officer who had won the presidential election with more than 60 percent of the vote. It was the first time in the hundred-thirty-year history of the Guatemalan republic that the presidency had been transferred peacefully and on time.

Arbenz became Latin America's youngest head of state at age thirty-seven. He was the son of a Swiss druggist who had emigrated to Guatemala and married a *ladina* from the country's Spanish-speaking white community. After his father died by suicide during an economic depression, Jacobo was enrolled in the national military academy, where he excelled as a student. Frustrated by a hidebound military structure that held back officers like him who were from a lower socioeconomic class, Arbenz gravitated toward reformist politics. He became an opposition leader and committed nationalist. Brilliant yet introverted and enigmatic, the handsome and fair-complexioned Arbenz, who had backed Arévalo throughout his administration, brought glamour to the presidency, with a beautiful and wealthy Salvadoran wife, María Cristina Vilanova Arbenz, who was always by his side at public appearances. A prominent American diagnostician, violating doctor-patient confidentiality, later told the CIA he had been summoned to Guatemala to investigate whether Arbenz had leukemia. The physician examined Arbenz and concluded that he was physically fit, just a hypochondriac. Another doctor who examined him reported that he suffered from neurasthenia, an ill-defined medical condition characterized by fatigue and irritability.

Intelligence reports the State Department prepared before Arbenz's assumption of the presidency described him as essentially a moderate and a definite improvement over Arévalo. The CIA likewise concluded that he was a smart and "cultured" leader. Washington hoped Arbenz would reverse what it considered Arévalo's extremist reform policies.

He would not. Arbenz pursued both industrial and agricultural reform with a passion beyond what Arévalo had displayed. Government should supervise Guatemala's social and economic modernization, the new president believed. He put together a wide-ranging legislative program to build factories, mine mineral resources, improve communications, take back from foreign control the country's transportation and electric power infrastructure, modernize banking, promote literacy in rural areas, and, most important, reform agriculture production. Among the initiatives he muscled through Guatemala's stunned congress was Decree 900, which expropriated 1.4 million acres of uncultivated land—407,000 of which had been owned by United Fruit—and redistributed it to some 100,000 poor families. Arbenz terrified the nation's vested interests—the landed elite, the Church, even most of the press opposed him—but the young leader, who brought hope to the poor, would not back down. A revolution began in Guatemala.

Was it a Communist revolution as Arbenz's political opponents in Guatemala charged and U.S. officials in Washington feared? Jacobo and his wife, María, had a complicated relationship with Communism. In the beginning they knew nothing about the ideology, so they read voraciously on the subject. And from what they read, the couple developed empathy toward the Soviet Union. Arbenz, however, did not believe a Communist state could soon be established in Guatemala; his country first had to go through "a capitalist stage," as one historian has termed it. Arbenz admired the undemanding and socially concerned members of Guatemala's tiny Communist party, the Partido Guatemalteco del Trabajo, or PGT, and he relied on the political skills of its Marxist leader, José Manuel Fortuny, a former radio broadcaster. But Arbenz, above all, was a nationalist, and as a nationalist, he accepted the backing of the Communists. After his election, he considered the PGT a legitimate part of his ruling coalition; it was a faction representing working people, as he saw it. The new president consulted Communist leaders regularly—but in terms of numbers, their party remained marginal. There was no evidence that Arbenz was under foreign Communist control or was a Communist "dupe."

As Guatemala's largest landowner when Arbenz assumed the presidency, United Fruit squealed the loudest—although it suffered little from the land it had to give back. In the United States, the company launched a large-scale political campaign to convince the White House, Congress, the CIA, the media, and even the Catholic Church that Arbenz was pro-Red and anti-American. Frank Wisner did not care a fig about United Fruit's business per se. He did not think that the company had to be returned to its old throne in Guatemala. Neither did other officers at the CIA. But what Wisner did care about was the spread of international Communism, and if United Fruit could be helpful in rolling back that spread, it was fine with him. A symbiotic relationship evolved between the company and the agency. United Fruit's Tommy Corcoran, for example, advised senior CIA officers on how to cultivate Democratic and Republican members of Congress, while United Fruit's publicizing the Communist menace in Guatemala carried water for the propaganda message the CIA wanted spread.

In the American business community, a few voices were raised to question whether United Fruit was the best ally for America's war against Guatemalan Communists. The president of Panocean Company Inc., a small U.S. lumber mill operating in Guatemala, warned the White House that United Fruit was clearly underhanded in its dealings with the local government and the Communists were scoring points because of this. The White House—and Wisner and Dulles, who received copies of the Panocean correspondence—ignored the warning.

Washington, instead, quickly considered its hopes dashed that Jacobo Arbenz would be just another opportunistic Latin leader willing to court the Americans. When just the opposite happened—when Arbenz strayed with his agrarian reforms, his willingness to work with local Communists, and his stubborn defiance of the United States—the Truman administration grew worried that the Central American nation was becoming a nightmare. The CIA's station chief in Guatemala City fanned the fire, cabling headquarters an exaggerated report that old-time Stalinists infested the country's government, gaining more influence in the regime by the day. The Truman administration "misjudged the new President," a later CIA analysis admitted. The reforms he planned actually "were modest, but he was determined to carry them out. Stiffening resistance from the United States and United Fruit led him to reassess his assumptions, adopt a more radical program, and find friends who shared his new opinion. . . . Ironically, the CIA supported the objectives of the Guatemalan reform." But irony was now lost on Wisner and his colleagues. They considered Guatemala a potential Soviet beachhead in the Western Hemisphere that threatened American security.

* * *

A little more than a year before Arbenz assumed the presidency, a thirty-six-year-old cashiered Guatemalan army colonel named Carlos Enrique Castillo Armas came to Wisner's attention. An officer in the CIA's Guatemala City station had transmitted a highly classified cable (kept secret from the rest of the U.S. embassy) about an interview one of his informants had had with Castillo Armas. The artillery colonel, who had been director of the army's military academy, was arrested in 1949 on a charge of illegally possessing arms, but he was later released on the personal orders of Colonel Arbenz, then the minister of defense under President Arévalo. As a civilian, Castillo Armas, who nursed a grudge against Arbenz for initially jailing him on a trumped-up sedition charge, began plotting an armed coup to overthrow the government. He claimed that he was disenchanted with Arévalo's and Arbenz's corruption of the military, and that a number of other active-duty officers and retirees shared his views.

Castillo Armas told the CIA source that he was in the "initial stages" of planning a military revolt. He said he had enough men in and out of the army to provide the manpower. He just needed weapons and was trying to obtain them from Nicaraguan dictator Anastasio Somoza and Dominican Republic strongman Rafael Trujillo. The colonel insisted that "the revolt he plans will be strictly Guatemalan and that no foreigners will participate in it," the CIA cable stated. "He said he also wanted to make it clear that he had no idea of establishing a military dictatorship in Guatemala." Professing to have "no personal ambition for power," Castillo Armas, who was in no hurry to launch his operation, claimed he would hold elections after a coup to establish "a true democracy." The CIA officer could vouch that from what other sources had told him, Castillo Armas appeared to be "well regarded." But it was an open question whether he could obtain the arms or keep his plot secret from the government's security service. The CIA assigned Castillo Armas the pseudonym "John H. Calligeris" and kept in touch with him.

He was not the ideal candidate to lead a coup, but there rarely is one. A small man with mestizo features and a thin Hitler-like mustache, Castillo Armas was the illegitimate son of a well-off landowner. Stubborn and closed-minded at times, he was an admirer of

Argentina's autocratic president, Juan Péron, but he seldom spoke about how he would govern Guatemala if he assumed power. Mixed reviews came to Wisner about Castillo Armas. Some CIA sources described him as an attractive candidate for Washington to back. An excellent cadet at the military academy and a highly capable officer with a reputation for bravery, he was fanatically ambitious and charismatic and a committed anti-Communist. Castillo Armas was also considered pro-American, having trained for eight months at the U.S. Army Command and General Staff School at Fort Leavenworth, Kansas. But Wisner also had reports that Castillo Armas was not popular with senior Guatemalan army officers, who would not be inclined to follow his lead. Some military colleagues thought he was an incompetent and weak leader.

Through the summer months of 1950, the CIA station in Guatemala City reported that Castillo Armas was continuing to perfect his plans for an armed revolt. The station officers could not tell Wisner how serious the ex-colonel was. Castillo Armas claimed he had military zones in the western part of the country supporting him, he planned to stage demonstrations in the capital, and he would have a force seize the National Palace and communications facilities. But numerous other coups had been plotted and discovered by Guatemalan security agents. Castillo Armas's biggest enemy, the CIA station believed, was a leak that would expose his operation. Meanwhile, Wisner's Latin America Division hatched a covert psychological warfare operation to combat the nation's Communists. A CIA agent posing as a student at an archaeological school in the country would secretly recruit Guatemalans to carry out the psywar campaign so it could not be traced to the U.S. government.

On November 5, 1950, while Jacobo Arbenz was in the last five days of his presidential campaign before the polls opened, Castillo Armas launched what amounted to a comically inept coup attempt. The colonel and seventy comrades attacked a military base in the capital, expecting it would spark a wider military revolt. But that did not happen. The coup attempt failed. Castillo Armas was severely wounded in a shoot-out with loyalist troops and carted off to a penitentiary. On June 11, 1951, he escaped from National Prison and fled to Colombia.

Several months later, United Fruit executives met with National Security Council staffers to offer their company facilities and employees in Guatemala to help with any anti-Communist operations the CIA might have been considering for that country. Dulles and Wisner responded that the agency was "very interested in this offer." By the beginning of 1952, CIA analysts viewed the Guatemala threat as "sufficiently grave," according to one agency history, to warrant a covert operation by Wisner's men to change its government. But the Truman administration "remained divided over whether Arbenz posed a threat dire enough to warrant such strong action." The CIA's Guatemala City station cabled headquarters that it continued to receive reports that a coup to oust Arbenz was "imminent," but the station could not tell if this was another move by Castillo Armas and, if so, whether he stood any chance of succeeding the second time around. Surely the Arbenz government "will take precautions," the CIA messaged the Pentagon.

Colonel Joseph Caldwell King, a West Point graduate, had lived in Latin America in the 1930s. He had built a condom factory in Brazil, ignoring business advice that it would be a poor investment in a Roman Catholic country. The factory prospered. King eventually sold it to Johnson & Johnson for shares in the medical company, which made him a wealthy man by the time he signed on with Wisner's operation as chief of his Western Hemisphere Division. Irreverent aides called J. C. King "Jesus Christ" behind his back because he was arrogant.

On January 11, 1952, King sent Wisner a dire memo warning that the Communists were gaining strength in Guatemala and that Arbenz was going along with them. At least three exile groups—one of them headed by Castillo Armas—were plotting against the Arbenz regime. Rumors also persisted that Arbenz "is ill with leukemia," King wrote. The Western Hemisphere chief was writing this inflated account off the top of his head. He saw no need to consult the CIA's best analytical minds on Latin America. Neither did Wisner. The covert action boys now overshadowed the analysts who might have offered conflicting or more nuanced views. Wisner sent King's memo to Dulles, who passed it along to Truman.

Three months later, Wisner and Beetle Smith (then the CIA director) ordered King to find out whether Guatemalan dissidents, with the help of dictators from neighboring countries, could topple Arbenz. King dispatched an operative to Guatemala City to search for organized opposition to the regime and determine if the CIA could buy support among the army, the Guardia Civil, and key government figures. The agent was sent on the scouting mission because Nicaragua's Somoza, previously considered a pariah by the U.S. government, had told Truman and State Department diplomats that if Washington provided the weapons, he, Trujillo, and Venezuela's government would "clean up Guatemala for you in no time." The Truman administration decided to give it a try.

The operation employing the dictators was code-named "PB-Fortune." "PB" was the agency digraph for Guatemala. Wisner decided to help Castillo Armas in his second coup attempt with weapons and sent a man to Tegucigalpa, Honduras, where Castillo Armas was holed up, to assess what kind of force he could lead and to give the cash-strapped colonel an initial $1,000 for expenses. The plan Castillo Armas had roughed out required $50,000 to arm six hundred fifty men, four hundred of whom would eventually attack key government facilities in the capital. The colonel envisioned his clandestine forces moving across the borders into Guatemala from Mexico, El Salvador, and Honduras, and from Amatique Bay at Puerto Barrios on the country's eastern coast. United Fruit offered its boats to help the CIA smuggle arms from the bay. A group of "professional gunmen" would also be employed to assassinate key Communists and to control labor unions, which were well armed. King estimated that Castillo Armas would need a total of $225,000.

Guatemalan sources warned the CIA station that they did not

believe the army could be bought off. The Arbenz government provided the officers with generous benefits. The army also had a well-organized espionage service with plenty of informants, which made soldiers distrust one another. Wisner was not deterred. He sent an officer to Guatemala with $50,000 to spend however he wanted on bribes; Wisner knew the money could go a long way. Guatemalan officials could be bought for small amounts. The CIA station began keeping close track of each Guatemalan Congress deputy to measure his susceptibility.

For a month beginning in July 1952, Dulles and Wisner were in a half dozen meetings to discuss the overthrow of Arbenz and the role the CIA might play in what was also called "Project A." The arsenal of arms to be shipped to Castillo Armas was "good stuff and in excellent condition," King told Wisner. Multiple two-hundred-pound boxes, with Spanish markings on the outside to disguise their contents as agricultural machinery, were packed with rifles, pistols, machine guns, ammunition, and radios. Along with the weapons came propaganda material prepared by a CIA group in Mexico City for the Guatemala station.

Another disquieting cable appeared in the traffic to CIA headquarters; it noted that rebel factions did not want Castillo Armas to be involved in a post-Arbenz military junta. King and his officers on the ground ignored the warning. They pronounced the Castillo Armas–led coup as "basically sound," according to one memo. The agency should stick with the colonel. His plot, which was scheduled to begin in September 1952, would succeed, the CIA station was convinced.

Truman in September formally authorized the CIA's backing of the coup. But Fortune lasted for barely a month. Dean Acheson, who had been kept largely in the dark about the CIA's project, learned about the full extent of the plot as a cargo ship loaded with arms for Castillo Armas sailed to Central America. Furious, the secretary of state stormed into Truman's office, convinced him that Fortune was a bad idea, and got him to redirect the ship to Panama,

where the weapons were off-loaded. Acheson, who had the full backing of his State Department, was justified in killing the project,
which was decidedly half-baked. The Guatemalan military had not
been subjected to months of CIA psychological warfare to soften it
up. The army's support for Arbenz was still firm. Moreover, Somoza
and his family had not been discreet about Nicaragua's and the
CIA's role in the planned coup. The agency's cover would soon have
been blown. Had Castillo Armas invaded, he would have been
trounced.

Smith gathered Dulles, Wisner, and other officers from the
Western Hemisphere Division into his headquarters office to deliver
the crushing news. "All plans for action" in Guatemala were canceled, he announced. Smith told the men he was "fully aware of the
dangers inherent in such a decision." But the State Department and
the Pentagon made policy, he reminded them. The CIA merely carried it out.

A CIA officer delivered the bad news to Castillo Armas: the
agency was forced to withdraw its arms support. The officer gave
the Guatemalan colonel a flimsy reason that was only somewhat
close to the truth. The CIA, the officer said, had been forced to call
off the weapons shipment after the U.S. State Department withdrew
the export permit, and State's decision came after Somoza and Trujillo made an "indiscreet approach to the Department," tipping off
its officials that the arms were being sent. To Castillo Armas, it was
all diplomatic double-talk. Any way he cut it, this was a huge setback
for his coup plot, the colonel realized. He would have "to rebuild
almost from the beginning," he told the CIA man.

The State Department and the Pentagon did make policy. But
Wisner's men were not shy about trying to trespass. They did so
now. After Acheson had Fortune shuttered, King asked Wisner for
$5,000 to continue a psywar campaign against Guatemala's Com-
munists, distributing handbills, for example, that accused them of
being part of a worldwide effort to harass Catholics. It would be
called the "Esplanade Project." Wisner and his aides continued to

have heated arguments with State Department diplomats blocking the arms the CIA wanted to deliver to Castillo Armas. Wisner argued, disingenuously, that the agency was merely carrying out the State Department's wishes. The diplomats weren't buying it. Wisner was going too far. The department refused to approve the arms export.

In the weeks after Fortune was canceled, events in Guatemala heightened U.S. anxieties. On December 11, the nation's Communist party opened its second congress, which senior Guatemalan officials attended. Eight days later Arbenz legalized the party so it could be a formal part of the regime's governing coalition.

PBFortune kept Castillo Armas in limbo from 1952 into 1953, putting the colonel on a $3,000-a-week retainer that allowed him to cling to a small force, with the CIA's arms held in the Panama Canal Zone in case the State Department freed them. Castillo Armas was given another code name, "Rufus." Wisner and King, meanwhile, continued to test how far they could proceed without State Department approval. And they waited for a new administration.

* * *

Eisenhower began his presidency largely passive on the subject of Guatemala, save for having a vague feeling, which was reinforced by his National Security Council, that all was not well in Latin America. Like his predecessor, Dean Acheson, John Foster Dulles knew little about Latin America beyond his exposure to the region through his law work. Foster, however, did believe that America's best friends in the Western Hemisphere were its dictators.

Not interested in Latin America except for making showy drop bys at hemispheric conferences, Foster left day-to-day U.S. foreign policy toward the region to Beetle Smith, his new undersecretary. Guatemala became the general's pet project. A devout Catholic, Smith milked Church contacts for information on developments in the country. Given its preoccupation with defending both its own wealth there and its grip over Guatemala's congregations, the Catholic Church was hardly a source of unbiased intelligence.

Smith kept the CIA's Guatemalan project afloat until the coup in Iran convinced Ike that covert operations could inexpensively topple unfriendly regimes. United Fruit's Tommy the Cork stepped up his lobbying to persuade the new president's inner circle that the Guatemalan government was an enemy worth the effort. As Ajax reached its denouement, J. C. King and an aide, Hans Tofte, began drafting a rough outline for a new operation to oust Jacobo Arbenz. A Danish refugee, Tofte had worked for Donovan resupplying Yugoslav partisans during World War II and afterward had joined Wisner's outfit, serving on his Psychological and Paramilitary Operations staff. A week after Mossadegh fell in Iran, Smith met with Wisner and King and gave them the okay to remount the Guatemala coup. The code name for the now high-priority operation was changed from PBFortune to PBSuccess (considered more morale building for the operatives).

Four powerful men—Allen Dulles and Frank Wisner at the CIA, Foster Dulles and Beetle Smith at the State Department—were now in place to pursue a covert remedy to the Guatemala problem, and to see that the project was not derailed a second time. The four knew relatively little about the enemy they now faced. The Guatemalan Communists, who had numbered in the inconsequential hundreds through the end of the 1940s, now totaled no more than five thousand, or about a tenth of a percent of the population. Most were ideologically illiterate, knowing next to nothing about Marxism-Leninism. The number of skilled activists who did was tiny, though they managed to exercise a somewhat outsized influence in parts of Arbenz's government. The CIA did its best to compile a list of several hundred influential Communists in the country, and its station had managed to plant a mole in the Communist PGT. But the agency could never be sure about the reliability of their mole.

American politicians voiced an unshakable conviction that the

Communist world was hegemonic and that Guatemala was on the brink of becoming a threatening arm of the Soviet empire. There is no "homegrown communism," the chairman of the Senate Foreign Relations Committee declared. All Communism "takes orders" from Moscow. Guatemalan Communist party leaders, however, had only limited contact with West European and East Bloc countries. They were not invited to Soviet party functions. They received little help from foreign Communist parties or front organizations. Only once did a Russian commercial attaché from Mexico attempt to develop ties with the country, and nothing came of the effort. Even Wisner's Western Hemisphere Division admitted it needed far more information to prove a Guatemalan connection with Moscow and international Communism. Alarmists claimed the Kremlin was pouring hundreds of agents into Latin America to serve as spies, saboteurs, and propagandists. But there was no hard evidence of Moscow doing that from thousands of miles away. The CIA compiled flight data on official Soviet Bloc travelers going to and from Guatemala. There were not a lot making the trip.

The Central American nation, however, showed a glaring disregard for optics, which only reinforced American prejudices. Some eighty Guatemalans demonstrated in front of the U.S. embassy in the capital on behalf of Julius and Ethel Rosenberg. After Stalin died, the Guatemalan Congress observed a minute of silence as tribute.

Dulles had been enthusiastic from the start about a coup in Guatemala. So had Wisner. Though he reserved the right to change his mind before H hour, Eisenhower came on board as well. He asked Dulles what the chances were for success in Guatemala. Forty percent, the CIA director replied. That was good enough for the president.

Wisner huddled with King on PBSuccess at the end of August 1953, repeating the marching orders Dulles had given him. The CIA would be "the marshal of the procession," Wisner declared. With Ajax in Iran over, Dulles had told him clearly "that Guatemala is now the number one priority of the Agency" and King would be responsible, Wisner said, "for getting the show on the road." Above all, they must do all they could to protect the security of the operation and shield the U.S. role in it.

Planning for PBSuccess was kept highly secret. Only Ike, the Dulles brothers, Wisner, and a few top CIA and administration officials knew its details. Smith ordered Wisner to deal directly with him or with just two other people in the State Department on the operation. King moved to curtail access to PBSuccess within the CIA, with top officials in the agency's intelligence-analysis directorate not knowing about it and a clandestine unit inside his Western Hemisphere Division roped off to carry it out.

Wisner believed the operation would be extremely difficult and require a "considerable period of buildup," he told Dulles. Ajax had taken less than six weeks to pull off in Iran. Wisner's planners warned that Success in Guatemala could take a year or more. The key for the coup was turning the Guatemalan army against Arbenz, Wisner's men knew. That would not be easy.

* * *

The CIA soon had an accurate count for the strength of Guatemala's army (some 6,200 poorly trained and equipped soldiers), of the country's Guardia Civil (nearly 3,000 men), and of the police force (about 3,500). Wisner's officers also had a list of all the military bases and weapons stockpiles, plus thumbnail sketches for top officers who might be important in a coup. The agency knew little so far about the capability of Arbenz's intelligence service.

Wisner's planners saw cracks in the military support Arbenz enjoyed. They might be exploited. King noticed that relatively few high-ranking officers were then well paid. The CIA station had picked up intelligence that Arbenz had to transfer some officers suspected of being disloyal to remote posts, which indicated to King that the army's complete loyalty to the regime could not be guaranteed and Arbenz was not all-powerful. Many Guatemalan officers had cordial diplomatic and social relations with American military attachés in the U.S. embassy. Wisner wanted to look for ways the attachés could provide "chicken feed" (small gifts or favors) to their Guatemalan colleagues.

One of the early items the clandestine service chief attended to was the American ambassador to Guatemala. Wisner, who had long been irritated by overcautious diplomats stymieing his psywar plans in Guatemala, thought the current U.S. ambassador there, Rudolf Schoenfeld, was too passive for the unfolding operation. The CIA arranged with the State Department to have Schoenfeld packed off to the embassy in Bogotá, Colombia. In his place, Wisner picked Jack Peurifoy, who did not speak Spanish but was a hard-liner he thought better suited for a covert operation. Peurifoy, who sported flashy shirts and a bright green Borsalino instead of a diplomat's pin-striped suits and homburg, was an admirer of Senator Joe McCarthy and proudly went by the nickname "pistol-packing Peurifoy" because he often carried a revolver in a shoulder holster. Peurifoy, who had worked well with the CIA when he was ambassador to Greece, was eager now to please Wisner in Guatemala, convinced before he even set foot in the country that Arbenz had to go.

The ambassador and his pistol arrived in Guatemala City on October 29 with few in the embassy knowing of his secret coup mission. The CIA station set up a classified communications channel so the new envoy and CIA headquarters in Washington could exchange messages without anyone else in the embassy seeing them. Peurifoy's cryptonym on the cables became "Jmblug." Among the secret reports he sent to Wisner was an account of the only serious conversation he ever had with Arbenz during his ambassadorship. "I am definitely convinced," Peurifoy wrote, "that if the [Guatemalan] President is not a communist, he will certainly do until one comes along."

Wisner and Dulles's next decision was to settle once and for all on whom the U.S. government should pick to lead the rebellion.

There were two other candidates besides the Truman administration's man, Carlos Enrique Castillo Armas: coffee grower and former interior minister Juan Córdova Cerna and retired general Miguel Ydígoras Fuentes. Córdova Cerna, however, had been diagnosed with throat cancer and Ydígoras Fuentes was judged too right-wing, prickly, and corrupt. That left Castillo Armas. He had no strong political beliefs beyond being a nationalist and an anti-Communist. Not a particularly bright man, Castillo Armas was determined by the Eisenhower administration and United Fruit to be easy to deal with and malleable.

A CIA officer met with Castillo Armas to inform him that the United States had anointed him to be Guatemala's liberator. It would be Castillo Armas's third try, this time with full U.S. backing. (The officer also put "Rufus" under strict orders to maintain the fiction that the U.S. government was not helping with the arms soon coming to him.) Castillo Armas and the agency immediately began plotting psychological warfare operations that would have to be mounted to prepare the country for the rebellion. The CIA was sold on the newfound science of advertising, which Madison Avenue used to market soap and which Wisner's men thought could turn off consumers to Arbenz and Communism. Radio stations would be scouted to capture and mount propaganda broadcasts. Six hundred thousand colored stickers and one million stamps would be distributed with the Castillo Armas slogan "God, Country, Liberty" printed on them. Thirty thousand anti-regime comic books would be published. No idea was considered too outlandish for scaring Guatemalans, their army, and the rest of Latin America into believing a Red wave was coming. Agents skilled in spreading rumors would be infiltrated into the country to spread discontent. Among many poison-pen letters to be circulated would be a document purporting to be a plan by the Communists to take over the Guatemalan government. Even cookies with Communist symbols stamped on them would be baked.

Wisner's men never completely trusted Castillo Armas, however.

He had no guerrilla warfare experience, they could see, and his organization definitely needed to tighten security so Communist agents couldn't infiltrate it. Agency officers on the ground also picked up rumors, circulated by the colonel's rivals in the opposition movement, that he was not genuinely opposed to the Arbenz regime and that he was, in fact, a cunning double agent Arbenz was secretly paying $1 million to undercut any planned revolution. The CIA could find no evidence to support that charge or another report that Castillo Armas was secretly on United Fruit's payroll. The company's local manager kept the CIA's station chief in Guatemala City posted on his movements in the country—or at least the station chief thought he was being kept fully informed.

Wisner sat down with his deputy, Richard Helms, and his Latin America chief, J. C. King, and began roughing out a coup plan for Guatemala, a draft of which they sent to Dulles on September 11. They could paint only in broad brushstrokes at that point, Wisner knew. It was impossible to anticipate or plan for every twist and turn the covert operation would take. Those were fluid undertakings. As he had been taught in his first week of OSS spy training, Wisner did not regard the unknown "as a particular drawback" since adjustments could be made as the operation unfolded, he wrote.

Wisner estimated that the cultivation phase of the operation would take no more than eight months and would cost $3 million. The ground for the coup had to be carefully tilled by many hands, he believed. With the CIA leading a government-wide operation, PBSuccess relied on the State and Defense Departments "to isolate Guatemala diplomatically, militarily, and economically," according to one agency history.

Officers in the CIA's Guatemala City station probed for any weaknesses they could find and exploit in the Arbenz regime's finances, such as inflation indicators, difficulties in paying government salaries, and unreported movements of gold. From their findings, Wisner crafted a broadscale economic war to throttle Guatemala's economy. He decided to pressure suppliers to interrupt or slow down oil shipments to the country and at the same time proposed sabotage attacks against fuel storage facilities and pipelines. King secretly consulted top business executives on economic moves that could be made and their effects, such as choking off exports of newsprint and ink to Guatemala to stifle the press, and cutting back U.S. imports from the hundred million pounds of coffee beans Guatemala produced. (The businessmen advised that halting newsprint, ink, and the coffee trade wasn't feasible.) After discovering that Arbenz's finance officials had managed to secretly transfer almost $5 million from the U.S. to Switzerland, Wisner moved to have New York banks block transactions by Guatemalan government accounts.

The Guatemalan army remained key for the revolt, Wisner, Helms, and King decided, and Guatemala City (the nation's capital) was the most important target. Preparations there "for subversion and defection of Army leaders, as well as government officials and political personalities, are in progress," the three men wrote Dulles. The actual armed force that the CIA could field at the moment consisted of only about three hundred rebels Castillo Armas had camped in the jungles of Honduras. The plan Rufus had formulated to use them in a coup during the Truman administration was now "substantially obsolete," Wisner told Dulles, and it needed to be "radically readjusted to meet a more adverse situation." The arms cache in Panama now had to be quickly sent to Castillo Armas's Honduran base to help him train his men. Military aid would also have to be secretly provided to Nicaragua, Honduras, and El Salvador to keep them amenable to basing Castillo Armas's guerrillas on their soil. Washington's public criticism of the Arbenz government would have to be stepped up, along with moves to discredit it in international forums like the Organization of American States.

The CIA, at the moment, had only twenty-five officers working in embassies or in the field in Guatemala, Honduras, and Panama—by Wisner's count, a "negligible" number, which he began expanding. More secret agents operating under "non-official cover" (that is, not posing as embassy employees enjoying diplomatic immunity if they were caught) would be inserted, Wisner decided. King created the "K-Program," which, for example, sent a CIA agent code-named "Page" to Guatemala for ninety days to pose as a wealthy American businessman with a wad of cash to encourage defections from the Arbenz government and from trade unions. Castillo Armas also contributed three of his spies to roam Guatemala and penetrate the military. Wisner's field officers called them "Semantic," "Secant," and "Sequin."

The American embassy in Guatemala City was a six-story building on the corner of busy Eighth Avenue and Twelfth Street near the Guardia Civil headquarters, the National Palace, and the Central Plaza. The "Terrace" (one of the building's cryptonyms) had become a veritable fortress: difficult to storm, with padlocked, heavy steel-grilled doors at all entrances to the walled compound and its building; a large contingent of armed Marines; and enough food and water stockpiled to sustain the staff for three or more weeks (the time the CIA station estimated for a revolt to take place).

The CIA station's offices, which accommodated fifteen intelligence operatives and secretaries, were housed on the guarded fourth floor next to the ambassador's suite. The station had set up procedures it hoped would prevent exposure, such as Guatemalan agents calling in to one of its fourth-floor phones never giving their real names over the line, meetings with snitches always held away from the embassy, and CIA officers always on the watch for Guatemalan agents trailing them when they left the compound. The agency found that officers who had brought their wives with them actually attracted less attention when the couples strolled the streets. One paranoid officer, however, fearing a government security detail was about to close in on him, chewed up and swallowed a sensitive document during a walk.

Dulles approved Wisner's September 11 draft plan four days later. On his own, Wisner checked with the White House to see if anything approving his draft had been put in writing. Nothing had.

Green lights from higher-ups would now be mostly verbal to keep any paper trail from leaking. The only tweak Dulles asked for was the setting up of an international foundation devoted to freeing Guatemala from Communism. It would be a front group for distributing "black" propaganda throughout Latin America. The foundation faced the daunting task of changing the minds of many Central Americans, who rightly worried that dictators like Somoza and Trujillo were bigger problems for the region than Arbenz. Whiting Willauer had been made ambassador to Honduras and Thomas Whelan the top envoy for Nicaragua—the CIA judged both to be aggressive team players.

Three days later, on September 18, Dulles formally approved $3 million for PBSuccess and arranged for a secret money draft from the Bureau of the Budget. The first $50,000 check was cut immediately. *Move quickly*, the CIA director ordered his clandestine service chief. All Dulles wanted now were periodic progress reports. Wisner saluted and conveyed the sense of urgency to his operatives.

Chapter 21

OPERATION SUCCESS

JUST BEFORE CHRISTMAS 1953, the CIA set up its operational headquarters for PBSuccess at Opa-Locka, Florida, a sleepy little town in northern Miami-Dade County, where a U.S. Navy intelligence arm worked out of a largely abandoned Marine air base, not doing much of anything. The base's admiral was curious why the CIA wanted to take over a vacant operations building, a communications station, and three sets of quarters on an isolated part of the installation for the next six to eight months. King's representative would put nothing on paper and told him only that the CIA was fulfilling a mission from the National Security Council that the State Department and the Pentagon deemed "high priority." If anybody asked, the admiral was to say only that a Defense Department task force had set up a field station on the base for scientists and technicians doing unspecified research.

Outside the headquarters building, eight post office boxes were set up to receive propaganda material Washington mailed to Opa-Locka. New locks were put on the only entrance door, which opened up to a locked reception room where two-way mirrors had been installed. In the operations room, maps and complex charts were plastered on a forty-foot wall to track the project's many moving pieces. A dozen officers manned the Opa-Locka facility, which was given the code name "Lincoln." It became the command center for the more than a hundred case officers and support personnel beginning work on PBSuccess in Guatemala and other Central American countries. Wisner and Dulles also briefed Hoover on Lincoln, assuring him they were not treading on his turf and spying on Americans. They wanted no trouble from the FBI director, and he never gave them any.

A bureaucratic tangle over who ran the covert operation had to be unsnarled. J. C. King had overseen PBSuccess from its inception, but by late fall, Wisner had become disenchanted with the abrasive officer's leadership. "Jesus Christ" was pushed aside. Wisner then took the unprecedented step of assuming control over the entire program and running it himself. He tried to play down the import of what he was doing, but it was a major move on his part. The clandestine service chief, who was responsible for CIA operations around the world, was now conferring with agency officials practically every other day of the week on the covert program for one small Central American nation. Wisner involved himself in every aspect of PBSuccess's planning and implementation, keeping close tabs on its progress and meeting the Dulles brothers regularly to monitor their pulses. Wisner left Helms, who was privately skeptical about PBSuccess, to run the rest of the plans directorate's initiatives globally while he plunged into the Guatemala coup.

To run day-to-day operations at Opa-Locka, Wisner had Allen Dulles bring in Al Haney, a six-foot, ruggedly handsome former Army colonel who had been station chief in Seoul and who was now eager to take field command of what he could see was the CIA's hottest operation. Wisner, however, left King in control of the Western Hemisphere Division, where the jilted chief kept up a civil war with Haney over control of PBSuccess. It was a bureaucratic stew Wisner could blame only himself for mixing. Moreover, from the minute he hired him, Wisner had qualms about the hard-charging "Brainy

Haney," as he was not too affectionately called by others. Suspicious that the former Seoul station chief would stray from orders, Wisner dispatched Tracy Barnes, his psychological and paramilitary warfare chief, to Opa-Locka to keep watch on Haney and to referee squabbles King had with him. Finally, Richard Bissell, who had earlier slipped Marshall Plan funds to Wisner and whom Dulles had recruited as a special assistant, was put in charge of overseeing PBSuccess administration and logistics, chores that did not interest Dulles or Wisner.

Using the code name "Harold S. Whiting" in his cables, Wisner fired off hundreds of orders to Opa-Locka and the CIA station in Guatemala City. He had instructions for selecting the twenty-eight most dangerous Communists as "targets for character assassination," monitoring Communist activities in bordering El Salvador, and assembling weapons like rifles, grenades, napalm, and piano wire. No detail was too small. The rocks hollowed out for messages at dead drops should be volcanic pieces indigenous to the countryside. The challenge for an agent determining the bona fides of another agent he was meeting should be: "Are you a friend of Tommy Tompkins?" The response from the other agent should be: "An old bragging and lying acquaintance."

Just because Eisenhower had ordered a covert operation did not mean the national security bureaucracy would jump up and carry it out. Wisner faced a number of interagency snarls he had to untangle. He asked for military aid to be sent to Nicaragua, Honduras, and El Salvador to reward their cooperation with PBSuccess. He wanted Somoza, in particular, to pad his arms request so part of the U.S. shipment could be secretly skimmed off and delivered to Castillo Armas in Honduras. But the Pentagon's Joint Chiefs, who had not been briefed on the covert operation, questioned why those shipments were needed, and balked at sending them. The Defense Department also wanted to remove their attachés from the Guatemalan embassy, believing they were no longer needed there since the Pentagon had been ordered to cut off military-to-military dealings with Guatemala. Those officers, however, could be valuable in gleaning intelligence from and planting disinformation with their old Guatemalan contacts, Wisner believed. He convinced Beetle Smith to lobby his military contacts to keep the attachés there. The Army and the Air Force agreed to retain their missions at the embassy—although the Air Force resisted having its attachés engage in spy work.

During the first two weeks of February 1954, Wisner took leave to drive to his home in Laurel and then on to Florida. It was a much-needed respite from his crushing workload in Washington. Most Saturdays and Sundays he had been chained at his desk, laboring over PBSuccess, with no time to tend to chores on the farm. Dulles had become relentless in his prodding Wisner to move quickly on the operation, repeating in meeting after meeting in Washington and during his occasional trips to Opa-Locka how high a priority this mission was. "I am under pressure by others to get on with this!" the harried CIA director scolded Wisner.

Dulles wanted the CIA's best brains put on PBSuccess to make sure it succeeded. Tofte assured Wisner that "well-qualified, enthusiastic people were being assigned to the team." To bring the agency's top talent to bear, Wisner finally decided to cut more people in on the secret operation, which had always made him nervous when he had had to do so in the past. In his office safe, he kept two lists. The first one was of officers like himself, Dulles, Helms, and Deputy CIA Director Charles Cabell, who had complete knowledge of PBSuccess. The second list was of those who were given only the information they needed to know in order to do their PBSuccess jobs—although Wisner realized the need-to-know folks were probably smart enough to guess the full extent of what was happening.

Widening the circle inevitably brought in criticism of the plan Wisner was devising. A CIA officer just read in on the operation in late January worried in a memo to King about the blowback for the U.S. government if its involvement in the coup were exposed, which the officer feared was possible. Security was poor on Castillo

Armas's end of the project; far too many people in the region knew about the plot. Wisner ignored the pessimists.

He ignored the optimists as well. He had been told that gossips in Washington's high government circles speculated that the anti-Arbenz political climate in Guatemala was such that a spontaneous revolt might overtake PBSuccess or that the operation the CIA planned to launch might be much easier to carry out than originally suspected. That kind of loose talk should be squelched, Wisner said. PBSuccess would be a difficult operation. He became leery when good news from the project seemed too good. When a Guatemalan source, code-named "Essence," passed along an overly rosy report, Wisner snapped: "Is he off his rocker, or is there some substance to his statements? If even 50% of what he says is true—then matters are twice as far advanced (favorably) as I have ever heard."

* * *

Castillo Armas's rebels trained on firing ranges and in rudimentary combat maneuvers at camps in Honduras and Nicaragua, with some diverted secretly to Opa-Locka for specialized instruction. Honduras, where Castillo Armas claimed to have a hundred men, was the most important site because it would be the launching pad for his invasion. Honduran president Juan Manuel Gálvez wanted Arbenz ousted, but fear that Castillo Armas might fail had made Gálvez and his senior advisers weak-kneed. Whiting Willauer, a veteran of anti-Communist activity in Asia, arrived just in time to bully Gálvez into showing more resolve.

Two CIA contractors with military experience were dispatched to the Honduran camp to begin training guerrilla combat leaders on the first day of 1954. Another CIA officer, posing as an American advertising consultant, was sent to Tegucigalpa, where Castillo Armas and a group of his followers had established their headquarters in a two-story house downtown. The Guatemalan colonel also had several safe houses and a small farm outside the city. The CIA officer and those who followed him set themselves up in one of the safe houses with a radio for communicating back to Opa-Locka. In addition to advising Castillo Armas, the CIA officers scouted out the security measures at the Guatemalan embassy in Tegucigalpa in case they had to break into the compound to steal documents.

The CIA had no trouble keeping the eager-to-please Somoza in the program. The Nicaraguan dictator let the agency use his plantation at El Tamarindo, where a hundred fifty men were trained in sabotage and demolitions, and the volcanic island of Momotombito in Lake Managua, where another hundred fifty were instructed in firing weapons. About a dozen Guatemalan pilots trained for Castillo Armas's small air force at an abandoned airstrip near Puerto Cabezas on the Caribbean coast, and a handful of radiomen received instruction on broadcasting propaganda near the capital Managua.

There was one other training operation, and Wisner's officers went to great lengths to keep it distant from the United States government.

* * *

The first week in January 1954, a CIA paramilitary officer pretending to be a soldier of fortune and small-time arms dealer boarded a LANICA Airlines flight that was headed from Miami to Managua. His mission was to set up a two-month commando-training program for the best prospective fighters the agency could find among the mercenaries and Guatemalan expats in the Nicaraguan capital. Those men would be "the pick of the crop," a secret memo told him.

Stripped of all identifying documents except for his American passport, the CIA officer was ordered to have no contact with any U.S. officials in Nicaragua. After arriving in Managua, he was to check into the designated hotel. A Nicaraguan would knock on the door to his room, identify himself only as "a friend of Pablo's," and take him to the training camp. Among the thirty guerrillas the CIA man was to instruct, the agency wanted two of them to have eight hours of training as "assassination specialists who in turn will instruct assassinations teams at a separate site for special assassination jobs," the memo ordered.

The hit men, skilled in picking off targets using knives, drugs, and pistols and rifles with silencers, would be designated "K Team personnel." PBSuccess planners envisioned that fifteen days before the start of the coup, the K Team leaders would receive their assassination instructions. Wisner's directorate considered targeted killings to be "an extreme measure," as one agency training document put it. Preferably any hit should have been carried out by a foreign team instead of an American unit. A U.S. official should never have to put his name on a piece of paper that actually ordered an execution.

For more than two years, however, Wisner's officers had been drawing up lists of hostile government officials, Guatemalan Communist party members, and Communist sympathizers whom the rebels should jail or kill before or after a coup. The "Category I" persons, who would be "disposed of through executive action" (the agency's sterile jargon for "murder"), totaled fifty-eight by September 1952. Many more were added to the list over the next eighteen months. Wisner's station chief in Guatemala City at one point cabled Washington that he had "professional gunmen" he could hire in the capital who could "eliminate some of the best commies . . . for $2,000 a head." Trujillo offered Castillo Armas his trained pistoleros to knock off up to twenty government leaders under Arbenz in exchange for the colonel's rebels killing four Dominican political opponents exiled in Guatemala. Castillo Armas said he would add the four to the K Team's hit list the day the coup was launched.

Wisner drew the line at using amateurs for executive action. He balked at a Lincoln station plan to enlist campesinos in the killing of Guardia Civil members. This could result in "large-scale bloodletting," he cabled Opa-Locka, and could make Castillo Armas's rebels look like terrorists.

The CIA had evidence that the other side was planning assassinations—and already had blood on its hands. Agency officers in the field received numerous reports from their sources that Guatemalan government assassins were infiltrating into Honduras to kill Castillo Armas and kidnap his wife. An alert was sent out to all the CIA stations in Latin America to be on the lookout for Guatemalan hit teams targeting political refugees who had fled the country. Rattled by the agency's psywar, Arbenz's beleaguered government in early June 1954 suspended constitutional guarantees, imposed media censorship, and began waves of arrests. Several hundred suspects were detained, prisoners were tortured, and at least seventy-five were executed, prompting outrage among American reporters and congressmen. Communist leaders in Guatemala City didn't help the regime's image any when they publicly warned that anti-Communists would be beheaded if rebels attacked.

Ultimately the threat of assassinations became more a propaganda weapon than a real one. For all the paperwork the CIA produced and all the planning and training that it did, there was no record of the agency ever conducting any assassinations in Guatemala. No Arbenz officials or Guatemalan Communists were killed.

* * *

Pilots from Civil Air Transport, the CIA's air arm, were enlisted to fly tons of weapons and supplies from stockpiles in a New York City warehouse and the Panama Canal Zone to Castillo Armas's camps in Honduras and Nicaragua. The cargo was described on bills of lading as mining equipment. The aviators were paid handsomely, they wore nothing that would identify them as being from the United States, and their C-47 transport planes were stripped of all American markings. Believing that airpower was the key to shocking Arbenz, Tracy Barnes set out to create a private air force of thirty war-surplus fighter planes and bombers that Castillo Armas's pilots could fly from Honduras, Nicaragua, and Panama to control the skies and attack Guatemalan targets.

The "Liberation Air Force," as it came to be called, was tiny.

Fortunately, it faced an equally weak Guatemalan government air force. An air attaché in the U.S. embassy estimated that Arbenz's air force had thirty-eight planes, only fourteen of which were combat-worthy, and forty-six pilots, most of whom were unreliable and had no desire to fight. Several had already sought asylum in foreign embassies and the remaining few were grounded to prevent any more from deserting with their aircraft. Barnes and the other air strategists at Opa-Locka still worried that Arbenz had enough airpower to intercept rebel bombers flying over Guatemala City, to spot Castillo Armas's base camps in Honduras, and to drop bombs that might wipe them out. The Lincoln station compiled a long and detailed list of Guatemalan rail facilities, radio broadcast stations, airfields, and utilities the Liberation Air Force could attack with bombs fashioned from blocks of TNT surrounded by concussion grenades. Worried about collateral damage, Dulles ordered the Lincoln station to scale back the ordnance it wanted to dump on the capital. Anything dropped from the air, a CIA cable noted, often ended up hitting "the nearest church, hospital or expectant mother."

* * *

For five months, Arbenz and Wisner moved diplomatic initiatives and counter-initiatives like pieces on a chessboard. United Fruit was asked to put up $100,000 for delegates to attend a CIA-backed First Great Continental Anti-Communist Congress in Mexico City. The Guatemalan government released a white paper alleging a vast international conspiracy was planned to undercut the incumbent regime—a charge that was largely true. Wisner publicized former Belgian king Leopold III's not making Guatemala one of his stops during a Caribbean tour as an intentional omission because the country was Communist controlled.

The Lincoln station, meanwhile, asked its officers in Guatemala City to send Opa-Locka the addresses of all of Arbenz's official and private residences, along with the percentage of time he spent in each of them. Lincoln asked for diagrams of every house and hide-away plus detailed descriptions of their security and communications systems. The agency wanted to see if there was a pattern to Arbenz's movements so it could predict where he would be at any time. That would be important intelligence during Guatemala's rainy season in late spring and early summer when Castillo Armas was thinking about launching his coup with an attack on nine key military and civilian targets in the country.

* * *

For PBSuccess to succeed, Wisner also needed the U.S. Congress and the American media to cooperate. Capitol Hill proved to be no problem. If anything, representatives and senators were more forward leaning than Eisenhower and demanded that he do everything short of war to stop what they feared would be a Soviet takeover of Guatemala. Dulles quietly approached key committee chairmen and assured them that Arbenz was receiving the administration's close attention. He said he could not go into detail because the matter was "extremely delicate." Many in Congress took the wink and nod as a signal that the CIA was involved in Guatemala in some way, which they appreciated.

For the most part, the CIA got the help it needed from the American media. Most of the reporters and editors accepted what the U.S. government fed them without questioning it. Like Congress, the press grew alarmed that Guatemala was becoming a Soviet puppet. A dark view of the Arbenz government interested American readers. *Time* magazine rewrote correspondents' files from the region so their stories would be more hard-line. The *Washington Post* ran anti-Arbenz editorials. Wisner's officers fed anti-Communist leads to *Look* magazine and in the region distributed stills from an NBC documentary on Communist infiltration of the Guatemalan government. Even the cantankerous Walter Winchell broadcast on the Red menace in Central America. So hostile was the press toward Arbenz, United Fruit's public relations flacks kept a light touch on U.S. coverage. American reporters did the banana company's work for it. There were hints in some news stories of an American role in Guatemala's opposition movement. But James Reston, one of those who suggested it, did not criticize the CIA or Dulles if they were involved.

Not every journalist cooperated. A handful of British newsmen were hostile to U.S. policy toward Guatemala. Wisner convinced the State Department to complain to Churchill. But Wisner's biggest headache was in the American media with Sydney Gruson of the *New York Times*. Born in Dublin and reared in Toronto, the highly respected foreign correspondent had written objective stories on Arbenz that got him expelled from the country in November 1953. One of Gruson's pieces had even been favorable toward United Fruit. But Gruson had developed good contacts in the Guatemalan government, and he used them to be admitted back into the country. Beginning in 1954, the *Times* reporter started filing reports that strayed from the CIA line and questioned U.S. policy toward Guatemala. Agency officers in Guatemala, Opa-Locka, and Mexico City accused him of being a leftist whose articles were "highly detrimental [to] our cause," as one cable complained. Stewart Alsop joined in the smear, whispering into Wisner's ear that he had known Gruson for many years and that the reporter had always been a distinct "fellow wanderer."

Wisner heartily agreed. He suspected that Gruson and his wife, Flora Lewis, who was also a foreign correspondent, were Soviet agents. CIA officers began feeding stories to friendly publications, such as *Time* magazine, to counter the articles Gruson wrote that they claimed were Communist-inspired. Wisner also launched a full-scale CIA investigation of the couple. All of Gruson's stories were carefully analyzed to uncover a pro- or anti-American pattern to his reporting. The investigators concluded that Gruson's stories "are definitely unfriendly to U.S. policy."

Dulles finally played hardball. Practically accusing Gruson of being a Communist dupe, the CIA director talked *New York Times* publisher Arthur Hays Sulzberger into removing the reporter from the Guatemala beat.

* * *

Wisner soon found that security was the most vexing problem with this project. Castillo Armas had a loosely bound intelligence service. Made up mainly of snitches passing him tips, it could hardly be called a service. He had no counterintelligence capability to ferret out hostile spies in his organization. The colonel's secret operation in Honduras leaked like a sieve. The Lincoln station in Opa-Locka cabled Wisner reports of one security breach alert after another that forced its officers to move radios in the Honduran jungle, destroy code pads they feared had been compromised in one instance, and dump communications equipment in a lake in another. By February, Wisner's men at Opa-Locka worried that Arbenz's agents had thoroughly penetrated PBSuccess. The Guatemalan government, in fact, had already exposed a number of the CIA's operational details and published them in the nation's newspapers.

There was likely a high-level leak in Castillo Armas's Honduras organization. A CIA memo declared, "We must find it." Headquarters in Washington rushed a polygraph team to Central America to "flutter" Castillo Armas and key members of his staff. Castillo Armas passed his test. But five senior aides were caught lying to the examiners and suspected of working for Arbenz. Polygraph testing in Nicaragua uncovered two more Guatemalan government agents. All seven were immediately cut off from operations. But even the men the polygraphs cleared could be problems in the future if they were bribed with enough money to talk, Wisner's officers feared. Suspicious cases continued to turn up, like what seemed to be an agitator at one of the Nicaraguan camps who tried to sow discord among other trainees. He was whisked off to Honduras. Castillo Armas also had a big mouth, and he bragged to others about the help the United States was giving him.

The security breaches weren't confined to the rebel bands. There were embarrassing slipups in Wisner's organization. Tracy Barnes was sloppy with security, which irritated Wisner. One CIA officer left five cables dealing with PBSuccess unattended in his Washington hotel room—"an unpardonable" lapse in judgment, an agency investigation concluded. Another officer left in his Guatemalan apartment six sensitive cables with sources-and-methods information and a list that identified the real names behind different cryptonyms. The agency sent the officer home for interrogation and had to assume that this intelligence was in the hands of the Guatemalan government.

A suspicious person was spotted with his ear pressed to the keyhole of the door to one of the Lincoln station's safe houses on the Opa-Locka base. It was clear to Lincoln's security officer that Opa-Locka was under "heavy surveillance" from some Latin American intelligence service. He couldn't tell which one. CIA technicians in the Guatemala City embassy discovered that one of the agency's phone lines had been tapped. The technicians decided to leave the tap as it was so the line could be used to feed Guatemalan intelligence disinformation. Wisner told his PBSuccess staff he feared hostile agents had the U.S. embassies in Managua and Tegucigalpa under "technical surveillance."

Wisner's aides also suspected that Whiting Willauer, the U.S. ambassador in Tegucigalpa, might have revealed to Honduras's president and his senior aides too much about American involvement in the Guatemalan coup plans. Willauer adamantly denied doing so, but Wisner fired off to the envoy a pointed cable ordering him to keep quiet. Wisner sent a CIA secretary to the Tegucigalpa embassy to help with dictation and typing—and to keep an eye on her boss. He also began carefully reading all the messages Willauer was cabling to the agency in Washington, worried that the ambassador was under too much pressure.

The CIA concluded that Arbenz did not have any documents clearly showing that Washington had a covert operation to overthrow his government. But the agency believed he likely did have enough intelligence to make him suspicious that the U.S. was involved in something nefarious, and his spies were no doubt working hard to find solid proof. Leaders in many Latin American countries were already satisfied that the gringos were involved in a coup effort, and some were pleased rather than alarmed. Concluded a secret CIA report: "We have been, are now and will continue to be vulnerable to being caught in the act."

The Lincoln station ordered officers in the Guatemala City station to plumb their sources on how much Arbenz knew about PB-Success and what moves he was considering "to counteract opposition plans." Contingency plans had to be made if the operation was blown. Wisner drafted a cover-and-deception directive with forged documents to be leaked, which would hide U.S. involvement by implicating other countries, such as the Dominican Republic, Venezuela, and Argentina. That false narrative shouldn't have been too hard to sell, Wisner calculated. Arbenz had hostile neighbors.

* * *

On April 28, 1954, Wisner, Barnes, and Bissell gathered with nine Lincoln officers in a makeshift war room that had been fashioned in their Opa-Locka headquarters. Wisner meant the meeting to be something of a pep talk. He had received a report that operatives at the Lincoln station were "showing signs of overwork and strain." Wisner was proud of the energy and enthusiasm the Lincoln officers had shown, but he worried that "they were driving themselves so hard they could crack up if they continue at their present forced pace." Morale was also low in the harried CIA station in Guatemala City, where officers faced increased government police activity that made their operations more difficult to carry out. Large egos were at play there and Wisner knew he had to placate them. Sensing some unease in the ranks over the controversial work they were doing, he sent all the members of the PBSuccess team a reassuring message that their service in that covert operation would not jeopardize their careers or future promotions in the CIA.

Wisner was the first to speak at the April 28 meeting. "We have the full green light and the go-ahead," he told the assembled CIA men. Guerrilla tactics, propaganda, air cover . . . it all had the okay of headquarters, Wisner said, adding that he knew the officers in the field would need "a sufficient degree of flexibility in their approach to this thing." All covert work involved some operating on the fly. That said, he wanted every person in the room to do all they could to minimize the chance of the coup "being pinned on the U.S." If that proved impossible, Wisner hoped that in the coup's aftermath, there would be so much confusion that "it can't be sorted out" who was responsible for what.

Dulles, as was always the case with the CIA director, had the final say on whether or not the agency launched the revolt. "The boss has to be satisfied that we have what it takes" and that the CIA officers and the Guatemalan guerrillas in the field were ready and strong enough to carry out PBSuccess, Wisner said. Dulles didn't care about whether what the men in that war room were doing was right from a foreign policy perspective, Wisner said. Others in the administration considered those kinds of geopolitical questions. Allen Dulles was "interested only in the success of the operation." At that moment there was no CIA mission as important as that one, Wisner told the officers, "and no operation on which the reputation of the agency is more at stake."

Wisner said it appeared to him that the coup would be ready for launching "during the month of June." The Lincoln station officers agreed. They were already circulating rumors in the Guatemalan countryside that Arbenz and his top lieutenants were transferring their private funds to Switzerland and readying a plane to fly them to another country. Wisner was bursting with ideas and orders at the Opa-Locka meeting. In case Arbenz did, in fact, plan an escape, Wisner wanted airports seized and aircraft the president might use sabotaged. He asked the Lincoln station officers to prepare two maps he could post on a wall in his Washington office: one of Guatemala and the surrounding countries; the other depicting in detail the nation's road-and-rail network, its telephone lines, and the location of its nine garrison towns.

Bissell was struck by the show of enthusiasm Wisner put on during their Opa-Locka meeting. The clandestine service chief, as everyone knew, was a disciple of bold covert action, but Bissell had been perplexed by what seemed to him to be Wisner's continuous unease with PBSuccess in the previous months. He had constantly second-guessed his field commanders and had been excessively worried, or so it seemed to Bissell, about failure. Bissell later thought Wisner's agitation over Guatemala might have signaled the beginning of his mania, which was bound to surface under stress. But Wisner had good reason to be edgy. He had always been wary of big covert operations, and PBSuccess had evolved into a huge one. He knew that State Department officials, including Foster Dulles, were inclined to scuttle the CIA project if a diplomatic solution could be found for Guatemala. Also, with all the security breaches, operational failure and severe embarrassment for the United States were distinct possibilities that kept him up at night.

* * *

The rumormongering that Wisner was briefed on at his Opa-Locka conference was just a small part of a much larger bare-knuckle campaign he now wanted stepped up to prepare Guatemala for the coup. The agency found a way to blame Guatemalan-linked Communism for the four Puerto Rican nationalists who shot thirty rounds onto the House of Representatives floor in 1954. The number "32" was painted on public walls to signify Article 32 of the Guatemalan constitution, which prohibited international political parties, like those for the Communists, from operating in the country. Stickers reading, "A Communist lives here," were slapped on doors. Fake death notices for Arbenz and his top advisers were published in newspapers. For a government-sponsored May 1 parade, CIA agents slipped "stench vials" into the cars of high-ranking officials being driven in the event.

Gauging the effect of the propaganda campaign was difficult for the CIA station in Guatemala City. It published a weekly "Psychological Barometer," which reported "a general feeling of hopelessness" among the public, but the survey, which was compiled by CIA officers after they talked to the few people they could buttonhole outside the embassy, was unscientific. The station could see more clearly that the country's upper class was beginning to desert Arbenz. There were also signs that the loyalty of the army had been faltering for months. An operation code-named "Kugown" hoped to nurse that disaffection, as did a purported government phone bank used to call the servants of senior officers and demand that they pay exorbitant union fees to work in the homes.

The Arbenz government tried mudslinging of its own, accusing the United States of employing bacteriological warfare against the country. The regime's effort was puny compared to the propaganda machine Wisner had cranked up.

To oversee the Lincoln station's propaganda program, Barnes had recruited the flamboyant E. Howard Hunt, who had established the CIA's station in Mexico City, where he had overseen propaganda by the agency's Guatemalan Anti-Communist Committee. Envisioning the Lincoln station's psywar effort as something akin to a terror campaign to intimidate Arbenz and his troops, Hunt had as his deputy David Atlee Phillips, a Spanish-speaking former actor from the CIA station in Santiago, Chile. On a hillside near Managua, Phillips supervised a clandestine radio station code-named Sherwood that beginning on May 1 beamed daily propaganda programs into Guatemala from seven o'clock in the morning until ten p.m. at night.

Sherwood was a risky operation for Wisner, who constantly worried that Guatemalan government agents with radio-direction-finding equipment would locate the facility and blow the CIA's cover. No way could the Eisenhower administration then plausibly deny involvement in the coup.

With its recordings flown in from Opa-Locka, La Voz de la Liberación combined popular music with bawdy jokes and antigovernment propaganda. The only rules it followed were that the shows would not tread too close to official U.S. positions, the jokes could not be too off-color, threats of an American invasion would not be made, and the theme hammered away at constantly would be "work, bread and country." If actual news items were not available, fake news could be substituted. The Lincoln station asked the CIA station in Guatemala City to supply it with a fifteen-minute recording of Arbenz's voice, which could be spliced and inserted into broadcasts. For another show, CIA officers used an unwitting Guatemalan pilot who had defected with his plane; they got him drunk one night and secretly recorded his rants against the Communists.

Sherwood had its problems. The CIA's Guatemala station complained that the broadcast signal was too weak to be heard in the capital. La Voz de la Liberación could be easily jammed. Also, there were only seventy-two thousand radio sets among the more than three million Guatemalans, so Sherwood's propaganda was not reaching the masses. But the Guatemalan government knew that well-off citizens, including the officer corps, were being reached, so it launched an aggressive effort to find the radio station in Nicaragua and destroy it.

One propaganda victory dropped into Wisner's lap that spring. Since the beginning of 1954, the Arbenz regime and he had been playing a cat-and-mouse game over arms shipments. The Guatemalan government had tried a number of times to buy arms on the international market. The CIA had succeeded in blocking the sales and at the same time had launched a counteroffensive code-named "Washtub" to convince Latin nations that the Soviets were finding ingenious ways to sneak weapons to Communists in the region. On May 16, the Lincoln station cabled Wisner the news that the Swedish freighter SS *Alfhem*, packed with two thousand tons of arms the

Guatemalan government had bought from Czechoslovakia through middlemen, had succeeded in evading U.S. Navy surveillance ships and was off-loading its cargo at Puerto Barrios on Guatemala's eastern coast.

The arms, in crates labeled as carrying optical and laboratory equipment, had cost the Arbenz government $4.86 million, which CIA analysts suspected the Soviets helped finance. The weapons consisted of World War II–vintage rifles, machine guns, howitzers, mortars, and mines of poor quality. But the shipment's propaganda value for the Americans was priceless. The *Alfhem*, whose owner slipped the CIA a bill of lading on the cargo, silenced PBSuccess doubters in the State Department. Foster Dulles exaggerated the potency of the cargo, claiming that it would enable Guatemala to triple the size of its army and become a regional power capable of crushing its neighbors. Capitol Hill erupted with resolutions giving the Eisenhower administration carte blanche to keep Communism out of the Western Hemisphere. The media plunged into a frenzy. One reporter asked Dulles to confirm a report that the *Alfhem* cargo included atomic bombs. Dulles said the CIA had no evidence of that.

The arms would be transported by train to Guatemala City, so Castillo Armas dispatched three sabotage teams to try to derail the hundred twenty-five cars loaded with weapons, but the teams failed. Arbenz tried his best to contain the PR damage but to no avail. To rattle Guatemalan officers, the Sherwood station broadcast that most, if not all, of the *Alfhem* weapons were intended not for the army but instead for friendly labor unions, peasant cadres, and Communist activists—a charge that turned out to be not too far from the truth.

* * *

By the beginning of May, PBSuccess was ready to put maximum pressure on Jacobo Arbenz. The operation, a CIA memo explained to Eisenhower, depended "on psychological impact rather than military strength." Arbenz commanded the most formidable army in Central America. Without massive external aid, including U.S. troops, Castillo Armas had no hope of winning an armed conflict. Wisner and his psywarriors instead had to deceive Arbenz and his military leaders into believing that Castillo Armas headed a major guerrilla force with the United States military waiting in the wings. It was a sophisticated battle plan, and until the coup was actually underway, Wisner knew it would be hard for him and his team to measure whether they were succeeding at the complicated amalgam of propaganda, sabotage, airpower, intimidation, and raids by a rag-tag band of insurrectionists.

By the end of May, the signs were obvious to Arbenz and his inner circle that an attack was coming. Castillo Armas's invasion plans became Guatemala's worst-kept secret. His soldiers "swaggered around the streets of Tegucigalpa," according to one news article. Reports that the country's president was feeling increasingly stressed and depressed flowed into the CIA's Guatemala City station, with one source even predicting that he would resign "this year." Lincoln cabled orders to the Guatemala station to ramp up spying on the Arbenz government, its army, and Communist groups. "We need accurate information in order to successfully counteract the enemy moves," Lincoln messaged. CIA officers in Guatemala City interviewed anyone they could find who had visited the palace and might give the CIA insights on Arbenz's mental condition.

A detailed flowchart was drafted to show how PBSuccess would unfold each week up to D-Day, which was envisioned for mid-June. Timelines were plotted for sabotage teams, Sherwood broadcasts, aircraft missions, and guerrilla attacks. The CIA station in Guatemala City compiled a detailed political chain of command for the capital—although very little policymaking was now done below the presidential level, the station advised. An operational plan with lists of all the army forces and their garrisons in the city was put together; it also had the targets the coup plotters were assigned to take down. The Lincoln station reported to Wisner that combat training was proceeding smoothly at the Honduran and Nicaraguan camps. Morale was high among the trainees, and ninety tons of arms and equipment were now in place. The one worry CIA officers in Guatemala had was that an increasingly nervous Arbenz would now try to provoke opposition circles into a premature uprising that the government could easily crush. The opposition shouldn't take the bait.

Wisner didn't intend to. He kept a short leash on Lincoln, not wanting its officers in the field jumping ahead. They must stick with the psywar measures for now, he ordered. Wisner could not be sure that Castillo Armas or one of his guerrilla leaders would not launch an attack too early, so he drafted contingency plans for how the agency would deal with that kind of mess.

On May 11, Barnes sat down with Wisner and briefed him on Castillo Armas's attack plan, his military buildup, and his forces' readiness. Wisner was in a nervous and irritable mood. He had reports that Castillo Armas continued to shoot his mouth off about U.S. backing. Opa-Locka was slow in responding to his queries, Wisner griped. He kept worrying that the Guatemalan army and public would not rally behind the rebels. The Sherwood station had been dogged with problems. On May 4, the broadcast was jammed, with a loud whistle sound drowning out the program. The voice of one announcer was recognizable, endangering his family in Guatemala. Wisner finally convinced the State Department to allow a plane to fly over Guatemala City and drop leaflets announcing that liberation was at hand, but one bundle thrown from an aircraft did not open and bounced off the roof of the presidential palace. There were unconfirmed reports as well that Guatemalan government agents had infiltrated into Honduras to hunt for Castillo Armas's forces.

Lincoln conjured up more dirty tricks. To make Arbenz's armed forces think that the Red Army was coming, it had a cable reserving rooms for a Soviet military delegation for three months sent to Guatemala City's Hotel Colonial. The CIA station spread a rumor that Rogelio Cruz Wer, chief of the Guardia Civil, had had to return his

Buick to the dealer eight months earlier because he could not make the payments. But now he was negotiating to buy a Cadillac—the inference being that new bribe money had arrived. Lincoln's psy-warriors also circulated gossip they picked up that Guatemala's army chief had found his wife in bed with the chief of the air force and the army man had fired several shots into the air to chase away the airman.

* * *

At the beginning of June, the CIA decided that five days before the start of the revolt, two command posts would be set up in Honduras—one for Castillo Armas, the other for his second-in-command. That way, if one leader were taken out, the other would be alive to continue the military operation. It would also boost the morale of the men by having a leader close by their side. Wisner still prohibited more CIA officers from moving to the field, fearing the Americans would stand out and possibly compromise security.

Wisner remained on edge, and now even the usually optimistic Tracy Barnes began to worry that the operation might fail. He thought the boss should consider an alternate plan. PBSuccess depended on careful timing and so many elements succeeding. Security failures could still backfire on the CIA. The Lincoln station was growing increasingly unimpressed with what it saw as Castillo Armas's weak leadership. The CIA station in Guatemala City reported that its project to recruit Guatemalan army defectors was stalled. Although the station continued to pick up "insistent rumors" of dissatisfaction in the officer corps, the station reported that it stood "not a ghost of a chance" at the moment of moving a high-level commander to the rebel cause. If there was a piece of good news—and it was a small piece—it was intelligence that Arbenz had sent his children to Mexico City, a sign that he thought his enemies might succeed. But perhaps the operation should adopt a go-slow approach, Barnes wondered.

At a press conference Ambassador Peurifoy held in Guatemala City, Wisner planted a question that threw cold water on Arbenz regime claims that the U.S. government was a lackey for United Fruit. In fact, Barnes found Corcoran, the company's Washington lobbyist, to be a pest seeming always to be trying to stir up trouble on Capitol Hill. Barnes ordered that nobody at the CIA talk to Tommy the Cork without Dulles's approval. Wisner also found a way to gain propaganda points by the U.S. government turning on United Fruit. He proposed a scathing publicity campaign blasting the Arbenz regime for reaching a strike settlement with United Fruit that screwed the workers. To counter the claim that Castillo Armas was also a United Fruit puppet, Wisner had the colonel condemn the deal as well.

* * *

On June 15, the Dulles brothers and other top security advisers held a breakfast meeting on the Guatemala operation with Eisenhower. The president was blunt, telling Allen Dulles and the others to be "damn good and sure you succeed. . . . When you commit the flag, you commit it to win." Later that day, a Lincoln station order was radioed to Castillo Armas to invade. He had divided his band of just under four hundred eighty men into four small groups that now marched or were flown by the CIA's DC-3 transports to their staging areas near Guatemala's border at the Honduran towns of Florida, Nueva Ocotepeque, Copán, and Macuelizo. In the dead of night on June 17, the four rebel contingents would make five separate incursions into Guatemala. Dividing a force like that violated sound infantry tactics, but Castillo Armas, riding over muddy trails to the border, was launching a psychological warfare—not a military—operation. He wanted his small army to seem like a big one that would supposedly strike fear into any government force. Ahead of the invading soldiers, ten trained saboteurs would fan out into the countryside, blowing up railroad tracks and cutting telegraph lines.

Barnes, who moved to Opa-Locka for the beginning of the revolt, assured an uneasy Wisner that the Lincoln station intended to
control the big decisions that had to be made in the attack. The boss
still worried about Castillo Armas's "lack of competence and apparent incapability" to make decisions. To the PBSuccess officers who
had close contact with the Guatemalan colonel, it was evident as well
that he was not an intelligent man, that he lacked administrative
ability, and that he was easily influenced by the last person who had
talked to him.

In the final forty-eight hours before D-Day, Wisner, and even
Dulles, tried at times to micromanage from Washington, issuing
orders on the timing of air attacks over Guatemala City and on the
type of ordnance that could be dropped, and sending instructions
on the final propaganda messages they wanted Sherwood to broadcast. But Wisner realized that all he could really do at that point was
sit and wait. He found that for him it was the most difficult part of
any covert operation. On June 16, he cabled the Lincoln station a
final broad piece of guidance: "this appears [the] time for calculated
risk taken with eyes open in order [to] obtain maximum results."

* * *

A CIA history of what happened next was unsparing. "Even before
H-hour, the invasion degenerated from an ambitious plan to tragi-
comedy." Castillo Armas's contingent that was supposed to dip
south into El Salvador and cross northwest at San Cristóbal to the
Guatemalan town of Jutiapa was spotted by Salvadoran policemen
the afternoon of June 17, arrested, and relieved of its weapons. Castillo Armas eventually got his men released but without their weapons. Several hundred rebels, meanwhile, crossed the border farther
north that day and headed slowly toward Zacapa and Puerto Barrios.
It was an inauspicious start, to say the least, and the Lincoln station
cabled Wisner it feared Castillo Armas's headquarters was already
"demoralized, frightened into inactivity, or badly disorganized by

commie police efforts and arrests." But Lincoln told Wisner that the rebel commander should personally "move out as planned" the next day, on the theory that his doing so would force Arbenz's hand.

Wisner grew panicky. He cabled Opa-Locka, anxious to know where all the CIA officers in the field would be when the other guerrilla contingents moved out on June 18. He and Dulles worried that their officers with their "pale faces" might be spotted by reporters covering the invasion and, even worse, rounded up by Arbenz's forces. Wisner need not have been anxious about the press. Most correspondents in the region had no idea what was really going on. Castillo Armas had kept them at arm's length, and the media had swallowed the line that this was a David-and-Goliath battle between an intrepid band of rebels and a powerful Communist army.

The night of June 18, Castillo Armas, sporting a leather jacket along with a checked shirt, drove a battered station wagon across the border south near the Salvadoran line. He led a detachment of slow-moving foot soldiers weighed down with weapons and supplies; they were headed for Chiquimula in Guatemala. He encountered no resistance, but also no outpouring of support, so the Lincoln station ordered him to stop two days later after he captured Esquipulas, six miles inside Guatemala. He was to avoid any more battles and wait for further instructions. Recruits did eventually join Castillo Armas's force, but only in places where his *liberacionistas* met no resistance. In places where Castillo Armas had to fight, no recruits materialized, and the colonel faced desertions among his own ranks.

In Guatemala City, Peurifoy strutted about his embassy the night of June 17, wearing his shoulder holster and pistol and bragging to his staff: "Well, boys, tomorrow at this time we'll have ourselves a party." The CIA's makeshift air force of F-47 Thunderbolt fighter planes began dropping grenades and dynamite sticks and firing .50-caliber machine-gun rounds on targets in Guatemala City and on spots Castillo Armas's guerrillas were attacking just across the Honduran border. Most of those were harassing raids—like the tear gas canisters one plane dumped on the presidential palace, where Arbenz was holding a meeting—and Wisner and Dulles wanted to keep them that way. They refused to allow aerial bombing of Guatemalan army garrisons for fear of uniting the military behind Arbenz. For the moment, the harassing attacks had their effect. The night of June 18, Arbenz ordered a blackout in the capital, which only further frightened parents and children.

But by June 19, Success began to teeter toward failure, as Ajax had. Arbenz thought Castillo Armas's incursions from the Honduran border were a sideshow. The key battle, the president believed, was in Guatemala City, where many residents were fleeing in cars and horse-drawn carts because of rebel air attacks. Arbenz did not even consider going to the southern front to lead his troops against Castillo Armas's puny band. He remained in the capital and asked Colonel Carlos Enrique Díaz, his armed forces chief, to select men who would lead the troops against the rebels. Arbenz intended to let rebels penetrate the interior of the country unopposed, but then to attack and destroy the Castillo Armas force in a counteroffensive launched from Zacapa, which was thirty miles west of the Honduran border.

By June 20, the initial panic over the invasion and the air attacks began to wear off. The Lincoln station instructed Sherwood to convey in its broadcasts the impression that the country was "in uproar," but that was not how the country felt at that point. The Guatemalan government was "recovering its nerve," the CIA station in the capital reported. Ambassador Peurifoy had lost his swagger and the CIA station cabled Wisner that the envoy's life was now in danger "from commie-controlled mobs of drunken Indians and other irresponsible persons." Castillo Armas's ground offensive at Esquipulas stalled. His soldiers were defeated at Gaulán and the next day at Puerto Barrios. Meanwhile, more than two thousand government soldiers had assembled at Zacapa—the only saving grace for the rebels was that the soldiers' commander delayed launching them against the insurgents. Rebel planes controlled the skies over Guatemala City but faced effective antiaircraft fire from

Arbenz's forces on the ground. Al Haney, who was overseeing day-to-day operations, phoned Dulles from Opa-Locka and informed him that three planes had been lost so far—the number was significant considering the rebels now had only two dozen aircraft in their arsenal. There were also botched missions among the sorties, such as the one by the rebel pilot who destroyed an evangelical radio station instead of the government station he was supposed to hit nearby. Wisner's goal of creating the impression that the Arbenz regime faced a juggernaut was unraveling. Somoza in Managua became more anxious. He had never liked Castillo Armas and now he grumbled that the "little prick" was fouling up the revolt.

With rebel soldiers beginning to desert Castillo Armas's band and with Wisner still vetoing Lincoln station proposals to step up air attacks against antiaircraft batteries and army garrisons—he continued to fear doing so would only harden Guatemala's armed forces against the rebels—Allen Dulles delivered a blunt memo to Eisenhower on June 20. "The outcome of the efforts to overthrow the regime of President Arbenz of Guatemala remains very much in doubt," the CIA director told the president. Everything depended on which way the nation's armed forces went, which was difficult for the agency to discern at that point because "the position of the top-ranking military officers is constantly shifting."

The next day, the news from Puerto Barrios was even more dire. The defeat for the rebel force there was "colossal," according to one CIA history. Castillo Armas lost nearly half his regular army to a counteroffensive by police and hastily armed dockworkers. Haney at the Lincoln station cabled Wisner, pleading for three more F-47 fighter aircraft for the dilapidated rebel air force. He also wanted the green light to use more aerial firepower on the enemy. Wisner remained hesitant to launch a broader air campaign and he was losing confidence by the day in Castillo Armas's leadership. The insurgents had occupied only limited and unimportant territory, the populace was still slow to join their cause, and Castillo Armas was getting nowhere with convincing government troops to desert. Bissell cabled Lincoln that Eisenhower would have to approve the dispatch of more Thunderbolts.

On June 22, Allen Dulles and Henry Holland, the assistant secretary of state for inter-American affairs, met with Eisenhower in the White House. Holland strongly opposed sending two F-47s to replace a couple that had been lost, arguing that the move would be sure to confirm to the world that the United States was involved in the revolt.

After Holland made his case, Ike turned to Dulles. What chance would the rebels have of succeeding without those planes? he asked.

"About zero," Dulles replied.

"Suppose we supply the aircraft," Eisenhower continued. "What would be the chances then?"

"About 20 percent," Dulles answered.

Eisenhower approved sending the two fighters. He later told Dulles that if the CIA director had predicted success at 90 percent, "I would have had a much more difficult decision" because he would have known Dulles was sugarcoating his estimate.

But Dulles could have upped his odds for success—although he didn't know it at the time. Luck began to turn Castillo Armas's way on June 23. He established a provisional government in Esquipulas, six miles from the Honduran border. More important, the large contingent of government troops sent to Zacapa to mount a counteroffensive refused to fight, fearful that American soldiers were waiting in the wings to counterattack. Arbenz grew uneasy. Guatemala City was swirling with rumors that the numbers in rebel contingents were increasing by the hundreds as volunteers came forward from each town liberated. It wasn't the case, but that was what many in the government believed. The CIA had a report that Arbenz's wife, María, was now in El Salvador. Sensing a shift, Wisner cabled the station in Guatemala City to have the embassy's military attachés roam the capital to gauge the mood of the officer corps.

The extra planes arrived—CIA officers told reporters they were Venezuelan aircraft—and they were put to work strafing trains and military barracks at Zacapa. Bissell cabled Opa-Locka that Wisner had approved more targets in Guatemala City to be bombed, such as petroleum tanks, and the pilots should follow up with leaflets explaining why they had been hit. Wisner told the Lincoln station that he expected "discipline in the air ops," but he didn't always get it. An overeager aviator mistakenly sank the British freighter *Springfjord* at Puerto San José: the error later cost the CIA $1 million in restitution.

Knowing it would rattle the Arbenz regime, Wisner convinced the State Department to announce on June 24 the evacuation of nonessential embassy employees and Americans wishing to leave Guatemala. That same day, the Sherwood station was ordered to broadcast a "flash announcement" that government troops in Chiquimula and Zacapa were "defecting to the liberation movement in large numbers"—which was not completely true. CIA paramilitary officers were authorized to bribe Guatemalan officers into defecting, which netted one commander $60,000 when he surrendered his troops, but Castillo Armas still had to hire drivers for his supply trucks because volunteers could not be convinced to serve.

* * *

The Lincoln station continued to complain to Wisner about the lack of air support for rebel troops in the field, but by June 25, the pounding from the sky had begun to take its toll in Guatemala City, where the bombings became known as the *sulfatos* for the laxative effect they had on Arbenz and his top people. A Communist party official and later a colonel Arbenz trusted drove to Zacapa and both reported back to the president that the demoralized officers there, fearing the arrival of the Americans, wanted Arbenz to resign. If he didn't, "the army will march on the capital to depose you," the colonel warned. Arbenz summoned his cabinet, party officials, and union leaders to the presidential palace to inform them the army was in revolt and the only hope was to arm the populace. But that plan never materialized. Only a handful of citizens showed up for weapons and the army refused to give them any.

Arbenz correctly judged that Castillo Armas's force was militarily insignificant. As long as the United States did not join in, Arbenz thought he could depend on the army's loyalty to repel an attack by exiles. Ultimately what turned the tide in the rebellion was not rebel air raids or the Sherwood broadcasts but instead the Guatemalan army officers' fear that defeat of the motley rebel force would be followed by an American invasion. Arbenz privately began to fear that outcome as well. Morale plummeted in Guatemala City. Guatemalan authorities became greatly disturbed when the CIA planted rumors that Castillo Armas was gathering thousands of volunteers as he marched toward the capital. His numbers actually remained at around four hundred at the border. The international press corps did nothing to correct the fiction that he commanded a massive army.

The CIA situation report for June 26 pleased Wisner as he read it in his Washington office. Castillo Armas's forces "are beginning to have some significant successes in the field," he cabled Opa-Locka. Wisner sent Dulles's congratulations to "all hands." The CIA station in Mexico City reported from its sources that Arbenz had "at long last seen the handwriting on the wall" and was making arrangements to flee Guatemala "with $8 million worth of loot." This was only hearsay, but it was enough to prompt Wisner to once again try to block fund transfers in New York banks and to have the Sherwood station publicize any financial moves by Arbenz.

For all of PBSuccess's missteps, covert action had finally beaten down Jacobo Arbenz. Hunkered in his palace office throughout June 26, receiving nothing but discouraging reports that his army was near mutiny, he mulled stepping down until José Manuel Fortuny, the PGT leader, convinced him that night to arm a hundred Communists for a last-gasp stand. The Communists, however, had no idea how they could seize weapons from the army and defend the capital.

Like Arbenz, Wisner was exhausted from near-twenty-four-hour workdays. He confided to others that he feared fatigue might cause him to make bad decisions. He wanted Peurifoy in the Guatemala City embassy and the Lincoln station officers in Opa-Locka to point out if he was making errors in judgment.

Sunday morning, June 27, broke rainy and cool over Guatemala. Fighting continued near the Honduran border, with rebel forces winning some skirmishes yet still losing others. Castillo Armas's planes continued bombing and resupply missions in the bad weather with mixed results, and the Sherwood station kept up broadcasts. One appealed to the "women of Guatemala: Don't let your menfolk fight on the side of the Communists and traitors." Wisner recommended that Sherwood also take more potshots at United Fruit, which he knew was a perfect propaganda foil. Now emotionally shaken and drinking heavily, Arbenz could see that he had lost the support of key groups in Guatemala, such as the upper class, the middle class, the Catholic Church, and the army. Only a small Communist minority and the nation's politically powerless poor supported him.

On Sunday afternoon Carlos Enrique Díaz, the armed forces chief, summoned Peurifoy to his home, where the colonel sat in his living room with four confederates. The officers told the American ambassador they planned to force Arbenz to resign that evening. Díaz would become president and would immediately outlaw the Communist party and exile its leaders. In return, Díaz wanted Washington to dump Castillo Armas. Díaz and his cabal refused to deal with the renegade colonel. A suspicious Peurifoy told the officers he could not guarantee anything since he did not control Castillo Armas's forces—which certainly shaded the truth.

Díaz then motored to the presidential palace and told Arbenz he had to resign in favor of Díaz taking over. The colonel attached a sweetener to the order: he vowed never to negotiate with Castillo Armas. With that promise, Arbenz acquiesced and said he would announce his resignation decision in a radio broadcast at nine o'clock that night. Arbenz did not quit as a frightened man. Díaz had lulled him into believing that the hated Castillo Armas would be blocked and a President Díaz would preserve many of Arbenz's reforms.

The president next informed his cabinet he intended to step down. He then taped a speech that was broadcast on the radio at nine. Arbenz announced that he was turning power over to Colonel Díaz. Arbenz denounced Castillo Armas's revolt and predicted that Díaz would quickly route the rebel forces. After Arbenz signed off, Díaz came on the air, proclaiming that he was seizing power and that he would continue to fight Castillo Armas.

Peurifoy listened to the broadcasts in disbelief. "We have been double-crossed," the ambassador immediately messaged the State Department. He recommended to Washington that Guatemala City be quickly bombed. The CIA agreed. Charles Cabell, the agency's deputy director, cabled orders to the Lincoln station that the Guatemala City radio station should be struck so Díaz could not get back on the air, and that the Guatemalan field army should be strafed so it didn't return to the capital intact. The U.S. had not launched Castillo Armas's invasion in order to hand the presidency over to one of Arbenz's pals—particularly not to someone the CIA suspected had Communist leanings. Washington wanted its own man in the presidential palace—a staunch and malleable American ally. The United States had to "crack some heads together," said Foster Dulles, and Peurifoy was perfect for that job.

Late that Sunday night, two CIA officers barged into Díaz's headquarters office and one of them arrogantly told him: "Colonel, you're just not convenient for the requirements of American foreign policy." The CIA men then escorted the armed services chief to Peurifoy's residence, where the grumpy ambassador told him the same thing. Díaz exited with his tail between his legs.

He returned later and proposed ruling in a three-man junta that included Colonel José Angel Sánchez (the defense minister) and Colonel Elfego Monzón, an ambitious senior officer. Peurifoy continued to insist that Díaz must resign. "In the eleven days after Arbenz resigned five successive juntas occupied the presidential palace," a later CIA history noted, "each one more amenable to American demands than the last." Finally, Peurifoy and the State Department accepted a pact to jointly rule the country that Castillo Armas and Monzón signed on July 2.

Their business concluded, PBSuccess officers in Opa-Locka and Central America began making their way back to Washington. Wisner sent a CIA–State Department team to Guatemala City to "snatch" 150,000 Arbenz government documents so the agency could reconstruct the Communist party complex in the nation and trace Soviet connections to it in a project code-named "PBHistory." But the documents turned up no smoking-gun evidence the Soviets had been controlling the local Communists. The CIA sifted through personal possessions Arbenz left behind after he fled to Mexico's embassy in the capital. They found a volume of Mao's writings and a biography of Stalin. The agency also laid plans for how the CIA might work with the new Guatemalan government to reorganize its intelligence service under Washington's control.

On July 3, 150,000 demonstrators turned out in Guatemala City to welcome the arrival of Castillo Armas with firecrackers distributed by CIA officers. A worn-out Wisner took the next day off and spent a fun Fourth of July at Paul Nitze's south Maryland farm. At times, friends began noticing Wisner being in peculiar moods that they had trouble describing but that they believed to be more than just the result of overwork.

On July 8, with CIA bribe money greasing the way, the junta picked Castillo Armas to be the provisional president. Washington granted official recognition of his government five days later. With Peurifoy pulling more strings, Castillo Armas became full president of Guatemala on September 1.

Wisner sent congratulatory messages to the Guatemala City and Opa-Locka stations. But he knew PBSuccess was not a complete victory. In the chaotic week after Arbenz's resignation, most of

Guatemala's Communist leaders had managed to escape the country or take refuge in foreign embassies. Wisner ordered that the CIA station put the foreign compounds under "careful surveillance" and have any Communists straying from their premises arrested immediately. The agency had reports that Arbenz was packed into the Mexico embassy with his top people and perhaps two hundred Communists or Communist-sympathizer friends. Wisner ordered that the station try to slip "phony commies" into the compound to spy on the guests.

* * *

In mid-August, Eisenhower summoned PBSuccess's managers to the White House for a formal briefing on the operation. At Dulles's home, Dulles, Wisner, and the operation's other leaders rehearsed what they planned to say. The CIA director was a demanding stage director, at one point dismissing the script for one officer's remarks as "crap" and ordering that it be redone.

At the White House, the Success team set maps on an easel and loaded a projector with slides for the presentation. Their audience included not only Ike, but also Nixon, cabinet officers, and even members of the First Family, all of whom listened raptly. This was a triumphant moment for Wisner and his clandestine service. At the end of the presentation, Eisenhower asked how many men Castillo Armas had lost.

"Only one," the briefer answered.

"Incredible," the president murmured.

The briefer had lied. There were at least forty-three rebels who died at Puerto Barrios and Gualán. Another seventy-five members of the civilian opposition had been killed in Guatemalan jails. The briefer also did not dwell on the many problems PBSuccess had encountered.

As it had with Ajax in Iran, the CIA compiled a highly classified in-house assessment of the operational lessons learned and the errors made in PBSuccess. But those mistakes were considered technicalities in the minds of the agency reviewers. The CIA and the administration officials who were cleared for access to PBSuccess were ecstatic about the outcome of the operation. Eisenhower considered the elimination of the Communist threat from Guatemala one of his proudest foreign policy accomplishments. In his office, Foster Dulles hung a framed political cartoon showing him and a collection of spies dressed in black toppling the government of Guatemala. Polly saw her social status in Republican Washington soar— although she didn't know exactly why because her husband remained quiet about PBSuccess. At her P Street house, she hosted a fancy luncheon for Mamie Eisenhower with luminaries like Clare Boothe Luce attending. Ike had made Clare, the wife of *Time* publisher Henry Luce, his ambassador to Italy.

Almost every CIA officer involved in PBSuccess received an award or commendation. Ever the self-promoter, Peurifoy lobbied his State Department bosses and Wisner for a Legion of Merit for his part in the operation. After Castillo Armas arrived in the United States on October 31, he was honored with a twenty-one-gun salute in Washington and a ticker-tape parade in New York City.

Wisner worked hard to shape narratives after the coup. He ordered the CIA station in Guatemala City to slip material to Representative Charles Kersten, chairman of the House Select Committee on Communist Aggression, to help the panel's investigation of Communism in the country and to make sure the congressmen did not bump into PBSuccess. Wisner tried to coax the British embassy in Washington to have the Foreign Office in London produce a white paper that would detail events leading up to the Guatemala coup and paint the United States in a positive light. He proposed that the CIA secretly back the publication of a paperback on "Russian intervention in Guatemala." A two-to-three-man agency team would gather research for the book, which would be serialized in newspapers. Wisner helped arrange for an MGM film crew to visit Guatemala for a documentary on Communist atrocities there. Allen

Dulles also had some repair work to do with *New York Times* publisher Arthur Hays Sulzberger, who now regretted that he had pulled Sydney Gruson from Guatemala. Sulzberger, who was unhappy about the way his paper had been manipulated, told Dulles he had some explaining to do.

Wisner's postcoup propaganda blitz turned out to be overkill. Congress and the American press were still cheering sections for the administration. There was hardly any public outrage among Americans over the Guatemala coup. Few Americans knew what had actually happened, and what little they did know left them convinced that there had been a successful outcome to the crisis in Central America. American reporters played down rumors of U.S. involvement in the revolt. The cover was never blown. Eisenhower's approval rating stayed at 60 percent or higher.

Ignored by Americans was the ferocity of international protests after the fall of Arbenz, which shocked CIA and State Department officials, who closely monitored it. In Latin America, the bitter taste remained for generations. The fall of the Arbenz regime helped stoke "an enduring legacy of anti-Americanism," a later CIA study concluded. The agency's "victory over Arbenz proved to be a lasting propaganda setback" for the United States.

* * *

Castillo Armas allowed his predecessor to leave the country on September 11. He ordered Arbenz to be stripped-searched before he boarded a plane at the airport. The ex-president and his wife flew to Mexico, where he received a chilly welcome. In December he flew to Europe. Mexico refused to allow him back in a few weeks later. For the next seventeen years, he wandered through France, Czechoslovakia, Uruguay, Switzerland, Cuba, and finally Mexico. He was a lonely man, reviled by former supporters and Latin American leftists for surrendering to the Americans rather than fighting.

Into the late 1950s, the CIA continued to monitor Arbenz's

movements and intercept his mail. In 1957, the agency decided to pile on by leaking a psychiatrist's interview with him to show he was unfit for public office. Arbenz died on January 27, 1971, reportedly drowning in a bathtub.

* * *

Foster Dulles wanted a sweetheart deal for American businesses in Guatemala. Castillo Armas obliged and returned to United Fruit practically all the land the Arbenz government had expropriated from the company, and he abolished the tax on the interest, dividends, and profits that foreign investors received. He also dismantled Decree 900 and ensured that only undeveloped, inaccessible, or poor-quality land would be available for distribution. The end result: 2 percent of Guatemala's population continued to own more than half the country's land.

Beetle Smith was put on United Fruit's board of directors in 1955 after he left the State Department. The general wanted to be the company's president, but the board rejected that, pointing out that Smith knew nothing about the banana business.

United Fruit, however, did not thrive after PBSuccess. The privileges Castillo Armas granted the company ended up being worth less than they had been before, American consumers ate less fruit in the 1950s, other businesses cut into United Fruit's market share, and it managed Guatemalan land poorly, resulting in declining yields. Once United Fruit's usefulness to the covert operation ended, the State Department, wanting to improve relations with Latin America, demanded that the company pay higher wages in the region, and the administration proceeded with a separate antitrust suit against the company. Corcoran complained to J. C. King and other officers in Wisner's plans directorate about what the company considered shabby treatment. But United Fruit's business continued to decline during the 1960s and the firm sold off the last of its Guatemala land in 1972.

* * *

Estimates of the total cost of PBSuccess ranged from $5 million to $7 million. The Eisenhower administration considered it a bargain even at the higher price. The covert operations in Guatemala and Iran pumped up self-confidence within the CIA. Wisner's directorate was now treated as a highly successful and low-cost fifth armed service—besides the Army, Navy, Air Force, and Marine Corps—that Eisenhower had at his disposal. Cheap victories in Iran and Guatemala stirred within the CIA a dangerous delusion that strongmen could be frightened out of power, that Ajax and Success could be repeated in other nations the United States found objectionable. The CIA would never be the same after those operations.

Buoyed by his triumphs in Iran and Guatemala, Wisner proposed setting up an "Action Operations Unit" composed of fifty men trained in all aspects of covert operations; they would be available to swoop into a country and carry out a coup, as with PBSuccess.

The long-term cost of the Guatemala operation proved to be far higher than estimated. Castillo Armas did not produce the stable non-Communist government Washington had been looking for. His regime was embarrassingly inept—worse than what CIA officials had feared. The colonel lunged to the right with repressive and corrupt policies that soon polarized Guatemala and fueled a renewed civil conflict. Guatemala quickly came to depend on aid handouts from the United States, which ended up underwriting a ballooning government deficit aggravated by corruption and mismanagement. In 1957, Castillo Armas was assassinated by a member of the presidential guard. The U.S. Information Agency claimed it was a Communist plot.

Allen Dulles and Henry Holland, the assistant secretary of state for Latin America, privately worried early on that the governments following Arbenz's might "commit excesses" in their efforts to root out Communism and that they might carry out unwarranted executions. Wisner was not persuaded. He ordered that a crucial paragraph in a CIA analysis of the aftermath of PBSuccess be cut. The paragraph pointed out that there had been many analysts and desk officers in the CIA and the State Department who disapproved of the covert operation. Those dissenters believed that the method used to eliminate Communist influence in Guatemala would trade short-term advantages "for grave long-term risks." PBSuccess would produce new problems for the United States in the hemisphere. Wisner did not want to hear that kind of criticism.

But history more than validated the dissenting paragraph. For nearly four decades after PBSuccess, a succession of brutal military dictatorships fought a Communist insurgency with waves of repression and terror. Government-backed death squads killed more than 200,000 Guatemalan peasants and "disappeared" some forty thousand more. That abysmal human rights record was unmatched by any nation in Latin America at the time. A peace agreement signed by the Guatemalan government and the guerrilla movement on December 29, 1996, finally ended one of the longest wars in Latin American history.

Poor Guatemala.

Chapter 22

INVESTIGATIONS

BY THE SUMMER OF 1954, Frank Wisner felt under siege. Hoover continued to dog him over the Tanda Caradja affair. For the next two years, bureau agents kept collecting informants who peddled dirt on the CIA's clandestine service chief. Wisner's growing FBI file noted that "outwardly" he appeared "friendly towards the bureau." But the reports always accused him of being "somewhat of a controversial figure"—which Hoover agreed was the case.

The charges that resurfaced could almost all be traced back to Nicolae Malaxa, the shady Romanian industrialist and longtime Wisner enemy. Allen Dulles's "right-hand man," according to the latest rumors that reached FBI agents, was actually "a Russian spy" still working in Austria with Tanda, who was a "dangerous" Soviet agent. Again, the CIA launched an intensive investigation, and again, the agency found nothing, reporting in a May 1955 letter to Hoover that these warmed-over allegations against Wisner "are based on fabrication, distortion of fact and Romanian gossip."

The surveillance worked in reverse, too. Wisner's men kept a close watch on the FBI, especially the agents Hoover sent overseas, to make sure they were engaged in legitimate law enforcement work and not spying, which was the CIA's job. Wisner also urged Dulles to get tough with Hoover's pals in the press, who published "smear stories" attacking the CIA. The two agencies did occasionally cooperate in the surveillance of foreign diplomats in the United States, and Hoover was willing to share intelligence with the CIA in some cases—although he became testy when Wisner's men dismissed FBI's leads as worthless. Hoover pointedly ordered that any agent encountering Wisner should be "most circumspect with him."

By the summer of 1954, Wisner no longer had to worry about Joe McCarthy. The senator's aides had boasted that after he finished with his investigation of Communists in the U.S. Army, his next target would be the CIA. But McCarthy imploded politically before he could go after the intelligence agency. The televised Army-McCarthy congressional hearings from April to June exposed the senator as a drunken bully. Hoover cut off McCarthy's access to bureau information, the Senate eventually censured him, and the press now ignored his rants. As for the rest of Congress, Dulles and Wisner continued to be able to charm its members and fend off aggressive oversight.

The two men, however, faced far more serious probing from inside the Eisenhower administration. Ike feared that the CIA had gotten too big. He was uneasy with the way Allen Dulles managed it, aware from his own sources that the Guatemala operation had had its problems. Eisenhower regarded as deadly serious the threat the Soviet espionage network posed to the United States. He was willing to go to great lengths to counter it. But he wanted the job done right.

On June 26, 1954, as the Guatemala operation lurched toward success, Eisenhower summoned retired general James Doolittle to his office and asked him to set up a panel to study the CIA's covert operations and to deliver directly to him a top secret report on what he found. The charismatic leader of the first American air raid over Japan in 1942, Doolittle had served under Eisenhower in England and was well-versed in military special operations. Wisner, who had suffered through these kinds of investigations before, realized the potential for embarrassment with the latest one. But in that case, he was cheered by the fact that Doolittle was an old friend. The general, he believed, would not be a problem.

As Wisner was busy tying up loose ends in PBSuccess, the Doolittle committee took over a suite of offices he had in one of the CIA buildings to conduct its six-week inquiry. Though consumed by Guatemala, Wisner kept close track of Doolittle and his probe. He tried to exercise some control over the general's line of inquiry and head off gripes the panel might hear from assistant secretaries in the State Department who accused him of not clearing his covert operations with them, inferring that at times he went rogue. Wisner, who adamantly insisted that he worked only to promote U.S. foreign policy, sometimes claimed he had received clearance for operations from senior officials above the assistant secretaries, who had been intentionally kept out of the loop by their department.

Doolittle issued his top secret report at the end of September and its findings were not what Wisner expected from his old friend. American covert operations, the Doolittle panel concluded, must be "more effective, more unique and, if necessary, more ruthless" than the enemy's. The United States faced an "implacable" foe "bent on world domination." The American concept of "fair play" must be tossed out the window, the U.S. government must be ready for a dirty war, and the public must "understand and support this fundamentally repugnant philosophy." Wisner had no quarrel with that conclusion, nor with the Doolittle panel's declaration that the CIA was "doing a creditable job" in the dirty war.

But the panel also found that Wisner's plans directorate had "ballooned" into a "vast and sprawling" organization, with sensitive positions being filled by officers with "little or no training for their jobs." The deadwood needed to be cleared. Wisner's clandestine service, with its more than forty major units, was an organizational mess, the panel reported. One thousand persons could be cut in a reorganization. The directorate's elaborate staff structure could be simplified. Wisner's men continued to take on too many projects. The nonessential ones needed to be trimmed back.

In a private meeting with Eisenhower, Doolittle was even more blunt. Dulles was a poor organizer who surrounded himself with loyal but not particularly competent people, the general told the president, implying that Wisner was one of them. The CIA lacked discipline. Security needed to be improved. Too much information was being leaked at cocktail parties. (Doolittle did not identify which parties, but the Georgetown set was clearly what he had in mind.) The general was also critical of the fact that the Dulles brothers controlled both the State Department and the CIA. (Ike, who had made that choice, was not bothered by it.) Eisenhower did not argue with Doolittle's assessment that "Frank Wisner is a chap of great promise but not a good organizer." The president acknowledged that the panel's criticism of Wisner—and of Dulles's deputy, Charles Cabell—did "disturb" him. Eisenhower concluded that the CIA was no different from other federal bureaucracies, for which he had found it hard to recruit good administrators.

For both Dulles and Wisner, Doolittle's criticism stung. Wisner by then was more than an overseer of covert programs to bribe foreign officials or topple governments overseas. As deputy director for plans leading the CIA's entire clandestine service, he also supervised sensitive espionage operations to steal secrets abroad, which usually involved breaking a foreign country's laws; counterespionage operations to protect the CIA from being penetrated by hostile agents; and "liaison operations"—as they were called in the spy business—to enlist the help of foreign secret services in the CIA's spying. It was a big job, and particularly in the case of liaison operations, Wisner was breaking new ground in putting together a system to exploit the capabilities of the friendly foreign services.

Dulles and Wisner immediately began damage control, which they had always been good at in those situations. Five months after the damning report, Dulles and Wisner hosted a dinner for Doolittle and his staff to tell them the progress the CIA had made in

implementing the panel's recommendations. The plans directorate
had been streamlined and a new review committee had been set up
to do a better job of vetting operations and weeding out less essential projects than the old one had. Wisner also moved to improve not
only the screening of applicants for his clandestine service but also
their training at Camp Peary, a secret facility near Williamsburg,
Virginia. (In the past he had dumped his poorly performing officers
on the camp to be instructors.) Dulles won over Doolittle with a
heavy dose of the flattery he was famous for, and he persuaded the
general to pay another visit to Ike to tell him the CIA director was
being a good team player and deserved a pat on the back for adopt-
ing the panel's reforms.

But the investigations continued. A year after the Doolittle investigation, the Hoover Commission, set up with former president
Herbert Hoover as chairman to examine the organization of the
Executive Branch, received a report from former World War II and
Korean War general Mark Clark, who led a task force on intelligence activities. The Clark Task Force recommended reforms in the
$800 million spent annually on intelligence operations. Wisner
lashed back that time, adamantly insisting to the task force that
operatives "were not inexperienced, uncontrollable and freewheeling." On the whole, the Clark Task Force was good to the
CIA, Wisner felt. It refuted McCarthy-like charges that Communists and subversives had penetrated the agency. The CIA had
"successfully withstood the acid test of these unprecedented investigations," Wisner declared in a memo.

A year later, however, David Bruce, who had been Donovan's
OSS station chief in London, and Robert Lovett, a former defense
secretary, produced a report as scathing as the Doolittle report,
blasting the CIA for dabbling too much in Third World intrigues at
the expense of collecting hard intelligence on the Soviet Union.
That report had to come as a shock to Wisner, who considered
Bruce another old friend. At one point the two men had even discussed forming a syndicate to buy an $875,000 piece of property.

Within his own agency, Wisner also had to deal with what he considered unwanted intruders. The CIA by the end of 1955 had an expanded staff of auditors checking how money was spent and property was used in clandestine operations. Wisner's station chiefs found that giving the auditors access was a pain, but it forced the chiefs to become more responsible in managing spending, which was always in cash, not checks. They were also able to make some of their ultrasecret activities exempt from auditor review.

Wisner hated Lyman Kirkpatrick, the CIA's inspector general, who detested him just as much and was always eager to investigate anything he thought amiss in Wisner's clandestine service. Wisner did not want Kirkpatrick's IG officers snooping freely around the directorate's programs and reporting to Dulles behind his back. It took the two men all of January and February 1955 to negotiate the ground rules for Kirkpatrick's teams to go into Wisner's directorate to inspect for wrongdoing and other problems. The agreement they arrived at was wordsmithed as if it were an arms control treaty; Dulles had had to jump in at times to referee. And even after the accord was hammered out, Wisner continued to quibble over inspector general findings from their probes of his shop.

* * *

In September 1955, the CIA delivered to the White House secure communications equipment, along with a four-unit switchboard, so the president, Foster Dulles, the chairman of the Joint Chiefs of Staff, and Allen Dulles could talk to one another on a line that scrambled their calls. But the technology—along with the briefings the CIA director gave to National Security Council meetings the president chaired each week—were not enough to control the agency's covert operations and prevent embarrassing surprises. The different reports from Doolittle, Clark, and Bruce convinced Ike that, notwithstanding Wisner's protestations, the CIA under Dulles's lax management was in danger of becoming a rogue elephant in desperate need of oversight of its secret activities. Eisenhower did not have the time to be briefed on the details of all CIA operations—and for some operations he preferred not to know the details. But he recognized that he had to have someone or some group he trusted oversee what the CIA was doing.

He decided to create the President's Board of Consultants on Foreign Intelligence Activities, which would be made up of leaders in academia, industry, foreign policy, and the military who would advise him on overall intelligence policy. To approve major covert operations of the CIA or of any other government agency, Eisenhower had earlier replaced the Psychological Strategy Board, which had been ineffectively doing that job, with what was called the Operations Coordinating Board. But the Operations Coordinating Board ended up being as ineffective as its predecessor. The new board's members were in no better position than the old board's members to evaluate the CIA's capabilities or to determine whether the results of a covert operation were worthwhile. Dulles and Wisner continued to be reluctant to discuss sensitive programs with such a large group. Dulles was also still the one who decided if a project was large enough to be worthy of review by the Operations Coordinating Board. The bottom line remained that there were subtle ways the CIA could operate covertly on its own and end up making foreign policy.

Ultimately, the problem Eisenhower saw with the CIA boiled down to Allen Dulles. The review boards he had appointed told the president so. Ike appreciated the intelligence reports the agency's experts produced as well as its clandestine capabilities, which he had seen on full display in Iran and Guatemala. But he recognized the CIA's shortcomings and complained that the CIA's analysts sometimes overestimated the threat posed by the Soviet Union, and that Wisner's covert operations fell short of what he wanted. The big-picture experts on the President's Board of Consultants recommended to him that Dulles detach himself from day-to-day CIA activities and concentrate instead on his broader role as director of central intelligence, in which he advised the president on overseas threats and coordinated the spying activities of all the federal agencies along with the reports that poured out of them.

But administration was not in Dulles's DNA. His administrative shortcomings, which had first surfaced when he led the World War II OSS station in Switzerland, remained. He still had what one biographer described as a "little-boy fascination with covert operations." "I'm not going to change Allen," Ike finally told Gordon Gray, who now served as his special assistant for national security affairs. He could fire his CIA director and appoint someone who would assert more authority. Or he could keep Dulles with his flaws. Eisenhower chose to do the latter. Dulles's pluses as a charismatic spymaster with a loyal following in his agency outweighed his minuses as an administrator, Eisenhower decided. "I'd rather have Allen as my chief intelligence officer with his limitations than anyone else I know," the president told Gray.

* * *

Wisner managed to escape the Washington investigations with occasional trips overseas. He toured CIA stations in the Far East during the fall of 1954. In Tokyo he attended a black-tie dinner with U.S. embassy diplomats and senior American military officers in the region. Wisner made stopovers in Manila and Saigon for close-up views of problems in those cities. When he returned to Washington, he lobbied Joe Alsop to write a column on the success of U.S. policy toward Vietnam and Ngo Dinh Diem's leadership in the south—though neither would later prove to be a success. Wisner also pumped an extra $190,000 into Project DTPillar to fund anti-Communist groups operating in Southeast Asia.

Polly joined Frank the next year when J. C. King escorted him on a fact-finding trip through Latin America in October and November. Wisner managed to wedge in some vacation time with his wife after he finished inspecting the hemisphere's CIA stations. The agency had no problem with Polly joining Frank on the trip. In fact, it was often encouraged. The CIA had become more family oriented—as much for operational reasons as anything. The CIA by the mid-1950s recognized the realities of intimacy between couples and began conducting security investigations of spouses on the assumption that there was no way an officer could or would keep everything he did secret from his wife. Though he had failed in his own marriage, Dulles was particularly sensitive to the importance of family in his workforce, granting, for example, one officer thirty days of paid leave to tend to an ailing wife. In 1955, the CIA also began hiring the children of its officers for clerical jobs in the summer. The teenagers were given clearances to see documents stamped "SECRET."

* * *

By the summer of 1955, Wisner was back on the offensive and intent on bucking up morale after what he considered a string of mudslinging investigations. He hunted for more Washington office space for the men and women planning his operations. Cabell approved his request to buy and rent IBM computers to manage the nearly ten million pages of personnel files, classified documents, and reference cards stuffed in his directorate's filing cabinets. And as investigative panels poked into the CIA's insides, the agency scored an intelligence triumph from digging a hole.

The year before, the CIA and Britain's Secret Intelligence Service had launched an audacious joint project, code-named "Operation Gold," to dig a 1,476-foot tunnel into the Berlin sector that the Soviets occupied because the agencies wanted to tap three underground telephone cables that Russian occupation forces in the city used to talk to military facilities throughout the East Bloc. The nearly $30 million project was the most elaborate and costly secret operation the CIA had ever tried in Soviet-occupied territory. Experiments in tunnel construction had been secretly conducted in

New Mexico and Surrey, England. The thirty-one hundred tons of dirt that were dug out had to be hidden in a nearby warehouse with a deep basement, a rubber solution was sprayed on the hundred twenty-five tons of steel plates lining the tunnel so East German border guards aboveground would not hear metal clanking at their feet, and six hundred tape recorders had to be bought to record the conversations over the some hundred fifty voice and telegraphic circuits the three cables carried.

The tunneling was finally finished in February 1955 and conversations began flowing into the CIA's recording machines by the summer. Wisner, Dulles, and Helms were the only senior U.S. officials who knew everything about Gold. Wisner considered the tunnel an extraordinary achievement in intelligence collection.

The KGB, however, had known about the operation early on. There was only one security leak among the fifteen hundred persons involved in the operation, but it turned out to be a serious one. George Blake was a British MI6 officer involved in Operation Gold's planning. He was also a Soviet mole, and he tipped off the KGB to the tunnel. A small KGB team was formed to secretly locate the tap, which it did in late 1955. Early in 1956, the Soviet security service developed a plan for the electronic interception to be accidentally discovered; they activated it on the night of April 21. A special Russian signal corps team, pretending to be conducting routine maintenance on the communications lines, began digging and, by two a.m. the next morning, reached the underground chamber where the taps were located.

Why had the Soviets permitted the tunnel to be dug and then the phone intercept to operate for nearly a year? Although the KGB had no doubt been aware of the potential importance of the tap, its priority was protecting George Blake, its prized source in MI6. Neither the GRU (the Soviet military's intelligence arm) nor the East German intelligence service (Stasi) was informed of the KGB discovery. Over the years many reporters and ex–CIA officers have claimed the KGB planted insignificant information or disinformation on the phone circuits to fool the agency. The CIA, however, later concluded that the information vacuumed from the cables was genuine. The KGB might have concluded that the tap was not a direct threat to its organization. Locating the tunnel took time. Also, halting phone communications over the cables or planting convincing disinformation would have been a major undertaking, far easier said than done, that Moscow likely could not have kept secret.

Wisner and others in the CIA thought the Soviets would keep their discovery of the tunnel secret so they would not lose face over having had the Americans listening in on their phone calls. But for some strange reason, the acting Soviet commander in Berlin briefed the city's reporters and gave them a tour of the tunnel without checking first with Moscow. The tunnel's discovery ended up being a propaganda triumph for Wisner and the CIA. The *Washington Post* hailed it as an example of "Yankee ingenuity."

After the tunnel was shut down, it took the CIA another two years and five months to transcribe, translate, and evaluate all the messages that had been intercepted. About forty thousand hours of telephone conversations and six million hours of telegraph traffic had been recorded. The intelligence haul from the intercepts included reports on the strength of Red Army units, background on the reorganization of the Soviet Defense Ministry, revelations about the nuclear capability of Soviet aircraft, Russian plans for East Germany and Poland, and the identities of several thousand Soviet officers and several hundred employees of the Soviets' atomic energy program. Even the idle gossip that was recorded sometimes provided insights on political maneuvering among Kremlin leaders.

*   *   *

By August 1955, Dwight Eisenhower did not intend to run for reelection. His health had been poor. He suffered a heart attack in September. But in the mid-1950s, when the two superpowers built the hydrogen bomb (even more powerful than the atomic bomb and soon to be carried to its target in about a half hour by the intercontinental ballistic missile), Ike had become a reassuring presence guiding the country through tense times. He changed his mind and decided to seek a second term, intent on winning by a large margin to give him a mandate.

By then the CIA had largely given up on successfully infiltrating agents into East Bloc nations like Albania to organize resistance movements, although Wisner and Dulles still held out faint hope that agency operations could loosen the tight grip of the Communist regimes. Announcers at Radio Free Europe and Radio Liberty were under orders not to provoke premature revolts among the populations there with hints on the air that the Western powers would come to the rescue. It would be a promise that could not be kept. Though it was difficult for the CIA to judge the impact that the radios had had in the Soviet Union and its satellites over the past two and a half years, the agency continued to believe they were an effective propaganda tool, if for no other reason than the fact that Moscow had tried its best to shut down the broadcasts through jamming and having East Bloc secret police intimidate the exile staffs who ran the programs.

Wisner made course corrections in his thinking about propaganda. Though in the past he had thought that Dulles enjoyed the limelight too much for a spymaster, by the beginning of 1955, Wisner believed that his boss shouldn't be the only one promoting the agency. The CIA needed to improve its public relations "at all levels," he told his aides. Though he had no background in the subject, Wisner also began to insert himself and the CIA into the fine arts, becoming something of an aficionado on their value as a propaganda tool.

New York millionaire Nelson Rockefeller, who was serving as a special assistant for foreign affairs in the Eisenhower White House, occasionally lunched with Wisner to discuss the CIA's propaganda programs. At one luncheon in April, the Rockefeller family scion asked the clandestine service chief what he thought about the U.S. government letting George and Ira Gershwin's *Porgy and Bess*, which had been garnering stellar reviews on its American tour, perform in Moscow if invited. Washington had not received an invitation, but a Polish cultural attaché had put out a feeler on it.

Wisner was intrigued. Three years earlier, he and Polly had reserved a block of orchestra seats for friends and relatives to attend the opening night of a revival of the Black opera at Washington's National Theatre and to watch Leontyne Price perform in the lead role of Bess. Wisner considered the African American spinto soprano, who was born in Laurel, a family protégé. Leontyne's aunt had worked as a laundress for Wisner's mother, and Leontyne had later played with the children of Wisner's sister Elisabeth. Elisabeth and her husband, Alexander Chisholm, had been among many who encouraged the young girl's obvious singing talent and helped pay the tuition for her to attend Juilliard in 1948. The financial support Elisabeth and Alexander gave to educate Leontyne and other Black children in Laurel earned them threatening phone calls from the Ku Klux Klan.

Wisner polled his sources in Europe, where the *Porgy and Bess* company had performed earlier. They heartily endorsed a Russian tour—an ideal "cultural persuader," his Rome station chief, who had seen the show, cabled back. With Wisner's help a delicate diplomatic dance ensued to secure a Russian invitation and U.S. acceptance. The play premiered in Leningrad at the end of 1955.

Wisner, however, balked at ballet, an art form about which he knew little. He rejected Rockefeller's proposal to send the New York City Ballet to tour Russia in exchange for the Bolshoi Ballet performing in the United States. Russian dancers outclassed American dancers, as Wisner saw it. An exchange program in that art form would "show us up in an unfavorable light," he said. Beetle Smith at the State Department agreed with him, as did practically every other national security official Wisner polled on the subject. The U.S. should stick to exporting Broadway hits it knew the Russians couldn't match, like *Oklahoma!* and *Kiss Me, Kate*, Wisner said. Rockefeller thought the espionage chief was full of himself.

* * *

Oxford philosopher and historian Isaiah Berlin not only passed along to Wisner his analysis of Kremlin maneuvers. He also advised the spymaster on how to set up the Betting Book. It was a British party game in which guests recorded small wagers on whatever anybody could dream up to bet on. Wisner kept the entries for his Betting Book in a leather-bound volume, in which notations on the bets were meticulously recorded.

The book was a hit with Georgetown set friends as well as with relatives. Clark Clifford bet $5 to Joe Alsop's $1 that Chief Justice Earl Warren would not permit himself to be a candidate for the GOP presidential nomination in 1956. (Clifford won.) Asia scholar George R. Packard bet Wisner $1 that the Brooklyn Dodgers would blow the 1955 World Series to the New York Yankees. (The Dodgers won.) Frank II bet his mother fifty cents that his friend Bowman Gray III from the tobacco company family would not matriculate at the University of Virginia. (Polly won. Gray went to UVA.)

* * *

By the mid-1950s, Joe Alsop considered Wisner his closest friend in Washington. That distinction did not sit too well with Eisenhower. The president launched an intensive leak investigation in spring 1955 when he suspected a National Security Council document on Soviet satellites had been slipped to the Alsop brothers. Dulles thought he had convinced Ike that the brothers, whose column reached twenty-five million readers by 1955, were not guilty in that case. The column in question was just based on speculation by Stewart Alsop, not an NSC paper. But Eisenhower continued to simmer over the pair. After Joe returned from an Asia trip that spring,

Dulles ordered Wisner to cancel his plans for a welcome-home party at the Locust Hill farm. The president was still angry about the column.

Frank and Polly by the mid-1950s were mentioned regularly in the society columns of Washington's newspapers. The Wisners and the Grahams, along with the Nitzes and the Bissells, hosted a lavish dance party for a hundred fifty guests that they called the "Bankruptcy Ball" because the country was still recovering from a recession. Phil Graham invited Wisner to the Gridiron dinner for Washington's media and political elite.

Increasingly Kay was having to make excuses for Phil's erratic behavior at the parties. He drank too much at the Bankruptcy Ball and had an embarrassing fight with his wife. To cheer her up, Polly organized a surprise party and dance at the P Street house to celebrate Kay's thirty-ninth birthday.

After the intensive Guatemala operation, Wisner began to spend more weekends at Locust Hill. He changed his registration for voting to Maryland and drew even closer to the rural life. He joined the habitat conservation group Ducks Unlimited—his passion for hunting the waterfowl never dimming. After he became close friends with a couple who operated a nearby vegetable farm, he frequently dined with them on platefuls of fresh spinach, peas, and broccoli. Billy Sigman never forgot the day Wisner and he were leaning on a fence rail in the orchard and the Locust Hill farm manager said he eventually planned to buy a house. Wisner said he would put down cash for the home so Sigman could invest his money "in something that's going to make you money." It was an incredibly generous offer, yet one Wisner could afford. Polly and he continued to receive sizable amounts of money bequeathed to them by their families.

* * *

Dulles and his deputy, Charles Cabell, consistently gave Wisner glowing reviews in his fitness reports—a "superior" senior aide, one evaluation declared; "one of the most outstanding officers of this agency" or, for that matter, "in this line of business," another report stated. Along with the praise came hefty salary increases—to $20,000 in the summer of 1956 (more than $220,000 today). Yet beginning in 1954, a caveat was repeatedly inserted in Wisner's evaluations. The clandestine service chief was too thin-skinned, his CIA bosses noted. The flaw was "very minor," they insisted, but they felt compelled to bring it up. "His principal weakness is an oversensitiveness to criticism," Cabell and Dulles wrote. Dulles and Wisner respected each other, but their relationship began to have moments of uneasiness. While Dulles found Wisner to be too touchy and excitable, Wisner found just as irritating the director's sloppy administration and his carelessness in handling secrets.

There had begun to be what might be called "episodes" in Wisner's behavior. The episodes were spaced out in time, so they did not raise serious alarm bells. But Dulles noticed the episodes, so did Wisner's coworkers, and so did his family. Dulles pushed for more and larger operations. Wisner was a workaholic and a detail man who took seriously the job of running thousands of covert projects overseas. In that kind of pressure cooker, who wouldn't have been a little erratic at times? his colleagues rationalized. They were reluctant to harp on Wisner's weird moments. The episodes were like intermissions between weeks, even months, of calm and cool behavior during which State Department and Pentagon officials found Wisner mentally sharp and inventive when they needed something from him or his agency. Wisner also remained orthodox—a hawk as other top officials were when it came to the Russians.

But those episodes . . . They soon became hard to ignore. In Vienna, at an early-1955 meeting with station chiefs, Wisner burst out with a complaint about the proliferation of operations that had no end to them—an odd gripe, the others thought, considering he was the man who had launched those operations and sometimes kept them going past their prime. Wisner began to grumble openly that people were out to get him no matter what he did—perhaps his paranoia was understandable, considering the investigations by Hoover and others in the administration. He snapped at Phil Graham about a "muckraking" *Washington Post* reporter investigating corruption in Thailand—uncharacteristic behavior toward his old friend. At an agency dinner, Wisner tried to give a humorous speech impersonating a Soviet general, which his senior aide, Frank Lindsay, thought was odd. Peter Sichel and Larry Houston with the CIA and Gordon Gray at the White House began to notice an edginess about their friend.

Wisner became a chain-smoker. In the old days, he could nurse a glass of bourbon for most of a party. Now he began refilling his drink more often. Polly found herself having to calm her husband down when he became too rowdy at their parties, which began to spark squabbles between them after the guests had left. Another source of irritation between the couple was Frank's excessive spending on Greek artifacts, which Polly tried to curb. Frank II and Ellis were away most of the time at boarding school and did not see their father's early erratic behavior. Graham and Wendy were at home to witness some of it, but they were too young to understand what they were seeing. Graham recalled being shocked and perplexed over his father blowing up at him when he was around six years old for acting too eager as Wisner was negotiating to buy a schooner on the Eastern Shore.

In Wisner's day, relatively little was known about bipolar disorder, which then was called "manic depression," or about how to spot the disease in its early stages. Mania and depression, however, have long been prevalent among the political elite. Recently, a scientific journal article calculated that nearly half of the thirty-seven U.S. presidents between 1776 and 1974 suffered from depression, anxiety, bipolar disorder, or alcohol abuse.

Part of the problem with the diagnosis of the disease in the mid-1950s—and today as well—was that "manic episodes differ from person to person and in the same individual from time to time," according to one psychiatric textbook. Symptoms also vary widely as the mania progresses through its various stages. Wisner, at that point, could have been among the many people who have bipolar disorder but never suffer a major manic episode. In mania's early phase, a person may feel euphoric, mentally sharp, and tremendously self-confident. Wisner might have gone through this state of "grandiosity," as psychiatrists call it, in his early CIA years. But the feel-good stage of mania might not last long, and the patient can begin to have angry and irritable moods, which now seemed to be happening with Wisner as 1955 ended and 1956 began. Bipolar disorder can cause individuals to smoke more and to abuse alcohol, which Wisner was beginning to do. Impulsive or irrational buying, as Wisner was engaging in, is also often common in the manic state.

Wisner's wife and his friends were not trained to deal with a disease about which they knew next to nothing. Polly could not expect her husband to just "snap out of it," which a person with bipolar disorder cannot do. Polly could also have erred in the other direction—interpreting her husband's every emotion as symptoms of the ailment when they sometimes were not. Bipolar disease requires sophistication and nuance in a spouse's behavior that Polly could not have hoped to have. To complicate matters further, Wisner appeared to be among a sizable minority with bipolar disorder who at the outset show symptoms of hypomania and then mania but not depression. But one thing became certain: Wisner's episodes were growing more frequent over time.

Chapter 23

HUNGARY AND THE CANAL

THE BESTSELLERS *PEYTON PLACE* and *The Man in the Gray Flannel Suit* (on the tensions of small-town and suburban life, respectively) were among the most influential American novels in the mid-1950s. Betty Friedan began writing *The Feminine Mystique*, which in the next decade would become the bible for the country's feminist movement. But books paled compared to the growing power of television. Americans glued themselves to TV family sitcoms like *The Adventures of Ozzie and Harriet, Leave It to Beaver,* and *Father Knows Best.* In New York, Ed Sullivan hosted the most successful television variety show in the nation and became the country's arbiter of culture. On the West Coast, Marilyn Monroe, perennially cast as a dumb blonde in her films, proved to be far smarter and talented than she was given credit for. The IQ game shows *The $64,000 Question* and *Twenty-One* became huge successes until it was revealed the brainy contestants had been coached on the questions, which traumatized viewers.

Wisner continued to dress like a sophisticate of the world. While he still bought his suits from a London tailor, he had his CIA station in Bangkok shop for silk sport shirts to send to him. Outside the hundreds of pages of classified documents he consumed at the office each day, most of Wisner's reading at home was not novels like *Peyton Place* but instead histories—the more arcane the better.

Wisner did appreciate the visual medium's power. He learned that a Hollywood studio was considering producing a television show taken from World War II OSS files and got Dulles to approve his assigning an officer to "covertly" watch the production and make sure no classified information that might harm current CIA operations was aired. In May 1956, Wisner and Dulles were also intrigued with the idea of the CIA secretly funding a film on what Nikita Khrushchev had said about Joseph Stalin three months earlier.

* * *

Khrushchev delivered the speech while Frank and Polly luxuriated aboard the yacht *Camargo III*, which their old friends Julius and Dorette Fleischmann owned and sailed out of Nassau. Wisner had so looked forward to this Caribbean cruise. "I find that after some eight years of work I am in need of having my physical and spiritual batteries recharged," he wrote a friend. During his month of ocean leisure, "so complete was my relaxation," he told Junkie Fleischmann later, "that I found it somewhat difficult to readjust to the activities and requirements of 'real life.'"

It was on February 25, 1956, while Wisner sunned himself on the deck of the *Camargo*, that more than five thousand miles away, in snow-covered Moscow, Khrushchev delivered a fiery speech denouncing Stalin to members of the Twentieth Congress of the Communist Party. The formal address to the fifteen hundred delegates in the Great Hall of the Kremlin was twenty thousand words long and took the Soviet first secretary half a day to deliver. Khrushchev accused his predecessor of being a remote and gullible World War II leader who had allowed the Germans to invade and had purged the Red Army of its best leaders. Throughout his brutal dictatorship, Stalin had carried out the "cruelest repression" against anyone who disagreed with him, Khrushchev railed. "Many thousands of honest and innocent Communists" were summarily executed in a program of "mass terror." On a personal level, "Stalin was a very distrustful man, sickly suspicious," Khrushchev maintained, and Lenin thought that he "was excessively rude" and that his "persecution mania reached unbelievable dimensions." "Comrades! We must abolish the cult of the individual decisively," Khrushchev thundered to his stunned audience, who at the end broke into prolonged applause.

Speculation swelled over whether the speech signaled a move to a more liberal and rational Soviet system of government. That quickly proved to be wishful thinking, a later CIA report concluded. Khrushchev's exercise of power soon differed little from Stalin's. Khrushchev conducted his share of purges, imprisonments, and executions to assume unquestioned control of the Soviet state. He also encouraged a cult of personality for himself. Wisner, who had a vigorous debate over what the Soviet leader's denunciation really meant with George Kennan and Chip Bohlen, believed that Khrushchev was a more wily and skillful leader than Stalin but still an enemy of the United States as committed as Stalin was to America's downfall.

The CIA quickly began to pick up hints of the explosiveness of what Khrushchev had said behind closed doors to the Party Congress. Dulles dearly wanted a copy of the Russian leader's speech. At a meeting with Wisner and other top officers, the CIA director offered a $500,000 reward to whoever brought him one. The offer was just for show. Dulles didn't have the money or authority to post a $500,000 reward. He dangled the cash offer just to demonstrate how enthusiastic he was about getting his hands on the prize.

It took almost two months for the CIA to secure the speech text—a surprisingly long time considering that more than fifteen thousand copies of it had been printed and distributed within the Soviet Bloc. By April three copies—one from a Polish Communist source, the second from Israeli intelligence, and the third from an

Italian leftist—sat on Wisner's desk in Washington. At first, he was nervous that the transcripts he had might be phonies planted to embarrass the agency. But CIA analysts soon verified the copies were genuine.

What to do with the prize? Wisner wanted to feed bits of it slowly to the East Bloc, along with disinformation, to stir unrest, but Dulles overruled him. With Eisenhower's approval, the CIA director gave the entire transcript to the *New York Times*, which published it on June 5.

The *Times* story was an international bombshell. The BBC soon began broadcasting excerpts from the speech in Russian into the Soviet Union. Wisner was happy to see that the broadcasts were not jammed. Radio Free Europe and Radio Liberty aired excerpts as well. Wisner's psychological warfare officers salted the version leaked to the *Times* with doctored paragraphs containing disinformation that they hoped would stir up disenchantment when they were spread among the satellites' Communist parties. Wisner also found a publisher to turn out the speech in book form. He liked to tell a joke that a Politburo member said after the speech: "I thought he was going to talk about desalinization." Wisner tried, unsuccessfully, to get Herblock at the *Washington Post* to draw an editorial cartoon using the pun.

Even before the June *New York Times* publication, shock waves from Khrushchev's speech had coursed through the East Bloc. In Hungary, where reports of the speech spread by word of mouth, pressure had been building against the country's repressive regime for years. Yet despite the ferment stirred, few Western observers predicted that violent upheaval would occur or that there would be any significant challenge to Communist governments. The State Department's intelligence and research bureau concluded that Soviet controls would easily endure.

But revolts in Eastern Europe did occur and Wisner had to deal with them. In Poland, the whispered conversations about the speech had already created factions among the nation's ruling Communist elite, which became emboldened in their criticism of the party's higher echelon. Their grumbling encouraged Polish society in general to begin challenging the Communist system's basic tenets. The spark was lit in Poland on June 28.

Fed up with poor pay and working conditions, factory employees in the western city of Poznań rioted that morning. Four Polish armored and infantry divisions began moving into the city during the afternoon to battle a rampaging crowd that had swelled to 100,000. Most of the fighting occurred on the first day, June 28, but sporadic confrontations lasted for three more days. In the end, fifty-seven protesters were killed, some six hundred were wounded, and more than seven hundred were arrested. Foster Dulles talked tough after the uprising, but ultimately the U.S. government's response was mild: expressing shock at the shooting of protesters, showing sympathy for the families of the fallen, and offering food aid.

The Poznań riot shook the Polish government and reverberated throughout Eastern Europe, whose Communist leaders blamed the West, and Allen Dulles in particular, for instigating the revolt. But although U.S. propaganda had aimed at loosening the control those regimes had over their populations, Washington had had nothing to do with starting or encouraging the violence. Wisner, however, was privately delighted that it had occurred. So was Dulles, who coldly calculated that a little bloodshed in the satellite nations was good. He pressed Wisner to step up the CIA's penetration of Communist parties in the East Bloc. "You can't make an omelet without breaking eggs," the CIA director said. Eisenhower, however, was more circumspect and not eager to spark violent unrest in the egg breaking.

After the Poznań riots, Polish Communist leader Władysław Gomułka launched a rapid de-Stalinization program in his country. It terrified the nation's old guard Communists, who on October 19 called on the Russians to send in the Red Army to contain what they feared would soon be a revolt. Khrushchev denounced the changes

Gomułka wanted, mobilized Soviet troops, and flew to Warsaw that same day to strong-arm the Polish leader. Gomułka, however, would not be bullied. He delivered a fierce attack on Stalinism to a crowd of 400,000 and promised even more reforms. In a tense meeting with Khrushchev at the Warsaw airport, the Polish leader demanded that the Red Army advance on Poland be halted. Fearing a tough fight with the Polish militia, not to mention the population in general, Khrushchev backed down, halting the Soviet tank divisions at the Polish–East German border in exchange for assurances from Gomułka that Poland would remain a loyal Soviet ally. The crisis passed.

* * *

By late fall 1956, Wisner's clandestine service still had little means to spark a revolt in Eastern Europe. Even if he had been able to incite violence, Wisner wondered whether it would have been a good idea for the U.S. government to be doing something like that. It was a question he had been asking himself and privately posing to others in his business for about three years now. In August 1953, Wisner had joined Barnes and Helms in raising the touchy question. "What is our ultimate objective in stirring up trouble in East Germany and the satellites," Wisner asked Dulles, "and what major over-riding policy are we working [to support]?"

Eisenhower's loose liberation talk in the 1952 presidential campaign, promising to help free the Russian satellites, had earned him political points at home and raised hopes in East Europe. CIA analysts had concluded, however, that the Communist regimes would not be toppled by just internal unrest, and if a revolt did break out spontaneously, Barnes, for one, said that Washington "should be extremely cautious" about giving it too much encouragement. Wisner believed that he and the other spy leaders had a responsibility as covert operators to press Washington's political leaders to be crystal clear in the policy guidance they gave the CIA. But he could see that the members of the new administration were reluctant to face the question of what the U.S. position should be if Communist regimes in East Europe could not keep control of their countries, even though he urged them to deal with that dilemma.

As near as Wisner could tell, his marching orders were to "keep the pot simmering," he told Dulles in one memo, "but to avoid boiling it over." Those were horrible instructions, but that was the reality. The United States was not as intent on challenging Russian control of Eastern Europe as it was on trying to make life miserable for the Soviet occupiers. If an East European country tried to revolt on its own, Wisner could see that the United States would just have to stand by and wring its hands.

In March 1953, Wisner brought up this thorny issue when a senior CIA officer sent Dulles a proposal to organize cells in East European factories to stage strikes and demonstrations. Fine, Wisner told Dulles, but suppose the factory revolts are successful and the violence that breaks out is large enough to "pose the kind of challenge to the Russians that would require them to move in on the situation with massive (military) repressive measures. The question is—what do we do then?" The unspoken answer to that question, Wisner and his top men knew, was nothing. The United States was not about to intervene with military force to support such a rebellion and risk nuclear war with the U.S.S.R. Peter Sichel, one of Wisner's top aides, was brutally candid about the reality. The CIA's infiltration operations into the East Bloc, he believed, were grounded on a lie the agency was telling the infiltrators: their operations were being launched to liberate Russia and its satellites. Perhaps it was appropriate that one of the cryptonyms for the CIA's East European operations was "BGWoeful."

* * *

On October 20, the day after Khrushchev brokered a deal in Warsaw to defuse the Polish crisis, a special plane Wisner had arranged to fly him to Europe landed at Bovington, an old wartime operational airfield about an hour's drive southwest of London. Rolfe Kingsley, one of his most trusted aides, was the only person from his Washington staff who was with him. Bronson Tweedy, the deputy chief at the CIA's London station, was there to greet him and take him to the raft of appointments Wisner had booked for the London leg of his trip.

Wisner had been planning this journey since August. In London, he wanted to talk to the British about a new Western relationship toward Africa, where an explosion of independence movements was beginning. Wisner also managed to wedge into his packed schedule a rushed side trip to the ancient Rugby School in Warwickshire, where his son Frank II, then seventeen, was a student. Covered in mud, Frankie was shocked to see his father standing on the sideline of the rugby field. He ran over and gave him sort of a hug. Wisner had not told him he was coming. "I'm here," was all Frankie's father said. "I don't have long. I came up from London to see you. I cannot stay. I just wanted to lay eyes on you." And that was it. Wisner turned around and left the field, with Frankie standing there totally perplexed.

When he boarded the flight to England on October 20, Wisner was wrung out from the Washington grind. Helms believed that overwork had begun to seriously affect his boss's health around the time of the Poznań riot in June. The February Caribbean cruise had been rejuvenating, but by summer Wisner could not seem to pace himself and the strain began to show. There was at times a ferocity about him, with more brooding, more suspiciousness. Friends like Helms worried he was seriously ill. From the minute Wisner stepped off the plane in Bovington, he seemed to Tweedy "very high strung," as the aide recalled later.

From London, Wisner wanted to fly to France and then to Southeastern Europe, including Greece. Typical of him, he had booked nonstop rounds of meetings at each stop. The Polish crisis added to a vast amount of work Wisner had already planned in

London. So did two more political explosions—in Hungary and at the Suez Canal.

* * *

After World War II, Stalin imposed a brutal occupation over bombed-out Hungary, which had allied with Nazi Germany. The Kremlin put Mátyás Rákosi in power. The sadistic Communist dictator, who was called "Arsehead" behind his back, transformed the nation into a model Stalinist state and ruined its economy. Organized like the KGB, the viciously efficient Hungarian security service, the Államvédelmi Hatóság, or ÁVH, became the most feared government unit in the country. By 1950, political opposition had been destroyed and over the next three years more than 1.3 million Hungarians were prosecuted, jailed, or executed in political purges.

Radio Free Europe broadcasts, which regime jamming never succeeded in silencing, became hugely popular. Wisner's officers targeted Hungary with other small-scale psychological warfare operations, such as circulating anti-Communist chain letters and publications. Balloons that were floated over the country dropped millions of leaflets trying to convince Hungarians that the Communist regime "is weaker than you think," as one message stated.

It wasn't. Hungary was hostile territory for CIA covert operations in the early 1950s. The ÁVH was surprisingly efficient at rounding up the Hungarian agents the CIA sent in, leaving the country barren of organized resistance groups. By 1953, the Hungarian border had become progressively more difficult to penetrate and potential Hungarian operatives had become more reluctant to collaborate with the CIA. A January 1956 U.S. Army report concluded that in Hungary—with its flat terrain, which offered little cover and concealment in most places—it would not be easy for American-trained guerrilla forces to infiltrate the country and sustain themselves. What resistance that did exist was largely passive, such as workers deliberately slacking off on the job.

Disenchanted with Rákosi's inept rule, Moscow's post-Stalin collective leadership in June 1953 replaced him as prime minister with Imre Nagy, an honest, plainspoken, and loyal Communist who promised a "New Course" that would rid the nation of the more odious aspects of Rákosi's dictatorship. Hungarians were joyful but not for long. Nagy's New Course failed to live up to expectations, while Rákosi hung around and worked tirelessly to sabotage Nagy's premiership and grab back power. Moscow soon encouraged a rivalry between the two leaders to see who would come out on top. Over time, Rákosi resumed being the favorite of the Soviets, who grew disenchanted with Nagy.

By spring 1955, Nagy was out and Rákosi was back in with a loyal underling whom he installed to replace Nagy as prime minister. Nagy was expelled from the Communist Party, but he became widely popular among ordinary Hungarians. Then came Khrushchev's Twentieth Party Congress speech denouncing Stalin, which posed a problem for Rákosi. If Stalin was now a criminal, what did that make Rákosi, his protégé? In Budapest's sophisticated Communist Party circles, Rákosi was mocked. By the summer of 1956, he was openly called a murderer, and the ÁVH did not have the power it once had to extinguish such heresies.

During all the intrigues, U.S. intelligence about Hungary was paltry. American diplomats in Budapest had few contacts with senior Hungarian officials. The American legation minister had rotated out in August 1956 to take a new assignment. By the time Wisner flew to London on October 20, his agency had just six analysts on its Hungarian desk in Washington and no spy network to speak of in Hungary. There was only one CIA representative in Budapest and his was mainly support work, such as mailing letters and buying stamps and stationery.

Once more, the Kremlin became anxious. It had seventy-five thousand Russian ground troops and airmen in Hungary. Soviet military commanders in the country began to notice that Hungarians were more standoffish, even hostile, toward their soldiers. In

July, the Soviets had replaced Rákosi with Ernő Gerő, another inflexible Stalinist with blood on his hands from Rákosi's reign of terror. He turned out to be a terrible choice.

Hungarians became as unhappy with Gerő as they had been with Rákosi. On October 6, one hundred thousand people turned out for the reburial of five Communists who had now become popular only because they had been hanged by the Rákosi regime seven years earlier. Later that evening, some five hundred university students marched to a monument in Buda, shouting anti-Communist slogans. Police broke up the small demonstration quickly and peacefully. Khrushchev, however, soon became disenchanted with Gerő, whom he judged to be a lazy leader with no appreciation of the crisis unfolding before him.

On October 22, Dulles, who was still preoccupied with what Khrushchev was up to in Poland, sent to Wisner in London a cable with Washington's latest intelligence on the crisis in Warsaw. Dulles and Wisner soon had to change their focus. On that same day, five thousand Hungarian students crammed into a lecture hall at Budapest Technological University and drafted what amounted to a sixteen-point manifesto for a revolution. They planned to march the next day in support of the Polish revolt. The fuse was set.

* * *

Completed in 1869 and initially owned by a French and British company, Egypt's Suez Canal became the key sea transport route between Asia and Europe, giving Britain and France access to Persian Gulf, Indian, and Far East markets without their ships having to sail around Africa's Cape of Good Hope. Sixty-seven million tons of oil and sixty thousand British troops passed through the waterway each year. By the 1950s, however, the canal was entangled in Cold War and postcolonial politics. Gamal Abdel Nasser, the Egyptian nationalist who had seized power in 1954, was intent on playing Britain, France, the United States, and the Soviet Union against one another to further his goal of transforming his country into an independent modern state. Nasser hoped to cultivate cordial relations with the United States to obtain financing for development projects such as the Aswan High Dam across the Nile River, and to counter the British and French, whose imperial designs he did not trust. In a double bank shot, the Egyptian president was also receiving arms from Czechoslovakia. Although the aid did not come with enough training and technical support to materially improve Nasser's fighting power, it alarmed the Israelis.

In 1955, Prime Minister Anthony Eden—who ruled his cabinet with more of an iron hand, particularly on foreign policy, than Churchill ever had—believed he could handle Nasser. Along with France, Britain held out hope that conciliation on their part would make the Egyptian president a team player. By spring 1956, Eden knew that appeasing Nasser had failed. Believing the West was no longer interested in proceeding with the Aswan High Dam, Nasser on July 26 nationalized the Suez Canal, taking over its company operations from the British and French purportedly to generate funds for the dam project.

Dulles and an aide drove to the Locust Hill farm that day to brainstorm with Wisner on what countermeasures the United States should take, if any. The British government, which owned a controlling interest of 45 percent of the shares in the Suez Canal Company, was ready for tough countermeasures. "The Egyptian has his thumb on our windpipe," Eden declared, while the British press proclaimed "no more Hitlers." Egged on by France's more militant premier, Guy Mollet, Eden warned in a telegram to Eisenhower that "we must be ready, in the last resort, to use force to bring Nasser to his senses."

That was not the kind of talk Ike wanted to hear from America's closest ally. Washington's strategic goal in the Middle East was to prevent the Soviets from gaining any foothold there. At the same time, CIA analysts recognized that imperialism drove British and French foreign policy toward the region, which did not necessarily square with American objectives. Believing Nasser was well "within his rights" to nationalize the waterway, Eisenhower opposed any British or French military takeover of the Suez Canal, and he had his State Department deliver that message to the two countries' ambassadors in Washington. The U.S. had little invested economically in the canal. Allen Dulles actually liked Nasser—so did his station chief in Cairo—but Foster did not.

Britain kept its invasion plans with the French secret from the United States. The two countries hoped—unrealistically—that the Americans would provide a nuclear umbrella over their operation to ward off the Russians. Eden and Mollet decided their militaries needed at least six weeks to prepare for an invasion. D-Day for the expedition, which was envisioned to be about the size of the Allies' World War II landing at Anzio, was put off until late September 1956.

CIA analysts floated the possibility in intelligence reports that the British and French might attack Egypt, but the reports were filled with so much uncertainty, they were largely useless to Eisenhower. But that possibility put Dulles on edge. He walked into a meeting with Wisner and his other deputies on Monday morning, August 13, and griped that when he had phoned agency headquarters over the weekend for the latest intelligence the CIA had on Suez, no one was there to field his query. He ordered Wisner and the agency's intelligence analysis chief to have men on weekend duty when there was an international crisis like that one. Wisner did so.

The CIA's equivocal reports were enough to worry Eisenhower. On September 2, he wrote Eden and flatly rejected using force in Suez, particularly with diplomacy not exhausted. The British prime minister gave him a saber-rattling reply. There was much personal animosity between Eden and Foster Dulles, who soon would be racked by colon cancer. The two men were barely speaking to each other at that point.

Soviet premier Nikolai Bulganin delivered a stiffer note to Eden and Mollet, warning that Russia would not stand idly by if there were an invasion of Egypt. There was a danger "that small wars can turn into big wars," Bulganin wrote. Russian foreign minister Vyacheslav Molotov assumed the United States was colluding with the British and French.

On September 22, Eden and Mollet announced they would put their case before the United Nations Security Council. It was a head fake. The invasion's D-Day was moved to October 8. Britain and France now had an important ally in their gambit—Israel, whose prime minister, David Ben-Gurion, was intent on launching a preventive war against Egypt and could now see the nationalization of the canal strangling Israeli shipping. After much private negotiating back and forth, the three countries agreed that Israel would attack Egypt at Suez first, giving Britain and France the excuse to intervene with their forces in an operation code-named "Musketeer" on the pretext of keeping the two belligerents apart and protecting the canal. Israel's code name for its part of the devious scheme was "Kadesh."

In the second week of October, high-flying American reconnaissance aircraft spotted signs that Israel was preparing for a military operation, but Washington assumed the attack would be on Jordan, not Egypt. "From this time on," Ike later recalled, "we had the uneasy feeling that we were cut off from our allies." Wisner was beginning to sense the same. Several days after Wisner's arrival in London, Sir Patrick Dean, the British chairman of the Joint Intelligence Committee, arranged for a formal dinner to be given in his honor. But when the time came to sit at the table, Dean was not there, and he did not show up until one a.m. The British intelligence chairman had likely been at Sèvres, France, signing on behalf of the United Kingdom the final Anglo-Franco-Israeli operational agreement for the attack on Suez. Wisner, who thought Dean's absence odd, had already become suspicious that his MI6 cousins were keeping a secret from him. "Something is burning," he cabled back to Washington.

"Out from under every door that he passed there were escaping scents of plots for Suez," Frank II recalled his father saying later.

* * *

The Hungarian revolt on October 23 took Wisner by surprise. It took the U.S. mission in Budapest by surprise. Back in Washington, it took the White House, the State Department, and the CIA by surprise. The revolt also took Moscow, which had extensive intelligence assets in Hungary, by surprise. And the suddenness of the revolt took Hungarians by surprise.

As Wisner prepared to begin his long-scheduled tour of CIA stations on the European continent, scattered protests began in Budapest. Twelve thousand students marched on the Pest side of the river at the Petőfi Statue. Eight thousand students gathered at the Technological University. Hammer-and-sickle emblems were cut out of Hungarian flags. Twenty-five thousand crammed into Bem Square. On the streets an informal alliance formed between workers and intellectuals. The mood everywhere in the capital grew angrier, with protesters shouting: "Russians, go home!"

At five o'clock that afternoon, Gerő, Hungary's strongman, asked the Soviet ambassador and military attaché in Budapest for Russian troops to halt the demonstrations, a request the local Red Army commander balked at fulfilling until Marshal Georgy Zhukov, the Soviet defense minister, ordered him that evening to prepare for combat. As dusk fell over the capital, the crowd of protesters outside the parliament grew to two hundred thousand. Nagy drove to the demonstration, while Gerő delivered a radio broadcast scolding the protesters, which sparked an explosion of public outrage. By eight forty-five p.m., another demonstration erupted at Budapest's prominent Heroes' Square, where a crowd knocked down a bronze statue of Stalin. Meanwhile, Nagy, who had seriously misjudged the national mood, appeared at Kossuth Square, where he praised the demonstrators but begged them to go home. They refused.

Hungarian troops were dispatched to the Radio Budapest building to restore order and crush the demonstration, but they refused to attack the students. Some soldiers joined the crowd in fighting the hated ÁVH men at the scene; some handed their weapons and ammunition over to the protesters, while most returned to their barracks. The balance of power had shifted in favor of those new rebels. Their protest had now become an armed insurrection. Yet, while the insurgents finally captured the radio building just before dawn of October 24, the government kept broadcasting from a duplicate transmitter at the Interior Ministry, denying the freedom fighters control of the airwaves.

Soon Radio Free Europe's monitoring equipment in West Germany began picking up the transmissions of low-powered stations the rebels had seized around Hungary, and the RFE staff started relaying back to the CIA in Washington English translations of the broadcasts. They gave the Eisenhower administration its first inkling that the Budapest street fighting was evolving into a national revolution. Allen Dulles huddled with his top advisers at agency headquarters to determine what had happened in Hungary. With no contingency plans on the shelf for dealing with such a revolt, the CIA men began brainstorming the responses the United States might make, such as infiltrating trained saboteurs into the country to help organize the revolt, smuggling in weapons to the new insurgents, or intervening with Western military forces. But no such responses would be made and Wisner, now sitting in London watching events in Hungary unfold, knew they would not be made.

The Kremlin strongly suspected that the CIA was actively involved in the Hungarian revolt, but the fact was no agency guerrilla organizers would be smuggled into the country. Hungarian rebel tactics "were improvised on the spot," Wisner would note in a later memo, and leadership of the revolt "did not develop until several days after the outbreak of fighting." A transfer of arms to the Hungarian rebels was never seriously contemplated in Washington. Wisner would later insist in that same memo that not a single weapon the Hungarian rebels used had been manufactured in the West. Besides, the rebels had all the arms they needed from Hungarian soldiers who defected with weapons or gave freedom fighters the keys to their armories. Sending in American troops was also out of the question. Hungary was surrounded by Communist countries and neutral Austria, which did not make U.S. military intervention easy. Robert Amory, a top intelligence-analysis officer at the CIA, tossed out the idea of the United States using nuclear weapons to interdict Soviet reinforcements pouring into the country. Amory admitted later his idea was "lunacy."

The U.S. response, instead, was cautious, and Wisner knew it would be cautious. It grew, as he also well knew, out of the Eisenhower administration's policy of keeping the pot boiling in Eastern Europe without having it boil over into a possible nuclear conflict. Senior American officials publicly expressed sympathy for the Hungarian people and offered general support for the revolution's goals. The United States took the lead in raising the issue in the U.N. Security Council. The administration held out the prospect of limited economic assistance to Eastern European governments if they achieved a measure of independence from Moscow, but at the same time, U.S. diplomats assured their Soviet counterparts that America was not seeking a military alliance with Hungary or other East European countries. In other words, Washington's response was tepid.

Under orders from Khrushchev, Gerő brought Nagy back into the government, appointing him prime minister once more as a fig leaf. But Nagy refused to ask the Soviets to send in troops to restore order. The Red Army came anyway, with six thousand soldiers and seven hundred tanks entering Budapest in the early-morning hours of October 24. They found themselves in an intense urban war with an unorganized yet determined and inventive enemy showering them with gunfire and Molotov cocktails. Khrushchev, however, was confident the Gerő-Nagy regime could restore order because his military advisers were assuring him that Russian troops were mopping up "pockets of bandits" and would soon have Budapest under control.

Nagy spoke on the radio at midday, pleading with his countrymen to stop fighting and promising reforms. The revolutionaries, as well as a majority of Hungarians, ignored him. In Budapest, about three thousand freedom fighters took up arms on October 24, suffering eighty killed and four hundred fifty wounded, and the revolution spread throughout the rest of the country. Hungary's one-party rule was unraveling. At the end of the day, Khrushchev was told the bad news: sixty Russian soldiers had been killed or wounded, eight tanks and armored vehicles had been destroyed, and Soviet forces did not control Budapest. The Russian leader, who had been reluctant to send in the Red Army, was now ready to unleash it.

The morning of October 25, a regime radio broadcast claimed that Soviet troops had liquidated the rebel insurrection, but that was a lie. Street fighting continued. The rebels used hit, run, and hide tactics against Soviet T-34 tanks, with teenagers and even children attacking them. The freedom fighters calculated that if they could keep Russian soldiers, who had not been trained in counterinsurgency combat, bogged down in a war of attrition, it would raise Hungarian spirits, the West would rally behind the rebellion, and Moscow would negotiate an end to the conflict or just evacuate its forces. The Red Army, however, was in an ugly mood. Soviet soldiers and ÁVH sharpshooters opened fire on five thousand demonstrators at Kossuth Square on October 25, leaving seventy-five of them dead and 282 wounded. The public mood after the massacre changed "from exhilaration and excitement to bitterness and despair," according to one chronicler of the revolt.

Several hundred Hungarians converged on the U.S. legation building near Kossuth Square and begged for American military aid. Legation officers told the crowd only that they would pass along the pleas to the U.S. government. With military aid ruled out, Wisner's psychological warfare officers back in Washington debated on October 25 how far Radio Free Europe should go in a propaganda offensive. So far, RFE had confined itself to reporting only straight news on the Hungarian revolt and had limited its commentary to condemning the Soviet military intervention and supporting demands for the withdrawal of the Red Army. The dilemma, the CIA propagandists realized, was how the radio could convey U.S. support for the rebels without provoking an even harsher response from the Soviets. At a minimum, Radio Free Europe should have been allowed to offer "sympathy and admiration for the courage and spirit of the embattled rebels," a CIA memo recommended. Should RFE go further and offer advice to insurgents on how to carry out their battles with the Soviets? Should RFE offer suggestions to "the Hungarian people generally, such as urging that they cooperate in cutting off food and other supplies from the Soviet troops?" the agency memo asked. Wisner's psychological warriors didn't have answers to those questions yet.

On October 25, the Kremlin cashiered Gerő and fished into the second ranks of the Hungarian Communist structure to make a quiet ascetic named János Kádár the party's first secretary. Nagy remained as prime minister, but his dream for a Hungary with reformed Communism was marginalized.

* * *

Meeting secretly in Paris on October 24 and 25, British, French, and Israeli officials made final plans for the invasion of Egypt. The Israeli attack would begin at dusk on October 29. Britain and France proposed to launch their operations on October 31. London insisted that appearances be maintained. At all times, the Anglo-French contingent should be seen as defending the canal against threats by both the Israelis and the Egyptians. The Israeli attack could not simply look like a border raid, the British insisted. Anything short of a full-scale war launched by Tel Aviv would not be viewed by the international community as a threat to the canal that would justify Britain and France intervening militarily to protect the waterway.

* * *

On October 26, Allen Dulles, who made a point of trying to entertain Eisenhower at National Security Council meetings, told him a story about a cable writer at the U.S. legation in Budapest penning his report while lying on the floor of his office to avoid being hit by bullets flying in from the outside. At that point, Dulles did not bother with offering proposals to the council for paramilitary operations in Hungary. Eisenhower was not interested in them. The president by that time had moved on from a cautious wait-and-see approach to "active non-involvement" in the Hungarian revolt, as one historical account phrased it. He worried that, threatened with the loss of control of the satellites, Khrushchev might lash out militarily as Hitler had toward the end of World War II. Ike might have had the Russian leader pegged wrong at that point. Chip Bohlen in Moscow cabled Washington that he had just seen Khrushchev and Bulganin at a reception. The ambassador had never seen them looking so grim.

Eisenhower was not alone in putting the brakes on a Western response to Hungary. Europe's North Atlantic Treaty Organization moved even more deliberatively than Washington's National Security Council. In New York, the U.N. Security Council slow-walked the convening of a meeting on Hungary. Cord Meyer, a CIA psywar director, later insisted that he kept churning out to Radio Free Europe newscasters policy directives instructing them to tiptoe in their broadcasts between encouraging the Hungarian rebels and not inciting them to revolution.

* * *

Photos taken over British bases in Cyprus by the CIA's new high-flying U-2 plane revealed a large number of British and French bombers and transport planes parked near runways on October 27. Another U-2 spotted a squadron of French fighter-bombers at an Israeli airfield. But the three countries, all expert in deception, continued to succeed masterfully in hiding from the CIA what they intended to do with those air assets.

* * *

The morning of that same day, bloody fighting was leaving parts of central Budapest in ruins. The public paid no attention to the new cabinet announced by Nagy, who was lagging behind the revolution. By midday October 27, a column of Soviet tanks and artillery battled a hundred fifty rebels to a draw at the Kilián Barracks and Corvin Passage in the most furious fight of the revolution. Rebel morale was high, while the Russians licked their wounds. Not all of them had a stomach for urban combat, and at times they fought among themselves. The Hungarian army, meanwhile, played a confusing role. Its commander was hard-line, but he could not rely on his troops, many of whom continued to join the insurgents. Dulles that day sent an equivocal cable to Wisner in London. It appeared intended to keep him calm but likely only left him confused. "These are dramatic days and we must weigh carefully all our actions," the CIA director wrote his clandestine service chief. "However, I'm not one of those who believes we should be hindered by undue caution."

By nightfall on October 27, Nagy decided to step in front of the revolution and accept nearly all the insurgents' demands for reform. Party chief János Kádár joined him in pressing Khrushchev to agree to a settlement and an end to the fighting. By midday on October 28, a shaky cease-fire was announced over government radio. The next day, Soviet forces began withdrawing from Budapest, although they remained stationed outside the city while other divisions stayed in place in the countryside. Throughout Hungary, jubilation spread because the revolution had triumphed.

On Monday morning, October 29, as Red Army tanks rumbled out of Budapest, Wisner flew from London to Paris, where he checked into the Hôtel de Crillon. He plunged into a furious round of meetings with NATO officials and his station chiefs who had gathered in the French capital to brainstorm with him a strategy now for stabilizing Hungary.

About five hours after Wisner arrived at the Hôtel de Crillon, Israel, with the French providing air support, launched a surprise attack on Egypt, then rapidly occupied the Sinai Peninsula over the next few days. Following their deception plan, Britain and France on October 30 delivered ultimatums to Egypt and Israel to stay clear of the Suez Canal. Israel complied, as prearranged with London and Paris. But Egypt, as the British and French expected, had to reject the demand in order to move military formations and supplies across the canal to counter the Israelis in Sinai. British and French bombers and warships then attacked Egyptian military targets over the next week, followed by their paratroop and amphibious forces landing at the Mediterranean end of the canal and occupying a zone on either side.

Eisenhower was totally blindsided by the attack and not too happy with Allen Dulles and the CIA for failing to warn him of it in advance. From the president on down, every senior official was absolutely furious with the British and French for pulling off that stunt—no one more so than Frank Wisner, who was outraged the two countries would divert global attention and sabotage what he considered the best chance to peel off an East European country from the Soviets' grip, just to satiate their imperial appetites.

Wisner had never trusted the French secret service. He did not expect them to be candid with him. But the British? That was a different matter. The American CIA and Britain's MI6 were unusually close—more than "cousins," as they were commonly called. Wisner had many old friends in British intelligence. That they would deceive him like that hurt deeply.

* * *

By the time he had arrived at the Hôtel de Crillon, Wisner appeared unduly agitated to the CIA officers who greeted him there. He had quiet moments. At other times he was volatile: pent up with anger, screaming at aides, and trying to micromanage the work of his stations.

Agency officers in Europe and back in Washington believed the crushing workload Wisner had endured for so many years had finally caught up with him. The zeal and intensity the boss displayed in running the CIA's clandestine operations "imposed unquestionably an abnormal strain on his vigorous physique," Helms said. Al Ulmer, a Far East Division chief in the CIA, voiced the refrain of many agency officers: Wisner had just "burned himself out." The twin crises in Hungary, where he had been helpless to aid the rebel revolt, and in Suez, where he had been betrayed by the British, had finally broken him mentally.

Colleagues became even more expansive in their armchair psychoanalysis. "Wisner's hopes for the world were crumbling around him," opined Bronson Tweedy, the London station's deputy chief. Gerald Miller, another headquarters officer, believed Wisner had long suffered "Iron Curtain phobia" left over from his Romania days early in the Cold War. He broke down from what he saw in Hungary as a "fracture in the Iron Curtain and he couldn't do anything about it." There was even speculation that the moral ambiguities of his "life in secrets" had finally done him in.

They were all interesting theories, but they were nowhere near the truth. The real story was different. Frank Wisner was having a mental breakdown not because of his workload or because of the international crises unfolding before him or because he could not change the course of the Cold War. He was breaking down mentally because he suffered from a complex disease caused by a biological malfunction in his brain that for many people was genetically inherited. The hypomania that he had experienced for so many years and that had made him appear almost superhuman in his government work and private life had now transformed into full-blown mania, which had kicked in by the time he arrived in Europe. Hungary and Suez appeared to be trigger events that helped set off the manic attack.

Wisner would not have had a breakdown if he had not suffered from bipolar disorder. He was a savvy government operator. He knew full well that there was no chance the Eisenhower administration would intervene in Hungary; the mild U.S. response could not have surprised him and would not have made him so distraught that he would begin suffering an emotional collapse. The same with British duplicity in Suez, which angered him but would not have caused him to become unhinged if he had been healthy. Yes, he had a crushing workload, but other CIA officers did as well during that tumultuous period and they did not go off the rails. Besides, Wisner was able to rejuvenate himself with vacations and outdoor work at the farm. Bottom line: a disease—not his job, as his colleagues thought—felled him.

The onset of a manic episode can be abrupt, developing over a few days, or it can take time to unfold. Although the symptoms might be almost imperceptible at first, they gradually become "more extreme, more unpleasant, and more unmistakably pathological," according to one psychiatrist. That appears to have happened in Wisner's case. Bipolar disorder has been described as the "chameleon" of psychiatric diseases. It can sneak up on its victim with symptoms that are different from patient to patient. Wisner began exhibiting classic manic symptoms, such as irritability that turned into explosive anger at times; paranoia; agitation and churning in his mind; bursts of energy; and a decreased need for sleep. In his day, people afflicted with that mood disorder were often given by friends, family, and even doctors "the covert message" that they were to blame for their odd behavior—or, in Wisner's case, that overwork and multiple international crises were the culprits. *Just take a rest, pull yourself together, figure things out,* patients were told in so many words.

Yet while the external stress of Hungary and Suez might have helped precipitate his initial episode of bipolar disease, eventually the illness he suffered would take on a life of its own. Later manic-depressive episodes would begin without obvious events sparking them. Wisner would soon find the condition maddening not because he got into that disturbed state of mind but because he could not stop from getting into it. There would be no end to the disease. Wisner did not realize it when he flew to Paris, but he was entering a dark period of his life.

* * *

On October 31, *Pravda* posted a declaration promising greater equality in Moscow's relations with its East European satellites and

announcing that the Soviet Union was prepared to enter into negotiations with the Hungarian government on Red Army troop levels
in the country. An optimistic Allen Dulles called it a "miracle," telling Eisenhower the crisis appeared to be on the verge of being resolved. Ike was skeptical. The news seemed to him to be too good
to be true.

It was. On the same day of the *Pravda* declaration, the Kremlin
leadership—racked by uncertainty, indecision, and confusion—
reversed itself and decided to have the Red Army take over Hungary. What the world saw as hopeful signs, Khrushchev saw as a
defiant satellite remaining in turmoil. Nagy had released some eight
thousand political prisoners and announced the formation of a mul-
tiparty democracy—moves he knew Moscow would find unacceptable. The earlier Soviet troop evacuation of Budapest had left volatile
security vacuums. The morning of October 30, fighting broke out
between insurgents and ÁVH officers in the Pest commercial district's Republic Square for control of the Greater Budapest Communist Party headquarters. The gun battle escalated into a brutal
three-hour siege, horrifying Soviet envoys in the Hungarian capital,
who telegrammed Moscow that the situation in the country "is getting worse."

Khrushchev and the Soviet leaders around him now believed the
rebellion threatened Communist rule over Hungary. The West would
see a lack of response by Moscow as a sign of weakness, especially after the British-French-Israeli strike against Suez. Anti-Communist
sentiment in Hungary threatened the rule of neighboring satellite
leaders. In the Soviet Union, party members would not understand a
failure to respond with force in Hungary. Khrushchev did not want
to be the man who lost that country. He coldly calculated that the
upcoming U.S. presidential election, the Anglo-French invasion of
Suez, and the obvious rupture of relations among Western allies left
him room for maneuver to crush the Hungarian revolt and suffer little
more than political repercussions. Watching events from Paris, Wisner believed Khrushchev would succeed.

Soviet leaders decided that their second invasion of Hungary "would be done ruthlessly, efficiently, and without mercy," according to one historical account. Khrushchev's generals told him it could be accomplished in three days. "We'll do it, then," the party first secretary decided, ordering that Nagy's government be kept in the dark about it as long as possible so Hungarians would not have time to organize a defense.

On November 1, Red Army troops and tanks started pouring across the Ukrainian and Czech borders into Hungary in "Operation Whirlwind." The Hungarian air force remained grounded as Soviet troops surrounded airports. Nagy frantically phoned Moscow but could not connect with Khrushchev, who prepared to fly out to brief other satellite leaders of his invasion decision. Kádár, meanwhile, betrayed the revolution and was flown to the Russian capital to declare his cooperation.

As the Red Army's tanks rolled into Budapest once more, Wisner sent friends back in Georgetown long, rambling letters expounding on the evils of Communism. James Reston received one of the alarming notes, which sounded like it had been written by Joe McCarthy.

* * *

The morning of November 1, Eisenhower and the other members of his National Security Council pulled their chairs up to the long table in the Cabinet Room. The president began by announcing that he wanted to focus on the Middle East instead of the Hungarian revolt. Suez was more important to American security interests, Eisenhower had decided. Hungary was old news, the country's fate already settled, and the United States could not change what was happening there. Suez now represented the larger threat in Ike's mind. He worried about the Soviets injecting themselves militarily into the crisis. Was it possible the Russians had already "slipped" the Egyptians a half dozen atomic bombs? Eisenhower asked. Bulganin had made a veiled threat to use nuclear weapons if hostilities continued there. Admiral Arthur Radford, chairman of the Joint Chiefs, said he doubted it. The Soviets, in fact, were bluffing. Khrushchev had no intention of becoming mired in the Middle East muddle, saying at one point: "The English and the French are in a real mess in Egypt. We shouldn't get caught in the same company."

Allen Dulles, who had been loath to shut the door completely on some type of CIA aid to the Hungarian revolt, cabled Wisner in Paris that Washington was firmly locked into doing nothing. Egypt, rather than Hungary, was now the U.S. priority. Radio Free Europe continued to be under orders to report only military developments and insurgent demands and not to take a position for or against any Hungarian political party or leader so as not to provoke the Soviets.

*　*　*

The Hungarian tragedy continued to play out. Realizing resistance was futile, Nagy made no move to throw the Hungarian army into the fight against the Soviet invasion. On November 3—as Foster Dulles was rushed to Walter Reed hospital for emergency cancer surgery—150,000 Soviet troops and 2,500 tanks closed in on Budapest and other key Hungarian towns. Rebel bands that had started the revolution twelve days earlier offered the only resistance, fighting hard and courageously. But that time, the Russians mounted a savage and ruthless war with overwhelming ground and air forces that made quick work of the resistance. Imre Nagy fled to the Yugoslav embassy and János Kádár was brought back from Moscow to head a new government.

*　*　*

On the morning of November 3, Wisner flew to Germany. That day he visited CIA outposts in Bonn, Heidelberg, and finally, by late afternoon, Frankfurt, where he stayed with Tracy and Janet Barnes at their villa. After the Guatemala operation, Barnes had been rewarded with a transfer to Frankfurt to head the large CIA operational headquarters there. Wisner was not surprised by the second Soviet invasion, and he knew the West could do nothing to stop it. His disease, however, had put him in a manic state. Over the days he was in Germany, he ran from one appointment to another, meeting American military officers and diplomats as well as key Germans like intelligence chief Reinhard Gehlen. He stayed up half the night talking to Barnes, then started up early the next day with only two to three hours of sleep. A man who dominated any conversation in normal times, Wisner now made it impossible for others to get a word in. Tracy and Janet found him to be irrational as he rambled on. Wisner also went on shopping sprees—another manic symptom—buying two electric train sets for his children and a variety of ceramic articles.

The stress Wisner put his body through was clearly not good for the disease in his brain. He was not eating a healthy diet or exercising, he was smoking and drinking too much, and he was not getting a good night's sleep—all of which were harmful for a person with bipolar disorder.

* * *

On November 6, Eisenhower handily defeated Democrat Adlai Stevenson once more to win the mandate he wanted for a second term in the White House. (Wisner later recorded in the Betting Book that Washington journalist Rowland Evans paid him $5 for losing his wager that Stevenson would beat Ike.) U-2 flights on November 6 discovered no Soviet forces moving toward Egypt as an Anglo-French armada began bombarding Port Said at the northern end of the canal into submission. World War III was not about to commence. The Eisenhower administration finally pressured Israel to move back to its old borders, and Britain and France to accept a U.N.-policed cease-fire and withdraw their forces from Egypt.

Anglo-French dreams of a "great expedition" to restore national pride and internationalize the canal lay in tatters. Israel could now never expect the waterway opening to its vessels or the sporadic violence along its borders ever abating. Israel's invasion made Arab states even more eager for its expulsion from the Middle East. The only nation to benefit from the Suez crisis was the Soviet Union, which saw Third World hostility toward its invasion of Hungary reduced by what Britain and France had done in Egypt.

* * *

On November 7, Wisner flew to Vienna, where he spent the next five days observing Hungarian refugees streaming across the border into Austria. He felt cut off from Washington's power centers, to which he usually had ready access as one of the capital's important players. It frustrated him.

After two days of brutal bombardment, Hungarians began to crawl out of their hideouts on November 7. Some Budapest commercial districts lay in ruins. One by one the Red Army had crushed the main resistance centers. In the revolution, about two thousand Hungarians were killed, including Nagy, who had been lured out of the Yugoslav embassy and hanged. Into the U.S. legation in Budapest soon trickled reports that the Soviets were engaged in a favorite tactic they had practiced in past military occupations: loading thousands of Hungarians, many of them women and children, onto railcars headed to Russian prison camps.

The U.S. embassy in Vienna and the relatively small CIA station inside it were in a chaotic state when Wisner arrived. The bulk of the reports CIA headquarters in Washington had received on Hungary during the revolt had come from border areas near Austria—but that input was meager. Before the start of the revolution, the agency's Vienna station had had no cross-border intelligence-collection operations inside Hungary and no Hungarian speakers among its officers. It was little wonder that the Vienna station had never seen the Hungarian revolt coming. At the outbreak of the revolution, the station "was not facing in the direction of Hungary," a secret CIA after-action report concluded.

The Vienna CIA chief threw everyone he had available into covering the revolt when it erupted. Wisner rushed in seven Hungarian speakers. But it was a hit-and-miss enterprise. There was no plan for how to deploy the new people except to dispatch them to the Hungarian border to observe and report. Some were ordered to sneak into Hungary and send back what they saw among Soviet forces. But those spies managed to cover only what was going on in western Hungary. The station knew little about what was happening in Budapest.

The U.S. ambassador in Vienna was Llewellyn Thompson, a timid man so obsessed with not upsetting the Russians that he ordered embassy wives donating blood for wounded Hungarian freedom fighters not to reveal at the donation site that their husbands worked at the embassy. Wisner borrowed a bed in Thompson's residence but slept in it little, sitting up until five a.m. each night while he was in the city. He set up what amounted to a field headquarters in the embassy, demanded to see all the cable traffic that arrived from Budapest, and micromanaged every move his station was making, which was impossible for one person to do. CIA officers at the embassy were dumbfounded by the work overload Wisner piled on himself. Wisner admitted to Thompson that he was acting erratically, but he could not stop himself. He became obsessed, for example, with a report that Mongolian soldiers in the Red Army units in Hungary had defected and were hiding in Vienna; it turned out to be false. Regulars in the Vienna station chafed at an outside bigwig like Wisner swooping in to take over their spy business. But Wisner was determined to get operations—any kinds of operations—going.

Unable to sit still, alternating between bouts of anxiety and depression over the revolt, Wisner hopped into an agency car the first chance he got and had the driver take him to the Austro-Hungarian border. The more than two-hundred-mile stretch had become largely porous after the Hungarian government removed barbed wire and mines along its path in the spring and summer. Thompson had ordered his embassy staff to stay away from the border, fearful of antagonizing the Austrians on his side or the Soviets on the Hungarian side, but Foreign Service officers defied him and visited it anyway.

Wisner found a chaotic spectacle when he arrived at the border. More than 150,000 Hungarians were pouring across it and beginning to swarm all over Vienna. Wisner and his CIA officers already there trying to collect intelligence found themselves competing with hordes of nosy newsmen, Austrian welfare workers, gawking tourists, spies from other intelligence services, and American VIPs on junkets, like Wild Bill Donovan and Vice President Nixon. For Wisner it was largely a waste of time. The CIA officers, all under strict orders not to reveal they were agents of the U.S. government, found that few of the refugees came from Budapest and those who did had little reliable information about what was happening in the capital.

Wisner saw hundreds of freedom fighters come across, some still carrying their weapons and "wearing their gallant little cockades," he recalled later. He saw laborers as well as boys as young as fourteen who had been battling tanks and wanted to return to resume the fight. Several begged him for liters of gasoline they could take back to fuel Molotov cocktails they would throw at armored vehicles.

Witnessing the Hungarian revolt up close from Vienna, Wisner grew more frustrated over what he said was "a lack of comprehension in Washington as to the true significance of the Hungarian revolt." Because of the disease taking hold of him, his rational understanding of the limits of the Eisenhower administration's response changed to a burning rage over those limits. The administration was too preoccupied with the Suez crisis, he railed at others in the embassy. The U.S. government had its eye off the ball. Wisner now believed he had to do all he could to awaken Washington to the crisis among the satellite nations. Other CIA officers in the Vienna embassy felt as he did. But overtaken by his manic attack, Wisner made a poor case for U.S. action in the cables he sent back to Washington.

The ever racing and jumbled thoughts in his mind, typical of the mania he suffered, led to an outpouring of frenzied writing in his dispatches to CIA headquarters. Helms found some of them so nonsensical that he had them pulled from agency records. In one weird cable that Helms failed to delete, Wisner recounted a focus group of seven that he had convened; it purportedly included U.S. embassy officials, a few of their wives, and what he said were two "quiet Americans" (borrowing from the Graham Greene novel he must have read the year before). He called the panel his "Dramatis Personae" and gave each member a letter instead of using a real name. For five single-spaced pages of type filled with long paragraphs and run-on sentences, Wisner recounted his focus group's debate over whether Radio Free Europe, Voice of America, and the BBC should have been blamed for inciting the Hungarian revolt—although it was unclear whether that debate was among the group or in his own addled mind.

Walter Ridder, a member of the Ridder newspaper family and head of the chain's Washington bureau, had decided to fly with his wife, Marie, also a journalist, to Europe to witness the Hungarian revolt firsthand. They arrived in Vienna after a stop in Budapest. In reports filed back to his newspaper chain, Ridder lamented the "tragic loss of United States prestige among the peoples of Central Europe." Ambassador Thompson, an old friend of the Ridders, arranged for them to meet Wisner for dinner at a tiny inn on the outskirts of Vienna near the Hungarian border. The Ridders and the Wisners had socialized in Washington, although Marie found Polly somewhat intimidating.

Wisner seemed calm and collected to Walter and Marie when their cab picked him up at Thompson's residence and on their drive to the restaurant. Over plates of schnitzel in the inn, Wisner quizzed the couple on what they had seen in Budapest. But then out of the blue, Wisner stood up and announced in a loud voice to the other diners that Russian tanks had assembled at the border and would storm into Austria at any time. His declaration stunned Walter and

Marie, who knew that was not the case. Fearing that what Wisner had just said might spread quickly from the inn and send Austria into a panic, Walter, who spoke German, stood up immediately and told the wide-eyed diners that his wife and he had just crossed the border and no Soviet tanks were poised there to invade.

The coupled hastily paid the bill and hustled Wisner, who did not seem to realize the furor he had stirred up, back to the ambassadorial residence, where Thompson met them at the front door. The envoy shook his head after Walter told him what had happened. "I'll take care of it from here," he whispered to Walter, and guided Wisner into the residence.

Wisner flew to Rome the evening of November 12. An embassy car whisked him from an airfield outside the city to a dinner at the U.S. ambassador's residence, Villa Taverna. Clare Boothe Luce was a big fan of the CIA who kept a close watch on agency operations run out of her embassy; she now wanted to hear Wisner's take on the Hungarian revolt. Influential in conservative Republican politics, the glamorous Clare was decisive, blunt spoken, confident, and not easily scared; she had been intent on taking charge of U.S. foreign and military policy toward Italy over the past three years. Eisenhower and Foster Dulles, however, were inclined to ignore her diplomatic advice. Allen Dulles had made it no secret that Mrs. Luce turned him on.

Also attending the Villa Taverna dinner was William Colby, a low-key yet energetic covert officer in the CIA's Rome station. Colby, in charge of the agency's largest political action program overseas, was secretly backing Italy's center-democratic parties campaigning to prevent the Communists from winning national elections in 1958. He considered the CIA's illegal funneling of $30 million a year into the Italian elections morally justified, seeing as how the Soviets were pumping $50 million a year into the Italian Communist Party.

Wisner's appearance and behavior at the Luce dinner shocked Colby, who later said he thought the boss "was near a nervous breakdown." Wisner drank heavily. He ranted and raved all through the meal, which lasted until two thirty in the morning. He was so wound up, he talked nonstop. He was distraught about the refugees he had seen fleeing to Austria; some of them had been gunned down at the border by Soviet troops while he stood by helplessly, he told the ambassador. Yet Wisner, at the same time, lashed out at others, such as American journalists in Budapest who denounced the U.S. failure to aid the freedom fighters. Before the revolution, Wisner rattled on to Luce, U.S. policy toward East Europe had been to keep up "various forms of pressure" and to dial up that pressure on "weak points as they develop" but to avoid "extreme forms of provocation." But now all of that was up in smoke. Colby agreed with the basic point Wisner was making. The United States could have intervened in Hungary during the crisis in a way that would not have involved going to war with Russia, he thought. But Wisner was making a horrible hash of his presentation to Luce. At one point, he broke down and wept before the ambassador.

Luce could clearly see that her old friend was mentally collapsing. The next morning, she found him practically in a drunken stupor, still upset and disoriented. But Luce put on a show of being fascinated by Wisner's account of the Hungarian revolt. She brainstormed with him on ways her embassy might lend a hand to the besieged Vienna mission, and she drafted a letter urging Eisenhower to be more forceful on Hungary; Wisner later reviewed it.

After three and a half days in Rome—"working at top clip day and night," as he later put it in a memo—Wisner flew to Athens, where he spent another five days meeting with his station officers and Greek officials on Hungary and the Middle East. From there, he flew to Turkey, still never finishing his meetings before four a.m. He drafted a memo he later cabled to Nixon, who was back in Washington after his Vienna trip; in the memo, Wisner insisted that Americans should feel "a special pride in our country"— a contradictory sentiment for Wisner, who in front of Luce had not been too proud of the way Washington had acted during the revolt.

Then it was back to Athens for another ten hours of intense conversations with Greek officials over two days. Between meetings, Wisner continued to compulsively buy figurines and Greek sculptures from Athens dealers and have them shipped back to his Georgetown home. On the evening of November 17 in Greece, he visited a small restaurant near the waterfront in Piraeus on the east coast of the Saronic Gulf. Wisner dug into a plate of small shellfish—they were limpets or cockles; he couldn't tell which. Something about them tasted funny, but he ate the seafood anyway. Clare Boothe Luce was later convinced that KGB agents had contaminated his meal. That was not the case. Wisner had simply eaten bad shellfish. But it would take a while for him to feel the effects.

On Tuesday afternoon, November 27, Wisner finally boarded a TWA plane in Athens for the trip to New York City. Exhaustion overcame him, along with a serious case of laryngitis from nonstop talking in Greece and Turkey. He slept the entire flight back.

PART FOUR

SIDELINED

Chapter 24

BREAKDOWN

A LITTLE AFTER FOUR o'clock on Sunday afternoon, December 16, Wisner pulled his car up to the curb at the P Street house in Georgetown, returning from a weekend of duck hunting near his farm. The shoot had been a much-needed break from the hectic three weeks he had spent since he flew back to the United States. Though he continued at times to display bipolar symptoms—friends found him occasionally excitable, overtalkative, and hyperactive immediately after his return—Wisner plunged back into grueling rounds of Washington meetings and briefings on his European trip for Dulles and other U.S. officials.

The frustration and despair that had gripped him in Rome was now replaced by unbounded optimism that the Soviets were on the defensive after Hungary and that America would ultimately win the Cold War. Wisner appeared to be back to his old combative self, donating to Red Cross relief for the Hungarians and helping Polly organize a benefit for the refugees. Four days earlier he had even managed to place in the Betting Book a complicated two-part wager on the Suez crisis that had a bottle of French champagne as the prize.

Recriminations and finger-pointing nevertheless began when he returned home on November 27. Wisner found Washington in an ugly mood. Rarely had he seen a time of such "internal bickering and unpleasantness," he wrote his brother-in-law, Alexander. Wisner felt alone, unsupported in his foreign policy initiatives. It seemed to him more difficult to get anything done in the government. The CIA came under withering fire for failing to anticipate the Polish and Hungarian revolts and the British-French-Israeli attack on Suez. Allen Dulles worked his congressional and press pals hard, trying to convince them that those crises had not caught his agency completely by surprise. Yet Eisenhower, who suffered a minor stroke later in 1957, was becoming more irritated with all his aides, and particularly with Dulles and his failure to direct what was becoming a billion-dollar-a-year complex of civilian and military intelligence.

Even more serious for Wisner, his field officers in Europe and his Radio Free Europe broadcasters in Germany were being accused of deliberately inciting the Hungarian uprising and then, after the freedom fighters revolted, of giving them the false impression that the Western powers would come to the rescue. A postmortem by General Lucian Truscott, a favorite Eisenhower troubleshooter, blamed CIA operatives on the ground for leading the Hungarians on.

But the truth, as always in the case in agency operations, was more complicated. The Hungarian revolt had been provoked not by Radio Free Europe broadcasts or the machinations of the few clandestine officers on the ground, but instead by a decade of brutal Communist rule in the country. If there had been an outside factor at play, it was more the Polish revolt, which had inspired Hungarians to believe they could challenge Soviet rule as well.

Overly enthusiastic Radio Free Europe announcers had occasionally gone off script, broadcasting suggestions on tactics and weapons the insurgents might use, along with claims that their fighting had left the Soviets on the ropes. There had also been hints that Western support was imminent. But for the most part, RFE broadcasts had stuck to reporting straight news and not inciting violence or promising Western aid. Moreover, the inflammatory programs that had slipped in had not altered the battle dynamics on the ground; guerrilla leaders had had vague hopes that the West would intervene but they had been determined to fight on no matter what Washington did. Wisner thought the charge that he and the CIA had "stirred up the whole affair" in Hungary was nothing more than Soviet propaganda that unethical Western reporters had swallowed, and it infuriated him. Indeed, although he did not realize it, accusing the CIA of losing Hungary in many ways reflected American hubris. Hungary had never been the CIA's to lose.

Under White House orders, Truscott began to dismantle the CIA program to roll back Communist regimes in Eastern Europe. Tighter controls were also slapped on Radio Free Europe broadcasts. An operation to liberate Czechoslovakia from the Kremlin's grip that Wisner later pushed went nowhere. With the crushing of the Hungarian revolt, the goal of covertly using European émigré groups to break up the Soviet Bloc was abandoned. Some CIA money continued to trickle into the National Committee for a Free Europe for the exiles to use. But the Eisenhower administration had now resigned itself to gradual reform in East Europe. The National Security Council soon decreed that CIA and State Department officials should no longer work so closely with exile committees and it discouraged radio outlets such as RFE, Voice of America, and Radio Liberty from being used to broadcast the messages of exile leaders, who did not seem to have any significant followings in their homelands.

As Wisner parked his car on P Street that Sunday afternoon, he felt the first chill course through his body. He had experienced what seemed to be a small flush of fever, or something like it, a half hour earlier, but he dismissed it as inconsequential. But when he climbed out of the car and staggered into his house, the chill struck him with such force and caused him to shake so badly that it was almost impossible for him to hold on to the stair banister and crawl to his bedroom on the second floor.

Polly piled an electric blanket and other covers on top of her husband to warm him and stop the violent cold and shaking he was experiencing. The chills were followed by a fever that ran up to 102 degrees that afternoon. During the next two days, Wisner alternated from chills, to violent fevers, and then to sweats that became so pervasive that he was forced to change pajamas and bed linens with each cycle. By Monday afternoon, his fever hit 105 degrees. Polly rushed him to Georgetown University Hospital, where his temperature on Tuesday, December 18, reached 106. Wisner could see that his mind was in a fog. He could not make clear decisions, but as best as he could, he tried to articulate the disorientation he was feeling to the doctors attending to him.

On the evening of December 20, a Georgetown Hospital specialist took over Wisner's case, interviewing him extensively and putting him through more lab tests. Two days later the specialist arrived at his diagnosis. His patient had "fulminating infectious hepatitis," a particularly rare, virulent, and dangerous form of the viral disease that came on more violently than normal hepatitis and that could cause significant liver damage. Doctors pumped Wisner full of antibiotics. They also tried cortisone, then an experimental drug, not realizing the steroid made a patient with bipolar disorder (a disease that Wisner had not yet been diagnosed as having) even more agitated. On their Christmas break from school, Frank II and Ellis visited their father in his hospital room. In periods of lucidity, Wisner admitted to the boys that he was mentally unwell.

He became a difficult patient for the medical staff. At two o'clock one morning, speaking in French, he bullied a nurse into letting him phone Phil Graham so he could lobby the publisher to have Herblock draw a Hungary cartoon with blood dripping down from Khrushchev's elbows. Billie Morrone began to visit his hospital room. Wisner wanted to dictate letters, but in the beginning, he could not get past the first sentence. Among national security officials and journalists, word spread quickly in Washington and in U.S. embassies overseas that the leader of America's clandestine service—who oversaw "one of the hardest and most important jobs in government," as one White House aide put it—had been stricken with hepatitis.

Wisner became convinced the liver ailment had caused the manic symptoms he exhibited during his European trip. He rationalized that at any stop on his journey, he could have picked up the disease, which had as much as a thirty-day incubation period. The sense of gloom, the agitation, the feeling of abandonment he felt, could all be explained by the hepatitis he had contracted, Wisner ardently believed. He considered the infection and the mental breakdown caused by it job-related injuries, so he filed a compensation claim with the CIA for his $1,006.75 in medical bills. On January 4, 1957—in an attempt to contain the damage being done to his professional reputation—Wisner wrote to the doctors at Georgetown Hospital and the CIA a lengthy memo offering his theory for how hepatitis had fried his brain. The doctors went along with that explanation. At that point, no one—not Wisner, nor his physicians, nor his family and friends—suspected that he was suffering from bipolar disorder on top of hepatitis. Just hepatitis, at that point, seemed to everyone to be a satisfying explanation for his odd behavior.

* * *

For about a month, Wisner lay on his back at Georgetown Hospital—he called it the "pest house"—and then in bed at his P Street home. He hated that his doctor had ordered him not to drink alcohol for a long while. George Kennan, Dean Acheson, Allen Dulles, and Joe Alsop dropped by with books for him to read and pleas that he not rise too soon from his bed. This disease was known to require a long convalescence.

On January 18, 1957, Frank and Polly flew down to Albany, Georgia, for what was supposed to be a lengthier convalescence. But Wisner substituted CIA work with family business, scouting expensive real estate he and friends might buy. The couple next spent two weeks at a harborside bungalow Junkie Fleischmann owned in Naples, Florida. After that, they motored to Laurel to explore more real estate buys and inspect a new oil field just discovered on family property.

By the end of February, Wisner was back at his CIA office in Washington—at first for only a couple hours each day, then gradually increasing his workload to a full day. Friends said he had returned to work too soon. Wisner later agreed. He thought he should have taken a year off.

* * *

In the beginning, CIA officers in the hallways and meeting rooms gave Wisner furtive glances when he returned to work. But weeks passed and he seemed to be his old self. Wisner returned to Georgetown Hospital and his doctor's office regularly for blood and urine tests, but he ignored medical advice to get plenty of rest and stop drinking. In the deputies' meetings Dulles chaired each week, Wisner acted normally, as if nothing had been wrong. He raised concern about a deteriorating situation in Indonesia, waded into complicated arms control issues, hatched anti-Soviet propaganda projects, delivered reports on turmoil in the Middle East, and discussed ways to streamline the CIA's daily intelligence bulletin sent to other agencies. Dulles, who had recommended Wisner for membership in Washington's Metropolitan Club, felt comfortable enough with his deputy's job performance to have him represent the CIA in sensitive Budget Bureau meetings on its spending. Wisner even joined CIA staff conferences to grapple with the ballooning number of agency employees deemed "psychoneurotic"—fifteen, as of September 1957; they were eating up a considerable amount of the medical and personnel offices' time.

Still maintaining his special clearances, Wisner on June 25 flew to a Nevada nuclear test site to observe an aboveground explosion. The Soviets, who hoped to score diplomatic points by floating proposals for a nuclear test ban, stunned the world almost four months later by launching an intercontinental ballistic missile with the Sputnik satellite atop it.

Wisner also smoothly handled one socially touchy case. On a reporting trip to Moscow in February 1957, Joe Alsop had been caught in a "honey trap" by the KGB, which secretly photographed him having sex in a hotel room with one of the Soviet service's male agents. Alsop refused to be blackmailed by the KGB into working for the Russians and told the U.S. embassy in Moscow and Wisner in Washington what had happened.

Wisner advised his friend to also report the incident to Hoover, who already had a growing file on the Alsop brothers. All of top Washington, including Polly and others in the Georgetown set, soon knew about the tryst. But the KGB never leaked the photos to the press. Under orders from Wisner, Helms dispatched an officer to New York City to tell the KGB resident there to knock it off or the CIA would retaliate with honey traps against Soviets. Joe Alsop, who became an even more intense anti-Communist, remained forever grateful to Wisner, who he thought had saved his life.

Memories of Wisner's earlier breakdown faded quickly. Throughout D.C., it was still recognized that the clandestine service chief commanded "the dynamic people" in the CIA, said one outside investigator.

* * *

Bipolar disorder, however, can be a frustrating disease that does not have a straightforward beginning, middle, and end. The illness can have many beginnings, many endings. It "can develop within an individual, and then, *without any treatment at all*, the symptoms may go away for years at a time," writes one psychiatrist. If the disease is untreated, the length of time between bipolar episodes varies widely. All Wisner's son Ellis could say was that his father's manic depression "would ramp up and then down."

By the beginning of 1958, Wisner began to ramp back up. He gained weight and became increasingly dumpy-looking, with alcohol sometimes on his breath in the morning and dark circles under his eyes from lack of sleep. At agency meetings, when he disagreed with colleagues, the tone of his voice and the look in his eyes could be off-putting. He became shrill at times, lashing out at others, accusing them of being "commies." He interrupted his officers' briefings with scatological stories about the Russians. At times, he alternated between belaboring inconsequential points and remaining in unhappy silence on important subjects.

Wisner continued to have his moments of rational calm, for example, in the summer writing to Lansdale, his Philippines expert, a thoughtful and incisive letter evaluating the colonel's ideas for the Cold War intelligence the U.S. government would need. But more and more, the calm moments became only brief interludes. Wisner began writing long, argumentative letters to others. He thought coworkers were trying to push him aside and Russian agents were following his every move, even when he was bird hunting. At social gatherings, it was clear to Nitze, Bissell, and other friends that Wisner was losing all connection with reality. On a visit to Washington, Chip Bohlen stayed up partying with Wisner until three a.m. Arguments with Joe Alsop, always a lively staple of Georgetown set gatherings, now became more heated. Wisner almost had fistfights with other partyers. Guests sometimes found him outside in his garden rehearsing what he wanted to say to the others when he returned inside.

Phil Graham, who had been on the cover of *Time* magazine in 1956, also began showing symptoms of manic depression the next year, around when Wisner suffered his first breakdown in Europe. Kay did not believe that stress in her husband's job caused it, as everyone thought was the case with Wisner. She had long suspected a latent disease had always been present in Phil's body. But in August 1958, the *Washington Post* publisher was lucid enough to talk his friend out of a crazy idea. Wisner became obsessed with the notion of becoming president of the University of Virginia. He lobbied the school for the top job and enlisted friends to send recommendations. Phil, who must have known about Frank's condition, gently persuaded him to withdraw his application. Wisner did but never gave up the idea of one day becoming UVA's president.

The madness all unfolded before Polly, and she did not know what to do. Mental illness, particularly bipolar disorder, was difficult for anyone in the 1950s to fathom, and Polly did not understand the disease now tormenting her husband. She was deeply worried about—plus deeply embarrassed by—Frank's erratic behavior. Polly and the family became closemouthed about the disease. To be open about it with others could mean Frank losing his job and suffering public humiliation, they feared. Behind Polly's back, Washington gossips sniped that she was interested only in protecting her social standing.

It was a cheap shot. Polly was indeed a highly controlled woman who kept a stiff upper lip. That was her nature. She had held the family together when Frank was away during World War II, but she was not prepared for holding the family together when her husband was losing his mind. Polly was a proper Southern woman. To be mentally ill was considered almost inexcusable.

She did her best. But she was always tormented that what she did was too little too late. Wisner grew furious when Polly locked the liquor cabinet to try to curb his drinking and when she tried to restrict his acquiring new plots of land and his spending sprees on Greek antiquities, Thai silk, and model boats from various shops. Frank became verbally abusive toward Polly. Their marriage went downhill. It got to the point that he browbeat her so much that she could not talk to him anymore. Polly reached out for help to Frank's sister Elisabeth, who still held considerable sway over her brother. In the summer of 1958, Elisabeth flew up from Mississippi and stayed at the farm several weeks to help Polly deal with the family crisis.

Polly also turned to Richard Helms, who had served as acting chief of the plans directorate when Wisner was on his European trip and then on sick leave because of the hepatitis. Quiet, cautious, expert in bureaucratic survival, and an aficionado of patient intelligence gathering, Helms had been Wisner's loyal number two man. His code name was Fletcher M. Knight.

Polly trusted Helms to protect her husband, which Helms was intent on doing. CIA officers began coming to him, too, worried that something was seriously wrong with Frank Wisner. The agency had to do something about it. But Helms, who could see for himself that his boss was becoming more erratic, did not want to stick his neck out and force Wisner's removal as head of the clandestine service. What if he was wrong and Wisner was just suffering a brief relapse of hepatitis? Wisner still had important allies in Congress, the State Department, and the Pentagon. If Helms moved preemptively on the man, he could ruin his chances for promotion. So he temporized.

But officers worried about Wisner's condition were going to Dulles as well. The CIA director had already had to phone the target of one of Wisner's senseless rants, a newspaperman, to smooth ruffled feathers. Dulles had a deputy send a message to Polly that he thought her husband needed a break.

Wisner was nudged into taking extended sick leave beginning on August 1; he would spend most of the leave resting at the farm, where friends and relatives believed he could recover from whatever effects of the hepatitis were still bothering him. Billie Morrone continued to do secretarial chores for him, shuttling at times between his CIA office and Locust Hill with letters for him to sign. Wisner also thought that "taking some much-needed leave" and tending to farm chores were just what he needed, he wrote a friend.

The change of venue, however, did not help. The manic depression reared up with a vengeance once more. Wisner's illness began scaring the children. Back from college in the summer of 1958, Frank II realized for the first time the full extent of his father's despair. He saw Wisner talking nonstop during the day but making no sense in what he said; walking around at night restless yet showing no signs of excessive fatigue; and becoming paranoid about money and perceived enemies. Things became worse as August passed. Wisner's condition had a profound effect on Frank II, who became confused and upset tending to chores at the farm during the day and sitting up late at night with his dad. He could find his father calm for long periods, but when his dad's volatility grew, Frankie knew to back away.

Wisner also became unusually angry with Ellis over business matters—blowing up at him, for example, when farm manager Billy Sigman left for a better job and Ellis supported Sigman. Polly tried to shield young Graham and Wendy (who was a rambunctious and independent-minded child) from their father. Graham would later be packed off to St. Paul's, an elite boarding school in Concord, New Hampshire, that he hated.

Convinced that he alone could solve foreign policy problems, Wisner began to worry constantly about mistakes leaders in Washington were making in the Cold War with Russia. He appeared to be power hungry, willing to fight anyone to be the top man in any organization. He knew he had incurred the wrath of countless people in the U.S. government, but he didn't care. He was the lead actor. The world was his stage. Several times, he referred to himself as "the Great Frank Wisner."

Polly counted that her husband had thirteen real estate deals pending. He became paranoid that the farmhands he employed at Locust Hill were stealing from him. He envisioned himself as a member of the landed gentry dispensing largesse to poor people at huge parties. He was convinced he would strike it rich from oil fields the Wisner family owned in Mississippi, he wanted to recondition an old yacht (Polly knew it could cost a fortune), and he began running up bills behind her back. He believed he could fund his own "clean" hospital with a dozen psychiatrists and nurses.

Wisner unloaded on Polly. He felt he was closer to his sister Elisabeth now than to his wife. He still loved Polly, he insisted. He depended on her. Yet *he* wanted to control *her*, and he knew he wasn't succeeding. He didn't know if he could cope with the constant friction that had developed between them because of his illness. He resented female domination, but at the same time, he had no respect for female passivity. At one point Wisner claimed that Polly had beaten and kicked him, leaving black-and-blue marks all over his body. It wasn't true. Wisner also claimed Polly constantly "grated" on him. The opposite was the case.

It became obvious to Polly that quarantining the problem at the farm was only a stopgap measure, not an answer. With the psychiatrists she had enlisted unable to treat her husband's disease while he remained at Locust Hill, Polly finally convinced Frank that he needed institutional care. His sister Elisabeth and old friends—like the CIA's Desmond FitzGerald, neighbor Henry Sears, Atomic Energy Commission member John Graham, and White House national security aide Gordon Gray—urged him as well to enter a mental asylum.

Frank checked into the nearby Sheppard Pratt Hospital on September 12. Polly signed the commitment papers the next day, hoping her husband would be cured and released by the end of the year.

Chapter 25

SHEPPARD PRATT

THE SECOND WEEK OF December 1958, Allen Dulles pulled up in his new chauffeured Cadillac to the front entrance of the Sheppard Pratt Hospital's main A and B Victorian buildings, which had been constructed in 1891. The CIA had wanted to have bulletproof glass installed in the new limousine, but that would have driven up the cost and delayed delivery, so the agency ordered it without the security alterations and assumed that the director was safe driving around Washington.

Dulles climbed out of the backseat and CIA security agents whisked him up the steps to a foyer off the entrance where Wisner sat. He wore a gray wool suit and vest with a white shirt and a necktie that Polly had brought him, along with an electric shaver and aftershave lotion for his beard. Wisner looked as if he were ready to head off to work.

The *National Review*, a conservative editorial magazine, had recently noted cryptically in its "For the Record" column that a "major scandal" might be under the CIA rug—"the complete nervous breakdown of a top intelligence officer." Dulles hoped such vague references would be all that leaked about the Wisner commitment for now.

This was another bleak visit for the CIA director. Many of the anchors in his life were beginning to break away. Within months, Wild Bill Donovan would be dead from arteriosclerotic atrophy of the brain and Allen's brother, Foster, would succumb to cancer. About to turn sixty-five, Allen Dulles could no longer act as the freewheeling spymaster. America's intelligence apparatus was becoming too large, and he was losing his grip on it. With all the job's bureaucratic headaches, he was finding it less fun. Eisenhower had begun to exclude him from his inner circle. And now Frank Wisner—his loyal, enthusiastic partner in pioneering America's covert action capability—was confined to a mental institution and would have to be cast away, which many top U.S. officials thought would be a blessing.

Lucien Truscott, who after being appointed deputy CIA director for coordination was in charge of working with other intelligence outfits, warned Dulles that his cherished covert operations to topple foreign governments and influence politics abroad simply took up too much of the agency's time, effort, and money at the expense of traditional spying. The White House believed that Wisner's commitment to Sheppard Pratt meant it was unlikely he would return as head of the plans directorate. Perhaps that would be "beneficial," Truscott told Dulles. With Wisner out of the picture, a better balance could be restored between covert operations and intelligence collection, White House aides thought. Ike agreed. With Wisner's departure, the president wanted a shake-up in the CIA's clandestine service.

Eisenhower's group of wise men—the Board of Consultants on Foreign Intelligence Activities—had concluded that Wisner had run the clandestine service without any meaningful outside evaluation. Basically, he had been self-evaluating, which the wise men concluded was intolerable. The board told Ike bluntly that it was dangerous entrusting so much power over American foreign policy to a man now found to be insane. Wisner's commitment to Sheppard Pratt gave the White House the opportunity to reorganize the CIA's plans directorate and put in more oversight of it.

Dulles predictably resisted the reform. He was at Sheppard Pratt that day to tell Wisner how he planned to head off the consultant board. Settling into a comfortable chair across from Wisner, Dulles could see that his deputy had improved considerably in the three months he had been confined to the institute. Wisner appeared calm and in control of his emotions. Dulles was always pleased when he received reports that one of his men had recovered from a nervous condition and he thought it was important for those officers to know that the agency was standing behind them. But Polly, who had kept in close touch with Dulles since the commitment, warned him that the doctors had told her that Frank still had a way to go. Dulles could now see for himself that his frail-looking deputy was "still quite sick," he later told aides.

Wisner as well recognized that he was not ready to leave the institute. He was also savvy enough to know that when he did check out of Sheppard Pratt, he would not be returning to his old job as head of the CIA's clandestine service. Reinstating emotionally troubled case officers to their positions was one thing; a return to a high-profile, high-pressure job like the one Wisner had had was not going to happen, he knew. That was why what Dulles had to tell him first—that when Sheppard Pratt released Wisner, he would take some undefined job in Dulles's personal office at his old salary—did not surprise him. Wisner did not put up a fight over that move.

But it was the second piece of news that Dulles had that upset him. As of the beginning of 1959, the CIA director said, he was replacing Wisner with Richard Bissell as head of the plans directorate. Since 1954, Bissell had overseen the U-2 spy plane program, a highly successful operation that had revolutionized the collection of Soviet military intelligence and made him the "golden boy" of the CIA.

Wisner, however, dearly wanted his loyal deputy, Richard Helms, to be the new clandestine service chief. Helms, who thought he had the inside track for the job since he had served as acting head of the plans directorate during Wisner's absence, was bitterly disappointed that Dulles passed him over. Helms hated Bissell and considered him an amateur at clandestine operations. Helms was made Bissell's deputy. The two men would never get along.

Dulles never considered Helms fully on board with covert operations, while he was sure Bissell would be. Bissell, moreover, instituted a number of changes in the way covert operations were run and evaluated that Dulles thought would keep the consultants' board off his back.

Dejected after Dulles left, Wisner returned to the work of healing his mind.

* * *

Wisner's admitting card at Sheppard Pratt listed him as "Patient Number 14,811." He arrived at the institute on September 12 with only his wristwatch and $2.16 in his pants pocket. Polly later brought a brown suitcase with a complete wardrobe for him to wear.

At any time, the institute averaged about two hundred forty patients, which was sixty patients under its capacity. It had twenty-five full-time or part-time psychiatrists and a total of 461 nurses, orderlies, clerks, building workers, and groundskeepers. Sheppard Pratt looked like a small elite college, with its cluster of stately brick buildings, manicured lawns, old trees, and lush gardens. Vegetables were grown and livestock was raised on the grounds to feed the patients. The Pinkerton Service provided guards for the facility.

The patient shortage meant lost income, but the institute still considered itself fortunate—if for no other reason than that it had had no suicides in the past year. Sheppard Pratt had the reputation for being a good place to go to if you were well-off. It was not cheap. The charge for just Wisner's room and board was the top rate of $150 a week (more than $1,600 in today's dollars). In addition to that bill, Polly paid for laboratory services and outside medical specialists brought in on her husband's case.

Wisner's sister Elisabeth, who rode in the backseat of the car that took him to Sheppard Pratt on September 12, succeeded in keeping her brother calm as the two psychiatrists in the vehicle continued to interview him. When they arrived at the institute, the psychiatrists had the staff car take Elisabeth back to the Locust Hill farm and escorted their new patient into the facility. Wisner was angry, resentful, humiliated, and unhappy about being in a place where he did not want to be—locked up against his will, or so he thought. The Sheppard Pratt staff and the patients who encountered him that first day found him haughty, hard to deal with, and out of control.

His surly behavior, however, did not surprise the doctors and nurses who were the first to meet him in the admitting room and who were guided by what the staff called the "Ten Commandments" for dealing with new patients and their relatives. (Commandment 1: "Take care of your patients' immediate needs." Cures didn't come quickly. Commandment 3: "Don't try to dispense 'insight.'" It could not be given in an IV.) The institute's admitting doctors were trained to consider the first half hour that new patients spent at Sheppard Pratt to be their most important time there. The institute believed it was critical that its doctors get acquainted with Wisner before other patients talked to him and "poisoned" his head with wrong information, like "If you tell them you hear voices, you will never get out of this place."

The psychiatrists knew Wisner would be concerned more with what they were going to do *to* him rather than *for* him. They expected that Wisner would not be cooperative. They knew that, like most of their patients, he did not want to stay at Sheppard Pratt. They guessed that Wisner was likely no different from most of the mentally ill patients they saw—who "have an unconscious insight that there is something quite odd about themselves," said one Sheppard Pratt psychiatrist. "If you avoid getting into a fight with them, they will go along for some time accepting that they are patients." The approach soon disarmed Wisner.

Since September 12 was a Friday, a senior psychiatrist making his normal rounds that day was in the admitting room and was the first to talk to Wisner. The CIA man was given a complete physical examination and doctors probed as much as they could to compile a personal history on him—or as much of a history as Wisner would divulge. He was given a battery of six psychological tests, such as the Stanford-Binet to measure intellectual ability and the Rorschach, which analyzed a patient's perception of inkblots. The staff determined Wisner's IQ, which was high. Patients like him, who were extremely irritable and excited, were first kept in the "disturbed ward." The highly agitated ones were given hydrotherapy with warm baths and showers, which had a soothing effect. Some were also put in cold, wet sheet packs to control their overactivity and to protect others from their physical attacks. Massage therapy, along with special diets and exercise, was tried. For the severe insomnia that had kept Wisner up to all hours of the night, the nurses treated him with the sedative sodium amytal and turned off all lights in his room at night to put him back into a normal sleep pattern.

And to jolt Wisner out of the acute manic state he was in, doctors quickly decided he needed electroconvulsive therapy, commonly known as shock treatment. Sheppard Pratt was considered an innovator in trying to move beyond the old Freudian psychoanalysis of mental patients on the couch and to begin experimenting with antipsychotic drugs that might treat the biological causes of mental illness. During the 1930s the institute began experimenting with the convulsive drug Metrazol as well as with an insulin shock treatment that it used on schizophrenic patients.

In 1940, Sheppard Pratt bought its first shock treatment equipment and began using it instead of Metrazol or insulin on suicide-prone manic-depressive patients. Doctors found immediately that administering the shock treatment was simpler and caused fewer side effects than Metrazol did. An electric current that was sent into the brain by way of electrodes attached to the temples shocked the patient into convulsions that altered brain chemistry in a helpful way. Patients emerged from the electroconvulsive treatment "quite happy," according to one Sheppard Pratt report, and they had no recollection of what had been done to them. By 1941, 40 percent of the institute's patients treated with electric shock were able to go home. Other mental hospitals reported the same success with the treatment.

For decades, though, a popular myth—fueled by movies like *One Flew Over the Cuckoo's Nest* in 1975—prevailed that electric shock treatment was a barbaric, medieval-like procedure extremely painful for patients, and it electrocuted brains, wiped out memories, and created zombies. Wisner's sons assumed their father had undergone a ghastly procedure. Phil Graham was horrified when he learned his friend had been shocked. Rumors circulated in CIA circles that Wisner had told colleagues the shock treatment he received had been torture. Wisner said nothing of the sort, because the shock treatment he received was not painful and the beneficial results came quickly after he underwent the procedure.

Medical practitioners since the sixteenth century had been experimenting with potions with ingredients such as camphor to produce convulsions they thought might cure lunacy. By 1938, electricity was being applied to the brains of schizophrenics. In the more than eighty years since, electroconvulsive therapy has proven to be highly effective—almost miraculous in some cases—for the treatment of depression and mania. The patient usually feels better after a few shocks. Even today, electroconvulsive therapy remains one of the most effective treatments for bipolar disorder.

Moreover, in Wisner's day electric shock was the only effective treatment available for him. When he entered Sheppard Pratt in 1958, the modern era of psychiatry was dawning. Bipolar disorder and other mental maladies were beginning to be recognized as diseases to be treated with drugs. An Australian doctor's 1948 discovery that lithium could dramatically settle down manic patients did not make its way to the United States until the 1970s, when the Food and Drug Administration approved the medication.

Because of shock treatment's promise, it was often overprescribed and abused in the mid-1940s, administered to patients for drug addiction, alcoholism, and homosexuality, or to discipline and control the unruly ones. Sheppard Pratt used electric shock on its patients sparingly, mainly because its doctors did not know why the treatment worked so well. For patients with bipolar disorder like Wisner, a half dozen to a dozen shock treatments were administered over several months. Sheppard-Pratt policy also required Polly to give her approval for the shock therapy.

Two electrodes attached to Wisner's right and left temples were connected to a sine wave device that delivered the electrical charge for several seconds. To avoid violent muscle contractions and bone fractures from the machine-induced seizure, he was given the relaxant succinylcholine, along with a barbiturate anesthesia to put him to sleep. So he would not break his teeth or bite his tongue when the electrical charge caused his jaw to clamp shut, a bite block was inserted into his mouth.

The entire procedure lasted no more than an hour and Wisner woke up foggy-minded with a headache but clueless about what he had been through. Shock treatments could cause memory loss, but in most cases, it was short-term. Rarely did a patient lose his memory for a long time. Wisner never complained of any memory loss from the institute's treatments.

The immediate danger of Wisner dying from acute mania soon passed because of the early shock treatments. When he calmed down and became more comfortable with the resident physician handling his case, Wisner was moved to the "less disturbed ward," where he had more freedom to wander from his room. Polly sent a framed family photo to set on his dresser. Wisner received letters from friends wishing him well and offering their own home remedies. Admiral Felix Stump, who had just retired as commander of the U.S. Pacific Fleet, wrote him that he was a war casualty and his absence from the CIA "is being suffered by us all who are interested in fighting Communism." Turkey's defense minister sent him a box of figs, insisting they were good for his mental health.

Wisner had a long stay at Sheppard Pratt in store for him. The average length of the stay for a patient in his condition was five months. Convalescing from the shock treatments took a while. Also, psychoanalysis and psychotherapy still dominated the medical profession, so there would be a lot of time spent talking. A patient could not truly heal until he had worked with his therapist through the things that were really bothering him, or so the thinking went. It was an open question whether the months Wisner spent talking to a psychiatrist really helped, but he dutifully sat through the sessions.

Sheppard Pratt had in place a routine in which daily rounds were conducted by the resident assigned to Wisner's case and by a senior psychiatrist who visited him to talk. Several outside doctors were also consulted; one of them was an orthopedist who prescribed Wisner weights for leg exercises. Sheppard Pratt was as much a resort spa as a mental facility, and when Wisner was permitted to roam about, he joined in the many activities. The institute had what it called the "Ivy Nook," where patients could order snacks and milkshakes and chat with other patients in a relaxed atmosphere. There was also a tea and gift shop, where patients could socialize with relatives. Billie Morrone, who helped manage the family finances, put $50 in Wisner's account at the facility so he could sip tea and buy cookies and cigarettes at the shops.

Patients put on plays in a small theater on the grounds, performed in an orchestra, tended to a garden in the greenhouse, and joined a fishing club. Sheppard Pratt also had tennis courts, a shuffleboard court, a small golf course, and a swimming pool. Polly sent her husband his golf clubs, three tennis rackets, and four cans of tennis balls. Occupational therapy was an important part of rehabilitation for patients like Wisner. Polly sent paint and drawing supplies for him to use in the art shop. He hadn't drawn or painted since he was a boy. She also sent him furniture he could repair in the woodshop. Wisner had always been a good carpenter.

Sheppard Pratt had a well-stocked library of 6,443 books and magazines. The *New York Times* was delivered daily, and Wisner read it devotedly with his morning tea. Polly also kept a stream of books flowing to Frank, who continued to be a voracious reader. She sent him the English version of Boris Pasternak's Nobel Prize–winning *Doctor Zhivago*, which Frank was eager to read for an operational reason. *Doctor Zhivago*, which told the story of a physician-poet during the tumultuous 1917 Russian Revolution, had been considered heresy by Soviet authorities and banned in Russia. The CIA in 1958 helped arrange for the eight-hundred-page manuscript to be published. More than ten thousand copies of a Russian-language edition were eventually sneaked back into the Soviet Union for readers there, all part of a highly successful agency Cold War program that distributed ten million banned books and periodicals inside the East Bloc.

Polly did her best to keep the family functioning during Frank's absence. She also tried to carve out a life for herself, traveling with the Grahams on trips to Cape Cod and attending a National Cathedral Christmas service by herself. Frank joined other patients in stringing popcorn, cranberries, and raisins on long cords hung from trees outside their windows for the holidays. Wisner was showered with gift packages to open in his hospital room on Christmas Day. Billie Morrone bought a small model steam engine set for Wisner to give to Graham.

Wisner's absence from his children's lives became heart-wrenching. Polly did not allow them to visit their father and she was guarded about the details of his illness that she shared with them. For Wendy the separations from her father became especially painful. Seven years later, as her coming-out party began, Wendy was told that her father would not be attending. Wisner had again been hospitalized because of his mental illness. His absence crushed her. Wendy so adored her dad. In front of the guests, she crumpled to the floor sobbing—the weight of this disease finally overcoming her.

Beginning in February 1959, however, Wisner's condition improved enough that he was allowed to go home on weekends. He felt "fully restored and recharged," he wrote *New York Times* correspondent Cyrus Sulzberger, "presently approaching the point of return to civilization."

On March 4, 1959, Wisner checked out of Sheppard Pratt, sooner than he had expected. He had stayed at the institute for 172 days. Rumors that Wisner had been miserable at the institute spread in the CIA, but those reports were false. "I think that the hospital did, in the over-all, a very fine job in my case," he wrote attorney Ambler Moss, who had done legal work for the family. In his final months at Sheppard Pratt, Wisner believed his "improvement progressed very rapidly and in the latter stages of my time at the hospital things were not unpleasant for me."

The CIA granted him another thirty days of sick leave. He intended to take his time returning to work. He did not want to make the mistake he had made after his hepatitis attack and rush back. Once more, Polly and he retreated to Junkie Fleischmann's cottage in Naples for three weeks of golf, tennis, and beachcombing. After Florida, the couple spent ten days in Laurel and then returned to Washington in the latter part of April. The four children visited them during their spring breaks and found their father subdued, quiet, and withdrawn. But Wisner felt much better than he appeared to the kids. "I am recovered," he proudly wrote to a friend. "Actually, I'm in wonderful shape and expect to stay that way." But he planned to "discipline" himself. He would keep his summer quiet and wait until fall to "enter into greater activity."

Wisner did not know what the future held for him, but he was optimistic. After his Florida vacation, a friend told him that he looked "tanned and in good spirits and health." Angleton, the CIA's counterintelligence chief, informed the FBI that Wisner was fully recovered and that the doctors had approved his return to work. The bureau, however, remained suspicious that that was the case.

Frank II said he found the next two years "a period of respite." Wisner displayed none of the symptoms of bipolar disease. Frank II considered the time the best two years he had with his father.

But what Wisner was experiencing was only a lull. Sheppard Pratt had a social worker sit down with Polly to counsel her on the symptoms to look for that might indicate Frank needed to return to the hospital, such as being unable to sleep at night. Wisner was told to watch his diet and get more exercise (both of which he was willing to do) and to cut back on alcohol (which he only grudgingly agreed to for the moment). The Sheppard Pratt doctors also thought Wisner should continue meeting regularly with a psychiatrist.

The institute tried to keep in touch with Polly. But for the most part, she was left pretty much on her own. Sheppard Pratt's leaders recognized that their aftercare program for patients and their families was inadequate. Shock treatments made a manic-depressive patient like Wisner feel better quickly, but they did not have a long-term effect as a mood stabilizer. The relapse rate was high. Bipolar illness, writes one psychiatrist, seems merely to "hibernate." To keep the disease's symptoms from returning, Wisner needed monthly "maintenance" shock treatments or effective drugs like lithium. But in the late 1950s, the only treatment available for the disease after he left the hospital was talking to a psychiatrist while lying on a couch.

Chapter 26

LONDON

WHEN HE RETURNED TO work in the spring of 1959, Wisner was given what he described as a "very pleasant office" at CIA headquarters in downtown Washington, where Billie Morrone helped him tend to a pile of official and personal paperwork. Wisner began mixing with old colleagues, who approached him haltingly. He was trying to catch up with what had happened at the agency in his absence—"breaking the ice," as he put it in a letter to his brother-in-law, Chis.

The CIA was a paternalistic organization that prided itself on looking after its people. Polly was touched that Dulles wanted to do "something nice" for her husband; he asked Wisner to be the CIA's chief of station in London.

The appointment made sense to Dulles. Wisner could not return to the pressure-packed job of deputy director for plans. The London station was a far less demanding post, its work largely diplomatic. The station chief did no spying. He mostly served as a liaison helping manage the flow of intelligence between the American and British services, which still worked together closely despite the Kim Philby and Suez debacles. Wisner already had many professional contacts in London. He would be among longtime friends, acting like an ambassador circulating in high society. That did not sit too well with the Foreign Service officers at the embassy, who grumbled that their CIA colleagues were too much like diplomats and intruded on the foreign policy work the State Department's representatives should have been doing. Dulles, who could not have cared less about mussing up bureaucratic feelings, offered Wisner the London post at his old executive salary of $20,000 a year (more than $214,000 in today's dollars). It would make him the highest-paid station chief in the CIA network.

Wisner mulled over the offer for a while. After he was discharged from Sheppard Pratt, he had considered resigning from the agency and taking up business interests. Locust Hill had never looked lovelier to him when he returned to it and he did not know if he could keep the farm going if he moved to London. On the other hand, Wisner did not want his mental breakdown to be his reason for leaving the agency he so loved. He thought the London post was an important one that would give him the opportunity to contribute to the CIA in a significant way—and he knew it wouldn't be as stressful as his old job.

Frank and Polly both liked the idea of spending a couple years of their lives abroad. Who knew what might happen after that posting? Wisner thought that if he did well in London, he might have a chance at another top CIA job, perhaps the directorship.

Wisner started making plans for the move. Frank II came down from Princeton University during a school break to oversee work at Locust Hill for a while until a caretaker could be hired to handle farm business. A renter was found for the Georgetown home and India's ambassador to the U.S. leased the farmhouse in Galena. As a side job from her CIA secretarial work, Billie Morrone was hired to help Wisner handle his personal finances in Washington and his investments in Laurel. Wisner also had one of his physicians in Baltimore send to the CIA's doctor a letter certifying that he was physically and mentally fit to assume the station chief's job.

Frank and Polly took their time getting to the new posting in

London, setting sail on the SS *America* out of New York on August 7. After landing in Southampton, England, they flew to Greece for a nearly three-week vacation with Frank II, Wendy, and Graham. Wisner began work in London on September 21.

Within months, the CIA station moved to the third floor of the new U.S. embassy at 24 Grosvenor Square. The six hundred rooms in the just completed building still had quirks to be worked out, such as kitchenette faucets tilted sideways and a one-way mirror for the CIA station's ladies' restroom installed backward. For their quarters the couple first moved to a large house at 11 Wilton Crescent near Belgravia Square and then later to a house just as big at 48 Hyde Park Gate. Wisner wanted spacious residences with rooms for three servants to handle the heavy entertaining he and Polly planned.

An Anglophile, Wisner loved his posting in London. Becoming a regular customer at Court Tailors & Breeches Makers, he dressed like a British gentleman and wore knickers when he trekked out on the moors. He bought a Jaguar to drive around the city; joined the Brooks's Club, the St. James's Club, and the New Zealand Golf Club; and enjoyed attending horse races and Oxford-Cambridge rugby matches. He spent many weekends in Scotland on bird-hunting trips—although Polly hated those excursions because they were usually stuck in cold, drafty country houses. Eric Sevareid, the CBS correspondent based in London, became a shooting companion. Wisner also kept up a friendly correspondence with Ian Fleming, whose James Bond novels he enjoyed reading.

At first, the deputy CIA chief in London handled much of the station's duties as Wisner became acclimated to his new job. But soon Wisner took over with the hands-on management for which he had been famous while running the plans directorate; he insisted on seeing all the cable traffic that came in. As he had in Washington, Wisner demanded a lot from the men and women who worked for him in London. Yet along with the seriousness, much of the old gentleness and playfulness returned to him.

In London Wisner soon had a secretary on whom he relied as much as he had on Billie Morrone in Washington. Though not particularly beautiful, Tish Freeman was articulate, impeccably dressed, well-mannered, and, like Morrone, extremely efficient. She had joined the CIA in 1951, then worked her way up from the steno-graphic pool to serve as the personal secretary for the demanding James Angleton, with access to his most sensitive counterintelli-gence projects. Angleton fought losing any of his valued subordi-nates, but he willingly went along with Freeman's transfer to his old friend in London.

Tish worried about what she might be getting into. She had heard about Wisner's fearsome reputation as clandestine service chief and she knew he had been institutionalized for mental illness. Angleton gave her two pieces of advice. First, Wisner was likely not completely over his illness, so if he lost his temper with her, she should not take it personally. Second, if she could win over Polly, she would "have it made" in the job.

Tish found Wisner to be a gracious gentleman who dazzled her with his wide range of London contacts and what she considered a razor-sharp mind. She also discovered that he was an exacting boss who could spot minor errors in the reams of documents she typed for him. Tish also cultivated Polly, who became a close friend. She grew as devoted to the couple as Billie Morrone was.

* * *

Polly was soon entertaining in London as she had in Georgetown. British intellectuals, politicians, and aristocrats regularly dined at the Wisner table. Frank resumed his close friendship with the Ox-ford don Sir Isaiah Berlin, and Polly went on regular shopping trips with Lady Berlin. Wisner became close to George Brown, the num-ber two man in the Labour Party, who, Wisner once joked, had a "sparrow belly." A little liquor in it had a big effect on Brown, Wis-ner found.

The Wisners also imported the Georgetown Sunday suppers, sometimes with the same unpredictable results. During one week-end meal, novelist Arthur Koestler was sitting at the table next to journalist Martha Gellhorn, the ex-wife of Ernest Hemingway, and Gellhorn shouted: "Arthur, get your goddamned hand off my thigh!"

Gossip that stung Polly soon spread that she was again wearing Frank down mentally with a punishing social schedule. The fact was, Frank wanted the social whirl as much as Polly did.

* * *

Less than a month after taking over the CIA station in London, Wisner flew back to Laurel for his mother's funeral. Frail, living in a little apartment with a caregiver, and having suffered numerous falls, Jeannette Wisner died on October 13, 1959, at the age of eighty-four. Her passing was big news in Laurel. "She was dearly loved and her friendship was greatly treasured by those who had known her," an editorial in the *Laurel Leader-Call* declared.

Over the years, Wisner's relationship with his mother had grown distant. Jeannette always called her son "Brother." But the two had different interests. In her later life, Wisner found himself sitting in awkward silence when he was with his mother.

* * *

When Wisner returned to London, much of his station work continued to be routine: delivering letters from Dulles to senior British officials, meeting with Foreign Office diplomats to discuss Radio Free Europe, and receiving a long line of visitors passing through the city. Helms and his wife, Julia, visited Frank and Polly. Bissell stopped by. Balkan comrades from World War II arrived to reminisce over bottles of champagne. A parade of station chiefs who had served under Wisner also came through; Tish invariably heard them say, "Hello, boss!" when they walked into his office.

The one covert operation Wisner had a bit part in was trying to secure London's help in a CIA plot to oust Cheddi Jagan, British Guiana's nonaligned leftist prime minister who the U.S. government was convinced was a closet Castro Communist. But cloistered in London, Wisner was no longer a player in the big events of the day, such as in 1961 when the Soviets built the Berlin Wall separating East Germany from West Germany.

Wisner was also detached from future CIA failures and seamy operations. Eisenhower and an inattentive Dulles let Bissell launch one too many U-2 flights over the Soviet Union to photograph strategic weapons sites. On May 1, 1960, the Russians shot down one of the aircraft and captured its pilot, Francis Gary Powers, forcing an embarrassed Ike to admit he had been spying after his administration had at first publicly denied it. Under White House orders the president could plausibly deny he had ever issued, the CIA hatched plans to assassinate four foreign leaders found distasteful: Cuba's Fidel Castro, the Belgian Congo's Patrice Lumumba, Iraq's Abd al-Karim, and the Dominican Republic's Rafael Trujillo. A later Church Committee investigation of CIA abuses concluded the agency never carried out any of its plots.

Frank and Polly were delighted when John Kennedy was elected president, as were many other top CIA officials who liked the committed cold warrior and the eager young advisers he brought with him. Upon becoming president, Kennedy quickly reappointed Hoover and Dulles to their positions—a move he came to regret in the case of Dulles. The president gave the green light for 1,400 CIA-trained Cuban exiles to land on the western shore of Bahía de Cochinos (the Bay of Pigs, as it became known in English) on April 17, 1961. The CIA believed Castro could be toppled as Arbenz had been in Guatemala. But the Cuban dictator was far stronger. His defense forces in short order swept up the poorly armed invaders at the beach. Kennedy publicly accepted responsibility for the debacle, but after an appropriate interval, he fired Dulles. Bissell, who had organized the invasion, resigned.

Wisner believed the Bay of Pigs operation had grown much too large to be carried out covertly. A project that size should have been given to the military, not the CIA, which had made a mess of it, he thought. Even so, he was distraught that Dulles had been cashiered and tried to help him secure a British publisher if he chose to write his memoirs. Wisner even felt badly for Bissell, who was the most responsible for the botched mission. He was delighted, however, when news reached him that Helms would replace Bissell as director of the clandestine service.

Dulles spent his final months as CIA director overseeing the building of a permanent $46 million headquarters on a hundred forty acres of farmland in Langley, Virginia, outside Washington. Wisner had long opposed building the CIA headquarters in Langley, worrying that it was too big, too flashy, and too visible. He preferred the anonymity of the nondescript structures along the Reflecting Pool (much like the British MI6 model) that placed the CIA close to the federal centers of power.

In 1959 and 1960, Wisner received glowing fitness reports for his London service. Helms wrote him that he appreciated "the calm, constructive and effective way" he had carried out his duties there. Headquarters recommended that his two-year tour be extended to February 1962. With Dulles leaving, there was even talk among friends like Kennan, Harriman, and Bohlen, who were now all in the Kennedy administration, that with Wisner appearing to be his old self again, he might even be a contender for the CIA directorship.

Polly was joyful that she and Frank were once again enjoying each other's company as husband and wife. Frank was doing "so well," Polly wrote in early 1961 to Kay Graham, who had kept her regularly posted on Washington society news. "I do admire him and think he has shown such guts and character." A Scottish doctor who had been seeing Frank regularly "is also pleased with him," Polly added. They had talked about Frank retiring and their living permanently at the farm if there was not a senior position for him at the agency when they returned from London. Life was back to normal, Polly thought.

But then the disease returned from its hibernation. Frank and Polly flew back to the United States in the first week of June 1961 to attend Frank II's graduation from Princeton. (They had received the welcome news that their oldest son had been admitted into the Foreign Service and would be joining the State Department after college.) The couple stopped off in Washington, where Wisner reunited with friends like Chip Bohlen and met with Helms, who filled his old boss in on the Bay of Pigs fiasco and assured him that "the outfit you put together has quite some resilience and discipline" and would survive. There were late-night parties in Georgetown, where Wisner seemed to friends to be vibrant once more, knocking back drinks as he had done in the old days.

As the couple prepared to head back to Great Britain, Secretary of State Dean Rusk asked Wisner to accompany him on a diplomatic mission to Geneva. Wisner was delighted to tag along. But when he flew back to London afterward, Polly could immediately see as Frank stepped off the plane that he had returned to his old manic state.

Back at work, Wisner became obsessed with propaganda projects and began berating British officials who did not agree with him. In letters to news friends like Stewart Alsop, he vented about leaks of classified material to reporters, which helped the Russians. He had to write apologies to the Brits for his erratic behavior at social gatherings. At one point, he phoned a member of the British cabinet after two a.m. to dictate a press release he wanted him to release.

As they had with past episodes, Polly and the CIA tried to quarantine Wisner so he did not do any more damage. Wendy and Graham were sent to American boarding schools. Wisner was kept at home. Cables were brought to him to read, and aides took the increasingly irregular orders he issued and toned them down. Increasingly, his deputy ran the station. No one wanted to tell Wisner that he had tipped over the edge once more.

Two London doctors (one a psychiatrist, the other a general practitioner) were brought in on his case. A nurse was summoned to the Hyde Park Gate home to help Polly. The doctors theorized that Wisner was now suffering from a thyroid condition on top of his manic depression. Realizing that the electroconvulsive therapy

Sheppard Pratt had administered had stabilized Wisner, the British doctors began the same for him. He received shock treatments twice a week for the next five and a half weeks.

Word spread quickly back at the CIA and in Georgetown that Wisner was suffering from another manic attack. Helms tried to cover for his old boss. The CIA medical staff was alerted and an agency doctor flew to London to work with the British physicians.

On September 27, 1961, Kennedy announced that he was picking as the next director of central intelligence John McCone, who was sworn in two months later. Liberals in the administration were appalled that JFK had chosen a conservative Republican for the post. A wealthy California businessman trained as an engineer, McCone had served briefly as an Air Force undersecretary during the Truman administration. Wisner had known him quite well when the two of them worked in Washington. They had socialized together with their wives. Wisner told Helms that the new director was able and tough. Bleeding-heart liberals shouldn't write him off, he said.

Agency staffers soon gave McCone the nickname "Jolly John," which he decidedly was not. A forceful and curt leader, McCone became more interested in intelligence analysis and technical collection by spy satellites than in cloak-and-dagger operations. Jolly John was outraged when he learned that his London station chief was being kept on the job while in the middle of a nervous breakdown, and he became worried when he discovered that British doctors not cleared by the CIA were treating Wisner. McCone ordered that Wisner come home as soon as he was able to travel.

By fall 1961, Wisner's London doctors were satisfied that the shock treatments had stabilized their patient and he could return to work. Wisner, they believed, was on the road to recovery. Their patient thought so as well, and he continued to blame overwork for his problems. "I simply overdid and overextended myself," Wisner wrote Bob Joyce, "and had to pay the price. I suppose that this time I should have learned more precisely what my limits of energy and endurance are." Wisner never considered that the London station job had not been strenuous and that something else was causing his mental breakdown. He continued to try to put a brave face on his troubles, telling a friend that London had been a "very happy and interesting tour."

On March 9, 1962, the CIA issued a press release announcing that Wisner was returning to Washington to be a "special assistant" to McCone. Wisner considered it an important job, although he was not clear on what exactly a special assistant would do. McCone thought he could use Wisner's formidable Washington media contacts to his advantage.

Archibald B. Roosevelt Jr., a grandson of Teddy Roosevelt and a career CIA officer, replaced Wisner as station chief. Wisner passed along to him his notes on his key contacts in London. Roosevelt later told colleagues that Wisner's personal files represented "the work and thoughts of a madman." Polly grew angry with Archie and his wife, Lucky, who she thought were trying to muscle them out of London.

In mid-May 1962, Polly phoned Tish Freeman from a country house in Wiltshire where Frank and she had been spending their weeks before leaving London. She asked Tish if they could stay at her mews flat for a few days before they flew to Washington. Tish readily agreed. Staffers in the London station were truly sad to see Wisner go, no one more so than Tish. She had never known a kinder and more understanding boss, and she had become close friends with Polly.

On the morning of their departure, Wisner pulled Tish aside at the curb where cars dropped off passengers at London Airport. "He then thanked me for everything I had done for him," Tish recalled. Wisner "hoped we might work together again one day, but if not, he wanted me to know he would do anything he could to help me in the future." Aides gathered up the couple's bags and escorted them to the gate for their plane, leaving Tish at the sidewalk emotionally drained.

Chapter 27

OUTSIDE

IN SUMMER 1962, WISNER settled comfortably into a spacious office at the new CIA headquarters in Langley. He was afforded a number of "status symbols," as he called them: a parking space in the building's basement and a key to McCone's private elevator, plus Billie Morrone and another secretary to handle his correspondence. "Big John" (another not-to-endearing nickname Billie gave the director) also allowed Wisner to keep receiving his executive salary of $20,000 a year.

In the beginning, he had several long talks with McCone and attended the agency's Executive Committee meetings. But the director and his deputies had few jobs for a man they deemed to be worn-out. Quickly realizing he would no longer be involved in covert operations or have any kind of meaningful access to the CIA's other secret work, Wisner resigned from the agency on August 31. The CIA kept his departure a closely held secret. In a private ceremony in the director's conference room, McCone presented Wisner with the agency's Distinguished Intelligence Medal. Wisner, who looked older than his fifty-three years, was deeply touched by the award.

He did not cut the cord completely. For the next three years, he worked off and on as a $50-a-day consultant for the CIA, which enabled him to keep his top secret security clearance. Occasionally he was interviewed for his recollection of past events in CIA history and senior agency officers sometimes solicited his advice over long lunches. But the consulting days became more infrequent over the years. After retirement, Wisner never talked about missing the agency. It was clear to him that his spy life was behind him. He was now no more than a spectator to international crises like the October Cuban missile standoff, when the CIA accurately warned, based on intelligence from its agents and photos from its U-2 flights, that Soviet rockets were coming to the Caribbean island.

* * *

After repairing damage the renters had done to the Georgetown and Locust Hill homes, Polly reestablished herself as one of Washington's best social networkers. Soon the P Street house was again being mentioned in society columns as one of the city's premier party spots. But Polly never shook off the embarrassment she felt when Frank had his manic attacks. When they returned to the United States, she became the dominant figure in their house, highly protective of her husband. Frank at times felt suffocated by her oversight.

The strains in the marriage returned after Frank left the CIA. It was no surprise. Divorce rates are high among couples in which one spouse has bipolar disorder. Polly and Frank stuck together. But the love and affection that had returned for a while in London dissipated after the breakdown there.

* * *

Except for the fact that he wanted to stay busy, Wisner was somewhat unfocused in retirement. Since he had graduated from law

school, he had cared about little except work. His only outside interests had been hunting, gardening, and cooking. Since he had left
Sheppard Pratt, he had also shown some talent as a sketch artist.
Richard Bissell and he considered setting up a business partnership
to promote nuclear power, but the idea went nowhere. Finally, Wisner decided to establish a consulting firm in space a law firm offered
him in their downtown Washington office on Eighteenth Street
Northwest.

He formed a loose partnership with John Graham, a University
of Virginia law school classmate who was winding up his five-year
term as a member of the Atomic Energy Commission. Wisner and
Graham, who had talked for many years about working together in
some venture, became savvy entrepreneurs. They bought stock in
businesses like Southern Industries and Great Northern Paper
Company and used the purchases as entrées to do consulting work
for the firms. As a good intelligence officer would, Wisner became
skilled at stirring up new accounts just by keeping in touch with
companies. At a dinner party, he pumped Clare Boothe Luce for
information on Italian politics, then took a trip to the country to
scout it out. Back home, he wrote a lengthy memo on Italy. He
dropped off one copy at the National Security Council and another
with Charles Adams, president of Raytheon Company, which had
been doing a lot of business in Italy.

Wisner's probes were not always successful. He tried to convince the R. J. Reynolds Tobacco Company to diversify and buy the
Fannie Farmer candy manufacturer with him being the middle-
man brokering the deal. Reynolds wasn't interested. But other ventures paid off. Frank Lindsay, an old CIA comrade, hired him as a
$300-a-day consultant to use his Pentagon and CIA contacts to
smooth the way for Lindsay's company to snare a contract to build
aerial reconnaissance equipment.

The CIA, meanwhile, kept a loose watch on Wisner's contacts
with foreign officials. Occasionally, Wisner wrote a flattering letter
to J. Edgar Hoover, hoping to ingratiate himself with his old

nemesis. Hoover wrote back polite but perfunctory notes—and still had his agents keep an eye on Wisner.

* * *

Wisner also took up a number of worthy causes. He became a contributor to the Johns Hopkins School of Advanced International Studies and a member of its advisory council. He joined a committee McCone organized to pay the college expenses for children of CIA employees, and donated $3,000 over three years to its scholarship fund. He became a prodigious fundraiser for his old British friend Bill Deakin, the warden of cash-strapped St. Antony's College at Oxford, which had a foreign studies graduate school, a majority of whose students were American.

In 1963, Wisner joined the board of trustees of the Conservation Foundation, which had been set up to protect natural areas and their wildlife, and he raised money for the organization. He also lobbied the Weyerhaeuser Company, where he had many contacts from family business in Laurel, to support the foundation's advocacy of forest conservation. It was an unusual interest for a spy, but Wisner had always been a conservationist. He asked, however, that the foundation not share his CIA background too widely.

* * *

Wisner became a literary publicist of a sort. He sent friends recommendations for books he liked—such as the World War II adventure *Von Ryan's Express*, whose movie version starred Frank Sinatra—and warned colleagues of films he didn't like, such as Stanley Kubrick's satirical Cold War comedy, *Dr. Strangelove*. For some books, Wisner became an aggressive marketer, such as for Nicholas Henderson's historical biography, *Prince Eugen of Savoy*. He wrote a fawning review of Allen Dulles's *The Craft of Intelligence*, which he distributed widely to associates in the United States and Great Britain, and for which he plotted media counterattacks against reviewers who panned the book. He also dabbled in the entertainment industry, agreeing to serve as a technical adviser to a Hollywood company considering a World War II espionage movie.

Wisner became good friends with Scottish-American spy novelist Helen MacInnes, whose book *The Venetian Affair* he considered one of the best fiction works on espionage. He became an informal adviser to MacInnes and her Harcourt, Brace editor on future projects, opening doors for the author in Washington's national security community. He arranged for MacInnes to tour the FBI's headquarters, for example, and promoted her writing in media and intelligence circles. MacInnes, who enthused that she was "terrifically impressed" with Wisner's editorial suggestions, believed he had "a really brilliant mind."

* * *

For the country, and for Wisner personally, 1963 was a sad year.

In early August he was on a grouse hunt with more than a dozen others in the chilly damp moors of Scotland. Wisner's son Graham had joined his father along with one of his cousins in walking ahead of the hunting party as "beaters" to roust the birds. During a lunch between shootings, someone handed Wisner a newspaper that had a report that Phil Graham had killed himself. Wisner was devastated, although he kept his feelings hidden from the others. Frank II had had a premonition that something bad was going to happen to Graham, who had become a mentor to him. Stationed at the U.S. embassy in Algiers, Frankie had received a letter from Phil asking his young friend not to think poorly of him and to remember the man he was, not what he had become.

Wisner and Graham up to that point had followed similar medical paths. Phil had been hypomanic since 1957, but neither Kay nor his friends recognized it at the time. In late October 1957, a little less than a year after Wisner's breakdown in Europe, Graham had his own mental collapse and began seeing a psychiatrist. Like Polly, Kay did not know enough about the disease to realize that though the talk therapy the doctor practiced with the publisher briefly stabilized him, it was inadequate to treat his disease. Shortly after he bought *Newsweek* in 1961, Phil's manic-depressive episodes resumed with a vengeance. He went into and out of extramarital affairs, began drinking heavily, bought compulsively, and exploded in anger at Kay. He refused to take shock treatments (the only clinically effective therapy for bipolar disorder at the time), believing they had scrambled Frank Wisner's brain. As with Polly, each time Kay thought her husband was recovering, he would relapse into a manic episode. On August 3, Graham grabbed a 28-gauge shotgun from the rack of rifles kept at their country home, Glen Welby, pointed it at his head, and pulled the trigger.

Wisner continued each month to visit Sibley Hospital psychiatrist Zigmond Lebensohn, who had treated him before his commitment to Sheppard Pratt. He enjoyed just talking to Lebensohn during the sessions. At one point he sent Lebensohn a copy of *Prince Eugen of Savoy*, which he thought the psychiatrist might enjoy reading.

Frank and Polly hosted Raytheon president Charles Adams and his wife at the farm over the weekend of November 23 and 24, 1963. But it was a grim outing, with nobody wanting to do much of anything except watch network news coverage of John Kennedy's assassination in Dallas on November 22. Wisner, who witnessed the funeral procession from his Washington office window on November 25, had not known Kennedy personally, but he was crushed by his death. It was a terrible blow for the country, he thought. Wisner was appalled by what he called the "squalid performance" of the Dallas police force after the assassination, when nightclub owner Jack Ruby was able to kill Lee Harvey Oswald right in front of their officers, snuffing out any chance authorities would have had to unravel the facts behind the assassin's heinous act. Frank believed Oswald was the single killer, but he remained curious about the loose connections Oswald had with Russia.

* * *

Frank and Polly spent the evening of February 9, 1964, at Kay Graham's house to play bridge and to watch the Beatles perform on *The Ed Sullivan Show* for the first time. Polly did not think the British rock group would last long, but Wendy told her she would be proven wrong.

Wisner and his wife rented a house in Atlantic City, New Jersey, in late August to witness Democrats at their party convention nominate Lyndon Johnson for president and Hubert Humphrey as his running mate. Wisner believed LBJ was "a man of great experience and considerable wisdom," he told his children. The country would be in good hands, he thought.

Wisner wholeheartedly backed Johnson escalating U.S. military involvement in Vietnam and he was overjoyed when Frank II was transferred to the U.S. embassy in Saigon. Wisner soon had fierce debates with Wendy and Graham, who opposed the Vietnam War. He sent a memo to the CIA and the White House on a two-hour chat he had had with a British Asia expert who was pessimistic about the chances of any Western power defeating North Vietnam or the Viet Cong in the south except with massive military force. Wisner never indicated whether the analysis swayed him. Instead, he fretted over the growing number of anti–Vietnam War news articles and books being published, which he warned could "collectively contribute much to the confusion of the public mind."

Wisner rabidly defended the CIA's anti-Communist operations in Vietnam. In October 1963, he sent to the agency's deputy director a melodramatic memo that he said was "top secret" and for the deputy's "eyes only." In it, Wisner claimed that a vast network of government leakers, led by several top State Department officials, was feeding salacious stories to reporters eager to vilify the CIA. That was a bit too conspiratorial even for Langley. A note scribbled by an agency officer on Wisner's memo read: "Suggest that we cool off on this."

* * *

By summer 1964, family and friends began to notice Wisner's erratic behavior increasing once more. Realizing he had again begun
to slip, Wisner admitted to his son Ellis, who had returned during
a summer break from studying abroad in England to work on the
farm, that he could not give Polly the emotional support she deserved. He needed Ellis's help.

A friend noticed that Frank seemed oddly withdrawn at a luncheon Polly hosted. Again, there were more outbursts at home and
during parties. British MP George Brown told Wisner a letter Frank
had sent him on Cuba was irrational. "Some of your comments are
oddly unlike you," Brown wrote his old friend. Billie cabled Tish in
London that the boss was in trouble. It did not help that on top of
his next unraveling, Wisner had to enter the hospital in March 1965
to undergo surgery for a painful stomach hernia, which turned out
to be more complicated than he had expected.

Wisner began to nurse obsessions. He mounted a letter-writing
campaign to stir up hostile book reviews of *The Ambassador*, a novel
written by prominent Australian author and playwright Morris
West that Wisner insisted painted an unfair picture of the CIA. The
Alsop brothers ignored him. Sherman Kent, who led the CIA's
Board of National Estimates, told Wisner he thought *The Ambassador* was actually a good book. Dean Acheson liked it as well and told
Wisner he shouldn't be so "unduly disturbed" about the novel. Wisner would not give up. Almost like a literary stalker, he kept a de-
tailed "Box Score," listing in three columns the reviews that were
"Against the Book," "Favorable to the Book," and neutral on it.

Wisner also became fixated on Martin Bormann, Hitler's private secretary, who had been determined to have killed himself in
Germany as the European war ended in May 1945. But into the
1960s, there continued to be Bormann sightings all over the world.
Wisner, who collected the speculative stories, became convinced
that the top Nazi had fled to South America. He tried to enlist

Howard Hunt into collaborating with him to write a book on the evidence Wisner believed he had that Bormann was hiding in Latin America, but Hunt wasn't interested. Wisner invented a new game he called Bormann Schmormann—Who's Got the S.O.B.? complete with rules for the treasure hunt that he sent to friends and relatives. He wrote a detailed memo to Desie FitzGerald at the CIA, pressing him to have the agency join in the hunt. FitzGerald ignored him.

FitzGerald wasn't the only one shunning Wisner. By 1965, bipolar disease fatigue had begun to set in among the people around him. Wisner progressively lost many friends who did not have the time for him or who just didn't want to deal with his breakdowns any longer. The guest book at the farm had no entries after June 1965. Moreover, Wisner's sister Elisabeth, who had been a stabilizing force for him in the past, was not available to help Polly. Elisabeth since mid-1964 had been having difficulty recuperating from a serious operation. It all left Wisner more isolated, pushing him further into depression.

Dr. Lebensohn suggested he try coping mechanisms, such as recognizing the "lumps" that were causing his "mental indigestion." The psychiatrist also had Wisner check into Sibley Hospital in spring 1965 for more rounds of shock therapy. Wisner was no longer the haughty patient he had been when he showed up on Sheppard Pratt's doorstep. He arrived at Sibley far more humble. He knew he needed help. The Sibley medical workers had no idea what Wisner had done for a living. They saw only an unusually kind and thoughtful man who encouraged them to press on with the grim work of caring for those with mental illness. "He never failed to try to cheer us," one hospital employee later wrote Polly. Wisner, in particular, befriended a young woman in the ward suffering from manic depression. When doctors could not, he was able to communicate with the girl. She became happy talking to him, more in touch with reality from her conversations with the kindly man than those she had with anyone else.

Before flying to Vietnam, Frank II visited Sibley. He took his father out on a car ride for some fresh air, stopping at one point on the edge of Rock Creek Park. Slumped on a park bench, his father appeared to him to be in utter despair. Wisner had reached the point of not wanting to go further in life. He was a sick man who complained that Polly was pushing him too hard to get over his problems. He also told his son he was now worried the constant shock treatments were causing his memory to erode.

Wisner checked out of Sibley at the end of July 1965 and headed to the farm to complete his recuperation through the month of August. Once more he was optimistic about his prognosis. But August passed and Wisner realized his mental state continued to be precarious. Lebensohn urged him to cut back on work. On September 22, 1965, Wisner sat down with Helms for lunch and told him he would not be renewing his consulting contract with the agency. He was severing his last tie with the CIA.

Chapter 28

A LIFE CUT SHORT

WISNER SO WANTED TO go with friends to a partridge shoot he had organized outside Madrid. He had put together a previous hunting trip to Spain in the fall of 1964 and enjoyed it thoroughly. Wisner had had his special shotgun repaired in London for that hunt, and he had attended a school there to train in shooting Spain's elusive red-legged partridges. Before the outing, he had stopped in Paris for a wonderful visit with Chip Bohlen, whom Kennedy had appointed ambassador to France. Though the number of birds he bagged on the 1964 trip had been modest, he had never experienced a better shoot or more pleasant surroundings and companions for it, such as Henry Morgan of Morgan Stanley—although others in the party, who knew Wisner's medical past well, worried on that trip about him wandering through the thickets with a loaded weapon.

Wisner wanted to replicate that fabulous 1964 trip in 1965. He spent seven months organizing the outing and lined up old friends like Henry Sears to join him. He secured a permit from the Spanish embassy in Washington to take two shotguns into Spain. He made reservations for the group to stay at the Ritz Hotel in Madrid before being chauffeured out to the countryside by a guide.

But when Frank and Polly boarded the plane for Paris on October 11, 1965, he was struck with another manic-depressive attack. The usual symptoms returned: tenseness, anxiety, paranoia, anger over restrictions Polly imposed on him, and fear that he was losing his mind. Their six days in Paris at the ambassador's residence were agonizing for Polly as well as for Chip and Avis Bohlen. At a dinner party the ambassador threw for the couple, Wisner was wound up tightly, talking endlessly, seeming constantly on edge.

The Wisners flew to London on October 17 and checked into the Ritz Hotel in Piccadilly for a short stay. Ellis took the train to London from Oxford, where he was finishing his thesis. He found his father lethargic, despairing, and dead set against leaving his hotel room. Wisner was in what psychiatrists call a "depressive stupor." He did not have the energy to do anything. He could hardly climb out of the lounge chair in his hotel room and he rambled on about running out of money. To give his emotionally worn-out mother a break, Ellis talked his father into walking to a nearby museum. But they stayed there only briefly. Back at their hotel room, Wisner sank into the chair exhausted. Ellis could see that he had gained weight, that his cheeks were puffy, and that the sad look on his face never left.

Spain was out of the question. Polly booked a flight back to the U.S. for them on October 22.

* * *

A week later, on October 29, Polly helped Frank into the car for the drive from their Georgetown house to Locust Hill. Margaret Weller, their interior decorator, joined them at the farm to advise on furniture arrangements. Before she left Georgetown, Polly had phoned George Long, who had succeeded Billy Sigman as their farm manager, and asked him to gather up the rifles at Locust Hill and lock them up outside the farmhouse so her husband couldn't get his hands on them. Doctors or friends who could see that Wisner looked miserable might have warned her to keep the firearms away from him. Or Polly might have had a premonition that something bad might happen if her husband had access to them.

Long and his assistant, Richard Rhodes, collected what they thought were all the guns at the farm. But they missed one weapon—a 20-gauge Ferlach double-barreled shotgun that Wisner had had shipped from Austria to give to Frank II over a decade earlier. It was propped up out of sight in the closet of a second-floor room. The Ferlach was not a gun that was regularly used, so it was easy for Long and Rhodes not to account for it. Or Wisner might have hidden the weapon in the closet. The family never knew.

A friend who saw Wisner just before he climbed into the car for the trip to Locust Hill noticed that he was quiet, but he appeared to be in a good mood. When he arrived at the farm that afternoon, Wisner pleasantly told Long and Rhodes, who were out in the barn, that he would join them after he went upstairs in the farmhouse to change from his city clothes into his work clothes. That was the first thing he always did when he came to Locust Hill.

Less than an hour later, Polly and Margaret, who were downstairs in the kitchen, were jolted by the sound of a shotgun blast from the second floor. Polly knew instantly what had happened and she stayed in the kitchen. Margaret hurried upstairs and returned within seconds. "He's gone," she told Polly.

Long and Rhodes arrived quickly. The two men bounded up the stairs to the second-floor room where the sound had come from. They opened the door and choked on the gunpowder smoke that filled the room from the shotgun blast. Wisner lay on the floor, the Ferlach shotgun across his leg, with blood soaking the carpet. He had put the end of the shotgun barrel to his right temple and pulled the trigger. The discharge from the weapon had blown practically half his head off.

Long rushed downstairs and told Polly what had happened. She did not go upstairs to see for herself. She couldn't bear to view the grisly scene. Instead, she told Long to go back up and cover her husband with a sheet.

An ambulance and deputies from the Kent County Sheriff's Department arrived shortly before five p.m. and declared Wisner dead on the scene. No autopsy was performed on the body. It was clear to deputy medical examiner Robert Farr how Wisner had died.

Wisner's brother-in-law, Chis, and his business partner, John Graham, identified the corpse at the morgue, sparing Polly that ordeal. Funeral director Edward Fellows from Millington, Maryland, took away the body, which was eventually transported to Joseph Gawler's Sons funeral home in Washington. Polly ordered the funeral home not to attempt to embalm Frank because of the damage to his head. The casket would remain closed.

* * *

The CIA refused to divulge to journalists piecing together their stories the night of October 29 what exactly Wisner had done for the agency. The *Washington Post* quoted what it reported was a "close friend" saying that Wisner had been "one of the founders" of the agency's covert operations capability—"one of a half dozen of the most important men in Washington during his CIA career." A group of Wisner's closest agency friends later that night released a statement that read: "Frank Wisner, in the most literal sense, gave his life to public service."

An editorial in the Communist newspaper *The Worker* printed a crude headline: "One Head Less in the CIA." The paper branded Wisner an international criminal. Some stories in American and international publications speculated that CIA assassins had murdered Wisner because he was about to write a tell-all book about the agency. A Mexico City magazine article claimed Wisner's demise was part of a "dark struggle of the secret services." The conspiracy theories never ended. A friend told Frank II many decades later that he still suspected the CIA gave Wisner shock treatments to wipe from his mind the sensitive intelligence he knew.

* * *

As soon as he learned of the suicide, Angleton rushed to Wisner's Georgetown home to make sure no classified documents had been left out in the open, where they could fall into the wrong hands. Billie Morrone's first phone call was overseas to Tish Freeman in London. "Brace yourself," Billie told Tish. "He's done it."

* * *

Why did he do it? Why did Frank Wisner kill himself? His family asked that question over and over for years to come. They could offer only imperfect theories: their father was a casualty of the clandestine service; he had been caught up in the Hungarian revolt and the Suez crisis; he didn't take care of himself following the acute attack of hepatitis; the aftereffects of that disease caught up with him; he was humiliated by his fall from power; Hoover dogged him over the Caradja affair; he could not take the horror of falling apart in front of everyone; the depth of despair closed in on him like black walls.

Wisner left no suicide note. The fact that his father had appeared calm and collected talking to Long and Rhodes before he went upstairs and shot himself—perhaps it meant that he had not been 100 percent committed to taking his life, his son Ellis later speculated. "Maybe there was a little two percent in him saying, 'Don't go ahead with this,'" Ellis said.

That was not likely the case. For a person afflicted with bipolar disorder, the symptoms can become so painful, so unrelenting, that suicide can seem the only means of escape. It is not uncommon for such a person to be calm and in good spirits before taking his life— even acting that way in front of his psychiatrist. Wisner might have felt at peace with himself once he made the decision to die. Or he might have been deceiving others so he could carry out his final act.

"Patients with depression or with manic depression are far more likely to commit suicide than those with other psychiatric or medical illnesses," particularly if the disease is untreated or inadequately treated, according to one medical textbook. Also, a majority of people with bipolar disorder who kill themselves have been in contact with a health care provider in the months leading up to their deaths, as was the case with Wisner. And there are almost always warning signs in the weeks preceding a suicide—although they often become obvious only after the fact.

* * *

When Frank killed himself, Polly did not shed a tear. Yes, she was as shocked and devastated as the rest of the family. But not completely shocked. Since her husband's commitment to Sheppard Pratt, Polly had always had an inkling that something like that might happen. Polly had been a stoic. By nature, she was a strong woman, never one to show her emotions. She was not prepared to take her children in her arms to comfort them with love and affection.

Her husband's bipolar disorder had also exhausted her. Friends suspected she had had it with Frank. It is not unusual for the spouses of people with bipolar disorder to be fed up. Marriages can unravel. A spouse can start out concerned and caring but end up impatient and resentful—which the sick person often sees as rejection and lack of sympathy. When researchers asked couples whether they would have married if they had known the illness would invade their lives, 5 percent of the bipolar patients said they would not have. But 53 percent of the spouses—ten times as many—said they would not have.

Ellis was in Oxford when Bill Deakin at St. Antony's College phoned him with the news that his father had died. He caught the first flight back to the United States that he could book.

Wendy was at Sarah Lawrence College in New York when the news arrived. She was stunned and heartbroken. Just four months earlier, her parents had thrown a party for her, and nothing had seemed out of the ordinary with her father. She blamed the CIA and its cold war for wearing down her father and killing him.

William Porter, who had just been made deputy U.S. ambassador in Saigon, brought Frank II to his residence and gave him the news he had received that his father was dead. "Get yourself organized to go back home to be a part of the funeral," Porter told his new aide. The job on his staff would be waiting for him when he returned. Much later, CIA doctors told Frank II that if his father had hung on for another five years, the early drugs that were coming to the market for bipolar disorder could have saved him.

The headmaster of St. Paul's School in Concord, New Hampshire, summoned Graham, whom he knew to be a troubled child. Showing no empathy, he brusquely told the boy only that his father had died and that he should pack a bag to go home. Graham felt like he had been hit by a truck. He knew nothing about his father's torment, regarding him still as an "awesome figure," he said. When he arrived at the Georgetown house, Graham and Wendy went up to a second-floor bedroom and locked the door behind them. They read the *Washington Post* account of their father's death and learned for the first time that he had shot himself.

* * *

November 2 was a chilly, sunny day for Wisner's funeral at Washington's National Cathedral. Wisner had joined Polly in contributing $250 to the All Hallows Guild garden on the cathedral grounds at the request of an Oklahoma senator, and he had bequeathed a larger gift to the Cathedral School. The hundred fifty seats for the service in the lower-level Bethlehem Chapel filled up quickly and a long line of relatives, friends, and intelligence colleagues snaked to the outside. The CIA officers attending—they included Allen Dulles and Richard Helms—had grim looks on their faces, but Wisner's passing had not surprised many of them. The congregants were asked to give thanks for the gifts God had given Wisner—"his unshakable integrity, his sensitivity, and determined strength."

After the funeral, Polly sent the altar flowers to the Washington Home for Incurables. About one hundred cars lined up with two motorcycle policemen as escorts and proceeded to Arlington National Cemetery. Two FBI agents kept watch at the cathedral and at the cemetery for any foreign agents snapping photos of U.S. intelligence officers attending the services. The bureau reported no suspicious activity.

Wisner was buried a short walk from the sites of World War II leaders such as George Marshall and Beetle Smith. The three-volley rifle salute given to veterans startled the children. There was a Wisner and Chisholm family grave site in Laurel, but Polly wanted Frank buried next to his war comrades, with his gravestone simply noting that he had been a commander in the U.S. Navy.

The reception at the Georgetown home was packed after the burial. The Wisner children found a patch of floor to squat on while they munched finger food and talked. There was nowhere else to sit.

* * *

Hundreds of condolence letters poured in after Wisner's suicide. As many came from his British friends as from his American ones. A lot of the writers were truly shocked, while others had seen signs over the years that he had not been well. Letters from senior U.S. officials contained boilerplate condolences. The more revealing notes came from Wisner's coworkers, who were truly grief-stricken at the loss of a man they considered kindhearted, self-effacing, and engaged in a dirty business for which they thought he had not been really suited. "None of us will be quite the same again," Tracy Barnes's wife, Janet, wrote Polly. Agency deputy director Charles Cabell insisted Wisner was "as much of a casualty in the struggle against the evil force of Communism as any soldier felled by an enemy bullet in Vietnam." Wisner's country had "squandered" his life, claimed *New York Times* correspondent Arthur Krock. "We went through some thick times over the years," Helms wrote Polly, but never "did we ever exchange an angry word." Even the FBI's Sam Papich, who had spent many years tracking Wisner's movements for the bureau, admitted to Polly that he always liked the man. "In this complex and mad world," Papich wrote her, "I was fortunate to live a significant part of our country's history with Frank."

Polly kept detailed records on the letters, noting when each had been answered.

The sniping behind Polly's back continued. Her overloading Frank's social schedule had driven him to suicide, gossips whispered. Carmel Offie was particularly cruel, claiming Polly was sexless, which drove Frank mad. Offie also became a target of snide remarks; others accused the fast-talking CIA aide of constantly prodding the overworked Wisner to cut ethical corners on operations.

* * *

Polly Wisner and Katharine Graham now shared an unenviable bond. Their husbands' suicides some two years apart were strikingly similar. The deaths of two such formidable men were equal shocks to political and social Washington. The two widows talked for hours about why those tragedies had befallen them.

Polly at one point told Kay she did not think that Frank or Phil "could have borne life as kind of doing nothing."

Kay agreed. "I think Phil had that figured out and Wiz did, too," she told Polly.

Said Polly: "They just could not bear *not* being in the center" of the country's affairs.

* * *

The final accounting of the estate Wisner left behind showed that he was considerably well-off. Its gross amount before expenses was a little more than $1.9 million (over $18 million in today's dollars). Polly, who had considerable assets from Knowles family money, received the bulk of the inheritance, but Wisner bequeathed about $65,000 (more than $640,000 in today's dollars) in stocks and cash to each of his children.

For the next eighteen years, little was publicly known about

Wisner's work as a CIA operative. One aspect of his clandestine life, however, was revealed several months after his death: the fact that he had been a member of the secret Seven Society at the University of Virginia. By tradition, a wreath of black magnolias in the shape of a "7" appeared at his Arlington National Cemetery grave site.

EPILOGUE

JOHN GRAHAM HELPED POLLY with family business affairs after Frank's death, but Polly dived alone into many of the jobs that had to be tackled at Locust Hill. In the past, she never had qualms about making big decisions, such as purchasing farm equipment and nearby land. She had rebuilt their herd of cattle, traveling to Canada to buy a bull, and had even become vice president of the Maryland Jersey Cattle Club. The Thanksgiving after Frank's death was grim and emotional for the rest of the family, but Polly refused to be downbeat. The children and she continued making wagers in the Betting Book that Wisner had so loved.

Back in Washington, she plunged into fundraising work for artistic institutions such as the Kennedy Center and the Phillips Collection. She served on a committee staging the Opera Ball in Washington. Her meticulously designed P Street garden was listed as a stop for Georgetown garden tours.

Polly continued her dinner parties with a passion. Newspapers routinely referred to her as one of the "Washington doyennes" who dominated DC high society. No one turned down her invitation. Her guest list almost always included a senior administration official, a couple of ambassadors, several senators, and lots of reporters. Guests were wedged around four or five round tables on the first floor, with one noted thinker, such as George Kennan or Henry Kissinger, designated to lead off the discussion.

Polly continued not to be shy about trading her social connections for political favors. She asked old friend Paul Nitze to check the promotion status of a loyal family friend who was a clerk in the Pentagon's adjutant general's office. Richard Helms, who was eventually elevated to CIA director, remained close to her. Polly reciprocated, helping Helms's second wife, Cynthia, navigate CIA mores for spouses and the unspoken rules of the Georgetown set.

Polly traveled a good bit. She visited her son Frank II in Vietnam and insisted that they not sit around pining over the loss of Frank Senior. Polly routinely sent her son news clippings on foreign policy issues she thought he should pay attention to. In 1967, she visited Moscow, where she stayed with Ambassador Llewellyn Thompson and his wife, Jane, who had taken in Frank during his Vienna breakdown. "At the U.S. Embassy in Moscow, it seems to be open house these days for Washington wives and widows who might once have been persona non grata because of their husbands' jobs," wrote *Washington Post* society columnist Maxine Cheshire. The Soviet invasion of Czechoslovakia the next year to snuff out liberalization reforms of the Prague Spring left Polly thinking about Frank's torment over Hungary a decade earlier. She was glad he was spared that second trauma.

Over the years, Polly and Katharine Graham became an inseparable team, each sustaining the other. Kay found much-needed joy in the intimacy the two shared. After Kay took over the *Post*, Polly helped her organize parties with senior Washington officials. In New York, the two ventured with Truman Capote to the "21" Club for cozy lunches and to Saratoga Springs for the mineral baths. Walking across a glacier on a ski trip in Switzerland, Kay told Polly she had decided how they should grow old gracefully: "We have to read a lot and not drink." Polly remained silent for what seemed like a long time, the only sound the crunching of their footsteps on ice. Finally, Polly asked in a deadpan, "When do we have to start?"

In 1975, Polly married Clayton Fritchey, a political journalist whose opinion column appeared in some hundred newspapers. For a long time a committed bachelor and ladies' man, Fritchey had pursued Katharine Graham off and on for the better part of a year, but when she resisted, he turned his attention to Polly. Lively and very smart, Fritchey, a committed liberal and lifelong Democrat who had once worked as Adlai Stevenson's press secretary, enjoyed lively debates with ideological opposites. Opposed to the Vietnam War, he had shouting matches with Joe Alsop, who was pro-war.

At first the Wisner children were hesitant about bringing Fritchey into the fold. But Clayton and Polly shared many friends and interests. He kept her busy. Clayton, who in short order was entering wagers in the Betting Book, always had a twinkle in his eye. He was quick-witted and a big tease. Soon he had won over the four children, who came to enjoy him as a stepfather. After their wedding, Clayton and Polly remodeled the P Street home, which earned them a glowing article in *Architectural Digest*.

Although Clayton never got along particularly well with Joe Alsop, Polly remained the columnist's loyal friend. "God knows, you have played a role in my life," Joe once wrote her. Polly frequently sent him notes on the columns she liked, though she agreed that he had grown increasingly "contentious" over the years, particularly on the Vietnam War. As he neared the end of his life and was stricken with lung cancer, Polly, Kay Graham, and Cynthia Helms visited Joe frequently to talk about art and archaeology instead of politics. He died on August 28, 1989.

Polly saw the 1980s as the beginning of the end for the Georgetown set. Jimmy Carter and his administration ignored their parties. The Reagans mingled with the Georgetown crowd but George and Barbara Bush stuck to their own circle of friends. The Bushes attended one of Polly and Clayton's Sunday suppers but didn't enjoy it and left early. Polly tried some matchmaking of prospective cabinet officers with the new Clinton administration. Until the end of her life, she remained a social force to be reckoned with in Georgetown. She died at her P Street home of a heart ailment at the age of ninety, about a year after Clayton Fritchey and Kay Graham both passed away. The *Washington Post*'s obituary reported that Polly had been among a small group of women who had "dominated high society in the nation's capital."

* * *

After graduating from Sarah Lawrence College, Wendy earned a PhD in American history from Boston University and taught at colleges in Maine and overseas. She wrote her PhD dissertation, which she later turned into a book, on the U.S. experience (and particularly her father's work) in Romania during World War II. If he had been alive to read it, Wisner would not likely have appreciated parts of the book that were critical of the American mission's performance in Bucharest. Wendy died in 2020 of complications from Alzheimer's disease.

Too young at the time to realize what was happening to his father, Graham could only imagine in later years the torment Wisner had gone through. He worshipped his father, dearly wishing he had had more time with him, and he never stopped asking why he had taken his life. When Graham was seventeen years old, he volunteered to work in a state mental hospital, hoping to gain some insight into the disease his father had suffered. After attending Antioch College, Graham earned a law degree from Georgetown University. He traveled the world as an attorney and worked for environmental causes.

Wisner wanted Ellis to go to law school, but his son had no interest in legal work, and he never wanted to follow his father into the CIA. Instead, Ellis taught high school English and Latin. He never kept his father's suicide secret from employers and coworkers. He got a wide range of reactions from people when they learned Frank

Wisner had killed himself. Like his brothers, Ellis wondered if his father's bipolar disorder would be genetically passed down. But he could only ask the question. He had no answer.

Since he was twelve years old, Frank II had wanted to join the Foreign Service. As a boy he could recite the names of every prime minister in the world. Wisner's oldest son ended up having a distinguished diplomatic career, serving as ambassador to Zambia, Egypt, the Philippines, and India. In Washington, he also served as an undersecretary in the State Department and Pentagon. He still holds warm and tender memories of his father as well as a deep feeling of gratitude for having had him as a parent. Being Frank Wisner's son, he always believed he had to live up to high expectations. "There is not a day in my life that I don't think of him, in some regard," Frank II says.

* * *

On January 29, 1971, nearly five years after the suicide, a closed memorial service was held in the auditorium of the CIA's Langley headquarters for Wisner's family and friends. Polly and her four children sat in the front row, along with Katharine Graham. CIA director Richard Helms presided. Frank Wisner "lived in the storm and strife of our profession," Helms said of his old friend. "He balanced his faith and hope for this society with a tough and sometimes melancholy realism. He was a big man who lived an uncompromising and full life."

The agency originally considered carving a star for Wisner on the Wall of Honor in the main entrance lobby of the headquarters building, which has stars for each CIA officer killed in the line of duty. But some CIA veterans objected. So did Frank II. Wisner was not a war casualty. He died from a disease. Instead, on one of the clandestine service's hallways, a glass display case was put up; it contained wartime photos of Wisner, medals he had been awarded, framed commendation letters, and a brass bust of him made by

American sculptor Heinz Warneke. A "Frank G. Wisner Award" was also established in the CIA's scholarship fund for children of employees; Polly contributed heavily to it. In 1997, on the agency's fiftieth anniversary, CIA director George Tenet named Wisner one of the agency's fifty "Trailblazers" for establishing "the doctrine for the use of covert action" and inspiring a cadre of future secret warriors. Wisner pioneered "some of the most intricate and challenging undertakings" of the CIA in its early years, his citation read.

The CIA bureaucracy's gratitude went only so far, however. Polly fought an agency ruling that since her husband had not been a full-time employee of the CIA when he shot himself, she was not entitled to any death benefits from his employment. Her lawyer argued that Wisner fell ill during his CIA service, which should have had a bearing on his widow's rights. The CIA also gave Polly a difficult time in collecting benefits from the retirement contributions Wisner had made. Polly received a lump-sum check in December 1965 for $15,860.45—the amount her husband had contributed to the Civil Service Retirement System. Polly did not deserve any more, the CIA ruled.

*　*　*

In 1967, William Bundy, then an assistant secretary of state for Asia, wrote Polly a touching letter maintaining that America's covert war in the 1950s "could never have happened" without her husband. "There must be only a handful of men at any period of our country's service about whom one can say that without his individual contribution enormous things would not have been done." Others agreed. "There has passed the greatest cold war soldier in American history," according to one newspaper editorial on Wisner's death. Frank II believes his father should be credited with helping shape America's intelligence capability, putting in place enduring building blocks in the national security system.

But to what end and at what cost? Wisner and the CIA officers

who served under him were not rogue operators. It would be grossly
naive to think they were. Presidents found the covert operations
Wisner's clandestine service would launch to be convenient shortcuts around the democratic process. The end of World War II saw
the Executive Branch beginning to make more foreign policy decisions in secret. The CIA, writes Arthur Schlesinger Jr., offered a
way for a president "to conduct foreign policy without diplomats,
carry out military actions without the armed forces, intervene at will
around the world without congressional authorization and scrutiny."
Administrations were never too bothered when the shortcuts sometimes led to questionable foreign involvements or unacceptable acts.

Wisner spent many hours briefing officials in the White House,
State Department, and Pentagon on his operations and asking for
their guidance. It was not in his nature to act as a rogue elephant,
insisted the CIA officers who worked with him. Wisner's view that
America needed an aggressive covert action program against the
Soviet Union was widely shared by top administration officials and
congressional leaders as well as by the press and the public. Wisner's
superiors ordered him to fight ruthless Soviet tactics with equal
American ruthlessness.

But it would be just as naive to believe that Wisner and his officers were mere obedient officials acting on the express instructions
of their president. Harry Truman, Dwight Eisenhower, and their
top aides gave them considerable leeway to operate, and they exploited that freedom for all it was worth. Truman and Eisenhower
knew only in broad brushstrokes what Wisner was up to. That
should come as no surprise. In wartime, a president gives his defense
secretary and top flag officers the objectives in general that he wants
in a military campaign. The president cannot be expected to know,
and in fact doesn't want to know, the nuts and bolts of how those
objectives are carried out at, say, the division, brigade, or battalion
level. So it was with the CIA, which was fighting what the agency
and the White House considered a war for survival against the Soviet Union.

Wisner fiercely resisted administration outsiders, or even insiders within his own CIA, meddling in the details of his operations. And no one was willing to challenge the independence he maintained or the legal and ethical corners he cut. Projects were concealed from high authority. But "more frequently it was the senior officials themselves who, through pressure for results, created the climate within which abuses occurred," a Church Committee report concluded. The Executive Branch, Congress, the courts, the media, and the American public backed what they knew, or thought they knew, that the CIA was doing against the Russians. They didn't mind not being told any more.

War with a hostile Soviet Union had seemed imminent to many in the U.S. government in 1948 when Wisner's highly secret Office of Policy Coordination was formed. He was ordered to begin covert operations before his organization was ready to launch them. The can-do lawyer from Mississippi was given many tasks he should have turned down. Even Wisner eventually realized this. The Defense Department pressured him to plunge into guerrilla operations better left to the military. Diplomatic initiatives more suited for the State Department were fobbed off on him. Wisner's secret organization—which had to ramp up its number of field officers too quickly, sacrificing quality for quantity—became "overused and misused," writes CIA veteran Harry Rositzke. In the beginning, it had to learn covert operations by trial and error, with the errors costing lives and wasting money.

Wisner's efforts to use émigré groups and to organize secret armies to topple East Bloc regimes failed, as did programs to infiltrate guerrilla operatives into the Soviet Union. Communist secret services had little difficulty scooping up most of the infiltrators. Unrealistic missions the Pentagon gave the CIA, such as placing guerrillas in front of the Red Army to slow it during a western advance or getting them behind the lines to rescue allied pilots in a "hot war," went nowhere. When the Hungarians did revolt and Soviet tanks brutally crushed the rebellion, the Eisenhower administration kept the CIA sheathed for fear of sparking a nuclear war between the superpowers.

The impact of Wisner's Mighty Wurlitzer to target East Bloc nations with propaganda broadcasts from the CIA's "freedom radios" was difficult to measure. CIA front operations were effective when they attracted the support of national groups, like the AFL and the CIO, that shared the agency's vision of American power in the world. The CIA-backed Congress for Cultural Freedom succeeded in refuting the Soviet lie that the arts could flourish only under Communism. The Soviets must have thought Radio Free Europe and Radio Liberty were effective; they went to inordinate lengths to jam the broadcasts. It was next to impossible, however, for the CIA to hide its backing of those large-scale radio operations. When the CIA's ties to the radios became public, it tainted the useful work they were doing winning hearts and minds. By 1976, RFE and Radio Liberty were operating separately from the CIA.

Finally, Wisner's officers succeeded in operations to topple democratically elected regimes in Iran and Guatemala. But the long-term, unintended consequences of those operations proved disastrous for American interests and the cause of human rights. Covert action was only one part of a wider clandestine service that Wisner pioneered for the CIA. Eventually, he also oversaw the agency's espionage and counterespionage operations as well as sensitive liaison operations involving foreign intelligence organizations.

* * *

America's shadow warfare did not end with Frank Wisner. Far from it. Controversial covert operations—in the name of national security or just plain expedience—continued with gusto. Assassinations were still plotted. Secret wars were waged in Laos and Cambodia. A democratically elected government in Chile was overthrown. The CIA and U.S. military conducted domestic spying on a massive scale. Mail continued to be opened illegally. Wisner's old colleague

E. Howard Hunt and another former CIA officer named James Mc-
Cord were part of a bungled attempt to plant listening devices in
the Democratic Party's national headquarters in the Watergate
complex.

With the *New York Times* and other news outlets exposing CIA
front organizations and agency spying on the anti-war movement,
public attitudes toward the CIA began to turn by the end of the
1960s. In the mid-1970s, the Church Committee in the Senate and
the Pike Committee in the House waged relentless probes of illegal
and unethical CIA activities. Covert action projects were scaled
back to a handful. Intelligence committees were established in the
Senate and House. Legislation requiring the White House to sub-
mit CIA covert action projects to congressional leaders for review
was passed. With multiple layers of oversight in Congress and the
national security bureaucracy, as well as a far more aggressive press,
Wisner's freewheeling operation could not have survived.

In the 1980s, William Casey, Ronald Reagan's CIA director, set
out to rebuild the agency's covert action capability, but he came
close to having it torn down after public exposure of his scheme to
sell Iran arms in exchange for hostages and to illegally divert the
profits to Nicaragua's Contra rebels.

On the day the Berlin Wall fell, November 9, 1989, Richard
Helms—who had left government service twelve years earlier after
pleading no contest to a federal charge of misleading Congress
about the CIA operation in Chile—sent Polly a handwritten note.
With the wall coming down, "I have thought often of Frank and
how delighted he would have been at the turn of the wheel," Helms
told Polly. "How vindicated he would have felt!" Helms remembered
"so vividly how pained he was by the course the Soviets took in
Hungary. . . . The TV picture of 1989 would have thrilled him."
Stewart Alsop went further, writing twenty years earlier that his old
friend "deserves a major share of the credit for the fact that the Cold
War was not lost."

Both men were being too generous. Ultimately, none of Wisner's efforts had had an appreciable impact on the Cold War, at least

in terms of defeating Soviet Communism. Broader forces were at work in the fall of the Soviet Union. The United States had formed a powerful postwar alliance with Britain and France and eventually with the defeated World War II enemies—Germany, Japan, and Italy—that proved too strong for the Soviet Union, especially after the defection of Communist China during the Nixon administration. The Soviet Union exhausted itself trying to head off and then compete with that coalition. The Russian government was overwhelmed by the burden of sustaining an empire abroad and maintaining a voracious military at home.

By the time party secretary Leonid Brezhnev died in 1982, "the economy of the Soviet Union was bankrupt, its ideology was sterile, and its policies were impotent," wrote William Hyland, former editor of *Foreign Affairs*. A huge nuclear weapons arsenal gained for it only an expensive arms race that American technology outpaced. America's containment policy, which succeeded more in Europe than in Asia, did play a part in Russia's losing the Cold War. But ultimately the Soviets lost that war because the Communist system on which their government rested proved fatally flawed.

Today, the CIA and the seventeen other intelligence units in different parts of the government give the United States a world-class spy operation, ahead of every other nation. This "intelligence community," as it is commonly called, spends about $2 billion a week snooping on others.

America's vast espionage apparatus still has its failures. The CIA insisted Iraq had an arsenal of mass-destruction weapons and gave George W. Bush's administration justification for invading the country in 2003. There turned out to be no such weapons. With the approval of the White House, the twenty-first-century intelligence community has continued to push the edge of the ethical envelope, as its 1950s generation did, detaining terrorists in remote sites overseas for "enhanced interrogation" (a euphemism for "torture") and assassinating their leaders with commando raids and drone strikes.

But there have also been triumphs. CIA and military spy agencies succeeded in uncovering dictator Vladimir Putin's Kremlin decision-making and military plans for the Russian invasion of Ukraine. American intelligence enabled Washington to announce what Putin would do before he could show the world. Since then, the United States and NATO have fed the Ukrainians important tactical intelligence to help them counter Russian advances on the battlefield.

Nearly three-quarters of a century ago, Frank Wisner was in on the founding of the CIA's clandestine service—for better or worse. He was on the front lines of the Cold War, a time today's young CIA officers know only from what they read in history books. It was a time when many feared American survival was at stake. Until a cruel disease felled him, that determined spy fought doggedly—or, as his critics say, fanatically—in that war. He tried.

ACKNOWLEDGMENTS

AS I'M SURE MY fellow authors who did it will agree, researching a book during the 2020–2022 COVID-19 pandemic was a daunting undertaking. During that dreary period, travel was difficult and archives across the country were closed as their employees rode out the infection storm, leaving historians cut off from repositories that housed boxes of documents important for their projects. At first glance the job would seem to be doubly hard if the subject of your historical biography was a CIA spymaster like Frank Wisner, whose government duties had been shrouded in secrecy. Fortunately, I found work-arounds.

I discovered that millions of pages of secret national security material from the 1950s, when Wisner led the CIA's clandestine service, have been declassified and can be raked up from the Internet with the click of a mouse button. The CIA has hundreds of thousands of declassified memos, reports, and meeting notes from that period on its website, cia.gov, which can be electronically culled using CREST, the CIA Records Search Tool. On its website, the FBI has a trove of documents from the 1950s made public because of Freedom of Information Act (FOIA) requests researchers have filed over the decades. In assembling the voluminous Foreign Relations of the United States (FRUS) series, which presents the official documentary historical record of major U.S. foreign policy decisions and significant diplomatic activity, State Department historians have brought to light thousands of national security documents that deal with Wisner's activities. Over the years, private research organizations, such as the National Security Archive and the MuckRock Foundation, have done yeoman's work filing FOIA requests to force the CIA to declassify multitudes of material from its controversial past. From these sources and others on the Internet, I was able to pluck more than fifty thousand pages of 1950s-era documents related to Wisner that when pieced together gave me a detailed picture of the man and his secret mission.

I benefited from the books of other authors who included Wisner in their histories. Evan Thomas, my boss when I worked at *Newsweek*, managed to negotiate with the CIA to get special access to classified documents for *The Very Best Men*, his groundbreaking account of four senior CIA officers who battled the Soviets in the shadows, one of whom was Wisner. I want to thank Burton Hersh, who included Wisner in his spy book, *The Old Boys*, for giving me access to intelligence documents he collected in his research. In *The Quiet Americans*, Scott Anderson wrote a commendable account of Cold War spying that also included Wisner. In *America's First Spy*, Romania diplomat George Cristian Maior authored a revealing history of Wisner's World War II spying in Bucharest, as did Elizabeth W. Hazard (Wisner's daughter) in her book, *Cold War Crucible*.

During the COVID shutdown, a number of archivists, librarians, and educators around the country hunted through their historical collections and sent me important documents dealing with Wisner. My thanks to officials at the Yale University Library, Princeton University Library, Georgetown University Library, Columbia University's Center for Oral History Research, the Harry S. Truman Presidential Library, the U.S. Army Heritage and Education Center, the Rockefeller Archive Center, the National Archives

United Kingdom in Kew, and King's College London who sent me documents on Wisner from their collections. When the National Archives at College Park, Maryland, reopened to researchers on a limited basis, archivist Suzanne Zoumbaris helped arrange for me to view a select group of boxes with documents on Wisner's OSS service. I also owe a special thanks to Jacob Geiger, director of strategic communications at Woodberry Forest School, who provided me with family correspondence from when Wisner attended the prep school, and to Randy Stevens, head of St. Timothy's School, who provided me copies of yearbook pages that mention Polly Wisner when she attended the school in 1930. I also want to thank Donald Graham for sending me transcripts of interviews Katharine Graham had with Polly for her autobiography.

As the pandemic eased, I was able to spend a week at the University of Virginia's reopened special collections library and its law library, where helpful staff members brought me boxes of family papers, correspondence, and academic records from the Frank Gardiner Wisner Papers. I was also able to visit the Library of Congress in Washington and the Hoover Institution Library and Archives at Stanford University, whose gracious staffs helped me find correspondence and interview transcripts of Wisner's comrades from the OSS and CIA.

I deeply appreciate the cooperation I received from Wisner's family for this biography. I spent about fifty hours interviewing Wisner's three sons: Ambassador Frank George Wisner II, Ellis Wisner, and Graham Wisner. They willingly answered all my questions, many of them dealing with the painful subjects of their father's descent into mental illness and his suicide. Ambassador Wisner shared with me declassified correspondence and personnel records of his father that the CIA turned over to him. Ellis Wisner, who serves as the family historian, allowed me to look at correspondence, medical records, and Wisner letters that had not been turned over to the University of Virginia. I also spent several days in Laurel, Mississippi, where Wisner's grandnephew, Alexander "Lex"

Lindsey, gave me a tour of Wisner's hometown and the family residence there. Lex also provided me access to the Chisholm Foundation Archive in Laurel, which contains family history records for Wisner and his sister Elisabeth Wisner Chisholm. A special thanks to Colleen Cagle at the archive, who found for me a transcript of Wisner's grades at Laurel's high school.

I had valuable medical sources to help me understand the bipolar disorder that tormented Wisner. Psychiatrist Dr. David Rubinow, distinguished professor and chair emeritus at the University of North Carolina at Chapel Hill's School of Medicine, suggested psychiatric textbooks I should study about that terrible disease. He then read my manuscript and spotted errors I needed to correct in the medical sections. Lisa Illum, archivist at the Sheppard Pratt Hospital, dutifully tracked down and provided me with copies of records on Wisner's stay at the psychiatric facility that remain. Lisa also put me in touch with John Rees, an archivist in the History of Medicine Division of the National Library of Medicine, where more Sheppard Pratt records are stored. John sent me reports and correspondence from that collection that helped me understand the hospital's procedures and atmosphere during Wisner's stay in the late 1950s. Dr. Harold Sackeim, who is a professor of psychology and radiology at Columbia University and an adviser to Sheppard Pratt on electroconvulsive therapy, briefed me on the type of shock treatment the facility administered when Wisner was a patient there.

I am grateful to CIA historian David Robarge for his help in navigating CREST on the CIA website. Intelligence historian Michael Warner read my manuscript, corrected errors, and offered important suggestions on ways to improve the biography. Of course, the book's conclusions and any errors that remain in it are all mine.

As she has been with all my books, my literary agent, Kristine Dahl, was a trusted adviser and good friend as I formulated the portrayal of Frank Wisner in my mind. At Dutton, I was blessed with a first-rate editorial team. Executive editor Brent Howard, who was in on the launch of the project, recognized, as I did, that *The*

Determined Spy needed a different approach from that of a straight biography. Executive editor Lindsey Rose's edit of the manuscript I submitted was superb. The structural changes, line edits, and trims she suggested greatly improved the drama and flow of the narrative. I want to thank editorial assistant Charlotte Peters, who attended to many details in bringing the work to publication. I also owe a debt of gratitude to Frank Walgren for his meticulous copyedit of the manuscript.

My books have always been family affairs. My wife, Judy, and my daughter, Colby, diligently proofread my manuscript. It is to my dear Judy, who has been at my side throughout this long writing journey, that I dedicate the book.

SELECTED BIBLIOGRAPHY

MANUSCRIPT COLLECTIONS
Abbreviations are used for manuscript collections in the source notes.
ADP Allen W. Dulles Papers
AHEC U.S. Army Heritage and Education Center
AKP Arthur Krock Papers
AP Joseph and Stewart Alsop Papers
AWP Albert C. Wedemeyer Papers
CFA Chisholm Foundation Archive
CIAGC CIA Guatemala Collection, https://www.cia.gov/readingroom/collection /guatemala
CMH U.S. Army Center for Military History
DEL Dwight D. Eisenhower Presidential Library
FBIW FBI file on Frank Wisner, https://archive.org/details/FrankWisnerFBI
FLP Franklin Lindsay Papers
GHP Gregg Herken Papers
GU Georgetown University Library Center for Special Collections
HA Hoover Institution Library and Archives
HSTL Harry S. Truman Presidential Library
KCL Kings College Library
LOC Library of Congress
M1642 Microfilm of Washington director's office
MEP Marvin R. Edwards Papers
MN MuckRock News
NA National Archives and Records Administration
NAUK National Archives United Kingdom
NLM National Library of Medicine
NRP Nelson Rockefeller Personal Papers
NSA National Security Archive

PGP Peter Grose Papers
PNP Paul H. Nitze Papers
PU Princeton University Library Special Collections
RAC Rockefeller Archive Center
RG226 Record Group 226, Records of the Office of Strategic Services
RG263 Record Group 263, Records of the Central Intelligence Agency
RHP Richard Helms Papers
RP Radio Free Europe–Radio Liberty Papers
RSP Richard Harris Smith Papers
SP Sheppard and Enoch Pratt Hospital Archives
UVA University of Virginia Albert and Shirley Small Special Collections Library
WCP William J. Casey Papers
WDP William J. Donovan Papers
WHP William Hood Papers

COLLECTION LIBRARIES
CFC Chisholm Foundation Collection on Frank Gardiner Wisner
DAP Dean Gooderham Acheson Papers, series 1, reel number 22
FWP Frank Gardiner Wisner Papers
LSM Frank Gardiner Wisner law school memorabilia, MSS-2014-02, Arthur J. Morris Law Library Special Collections
RJP Robert P. Joyce Papers
WCA Wilson Center Digital Archive
YU Yale University Library

PRIVATE COLLECTIONS
ALC Alexander Lindsey Collection
BHP Burton Hersh Papers
KGP Katharine Graham Papers with the Graham family
SPA Sheppard Pratt Archives
STA St. Timothy's School Archives
WFA Woodberry Forest Archives
WFC Wisner Family Collection

REMINISCENCES
Abbreviations are used for the oral history collections. For example, the reminiscences of Richard M. Bissell Jr. in Columbia University's Center for Oral History Research collection will be listed in the source notes as "Bissell, COH, [page number]."
CIAOHP CIA Oral History Program under the CIA history staff: Frank Lindsay
COH Columbia University's Center for Oral History Research collection: Sherman Adams, Dillon Anderson, Richard M. Bissell Jr., Charles E. Bohlen, Eleanor Lansing Dulles, Gordon Gray, Richard Helms (Foundation for Iranian Studies), James R. Killian, Arthur C. Lundahl
FAOH Association for Diplomatic Studies and Training, Foreign Affairs Oral History Project: Robert R. Bowie, Joseph N. Greene Jr., Thomas L. Hughes, James R. Lilley, Henry Loomis, Edwin McCammon Martin, William McAfee, James McCargar, William M. Rountree, John H. Stutesman, Harrison M. Symmes, Frank G. Wisner II

OHP OSS Oral History Project, National Archives and Records Administration, Record Group 263, Records of the CIA: David Crockett, Richard Helms, Arthur Schlesinger Jr.

SCS Smith Centennial Study, William Allan Neilson Library: Elisabeth Wisner Chisholm

UCB Regional Oral History Office, University of California, Berkeley: Turner McBaine

OTHER ABBREVIATIONS USED

AWD Allen Welsh Dulles
B Box for an entry or collection
CB Charles "Chip" Bohlen
CIA Central Intelligence Agency
CREST CIA Records Search Tool, cia.gov
DCI Director of Central Intelligence
DDCI Deputy director of Central Intelligence
DDE Dwight David Eisenhower
DDP Deputy director plans
E Entry for a collection
EW Ellis Wisner
F File
FBI Federal Bureau of Investigation
FGW Frank Gardiner Wisner
FGWII Frank George Wisner II
FOIA Freedom of Information Act
Fr Frames
FRUS Foreign Relations of the United States
HST Harry S. Truman
IG Inspector general
JA Joseph Alsop
JCS Joint Chiefs of Staff
JEH J. Edgar Hoover
KG Katharine Graham
NSC National Security Council
PG Philip Graham
PKW Polly Knowles Wisner
R Microfilm reel
RG Record group
RMH Richard M. Helms
S Series in a collection
SI Secret Intelligence
WJD William Joseph Donovan

AUTHOR INTERVIEWS

In the source notes, only the last name or the initials of the interviewee will be listed, followed by the date of the interview. For example, the author interview with Alexander Lindsey on July 14, 2020, will appear in the source notes as "Lindsey, July 14, 2020."

Elizabeth Winthrop Alsop, Avis Bohlen, Frances FitzGerald, Cynthia Helms, Fisher Howe, Rolfe Kingsley, Alexander Lindsey, Elizabeth McIntosh, Hugh Montgomery, Thomas Polgar, Charles Reeder, Marie Ridder, Harold A. Sackeim,

Peter Sichel, William vanden Heuvel, Ellis Wisner (EW), Frank George Wisner II (FGWII), Graham Wisner (GW)

BOOKS, PERIODICALS, DISSERTATIONS, BROCHURES, AND GOVERNMENT REPORTS
A work's full citation is given here. In the source notes, it will appear as a second reference. In most cases the source notes citation will give the author's last name and, if needed, the first name or book title to identify the work.

Abrams, Richard. *Electroconvulsive Therapy.* 4th ed. New York: Oxford University Press, 2002.
"Almost Successful Recipe: The United States and East European Unrest Prior to the 1956 Hungarian Revolution." U.S. Defense Department draft history released to the National Security Archive.
Alsop, Joseph W. *"I've Seen the Best of It":* Memoirs. New York: W. W. Norton & Co., 1992.
Alsop, Stewart. *The Center: People and Power in Political Washington.* New York: Harper & Row, 1968.
Ambrose, Stephen E. *Eisenhower: Soldier and President.* New York: Simon & Schuster, 1990.
———. *Ike's Spies: Eisenhower and the Espionage Establishment.* Jackson, MS: University Press of Mississippi, 1981.
Anderson, Scott. *The Quiet Americans: Four Spies at the Dawn of the Cold War—A Tragedy in Three Acts.* New York: Doubleday, 2020.
Atkinson, Rick. *The Guns at Last Light: The War in Western Europe, 1944–1945, Vol. 3 of the Liberation Trilogy.* New York: Henry Holt and Company, 2013.
Bayandor, Darioush. "Don't Just Blame Washington for the 1953 Iran Coup." *Foreign Policy,* Nov. 21, 2019. https://foreignpolicy.com/2019/11/21/dont-blame-washington-1953-iran-coup-mosaddeq/.
Bessel, Richard. *Germany 1945: From War to Peace.* New York: HarperCollins, 2009.
Bishop, Robert, and E. S. Crayfield. *Russia Astride the Balkans.* New York: Robert M. McBride & Co., 1948.
Bissell, Richard M., Jr., with Jonathan E. Lewis and Frances T. Pudlo. *Reflections of a Cold Warrior: From Yalta to the Bay of Pigs.* New Haven, CT: Yale University Press, 1996.
Bower, Tom. *The Red Web: MI6 and the KGB Master Coup.* London: Aurum Press, 1989.
Brown, Anthony Cave. *The Last Hero: Wild Bill Donovan.* New York: Vintage Books, 1982.
Burke, Michael. *Outrageous Good Fortune: A Memoir.* Boston: Little, Brown and Company, 1984.
Chambers, John Whiteclay, II. *OSS Training in the National Parks and Service Abroad in World War II.* Washington, DC: U.S. National Park Service, 2008.
Church Committee. Alleged Assassination Plots Involving Foreign Leaders. *An Interim Report of the Select Committee to Study Governmental Operations with Respect to Intelligence Activities, United States Senate, Together with Additional, Supplemental, and Separate Views.* Nov. 20, 1975; Foreign and Military Intelligence. *Final Report of the Select Committee to Study Governmental Operations with Respect to Intelligence Activities, United States Senate, Together with Additional, Supplemental, and Separate Views,* book 1. April 26, 1976; Intelligence Activities and the Rights of Americans. *Final Report of the Select Committee to Study Governmental Operations with Respect to Intelligence Activities, United States Senate, Together with Additional, Supplemental, and*

Separate Views, book 2. April 26, 1976, Supplementary Detailed Staff Reports on Foreign and Military Intelligence, book 4. April 23, 1976, Washington, DC: U.S. Government Printing Office.

Clay, Lucius D. *Decision in Germany: A Personal Report of the Four Crucial Years That Set the Course of Future World History*. Garden City, NY: Doubleday, 1950.

Colby, William. *Honorable Men: My Life in the CIA*. New York: Simon & Schuster, 1978.

Conboy, Kenneth, and James Morrison. *Feet to the Fire: CIA Covert Operations in Indonesia, 1957–1958*. Annapolis, MD: Naval Institute Press, 1999.

Cooper, Artemis. *Cairo in the War 1939–1945*. London: John Murray, 2013.

Corson, William R. *The Armies of Ignorance: The Rise of the American Intelligence Empire*. New York: Dial Press, 1977.

Crosswell, D. K. R. *Beetle: The Life of General Walter Bedell Smith*. Lexington: University Press of Kentucky, 2010.

Cullather, Nick. *Secret History: The CIA's Classified Account of Its Operations in Guatemala, 1952–1954*. Stanford, CA: Stanford University Press, 2006.

Currey, Cecil B. *Edward Lansdale: The Unquiet American*. Boston: Houghton Mifflin Company, 1988.

Darling, Arthur B. *The Central Intelligence Agency: An Instrument of Government, to 1950*. University Park: Pennsylvania State University Press, 1990.

Davidson, Jonathan R. T., Kathryn M. Connor, and Marvin Swartz. "Mental Illness in U.S. Presidents Between 1776 and 1974: A Review of Biographical Sources." *The Journal of Nervous and Mental Disease* 194, no. 1 (January 2006): pp. 47–51.

Dobbs, Michael. *Six Months in 1945: FDR, Stalin, Churchill, and Truman—from World War to Cold War*. New York: Vintage Books, 2013.

Dorril, Stephen. *MI6: Inside the Covert World of Her Majesty's Secret Intelligence Service*. New York: Free Press, 2000.

Elias, Alby, Naveen Thomas, and Harold A. Sackeim. "Electroconvulsive Therapy in Mania: A Review of 80 Years of Clinical Experience." *American Journal of Psychiatry* 178, no. 3 (March 1, 2021): pp. 229–39. https://ajp.psychiatryonline.org/doi/epdf/10.1176/appi.ajp.2020.20030238.

Ellis, Francis M., and Edward F. Clark Jr. *A Brief History of Carter, Ledyard & Milburn*. Portsmouth, NH: Peter E. Randall Publisher, 1988.

Eschner, Kat. "What We Know About the CIA's Midcentury Mind-Control Project." *Smithsonian Magazine*, April 13, 2017. https://www.smithsonianmag.com/smart-news/what-we-know-about-cias-midcentury-mind-control-project-180962836/.

Fink, Max. "Convulsive Therapy: A Review of the First 55 Years." *Journal of Affective Disorders* 63, nos. 1–3 (March 2001): pp. 1–15.

Finn, Peter, and Petra Couvée. *The Zhivago Affair: The Kremlin, the CIA, and the Battle over a Forbidden Book*. New York: Vintage Books, 2015.

Forbush, Bliss. *The Sheppard & Enoch Pratt Hospital 1853–1970*. Philadelphia: J. B. Lippincott Co., 1971.

———, and Byron Forbush. *Gatehouse: The Evolution of the Sheppard and Enoch Pratt Hospital, 1853–1986*. Baltimore: Sheppard-Pratt, 1986.

Forbush, Byron. *Seeing to the Future: The Story of Moses Sheppard and the Founding of the Sheppard Asylum*. Towson, MD: Sheppard Pratt, 2004.

Gardner, Lloyd C., Arthur Schlesinger Jr., and Hans J. Morgenthau. *The Origins of the Cold War*. Waltham, MA: Ginn-Blaisdell, 1970.

Garthoff, Douglas F. *Directors of Central Intelligence as Leaders of the U.S. Intelligence Community, 1946–2005*. Washington, DC: Center for the Study of Intelligence, Central Intelligence Agency, 2005.

Gleijeses, Piero. *Shattered Hope: The Guatemalan Revolution and the United States, 1944–1954*. Princeton, NJ: Princeton University Press, 1991.

Goodwin, Frederick K., and Kay Redfield Jamison. *Manic-Depressive Illness: Bipolar Disorders and Recurrent Depression.* 2 vols. New York: Oxford University Press, 2007.

Gotlib, Ian H., and Constance L. Hammen, eds. *Handbook of Depression.* 3rd ed. New York: Guilford Press, 2014.

Graham, Katharine. *Personal History.* New York: Vintage, 1998.

Greer, Kenneth E. "The Office of the Inspector General, January 1952–December 1971." Washington, DC: Historical Staff, Central Intelligence Agency, 2017.

Grose, Peter. *Gentleman Spy: The Life of Allen Dulles.* New York: Houghton Mifflin Company, 1994.

Halberstam, David. *The Coldest Winter: America and the Korean War.* New York: Hyperion, 2007.

———. *The Fifties.* New York: Random House, 1993.

Hazard, Elizabeth W. *Cold War Crucible: United States Foreign Policy and the Conflict in Romania, 1943–1953.* New York: Columbia University Press, 1996.

Helms, Cynthia, with Chris Black. *An Intriguing Life: A Memoir of War, Washington, and Marriage to an American Spymaster.* New York: Rowman & Littlefield, 2013.

Helms, Richard, with William Hood. *A Look over My Shoulder: A Life in the Central Intelligence Agency.* New York: Ballantine Books, 2003.

Herken, Gregg. *The Georgetown Set: Friends and Rivals in Cold War Washington.* New York: Alfred A. Knopf, 2014.

Hersh, Burton. *The Old Boys: The American Elite and the Origins of the CIA.* New York: Charles Scribner's Sons, 1992.

Heymann, C. David. *The Georgetown Ladies' Social Club: Power, Passion, and Politics in the Nation's Capital.* New York: Atria Books, 2003.

Hill, Lewis, and Frederic Worden. "Participant Teaching of Psychotherapy by Senior Physicians: A Hospital Program and Clinical Illustrations." *Psychiatric Quarterly* 26 (April 1952): pp. 228–43.

Holober, Frank. *Raiders of the China Coast: CIA Covert Operations During the Korean War.* Annapolis, MD: Naval Institute Press, 1999.

Hostler, Charles W. *Soldier to Ambassador: From the D-Day Normandy Landing to the Persian Gulf War—A Memoir Odyssey.* San Diego: San Diego State University Press, 2003.

Howe, Tony. "Growth of the Lumber Industry, (1849 to 1930)." Mississippi History Now. https://mshistorynow.mdah.state.ms.

Hunt, E. Howard, with Greg Aunapu. *American Spy: My Secret History in the CIA, Watergate & Beyond.* Hoboken, NJ: John Wiley & Sons, 2007

Hyland, William G. *The Cold War: Fifty Years of Conflict.* New York: Random House, 1990.

Immerman, Richard H. *The CIA in Guatemala: The Foreign Policy of Intervention.* Austin: University of Texas Press, 1982.

Isaacson, Walter, and Evan Thomas. *The Wise Men: Six Friends and the World They Made.* New York: Simon & Schuster, 1986.

Jackson, Wayne G. "Allen Welsh Dulles as Director of Central Intelligence, 26 February 1953–29 November 1961." 5 vols. Washington, DC: Historical Staff, Central Intelligence Agency, 1994.

Jacobsen, Annie. *Operation Paperclip: The Secret Intelligence Program That Brought Nazi Scientists to America.* New York: Little, Brown and Company, 2014.

Jamison, Kay Redfield. *An Unquiet Mind: A Memoir of Moods and Madness.* New York: Vintage, 1995.

Kaplan, Robert D. "The Antonescu Paradox." *Foreign Policy*, Feb. 5, 2016. https://foreignpolicy.com/2016/02/05/the-antonescu-paradox-romania-world-war-ii-hitler/.

Kettlewell, Caroline. "Famously Secret." *Virginia Living*, Sept. 13, 2019. https://virginialiving.com/culture/famously-secret/.

Key, David Stanton. "Laurel, Mississippi: A Historical Perspective." Master's thesis. East Tennessee State University, 2001.

Kinzer, Stephen. *All the Shah's Men: An American Coup and the Roots of Middle East Terror.* Hoboken, NJ: John Wiley & Sons, 2008.

Koch, Scott A. *"'Zendebad, Shah!':* The Central Intelligence Agency and the Fall of Iranian Prime Minister Mohammad Mossadegh, August 1953." Washington, DC: History Staff, Center for the Study of Intelligence, Central Intelligence Agency, 1998.

Laurie, Clayton D. "The Korean War and the Central Intelligence Agency." Washington, DC: History Staff, Center for the Study of Intelligence, Central Intelligence Agency.

———. "A New President, a Better CIA, and an Old War: Eisenhower and Intelligence Reporting on Korea, 1953." *Studies in Intelligence* 54, no. 4 (Extracts, December 2010): pp. 1–12.

Leary, William M., ed. *The Central Intelligence Agency: History and Documents.* Tuscaloosa: University of Alabama Press, 1984.

Lilly, Edward P. "The Development of American Psychological Operations 1945–1951." Washington, DC: Psychological Strategy Board, 1951.

Loftus, John. *The Belarus Secret.* New York: Alfred A. Knopf, 1982.

López-Muñoz, Francisco, Winston Shen, Pilar D'Ocon, Alejandro Romero, and Cecilio Álamo. "A History of the Pharmacological Treatment of Bipolar Disorder." *International Journal of Molecular Sciences* 19, no. 7 (July 23, 2018): p. 2143.

Lowe, Keith. *Savage Continent: Europe in the Aftermath of World War II.* New York: St. Martin's Press, 2012.

MacDonogh, Giles. *After the Reich: The Brutal History of the Allied Occupation.* New York: Basic Books, 2007.

Macintyre, Ben. *A Spy Among Friends: Philby and the Great Betrayal.* New York: Bloomsbury, 2014.

Maior, George Cristian. *America's First Spy: The Tragic Heroism of Frank Wisner.* Washington, DC: Academica Press, 2018.

Marchetti, Victor, and John D. Marks. *The CIA and the Cult of Intelligence.* New York: Dell, 1974.

Mark, Eduard. "The OSS in Romania, 1944–45: An Intelligence Operation of the Early Cold War." *Intelligence and National Security* 9, no. 2 (April 1994): pp. 320–44.

Marks, John. *The Search for the "Manchurian Candidate."* New York: W. W. Norton & Co., 1979.

Mauch, Christof. *The Shadow War Against Hitler: The Covert Operations of America's Wartime Secret Intelligence Service.* New York: Columbia University Press, 1999.

McCullough, David. *Truman.* New York: Simon & Schuster, 1992.

Meyer, Cord. *Facing Reality: From World Federalism to the CIA.* New York: Harper & Row, 1980.

Mondimore, Francis Mark. *Bipolar Disorder: A Guide for Patients and Families.* 3rd ed. Baltimore: Johns Hopkins University Press, 2014.

Montague, Ludwell Lee. "General Walter Bedell Smith as Director of Central Intelligence, October 1950–February 1953." 5 vols. Washington, DC: Historical Staff, Central Intelligence Agency, 1971.

Mosley, Leonard. *Dulles: A Biography of Eleanor, Allen, and John Foster Dulles and Their Family Network.* New York: Dial Press, 1978.

Murphy, David E., Sergei A. Kondrashev, and George Bailey. *Battleground Berlin: CIA vs. KGB in the Cold War.* New Haven, CT: Yale University Press, 1997.

"The 1956 Hungarian Revolution: A Fresh Look at the U.S. Response." Unpublished Defense Department historical study obtained by the National Security Archive. https://nsarchive.gwu.edu/document/22906-1956-hungarian-revolution-fresh -look.

Norfleet, Elizabeth Copeland. *Woodberry Forest: A Venture in Faith.* New York: Georgian Press, 1955.

Odell, Jonathan. *Laurel, Mississippi: City in a Bubble.* Bronxville, NY: Maiden Lane Press.

O'Toole, G. J. A. *Honorable Treachery: A History of U.S. Intelligence, Espionage, and Covert Action from the American Revolution to the CIA.* New York: Atlantic Monthly Press, 1991.

The Overseas Targets: War Report of the OSS, vol. 2. New York: Walker and Company, 1976.

Payne, Nancy. "Electroconvulsive Therapy: Part 1. A Perspective on the Evolution and Current Practice of ECT." *Journal of Psychiatric Practice* 15, no. 5 (Sept. 2009): pp. 346–68.

Petersen, Neal H., ed. *From Hitler's Doorstep: The Wartime Intelligence Reports of Allen Dulles, 1942–1945.* University Park: Pennsylvania State University Press, 1996.

Philby, Kim. *My Silent War: The Autobiography of a Spy.* New York: Modern Library, 2002.

Phillips, David Atlee. *The Night Watch.* New York: Ballantine Books, 1977.

Pierce, David. "America in the Postwar Period." *Inquiries* 1, no. 10 (2009): pp. 1–6.

Pisani, Sallie. *The CIA and the Marshall Plan.* Lawrence: University Press of Kansas, 1991.

Powers, Thomas. *The Man Who Kept the Secrets: Richard Helms and the CIA.* New York: Alfred A. Knopf, 1979.

Prados, John. *Lost Crusader: The Secret Wars of CIA Director William Colby.* New York: Oxford University Press, 2003.

———. *Presidents' Secret Wars: CIA and Pentagon Covert Operations Since World War II.* New York: William Morrow and Company, 1986.

———. *Safe for Democracy: The Secret Wars of the CIA.* Chicago: Ivan R. Dee, 2006.

"Project MKUltra, the CIA's Program of Research in Behavioral Modification. Joint Hearing Before the Subcommittee on Intelligence and the Subcommittee on Health and Scientific Research of the Committee on Human Resources, United States Senate, August 3, 1977." Washington, DC: U.S. Government Printing Office, 1977.

Pruitt, Sarah. "The Post–World War II Boom: How America Got into Gear." History .com, May 14, 2020; updated August 10, 2023. https://www.history.com/news /post-world-war-ii-boom-economy.

Ranelagh, John. *The Agency: The Rise and Decline of the CIA.* New York: Simon & Schuster, 1986.

Read, Anthony, and David Fisher. *The Fall of Berlin.* New York: W. W. Norton & Co., 1992.

Reed, Tish. "Moving Forward, Looking Back: Journey of a Small-Town Girl." Bethesda, MD: Print 1 Printing and Copying, 2015.

Richie, Alexandra. *Faust's Metropolis: A History of Berlin.* New York: Carroll & Graf, 1998.

Riebling, Mark. *Wedge: The Secret War Between the FBI and CIA.* New York: Alfred A. Knopf, 1994.

Robarge, David. "John McCone as Director of Central Intelligence, 1961–1965." Parts 1 and 2. Washington, DC: Center for the Study of Intelligence, Central Intelligence Agency, 2005.

Roosevelt, Kermit. *Countercoup: The Struggle for the Control of Iran.* New York: McGraw-Hill, 1979.

Rositzke, Harry. *The CIA's Secret Operations: Espionage, Counterespionage, and Covert Action.* New York: Reader's Digest Press, 1977.

Rubin, Barry. *Istanbul Intrigues.* New York: McGraw-Hill, 1989.

Ruffner, Kevin C. "Cold War Allies: The Origins of CIA's Relationship with Ukrainian Nationalists." File declassified by the CIA.

———. "Eagle and Swastika: CIA and Nazi War Criminals and Collaborators." Washington, DC: History Staff, Center for the Study of Intelligence, Central Intelligence Agency, 2003.

———. "Forging an Intelligence Partnership: CIA and the Origins of the BND, 1945–49." 2 vols. Washington, DC: History Staff, Center for the Study of Intelligence, Central Intelligence Agency, 1999.

———. "You Are Never Going to Be Able to Run an Intelligence Unit: SSU Confronts the Black Market in Berlin." *The Journal of Intelligence History* 2, no. 2 (winter 2002): pp. 1–20.

Schlesinger, Stephen, and Stephen Kinzer. *Bitter Fruit: The Story of the American Coup in Guatemala.* Cambridge, MA: Harvard University Press, 2005.

Sebestyen, Victor. *Twelve Days: The Story of the 1956 Hungarian Revolution.* New York: Pantheon, 2006.

Sichel, Peter M. F. *The Secrets of My Life: Vintner, Prisoner, Soldier, Spy.* Bloomington, IN: Archway Publishing, 2016.

Simpson, Christopher. *Blowback: The First Full Account of America's Recruitment of Nazis, and Its Disastrous Effect on Our Domestic and Foreign Policy.* New York: Weidenfeld & Nicolson, 1988.

Smith, Richard Harris. *OSS: The Secret History of America's First Central Intelligence Agency.* Guilford, CT: Lyons Press, 1972.

Snider, L. Britt. *The Agency and the Hill: CIA's Relationship with Congress, 1946–2004.* Washington, DC: Center for the Study of Intelligence, Central Intelligence Agency, 2008.

"Social Graces in Georgetown: Polly and Clayton Fritchey's Victorian Enclave." *Architectural Digest,* October 1987.

Srodes, James. *Allen Dulles: Master of Spies.* Washington, DC: Regnery, 1999.

Swartz, Martin Ben. "A New Look at the 1956 Hungarian Revolution: Soviet Opportunism, American Acquiescence." PhD diss., Medford, MA: Fletcher School of Law and Diplomacy, 1988.

Takeyh, Ray. *The Last Shah: America, Iran, and the Fall of the Pahlavi Dynasty.* New Haven, CT: Yale University Press, 2021.

Thomas, Evan. *The Very Best Men—The Daring Early Years of the CIA.* New York: Simon & Schuster, 1995.

Thomas, Hugh. *Suez.* New York: Harper & Rowe, 1966.

Viccellio, Robert. "Wrapped in Mystery." *Virginia Magazine,* spring 2012. https://uvamagazine.org/articles/wrapped_in_mystery.

Waller, Douglas. *Disciples: The World War II Missions of the CIA Directors Who Fought for Wild Bill Donovan.* New York: Simon & Schuster, 2015.

———. *Wild Bill Donovan: The Spymaster Who Created the OSS and Modern American Espionage.* New York: Free Press, 2011.

War Report of the OSS (Office of Strategic Services). New York: Walker and Company, 1976.

Warner, Michael, ed. *The CIA Under Harry Truman: CIA Cold War Records.* Washington, DC: History Staff, Center for the Study of Intelligence, Central Intelligence Agency, 1994.

———. "The Creation of the Central Intelligence Group: Salvage and Liquidation." Washington, DC: Center for the Study of Intelligence, Central Intelligence Agency.

———. "Hearts & Minds: Three Case Studies of the CIA's Covert Support of American Anti-Communist Groups in the Cold War, 1949–1967." Washington, DC: Center for the Study of Intelligence, Central Intelligence Agency, 1999.

———. "Origins of the Congress for Cultural Freedom, 1949–50." Washington, DC: Center for the Study of Intelligence, Central Intelligence Agency.

———. "Sophisticated Spies: CIA's Links to Liberal Anti-Communists, 1949–1967." *International Journal of Intelligence and Counterintelligence* 9, no. 4 (winter 1996–97): pp. 425–33.

Weinberg, Gerhard L. *A World at Arms: A Global History of World War II*. New York: Cambridge University Press, 1994.

Weiner, Tim. *Legacy of Ashes: The History of the CIA*. New York: Doubleday, 2007.

Wilford, Hugh. *The Mighty Wurlitzer*. Cambridge, MA: Harvard University Press, 2008.

Wilkie, Curtis. *When Evil Lived in Laurel: The "White Knights" and the Murder of Vernon Dahmer*. New York: W. W. Norton & Co., 2021.

Wolff, Robert Lee. *The Balkans in Our Time*. New York: W. W. Norton & Co., 1978.

Ziemke, Earl F. *The U.S. Army in the Occupation of Germany, 1944–1946*. Washington, DC: Center of Military History, United States Army, 1975.

SOURCE NOTES

In many instances a source note covers several paragraphs. Each source note lists material cited up to the previous source note. Some box numbers may have changed as archivists reconfigure their collections.

Prologue

2 **tormenting Wisner:** EW, July 15 and Oct. 20, 2020, Oct. 12, 2021, Jan. 12 and 27, 2021; Lindsey, July 14, 2020; FGWII, July 7 and 8, 2020, and Jan. 13, March 11, and April 1, 2021; Reeder, Aug. 20, 2020; Psychological Summary–Case No. 25835, WFC; Mondimore, pp. 21, 177–80; Goodwin and Jamison, vol. 1, pp. 60, 231; Elisabeth Wisner Chisholm to RMH, March 3, B: 3, RHP, GU; FGWII to Mommy and Daddy, July 2,1963, B: 2, FWP, UVA; GW, Sept. 16, 2020.

2 **"complete rest":** Gotlib and Hammen, pp. 15–16, 278; GW, Jan. 10 and Aug. 11, 2020; EW, Aug. 5, 2020; Goodwin and Jamison, vol. 1, p. 345; PKW letter to V. C. Georgescu, Sept. 26, 1958, B: 5, FWP, UVA; Evan Thomas, p. 10–11, 160; In Memoriam: Frank Gardiner Wisner, 1909–1965, Langley, Virginia, Jan. 29, 1971, WFC; JA to CB, Sept. 6, 1958, B: 14, JA, LOC; R. R. Roach to A. H. Belmont on FGW, Sept. 22, 1958, SAC, Baltimore to Director, FBI on FGW, Sept. 23, 1958, FBIW; Lyman B. Kirkpatrick diary entry, vol. III, Sept. 12, 1958, CREST for FGW.

4 **good facade:** Minutes for Deputies' Meeting, Jan. 8, June 12, June 25, July 9, and July 23, 1958, John S. Warner Memorandum for the Record, June 2, 1958, CREST for FGW; Sackeim, Jan. 18, 2022; FGWII, Oct. 18, 2012.

4 **in Hungary:** Evan Thomas, pp. 160–61; CB to JA, Sept. 12, 1958, B: 14, AP, LOC; Letter to FGW, July 7, 1958, B: 61, S: 2A, AKP, PU; Minutes for Deputies' Meeting, Aug. 29, 1956, CREST for FGW; Hersh, p. 305; EW, Oct. 6, 2020, and Jan. 12, 2021; 95. National Security Council Report, May 3, 1955, FRUS, Southeast Asia, vol. XXII, 1955–1957; Psychological Summary–Case No. 25835, WFC.

5 **$10 million:** FGW to Ellis Knowles, Feb. 1 and April 25, 1958, Ellis Knowles to FGW, April 23, 1958 B: 4, FWP, UVA; FGW to CB, Feb. 14, 1958, B: 1, FWP, UVA; P. E. Than to FGW, Sept. 7, 1959, B: 10, FWP, UVA; Discussion at the 333rd Meeting of the NSC, Aug. 1, 1957, DDE's Papers as President, NSC

Series, DEL; Hersh, pp. 416–17; Prados, *Safe for Democracy*, pp. 167, 177–79; Evan Thomas, pp. 158–59; Anderson, p. 465; Ranelagh, p. 334; Wisner Betting Book, pp. 54–55, WFC; L. K. White Certificate, Jan. 9, 1959, CREST for FGW; 2. Memorandum of Conversation, Jan. 2, 1958, FRUS, Indonesia, vol. XVII, 1958–1960.

5 **not improve:** FGWII, April 1, 2021; EW, March 17, 2022; Prados, *Safe for Democracy*, pp. 179–80; Evan Thomas, pp. 160, 162; FGW letter to Jane, July 15, 1958, B: 6, FWP, UVA.

6 **for Wisner:** Invoices for Dr. Eugene Meyer, October 1958, B: 5, FWP, UVA; Eugene Meyer obituary, *The Washington Post, Feb. 24, 1982*; Zigmond Lebensohn letter to Burton Hersh, May 3, 1988, WFC; Sackeim, Jan. 18, 2022; FGWII, Sept. 9, 2020, and Jan. 13 and 14, 2021; EW, Jan. 12 and March 17, 2021; EW interview with William L. "Billy" Sigman, Feb. 8, 2013, WFC; Mosley, p. 421; Herken, pp. 230–31; Marchetti and Marks, pp. 274–75; FGWII, April 1, 2021; CIA Support Services Historical Series: Overview of the Office of Medical Services 1947–1972, pp. 29–31, 37; DD/S Diary Notes, Oct. 15, 1957, CREST for FGW.

7 **usually there:** Marchetti and Marks, p. 274; Sackeim, Jan. 18, 2022; ADD/A Diary Notes, April 1, 1952, CREST for FGW; FGWII, Jan. 13, 2021; EW, Jan. 12, 2021; Forbush, pp. 9, 16–17, 20–21, 38, 46, 163; "Seeing to the Future," pp. 10, 22; Forbush and Forbush, pp. a, 12, 119, 151; Michael J. Halberstam, "Who's Medically Fit for the White House," *New York Times*, Oct. 22, 1972, p. 39; DD/S Diary Notes, July 11, 1961, cia.gov; Bissell, COH, pp. 9–10; GW, Jan. 12 and Dec. 10, 2020; Goodwin and Jamison, vol. 2, pp. 712, 905.

8 **human behavior:** Church Committee, *Final Report*, book 1, pp. 385–86, 423; Jacobsen, p. 365; Ranelagh, pp. 202–4; "Project MKUltra," p. 4; Marks, pp. 59–60.

8 **that mess:** Memo from H. Marshall Chadwell to FGW on Transmittal of Scientific Intelligence Memorandum, August 1954, CREST for FGW; Project Bluebird, Type–Operational Support, April 5, 1950, research project memo to CIA assistant directors, cc to FGW, Feb. 15, 1952, CIA Artichoke Files; Church Committee, *Final Report*, book 1, pp. 395–96, 407; Memo on MKUltra Sub-Project 28, principal researchers: Emory University, MKUltra Briefing Book, Jan. 1, 1976; Ranelagh, p. 207; "Project MKUltra," pp. 4, 42; Eschner, p. 2; Marks, pp. 79–80, 83; Director of Security memorandum for the record, Suicide of Frank Olson, Nov. 28, 1953, Memo to Colonel Edwards from Chief, SSD, on Olson, Frank, Dec. 2, 1953, Note to FGW and RMH from the IG on action to be taken in Frank Olson death, CIA Documents Concerning the Death of Dr. Frank Olson.

8 **Frankie why:** FGWII, Oct. 19, 2020, and Jan. 13, 2021; MKUltra Sub-Projects 77, 51, 52 on plant-based hallucinogens, MKUltra Briefing Book, Jan. 1, 1976.

9 **by shrinks:** Background Literature on Behavior Control and Drugs of Interest to Project Artichoke / Bluebird, CIA Artichoke Files; "Project MKUltra," p. 43; Marks, pp. 27, 113; R. L. Bannerman, Morse Allen interview, Feb. 25, 1952, CIA Artichoke Files; Sackeim, Jan. 18, 2022.

9 **the disease:** Psychological Summary–Case 25835, WFC; Goodwin and Jamison, vol. 1, pp. xxii, 3; Mondimore, pp. 25, 60–61; Sheppard and Enoch Pratt Hospital cards for FGW, SPA.

9 **that day:** Psychological Summary–Case 25835, WFC; Sackeim, Jan. 18, 2022; Elias et al., p. 229.

10 **be suicidal:** Psychological Summary–Case 25835, WFC.

11 **ten-year-old:** FGWII, Aug. 18, 2020; EW, Nov. 11, 2020, and Feb. 18, 2021; GW, Aug. 3 and Dec. 10, 2020; Reeder, Aug. 20, 2020; A Biographic Sketch of

Frank Gardiner Wisner by Arthur Jacobs, WFC; Evan Thomas, pp. 17, 133, 162; FGW Personal History Statement for the OSS, p. 2, WFC; Sichel, pp. 268–69; Herken p. 71; Stewart Alsop, p. 214; Psychological Summary–Case 25835, WFC; RMH Notes B: 1, WHP, GU; Elizabeth Alsop letter to PKW, Nov. 8, 1965, B: 13, FWP, UVA.

11 **follow soon:** Psychological Summary–Case 25835, WFC; EW, Jan. 27, 2021; Forbush and Forbush, pp. viii–ix; "Seeing to the Future," p. 22.

Chapter 1: Laurel

15 **the country:** Howe, p. 1; SouthBear's History of Laurel, Mississippi, https://msgw.org/jones/community/comlaurel2.html; Key, pp. 2, 20, 27–29.

15 **Civil War:** Key, pp. 25, 29; SouthBear's History of Laurel, Mississippi, http://sites.rootsweb.com; Wilkie, p. 5; Laurel / Jones County, Mississippi, brochure, B: 2, S: 226, JGCL, CFA; Chisholm, SCS, pp. 32–33.

16 **a conductor:** Wisner family photos and Gardiner family tree, CFA; "The Wisners in America and Their Kindred: A Family of Patriots & Pioneers," B: 5, S: 336, JGCL, CFA; Lyons High School Nineteenth Annual Commencement, June 27, 1889, Obituary notes for William Heupel, ALC; FGW biographic essay, CFA; "George E. D. Wisner in the Civil War," June 5, 2018, pp. 1–4, 6, 11, 18, 65–67, Wisner Civil War, FGED, CFA; Lindsey, July 14, 2020; FGWII, July 8, 2020.

16 **as "brilliant":** FGWII, July 8, 2020; EW, July 15, 2020; Lindsey, July 14, 2020; "Ten Young Maids: A Pleasing Old One—At the Odeon," play review newsclip, B: 3, S: 336, JGCL, CFA; Frank George Wisner biography, B: 6, S: 336, JGCL, CFA; Marriage license for Frank George Wisner and Mary Jeannette Gardiner, Sept. 27, 1897, "Wisner-Gardiner: Popular Lyons Young People and Happily Married," newsclip, B: 3, S: 336, JGCL, CFA.

17 **Mississippi business:** Laurel's Founding Families Historic Homes, Aug. 2, 2019, http://www.laurelmercantile.com/blogs/journal/laurels-historic-homes; Newsclips on Clinton lumber business and homes, *The Clinton Herald*, B: 2, S: 226, JGCL, CFA; Jeannette Wisner correspondence with Frank George Wisner in 1900, B: 6, S: 336, JGCL, CFA.

17 **finest in the South:** Guy M. Walker, "Laurel, Mississippi—the City of Co-Operation," B: 3, S: 226, JGCL, CFA; "Faith in the South's Future Exemplified," *American Lumberman*, Oct. 11, 1913, B: 20, FWP, UVA; Key, pp. 35, 42–43, 49–52; Odell, pp. 1–7.

17 **communities in the South:** Odell, pp. 1–7; Laurel's Founding Families Historic Homes, Aug. 2, 2019, http://www.laurelmercantile.com/blogs/journal/laurels-historic-homes; Key, pp. 5, 25, 56–57; Lindsey, Oct. 12, 2021; Howe, p. 1; SouthBear's History of Laurel, Mississippi.

18 **more marketable:** Photo of Frank George Wisner, Oversized Box P-39, FWP, UVA; "Worthy of Honor," newsclip, July 1908, B: 8, S: 336, JGCL, CFA; FGW biography, B: 6, S: 336, CFA; "Tribute Paid Frank Wisner Here Tuesday," newsclip, B: 6, S: 336, JGCL, CFA; EW, July 15, 2020, and March 26, 2021; FGWII, July 8, 2020; Lindsey, July 14, 2020.

18 **little hill:** Author tour of the Green Barn at 726 North Fifth Avenue; Photo of Frank George Wisner home in Laurel, B: 11, FWP, UVA; Lindsey, July 14, 2020, and Oct. 12, 2021.

18 **from depression:** "Mrs. Frank George Wisner: Green Gardens," Laurel, Mississippi, ALC; "Informal Opening Reveals Charming Garden," "Women's Auxiliary of St. John's Plans Lawn Party Saturday," newsclips, Elizabeth Craig to Jeannette Wisner, March 3, 1933, B: 4, S: 336, JGCL, CFA; "Mrs. Frank Wisner Dies; Funeral Rites Thursday," Oct. 14, 1959, *The Laurel Leader-Call*, Jeannette

Wisner File, CFA; Lindsey, Oct. 12, 2021; EW, July 15, 2020, Feb. 18, 2021, and March 26, 2021; FGWII, July 8, 2020; GW, Aug. 3, 2020.

19 **child survive?:** Newsclip on George and Louise dying, B: 10, Frank George Wisner biography, B: 6, Rt. Rev. Theodore Bratton to Jeannette Wisner, June 18, 1929, B: 2, Correspondence on the loss of George Brockway Wisner, B: 10, Baptism records, June 30, 1903, for Elisabeth Gardiner Wisner, B: 6, S: 336, JGCL, CFA; EW, Aug. 5, 2020.

19 **year later:** The State of Mississippi, Jones County, City of Laurel, sworn statement of Mary Jeannette Wisner on birth of FGW, Oct. 11, 1940, B: 11, FWP, UVA; EW, July 15, 2020, and Aug. 5, 2020.

19 **the disease:** Mondimore, pp. 161–62, 195–96; Goodwin and Jamison, vol. 1, pp. 185, 188, 217 and vol. 2, pp. 412, 418–19; EW, July 15, 2020, and Aug. 5, 2020; Gotlib and Hammen, pp. 223, 241, 316, 355, 364, 372, 382–83.

20 **busy kid:** EW, April 19, 2022; "Frank G. Jr." newsclip, B: 3, S: 336, JGCL, CFA; Gotlib and Hammen, pp. 220–22, 414; Goodwin and Jamison, vol. 1, p. 219; Reeder, Aug. 20, 2020; GW, Aug. 3, 2020; Evan Thomas, p. 18; Lindsey, Oct. 12, 2021; FGWII, July 8, 2020; EW, July 15, 2020, and Aug. 19, 2020; Mondimore, pp. 163–64; Goodwin and Jamison, vol. 1, pp. 176, 191–93 and vol. 2, p. 912; Psychological Summary—Case 25835, WFC; "Frank G. Wisner and Wife Injured," newsclip, March 1916, B: 10, S: 336, JGCL, CFA; photo of FGW as a boy in football gear, B: 11, FWP, and B: 1, CFC, UVA.

20 **for barracks:** EW, July 15 and Aug. 19, 2020, and March 17, 2022; *American Lumberman*, April 12, 1924, p. 85; *The Lumber Manufacturer and Dealer*, Feb. 15, 1917, p. 57; FGWII, July 8, 2020; Lindsey, July 14, 2020; "F. G. Wisner," newsclip, B: 6, S: 336, CFA; "Reforestration and Timber Conservation" paper by Albert R. Israel and Frank G. Wisner, B: 9; "Cooperators Confer with President Coolidge to Cut Down Forest Fire Loss," *American Forests*, pp. 679–80, B: 8, Letter from Frank George Wisner, File no. 12, B: 2, Frank George Wisner prepared statements before Congress, B: 6 and 8, "Meeting of Board of Directors, "Service Bulletin," "Business Interests Divided on Tax Cut," newsclip, B: 7, S: 336, JGCL, CFA.

20 **Gulfport, Mississippi:** Frank George Wisner letters to Jeannette Wisner, Nov. 12 and 13, 1917, B: 2, S: 336, CFA; War Industries Board check for one dollar to Frank George Wisner, Sept. 6, 1919, ALC; Income Tax Returns for Frank George Wisner (1919) and FGW (1926) B: 13, Frank George Wisner letter to Jeannette Wisner, B: 2, Purchasing documents on the American schooner *Phineas W. Sprague*, 1916–17, B: 10, S: 336, CFA.

21 **these absences:** Frank George Wisner letter to Jeannette Wisner, Sept. 29, 1917, B: 2, S: 336, JGCL, CFA; Psychological Summary–Case No. 25835, WFC; FGWII, July 8, 2020; EW, Aug. 5, 2020; Lindsey, July 14, 2020.

21 **manic depression:** Alexander Chisholm letter, Jan. 4, 1954, B: 4, FWP, UVA; FGW letter to Elisabeth Chisholm, Nov. 19, 1953, Elisabeth Chisholm letter to FGW, Dec. 14, 1953, FGW letter to Jeannette Wisner, Jan. 5, 1954, B: 4, FWP, UVA; Frank George Wisner letter to Jeannette Wisner, undated, B: 2, S: 336, JGCL, CFA; Gotlib and Hammen, pp. 244, 284–85, 417; FGWII, July 8, 2020; Psychological Summary—Case No. 25835, WFC.

22 **his deportment:** Photos of Elisabeth Wisner, ALC; EW, July 15, 2020; biographies of Elisabeth Wisner Chisholm, 1975 and 1981, B: 3, S: 446, JGCL, CFA; Elisabeth Wisner report cards for Laurel Graded School, B: 15, S: 446, JGCL, CFA; Lindsey, July 14, 2020; Psychological Summary—Case. No. 25835, WFC; Winchester Junior Rifle Corps certificate for FGW, B: 1, CFC, UVA; FGW letter to his parents from Camp Greenbrier, July 15, 1924, B: 4, FWP, UVA; Laurel High School grade transcript for FGW, provided to the author by the

Laurel school system; FGW drawings, B: 4, S: 336, JGCL, CFA; FGW drawings, B: 2, CFC, UVA; FGW fifth-grade report card for Laurel Grade School,
B: 11, FWP, UVA.

22 **Orange, Virginia:** FGW Laurel High School diploma, Oversized Box N-23,
CFC, UVA; Lindsey, Oct. 12, 2021; Odell, p. 4; Chisholm, SCS, pp. 4, 10;
Isaacson and Thomas, p. 48; EW, July 15, 2020; Gerald Cooper letter to Arthur
L. Jacobs, Nov. 20, 1969, WFA.

23 **yearbook proclaimed:** Norfleet, pp. 49, 71, 104; A Biographic Sketch of FGW
by Arthur Jacobs, WFC; Discover Woodberry, https://www.woodberry.org
/about/discover-woodberry; Letters to Mrs. Wisner, Feb. 19 and April 1, 1926,
WFA; FGWII, Oct. 19, 2012; "Capt. Motley Leads Trackmen to Decisive Victory over Fork Union," *The Woodberry Oracle*, April 21, 1927, WFA; Woodberry
Forest yearbook, WFA; Woodberry Forest School Athletic Association for
FGW 1927, WFA; Gerald Cooper letter to Arthur Jacobs, Nov. 20, 1969, WFA.

23 **a chance:** Jeannette Wisner letter to John Carter Walker, May 21, 1927, WFA;
A Biographic Sketch of FGW by Arthur Jacobs, WFC; FGW letter to John
Carter Walker, May 21, 1927, WFA; Norfleet, p. 65.

24 **of 1927:** Frank George Wisner letter to John Carter Walker, May 1927, John
Carter Walker letter to Frank George Wisner, May 23, 1927, WFA.

Chapter 2: University of Virginia

26 **on campus:** FGW letter to his parents, Oct. 20, 1929, B: 1, CFC, UVA.

26 **and "Sissie.":** Pisani, pp. 25–26; FGW letter to parents, Jan. 16, 1932, B: 1,
CFC, UVA; FGW letters to his parents during his European trip, June–August,
1928, B: 1, CFC, UVA; FGW letters to his parents, Oct. 9 and Nov. 16 and
28, 1932, B: 1, CFC, UVA; EW, July 15, 2020; A Biographic Sketch of FGW by
Arthur Jacobs, and FGW in World War II monograph by FGWII, WFC; Lindsey, Oct. 12, 2021.

27 **at a meet:** Transcript of FGW grades, 1927–1931, supplied to the author by
the Office of the University Registrar for UVA; News photo of FGW running
the hundred-yard dash, B: 20, FWP, UVA; Newsclips of FGW at track meets
from *The Daily Princetonian, Birmingham News,* and *The Times-Picayune,* 1929–
1931, University of Virginia General Athletic Association, V Certificate, B: 18,
FWP, UVA; J. H. Eddy letter to John C. Clark, May 29, 1931, B: 20, FWP,
UVA; "Alumni News," p. 2, Feb. 12, 1931, "Virginia vs. V.M.I," *The Woodberry
Oracle,* April 12, 1929, p. 1, WFA; Newsclips and "Track, 1929," *Corks & Curl,*
1930, article on FGW in track competitions, B: 11, FWP, UVA; FGW letters
to parents, Oct. 20, 1929, and Jan. 25, 1930, and FGW letter to his father, May
12, 1931, B: 1, CFC, UVA; EW, July 15 and Oct. 20, 2020, and Jan. 12, 2021;
Lindsey, July 14, 2020; A Biographic Sketch of FGW by Arthur Jacobs, WFC.

27 **he died:** FGWII, July 8, 2020; A Biographic Sketch of FGW by Arthur Jacobs,
WFC; Kettlewell, p. 3; FGWII, July 8, 2020; Viccello, pp. 1–27; FGW's Delta
Kappa Epsilon fraternity certificate, Oversized Box T-32, FWP, UVA; FGW
letter to his parents, May 19, 1931, B: 1, CFC, UVA; *Corks & Curls,* 1934, on
FGW memberships in UVA clubs, LSM, UVA; FGW letters to his parents,
Oct. 20, 1929, and Jan. 17, 1930, B: 1, CFC, UVA; Photo of FGW 1931 with
fellow members in UVA's IMP Society, Oversized Box P-39, FWP, UVA; FGW
letter to his parents, Oct. 16, 1932, B: 1, CFC, UVA.

27 **for life:** Hersh, p. 192; FGWII, July 8, 2020; Personal recollections of Arthur
Jacobs, B: 18, FWP, FGW letters to his parents, Feb. 1, 1931, and April 17, 1932,
B: 1, CFC, UVA.

28 **his parents:** FGW letters to his parents, Dec. 7, 1930, Feb. 7, May 7, and Aug.
25, 1931, and Jan. 5 and Feb. 1, 1932, B: 1, CFC, UVA.

28 **was reading:** Personal recollections of Arthur Jacobs, B: 18, FWP, UVA.
28 **the school:** EW, July 15, 2020; FGWII, July 8, 2020; Gotlib and Hammen, p. 9; Jamison, p. 42; Hersh, pp. 191–92.
29 **the office:** FGW letters to his parents, Nov. 11, 1930, and March 14 and 22, 1931, B: 1, CFC, UVA; UVA transcripts for FGW for 1929–1930 and 1930–1931 sessions, B: 2, CFC, UVA.
29 **"*Einfühlung* [empathy]":** FGW letters to his parents Feb. 16, Feb. 22, and May 22, 1931, B: 1, CFC, UVA.
29 **being accepted:** UVA transcripts for FGW for 1929–30 and 1930–31 sessions, B: 2, CFC, UVA; FGW letters to his parents Jan. 11 and 17, 1930, Sept. 21, 1930, April 11, 1931, and undated letter on Easter Sunday, B: 1, CFC, UVA; Professor's comments on FGW psychology quiz March 11, 1931, B: 2, CFC, UVA; FGW's Bachelor of Science diploma from UVA June 16, 1931, Oversized box T-32, FWP, UVA; UVA transcript for FGW for 1930–31 sessions, CFA.
29 **track coach:** FGW letters to his parents, Sept. 22 and 27, Oct. 29, and Dec. 13, 1931, B: 1, CFC, UVA.
30 **instructors stimulating:** Transcript of FGW's law school grades, 1931–1934, supplied to the author by the Office of the University Registrar for UVA; Office of the Dean report on FGW's grades for the 1933–1934 Law School session, WFC; To Whom It May Concern letter from Dean A. M. Dobie, Jan. 3, 1934, LSM, UVA; FGW letters to his parents, Feb. 7, 1931, Feb. 14, March 30, May 21, and June 9, 1932, B: 1, CFC, Office of the Dean letter to FGW on his being awarded the Samuel Baker Woods Jr. Memorial Award, June 29, 1933, B: 11, FWP, UVA.
30 **timber supplies:** FGW letter to his parents, Dec. 12, 1932, B: 1, CFC, UVA; GW, Aug. 3, 2020; EW, Aug. 5, 2020; FGWII, July 8, 2020; Key, pp. 61–62, 67–68; FGW letters to his parents, Nov. 3, 1930, April 25 and May 2, 1932, B: 1, CFC, UVA; Presidential invitation to Frank George Wisner for home-building conference, Dec. 2–5, 1931, B: 6, Frank George Wisner letters to Jeannette Wisner, undated, Sunday, May 1929, and March 5, 1932, B: 2, S: 336, JGCL, CFA; Frank George Wisner 1927 State of Mississippi Tax Return, Jeannette Wisner File, CFA.
31 **his son:** Wilkie, pp. 33–34; EW, Aug. 5, 2020; Odell, p. 6; Howe, p. 4; Key, p. 71; "Inventor of Masonite and New Plastic," *The Laurel Leader-Call*, April 14, p. 1, B: 4, Frank George Wisner letter to C. C. Sheppard, April 14, 1931, B: 6, S: 336, JGCL, CFC; Robert Hynson letter to Frank George Wisner, May 21 (no year), B: 21, FWP, UVA; Frank George Wisner memo on Russian cotton and lumber, WFC.
31 **he enjoyed:** FGW letters to his parents, May 7 and Dec. 10, 1932, B: 1, CFC, UVA.
31 **1933–1934 session:** George Eager letter to FGW on the Samuel Baker Woods Jr. Memorial Award, June 29, 1933, B: 11, FWP, UVA; George Eager letter to FGW, June 29, 1933, LSM, UVA; Transcript of FGW's law school grades, 1931–1934, supplied to the author by the Office of the University Registrar for UVA; Office of the Dean report on FGW's grades for the 1933–1934 Law School session, WFC; To Whom It May Concern letter from Dean A. M. Dobie, Feb. 13, 1934, B: 11, FWP, UVA; FGW letters to his parents, Jan. 28, Feb. 20, April 9, May 15 and 21 and June 1 and 16, 1933, B: 1, CFC, FGW certificate as a member of the board of editors of the *Virginia Law Review*, May 1933–June 1934, B: 18, FWP, UVA; Frank George Wisner note on U.S. Senate stationery to Jeannette Wisner, undated, B: 2, S: 336, JGCL, CFA; W. S. Rodman letter on Phi Beta Kappa induction to FGW, May 17, 1934, WFC; FGW Phi Beta

Kappa certificate, B: 18, FWP, UVA; FGW certificate of induction into the Raven Society, May 20, 1933, Oversized Box T-32, FWP, UVA; FGW certificate of induction into Phi Delta Phi, May 10, 1932, FGW certificate of induction into the Order of the Coif, June 12, 1934, B: 18, FWP, UVA; FGW Personal History Statement for the OSS, WFC.

32 **Phi Beta Kappa:** FWG's Bachelor of Laws degree from UVA, June 12, 1934, Oversized Box T-32, FWP, UVA; A Biographic Sketch of FGW by Arthur Jacobs, WFC; John Carter Walker letter to FGW, Aug. 10, 1933, WFA; Bishop of Jackson, Mississippi, letter to Frank George Wisner, May 26, 1934, B: 1, CFC, UVA; "Athletic Captains Win Scholastic Awards," *The Washington Post*, May 24, 1934, p. 1.

32 **that counted:** FGWII, July 8, 2020; Hersh, p. 192.

Chapter 3: New York

33 **lucrative jobs:** FGW Personal History Statement for the OSS, WFC; A Biographic Sketch of FGW by Arthur Jacobs, WFC; EW, July 15, 2020; Key, pp. 26, 62; "Eastman, Gardiner & Co. (1891–1937)," Mississippi Rails, https://www.msrailroads.com/EG&Co.htm; Odell, p. 6.

34 **Bar Association:** A Biographic Sketch of FGW by Arthur Jacobs, WFC; FGW's New York bar certificate, Oversized Box T-32, FWP, UVA; Ellis and Clark, pp. 9–11, 15, 17, 19, 21–23, 25–30.

34 **political causes:** FGW Personal History Statement for the OSS, WFC; Isaacson and Thomas, pp. 119–20, 130; Ellis and Clark, p. 75; FGWII, July 8, 2020; FGW Application for Commission in U.S. Naval Reserve, Oct. 16, 1940, B: 11, FWP, UVA.

34 **senior partners:** FGW Application for Commission in U.S. Naval Reserve, Oct. 16, 1940, B: 11, FWP, UVA; Hersh, pp. 192–93; Maior, pp. 35–36; Ellis and Clark, pp. 43–47, 75, 115; FGW Personal History Statement for the OSS, WFC; FWGII, July 8, 2020.

35 **in Europe:** FGWII, July 8, 2020; EW, July 15, 2020; A Biographic Sketch of FGW by Arthur Jacobs, WFC; Ellis and Clark, p. 184; Prados, *Safe for Democracy*, p. 43; FGW Personal History Statement for the OSS, WFC; Maior, pp. 33–34.

35 **intrigued Wisner:** FGWII, July 6, 2020; EW, Aug. 5, 2020; Alsop, Aug. 11, 2021; FGW letters to parents, Oct. 23 and Nov. 1, 1932, Jan. 22 and Feb. 5 and 15, 1933, B: 1, CFC, UVA.

36 **she could:** FGW Personal History Statement for the OSS, WFC; EW, Aug. 5, 2020; "George E. D. Wisner in the Civil War," June 5, 2018, Wisner Civil War, FGED, CFA; FGWII, July 7 and 30, 2020.

36 **his ancestry:** "Bishop Donegan Will Dedicate Chapel Sunday," *The Rye Chronicle*, undated, p. 8, B: 11, FWP, UVA; Robert Amory interview, B: 9, RSP, HA.

36 **her spunk:** FGWII, July 8, 2020; John Ellis Knowles letter to PKW, James B. Knowles, and John Ellis Knowles Jr., Dec. 14, 1953, B: 4, FWP, UVA.

37 **"social register":** FGW letter to John B. Hollister, Dec. 13, 1963, B: 5, FWP, UVA; *Tit Bits*, St. Timothy's School yearbook, June 1930, STA.

37 **other deeply:** GW, Aug. 3, 2020; FitzGerald, Dec. 2, 2020; EW, Aug. 5, 2020; FGWII, July 8 and Nov. 10, 2020.

38 **"Squirrel Eye":** EW, Aug. 8, 2020; FGW and PKW wedding photos, B: 1, CFC, UVA.FGW Personal History Statement for the OSS, WFC; FGWII, July 8, Aug. 19, and Oct. 19, 2020; FGW Application for Commission in U.S. Naval Reserve, Oct. 16, 1940, B: 11, FWP, UVA; GW, Aug. 3, 2020.

38 **half-mast:** "Frank Wisner Passes," *Jackson Daily News*, "Tribute Paid Frank Wisner Here Tuesday," newsclip, B: 6, S: 336, JGCL, CFA; FGW Personal History Statement for the OSS, WFC; FGWII, July 8, 2020.

38 **spy world:** FGW, July 8, 2020; EW, July 15 and Aug. 5, 2020; PKW to Jeannette Wisner, Friday, undated, B: 2, S: 336, JGCL, CFA; FGW letter to Ellis Knowles, May 22, 1940, B: 21, FWP, UVA; Psychological Summary—Case 265835, WFC.

Chapter 4: The OSS

41 **Naval Reserve:** FGW Personal History Statement for the OSS, WFC; FG-WII, Aug. 19, 2020; Evan Thomas, p. 19; FGW in World War II monograph by FGWII, p. 2, WFC; EW, Aug. 5, 2020; FGW Application for Commission in U.S. Naval Reserve, Oct. 16, 1940, B: 11, FWP, UVA.

42 **as a boy:** FGW Application for Commission in U.S. Naval Reserve, Oct. 16, 1940, B: 11, FWP, UVA; FGW's Data Card for All Naval Reserve Officers, WFC.

42 **the Navy:** FGW's Data Card for All Naval Reserve Officers, WFC; File no. 105905 from FGW, July 30, 1941, B: 11, FWP, UVA; Mortgage Department to FGW, Aug. 24, 1943, Green Lumber Company, Laurel, Mississippi, to FGW, May 15, 1943, WFC; FGW certificate of commission as a lieutenant junior grade in the U.S. Naval Reserve, April 3, 1941, WFC; News item that Jeannette Wisner placed in the *Laurel Leader-Call* on FGW commissioning, B: 11, FWP, UVA; A Biographical Sketch of FGW by Arthur Jacobs, WFC; FGW in World War II monograph by FGWII, p. 2, WFC.

42 **assign him:** Commandant Third Naval District letter to FGW, July 21, 1941, Appointment in Naval Reserve for FGW, May 2, 1941, Commandant Third Naval District letter to FGW, May 22, 1941, Officer Qualification Questionnaire for FGW, B: 11, FWP, UVA.

43 **for newspapers:** FGW Theater Service Record, Feb. 5, 1945, FGW Personal History Statement for OSS, FGW in World War II monograph by FGWII, p. 2, A Biographic Sketch of FGW by Arthur Jacobs, WFC; FGWII, Aug. 19, 2020; Officer Qualification Questionnaire for FGW, B: 11, FWP, UVA; John M. Templeton letter to FGW, Sept. 3, 1943, Federal Insurance Company invoices for PKW fur coats, WFC.

43 **subway riders:** FGWII, Aug. 19, 2020.

43 **Naval Intelligence:** Memo to W. Shepardson on Lieutenant Commander McBaine, March 1, 1943, Spencer Phenix memo to F. L. Belin, July 23, 1943, FGW memo to Spencer Phenix on Target Information, July 20, 1943, WFC; John Hughes memo to FGW, Oct. 7, 1943, B: 18, Franklin B. Atwood letter to H. K. Fenn, Oct. 1, 1943, B: 11, FWP, UVA.

44 **as well:** Church Committee, *Final Report*, book 1, p. 15; Leary, pp. 3–4; Waller, *Wild Bill Donovan*, pp. 58–83.

44 **those recruits:** Waller, *Wild Bill Donovan*, pp. 69–94; FGWII, July 8, 2020.

45 **on a ship:** Memo to W. Shepardson on Lieutenant Commander McBaine, March 1, 1943, Turner McBaine memo to Whitney Shepardson, Sept. 21, 1943, Turner McBaine memos to David Bruce April 7 and Oct. 19, 1942, FGW letter to AWD, Feb. 1, 1965, FGW letter to Naval friends, Jan. 21, 1945, WFC; Katharine Graham interview with Polly Fritchey, Oct. 10, 1989, p. 2, KGP; EW, Aug. 5, 2020.

45 **his organization:** W. T. M. Beale memo to security officer on FGW, Oct. 11, 1943, David Bruce to Commander Ravenel on FGW, April 21, 1942, WFC; W. L. Fox memo to J. R. Baine, March 14, 1943, B: 18, FWP, UVA.

45 **wrote him:** FGW Personal History Statement for the OSS, FGW one of seven Naval officers requested for the OSS, memo, Oct. 6, 1943, W. T. M. Beale to FGW, Oct. 16, 1943, WFC; EW, July 15, 2020; FGWII, Aug. 19, 2020.

46 **engraved on it:** W. T. M. Beale to FGW, Oct. 16, 1943, WFC; History of Schools and Training, OSS, Jan. 7, 1949, B: 2, E: UD 176, Instructions for Recruits, Jan. 19, 1944, B: 161, E: 136, RG226, NA.

46 **mouths shut:** Instructions for Recruits, Jan. 19, 1944, B: 161, E: 136, Student Mail Procedure, Training Directorate memo to All Geographic Desks and Administrative Officers, June 23, 1944, B: 223, E: A1 146, RG226, NA.

47 **as liaisons:** Chambers, pp. 238–39; Waller, *Wild Bill Donovan*, p. 73.

47 **he was told:** Desk Indoctrination memo for O.S.S. Basic Course, B: 265, E: 146, RG226, NA.

48 **spartan camps:** Chambers, pp. 6, 50, 54, 59, 61; History of Schools and Training, OSS, Jan. 7, 1949, B: 2, E: UD 176, L. B. Shallcross memo to John O'Gara, Information on Schools and Training Sites, Feb. 1, 1951, B: 7, E: UD161, Garland H. Williams memo to WJD, July 21, 1942, Fr: 479–80, R: 107, M1642, RG226, NA; *War Report of the OSS*, p. 232.

48 **field exercises:** Chambers, p. 61; L. B. Shallcross memo to John O'Gara, Feb. 1, 1951, Excerpts from History of Schools and Training, OSS, B: 7, E: 161, Layout of Area E-2, B: 13, E: 85, RG226, NA.

48 **shortened time:** Instructions to Students, Training Directorate memo to All Geographic Desks, Dec. 21, 1942, B: 161, E: 136, Basic SI-SO Course of Instruction, March 13, 1943, B: 163, E: 136, Manuals on spy tradecraft, the German army, and makeup of the OSS, B: 3 and 4, E: 161, Training Directorate memo to All Geographic Desks, Dec. 26, 1942, B: 223, E: A1 146, RG226, NA.

49 **operation alive:** Chambers, p. 243; *War Report of the OSS*, p. 234; Desk Indoctrination Memo for O.S.S. Basic Course, B: 265, E: 146, School Name list for Schools and Training, Sept. 29, 1943, B: 223, E: A1 146, RG226, NA.

49 **with detection:** Chambers, pp. 242–43; History of Schools and Training, OSS, Jan. 7, 1949, B: 2, E: UD 176, RG226, NA; *War Report of the OSS*, p. 234.

50 **sketch maps:** Chambers, pp. 71, 244–45; *War Report of the OSS*, p. 236; Waller, *Disciples*, pp. 111–14; Basic SI-SO Course of Instruction, March 13, 1943, B: 163, E: 136, RG226, NA.

50 **blocked off:** *War Report of the OSS*, pp. 234–35.

50 **the radio:** *War Report of the OSS*, p. 235; Complete Cipher Course for All Areas OSS, Double Transposition Cipher, B: 3, E: 161, RG226, NA.

51 **quick kill:** Chambers, pp. 190–93, 248–49; Louis Selenka Report on Projects, Division 19 Program as of Dec. 1, 1943, B: 207, E: 210, Enclosure: Amendments to O.S.S. 1942 Catalogue of Material, Fr: 1776–77, R: 14, Sylvester Missal memo to WJD, Feb. 16, 1944, Fr: 201–2, R: 73, M1642, "Gutter Fighting," Part II, "Unarmed," 2nd revision, SI: 3/25/44, B: 11, E: 90, RG226, NA.

51 **gain entry:** History of Schools and Training, OSS, Jan. 7, 1949, B: 2, E: UD 176, RG226, NA; Schools and Training, B: 158, E: 136, George A. Barnes memo to Patrick Dolan, Nov. 18, 1943, Fr: 853–57, R: 107, M1642, Kenneth P. Miller memo on Baltimore Schemes, Aug. 20, 1943, B: 163, E: 136, RG226, NA; *War Report of the OSS*, pp. 235–36; Waller, *Wild Bill Donovan*, p. 94; Waller, *Disciples*, pp. 114–15.

52 **20 percent:** *War Report of the OSS*, p. 236–39; History of Schools and Training, OSS, Jan. 7, 1949, B: 2, E: UD 176, RG226, NA; Chambers, pp. 73–74, 76, 244.

52 **"over-cautiousness."** Ezra Shine to Captain Miller, memo evaluating FGW performance at E-2, Nov. 26, 1943, WFC.

53 **would thrive:** *War Report of the OSS*, pp. 179, 235–37, 243; FGWII, Aug. 19, 2020; Philip K. Allen memo on Extension of the Basic E Course, April 26, 1944, B: 223, E: A1 146, RG226, NA.

53 **to Cairo:** Memo on FGW Requisition of Equipment and Supplies, Dec. 8, 1943, HJC memo to Colonel Sands and Harold J. Coolidge on FGW, Nov. 25, 1943, Forms for FGW request for supplies and equipment, Dec. 9 and 14, 1943, WFC; FGW Checklist for Military Personnel, purchasing $10,000 USGLI, Dec. 16, 1943, FGW orders for temporary duty in Cairo, Egypt, Dec. 10, 1943, B: 11, FWP, UVA.

Chapter 5: Cairo

54 **wrote Polly:** FGW travel orders for Cairo, Dec. 27, 1943, B: 11, FGW letter to PKW, Dec. 28, 1943, B: 20, FWP, UVA.

55 **Intelligence Branch:** Maior, pp. 47–48, 51; McBaine, UCB, pp. 54, 56; FGW letter to PKW, Dec. 28, 1943, B: 20, Turner McBaine letter to Whitney Shepardson, Sept. 21, 1943, B: 18, FWP, UVA; J. E. Toulmin letter to WJD, July 30, 1944, Fr: 319–20, R: 41, M1624, RG226, NA.

55 **Sharia Rustum:** HJC to Thomas Danberg et al., memo on Inoculations for Overseas, Dec. 9, 1943, WFC; Cooper, pp. 4–5, 26–27, 30, 35–36, 115–18, 119, 241, 258.

56 **considerable clout:** Cooper, pp. 6, 9–15, 17, 22, 25–26.

56 **the Axis:** Cooper, pp. 44, 54, 63, 67–68, 139, 198–99, 201, 204–7, 221–25, 238–40, 253, 268, 304–5; Rubin, pp. 140–41.

57 **colonial empire:** Cooper, pp. 36, 130, 133, 231–34, 269.

57 **over Cairo:** *The Overseas Targets*, p. 47; Rubin, p. 134.

57 **wrote Polly:** Waller, *Wild Bill Donovan*, p. 204; FGW letter to PKW, Dec. 28, 1943, B: 20, FWP, UVA.

58 **"upon me":** FGW letters to PKW, 1943 and Dec. 28, 1943, B: 20, FWP, UVA; Maior, p. 52.

58 **its secrets:** Chambers, pp. 296–97; *The Overseas Targets*, pp. 47–51; FGW Theater Service Record, Feb. 5, 1945, WFC; FGWII, Aug. 19, 2020; Maior, pp. 53–54.

59 **room table:** FGW letter to PKW, 1943, FGW photo album with photos from Egypt, B: 20, FWP, UVA; Percy S. C. Wood OSS personnel file, B: 851, Amariah G. Atwater OSS personnel file, B: 25, Stephen K. Bailey personnel file, B: 29, Walter Lowrie Campbell OSS personnel file, B: 104, Rolfe Kingsley OSS personnel file, B: 407, E: A1 224, RG226, NA.

59 **brass ashtrays:** Cooper, pp. 126–27; FGW letter to PKW, 1943, B: 20, FGW letter to PKW, 1944, B: 2, FWP, UVA.

60 **for him:** FGW letter to PKW, 1943, B: 20, FWP, UVA; Maior, pp. 52–53.

60 **sent there:** Atherton Richards memo to WJD, Sept. 30, 1943, Fr: 231–40, R: 41, M1642, RG226, NA; *The Overseas Targets*, pp. 47–48; Kingsley, Jan. 7, 2008.

61 **in Cairo:** FGW memo to Chief, SI, Report on Experience and Conditions Observed in the Field, March 27, 1945, WFC; Maior, p. 55; Reports Officer, OSS-Cairo, memo to Reporting Board, SI, OSS-Washington, April 30, 1944, B: 18, FWP, UVA.

62 **neighboring tables:** Maior, p. 51; Cooper, p. 127–28, 186, 259–60.

62 **Cairo station:** Kingsley, Jan. 7, 2008.

62 **of them:** FGW photo album with photos from Egypt, B: 20, FGW letter to PKW, 1944, B: 2, FWP, UVA; FGW letter to PKW, October 1944, WFC; Katharine Graham interview with Polly Fritchey, Oct. 10, 1989, KGP.

63 **March 1, 1944:** Reports Officer, OSS-Cairo, memo to Reporting Board, SI, OSS-Washington, April 30, 1944, B: 18, FWP, UVA; Maior, p. 55; FGW in World War II monograph by FGWII, pp. 5, 9, WFC; Citation for FGW to be an Honorary Officer of the Military Division of the Most Excellent Order of the British Empire, B: 20, FGW notification of appointment to lieutenant commander rank as of March 1, 1944, B: 11, FWP, UVA; FGW memo to Chief, SI, Report on Experience and Conditions Observed in the Field, March 27, 1945, WFC.

63 **the mess:** Waller, *Wild Bill Donovan*, p. 183; FGW in World War II monograph by FGWII, p. 9, WFC; FGW memo to Chief, SI, Report on Experience and Conditions Observed in the Field, March 27, 1945, WFC; Note to Colonel Buxton that WJD is in Cairo, Nov. 1943, Fr: 404, 407, R: 125, Fr: 120, 128, R: 84, WJD cable to Doering and Buxton, Dec. 18, 1943, Fr: 278, R: 88, Edward Dodd to E. J. Putzell, memo on Operational Problems of Istanbul Mission, March 3, 1944, Fr: 111–13, R: 79, M1642, RG226, NA.

Chapter 6: Istanbul

64 **wartime agencies:** Rubin, pp. 13, 17–18, 23, 120, 258.

65 **country's heart:** Rubin, pp. 12–21, 24.

65 **Germans invaded:** Rubin, pp. 5, 18–19, 26, 88–89, 114, 251–52, 255, 264–65; Rolfe Kingsley to Chief of Mission, OSS-Istanbul, memo on Activities of SI Branch covering period 1 August through 31 August 1944, WFC.

66 **in the war:** *The Overseas Targets*, pp. 51, 269; Rubin, pp. 25, 132; Waller, *Wild Bill Donovan*, pp. 155–57.

66 **from Germany:** *The Overseas Targets*, p. 269; Waller, *Wild Bill Donovan*, pp. 155–57; Rubin, p. 135; State Department–OSS documents establishing Lend-Lease cover for Lanning Macfarland, Jan. 23–Feb.18, 1943, Fr: 130–41, R: 118, M1 642, WJD memo to Lanning Macfarland, March 5, 1943, B: 340, E: 210, RG 226, NA.

66 **and Germany:** Kingsley, Jan. 7, 2008; *The Overseas Targets*, p. 269; Rubin, p. 166; Istanbul Office: First List of Code Names Under Flower System, Sept. 26, 1943, Folder WN 25870-72, E: 215, RG226, NA; Waller, *Wild Bill Donovan*, pp. 155–57.

67 **it was:** Lanning Macfarland letter to WJD, June 23, 1943, Fr: 1091–92, R: 79, M1742, Lanning Macfarland memo to Edwin J. Putzell with Interim Report from Chief, OSS Mission to Turkey, Nov. 13 and 22, 1943, B: 16, E: 211, RG226, NA; Waller, *Wild Bill Donovan*, pp. 155–57.

67 **the Germans:** Irving H. Sherman memo to Hazel Haight, Sept. 26, 1944, with "Report on My Istanbul Mission," Aug. 24, 1944, B: 16, E: 210, RG226, NA; Waller, *Wild Bill Donovan*, pp. 155–57; *The Overseas Targets*, p. 271.

67 **deemed worthless:** *The Overseas Targets*, p. 272; Rubin, p. 224; Maior, p. 67; John L. Riheldaffer memo to Silas B. Moore, Aug. 17, 1942, Fr: 75–76, R: 36, M1642, Cable to Harper and 550 from 154, July 3, 1944, and memo to A. W. Sulloway from Chief, SI, July 12, 1944, Fr: 1131–32, 1135, R: 79, M1642, RG226, NA.

68 **war facility:** *The Overseas Targets*, pp. 271–72; Waller, *Wild Bill Donovan*, pp. 191–99; WJD memo to JCS, Nov. 20, 1943, Forrest B. Royal memo to WJD, Dec. 5, 1943, B: 181, E: 210, Joint Report on Field Conditions by Florimond Duke et al., July 11, 1945, B: 27, E: 92A, RG226, NA.

68 **Macfarland's gang:** Kingsley, Jan. 7, 2008; AD/H memo to C.D., Feb. 14, 1944, ADH/255, with memo on Collaboration with O.S.S., Jan. 26, 1944, 1413/44 /18, NAUK; J. G. O'Conor memo to W. Shepardson, May 23, 1944, B: 16, E: 221, RG226, NA.

68   **too "casual.":** J. G. O'Conor memo to W. Shepardson, May 23, 1944, B: 16, E: 221, J. E. Toulmin letter to WJD, July 30, 1944, Fr: 319–20, R: 41, M1642, RG226, NA; Waller, *Wild Bill Donovan*, pp. 253–56.

69   **in Cairo:** J. E. Toulmin letter to WJD, July 30, 1944, Fr: 319–20, R: 41, Cable from Toulmin to Cheston, June 1, 1944, Fr: 1283–85, R: 39, M1642, RG226, NA; Istanbul File, Clothing Memo, FGW itinerary of travel from Cairo, Egypt, to Istanbul, Turkey, June 10–13, 1944, Tally Sheet Incoming for FGW, July 6, 1944, B: 11, FWP, UVA; Whitney Shepardson to WJD, memo on FGW, April 4, 1943; Rubin, pp. 21–22; Maior, pp. 58–59.

70   **"a Spy.":** FGWII, Aug. 19, 2020.

70   **"Sigma Sigma!":** Macintyre, pp. 61–62; SAINT Balkans to SAINT Washington, memo on De-Briefing Field Personnel, Sylvia Press, June 22, 1945, B: 200, E: UD 108-A, RG226, NA; Rubin, pp. 164–65.

70   **be disastrous:** Maior, pp. 57–58; FGW Theater Service Record, Feb. 5, 1945, WFC; FGW in World War II monograph by FGWII, p. 10, WFC; Hersh, pp. 195–96; FGW letter to Wallace Carroll, June 19, 1952, B: 2, FWP, UVA.

70   **of anger:** Harry Harper memo on the Dogwood Organization, July 17, 1944, B: 181, E: 210, RG226, NA.

71   **"from Central Europe":** Irving H. Sherman memo on "Report on My Istanbul Mission," Aug. 24, 1944, B: 16, E: 210, RG226, NA; Rolfe Kingsley to Chief of Mission, OSS-Istanbul, memo on Activities Report of SI Branch covering period 1 August through 31 August 1944, WFC; *The Overseas Targets*, p. 272.

71   **in Central Europe:** Rolfe Kingsley to Chief of Mission, OSS-Istanbul, memo on Activities Report of SI Branch covering period 1 August through 31 August 1944, WFC; R. H. I. Goddard memo to the Secretary of State, Aug. 12, 1944, B: 18, FWP, UVA; G. Edward Buxton memo to List S, Aug. 16, 1944, WFC; FGW memo to Chief, SI, Report on Experience and Conditions Observed in the Field, March 27, 1945, WFC.

71   **his children:** EW, Aug. 5 and Aug. 19, 2020; GW, Aug. 10, 2020; FGW photos for Istanbul, June–August 1944, B: 20, FWP, UVA.

72   **Nazis occupied:** *The Overseas Targets*, p. 269; Douglas Hartshorn memos to the Secretary of State, Aug. 30 and Sept. 6, 1944, Margaret Feldman memo to Douglas Hartshorn, Sept. 6, 1944, Fletcher Warren memo for Mr. Kimbel, Sept. 6, 1944, Rolfe Kingsley to Chief of Mission, OSS-Istanbul, memo on Activities Report of SI Branch covering period 1 August through 31 August 1944, FGW to Whitney Shepardson, memo on Relations with Office of War Information, April 13, 1945, FGW memo to Chief, SI, Report on Experience and Conditions Observed in the Field, March 27, 1945, WFC; *The Overseas Targets*, p. 272; R. H. I. Goddard memo to the Secretary of State, Aug. 12, 1944, B: 18, FWP, UVA.

72   **protection guarantees:** Kaplan, p. 4; Hazard, pp. 18–19; Wolff, pp. 183–84; Maior, pp. 50, 68–69; Hersh, pp. 196, 200; Rolfe Kingsley to Chief of Mission, OSS-Istanbul, memo on Activities Report of SI Branch covering period 1 August through 31 August 1944, WFC; Memo on Attempted Peace Negotiations with Allies, Aug. 7, 1944, BHP; Bernard Yarrow to WJD, Feb. 8, 1943, Summary of Recent Cables on Romanian Situation—The Possibilities of Rumania's Withdrawal from the Axis Partnership, Fr: 733–53, R: 104, M1642, RG226, NA.

73   **"purposes only.":** Memorandum of Information for the JCS, OSS Dispatch of Intelligence Team into Romania, July 12, 1944, B: 654, E: 190, RG226, NA; FGW to Whitney Shepardson, Aug. 26, 1944, memo on proposed forward operation in Balkans from Istanbul, B: 18, FWP, UVA; FGW cable to 154, Aug. 29, 1944, Fr: 12–13, R: 87, M1642, RG226, NA; For Donovan OSS to Deane,

Marshall, July 7, 1944, John R. Deane to P. M. Fitin, July 8, 1944, BHP; Memorandum for the President on OSS-NKVD Liaison, Nov. 5, 1943, https://cia.gov/static/Memoranda-OSS-NVKD-Liaison.pdf; FGW to John E. Toulmin, memo on Plan of Forward Operations in Balkans, B: 18, FWP, UVA.

73 **his detachment:** Maior, p. 71; Hazard, pp. 34–36; FGW memo to Chief, SI, Report on Experience and Conditions Observed in the Field, March 27, 1945, WFC.

73 **into Bucharest:** FGW to John E. Toulmin, memo on Plan of Forward Operations in Balkans, B: 18, FWP, UVA.

Chapter 7: Bucharest

75 **of Germans:** FGW memo to Charles Cabell, March 1, 1965, B: 8, Outline of activities and accomplishments of Lt. Comdr. Frank G. Wisner, USNR, (105905), as Chief of American Military Unit, Romania, B: 20, FWP, UVA; FGW memo to Chief, SI, Report on Experience and Conditions Observed in the Field, March 27, 1945, WFC; Maior, pp. 76, 80–81; Hazard, p. 44; FGW in World War II monograph by FGWII, WFC; FGW letter to R. W. D. Taylor, Oct. 1, 1946, WFA.

75 **were there:** Hazard, p. 41; Hersh, p. 197; FGW memo to Charles Cabell, March 1, 1965, B: 8, Outline of activities and accomplishments of Lt. Comdr. Frank G. Wisner, USNR, (105905), as Chief of American Military Unit, Romania, B: 20, Recommendation for Award, Wisner, Frank G., Feb. 4, 1945, B: 18, FWP, UVA; Report on the OSS (R&A) Bucharest Mission, September 1944, BHP; Rolfe Kingsley Activities Report of SI Branch, OSS-Istanbul, covering period September 1–30, 1944, Nov. 2, 1944, B: 18, FWP, UVA; FGW cable to Beale and Andrews, Nov. 26, 1944, BHP.

75 **charge him:** Maior, pp. 110–11; FGWII, Aug. 19, 2020; FGW in World War II monograph by FGWII, WFC; Report on the OSS (R&A) Bucharest Mission, September 1944, BHP; FGW Credit Slips for equipment B: 11, FWP, UVA; FGW letter to PKW, Oct. 13, 1944, WFC; FGW letter to PKW, Sept. 6, 1944, WFC.

75 **of "Ruritania.":** FGW memo to Charles Cabell, March 1, 1965, B: 8, Recommendation for Award, Wisner, Frank G., Feb. 4, 1945, B: 18, FWP, UVA; Katharine Graham interview with Polly Fritchey, Oct. 10, 1989, p. 2, KGP; FGW letter to PKW, Oct. 13, 1944, WFC; FGW letter to PKW, Oct. 13, 1944, B: 2, FWP, UVA; FGW letter to PKW, Sept. 6, 1944, WFC.

76 **that language:** FGW memo to Chief, SI, Report on Experience and Conditions Observed in the Field, March 27, 1945, WFC; Hazard, pp. 40, 44.

76 **oil fields:** FGW memo to Charles Cabell, March 1, 1965, B: 8, Outline of activities and accomplishments of Lt. Comdr. Frank G. Wisner, USNR, (105905), as Chief of American Military Unit, Romania, B: 20, Recommendation for Award, Wisner, Frank G., Feb. 4, 1945, B: 18, FWP, UVA; Hazard, p. 40; Memorandum of Information for the JCS on Activities of OSS unit in Romania, Nov. 18, 1944, BHP; Charles Cheston memo for General Arnold, Fr: 471, R: 20, M1642, RG226, NA.

77 **varnished fingernails:** Memorandum of Information for the JCS on Activities of OSS unit in Romania, Nov. 18, 1944, BHP; Recommendation for Award, Wisner, Frank G., Feb. 4, 1945, B: 18, FWP, UVA; Rubin, pp. 65, 67; Maior, p. 86; Report on the OSS (R&A) Bucharest Mission, September 1944, BHP; Edward Glavin memo to WJD, Sept. 11, 1944, Fr: 971–73, R: 86, M1642, RG226, NA.

77 **Royal Palace:** Maior, pp. 86–93, 117–19; Bishop and Crayfield, pp. 6, 173–74; Dobbs, p. 111.

78 **the Russians:** Report on the OSS (R&A) Bucharest Mission, September 1944, BHP; FGW memo to Charles Cabell, March 1, 1965, B: 8, FGW photos in Bucharest, B: 20, FWP, UVA; Maior, pp. 5, 80; FGW in World War II monograph by FGWII, WFC. Bishop and Crayfield, pp. 94–98; FGW in World War II monograph by FGWII, FGW memo to Chief, SI, Report on Experience and Conditions Observed in the Field, March 27, 1945, WFC; Hazard, p. 78; Hostler, p. 57; Dobbs, pp. 112–13; Memo to FBI director on FGW, Oct. 14. 1955, FBIW; Hostler, pp. 64–65; Memorandum on Caradja, Princess Catherine, https://www.archives.gov/files/declassification/iscap/pdf/2010-081-umissdoc8 .pdf; FGW memo to Charles Cabell, March 1, 1965, B: 8, FGW; photos in Bucharest, B: 20, FWP, UVA; Robert Bishop, Report on X-2 Activities in Bucharest, April 24, 1945, CIA FOIA; SAINT Balkans to SAINT Washington, memo on De-Briefing Field Personnel, Sylvia Press, June 22, 1945, B: 200, E: UD 108-A, RG226, NA.

78 **years later:** Maior, pp. 11, 111; Memo to FBI director on FGW, Oct. 14. 1955, L. B. Nichols to Tolson, memo on FGW, March 24, 1954, FBIW; Anderson, p. 48; Evan Thomas, p. 20; Dobbs, p. 112; Memorandum on Caradja, Princess Catherine, https://www.archives.gov/files/declassification/iscap/pdf/2010-081 -umissdoc8.pdf.

78 **"piece of work.":** FGW letter to PKW, Sept. 6, 1944, WFC.

79 **POWs landed:** FGW memo to Charles Cabell, March 1, 1965, B: 8, FWP, UVA; *The Overseas Targets*, p. 331; Maior, pp. 11–12; Report on the OSS (R&A) Bucharest Mission, September 1944, Letter to General Arnold from General Eaker, 1944, Russell Dorr and Philip Coombs memo to WJD, Sept. 27, 1944, WJD to Deane for Fitin, Sept. 29, 1944, BHP; Charles Cheston memo to JCS, Sept. 2, 1944, Fr: 118, FGW and WJD memos and cables on OSS exchanges with the Russians, Fr: 1122, 1259, 1260–61, 1269–74, 1276, R: 86, M1642, RG226, NA.

79 **the attacks:** *The Overseas Targets*, p. 331; FGW memo to Chief, SI, Report on Experience and Conditions Observed in the Field, March 27, 1945, WFC; Report on the OSS (R&A) Bucharest Mission, September 1944, BHP; Recommendation for Award, Wisner, Frank G., Feb. 4, 1945, B: 18, FWP, UVA; WJD memo to General Marshall, Aug. 11, 1943, Fr: 278–81, R: 7, FGW and WJD memos and cables on OSS exchanges with the Russians, Fr: 1122, 1259, 1260–61, 1269–74, 1276, R: 86, M1642, RG226, NA.

80 **had identified:** FGW memo to Charles Cabell, March 1, 1965, B: 8, FWP, UVA; Maior, p. 119; FGW photos in Bucharest, B: 20, FWP, UVA; FGW memo to Chief, SI, Report on Experience and Conditions Observed in the Field, March 27, 1945, W. L. Campbell memo to Commanding Officer, Sept. 18, 1944, WFC; *The Overseas Targets*, p. 332; FGW in World War II monograph by FGWII, WFC; Recommendation for Award, Wisner, Frank G., Feb. 4, 1945, B: 18, FWP, UVA; Edward Glavin to WJD, memo on OSS Activities in Romania, Sept. 11, 1944, Fr: 971–73, R: 86, M1642, RG226, NA; WJD cable to FGW, Sept. 22, 1944, BHP.

80 **it stopped:** FGW memo to Chief, SI, Report on Experience and Conditions Observed in the Field, March 27, 1945,WFC; WJD to Deane for Fitin, Sept. 29, 1944, BHP. FGW and WJD memos and cables on OSS exchanges with the Russians, Fr: 1122, 1259, 1260–61, 1269–74, 1276, R: 86, M1642, RG226, NA; WJD cable to FGW, Sept. 22, 1944, FGW to WJD via Joyce, Sept. 26, 1944, BHP.

81 **Royal Palace:** Maior, pp. 97–98; Edward Glavin to WJD, memo on OSS Activities in Romania, Sept. 11, 1944, Fr: 971–73, R: 86, M1642, RG226, NA; Report

on the OSS (R&A) Bucharest Mission, September 1944, BHP; FGW memo to Charles Cabell, March 1, 1965, B: 8, FWP, UVA; Robert Bishop, Report on X-2 Activities in Bucharest, April 25, 1945, CIA FOIA; Maior, pp. 99, 105, 115–17, 129–31, 143; Ellis and Clark, p. 76; FGW in World War II monograph by FG-WII, FGW memo to Chief, SI, Report on Experience and Conditions Observed in the Field, March 27, 1945, WFC; Hostler, 64.

81 **became "Typhoid.":** Hersh, p. 197; Maior, p. 13; Cable to Houck, Washington, and Horton, Paris, Feb. 15, 1945, FGW memo to WJD, March 30, 1945, Caserta, Italy, cable to OSS, Oct. 13, 1944, BHP.

82 **Western diplomats:** Rubin, pp. 65–66, 68; Dobbs, pp. 121–22; Wolff, pp. 194–95; Maior, p. 4; Bishop and Crayfield, p. 36; FGW memo to Chief, SI, Report on Experience and Conditions Observed in the Field, March 27, 1945, WFC.

83 **"the Russians.":** Maior, pp. 115, 124; Bishop and Crayfield, pp. 37–38; Hostler, pp. 63–65; Hersh, p. 201; FGW memo to Chief, SI, Report on Experience and Conditions Observed in the Field, March 27, 1945, WFC; WJD memo to Secretary of State, Oct. 14, 1944, Fr: 171, R: 26, M1642, FGW memo on Formation of New Romanian Government, Nov. 8, 1944, B: 26, E: A1 154, RG226, NA; FGW photos of Bucharest, B: 20, FWP, UVA; Joyce cable to WJD and Foster, Oct. 3, 1944, BHP.

83 **intelligence take:** Hersh, p. 201; FGWII, Aug. 18, 2020; Dobbs, p. 112; Maior, pp. 111–12, 114, 120, 123–24.

84 **from Jews:** Lindsey, July 14, 2020; Mark, p. 322; GW, Aug. 10, 2020; EW, Aug. 19, 2020; FGWII, Aug. 19, 2020; Reeder, Aug. 20, 2020; Hostler, p. 57; Bishop and Crayfield, pp. 101–3; Dobbs, p. 113; Hersh, pp. 204–5; Robert Bishop, Report on X-2 Activities in Bucharest, April 25, 1945, CIA FOIA; FGW letter to PKW, Oct. 13, 1944, WFC; SAINT Bari BB-007 memo to SAINT & DH/125 Washington, Dec. 2, 1944, F: JBX002 1944, E: UD 108A, RG226, NA.

84 **in mind:** SAINT Balkans to SAINT Washington, memo on De-Briefing Field Personnel, Sylvia Press, June 22, 1945, B: 200, E: UD 108-A, RG226, NA.

85 **"and misunderstandings.":** FGW memo to Whitney Shepardson, March 12, 1945, BHP.

85 **or Istanbul:** Recommendation for Award, Wisner, Frank G., Feb. 4, 1945, B: 18, FWP, UVA; Edward Glavin to WJD, memo on OSS Activities in Romania, Sept. 11, 1944, Fr: 971–3, R: 86, M1642, RG226, NA; Romania OSS Mission Assessment, Dec. 1944, B: 20, FWP, UVA.

86 **to Washington:** *The Overseas Targets*, pp. 331–32; Maior, p. 103; FGW memo to Chief, SI, Report on Experience and Conditions Observed in the Field, March 27, 1945, WFC; Recommendation for Award, Wisner, Frank G., Feb. 4, 1945, B: 18, FWP, UVA; Wilson, Rooks, and Glavin cable to FGW, Sept. 27, 1944, Aldrich cable to 109, Oct. 3, 1944, BHP; Saint BARI BB-007 to SAINT Washington, memo on Documents Uncovered in Bucharest with enclosures, Dec. 15, 1944, F: JBX002 1944, E: UD 108A, L. E. Madison to T. S. Ryan, memos on German Documents, Feb. 23 and March 17, 1945, B: 26, E: A1 154, Cables to WJD on FGW, September 1944, Fr: 1122, 1259, 1260–61, 1269–74, 1276, R: 86, M1642, RG226, NA.

86 **not to do:** Hersh, p. 202; Maior, pp. 140, 142; FGW memo to Chief, SI, Report on Experience and Conditions Observed in the Field, March 27, 1945, WFC; Bishop and Crayfield, pp. 95, 99, 141; FGW in World War II monograph by FGWII, WFC; Hazard, p. 43; *The Overseas Targets*, p. 332.

87 **the Russians:** FGW letter to his mother, Dec. 31, 1944, B: 2, Recommendation for Award, Wisner, Frank G., Feb. 4, 1945, B: 18, FGW memo to Charles Cabell, March 1, 1965, B: 8, FGW photos of Bucharest, B: 20, FWP, UVA; Robert

Bishop, Report on X-2 Activities in Bucharest, April 24, 1945, CIA FOIA; Joseph Rodrigo memo to WJD, Oct. 3, 1944, Fr: 965–66, R: 87, M1642, B. M. Bowie to FGW, memo on German Morale Questions, Nov. 3, 1944, B: 26, E: A1 154, RG226, NA; WJD cable to Deane, Sept. 29, 1944, BHP; FGW memo to Chief, SI, Report on Experience and Conditions Observed in the Field, March 27, 1945, WFC.

87 **neighboring homes:** Maior, pp. 97, 140–41; Hersh, p. 196; Memo to Sam Papich on FGW with enclosure, May 24, 1955, FBIW; John Deane letter to P. M. Fitin, Oct. 3, 1944, BHP; German Military Intelligence on Russia, L. E. Madison to H. Harper, memo on German Intelligence on Russian Equipment, Jan. 25, 1945, FGW memo to R. P. Joyce and Lieutenant Colonel Maddox, Nov. 2, 1944, B: 26, E: A1 154, RG226, NA; Bishop and Crayfield, pp. 142–43.

88 **put it:** WJD cable to Deane, Nov. 3, 1944, BHP; Hazard, p. 47; Caserta cable to Foster and Cheston, Sept. 21, 1944, BHP; L. E. Madison to H. Harper, memo on Attached Statement on Russian "atrocities," Jan. 23, 1945, B: 26, E: A1 154, RG226, NA.

88 **jail immediately:** Hazard, pp. 34, 47–49, 56; Wolff, p. 344; Green, Bari cable for FGW, Sept. 22, 1944, FGW cable to WJD via Joyce, Sept. 26, 1944, Report on Romania, Sept. 19, 1944, FGW cable to WJD, Oct. 13, 1944, BHP; FGW and WJD memos and cables on OSS exchanges with the Russians, Fr: 1122, 1259, 1260–61, 1269–74, 1276, R: 86, WJD to FDR memos on Soviet reparations and political moves in Romania, September 1944, Fr: 1167–75, R: 86, Fr: 311–13, 320, R: 24, M1642, RG226, NA.

89 **wrote Roosevelt:** Wolff, p. 278; Hazard, p. 63; WJD to FDR memos on Soviet reparations and political moves in Romania, September 1944, Fr: 1167–75, R: 86, Fr: 311–13, 320, R: 24, M1642, RG226, NA; Report on Russian activities; political alignment, Oct. 27, 1944, WJD cable to Deane, Sept. 24, 1944. Report on the OSS (R&A) Bucharest Mission, September 1944, BHP; FGW memo on Formation of New Romanian Government, Nov. 8, 1944, B: 26, E: A1 154, RG226, NA.

89 **two months:** FGW letter to PKW, Oct. 13, 1944, WFC.

90 **"off furniture.":** Wolff, pp. 279, 345; Memo on Romania: The Communist Party, Oct. 12, 1944, WJD cable to Deane, Oct. 3, 1944, BHP; WJD memo to Secretary of State, Sept. 26, 1944, R: 330–32, M1642, RG226, NA.

90 **"petroleum industry.":** Wolff, pp. 345–46; Report on Conditions Within Romania, Oct. 11, 1944, Caserta cable to Foster and Cheston, Sept. 21, 1944, BHP; FGW memo to R. P. Joyce and Lieutenant Colonel Maddox, Nov. 2, 1944, B: 26, E: A1 154, FGW cable to Joyce and Maddox, Nov. 5, 1944, Fr: 511–14, R: 87, M1642, RG226, NA.

90 **get the credit:** WJD memo to Secretary of State, Sept. 26, 1944, R: 330–32, M1642, RG226, NA; Summary of Soviet-Communist Tactics Employed in Gaining Political and Economic Control of Romania, FWP, UVA; Joyce cable to WJD and Foster, Oct. 3, 1944, BHP.

90 **from Istanbul:** Hersh, p. 209; Caserta cable to Foster and Cheston, Sept. 21, 1944, BHP; WJD memo to Deane, Sept. 24, 1944, BHP; FGW memo to R. P. Joyce and Lieutenant Colonel Maddox, Nov. 2, 1944, B: 26, E: A1 154, RG226, NA; John Maxson and George Britt memos to FGW, September 1944, B: 8, FGW memo to Whitney Shepardson and Stephen Penrose, April 13, 1945, B: 19, FWP, UVA.

91 **Soviet takeover:** FGW memo to R. P. Joyce and Lieutenant Colonel Maddox, Nov. 2, 1944, B: 26, E: A1 154, RG226, NA; Summary of Soviet-Communist Tactics Employed in Gaining Political and Economic Control of Romania,

FWP, UVA; Memo to FGW on Camp for German Women, Nov. 3, 1944, B: 26, E: A1 154, RG226, NA; WJD report to Deane, Sept. 20, 1944, BHP.

92 **that happened:** Maior, pp. 81, 109, 151; FGW in World War II monograph by FGWII, WFC; Bishop and Crayfield, pp. 95–96, 147–50; Summary of Soviet-Communist Tactics Employed in Gaining Political and Economic Control of Romania, FWP, UVA; WJD to FDR memos on Soviet reparations and political moves in Romania, September 1944, Fr: 1167–75, R: 86, Fr: 311–13, 320, R: 24, M1642, RG226, NA.

92 **security agents:** Bishop and Crayfield, p. 98; FGW memo to Charles Cabell, March 1, 1965, B: 8, FWP, UVA; BS by Army, Nov. 10, 1944, Fr: 517, R: 87, RG226, M1642.

92 **for intervention:** Maior, pp. 1–3, 125; Mark, p. 320, 325; Hyland, p. 35; Hazard, pp. 2–3, 58–59; Gardner, Schlesinger, and Morgenthau, pp. 7, 102; WJD memo to Secretary of State, Sept. 26, 1944, R: 330–32, M1642, RG226, NA; Yellow Book #4, p. 165, Verona files.

93 **she said:** FGW in World War II monograph by FGWII, WFC; Maior, p. 271; *The Overseas Targets*, p. 331; SAINT Balkans to SAINT Washington, memo on De-Briefing Field Personnel, Sylvia Press, June 22, 1945, B: 200, E: UD 108-A, RG226, NA; Robert Bishop, Lee Covington memo to D. C. Crockett, Jan. 20, 1945, CIA FOIA, vol. 2; FGW memo to E. J. Green, R. P. Joyce, W. L. Campbell, Sept. 15, 1944, WFC; Crockett, OHP, p. 36; SAINT Balkans memo to SAINT Washington, De-Briefing of Robert D. Brewster, July 21, 1945, B: 200, E: UD 108-A, RG226, NA.

93 **their reporting:** 109 cable to Glavin, Toulmin, and FGW, Oct. 2, 1944, BHP.

94 **more dire:** Maior, pp. 81, 139, 141; Smith, pp. 27–29; FGW in World War II monograph by FGWII, WFC; FGWII, Aug. 19, 2020.

94 **told Wisner:** J. E. Toulmin letter to FGW, Oct. 6, 1944, B: 8, FWP, UVA.

94 **to Roosevelt:** FGW cable to WJD, Sept. 26, 1944, BHP; Green, Bari cable for FGW, Sept. 22, 1944, Cable to 109, Relay of Bucharest to Caserta #57, Oct. 3 and 5, 1944, message on King Michael ammunition request, Glavin cable to WJD, Oct. 11, 1944, Reports Office cable to Cheston, Foster, and Belin, Oct. 4, 1944, BHP.

95 **security breaches:** Hersh, pp. 202–3; Maior, pp. 146–47; Hazard, pp. 55, 66, 99; Mark, pp. 328, 330, 334; FGW to Commanding Officer, Caserta and Recorder, Board of Officers, memos on promotion of Robert Bishop, Oct. 24, 1944, and Nov. 16, 1945, SAINT Caserta memo to SAINT Washington, Nov. 12, 1944, Roger Pfaff to Edward Glavin, memo on promotion of Major Robert Bishop, March 2, 1945, CREST for FGW; Robert Bishop, Sworn Statement of Lieutenant Colonel Walter Ross Against Major Robert Bishop, Sept. 25, 1945, CIA FOIA, vol. 2; FGW memo to Chief, SI, Report on Experience and Conditions Observed in the Field, March 27, 1945, WFC; Captain Louis Madison OSS personnel file, B: 474, Henry L. Roberts OSS personnel file, B: 650, E: A1 224, L. E. Madison memo to Lieutenant H. Harper, Jan. 29, 1945, B: 26, E: A1 154, Robert Bishop OSS personnel file, B: 58, E: A1 224, RG226, NA; Report of Investigation in case of Major Robert Bishop, Oct. 11, 1945, CIA FOIA, vol. 2.

96 **in Bucharest:** FGW letter to his mother, Dec. 31, 1944, WFC.

96 **up information:** Hazard, p. 64; Mark, p. 324; Maior, p. 99.

96 **"proven invaluable."** Hersh, p. 205; Maior, pp. 102, 132; Bishop and Crayfield, p. 146; Robert Bishop, Report on X-2 Activities in Bucharest, April 25, 1945, CIA FOIA; FGW cable to WJD, Nov. 1, 1944, Early cable to 109, Oct. 15, 1944, FGW memo to R. P. Joyce, Lieutenant Colonel Maddox, and

S. K. Bailey, Jan. 18, 1945, BHP; C. V. R. Schuyler letter of appreciation to FGW, Jan. 25, 1945, B: 11, FWP, UVA.

97 **enlisted men:** Maior, pp. 100, 132, 134; Maddox cable to FGW Nov. 22, 1944, Allied Force Headquarters, Caserta, Italy, memo to War Department Dec. 13, 1944, BHP; Schuyler memo to Gen. Hull, OPD Washington Dec. 10, 1944, B: 8, FWP, UVA.

98 **its removal:** FGW memo to R. P. Joyce, Lieutenant Colonel Maddox, and S. K. Bailey, Jan. 18, 1945, B: 18, FWP, UVA; Hersh, pp. 205–6; Maior, pp. 131, 135; Vassiliev Notebooks Concordance, note on General Cortland Schuyler, compiled by John Earl Haynes, 2008; 109 cable to Buxton, Jan. 10, 1945, FGW cables to Beale and Andrews, Nov. 25 and 27, 1944, BHP.

98 **one memo:** FGW memo to Charles Cabell, March 1, 1965, B: 8, FWP, UVA; Maior, pp. 9, 136, 154–55.

98 **a pioneer:** FGW letter to his mother, Dec. 31, 1944, WFC; WJD message to FGW, Jan. 10, 1945, B: 20, FWP, UVA.

99 **his warnings:** Maior, pp. 145–46.

99 **to a boxcar:** Maior, pp. 151, 156–57; Hazard, p. 68; Bishop and Crayfield, pp. 127–35; To the President, A Report upon Romania from Burton Y. Berry, B: 157, President's Secretary's File, HSTL.

100 **"can remember.":** Mark, p. 325; Katharine Graham interview with Polly Fritchey, Oct. 10, 1989, p. 3, KGP; Evan Thomas, pp. 19, 22; Hazard, p. 69; Maior, pp. 157–58; FGWII, Aug. 19, 2020.

100 **be approved:** Bishop and Crayfield, pp. 151–52; FGW receipts for pistol and canvas bag, B: 11, FWP, UVA.

101 **in the field:** FGW travel orders, Feb. 3, 1945, WFC; Hersh, p. 210; Travel itinerary for FGW, B: 11, FWP, UVA; FGW memo to Charles Cabell, March 1, 1965, B: 8, FWP, UVA; General Orders Number 68, Legion of Merit award for FGW, April 10, 1945, B: 18, FWP, UVA; FWG letter to Ellis Knowles, Jan. 14, 1946, B: 11, FWP, UVA; D. DeBardeleben memo to Executive Officer, SI, on FGW report, March 31, 1945, FGW Theater Service Record, Feb. 5, 1945, WFC.

101 **"and Vienna.":** Roy Melbourne's Report on the U.S. Mission to Romania, B: 20, FWP, UVA; William L. Cary memo to WJD, Jan. 22, 1945, BHP; Edward Glavin memo to WJD, Sept. 11, 1944, Fr: 971–73, R: 86, M1642, RG226.

101 **senior aides:** Hersh, p. 211; FGW memo to Colonel Glavin, R. P. Joyce, and S. K. Bailey on proposed addition to presidential stamp collection, Jan. 9, 1945, Fr: 226–29, R: 107, M1642, RG226, NA; FGW memo to WJD on Communication from King Michael of Romania to the President of the United States, March 1, 1945, with draft of proposed letter for WJD signature, BHP; FDR letter to FGW, Feb. 28, 1945, B: 20, FWP, UVA.

102 **test case:** Hazard, pp. 72–73, 92; Waller, *Wild Bill Donovan*, pp. 285–86; *The Overseas Targets*, pp. 331–35, 351.

102 **operating covertly:** Summary of Soviet-Communist Tactics Employed in Gaining Political and Economic Control of Romania, FWP, UVA; Cable for 109 only for Cheston, Feb. 1, 1945, Fr: 266, R: 87, M1642, RG226, NA.

102 **his children:** FGWII, Aug. 19, 2020; Hazard, p. viii; GW, Sept. 16, 2020.

103 **"so well.":** Maior, pp. 161, 163–64; GW, Dec. 1, 2020; Sylvia letter to FGW, Jan. 1, 1947, B: 1, FGW letter to Robert Alexander, July 23, 1947, B: 5, V. C. Georgescu letters to Wendy Hazard, Jan. 14 and April 7, 1993, B: 21, Letter to FGW, April 19, 1945, B: 11, FWP, UVA; D. DeBardeleben memo to FGW, July 5, 1945, F: WN24600–5, B: 4, E: A1 214, RG226, NA.

Chapter 8: Berlin

104 **"All is well.":** Interviewer's Report for FGW, FGW in World War II monograph by FGWII, WFC.

104 **no allergies:** FGW letter to friends, Jan. 21, 1945, WFC; Interviewer's Report for FGW, FGW letter to AWD, Feb. 1, 1965, WFC; Report of Physical Exam for FGW, B: 18, FWP, UVA.

105 **further duty:** Interviewer's Report on FGW, B: 18, FWP, UVA.

105 **to commander:** FGW memo to Stephen Penrose, Richard Southgate, and Charles Kate, April 18, 1945, John Magruder letter to Julius Holmes, March 20, 1945, William Maddox cable, Feb. 27, 1945, FGW top secret clearance, April 9, 1945, L. D. Flintom to Chief, SI Branch, on FGW promotion, June 1, 1945, WFC; James Forrestal memo to FGW, May 29, 1945, B: 11, FWP, UVA.

106 **immediate supervisor:** Evan Thomas p. 22; FGWII, Oct. 18, 2012; H. K. Heuser and E. W. Erne to R. B. MacLeod, memo on Post Collapse Intelligence Objectives, Aug. 12, 1944, B: 314, E: 190, RG226, NA; Philip Bastedo to AWD, memo on Status Report on OSS Mission to Germany, B: 276, E: 210, Cables to WJD approving OSS deployment to Germany, April 14 and 16, 1945, Fr: 964–68, R: 81, M1642, Memo to WJD from Executive Office on Suggested Introductory Remarks Concerning OSS Mission to Germany, March 31, 1945, Fr: 831–34, R: 81, M1642, RG226, NA.

106 **secret intelligence:** Ziemke, p. 320.

106 **and Czechoslovakia:** Waller, *Disciples*, p. 397; Hersh, p. 212; FGW memo to W. H. Shepardson, S. B. L. Penrose, and Walter Langsam, July 16, 1945, B: 4, E: A1 214, Recommendation for Oak Leaf Cluster to the Legion of Merit for FGW, June 26, 1946, B: 847, E: A1 224, RG226, NA; FGW letter to his mother, June 1, 1945, B: 1, CFC, UVA.

107 **German mission:** RMH to Chief SI, memo on German-Speaking Personnel in SI, Washington, Dec. 28, 1944, B: 57, E: 92, German Mission Progress Report, June 1945, B: 9, E: 99, RG226, NA.

107 **insecticide powder:** Schedule of Expenses and Itinerary of Traveler for FGW, April 26, 1945, Tally-Out packing and loading list for FGW, May 5, 1945, B: 11, FWP, UVA.

107 **a glass:** Waller, *Disciples*, p. 398; Richard Helms, pp. 53–54; Crockett, OHP, pp. 22–23; RMH officer club cards, B: 3, S: 4, Part 2, RHP, GU; Wiesbaden WWII photos, B: 1, MEP, HA; German Mission Progress Report, June 1945, B: 9, E: 99, RG226, NA.

108 **his mother:** Bessel, pp. 171, 273; Lowe, pp. 13, 48–49; MacDonogh, p. 1; Waller, *Disciples*, p. 406; FGW letter to his mother, June 1, 1945, B: 1, CFC, UVA; Memorandum T-4031A, Sept. 15, 1945, B: 489, E: 210, RG226, NA.

108 **forged papers:** *Occupation Forces in Europe Series, 1945–1946, Law, Order, and Security*, Historical Manuscript File, CMH; Waller, *Disciples*, p. 398; Lowe, pp. xiii, xvii, 5, 8, 9, 10, 13, 16, 24–28, 92; Clay, p. 276; Bessel, pp. 264–65, 274; Ziemke, p. 355; MacDonogh, pp. 315–16; Document No. 3, April 20, 1945, written by Stalin, B: 9, Russian and Eastern European Archive Documents Database, NSA.

108 **Army report:** Clay, p. 266; Survey of the Occupation of Germany Through November 1945, Beginning of the Occupation of Germany, CMH.

109 **nuclear device:** Waller, *Disciples*, pp. 401–2; MacDonogh, pp. 471–94; Weinberg, pp. 836–41; Polgar, March 19, 2013; Richie, p. 628; FGW memo to W. H. Shepardson, S. B. L. Penrose, and Walter Langsam, July 16, 1945, B: 4, E: A1 214, Robert Joyce memo on Report for the Month of July 1945, Aug. 23, 1945, B: 11, E: 99, RG226, NA.

110 **develop sources:** Waller, *Disciples*, pp. 402–5; Report on Berlin Operations Base, January 1946–March 1948, pp. 90–92, MN; Polgar, March 19, 2013; Black, Berlin cable to 110 and Schmidt, AMZON, Black, Berlin Memo to Canfield (Only), USFET, Aug. 18, 1945, B: 151, E: 88, RG226, NA; Letter to Colonel Harrison Gearhart, Sept. 5, 1945, Fr: 473–74, R: 44, AWD cable to WJD, March 16, 1945, Fr: 890, R: 81, M1642, RG226, NA.

110 **to him:** Kingsley, Jan. 7, 2008; Waller, *Disciples*, p. 405; Waller, *Wild Bill Donovan*, p. 400.

111 **his breakfast:** Hersh, p. 212; FGWII, Oct. 18, 2012; Petersen, p. 521; Helms, OHP, p. 22.

111 **occupied Germany:** Waller, *Disciples*, p. 406; Recommendation for Oak Leaf Cluster to the Legion of Merit for FGW, June 26, 1946, B: 847, E: A1 224, Lessons from the Resistance to the German Occupation of France, June 1945, B: 741, E: 190, RG226, NA.

111 **managing spies:** Waller, *Disciples*, p. 399; FGW memo to W. H. Shepardson, S. B. L. Penrose, and Walter Langsam, July 16, 1945, Gordon Stewart memo to S. B. L. Penrose, Richard Helms, and Harry Rositzke, March 30, 1946, B: 4, E: A1 214, Arthur Schlesinger Jr. Application for Federal Employment, B:683, Ides van der Gracht personnel file, B: 798, Virginia Rogers Murphy personnel file, B: 547, E: A1 224, RG226, NA.

112 **their own:** Waller, *Disciples*, p. 406; Mauch, pp. 206–8; Helms, OHP, p. 23; Report on Berlin Operations Base, January 1946–March 1948, p. 7, MN; FGW memo to W. H. Shepardson, S. B. L. Penrose, and Walter Langsam, July 16, 1945, B: 4, E: A1 214, Progress Report, R&A/Germany, August 1–31, 1945, B: 9, E: 99, Monthly Report to FGW of Steering Division, SI/Germany, Aug. 2, 1945, B: 4, E: A1 214, RG226, NA; 110, Berlin cable to Suhling, 476, Lee, and Hughes, AMZON, Aug. 11, 1945, B: 151, E: 88, Black USCON to 110, AMZON, cable Re: US 923, B: 15, E: 88, 110, Berlin cable to Bessermann, AMZON, Aug. 17, 1945, B: 151, E: 88, PMFS to Chadbourne Gilpatrick memo on George Wood, April 26, 1946, B: 453, E: 210, Crosby Lewis memo to Chief, SSU Mission to Germany, May 22, 1946, B: 2, E: A1 214, Black for Bratton USCON to Levin AMZON, Reur 839, B: 151, E: 88, RG226, NA; 110, Berlin cable to Lee and Hughes, AMZON, Aug. 11, 1945, BHP.

112 **civilian lives:** Report on Berlin Operations Base, January 1946–March 1948, p. 5, MN; Srodes, p. 365; Recommendation for Oak Leaf Cluster to the Legion of Merit for FGW, June 26, 1946, B: 847, E: A1 224, RG226, NA; FGW letter to his mother, June 1, 1945, B: 1, CFC, UVA.

112 **at Wiesbaden:** Schlesinger, OHP, pp. 38–39; Gerhard P. Van Arkel Theater Service Record, Oct. 22, 1945, B: 797, E: A1 224, RG226, NA; Gerhard Van Arkel interview, B: 1, RSP, HA.

113 **intelligence gathering:** Recommendation for Oak Leaf Cluster to the Legion of Merit for FGW, June 26, 1946, B: 847, E: A1 224, Progress report for FGW, July 1–31, 1945, Memorandum on OSS Mission for Germany as of 30 September 1945, B: 9, E: 99, RG226, NA.

113 **and Czechoslovakia:** Monthly progress report to FGW for July 1–31, 1945, B: 9 E: 99, Recommendation for Oak Leaf Cluster to the Legion of Merit for FGW, June 26, 1946, B: 847, E: A1 224, Edward Gamble memo to OPSAF, London, March 24, 1945, B: 203, E: 210, RMH to George Pratt, June 5, 1945, B: 283, E: 210, W. C. Reddick memo to WJD, May 28, 1945, B: 185, E: 210, L. Wurzel memo to Commanding General, Theater Services Forces, European Theater, Aug. 10, 1945, B: 4, E: A1 214, RG226, NA.

113 **Wehrmacht photographs:** Waller, *Disciples*, p. 401; Ides van der Gracht memo to FGW with July 1945 progress report, Aug. 3, 1945, B: 9, E: 99, Art Looting

Investigation Unit Final Report, B: 505, E: 92, RG226, NA; Gerhard Van Arkel interview, B: 1, RSP, HA.

114 **"the world":** Kingsley, Jan. 7, 2008; Waller, *Disciples*, p. 408; Cryptonym list, E: ZZ19, RG263, NA; Petersen, p. 525; Polgar, March 19, 2013; Monthly Report to FGW of Steering Division, SI/Germany, Aug. 2, 1945, B: 4, E: A1 214, T. J. Betts memo to A.C. of S., G-2 for 6th and 12th Army Groups, May 8, 1945, B: 20, E: 99, Emmy Rado memo to WJD, May 4, 1943, Fr: 1223, R: 104, M1642, F. L. Mayer memo on Russia, Dec. 11, 1944, B: 439, E: 210, WJD memo to General Marshall, Aug. 5, 1944, Fr: 492–94, R: 20, M1642, RG226, NA.

115 **new conflict:** Kingsley, Jan. 7, 2008; Schlesinger, OHP, p. 32–34; Hersh, pp. 158–59; Peter Sichel manuscript provided to author; Cynthia Helms, p. 107; FGWII, Sept. 9, 2020; Goodwin and Jamison, vol. 1, pp. 121, 124; Mondimore, p. 32; EW, Aug. 5, 2020; Arthur Schlesinger letter to FGW, Aug. 27, 1954, FGW letter to Arthur Schlesinger Jr., Feb. 16, 1945, B: 9, FWP, UVA; George Pratt letter to FGW, June 23, 1945, B: 114, E: 148, FGW memo to Whitney Shepardson, April 9, 1945, B: 439, E: 210, Intelligence Requirements on Russian Zone/Germany, Aug. 21, 1945, Nine Seven One memo to Paris and Caserta with enclosure, May 30, 1945, B: 439, E: 210, Franklin Canfield memo to AWD, June 7, 1945, B: 203, E: 210, RG226, NA.

115 **spy unit:** Peter Sichel manuscript provided to author; MacDonogh, p. 115; Polgar, March 19, 2013; SCI Seventh Army memo with enclosure, Dec. 4, 1945, B: 275, E: 108A, RG226, NA.

116 **Heinrich Himmler:** EW, Aug. 5, 2020; Waller, *Disciples*, p. 407; FGWII, Oct. 18, 2012; Passes to travel in Berlin, B: 3, S: 1, Part 2, RHP, GU; FGW letter to John Ellis Knowles with enclosure, Nov. 22, 1963, B: 4, FGW photo of his travel passes, B: 20, FWP, UVA; 110, Berlin cable to Canfield, Usfet Sept. 3, 1945, B: 151, E: 88, RG226, NA.

116 **per day:** Waller, *Disciples*, pp. 403–4; Richie, pp. 632–33; Lowe, pp. 7–8; MacDonogh, p. 118; Ziemke, p. 347; Clay, p. 21.

117 **their weapons:** Lowe, pp. 97–98; Ziemke, p. 349; Richie, p. 639; Read and Fisher, pp. 416, 438–39; MacDonogh, p. 211; Montgomery, July 17, 2012.

117 **labor camps:** Bessel, pp. 202–3, 296, 420–21; MacDonogh, pp. 202, 214; Richie, pp. 609, 622, 624–25, 641–43, 647; Lowe, p. 332; Report of Sachsenhausen Concentration Camp, Nov. 5, 1945, Notes on the Communist and Social Democratic Parties in Berlin, Sept. 15, 1945, B: 169, E: 108, STILT USCON cable to Tiger, AMZON WT NR 75, Black cable to 110 and Morse, AMZON, Aug. 8, 1945, B: 151, E: 88, 110 cable to Carib, Feb. 5, 1945, B: 15, E: 119, Russian Order for Requisitioning of Labor, Feb. 1, 1946, Fr: 1225, R: 1, M1656, RG226, NA.

117 **the plundering:** Richie, p. 612; Waller, *Disciples*, p. 411; Peter USCON cable to FGW and van der Gracht, AMZON, August 1945, B: 151, E: 88, RG226, NA; WJD memo to FDR, May 14, 1945, Fr: 314–15, R: 57, M1642, Memorandum T-4031A, Sept. 15, 1945, B: 489, E: 210, RG226, NA.

118 **missile program:** MacDonogh, pp. 239–40, 259; Ziemke, p. 315; Memorandum T-4031A, Sept. 15, 1945, B: 489, E: 210, RG226, NA; Memo on Project Paperclip, AG 231.2 GID-AGO, Feb. 21, 1949, National Archives Military Records Retain File, NA; Memo on Dismantling in the French Zone June 7, 1946, Fr: 206, R: 3, M1656, RG226, NA.

118 **Russian intelligence:** Murphy et al., pp. 6, 27–29; Ziemke, pp. 298–303, 305; Clay, pp. 26–27; Richie, pp. 609, 622, 627, 638; Polgar, March 19, 2013; Report on Berlin Operations Base, January 1946–March 1948, pp. 90–92, MN; Waller, *Disciples*, p. 412; Black USCON cable to 110 and Morse AMZON Message No. 5, B: 151, E: 88, Saint cable to Saint, DB1 on Russian Agents in Austria,

May 3, 1946, B: 1, E: A1 214, Preliminary Outline of the Russian Intelligence Service, Strategic Services Unit, B: 37, E: 211, RG226, NA.

119 **were fired:** Helms, OHP, pp. 25–26; Murphy et al., p. 19; Security Branch Progress Report, September 1–30, 1945, B: 9, E: 99, RG226, NA.

119 **keep quiet:** Weiner, p. 9; Murphy et al., p. 11, Waller, *Disciples*, pp. 407–8; Zuhkov message to Red Army commanders of the 1st Belorussian Front, April 24, 1945, B: 9, F: R11507, Russian and Eastern European Archive Documents Database, NSA; SSU Memo on Anti-American Literature, April 9, 1946, Fr: 79–80, R: 2, M1656, NA.

120 **bombed-out Berlin:** MacDonogh, pp. 8, 119, 228–30; Murphy et al., p. 8; Kingsley, Jan. 7, 2008; Waller, *Disciples*, p. 405; Peter Sichel manuscript provided to author; Report on Berlin Operations Base, January 1946–March 1948, pp. 90–92, MN; Peter Sichel to Gordon Stewart, memo on SI Activity in Berlin, March 19, 1946, B: 4, E: A1 214, Black USCON cable to 110 and Services, AMZON, Message No. 9, Black, Berlin cable to 110 and Services, AMZON, Message No. 15, Peter, No. 10, Berlin cable to van der Gracht and Wisner, AMZON, Aug. 9, 1945, B: 151, Helms, Berlin cable to van der Gracht, AMZON, Nov. 26, 1945, Helms, Berlin cable to van der Gracht, AMZON, Nov. 29, 1953, B: 152, E: 88, RG226, NA.

121 **attempting them:** Waller, *Disciples*, pp. 408–9; Helms, Berlin cable to van der Gracht, AMZON, Oct. 30, 1945, BHP; Philip Horton memo on needed documents and cover information, June 25, 1945, B: 4, E: A1 214, Progress Report, CD Germany, September 1945, B: 9, E: 99, CD Division, SI, OSS Mission for Germany, memo to OSS Units concerned, June 16, 1945, B: 4, E: A1 214, Memo to RMH on C&D Service, Aug. 12, 1946, B: 4, E: A1 214, Progress Report, CD Germany, July and August, 1945, B: 9, E: 99, Peter Sichel memo to Hoyt Irving, July 16, 1946, B: 4, E: A1 214, OSS/Mission for Germany, Progress Report, August 1–31, 1945, B: 9, E: 99, RG226, NA.

121 **the Balkans:** Waller, *Disciples*, pp. 406, 409–10; Schlesinger, OHP, pp. 35–36; Peter Sichel manuscript provided to author; Murphy et al., p. 421; Kingsley, Jan. 7, 2008; Recruiting of Wehrmacht officers by American Agents memo, July 20, 1948, Fr: 1036, R: 3, M1656, NA; Monthly Progress Report, X-2 Branch, May 1945, B: 276; E: 108A, Russian Deserters in the Berlin Area report, September 1945, B: 169, E: 108, The Red Army in Germany: Desertions, Crimes, Political Opinions report, April 1946, Fr: 264–65, R: 2, M1656, Survey of Berlin Operations, November 28, 1945, B: 1, E: 213, Richard Cutler memo to Crosby Lewis, Oct. 31, 1945, B: 2, E: 213, RG226, NA.

122 **a try:** Waller, *Disciples*, p. 409; FGW cable to 110, Berlin, Sept. 11, 1945, B: 9, E: 211, Bloomingdale Project Folder #9, AWD and FGW, AMZON cable to Chapin & Perry, Salzburg, Message No. 222, B: 160, E: 210, RG226, NA.

122 **spy service:** Waller, *Disciples*, p. 413; Murphy et al., p. 408; Memo to Secretariat, OSS Det. (Main), APO 413 on Code Names, July 11, 1945, B: 272, E: 210, RG226, NA.

122 **OSS memo:** Ranelagh, p. 137; Peter Sichel memo to Gordon Stewart, March 19, 1946, B: 4, E: A1 214, RG226, NA.

123 **its troops:** Monthly report to FGW of Steering Division, Sept. 5, 1945, B: 4, E: A1 214, Russian Financial Plans for Russian Zone report, Sept. 7, 1945, Report on Food Situation in the Russian Zone, May–Aug. 1945, B: 169, E: 108, Peter, Berlin cable to van der Gracht, Nov. 2, 1945, B: 152, E: 88, RG226 NA.

123 **stopped coming:** Monthly report to FGW of Steering Division, Sept. 5, 1945, B: 4, E: A1 214, 154 and 971 cable to Thayer, Chapin, and Perry, AMZON, Relay to Salzburg, Aug. 1, 1945, B: 192, E: 134, Monthly Report to FGW of Steering Division, SI/Germany, Aug. 2, 1945, B: 4, E: A1 214, RG226, NA.

123 **any mischief:** Monthly Report to FGW of Steering Division, SI/Germany, Aug. 2, 1945, B: 4, E: A1 214, Memo to FGW on SI/Steering Division—Report of August 1945, B: 9, E: 99, Notes on WJD meeting with aides, Jan. 4, 1945, B: 359, E: 210, Political Situation in the Russian and British Zones report, March 1946, Fr: 26–28, R: 2, M1656, Acting Chief, FBM and DH136, memo to Commanding Officer, SSU WD Mission to Austria, Oct. 9, 1946, B: 2, E: 215, Situation in the French Zone report, April 18, 1946, Fr: 329–30, R: 2, M1656, Saint, AMZON memo to Saint, Paris, Oct. 17, 1946, B: 3, E: 213, Memo on French Efforts to Recruit German General Staff Officers, Nov. 6, 1946, B: 3, E: 210, Memo on Project Marrietta, Nov. 4, 1946, B: 2, E: 213, RG226, NA; Waller, *Disciples*, pp. 411–12.

124 **as well:** Clay, p. 62; Ziemke, pp. 324–25; Lowe, p. 412; MacDonogh, p. 241; Waller, *Disciples*, p. 413; Helms, July 18, 2002; Peter Sichel manuscript provided to author; Sichel, March 11, 2013; Reeder, Aug. 20, 2020; Personnel Roster of SI/Germany as of September 15, 1945, B: 4, E: A1 214, RG226, NA.

124 **serious problem:** Richard Helms, p. 58; Ziemke, pp. 354, 421–23; Atkinson, pp. 544–45; Lowe, pp. 46, 57; Rumors in Russian Zone report, Feb. 7, 1946, B: 169, E: 108, RG226, NA; *Occupation Forces in Europe Series, 1945–1949, Morale and Discipline in the European Command*, CMH.

124 **enlisted subordinates:** *Occupation Forces in Europe Series, 1945–1949, Morale and Discipline in the European Command*, CMH; Clay, pp. 63–64; Ziemke, pp. 336–38; MacDonogh, p. 376.

125 **spy trade:** Waller, *Disciples*, pp. 414–16; Kingsley, Jan. 7, 2008; Sichel, March 11, 2013; Ruffner, "You Are Never Going to Be Able to Run an Intelligence Unit," pp. 15–16; Andrew Haensel and Gustav Mueller personnel and investigation files, B: 206, 303, 544, E: A1 224, Memo to FGW on Monthly Progress Report for SI/Production Division, Sept. 1–30, 1945, B: 9, E: 99, RG 226, NA.

126 **their zone:** Waller, *Disciples*, pp. 412–13; Recommendation for Oak Leaf Cluster to the Legion of Merit for FGW, June 26, 1946, B: 847, E: A1 224, OSS Mission to Germany, September Report, B: 9, Monthly Progress Report, X-2 Branch, September 1945, B: 9, Summary of OSS Activities During September 1945, B: 11, E: 99, RG226, NA.

126 **the SSU:** Number of personnel in OSS as of Sept. 30, 1945, FRUS, 1945–1950, pp. 206–9; Waller, *Wild Bill Donovan*, pp. 315–38; Waller, *Disciples*, p. 417; SSU as of mid-October 1945, memo to Assistant Secretary of War, B: 7, E: 99, Monthly report to FGW of Steering Division, Oct. 4, 1945, B: 4, E: A1 214, WJD cable to his overseas stations, Sept. 27, 1945, B: 192, E: 134, RG226, NA.

126 **Wisner said:** Richard Helms, pp. 61–62; Hersh, p. 213; Wisner cable to Suhling et al., Oct. 26, 1945, B: 192, E: 134, Wisner cable to aides in Germany, Oct. 29, 1945, B: 152, E: 88, RG226, NA.

127 **considered necessary:** Magruder cable to Bross, Oct. 5, 1945, B: 521, E: 210, RG226, NA; Cable to Cheston and Magruder from 110, Suhling, Wisner, Hughes, Lewis, and Black, Sept. 29, 1945, B: 193, E: 134, Franklin Canfield memo to John Bross and Lewis Gable, Sept. 11, 1945, B: 292, E: 190, RG226, NA.

127 **future hiring:** Waller, *Disciples*, p. 417; Report on Berlin Operations Base, January 1946–March 1948, p. 8, MN; Monthly report to FGW of Steering Division, Nov. 5, 1945, B: 4, E: A1 214, Magruder cable to 110 and Suhling, Oct. 4, 1945, B: 192, E: 134, RG226, NA.

127 **return home:** Waller, *Disciples*, pp. 417–18; Lewis and MacPherson cable to Yorker and Ream, Dec. 19, 1945, B: 608, E: 88, Hubert Will memo to James Murphy, Dec. 18, 1945, B: 3, E: 122, Secretariat memo to Douglas Dimond, Dec. 10, 1945, B: 203, E: A1 224, W. G. Suhling memo to AWD, Sept. 5, 1945,

Fr: 237–41, R: 74, M1642, 110, Morse, Black, Bastedo, Berlin cable to O'Malley and Suhling, AMZON, Sept. 2, 1945, B: 151, E: 88, RG226, NA.

128   **with Russia:** Waller, *Disciples*, pp. 417–19; Richard Helms, p. 63; Kingsley, Jan. 7, 2008; FGW memo to Whitney Shepardson, Aug. 28, 1945, WFC; Sichel, March 11, 2013; Evan Thomas, p. 23; Else and Bailey to FGW and Kingsley, AMZON, Sept. 5, 1945, B: 192, E: 134, Recommendation for Oak Leaf Cluster to the Legion of Merit for FGW, June 26, 1946, B: 847, E: A1 224, Cover Designation Authorized for Use by Strategic Services Unit, War Department, Mission to Germany, Feb. 19, 1945, B: 4, E: A1 214, SI, Salzburg cable to Penrose, Else, and Bailey Sept. 9, 1945, B: 468, E: 190, FGW memo to Whitney Shepardson, Stephen Penrose, and Howard Chapin, Dec. 6, 1945, FGW report of SI Operations—Berlin, Nov. 17, 1945, B: 4, E: A1 214, RG226, NA; FGW memo to Whitney Shepardson, Aug. 28, 1945, BHP; John Magruder memo to RMH, Dec. 20, 1945, B: 2, S: 1, Part 1, RHP, GU.

128   **as well:** Evan Thomas, p. 23; MacDonogh, pp. 172–73; Hersh, p. 214; FGW cable to Chapin, Nov. 21, 1945, B: 193, E: 134, RG22, NA.

128   **the idea:** Ziemke, pp. 407–10; MacDonogh, p. 497; Waller, *Wild Bill Donovan*, pp. 308–14; Waller, *Disciples*, p. 419; Richard Helms, pp. 64–65; Commander, U.S. Naval Forces, Germany, memo to FGW, Dec. 11, 1945, Travel orders to FGW and RMH, Dec. 11, 1945, Travel itinerary for FGW trip from Frankfort to Washington, DC, Dec. 11–16, 1945, B: 11, FWP, UVA.

129   **had done:** Maior, p. 173; FGW citation for Army Commendation Ribbon, B: 20, FWP, UVA; Recommendation for Oak Leaf Cluster to the Legion of Merit for FGW, June 26, 1946, B: 847, E: A1 224, RG226, NA; PKW letter to Mrs. Taylor, September 17, 1945, WFA.

129   **part of it:** Evan Thomas, pp. 10–11; FGW in World War II monograph by FGWII, WFC.

Chapter 9: Home

133   **richest nation:** McCullough, pp. 469–70, 520; Pierce, pp. 1, 4; Halberstam, *The Fifties*, p. x; Pruitt, pp. 2–4.

134   **not unwind:** Katharine Graham interview with Polly Fritchey, Oct. 10, 1989, p. 2, KGP; GW, Dec. 10, 2020; Evan Thomas, p. 353; FGW memo to the Chief of Naval Personnel, Dec. 29, 1945, and Chief of Naval Personnel reply, Jan. 5, 1946, B: 11, FWP, UVA.

134   **& Milburn:** Separation Process for FGW, Jan. 4, 1946, WFC; A Biographic Sketch of FGW by Arthur Jacobs, WFC; Elizabeth Cashell memo to Miss Mayer, Dec. 19, 1945, Chief of Naval Personnel memo to FGW, Dec. 20, 1945, U.S. Naval Personnel Separation Center (Officer) document for FGW, Jan. 8, 1946, B: 11, FWP, UVA.

134   **little Wendy:** Maior, p. 176; Hersh, p. 215; EW, Aug. 19, 2020; FGWII, July 8 and Sept. 9, 2020; E. J. Nofer letter to FGW, Sept. 8, 1947, B: 7, Dean Worcester letter to FGW, May 1, 1945, Alexander Chisholm letter to Dear "Col," April 12, 1947, B: 4, Secretary to Mr. Leeds letter to FGW, June 6, 1947, B: 7, FWP, UVA; "Obituary: Elizabeth 'Wendy' Wisner Hazard," *Portland Press Herald*.

135   **considering hiring:** Ellis and Clark, p. 75; FGWII, July 8, 2020; EW, Sept, 22, 2020; Evan Thomas, p. 23; Grose, pp. 258, 281–82; Mosley, p. 238; WJD memo to All Personnel, Sept. 13, 1945, B: 11, FGW letter to AWD, May 22, 1947, B: 3, FWP, UVA; Interview with PKW, B: 10, RSP, HA; RMH letter to Harry Harper, B: 455, E: 210, RG226, NA.

135   **the group:** Grose, p. 259; Anderson, p. 141; Walter Mallory letter to FGW, May 21, 1946, AWD letter to FGW, May 24, 1946, FGW letter to Walter Mallory,

Aug. 5, 1947, Philip Reed letters to Walter Mallory, Aug. 11, 1947, and to FGW, Aug. 11, 1947, B: 3, FWP, UVA.

135 **that resulted:** FGWII, Sept. 9, 2020.

135 **nuclear weapon:** McCullough, pp. 349–50, 355, 376–79, 496–97, 508; Halberstam, *The Fifties*, pp. 21–22.

136 **be conducted:** McCullough, pp. 463, 467, 512, 518; Leary, pp. 18–19.

136 **first impressions:** McCullough, pp. 399, 403, 409–10, 418–19.

136 **Russian threat:** McCullough, pp. 354—57, 375–76, 486; Ranelagh, pp. 102, 107–8; Leary, p. 18.

137 **him differently:** Hyland, pp. 4, 41–42; Rositzke, p. 14; Halberstam, *The Fifties*, p. 359.

137 **not do so:** Rositzke, pp. 14–15; Psychological and Political Warfare, Preface, Emergence of the Intelligence Establishment, from the Strategic Services Unit to the Office of Special Operations, FRUS, 1945–1950; 102. Memorandum from the Director of Strategic Services Unit, Department of War (Magruder) to Secretary of War Patterson, Feb. 4, 1946, FRUS, 1945–1950; Lilly, p. 19; Darling, p. 94.

137 **a president:** Warner, *The CIA Under Harry Truman*, p. 471; Corson, p. 273.

137 **a service:** Office of Policy Coordination 1948–1952, B: 4, S: 1, PGP, PU; Warner, *The CIA Under Harry Truman*, p. 7; Garthoff, p. 12.

138 **be messy:** Souers's Tenure as Director of Central Intelligence, Emergence of the Intelligence Establishment, FRUS, 1945–1950; Darling, p. 81; Warner, "The Creation of the Central Intelligence Group," p. 111; Garthoff, p. 11; 70. Memorandum from the Director of the Bureau of the Budget (Smith) to the President's Special Counsel (Rosenman), Jan. 10, 1946, FRUS, 1945–1950.

138 **spy service:** Ranelagh, p. 100.

138 **intelligence organization:** Warner, "The Creation of the Central Intelligence Group," p. 111; Leary, pp. 21–22; Ranelagh, pp. 103–4.

139 **Souers's organization:** Leary, pp. 20–21; Waller, *Wild Bill Donovan*, pp. 351–53; 68. Letter from Secretary of State Byrnes, Acting Secretary of War Royall, and Secretary of the Navy Forrestal to HST, Jan. 1, 1946, FRUS, 1945–1950; Ranelagh, p. 103; 105. Memorandum from the Fortier Committee to the Director of Central Intelligence (Souers), March 14, 1946, FRUS, 1945–1950; Souers's Tenure as Director of Central Intelligence, Emergence of the Intelligence Establishment, FRUS, 1945–1950.

139 **its country:** Prados, *Presidents' Secret Wars*, p. 80; Colby, p. 68; Leary, p. 24; Warner, *The CIA Under Harry Truman*, pp. 42–43, 66–67, 123.

139 **not working:** Leary, pp. 16, 21, 24–25; Warner, *The CIA Under Harry Truman*, pp. 85–86; Darling, pp. 75–76.

140 **he coveted:** Garthoff, p. 2; 149. Memorandum from the Director of Central Intelligence (Souers) to the President's Chief of Staff, May 7, 1946, FRUS, 1945–1950; Leary, p. 22; Corson, pp. 285–86.

140 **Special Operations:** Vandenberg's Tenure as Director of Central Intelligence, Emergence of the Intelligence Establishment, FRUS, 1945–1950; Darling, pp. 76, 98, 106a, 112–14, 120–21; Leary, pp. 23–26; Psychological and Political Warfare, From the Strategic Services Unit to the Office of Special Operations, Emergence of the Intelligence Establishment, FRUS, 1945–1950; 114. Memorandum to the Director of Central Intelligence's Executive (Wright), July 11, 1946, FRUS, 1945–1950; Church Committee, Foreign and Military Intelligence, *Final Report*, book 1, p. 102.

140 **it needed:** Darling, p. 106a; Ranelagh, pp. 108–9; Leary, pp. 22–23; Warner, *The CIA Under Harry Truman*, pp. 59–60; 198. Minutes of the Fourth Meeting of the National Intelligence Authority, July 17, 1946, FRUS, 1945–1950.

141 **intelligence agency:** Katharine Graham interview with Polly Fritchey, Oct. 10, 1989, pp. 2–3, KGP; FGWII, Aug. 9, 2020; GW, Sept. 16, 2020; EW, Sept. 22, 2020; Richard Helms, p. 114; Ellis and Clark, pp. 76–77.

141 **Latin America:** Stephen Penrose memo to Donald Galloway, Aug. 21, 1946, WFC; Stephen Penrose letter to FGW, March 3, 1947, B: 8, FWP, UVA.

141 **Washington forever:** Stephen Penrose memo to Donald Galloway, Aug. 21, 1946, WFC; Maior, p. 175; FGWII, Sept. 9, 2020; Hersh, p. 220.

142 **was dropped:** Evan Thomas, p. 24; Hersh, pp. 216–17.

142 **up doing:** EW, Sept. 22, 2020; Grose, p. 282.

Chapter 10: Washington

144 **in DC:** FGW letter to family, Oct. 1, 1947, B: 4, FGW letter to AWD, Oct. 1, 1947, B: 3, Milton Katz letter to FGW, Dec. 11, 1964, B: 2, FWP, UVA; AWD letter to FGW, Oct. 14, 1947, B: 59, ADP, PU; Rositzke, p. 1; McCullough, pp. 539, 547–48, 553–54, 561–65, 583; Katharine Graham interview with Polly Fritchey, Oct. 10, 1989, pp. 3, 48–49, KGP; Prados, *Safe for Democracy*, p. 44.

145 **their worlds:** Katharine Graham interview with Polly Fritchey, Oct. 10, 1989, pp. 1, 4, 5, 7, 11, 14, 18–20, KGP; Graham, pp. 19, 21, 24, 27, 31, 55, 58–59, 108–9, 110–11; 113–17, 121, 153–54, 157–58, 161–64, 183–85, 230–31; Miscellaneous Information on Mary (Polly) Wisner Fritchey, KGP; GW, Sept. 16, 2020; FG-WII, Oct. 19, 2020; "Polly Fritchey Dies," *The Washington Post*, July 11, 2002; OSS files on Philip Graham, B: 16, GHP, HA.

146 **three years:** Herken, pp. 16–17; Heymann, p. 53; Halberstam, *The Fifties*, pp. 132–37; EW, Oct. 6, 2020; FGWII, Sept. 9, 2020.

146 **cold war:** FGWII, Sept. 9, 2020; Isaacson and Thomas, p. 387; A Biographic Sketch of FGW by Arthur Jacobs, WFC; Office of Policy Coordination 1948–1952, B: 4, S: 1, PGP, PU; Darling, p. 250; 249. Report by an Ad Hoc Subcommittee of the State–Army–Navy–Air Force Coordinating Committee SANACC 304/11, Nov. 7, 1947, FRUS, 1945–1950; Attachment A, Deputy Assistant Secretary of State for Occupied Areas, WFC; Leary, p. 38; AWD letter to FGW, Dec. 23, 1947, and FGW reply, Dec. 30, 1947, B: 59, ADP, PU.

147 **for favors:** AWD letter to FGW, Dec. 23, 1947, and FGW reply, Dec. 30, 1947, FGW letter to AWD, March 10, 1948, B: 59, ADP, PU; George Kennan's "Long Telegram," Feb. 22, 1946, WCA; Evan Thomas, p. 24; EW, Nov. 11, 2020; Halberstam, *The Coldest Winter*, pp. 182–87; McCullough, pp. 490–91, 582, 751–60; Isaacson and Thomas, pp. 20, 103, 107; FGWII, Nov. 10, 2020.

147 **living rooms:** McCullough, pp. 548, 670.

147 **another's company:** FGWII, Sept. 9, 2020; Herken, pp. 7–8, 17–19, 25; GW, Sept. 16, 2020; Evan Thomas, pp. 26, 103.

148 **help her:** Graham, p. 164; EW, Oct. 6, 2020; FGWII, Oct. 19, 2020; Herken, pp. 29–30; Bohlen bio, B: 15, GHP, HA; Isaacson and Thomas, p. 21; Ridder, Sept. 7, 2021; Reeder, Aug. 20, 2020.

148 **the rocks:** GW, Aug. 8 and Sept. 16, 2020; FGWII, July 8 and Oct. 19, 2020; EW, Oct. 6, 2020, and Jan. 12, 2021, Ridder, Sept. 7, 2021.

148 **day after:** FGWII, Oct. 19, 2020; Reeder, Aug. 20, 2020; EW, Oct. 6, 2020; Richard Helms, p. 278; GW, Sept. 16, 2020; Hersh, p. 308; Herken, pp. 20, 27; FitzGerald, Dec. 2, 2020; Evan Thomas, p. 103.

149 **the pair:** OSS personnel documents on Stewart Alsop, B: 16, GHP, HA; FG-WII letter to Uncle Joe, July 28, 1965, B: 73, AP, LOC; Joseph Alsop, p. 264; Joseph W. Alsop Oral History Interview—RFK #2, 65/22/1971, B: 17, GHP, HA; J. Edgar Hoover note on Alsop brothers column, J. Edgar Hoover note on memo from L. B. Nichols to Tolson, Dec. 4, 1946, Aug. 4, 1942, FBI report on

Joseph Alsop, Memorandum for the Director, May 31, 1939, J. Edgar Hoover letter to Buel F. Weare, Aug. 21, 1947, M. A. Jones memo to Mr. Nichols, Sept. 2, 1947, FBI FOIA file on Joseph Alsop; EW, Oct. 6 and Nov. 11, 2020; FGWII, Oct. 19, 2020; Herken, pp. 13–14, 19, 22, 28, 35–37, 44–45, 90–92, 134, 153, 258; Alsop, Aug. 11, 2021; Joseph Alsop, pp. 387–88.

150 **the time:** EW, Sept. 22, 2020; Hersh, p. 227; Anderson, pp. 22–27; GW, Sept. 16, 2020; Evan Thomas, pp. 139–40; FGWII, Oct. 19, 2020.

150 **immeasurable pleasure:** EW, Aug. 5, 2020; GW, Aug. 3 and Sept. 16, 2020; FGWII, Sept. 9 and Oct. 19, 2020.

151 **the farm:** GW, Sept. 16, 2020; FGWII, Oct. 19, 202; Evan Thomas, p. 140; FGWII, Oct. 19, 2020; EW, Sept. 22, 2020; EW interview with William L. "Billy" Sigman, Feb. 8, 2013, WFC; Ridder, Sept. 7, 2021; Reeder, Aug. 20, 2020.

151 **with him:** FGWII, Sept. 9, 2020; EW, Sept. 22, 2020; GW, Aug. 3, 2020.

152 **were reading:** GW, Aug. 3, 2020; FGWII, July 8, 2020.

152 **"incipient Gestapo.":** Darling, pp. 183–88; McCullough, p. 741; 215. Memorandum for the Record, May 26, 1947, 217. Letter from the Director of Central Intelligence (Hillenkoetter) to the Chairman of the Senate Armed Services Committee (Gurney), June 3, 1947, FRUS, 1945–1950; Corson, pp. 288–89; Waller, *Wild Bill Donovan*, p. 352; McCullough, p. 476.

152 **own people:** Corson, pp. 292, 298; Ranelagh, p. 109; Organizational History of the Central Intelligence Agency, 1950–1953, pp. 29–33, MN.

153 **members ordered:** Cryptonyms for the CIA, File Unit, Textual Records, E: ZZ19, RG263, NA; 225. Minutes of the First Meeting of the NSC, Sept. 26, 1947, 231. Memorandum from the General Counsel of the CIA (Houston) to Director of Central Intelligence Hillenkoetter, April 7, 1948, 232. Memorandum for the Record, April 8, 1948, FRUS, 1945–1950.

153 **intelligence operations:** Darling, pp. 168a–169a; Organizational History of the Central Intelligence Agency, 1950–1953, pp. 26–27, MN; Ranelagh, pp. 194–95.

153 **first place:** Ranelagh, pp. 111, 117–19, 128; Leary, pp. 37–38.

154 **Naval operations:** Waller, *Wild Bill Donovan*, p. 353; Darling, p. 193a; Ranelagh, pp. 112–13; Warner, *The CIA Under Harry Truman*, p. xvii; 205. Memorandum for the Record, Washington, undated, FRUS, 1945–1950.

154 **in Washington:** "A Look Back . . . Roscoe Hillenkoetter as DCI," CIA News & Information, cia.gov; Richard Helms, p. 81; Darling, p. 285; Corson, p. 298; Snider, p. 44; Warner, *The CIA Under Harry Truman*, p. xvii; Ranelagh, p. 166; Leary, p. 23; The DCI Historical Series, General Walter Bedell Smith as Director of Central Intelligence, October 1950–February 1953, vol. 1, pp. 1-2, 1-3; FGWII, Nov. 10, 2020.

155 **the operation:** Darling, p. 246; Leary, p. 38; Report by Dr. E. Lilly, Dec. 21, 1951, pp. 34, 68, NSC Staff Papers, OCB, Secretariat Series, DEL; Office of Policy Coordination 1948–1952, B: 4, S: 1, PGP, PU; Maior, p. 178; Evan Thomas, pp. 25–28; Wilford, p. 30; Ruffner, "Cold War Allies," pp. 34–35; Ruffner, "Eagle and Swastika," pp. 222–29; Letter to FGW from London, June 2, 1948, B: 2, CFC, UVA.

Chapter 11: Wiz's Secret War
156 **months earlier:** Photo of Truman and NSC members in the Cabinet Room, Aug. 19, 1948, Accession No. 73-2703, HSTL; 299. Memorandum for the President of Discussion at the 18th Meeting of the NSC, Aug. 1948, 300. CIA General Order No. 10, Aug. 27, 1948, 224. Memorandum from Acting Secretary of

State Lovett to Director of Central Intelligence Hillenkoetter, Sept. 23, 1947, FRUS, 1945–1950.

157 **satellite nations:** 292. NSC Directive on Office of Special Projects, June 18, 1948, 300. CIA General Order No. 10, Aug. 27, 1948, FRUS, 1945–1950; Warner, *The CIA Under Harry Truman*, pp. 213–16; Darling, pp. 246, 274; Hersh, pp. 226–27; Evan Thomas, pp. 29–30; Leary, p. 41.

157 **busy men:** Report by Dr. E. Lilly, Dec. 21, 1951, pp. 1–10, 12–13, 21, 25, NSC Staff Papers, OCB, Secretariat Series, DEL; Richard Helms, pp. 109–10; Lilly, p. 25; Hazard, p. 195; Leary, p. 43; Corson, pp. 303–4.

158 **a unit:** 269. Policy Planning Staff Memorandum, May 4, 1948, FRUS, 1945–1950; Office of Policy Coordination 1948–1952, DOC_0000104823, https://www.cia.gov/readingroom/docs/DOC_0000104823.pdf; Joseph Alsop, p. 307; Herken, pp. 30–38; Leary, p. 41; Warner, *The CIA Under Harry Truman*, p. xx; Psychological and Political Warfare, Introduction, From the Strategic Service Unit to the Office of Special Operations, Emergence of the Intelligence Establishment, FRUS, 1945–1950.

158 **performed poorly:** Darling, pp. 245a–246a, 253–57; Evan Thomas, p. 29; Ranelagh, p. 116; Leary, pp. 40–41; 276. Memorandum for the Director of the Policy Planning Staff (Kennan) to the Undersecretary of State (Lovett) and Secretary of State Marshall, May 19,1948, FRUS, 1945–1950; Michael Warner, "The CIA's Office of Policy Coordination from NSC 10/2 to NSC 68," B: 4, S: 1, PGP, PU; Warner, *The CIA Under Harry Truman*, pp. xx, 191–95, 201–3; Weiner, p. 26; 260. Office of Special Operations Directive No. 18/5 (Interim), Feb. 24, 1948, FRUS, 1945–1950.

158 **the admiral:** Leary, p. 42; Darling, pp. 246a, 275–76; Ranelagh, p. 134.

159 **that idea:** Office of Policy Coordination 1948–1952, *Studies in Intelligence* 17, no. 2-s (summer 1973); The Central Intelligence Agency and National Organization for Intelligence: A Report to the NSC by Allen Dulles, William H. Jackson, and Mathias Correa, Jan. 1, 1949, pp. 133–34; Darling, pp. 272–73; 277. Memorandum for the President of Discussion at the 11th Meeting of the NSC, May 20, 1948, 287. Attachment /3/ Memorandum from Director of Central Intelligence Hillenkoetter to the Assistant Executive Secretary of the NSC (Lay), June 9, 1948, 262. Memorandum from Secretary of Defense Forrestal to the Executive Secretary of the NSC, March 26, 1948, 367. Memorandum from FGW to Director of Central Intelligence Hillenkoetter, Feb. 14, 1949, FRUS, 1945–1950; Warner, *The CIA Under Harry Truman*, p. 204; Leary, p. 41; McCullough, pp. 603, 630–31, 647–48; Pisani, p. 59; Report by Dr. E. Lilly, Dec. 21, 1951, pp. 40–44, NSC Staff Papers, OCB, Secretariat Series, DEL; Murphy et al., p. 55; Document 132. ORE 46-49 Excerpt, May 3, 1949, The Possibility of Direct Soviet Military Action During 1949, p. 309, CIA Library, cia.gov; CIA's Analysis of the Soviet Union, 1947–1991, pp. 19, 21, 24–25, CIA Library, https://www.cia.gov/resources/csi/static/CIAs-Analysis-of-the-Soviet-Union-1947-1991-complete-collection-1.pdf; Lilly, p. 53; Hersh pp. 219–20; FGWII, Nov. 10, 2020.

159 **friend said:** Darling, p. 270; 248. Memorandum from the Deputy Director (Wright) to Director of Central Intelligence Hillenkoetter, Nov. 4, 1947, 294. Memorandum from the Director of the Policy Planning Staff (Kennan) to the Under Secretary of State (Lovett), June 30, 1948, FRUS, 1945–1950; Evan Thomas, pp. 30–31; Interview with PKW, B: 10, RSP, HA.

159 **secretary displayed:** Office of Policy Coordination 1948–1952, *Studies in Intelligence* 17, no. 2-s (summer 1973); Hersh, p. 227; Corson, p. 307; Ranelagh, p. 134; Powers, pp. 34–35; Weiner, p. 31.

160 **admiral's CIA:** Draft Working Paper, Chapter Seven, on CIA and Nazi War Criminals and Collaborators, Chapter 1–10, Draft Working Paper 0008, declassified by CIA; A Biographic Sketch of FGW by Arthur Jacobs, pp. 19–20, WFC; Warner, *The CIA Under Harry Truman*, p. 217; Darling, pp. 277–79; Maior, p. 184; Hersh, p. 227; Michael Warner, "The CIA's Office of Policy Coordination from NSC 10/2 to NSC 68," B: 4, S: 1, PGP, PU; 298. Memorandum of Conversation and Understanding, Aug. 6, 1948, FRUS, 1945–1950; FGW letter to Robert Blum, Aug. 11, 1948, with enclosed Memorandum of Conversation and Understanding, Aug. 10, 1949, draft on Implementation of NSC 10/2, WFC.

161 **as the CIA:** CIA Notification of Personnel Action for FGW on pay raise, Sept. 5, 1948, Hillenkoetter temporary security waiver for FGW, Aug. 26, 1948, WFC; Powers, p. 35; 381. Memorandum from FGW to CB, April 15, 1949, p. 352. Memorandum from FGW to Director of Central Intelligence Hillenkoetter, Sept. 13, 1948, 355. Verbatim Minutes of a Meeting of the Intelligence Advisory Committee, Dec. 3, 1948, FRUS, 1945–1950; Lilly, p. 25; OPC Cryptonyms, E: ZZ19, RG263, NA.

161 **"Organization X.":** Grose, p. 301.

161 **that country:** Herken, p. 80; Paul H. Nitze Oral History Interviews, Aug. 5 and 6, 1975, p. 74, HSTL; McCargar, FAOH, p. 77; 313. Letter from Secretary of Defense Johnson to Secretary of State Acheson, Oct. 7, 1949, Emergence of the Intelligence Establishment, 1945–1950, FRUS; Leary, pp. 46–47; Warner, *The CIA Under Harry Truman*, p. xxi; Robert Joyce Curriculum Vitae, WFC; George Kennan letter to Wendy Wisner Hazard, Jan. 25, 1995, B: 18, FWP, UVA; 310. Memorandum from FGW to Members of His Staff, June 1, 1949, FRUS, 1945–1950.

162 **for $1.20:** Phillips, pp. 47, 112; Darling, p. 280; Evan Thomas, p. 358; Herken, p. 99; FGWII, Oct. 19, 2020; Interview with Lyman Kirkpatrick, B: 10, RSP, HA; Memo to FGW, Dec. 16, 1952, on Director's Dining Room, B: 11, FWP, UVA; Photos of OPC and CIA buildings along the Reflecting Pool provided to the author by the CIA History Staff.

162 **legal skills:** History of OPC/EE-1, Sept. 1948–January 1952, 114.5, CREST for FGW; Evan Thomas, pp. 15–16; Hersh, p. 228; Ridder, Sept. 7, 2021; Pisani, pp. 32–33.

162 **good friends:** Herken, p. 81; Frank Lindsay interview, July 26, 2000, CIA Oral History Program, CIA History Staff, pp. 3–7, 10–11, 13–15; FGW letter to Stewart Alsop, Jan. 22, 1964, Stewart Alsop reply, Jan. 27, 1964, B: 1, FWP, UVA; Frank Lindsay biographical material, B: 9, FLP, HA.

163 **through Billie:** FGWII, Dec. 11, 2020, and March 15, 2021; Director's Meeting minutes, Aug. 1, 1951, CREST for FGW; EW, Oct. 20, 2020; Project PBSuccess Daily Notes RE Arms Shipment to Guatemala, April 7–June 29, 1954, notes for April 27, 1954, https://www.cia.gov/readingroom/docs/DOC _0000934420.pdf; Correspondence on Billie Morrone dealing with Wisner family financial affairs, B: 5, Tracy Barnes letter to Billie Morrone, Jan. 21, 1957, B: 1, FGW tape 1/29/57 B: 10, FWP, UVA.

163 **driver's license:** Evan Thomas, pp. 33–34, 85, 114; McCargar, FAOH, pp. 1–9, 56–57; Hersh, pp. 242–43; Harry Rositzke, "It Would Take More Than a Memoir to Explain E. Howard Hunt" (book review of Hunt autobiography), *Washington Star,* Jan. 19, 1975, CREST for FGW; Hunt, pp. 3–7, 9, 15, 23–25, 34, 39, 40–46; EW, Sept. 22, 2020.

164 **homosexual activities:** George Kennan report on Performance with the National War College in fall term, 1946, of Foreign Service Officer Carmel Offie, Notes on State Department investigation of Carmel Offie, William

Bullitt letter to Howland Shaw, Oct. 13, 1939, Investigative report on Carmel Offie with transcript of Q&A, Dec. 3, 1947, FBI memo for Tolson, Ladd, and Nichols, Feb. 4, 1953, B: 1, S: 1, PGP, PU; Evan Thomas, pp. 34–35; Hersh, pp. 42–43, 245–47, 252–55, 295; Anderson, pp. 179–82; FGWII, Oct. 19, 2020; EW, Oct. 20, 2020; Herken, p. 106; McCargar, FAOH, p. 87; SAC, WFO memo to Director, FBI, Dec. 9, 1952, on Carmel Offie Espionage—X, FBI file on Carmel Offie, MN.

164 **a jeep:** Phillips, p. 70; Prados, *Safe for Democracy*, pp. 45, 47; Herken, pp. 84–85; EW, Sept. 22, 2020.

164 **called them:** Daily Notes DD/S, June 17, 1955, DM-599; Minutes for Deputies' Meeting, Oct. 16, 1957, CREST for FGW; Deputy for Language Training to Chief, Language and Area School, memo on Weekly Activities Report, April 30, 1958, CREST for FGW; Weiner, p. 33; Wilford, p. 128; Corson, pp. 308–9; Herken, pp. 81–82; Prados, *Presidents' Secret Wars*, p. 35; Memo from Colonel White, Comments on Mr. Wisner's Paper on Mr. Kirkpatrick's "Ten Commandments," CREST for FGW; Prados, *Lost Crusader*, pp. 43–44.

165 **paramilitary training:** CIA Orientation Course to be conducted in the U.S. Agriculture Auditorium on Oct. 2–5, 1951, Outline for Office of Training Report, Memo to DCI on Survey of the Office of Training, April 22, 1954, A-DD/A Diary Notes, Aug. 19, 1953, CREST for FGW; Cryptonym for agent training program, E: ZZ19, RG263, NA; Prados, *Safe for Democracy*, p. 49; Prados, *Presidents' Secret Wars*, p. 36; Hunt, pp. 47–48; Colby, pp. 85–86.

165 **dragged on:** Ranelagh, p. 135; Hersh, p. 239; Warner, *The CIA Under Harry Truman*, p. 248; Evan Thomas, p. 63; Church Committee, *Final Report*, book 1, p. 23.

166 **the OPC:** DCI memo to Asst. Director for Policy Coordination of Fiscal Year 1949 Budget, Oct. 25, 1948; Bissell, pp. 68–69; FGWII, Oct. 19, 2020; Ranelagh, pp. 312–13; Pisani, p. 73; Warner, *The CIA Under Harry Truman*, pp. 321–22; Hersh, p. 235; Weiner, pp. 28, 35.

166 **in London:** Report of Efficiency Rating for FGW as of 3/5/49, B: 18, FWP, UVA; Report of Efficiency Rating for FGW as of 25 June 1950, CIA Notification of Personnel Action for FGW, 4/27/49, 10/28/49, and 12/8/49 on salary increases, WFC; Secretary to FGW letter to Bartley & Sons, Feb. 5, 1953, with invoice, B: 1, FWP, UVA; Office of Policy Coordination, 1948–1952, DOC_0000104823, https://www.cia.gov/readingroom/docs/DOC_0000104823.pdf; Hersh, p. 244.

167 **the boss:** Notes on Robert Joyce, B: 9, Interview with Lyman Kirkpatrick, B: 10, RSP, HA; A Biographic Sketch of FGW by Arthur Jacobs, WFC; Leary, p. 46; FGWII, Dec. 11, 2020; Evan Thomas, pp. 63–64; Powers, p. 34; Phillips, pp. 70–72; FGW cable to SR. REP., Guatemala City, July 2, 1954, FGW note, Sept. 8, 1953, on taking notes, CIAGC; Herken, p. 103; James Hanrahan, "An Interview with Former CIA Executive Director Lawrence K. 'Red' White," p. 7, CIA Library, https://www.cia.gov/resources/csi/static/Interview-With-Lawrence-White.pdf; Hersh, pp. 244–45; Howe, July 12, 2012.

168 **was hypomanic:** Mayo Clinic report on Bipolar Disorder, www.mayoclinic.org; Jamison, pp. 5–6; Goodwin and Jamison, vol. 1, pp. 37, 308, 381, 397, 402; Mondimore, p. xi; FGWII, Dec. 11, 2020; GW, Dec. 1, 2020; EW, Dec. 6, 2020.

168 **Hillenkoetter's CIA:** Annelise Kennan letter to PKW, Nov. 16, 1952, B: 7, FWP, UVA; Evan Thomas, pp. 39–40, 137–38; Herken, pp. 62, 73; Hughes, FAOH, p. 92; EW, Nov. 11, 2020; "Frank G. Wisner Dies; Former Official of CIA," obituary, CREST for FGW; O'Toole, p. 446; FGWII, Sept. 9 and Oct. 19, 2020.

168 **would do:** Bohlen, Nov. 17, 2020; Alsop, Aug. 11, 2021; FGWII, July 8, 2020; FitzGerald, Dec. 2, 2020.

169 **quality antiques:** Herken, p. 89–90; McCullough, p. 819; EW, Oct. 6, 2020; GW, Sept. 16, 2020.

169 **from Americans:** Herken, pp. 22, 60; Joseph Alsop, pp. 265–67; Katharine Graham interview with Polly Fritchey, Oct. 10, 1989, p. 2, KGP; Wilford, pp. 225–28; Evan Thomas, p. 105; EW, Oct. 6, 2020.

169 **the farm:** EW, Sept. 22, 2020.

170 **cattle feed:** FGWII, Oct. 19 and Dec. 11, 2020; Frank Lindsay interview, July 26, 2000, CIA Oral History Program, CIA History Staff, p. 37; EW interview with William L. "Billy" Sigman, Feb. 8, 2013, WFC; EW, Sept. 22, 2020; FGW and Charles Breckinridge correspondence, Sept. 12–30, 1947, B: 1, FWP, UVA.

170 **secluded setting:** EW, Oct. 6, 2020; Graham, p. 209; GW, Sept. 16, 2020; EW, Sept. 22 and Nov. 11, 2020; FGWII, Oct. 19, 2020; Ridder, Sept. 7, 2021; Bohlen, Nov. 17, 2020; Transcript of Kay Graham interview with PKW, Katharine Graham interview with Polly Fritchey, Oct. 10, 1989, pp. 14–15, KGP; FGW and RMH correspondence, June 29–30, 1947, B: 6, FWP, UVA.

170 **to the floor:** EW, Aug. 5 and Sept. 22, 2020, and Feb. 18, 2021; FGWII, Oct. 19, 2020.

171 **"eleven-year-old":** FGWII, Jan. 27, 2021; Reeder, Aug. 20, 2020; Lindsey, July 14, 2020; EW, Feb. 18, 2021; Alsop, Aug. 11, 2021.

Chapter 12: Albania

172 **be thin-skinned:** Hunt, p. 46; Evan Thomas, p. 41; 306. Memorandum for FGW to Director of Central Intelligence Hillenkoetter, Oct. 29, 1948, FRUS, 1945–1950; Darling, p. 280; Michael Warner, "The CIA's Office of Policy Coordination from NSC 10/2 to NSC 68," B: 4, S: 1, PGP, PU; Colonel Sheffield Edwards, I&S—Director, on phone call from an angry WJD, March 21, 1949, CREST for FGW; Prados, *Lost Crusader*, p. 38.

173 **two years:** Office of Policy Coordination 1948–1952, *Studies in Intelligence* 17, no. 2-s (summer 1973); Document No. 7, Weekly Summary Excerpt, 23 August 1946, Soviet Military Policy in Eastern Europe, CIA Library, https://www.cia .gov/resources/csi/static/5563bod1-EarlyColdWarDocuments.pdf.

173 **"French psychology.":** Office of Policy Coordination 1948–1952, FOIA for Peter Grose, pp. 11–12, B: 4, S: 1, PGP, PU, 307. Memorandum for the File, Nov. 16, 1948, FRUS, 1945–1950; Office of Policy Coordination 1948–1952, DOC _0000104823, https://www.cia.gov/readingroom/docs/DOC_0000104823 .pdf.

174 **greater good:** Draft Working Paper, Chapter Seven, on CIA and Nazi War Criminals and Collaborators, Chapter 1–10, Draft Working Paper 0008, declassified by CIA; Ruffner, "Eagle and Swastika," pp. 3, 6 of chapter 7, p. 17 of chapter 12; Murphy et al., p. 105; Bower, pp. 90–92; 301. Letter from Acting Secretary of State Lovett to Secretary of Defense Forrestal, Oct. 1, 1948, FRUS, 1945–1950; Evan Thomas, p. 37; 381. Memorandum from FGW to CB, April 15, 1949, FRUS, 1945–1950; Halberstam, *The Fifties*, p. 372.

174 **CIA history:** Church Committee, *Final Report*, book 1, p. 108; Prados, *Presidents' Secret Wars*, pp. 80–81; Hersh, p. 228; McCargar, FAOH, p. 77; Mosley, p. 245; Darling, pp. 280, 321–22, 371; CIA "History Highlights 1949–1974," CREST for FGW.

175 **OSO counterparts:** Corson, pp. 314–15; Montague, vol. 4, pp. 64–66; Leary, pp. 49–50; Warner, *The CIA Under Harry Truman*, p. xxi; Evan Thomas, p. 42; Murphy et al., p. 105.

175 **more money:** FGW memo of 15 September 1948 outlining relationship between OSO and OPC, WFC; Lilly, p. 48; CIA Organizational History in Brief, March 1975, p. 3, declassified by CIA.

176 **of power:** V. P. Keay memo to A. H. Belmont, Jan. 5, 1954, FBIW; Anderson, p. 250; Hunt, p. 45; Hersh, pp. 241–42; 375. Memorandum from FGW to the Under Secretary of State (Webb), March 18, 1949, FRUS, 1945–1950.

176 **David Halberstam:** David Ginsburg letter to Dial Press, June 26, 1978, B: 18, FWP, UVA; FGWII, Sept. 9, 2020; McCullough, pp. 699, 710, 714, 729–30; Halberstam, *The Fifties*, pp. ix–x, 80, 116–18, 132–37, 207, 214.

177 **mental illness:** McCullough, pp. 726, 734–36; Isaacson and Thomas, pp. 132, 324; GW, Dec. 1, 2020; Herken, p. 39; Halberstam, *The Fifties*, pp. 10–11.

177 **kind of time:** O'Toole, p. 440; Bower, pp. 1–47, 104; Evan Thomas, pp. 32, 66; Lilly, p. 48.

177 **start doing:** Anderson, p. 175; Warner, "Hearts & Minds," pp. 7–9; 308. Memorandum from the Director of the Policy Planning Staff, Department of State (Kennan) to FGW, Jan. 6, 1949, FRUS, 1945–1950; FGW memo on Policy Directive Governing Organization of Russian Refugees in Germany and Austria, Sept. 13, 1949, WCA.

178 **could use:** Corson, p. 314. Memorandum FGW to Joseph A. Frank of the OPC, Oct. 13, 1949, FRUS, 1945–1950; Powers, pp. 43–44, 47; Lilly, pp. 43–44; FGW memo to DCI on U.S. Air Force Interest in Escape and Evasion Intelligence, Nov. 15, 1948, CREST for FGW; 312. Memorandum from Secretary of Defense Johnson to Director of Central Intelligence Hillenkoetter, Oct. 6, 1949, FRUS, 1945–1950; Rositzke, p. 167.

178 **"to say, 'no.'":** Rositzke, p. 21; Frank Lindsay interview, July 26, 2000, CIA Oral History Program, CIA History Staff, p. 19.

178 **and preparation:** 302. Memorandum from Acting Director of Central Intelligence Wright to the Executive Secretary of the NSC, Oct. 8, 1948, FRUS, 1945–1950; Lilly, p. 49.

179 **"Penis Envy.":** Herken, p. 104; Prados, *Safe for Democracy*, p. 47; Phillips, pp. 74–75.

179 **secrets, agreed:** Evan Thomas, pp. 40, 65; Pisani, pp. 71, 76; Hersh, pp. 242, 291, 296; Leary, pp. 45–46; Corson, p. 31; Isaacson and Thomas, pp. 480–81; McCullough, p. 747; Document No. 145, Weekly Summary Excerpt, 30 September 1949, Soviet Union: Atomic Explosion, CIA Library, https://www.cia.gov/resources/csi/static/5563bod3-EarlyColdWarDocuments.pdf; Warner, *The CIA Under Harry Truman*, pp. 327, 330; April 7, 1950, A Report to the President Pursuant to the President's Directive of Jan. 31, 1945, FRUS, 1945–1950, Foreign Economic Policy, vol. 1; Memo to Mr. Rosen on FGW clearance for Atomic Energy Act secrets, July 19, 1949, B: 18, FWP, UVA.

180 **behind the scenes:** Outline of the Understanding Between OPC and National Committee for a Free Europe, Oct. 4, 1949, WCA.

180 **ever launched:** Warner, "Hearts & Minds," p. xiii; Evan Thomas, p. 60; Wilford, p. 7; FGWII, Nov. 10, 2020; Ranelagh, p. 218.

180 **would suffice:** Warner, "Hearts & Minds," p. 2; Lilly, pp. 21–22; Rositzke, p. 163.

181 **staged there:** Office of Policy Coordination 1948–1952, B: 4, S: 1, PGP, PU; Warner, "Hearts & Minds," pp. 2, 11–12, 17; Wilford, pp. 70–71, 78; Warner, "Origins of the Congress for Cultural Freedom," pp. 89–98; Lilly, p. 29; Warner, "Sophisticated Spies," p. 428; Office of Policy Coordination 1948–1952, *Studies in Intelligence* 17, no. 2-s (summer 1973); Office of Policy Coordination 1948–1952, DOC_0000104823, https://www.cia.gov/readingroom/docs/DOC_0000104823.pdf.

181 **Cultural Freedom:** Warner, "Hearts & Minds," pp. 21–22, 24–25; Wilford, pp. 1–5, 52–57, 71–72, 129; FGWII, Nov. 10, 2020.

182 **to cooperate:** "A Look Back . . . The National Committee for Free Europe, 1949," CIA News & Information, cia.gov; Hersh, pp. 256–57; Wilford, p. 31; FGWII, Oct. 19 and Nov. 10, 2020; Herken, p. 101; Memorandum of Conversation with J. Edgar Hoover, April 19, 1949, WCA.

182 **Iron Curtain:** Evan Thomas, p. 61; Herken, pp. 139–40; Wilford, p. 34; Office of Policy Coordination, 1948–1952, FOIA for Peter Grose, p. 15, B: 4, S: 1, PGP, PU; 310. Memorandum from FGW to Members of His Staff, June 1, 1949, FRUS, 1945–1950; Maior, p. 199; Photo with captions of the "Truth Beacons" and RFE balloons being launched, B: 3577, RP, HA.

183 **the country:** Rositzke, p. 186; FGWII, Dec. 11, 2020; GW, Dec. 1, 2020; Weiner, p. 35.

183 **covert operations:** Ruffner, "Cold War Allies," p. 19; Evan Thomas, p. 36; Maior, p. 206; Hersh, p. 256.

184 **the operation:** Hazard, p. 194; Ruffner, "Cold War Allies," p. 19; Memo to FGW and FGW memo on Policy Directive Governing Organization of Russian Refugees in Germany and Austria, Sept. 13, 1949, WCA.

184 **to as well:** Wilford, p. 30; Cryptonym list, E: ZZ19, RG263, NA; Hazard, p. 197.

184 **dangers as well:** Hazard, p. 195; Evan Thomas, p. 67; Maior, p. 207; Rositzke, p. 185.

185 **them up:** Maior, p. 209; Rositzke, p. 48; Bower, p. 91; Ruffner, "Eagle and Swastika," p. 14 of chapter 6; Paper Mills and Fabrication, CIA, February 1952, Chief, SR/2 to SR/COP, memo on AECHAMP Mission to Lithuania and NW U.S.S.R., July 21, 1953, E: ZZ19, RG263, NA.

185 **"BGFiend.":** Anderson, p. 204; Herken, pp. 109–10; Prados, *Safe for Democracy*, p. 59; Evan Thomas, p. 38.

187 **domino theory:** Irakli Koçollari emails to author and translation for author of selected chapters of his book *Secret Operations: Albania Under the Cold War*; Prados, *Safe for Democracy*, p. 58; Maior, pp. 209–10; Herken, p. 111; "Almost Successful Recipe," pp. 15–16; Project Outline for "BGFiend," June 22, 1949, CIA FOIA, cia.gov; FGW to Carmel Offie, June 22, 1949, memo on BGFIEND–Project Outline, CIA FOIA, cia.gov; Project Outline for "BGFiend," June 22, 1949, CIA FOIA, cia.gov.

187 **simple as that:** Project Outline for "BGFiend," June 22, 1949, CIA FOIA, cia.gov.

187 **Soviet Bloc:** Project Outline for "BGFiend," June 22, 1949, CIA FOIA, cia.gov; Kermit Roosevelt memo to ADPC on Revaluation of the Project BGFIEND, Nov. 29, 1949, CREST for BGFiend; CIA Draft on Project BGFIEND, July 17, 1952, CIA FOIA, cia.gov; Project Outline, BGDROVE, No. 1B—10.1, June 9, 1949, CIA FOIA, cia.gov; Prados, *Safe for Democracy*, pp. 58–59; Hersh, pp. 262–63; Dorril, pp. 370–71; SE Albanian Program—A Brief Historical Résumé, CIA FOIA, cia.gov.

188 **final approval:** Project Outline for "BGFiend," June 22, 1949, Budget Estimate Project BGFIEND, Memorandum for Chief, Confidential Funds Project BGFIEND, July 1, 1949, CIA FOIA, Absolute Aircraft Requirements BGFIEND June 22, 1949, cia.gov.

189 **on June 22:** FGW to Carmel Offie, June 22, 1949, memo on BGFIEND–Project Outline, FGW approval of Project BGFIEND on June 22, 1949, CIA FOIA, cia.gov.

189 **"easy reach.":** Weiner, pp. 542–43; Irakli Koçollari emails to author and translation for author of selected chapters of his book *Secret Operations: Albania Under the Cold War*; Herken, pp. 107, 109; Evan Thomas, p. 38; Prados, *Presidents'*

Secret Wars, p. 46; McCargar, FAOH, p. 81; Philby, p. 154; Memo to Chief, VLKiva on Transmittal of BGFiend Documents, Valuable/Fiend, Summary of Conclusions reached at a meeting on March 28 and 30, 1950, CREST for FGW.

191 **memo recommended:** SE Albanian Program—A Brief Historical Résumé, CIA FOIA, cia.gov; Kermit Roosevelt memo to ADPC on Revaluation of the Project BGFIEND, Nov. 29, 1949, CREST for BGFiend; Statement of Expenditures for July 1–Aug, 31, 1949, for BGFIEND, CIA FOIA, cia.gov; Memo for COP on Current Status of Project BGFIEND with Particular Reference to OPC Organization, Aug. 16, 1949, CIA FOIA, cia.gov.

192 **which he did:** Memo for CPP on Revaluation of the Project BGFIEND Sept. 7, 1949, CIA FOIA, cia.gov.

193 **he concluded:** Kermit Roosevelt memo to ADPC on Revaluation of the Project BGFIEND, Nov. 29, 1949, CREST for BGFiend; Evan Thomas, pp. 38–39; Irakli Koçollari emails to author and translation for author of selected chapters of his book *Secret Operations: Albania Under the Cold War*; Kermit Roosevelt memo to ADPC on Revaluation of the Project BGFIEND, Nov. 29, 1949, CREST for BGFiend; Herken, pp. 110, 122; Minutes of Meeting of the Joint Policy Committee for Operation BGFIEND, Nov. 21, 1949, CREST for FGW.

194 **the leaflets' messages:** Kermit Roosevelt memo to ADPC on Revaluation of the Project BGFIEND, Nov. 29, 1949, CREST for BGFiend; PW Annex to Project BGFIEND, Oct. 12, 1949, CREST for BGFiend; Memo for the Executive from FGW on Field Expenditures in excess of $5,000, Dec. 22, 1949, CREST for FGW.

194 **go that far:** Kermit Roosevelt memo to ADPC on Revaluation of the Project BGFIEND, Nov. 29, 1949, CREST for BGFiend.

194 **was possible:** Kermit Roosevelt memo to ADPC on Revaluation of the Project BGFIEND, Nov. 29, 1949, CREST for BGFiend; Draft of CIA paper on BGFIEND, July 17, 1952, CIA FOIA, cia.gov.

195 **Hoxha's spies:** Memorandum for COP, Dec. 15, 1949, CIA FOIA, cia.gov; Irakli Koçollari emails to author and translation for author of selected chapters of his book *Secret Operations: Albania Under the Cold War.*

195 **Nebraska Avenue NW:** Macintyre, pp. 23, 25, 29–30, 70, 118, 120, 129; McCargar, FAOH, pp. 82–83; Philby, pp. 26, 145; Burke, p. 152.

195 **Reflecting Pool:** Philby, p. 153; McCargar, FAOH, p. 84; Memo on FGW restricting British MI6 officers' access to OPC offices, Sept. 21, 1949, CREST for FGW.

Chapter 13: Asia and Eastern Europe

197 **self-proclaimed prophet:** FGWII, Nov. 20, 2020; Joseph Alsop, pp. 322–23; Halberstam, *The Coldest Winter*, pp. 23, 103–5, 163.

198 **the general:** Waller, *Wild Bill Donovan*, p. 323; Halberstam, *The Fifties*, p. 105; Halberstam, *The Coldest Winter*, p. 164; EW, Nov. 11, 2020; FGW letter to Charles Willoughby, Aug. 30, 1951, CREST for FGW; Jackson, vol. 2, pp. 123–24; Laurie, "The Korean War," p. 6; 43. Memorandum from Robert Joyce of the Policy Planning Staff to the Ambassador at Large (Jessup), Jan. 16, 1951; 12. Editorial Note, FRUS, The Intelligence Community, 1950–1955; Evan Thomas, p. 51; FGWII, Nov. 10, 2020; Interview with Lyman Kirkpatrick, B: 10, RSP, HA; Office of Policy Coordination, 1948–1952, DOC_0000104823, https://www.cia.gov/readingroom/docs/DOC_0000104823.pdf; FGW letter to Mr. and Mrs. Ellis Knowles, Feb. 24, 1964, B: 4, FWP, UVA.

199 **months later:** EW, Nov. 11, 2020; Richard Helms, pp. 102–3, 108, 359; Powers, p. 38.

199 **threat there:** Leary, pp. 47, 61.
199 **one-minute spots:** Halberstam, *The Fifties*, pp. 157, 163, 188–95, 201, 227–28, 282, 300–1, 305, 462, 473, 478–85, 500–2, 678.
199 **interest him:** FGWII, Oct. 19, 2020; EW, Oct. 20, 2020.
200 **"all types.":** 8. Memorandum by the Assistant Director for Policy Coordination of the Central Intelligence Committee, May 8, 1950, FRUS, The Intelligence Community, 1950–1955.
201 **operating-independently part:** 24. Memorandum from the Secretary of State's Special Assistant for Intelligence and Research (Armstrong) to the Under Secretary of State (Webb), Sept. 14, 1950, FRUS, The Intelligence Community, 1950–1955; Hersh, p. 253.
201 **service job:** 400. Memorandum from the Director of Central Intelligence Hillenkoetter to the Executive Secretary of the NSC (Souers), Oct. 7, 1949, FRUS, The Intelligence Community, 1950–1955; Mosley, p. 272; CIA Organizational History in Brief, March 1975, approved for release 2002/02/05; Darling, pp. 402–3; 398. Memorandum by FGW, May 8,1950, FRUS, The Intelligence Community, 1950–1955; 398. Memorandum from the Deputy Special Assistant (Howe) to the Secretary of State's Special Assistant for Research and Intelligence (Armstrong), Sept. 8, 1949, FRUS, 1945–1950; FGW memo for the Director of Central Intelligence, Feb. 14, 1949, WFC.
201 **an outcast:** Simpson, p. 226.
202 **with OPC:** Leary, pp. 42–43; Herken, p. 120; Grose, p. 293; 4. Memorandum from the Counselor of the Department of State (Kennan) to the Undersecretary of State (Webb) March 30, 1950, FRUS, The Intelligence Community, 1950–1955; Office of Policy Coordination, 1948–1952, B: 14, S: 1, PGP, PU; George Kennan letter to Wendy Wisner Hazard, Jan. 25, 1995, B: 18, FWP, UVA.
202 **social friends:** McCargar, FAOH, p. 77; 4. Memorandum from the Counselor of the Department of State (Kennan) to the Undersecretary of State (Webb), March 30, 1950, FRUS, The Intelligence Community, 1950–1955; EW, Oct. 6, 2020.
203 **off fireworks:** Herken, pp. 51–54, 115, 119–20; Isaacson and Thomas, pp. 350, 481–89; EW, Oct. 20, 2020.
203 **doing it:** A. C. Wedemeyer letters to FGW, Feb. 28 and March 10, 1950, B: 103, AWP, HA; FGW Memorandum for the Record, June 23, 1951, WFC; 94. Memorandum for the Files on a meeting at Mr. Barrett's home, Nov. 23, 1951, FRUS, The Intelligence Community, 1950–1955; 316. Memorandum from FGW to Mr. Miller of his staff, June 21, 1950, FRUS, 1945–1950; FGW memo to Deputy Director for Plans, CIA, Jan. 23, 1951, CREST for FGW.
204 **its headaches:** Grose, p. 325; Jackson, vol. 3, p. 103; Wilford, pp. 9–10, 36–37; Corson, p. 346.
204 **Korean War:** Warner, "Hearts & Minds," p. xiv; Ranelagh, pp. 250–52; Church Committee, *Final Report*, book 1, pp. 451–52; Wilford, pp. 130–35; Warner, *The CIA Under Harry Truman*, pp. 383–84.
205 **Industrial Organizations:** Wilford, pp. 56–68; Ranelagh, p. 249.
205 **and intellectuals:** Maior, pp. 196–98; Wilford, pp. 101–2, 117–19; Warner, "Origins of the Congress for Cultural Freedom," p. 89.
206 **they believed:** Wilford, pp. 83–84; Warner, "Hearts & Minds," p. 33.
206 **he was:** Warner, "Hearts & Minds," pp. xiv, 34, 41; Wilford, pp. 113–17.
206 **the rest:** Wilford, pp. 32–33.
207 **of leaflets:** Wilford, pp. 33–34; Richard Helms, pp. 355–56.
207 **not deliver:** Letter to DeWitt Poole, National Committee for a Free Europe, May 5, 1950, WCA.

208 **ethnic populations:** Memo to FGW on National Committee for a Free Europe, Oct. 19, 1950, WCA; Wilford, pp. 37–38.

208 **half dozen languages:** Meyer, p. 113; Rositzke, p. 157; Wilford, pp. 34–35; National Committee for a Free Europe, 1949, CIA News & Information, cia.gov.

209 **satellite nations:** Meyer, p. 112; FGW update on Radio Free Europe, Nov. 22, 1950, OPC Provides Propaganda Themes for Radio Free Europe, Aug. 10, 1950, Memo for Horace Nickels, March 16, 1950, WCA; Director's Meeting minutes, Sept. 19, 1951, CREST for FGW.

210 **empire as well:** Wilford, p. 35; Director's Meeting minutes, Aug. 7 and Sept. 17, 1951, CREST for FGW; Memorandum of conversation on Radio Free Europe, Nov. 20, 1951, Frederick Hier, "A Hungarian Diary," 1956, WCA.

210 **than the first:** Prados, *Presidents' Secret Wars*, p. 35.

211 **oppressed friends:** Wilford, pp. 40–41; Memo for FGW on Cinderella Discussion with Mr. Kennan, Aug. 21, 1950, George Kennan's Views on Radio Liberty, Dec. 21, 1951, WCA.

211 **bickering continued:** FGW memo on history of American Committee for Liberation, Aug. 21, 1951, OPC and Kennan Discussion of American Committee for Liberation, Aug. 21, 1950, George Kennan's Views on Radio Liberty, Dec. 12, 1951, WCA; Wilford, pp. 40–42.

211 **continuous jamming:** Radio Liberty Broadcasting Policy, March 28, 1952, Radio Liberty Aims and Objectives, Aug. 28, 1951, WCA; Meyer, p. 113.

212 **Russians attacked:** FGW courier certificate from the State Department, Aug. 17, 1950, FWP, UVA; AWD memo to J. D. Balmer, Nov. 19, 1951, CREST for FGW; Evan Thomas, p. 12; Burke, p. 156.

212 **the orders:** "Almost Successful Recipe," p. 4; L. C. Stevens to FGW, March 16, 1951, memo on Resistance Movements in Eastern Europe, CREST for FGW.

212 **East Germany:** Evan Thomas, p. 40; Minutes of meeting in Office of H. Freeman Matthews, July 31, 1951, CREST for FGW; Colby, pp. 81–88; Weiner, p. 47.

213 **Policy Coordination:** Evan Thomas, p. 356; Rositzke, pp. 167–68; Maior, p. 208; Ruffner, "Eagle and Swastika," pp. 233, 279–87, 405–9, 428–29; Letter to Wendy, Jan. 7, 1994, B: 1, RJP, YU; Lawrence Houston letter to Wendy, Jan. 7, 1994, WFC.

213 **one postmortem:** Rositzke, pp. 169–71; Memorandum from Robert P. Joyce of the Policy Planning Staff to the Deputy Undersecretary of State (Matthews), Dec. 31, 1952, FRUS, The Intelligence Community, 1950–1955; Evan Thomas, pp. 67–68.

214 **embarrass them:** Memorandum for: The BGSpeed File on Disposal of Yacht "JUANITA," CREST for FGW; Proposed Joint PW Policy Guidance for BG-Fiend, Aug. 3, 1950, CIA FOIA, cia.gov; BGFiend Project outline, Nov. 19, 1952, Brief Historical Résumé on BGFiend, Aug. 4, 1956, CIA FOIA, cia.gov; Memo for CPP, Review of BGFiend, Feb. 8, 1950, CIA FOIA, cia.gov; Herken, pp. 121–23; Memorandum for the Record, Meeting on Fiend of 27 February 1950, CREST for FGW; Statement of Agreement, Dec. 12, 1951, Notes for Discussion with Ascam, July 27, 1951, CIA FOIA, cia.gov.

214 **"immediate threat.":** Evan Thomas, p. 68; Herken, p. 145; "Almost Successful Recipe," pp. 17–18.

215 **two employers:** Dorril, p. 393; Philby, pp. 74, 100–1, 153; McCargar, FAOH, pp. 81–82; Prados, *Presidents' Secret Wars*, p. 51; Macintyre, pp. 36, 38, 52–53, 66–69, 102.

215 **to succeed:** Macintyre, pp. 101–3, 131, 154.

216 **in Albania:** Macintyre, pp. 135, 137; Ranelagh, p. 150; Irakli Koçollari emails to author and translation for author of selected chapters of his book *Secret Operations: Albania Under the Cold War*; Powers, p. 49; Dorril, pp. 394–95; McCargar, FAOH, p. 82; Lindsay, CIAOHP, pp. 22–23.

216 **the man:** David Ginsburg letter to Dial Press, June 26, 1978, B: 18, FWP, UVA; Mosley, pp. 278, 282; GW, Aug. 10, 2020; Anderson, pp. 259, 494; Macintyre, pp. 156–59, 184–85.

216 **Philby's betrayal:** Macintyre, pp. 155, 160–61, 164–68, 174–75; Philby, pp. 175, 181; Ranelagh, p. 157.

217 **to crack:** FGW memo on Status Report on the Albanian Project (BGFiend), Oct. 26, 1951, declassified by CIA, cia.gov: Country Plan Albania, CIA FOIA, cia.gov; Estimated Funds Required for Project Fiend—1 Jan. 1951–30 June 1951, CIA FOIA, cia.gov; BGFiend Project Analysis, June 22, 1951, CIA FOIA, cia.gov; Herken, pp. 142–43; Staff Conference minutes, March 19, 1951, CREST for FGW; Conversation with King Zog of Albania, memo for DCI, Aug. 16, 1951, cia.gov; Ranelagh, p. 157; Rositzke, pp. 171–73; Brief Historical Résumé on BGFiend, Aug. 4, 1956, CIA FOIA, cia.gov.

217 **back intelligence:** BGFiend Project outline, Nov. 19, 1952, Brief Historical Résumé on BGFiend, Aug. 4, 1956, CIA FOIA, cia.gov; Recapitulation of BG-Fiend Activities for the Period October 1950 to October 1951, Oct. 20, 1951, https://www.cia.gov/readingroom/docs/OBOPUS%20BG%20FIEND%20%20%20VOL.%202%20%28PROJECT%20OUTLINED%20REVIEWS%20TERMINATION%29_0033.pdf.

217 **Washington headquarters:** SE Albanian Program—A Brief Historical Résumé, CIA FOIA, cia.gov.

218 **same goal:** Dorril, pp. 398–99; Ranelagh, pp. 156–57.

Chapter 14: Korea and the Philippines
219 **their desks:** Joseph Alsop, pp. 306–8.

220 **no match:** Powers, p. 46; EW, Sept. 22, 2020; Peter Sichel manuscript provided to author; Halberstam, *The Coldest Winter*, pp. 1, 47–51, 76, 82–83.

220 **intelligence failure:** Halberstam, *The Coldest Winter*, p. 69; McCullough, p. 777; Corson, pp. 318–19; Ranelagh, p. 188; Darling, pp. 240–43.

220 **"my back.":** Warner, *The CIA Under Harry Truman*, pp. 265–68; Laurie, "The Korean War," pp. 4–10; Organizational History of the Central Intelligence Agency, 1950–1953, pp. 3–4, 11–18, MN; Halberstam, *The Coldest Winter*, p. 57.

221 **global war:** Halberstam, *The Fifties*, p. 69; McCullough, pp. 778–79; 181. Intelligence Memorandum 302, 8 July 1950, Consequences of the Korean Incident, CIA Library, cia.gov; Halberstam, *The Coldest Winter*, pp. 220–21.

221 **was tentative:** Halberstam, *The Fifties*, pp. 69, 74, 83; Halberstam, *The Coldest Winter*, pp. 11–12, 61, 102,138–50, 166–67; McCullough, pp. 793–94; EW, Nov. 11, 2020.

222 **active-duty job:** McCullough, p. 796; Darling, p. 347; "A Look Back . . . Roscoe Hillenkoetter as DCI," CIA News & Information, cia.gov: Montague, vol. 2, p. 7; Michael Warner, "The CIA's Office of Policy Coordination from NSC 10/2 to NSC 68," B: 4, PGP, PU; 375. Memorandum from FGW to the Under Secretary of State (Webb), March 18, 1949, 386. Memorandum from the Executive Secretary of the NSC (Souers) to HST, July 7, 1949, FRUS, 1945–1950.

222 **the choice:** Montague, vol. 2, pp. 1, 5; Leary, p. 23; Crosswell, p. 33.

223 **Dwight Eisenhower:** Crosswell, pp. 30–35; Montague, vol. 1, pp. 14–15, vol. 2, pp. 6, 11–12; Leary, pp. 23–24; Ludwell Montague, "The Organization of the

Clandestine Services," CREST for FGW; Laurie, "A New President," p. 3; Darling, p. 380; Snider, p. 45; Ambrose, *Ike's Spies*, p. 171.

224 **Policy Coordination:** Hersh, pp. 287–88; Montague, vol. 2, p. 20; Grose, p. 307; Press release on Allen Dulles, William Harding Jackson, and FGW, B: 1715, Official File, HSTL.

224 **in Asia:** Office of Policy Coordination 1948–1952, DOC_0000104823, https://www.cia.gov/readingroom/docs/DOC_0000104823.pdf; Office of Policy Coordination 1948–1952, B: 4, S: 1, PGP, PU; Lilly, p. 49; Grose, p. 324; Leary, p. 43; 26. Memorandum from [name not declassified] of the Office of Policy Coordination of the Central Intelligence Agency to Thomas A. Parrott of the Office of Policy Coordination, Oct. 10, 1950, FRUS, The Intelligence Community, 1950–1955.

225 **to expand:** Church Committee, *Final Report*, book 1, p. 23; Leary, pp. 43, 93; 8. Memorandum by FGW, May 8, 1950, FRUS, The Intelligence Community, 1950–1955; Minutes of meeting held in Office of H. Freeman Matthews, July 31, 1951, Minutes of the Eighth Meeting of the Psychological Strategy Board, Jan. 10, 1952, CREST for FGW; 71. Memorandum of a Meeting of the Senior Staff of the NSC May 28, 1951, FRUS, The Intelligence Community, 1950–1955; Memo to Chief, Far East Division, on WSBakery, July 24, 1951, E: ZZ19, RG263, NA.

225 **overnight visitors:** Interview with PKW, B: 10, Desmond FitzGerald biographical information, B: 9, RSP, HA; Corson, p. 320; Evan Thomas, pp. 43–50; Ranelagh, p. 223; FGWII, Oct. 19, 2020; Herken, p. 177.

226 **the Communists:** 12. Editorial Note, FRUS, The Intelligence Community, 1950–1955; "Two Prisoners in China, 1952–73," CIA Library, https://www.cia.gov/resources/csi/static/Two-CIA-Prisoners-China.pdf; Clandestine Services History: The Secret War in Korea, June 1950 to June 1952, July 17, 1968, https://www.cia.gov/readingroom/docs/CLANDESTINE%20SERVICES%20HIST%5B16049713%5D.pdf.

226 **had none:** Office of Policy Coordination 1948–1952, DOC_0000104.823, https://www.cia.gov/readingroom/docs/DOC_0000104823.pdf; Clandestine Services History: The Secret War in Korea, June 1950 to June 1952, July 17, 1968; Lilley, FAOH, pp. 1–17; O'Toole, p. 450; Evan Thomas, p. 51; Weiner, p. 55.

226 **bribe money:** Clandestine Services History: The Secret War in Korea, June 1950 to June 1952, July 17, 1968.

227 **United Nations control:** Weiner, pp. 53–56; Evan Thomas, pp. 51–55; Clandestine Services History: The Secret War in Korea, June 1950 to June 1952, July 17, 1968; Clandestine Services History: The Origins of CIA's Clandestine Organization in the Far East, 1945–1952, MN; Halberstam, *The Coldest Winter*, pp. 293, 303.

227 **not happen:** Halberstam, *The Fifties*, pp. 84–85, 378; Halberstam, *The Coldest Winter*, pp. 314–15, 364-67, 402, 424; Laurie, "The Korean War," p. 12; Warner, *The CIA Under Harry Truman*, pp. 349–51, 354.

228 **long overdue:** Halberstam, *The Coldest Winter*, pp. 467, 494, 591–94; McCullough, p. 834, 838, 840.

228 **American GIs:** Halberstam, *The Coldest Winter*, p. 625; McCullough, p. 859; Minutes of meeting in Office of H. Freeman Matthews, July 31, 1951, CREST for FGW; Marks, pp. 134–39.

229 **visited Washington:** Currey, pp. 69–72.

229 **on paper:** FGWII, Nov. 10, 2020; Anderson, pp. 78–89; Currey, pp. xii, xv, 11–23, 27, 32–34, 49, 56, 63, 68, 72–73; Lilley, FAOH, p. 20; Anderson, pp. 220–21.

230 **that country:** Currey, pp. 72, 78; Anderson, p. 267.
230 **by Magsaysay:** Currey, pp. 73–79, 92; Anderson, pp. 128–30, 269.
231 **a vampire:** Currey, pp. 38—40, 44–45, 83–88, 102–5; Anderson, p. 134.
231 **the story:** Currey, pp. 79–80, 89, 94–96, 113–14, 125–26, 130–32; Anderson, pp. 274, 278, 344–48; Joseph Alsop, pp. 379–80.
232 **Soviet Union:** HST letter to Secretary of Defense, Nov. 9, 1949, National Archives Catalogue, Identifier 205716735, File Unit Foreign Affairs File, 1940–1953, President's Secretary's File; McCullough, pp. 742–44; Hersh, p. 299; Halberstam, *The Fifties*, pp. 224–27; 98. Letter from Director of Central Intelligence Smith to Secretary of Defense Lovett, Dec. 11, 1951, FRUS, The Intelligence Community, 1950–1955; Lilly, p. 78; Holober, p. 7; Robarge, Part 2, p. 262.
232 **Party officials:** McBaine, UCB, pp. 185–91, 194–97; Prados, *Safe for Democracy*, p. 89; Prados, *Presidents' Secret Wars*, p. 83; Cryptonyms in Declassified CIA files, ZZ19, RG263, NA.
233 **"a bust.":** 98. Letter from Director of Central Intelligence Smith to Secretary of Defense Lovett, Dec. 11, 1951, FRUS, The Intelligence Community, 1950–1955; Prados, *Safe for Democracy*, p. 127; Evan Thomas, pp. 51–53; Lilley, FAOH, p. 17; "Two Prisoners in China, 1952–73," CIA Library.
233 **one meeting:** Prados, *Safe for Democracy*, p. 126; Weiner, pp. 58, 60–61, 553–54; Lilley, FAOH, pp. 16–17; Evan Thomas, p. 55; Minutes of meeting in Office of H. Freeman Matthews, July 31, 1951, CREST for FGW; Corson, pp. 321–22; Hersh, p. 300.

Chapter 15: Beetle's Bark
234 **grew up:** GW, Aug. 8 and Sept. 16, 2020.
235 **from family:** "Social Graces in Georgetown," pp. 188–91; Daniela Deane, "From P St. Salon to a Candidate's Makeover," *The Washington Post*, May 7, 2005, p. F1; FGWII, Aug. 19 and Sept. 9, 2020; EW, Sept. 22 and Oct. 6 and 20, 2020; "Georgetown Garden Tour to Aide Settlement House," newsclip, CREST for FGW; GW, Sept. 16, 2020.
235 **a stir:** William Simpson correspondence with J. Ellis Knowles, May 1951 to January 1952, B: 4, FWP, UVA; FGWII, Oct. 19, 2020; EW, Oct. 6, 2020; Heymann, p. 33; Herken, p. 187.
236 **his mistresses:** Grose, pp. 415, 498; Heymann, pp. 33–34; Katharine Graham interview with Polly Fritchey, Oct. 10, 1989, pp. 37–38, KGP.
236 **Alsop suppers:** Herken, pp. 20–23, 179; Miscellaneous Information on Mary (Polly) Wisner Fritchey, KGP; Graham, p. 207; Katharine Graham interview with Polly Fritchey, Oct. 10, 1989, p. 33, KGP.
236 **to Edwards:** Herken, p. 279; FGW CIA bio material on his and PKW's friendship with Joseph Alsop, Sheffield Edwards Memorandum for the Record on FGW report of his connection with Joseph Alsop, Sept. 2, 1953, WFC.
237 **attendees directly:** Evan Thomas, pp. 102, 106; Heymann, pp. 35–36; Interview with James Reston, B: 10, RSP, HA.
237 **unfavorable stories:** Wilford, p. 226; Minutes of Staff Conference, Sept. 12, 1955, Minutes of Director's Meeting, Sept. 7, 1951, CREST for FGW.
238 **his work:** Herken, p. 279; FGW CIA bio material on his and PKW's friendship with Joseph Alsop, Sheffield Edwards Memorandum for the Record on FGW report of his connection with Joseph Alsop, Sept. 2, 1953, WFC; Graham, p. 210; Katharine Graham interview with Polly Fritchey, Oct. 10, 1989, p. 8, KGP; Wayne Jackson letter, Nov. 7, 1951, B: 6, FWP, UVA.
238 **the possibility:** Letter to A. G. Atwater, Nov. 15, 1952, B: 1, FWP, UVA; EW, Oct. 6, 2020; Miscellaneous Information on Mary (Polly) Wisner Fritchey, KGP; Kingsley, Jan. 7, 2008.

238   **Marshall Fund:** Hersh, p. 301; Minutes of Staff Conference, Oct. 27, 1952, Diary Notes on Director's Staff Conference with DD/P, May 4, 1951, Diary Notes on Director's Meeting, Dec. 18, 1951, CREST for FGW; Warner, *The CIA Under Harry Truman,* p. 449; 31. Memorandum for the Record by FGW, Nov. 2, 1950, FRUS, The Intelligence Community, 1950–1955.

239   **details secret:** Herken, p. 130; Minutes of Director's Meeting, Feb. 18, 1952, Minutes of Director's Meeting, Sept. 4, 1951, CREST for FGW; Warner, *The CIA Under Harry Truman,* p. 470.

239   **accomplish that:** Interview with Gerald Miller, B: 10, RSP, HA; Montague, vol. 1, p. 3.

240   **bottled up:** Interview with Lyman Kirkpatrick, B: 10, RSP, HA; Evan Thomas, pp. 42–43, 64–65; Martin, FAOH, p. 50; Hersh, pp. 301, 304; FGWII, Nov. 10, 2020.

240   **Dulles's home:** Interview with Kermit Roosevelt, B: 10, RSP, HA; Montague, vol. 1, pp. 13–14, vol. 2, p. 86; Grose, p. 325; Richard Helms, p. 101; Maior, p. 189; Mosley, p. 345.

240   **in mind:** WJD radio address transcript, March 18, 1951, B: 313, WJD memo to Bedell Smith on Russian defectors, B: 8A-2, WJD memos to Bedell Smith, Sept. 21 and Nov. 3, 1950, B: 1A, WDP, AHEC; 24. Memorandum from the Secretary of State's Special Assistant for Intelligence and Research (Armstrong) to the Under Secretary of State (Webb), Sept. 14, 1950, FRUS, The Intelligence Community, 1950–1955; Warner, *The CIA Under Harry Truman,* pp. 341–45: Vanden Heuvel, Jan. 7, 2008.

241   **instructed Wisner:** Montague, vol. 2, pp. 52, 56–57; Darling, pp. 410–11; Leary, p. 29; Warner, *The CIA Under Harry Truman,* p. 261; 29. Minutes of a Meeting of the Intelligence Advisory Committee, Oct. 20, 1950, FRUS, The Intelligence Community, 1950–1955; Ranelagh, p. 199; Crosswell, p. 33.

241   **to his office:** Montague, vol. 5, pp. 1–7; Minutes of Director's Meeting, Nov. 23, 1951, CREST for FGW.

241   **the way:** Corson, p. 323; Hersh, p. 289; Anderson, p. 310.

242   **Smith envisioned:** Darling, p. 413; Organizational History of the Central Intelligence Agency, 1950–1953, pp. 11, 89–91, MN; 29. Minutes of a Meeting of the Intelligence Advisory Committee, Oct. 20, 1950, FRUS, The Intelligence Community, 1950–1955; Darling, pp. 412–13; Montague, vol. 4, pp. 61–63.

242   **power centers:** Phillips, p. 13; Snider, p. 170; Richard Helms, 168; Leary, p. 55.

242   **for plans:** CIA Organizational History in Brief, March 1975, released by CIA Jan. 4, 2002, https://www.documentcloud.org/documents/22806874-cia-organizational-history-in-brief; Leary, p. 50; Hersh, p. 289; Evan Thomas, p. 43.

243   **clandestine service:** Montague, vol. 2, pp. 118, 122–23; Warner, *The CIA Under Harry Truman,* p. 385; Greer, p. 34.

243   **his division:** Thomas Braden Theater Service Record, May 7, 1945, B: 16, GHP, HA; Jackson, vol. 1, pp. 61–62, 69–70, vol. 3, pp. 102, 104; Prados, *Safe for Democracy,* p. 80; Wilford, pp. 62–65.

243   **the world:** Ranelagh, p. 190; 53. Memorandum from Director of Central Intelligence Smith to HST, Feb. 28, 1951, 55. Letter from HST to Director of Central Intelligence Smith, March 8, 1951, FRUS, The Intelligence Community, 1950–1955.

244   **covert operations:** Darling, p. 411; Montague, vol. 2, pp. 86, 94–96, 108–9; Hersh, pp. 298–99; Minutes of Daily Staff Meeting, Aug. 21, 1951, CREST for FGW.

245 **been Wisner:** Minutes of Staff Conference, Oct. 27, 1952, Transcript of Preliminary Staff Meeting of the National Psychological Strategy Board CREST for FGW; 107. Memorandum from Director of Central Intelligence Smith to the NSC, April 23, 1952, FRUS, The Intelligence Community, 1950–1955.

245 **with misgivings:** Memo to FGW on Albanian Operations, Oct. 11, 1951, Project BGFiend Review for DCI, Nov. 8, 1951, Project BGFiend Report, November 1951, CIA FOIA, cia.gov; FGW memo to Chief, EE Division, April 18, 1951, Excerpt from June 1, 1953, letter from accompanying attached memorandum, CREST for FGW; Herken, pp. 146–47.

246 **of success:** Sept. 6, 1951, CIA–State Department Reservations about Broadcasting to the Soviet Union, WCA.

246 **more trouble:** Organizational History of the Central Intelligence Agency, 1950–1953, pp. 11–27, MN; Herken, p. 138; Hersh, pp. 363–64; Weiner, p. 64; Evan Thomas, p. 66.

246 **little oversight:** Memorandum to the Director, Survey of Office of Policy Coordination by Deputy Director of Central Intelligence, May 24, 1951, CREST, cia.gov.

247 **their exposure:** Warner, *The CIA Under Harry Truman*, pp. 435–36, 441–43; 75. Memorandum from Robert P. Joyce of the Policy Planning Staff to the Director of the Policy Planning Staff (Nitze), June 21, 1951, 111. Memorandum from Robert P. Joyce of the Policy Planning Staff to the Undersecretary of State (Bruce), May 22, 1952, FRUS, The Intelligence Community, 1950–1955; Ranelagh, p. 218.

247 **dirty work:** Montague, vol. 4, p. 21–23, 35; 75. Memorandum from Robert P. Joyce of the Policy Planning Staff to the Director of the Policy Planning Staff (Nitze), June 21, 1951, FRUS, The Intelligence Community, 1950–1955.

248 **Smith approved:** Diary Notes on Director's Meeting, Dec. 18, 1951, Minutes for Deputies' Meeting, Aug. 22, 1952, CREST for FGW; Montague, vol. 4, p. 48; Leary, p. 48.

248 **the years:** Minutes of Director's Meeting, Nov. 14, 1951, Minutes of Director's Meeting, Nov. 23, 1951, Draft Revision of the Gray Report, March 4, 1952, CREST for FGW; The DCI Historical Series, Internal Audit of the Central Intelligence Agency, 1947 Through 1967, December 1972, CIA FOIA; Memorandum from the Secretary of State's Special Assistant for Intelligence and Research (Armstrong) to Secretary of State Acheson, Oct. 23, 1950, FRUS, The Intelligence Community, 1950–1955; Leary, p. 47; Montague, vol. 4, pp. 24–25, 50–51; Office of Policy Coordination 1948–1952, B: 4, PGP, PU; Jackson, vol. 3, pp. 16–18; Herken, p. 155; Prados, *Safe for Democracy*, pp. 79, 81–82; EW, Aug. 5, 2020.

249 **Smith said:** 71. Memorandum of a Meeting of the Senior Staff of the NSC, May 28, 1951, 75. Memorandum from Robert P. Joyce of the Policy Planning Staff to the Director of the Policy Planning Staff (Nitze), June 21, 1951, 76. Memorandum from the Acting Executive Secretary of the National Security Council to the National Security Council, June 27, 1951, FRUS, The Intelligence Community, 1950–1955; Memorandum for the Record of "Magnitude Conference," March 29, 1951.

250 **"be launched.":** Office of Policy Coordination 1948–1952, pp. 48–49, B: 4, S: 1, PGP, PU; 68. Memorandum from the Director of Central Intelligence (Smith) to the NSC, May 8, 1951, 75. Memorandum from Robert P. Joyce of the Policy Planning Staff to the Director of the Policy Planning Staff (Nitze), June 21, 1951, FRUS, The Intelligence Community, 1950–1955; FGW memo to

Deputy Director (Plans) on Recommendations to Accompany Magnitude Paper, April 23, 1951, WFC.

250 **could employ:** Montague, vol. 4, p. 39; Office of Policy Coordination 1948–1952, p. 48, B: 4, S: 1, PGP, PU; Prados, *Safe for Democracy*, p. 96; 108. Briefing Paper Prepared by the Chairman of the 10/5 Panel (Barnes), May 7, 1952, FRUS, The Intelligence Community, 1950–1955; Jackson, vol. 3, pp. 3–4; Warner, *The CIA Under Harry Truman*, p. xxvi; Ludwell Montague, "The Organization of the Clandestine Services," Memorandum on the Clark Committee Briefings, March 15, 1955, CREST for FGW; 70. Memorandum from the Secretary of State's Special Assistant for Intelligence and Research (Armstrong) to the Director of the Policy Planning Staff (Nitze), May 26, 1951, Annex 1, Memorandum from Brigadier General John Magruder to the Department of Defense Representative on the Senior Staff of the NSC (Nash), May 23, 1951, FRUS, The Intelligence Community, 1950–1955; Anderson, pp. 238–39.

251 **strategic plan:** 61. Paper Prepared in the Office of Policy Coordination of the Central Intelligence Agency, April 4, 1951, FRUS, The Intelligence Community, 1950–1955; Memo for FGW on OPC Strategic Planning, July 13, 1951, CREST for FGW.

251 **won 12–7:** Minutes for Director's Meeting, Sept. 25, 1951, AWD memo to J. D. Balmer, Oct. 26, 1951; Minutes for Director's Meeting, July 3, 1951; Minutes for Director's Meeting, Oct. 8, 1951, CREST for FGW; Warner, *The CIA Under Harry Truman*, p. 445; Interview of PKW, B: 10, RSP, HA; FGW letter to David and Evangeline Bruce, Nov. 20, 1951, B: 1, FWP, UVA.

252 **noble crusade:** Minutes on Staff Conference, Nov. 21, 1951, CREST for FGW; Leary, pp. 54–56; Office of Policy Coordination 1948–1952, pp. 24–25, B: 4, S: 1, PGP, PU.

252 **his game:** Ranelagh, p. 200; Hersh, p. 288; Montague, vol. 2, p. 87; Office of Policy Coordination 1948–1952, p. 9, B: 4, S: 1, PGP, PU; Notification of Personnel Action for FGW, 8/25/51, Promotion to Deputy Director (Plans), WFC; Request for Personnel Action for FGW, Dec. 19, 1952, for pay raise, B: 18, FWP, UVA.

253 **at times:** Minutes of Staff Conference, Dec. 18, 1950, Minutes for Director's Meeting, Aug. 27, 1951, Views of the Director on CIA Budget, as set forth on Nov. 23, 1951, Minutes for Director's Meeting, Jan. 24, 1952, CREST for FGW; EW, Sept. 22, 2020; Hersh, pp. 305, 383; Anderson, p. 402; McAfee, FAOH, p. 55.

253 **it out:** Official Diary, Aug. 17, 1951, Minutes for Director's Meeting, July 13, 1951, Minutes for Director's Meeting, March 19, 1952, Notes on Deputy Directors' Meeting, Dec. 29, 1952, Minutes of Director's Meeting, April 8, 1952, CREST for FGW.

253 **to increase:** Evan Thomas, pp. 138, 198–99; Hersh, p. 306.

Chapter 16: The Red Scare and the Black Book

254 **the South:** Halberstam, *The Fifties*, pp. xi, 119, 122–28, 172–79, 414, 442–43, 487, 496–99, 506, 570–75, 587, 636.

255 **no winners:** Halberstam, *The Fifties*, p. 27; McCullough, p. 746; Rositzke, pp. 1–12.

255 **domestic Communists:** McCullough, p. 521; Halberstam, *The Fifties*, pp. 9, 31, 59.

255 **the country:** Waller, *Wild Bill Donovan*, pp. 39–40; Halberstam, *The Fifties*, pp. 336–42; McCullough, pp. 521–22; 16. Letter from JEH to the President's Special Consultant (Souers), July 7, 1950, FRUS, The Intelligence Community, 1950–1955.

256 **intelligence officers:** McCullough, pp. 367, 673–74; Psychological and Political
Warfare, Introduction, From the Strategic Service Unit to the Office of Special
Operations, Emergence of the Intelligence Establishment, FRUS, 1945–1950;
22. Memorandum from Morton B. Chiles of the Federal Bureau of Investigation
to JEH, Oct. 2, 1945, 35. Memorandum from the Assistant Director for Administrative Management, Bureau of the Budget (Stone) to the Assistant Director,
Bureau of the Budget (Appleby), Oct. 26, 1945, 37. Letter from the Assistant
Director of the Bureau of the Budget (Appleby) to Attorney General Clark, Oct.
31, 1945, Emergence of the Intelligence Establishment, FRUS, 1945–1950; Minutes of Director's Meeting, Aug. 30, 1951, CREST for FGW; Riebling, p. 135.

256 **mounted overseas:** 157. Memorandum from C. H. Carson of the Federal
Bureau of Investigation to the Assistant Director of the Federal Bureau of In-
vestigation (Ladd), June 21, 1946, Emergence of the Intelligence Establishment,
FRUS, 1945–1950; 33. Memorandum from FGW to Staff and Division Chiefs,
Nov. 29, 1950, FRUS, The Intelligence Community, 1950–1955.

256 **"LCFlutter.":** 8. Memorandum by FGW, May 8, 1950, FRUS, The Intelligence
Community, 1950–1955, Ranelagh, p. 114; Powers, p. 72; Cryptonyms in Declassified CIA files, ZZ19, RG263, NA.

257 **as he did:** Riebling, pp. 113–15; Minutes for Director's Meeting, Aug. 10, 1951,
CREST for FGW.

257 **bureau headquarters:** Herken, pp. 107, 179; EW, Nov. 11, 2020; Memo from
Washington Field Office to D. M. Ladd, 2/15/51, Aull memo to Hennrich,
July 5, 1951, A. H. Belmont memo to D. M. Ladd, Feb. 14, 1951, Memo for Tolson, Boardman, and Belmont, March 28, 1957, FBI clipping file on Alsop
columns, FBI file on Joseph Alsop.

257 **six years:** Riebling, p. 99–100; Report on HTLingual, Mail Intercept Program,
Jan. 21, 1975, CIA release, Nov. 5, 2008.

258 **stopped growing:** Minutes for Director's Meeting, Aug. 22, 1951, Minutes for
Director's Meeting, April 25, 1952, CREST for FGW; Anderson, pp. 311–12.

258 **"the animals":** Halberstam, *The Fifties*, pp. 52–56, 233; McCullough, pp. 765–
66, 860–61; Anderson, p. 309.

259 **"much sleep.":** FGWII, Oct. 19 and Nov. 10, 2020; Rositzke, p. 87; Hersh, p.
326; Warner, *The CIA Under Harry Truman*, p. 455; Minutes for Deputies'
Meeting, Sept. 2, 1953, Excerpt from ADD/A (Colonel L. K. White) Diary
Notes, April 3, 1953, Minutes for Director's Meeting, Aug. 30, 1951, CREST
for FGW; Snider, p. 314; Ranelagh, p. 239; EW, Nov. 11, 2020; Joseph Alsop, p.
334; Herken, p. 123; Graham, pp. 193, 199; PKW letter to her mother-in-law,
FGW letter to his mother, June 4, 1954, B: 4, FWP, UVA.

260 **death sentences:** McCullough, pp. 651–52; Halberstam, *The Fifties*, pp. 40–42;
Minutes for Deputies' Meeting, Dec. 10 and 12, 1952, CREST for FGW.

260 **was noncommittal:** Halberstam, *The Fifties*, pp. 11–12, 332–33, 343–45,
350; EW, Nov. 11, 2020; FGWII, Nov. 10, 2020; A-DD/A Diary Note 87, Nov.
7–21, 1953, CREST for FGW; FGW letter to FGWII from London, B: 2,
FWP, UVA; FGW letter to Lewis L. Strauss, April 29, 1954, BHP.

261 **defense fund:** FGWII, Oct. 19 and Nov. 10, 2020; Herken pp. 159–60, 184–85;
Office of Policy Coordination 1948–1952, p. 10, B: 4, S: 1, PGP, PU; Grose, p. 344;
Powers, pp. 71, 73; Pforzheimer Memo for the Record, July 15, 1953, McCarthy
and Dulles correspondence, July 16, 22, and 27, 1943, CREST for FGW.

261 **a homosexual:** FBI file on Carmel Offie, MN; Powers, pp. 69–70, 368; D. M.
Ladd memo to JEH, Sept. 9, 1943, G. A. Nease memo to JEH, March 4, 1950,
V. P. Keay memos to A. H. Belmont, March 8 and July 20, 1950, Memo for JEH
on Carmel Offie, June 13, 1951, MN; R. R. Roach to A. H. Belmont, memo on

Joseph Alsop, 1957, FBI file on AWD; A. H. Belmont memo to D. M. Ladd, July 8, 1953, John Ford memo to JEH, July 8, 1953, FBI memo to Sherman Adams on Carmel Offie, Feb. 11, 1953, with attachment B: 1, S: 1, PGP, PU.

261 **tax evasion:** Guy Hottel memo to JEH on Carmel Offie, July 21, 1950, Washington Field Office memo to JEH, Sept. 1, 1950, SAC, New York memo to JEH, Oct. 13, 1950, SAC, Washington Field Office memos to JEH, Dec. 10, 1950, and April 2, 1951, Guy Hottel memo to JEH, Nov. 22, 1950, C. L. Trotter memo to Tracy, Feb. 16, 1954, Hennrich memo to Belmont, Dec. 11, 1950, FBI file on Carmel Offie, MN.

262 **a friend:** C. E. Hennrich memo to A. H. Belmont, Sept. 21, 1950, JEH memo to James M. McInerney, Dec. 19, 1950, FBI file on Carmel Offie, MN; Anderson, pp. 233–35; Pforzheimer Diary Notes on AWD Defense of CIA from McCarthy, CREST for FGW; EW, Nov. 11, 2020.

262 **hostile agent:** EW, Jan. 12, 2021; Riebling, p. 117; Herken, p. 185.

262 **the case:** Anderson, pp. 337–38.

262 **with him:** Wilford, p. 59; Evan Thomas, p. 368; McCargar, FAOH, p. 88.

263 **Wisner himself:** Anderson, p. 235; James McInerney memo to JEH, June 21, 1951, C. E. Hennrich memos to A. H. Belmont, July 14, 1951, and March 15, 1954, S. W. Reynolds memo to V. P. Keay, July 27, 1951, W. A. Branigan memos to A. H. Belmont, March 16 and 23, 1954, A. H. Belmont memo to D. M. Ladd, Feb. 19, 1954, L. B. Nichols memo to Tolson, Feb. 16, 1954, JEH memo to Warren Olney, March 24, 1954, FBI file on Carmel Offie, MN.

264 **Innsbruck, Austria:** Memo on Princess Catherine Caradja, www.archives.gov /files/declassification/iscap/pdf/2010-081-umissdoc8.pdf; C. H. Stanley memo to A. H. Belmont, May 21, 1952, L. B. Nichols memo to Tolson with attachment, May 9, 1952, FBIW.

264 **hated rivals:** Evan Thomas, pp. 138–39.

265 **"currency operations.":** Memo to file on FGW on meeting with an agent in the FBI Field Office, WFC; L. B. Nichols memo to Tolson with attachment, May 9, 1952, FBIW.

265 **intensive probe:** L. B. Nichols memo to Tolson with attachment, May 9, 1952, C. H. Stanley memo to A. H. Belmont, May 21, 1952, V. P. Keay memo to A. H. Belmont, May 29, 1952, JEH letter to Walter B. Smith, Nov. 28, 1952, FBIW.

265 **marry Moevs:** V. P. Keay memo to A. H. Belmont, May 29, 1952, Walter B. Smith letter to JEH, Dec. 24, 1952, FBIW; Larry Leisensohn letter to FGW, Jan. 10, 1947, B: 1, FWP, UVA.

266 **representing Ausnit:** FGW letter to William Deakin, April 2, 1952, B: 3, FWP, UVA; V. C. Georgescu letter to Wendy Hazard, Feb. 24, 1993, WFC; Walter B. Smith letter to JEH, Dec. 24, 1952, AWD letter to JEH, April 19, 1954, Sheffield Edwards letter to Sam Papich, May 24, 1955, BHP; C. H. Stanley memo to A. H. Belmont, May 21, 1952, V. P. Keay memo to A. H. Belmont, May 29, 1952, L. B. Nichols memo to Tolson, May 2, 1952, FBIW; Memorandum to Mr. Nichols, Dec. 19, 1950, FBI file on AWD.

267 **the case:** Evan Thomas, p. 139; FGWII, Nov. 10, 2020; EW, July 15 and Aug. 5, 2020; GW, Dec. 1 and 10, 2020; Assistant General Counsel memo to Director of Security, Jan. 5, 1955, WFC; Norman Farquhar letter to FGW, June 17, 1955, B: 1, FWP, UVA.

267 **and arresting:** Heymann, p. 46; GAO Report, May 15, 1978, "Widespread Conspiracy to Obstruct Probes of Alleged Nazi War Criminals Not Supported by Available Evidence—Controversy May Continue," p. 2; GAO Report, June 28, 1985, "Nazis and Axis Collaborators Were Used to Further U.S.

Anti-Communist Objectives in Europe—Some Immigrated to the United States," pp. 2–3.

268 **the Germans:** Loftus, pp. 9, 73, 78, 82, 89–90, 104, 158; FGWII, Nov. 10, 2020; EW, Nov. 11, 2020; Simpson, p. xiv; Draft Working Paper, Chapter Seven, Could He Not Be Brought to This Country and Used? and Chapter Twelve, Essential to the Furtherance of the National Intelligence Mission, CREST for FGW; William Casey letter to Edward Boland, May 26, 1982, with enclosed staff report on John Loftus allegations, CREST for FGW; John Bross letter to EW, May 9, 1986, WFC.

268 **Naturalization Service:** GAO Report, June 28, 1985, "Nazis and Axis Collaborators Were Used to Further U.S. Anti-Communist Objectives in Europe—Some Immigrated to the United States," p. 11; Simpson, p. 192; GAO Report, May 15, 1978, "Widespread Conspiracy to Obstruct Probes of Alleged Nazi War Criminals Not Supported by Available Evidence—Controversy May Continue," p. 40.

268 **"Third Reich.":** GAO Report, June 28, 1985, "Nazis and Axis Collaborators Were Used to Further U.S. Anti-Communist Objectives in Europe—Some Immigrated to the United States," pp. 10–11, 15, 20, 27–29; Simpson, p. 38; Jacobsen, pp. 282–85, 298, 450; Draft Working Paper, Chapter Eight, Cooperation Was an Unavoidable Evil, CREST for FGW; Ruffner, "Eagle and Swastika," pp. 146, 245.

269 **for the CIA:** Ruffner, "Eagle and Swastika," pp. 329–47, 404; Files, General Counsel, Entry, Residence, and Departure of Aliens, Dec. 7, 1948, CREST for FGW; Hersh, pp. 269–70; GAO Report, June 28, 1985, "Nazis and Axis Collaborators Were Used to Further U.S. Anti-Communist Objectives in Europe— Some Immigrated to the United States," pp. ii, 18, 26–27, 32–34, 40; Statement of Arnold P. Jones Before the Subcommittee on Immigration, Refugees, and International Law on Allegations of Nazi War Criminals Residing in the United States, Oct. 17, 1985.

270 **"one's club.":** Ruffner, "Eagle and Swastika," pp. 198–99, 203–4, 210, 218–20, 234; Ruffner, "Cold War Allies," pp. 41–42; Simpson, pp. 130–36, 266; GAO Report, June 28, 1985, "Nazis and Axis Collaborators Were Used to Further U.S. Anti-Communist Objectives in Europe—Some Immigrated to the United States," pp. 36–37; Loftus, p. 118; Cryptonyms in Declassified CIA files, ZZ19, RG263, NA; Grose, p. 314; Mosley, p. 238; Richard Helms, pp. 83–86; FGWII, Sept. 9 and Nov. 10, 2020; EW, Nov. 11, 2020; Ruffner, "Forging an Intelligence Partnership," vol. 1, p. xxix and Vol. 2, p. 12; Memo for DCI, Christmas Cards from General Gehlen, Jan. 20, 1955, CREST for FGW; Ruffner, "Eagle and Swastika," pp. 11, 290; FGW memo to AWD on Reinhard Gehlen, Nov. 6, 1953, CREST for FGW.

270 **war criminals:** Ruffner, "Eagle and Swastika," pp. 298, 321–25; Mosley, pp. 273–75; Richard Helms, p. 87; Ruffner, "Forging an Intelligence Partnership," vol. 1, p. xxviii.

271 **"too long.":** Ruffner, "Eagle and Swastika," pp. 324–27; Ruffner, "Forging an Intelligence Partnership," vol. 1, p. xxiii and vol. 2, p. 16; Richard Helms, pp. 86–87, 90–91.

271 **a year:** Warner, *The CIA Under Harry Truman*, p. 461; The Support Services, Historical Series, Supply Division 1951 Through 1970, CIA Historical Staff, September 1972, pp. 9–10; Richard Helms, p. 106; Grose, p. 417.

271 **literally, steaming:** Sept. 26, 1958, routing slip for FGW, Staff Conference minutes, Jan. 8, 1951, Minutes for Director's Meeting, June 2, 1952, DD/S Diary Notes, July 12, 1955, Minutes for Deputies' Meeting, June 26, 1952, May 11, 1953, and June 6, 1958, CREST for FGW.

272 **rarely succeeded:** John Magruder memo on Budget Bureau Report on Psychological Strategy Board, May 8, 1952, CREST for FGW; CIA's Analysis of the Soviet Union, 1947–1991, p. 35, CIA Library, https://www.cia.gov/resources/csi/static/CIAs-Analysis-of-the-Soviet-Union-1947-1991-complete-collection-1.pdf; Murphy et al., p. 42; Church Committee, *Final Report*, book 1, p. 558; Rositzke, pp. 74, 120–22, 127.

272 **potential recruits:** Rositzke, pp. 139–41; Minutes for Deputies' Meeting, Sept. 11, 1952, CREST for FGW.

273 **Helms believed:** Evan Thomas, pp. 36–37; David Frost interview with RMH, *Studies in Intelligence*, fall 1981, B: 8, E: 27, RG263, NA; ADD/A Diary, Feb. 25, 1953, CREST for FGW; Grose, pp. 328–29, 390.

273 **ever convened:** Church Committee, *Final Report*, book 4, pp. 128–32; Grose, p. 329.

274 **planet Jupiter:** Minutes for Deputies' Meeting, June 19, 1952, Minutes for Director's Meeting, May 26, 1952, Minutes for Deputies' Meeting, Nov. 28, 1952, Preparation for Jackson Committee, Wednesday, Dec. 3, Flying Saucers, (6), Official Diary (Acting DD/I), Dec. 12, 1952, CREST for FGW; 108. Briefing Paper Prepared by the Chairman of the 10/5 Panel (Barnes), May 7, 1952, FRUS, The Intelligence Community, 1950–1955; Warner, *The CIA Under Harry Truman*, pp. 459–60.

274 **legal trouble:** Minutes for Deputies' Meeting, Oct. 17, 1952, CREST for FGW; Attachment 1, Draft Memorandum by Director of Central Intelligence Smith, Oct. 8, 1952, Annex 2, Memorandum from Outerbridge Horsey of the Policy Planning Staff to the Deputy Undersecretary of State (Matthews), Jan. 26, 1953, FRUS, The Intelligence Community, 1950–1955; Grose, p. 327.

275 **Wisner thought:** Enclosure 1, Annex D to No. 6, "The National Psychological Program" of NSC 135, Aug. 1, 1952, FRUS, The Intelligence Community, 1950–1955; FGWII, Dec. 11, 2020; Prados, *Safe for Democracy*, p. 48; Minutes for Director's Meeting, March 4, 1952, CREST for FGW; Rositzke, pp. 28–29; "Almost Successful Recipe," pp. 18–19; Herken, pp. 174–75.

276 **his power:** Recording of Meeting in General Smith's Office Concerning Reorganization of DD/P, Approximate date July 15, 1952, Minutes for Deputies' Meeting, Oct. 2, 1952, Staff Conference minutes, May 26, 1952, Minutes for Deputies' Meeting, July 1, 1952, Minutes for Director's Meeting, March 6, 1952, Minutes for Director's Meeting, Jan. 25, 1952, Minutes for Director's Meeting, March 12, 1952, Minutes for Deputies' Meeting, Sept. 16, 1952, Minutes for Director's Meeting, Jan. 10, 1962, Minutes for Deputies' Meeting, Dec. 9, 1952, ADD/A Diary Notes, July 2–12, 1952, ADD/A Diary Notes, July 1, 1952, and Jan. 7, 1955, CREST for FGW.

276 **presidential election:** Minutes for Director's Meeting, Jan. 7, 1952, Minutes for Director's Meeting, March 18, 1952, Minutes for Director's Meeting, Feb. 25, 1952, Official Diary (Acting DD/I), Sept. 10 and Oct. 16, 1952, CREST for FGW; Crosswell, p. 43.

277 **no intellectual:** FGWII, Oct. 19, 2020, and Jan. 13, 2021; Mosley, p. 394; FGW letter to his mother, July 26, 1952, B: 4, FWP, UVA.

277 **became president:** Halberstam, *The Fifties*, pp. 244, 706; Ambrose, *Ike's Spies*, pp. 156–57, 256; Ambrose, *Eisenhower*, p. 288; Corson, p. 231; Laurie, "A New President," p. 3.

277 **be Eisenhower:** Katharine Graham interview with Polly Fritchey, Oct. 10, 1989, pp. 23–25, KGP; FGW letter to Mary Donovan, Nov. 25, 1952, and Mary Donovan's reply, Dec. 1, 1952, B: 3, FWP, UVA; Waller, *Wild Bill Donovan*, pp. 375–76.

278 **he did:** Ambrose, *Eisenhower*, p. 433; Minutes for Deputies' Meeting, Dec. 5, 1952, CREST for FGW; Herken, p. 159; FGW letter to Richard Stilwell, Nov. 13, 1952, B: 9, Sherman Adams letter to FGW, April 9, 1954, B: 1, FWP, UVA.

Chapter 17: Eisenhower

279 **Council meetings:** Adams, COH, pp. 166–67; Ambrose, *Eisenhower*, p. 323; Halberstam, *The Fifties*, p. 360; "Almost Successful Recipe," p. 96; Gray, COH, p. 26; Laurie, "A New President," p. 6.

280 **power overseas:** Ambrose, *Eisenhower*, pp. 321–23, 347, 437–38; Halberstam, *The Fifties*, p. 616; Anderson, pp. 330, 440; Leary, pp. 6, 146–49.

280 **with Ike:** Jackson, vol. 1, pp. 16–17; Montague, vol. 2, p. 4; Mosley, pp. 294–95; Organizational History of the Central Intelligence Agency, 1950–1953, pp. II—52, MN; Adams, COH, p. 167; Waller, *Wild Bill Donovan*, pp. 360–61; Minutes for Deputies' Meeting, April 28, 1953, CREST for FGW; Hersh, pp. 312–13; Interview with PKW, B: 10, RSP, HA.

281 **wide-ranging chats:** Mosley, pp. 288, 393; Waller, *Disciples*, pp. 17, 69, 72–76, 120; Philip Crowl interview with DDE, July 26, 1964, OH-14, Oral Histories, pp. 7, 10, DEL; Dulles, COH, pp. 94–95, 100.

281 **from the start:** Martin, FAOH, p. 62; Greene, FAOH, p. 29; Adams, COH, pp. 6, 20; Ambrose, *Eisenhower*, pp. 289, 302; Montague, vol. 5, pp. 112, 114, 116.

281 **her brother:** Avis Bohlen manuscript; Joseph Alsop, pp. 347–48; FGWII, Jan. 13, 2021; Anderson, pp. 318–19; Minutes for Deputies' Meeting, Dec. 23, 1952, CREST for FGW; Dulles, COH, p. 52.

282 **like them:** McIntosh, Aug. 29, 2007; Brown, pp. 826–88; Montague, vol. 5, p. 113; Srodes, p. 433.

282 **name, Pearre:** AWD Notice, April 23, 1953, CREST for FGW; Jackson, vol. 1, p. 73; Hunt, p. 69; Cryptonym list, E: ZZ19, RG263, NA; Corson, p. 377; Minutes for Deputies' Meeting, March 11, 1955, CREST for FGW; Mosley, p. 324; FGW letter to Charles Cabell, March 30, 1965, B: 2, FWP, UVA.

282 **around Washington:** Mosley, p. 345; Grose, p. 387; Interview with Wayne Jackson, B: 9, RSP, HA.

282 **house unlocked:** Minutes for Deputies' Meeting, Jan. 17, 1955, CREST for FGW; Waller, *Disciples*, p. 427; Minutes for Deputies' Meeting, March 9, 1953, CREST for FGW; Srodes, p. 452.

283 **officials occupied:** McIntosh, Aug. 29, 2007; Jackson, vol. 1, pp. 23–27; Grose, pp. 387–88; Richard Helms, p. 115; Ranelagh, p. 272; FGWII, Sept. 9, 2020; GW, Aug. 10, 2020; Interview with Wayne Jackson, B: 9, RSP, HA.

283 **his spies:** FGWII, Sept. 9, 2020; Grose, p. 417; Hersh, p. 32; Srodes, pp. 480–81; Interview with PKW, B: 10, RSP, HA; AWD Notice No. P-6-53, WFC.

284 **modern society:** Petersen, pp. 19–29.

284 **individual operations:** Jackson, vol. 1, pp. 71–72, vol. 3, p. 106; Richard Kovar, "An Interview with Richard Lehman," CIA Oral History Program, CIA History Staff, p. 53; Mosley, p. 324; Lundahl, COH, p. 591.

284 **stern brother:** Adams, COH, p. 168; Richard Kovar, "An Interview with Richard Lehman," CIA Oral History Program, CIA History Staff, pp. 52–53; Grose, p. 386; Anderson, COH, pp. 48–49, 69; Evan Thomas, pp. 185–86; Killian, COH, p. 22.

285 **the bureau:** Memorandum for Mr. Nichols on AWD, Dec. 18, 1950, R. R. Roach memo to A. H. Belmont on AWD, Nov. 4, 1958, Memorandum for Mr. Tolson on AWD, Aug. 7, 1953, Legal Attaché, Rome, to JEH on AWD,

Sept. 7, 1955, D. M. Ladd memo to JEH on AWD, March 3, 1953, Memo to L. B. Nichols on AWD, Dec. 19, 1950, FBI file on AWD.

285   **at the CIA:** Halberstam, *The Fifties*, p. 251; Ambrose, *Eisenhower*, pp. 308–9, 316; Jackson, vol. 1, pp. 46–47; Meyer, pp. 80–81.

286   **wife, Avis:** Bohlen, COH, p. 4; Herken, pp. 183–84; Joseph Alsop, pp. 349–50; FGW memo on the Development of a National Psychological Strategy, Jan. 2, 1952, WFC.

286   **senator posed:** FGWII, Nov. 10, 2020; Avis Bohlen manuscript; Bohlen, Nov. 17, 2020; EW, Nov. 11, 2020; Isaacson and Thomas, p. 575; Herken, p. 186.

286   **huge profit:** Letter to AWD, Nov. 3, 1953, V. P. Keay memos to A. H. Belmont, Nov. 3 and 9, 1953, and Jan. 5, 1954, FBIW.

287   **Soviet agents:** L. B. Nichols memo to Tolson, March 24, 1954, W. A. Branigan memo to A. H. Belmont, March 30, 1954, R. R. Roach memo to A. H. Belmont, Oct. 13, 1955, FBIW.

287   **smear campaign:** W. A. Branigan memo to A. H. Belmont, March 30, 1954, AWD letter to JEH, April 19, 1954, FBIW.

288   **the past:** Evan Thomas, pp. 138–39, 172; O'Toole, p. 451; Jackson, vol. 4, p. 96; Minutes for Director's Meeting, March 10, 1952, Minutes for Deputies' Meeting, July 25, 1956, FGW memo to DCI on Projected OSS Series, 1956, FGW memo to DCI on Congressional Contacts, Dec. 22, 1953, CREST for FGW; Herken, pp. 176–78, 218; Marchetti and Marks, pp. 334–35; Wilford, pp. 226–27, 231–32; Grose, pp. 338–39; Srodes, p. 433; Jackson, vol. 1, p. 51; Ranelagh, pp. 281–82; EW, Dec. 6, 2020; Hersh, p. 306–7.

288   **promotion policies:** Church Committee, *Final Report*, book 1, p. 145; Minutes for Deputies' Meetings, April 28 and May 21, 1953, Monthly Traffic Figures, June 1953, The Petticoat Panel: A 1953 Study of the Role of Women in the CIA Career Service, March 2003, CREST for FGW; Cryptonym list, E: ZZ19, RG263, NA; Memorandum from FGW to AWD Oct. 7, 1953, FRUS, The Intelligence Community, 1950–1955.

288   **more pixies:** Evan Thomas, pp. 37–38; 53. Report by the Psychological Strategy Board, July 29, 1953, FRUS, The Intelligence Community, 1950–1955; Warner, "Sophisticated Spies," p. 429; "Almost Successful Recipe," pp. 24–25; Powers, pp. 50–54; Anderson, p. 318; Herken, p. 175; 1953 BGFiend project continues on the same scale as 1952, Authorization of funds for BGFiend, Allotment Account No. 2100-019, CIA FOIA, cia.gov.

289   **action projects:** Waller, *Disciples*, p. 492; Richard Helms, pp. 102–7; Document No. 74, NSC 158, United States Objectives and Actions to Exploit the Unrest in the Satellite States, June 29, 1953, NSA.

290   **should be:** Hyland, p. 63; Confidential memo to AWD, FGW, and Charles Cabell on Stalin suffering a stroke, March 1–2, 1953; Grose, pp. 339–53; Mosley, p. 331; Isaacson and Thomas, p. 577.

290   **he said:** EW, Dec. 6, 2020; Minutes for Deputies' Meeting, March 23, 1953, FGW memo to DCI on psychological exploitation of Stalin's Death, March 1953, CREST for FGW; FGWII, Jan. 13, 2021.

291   **"long time.":** Khrushchev Personality Report issued after Stalin's death, CREST for FGW; CIA's Analysis of the Soviet Union, 1947–1991, CIA Library, https://www.cia.gov/resources/csi/static/CIAs-Analysis-of-the-Soviet-Union-1947-1991-complete-collection-1.pdf; Phillips, pp. 70–71.

291   **East Germany:** On the Front Lines of the Cold War: Documents on the Intelligence War in Berlin, 1946 to 1961, III. June 1953, CIA Library, cia.gov; Hersh, p. 377.

291   **Hill farm:** FGW letter to Chis, June 18, 1953, B: 4, FWP, UVA; Travel document for FGW and Tracy Barnes trip to Europe, June 19–July 10, 1953, B: 7,

FWP, UVA; Evan Thomas, pp. 75–85; EW, Oct. 20, 2020; Katharine Graham interview with Polly Fritchey, Oct. 10, 1989, p. 14, KGP.

292 **a hypochondriac:** FGW and Hardy Dillard correspondence, Oct. 27 and Nov. 2, 1953, B: 10, FGW and T. Munford Boyd correspondence, May 21–22, 1953, B: 1, Charles Stone letter to FGW, March 31, 1953, Neill Phillips letter to FGW, June 26, 1956, B: 5, FGW and Alexander Chisholm correspondence, April 15, June 17, and Dec. 31, 1953, B: 4, Laurel Realty Co. Balance Sheet, B: 4, FWP, UVA.

292 **fruitful results:** Travel document for FGW and Tracy Barnes trip to Europe, June 19–July 10, 1953, B: 7, FWP, UVA; Clandestine Services History: The Evolution of Ground Paramilitary Activities at the Staff Level, October 1949—September 1955, Nov. 1968.

292 **Kremlin walls:** FGW correspondence with Isaiah Berlin, July 22, Aug. 20, and Oct. 30, 1953, B: 1, FWP, UVA.

292 **the CIA:** Ambrose, *Eisenhower*, pp. 330–31; Halberstam, *The Coldest Winter*, p. 630; Halberstam, *The Fifties*, p. 360.

Chapter 18: Iran

293 **rolled back:** Halberstam, *The Fifties*, p. 396; Evan Thomas, p. 110; Ambrose, *Eisenhower*, p. 329.

294 **meeting notes:** Bowie, FAOH, p. 13; "Almost Successful Recipe," pp. a., 2; Warner, *The CIA Under Harry Truman*, pp. 219–32; Preparation for Jackson Committee, Central Africa, Friday, November 21, 1952 CREST for FGW.

294 **a target:** Symmes, FAOH, pp. 26, 30–31.

294 **pointed out:** Koch, p. 1.

295 **Persian Gulf:** Kinzer, pp. 18, 28, 31–40, 49.

295 **Peacock Throne:** Kinzer, pp. 42–45, 63–64; Takeyh, pp. 15, 28–29, 61; Helms (Foundation for Iranian Studies), COH, pp. 1–8; Halberstam, *The Fifties*, p. 363.

296 **back in:** Kinzer, pp. 65–66, 205; Documents Assessing the Soviet Threat, CIA Library, cia.gov; Takeyh, p. 39.

296 **the war:** Stutesman, FAOH, pp. 3–8, 14, 19–20; Halberstam, *The Fifties*, p. 363.

297 **London's benevolence:** Kinzer, pp. 67–68; Takeyh, pp. 55–58.

297 **"crude itself.":** Kinzer, pp. 68–70.

297 **supply them:** Kinzer, pp. 70–71.

298 **with him:** Kinzer, pp. xxvi, 53–61, 71; Stutesman, FAOH, pp. 12–13; Takeyh, pp. 67–68; 23. and 65. Despatches from the Embassy in Iran to the Department of State, May 4, 1951, and Feb. 16, 1952, FRUS, Iran, 1951–1954.

298 **six months:** Kinzer, pp. 71–75; 180. Progress Report to the National Security Council, March 20, 1953, FRUS, Iran, 1951–1954.

299 **Communist ideology:** Kinzer, pp. 77–78; 58. Memorandum Prepared in the Office of National Estimates, undated, 1. Despatch from the Embassy in Iran to the Department of State, Feb. 23, 1951, FRUS, Iran, 1951–1954; Stutesman, FAOH, p. 21.

299 **of Iran:** Kinzer, pp. 78–80.

300 **Iran's neighbors:** 4. Memorandum from the Plans Branch, Near East and Africa Division, Directorate of Plans to the Deputy Director of Central Intelligence, March 12, 1951, 5. Paper Prepared in the Directorate of Plans, Central Intelligence Agency, undated, 8. Memorandum from the Deputy Assistant Secretary of State for Near Eastern, South Asian, and African Affairs (Berry) to the Deputy Undersecretary of State (Matthews), March 15, 1951, 6. Draft Statement of Policy Proposed by the National Security Council, March 14, 1951, 61. Despatch from the Station in Iran to the Central Intelligence Agency, Jan. 20,

1952, 43. Despatch from the Embassy in Iran to the Department of State, Aug. 20, 1951, FRUS, Iran, 1951–1954.

300 **Dulles argued:** 11. Memorandum from AWD to Director of Central Intelligence Smith, March 28, 1951, FRUS, Iran, 1951–1954.

300 **out to be:** 13. National Intelligence Estimate, April 5, 1951, FRUS, Iran, 1951–1954; Kinzer, p. 205; Takeyh, pp. 72, 84, 102–3.

301 **told her:** 10. Memorandum from the Chief of the Near East and Africa Division, Directorate of Plans (Roosevelt) to AWD, March 26, 1951, FRUS, Iran, 1951–1954; Koch, p. 22; Prados, *Safe for Democracy*, p. 98; Roosevelt, pp. 23–24, 35–36, 46, 48, 51, 58–59; Kinzer, pp. 4, 148; EW, Oct. 20, 2020; FGWII, Oct. 19, 2020, and Jan. 13, 2021; GW, Dec. 1, 2020.

302 **despised them:** Kinzer, pp. 81–84, 91.

302 **"by decree.":** 20. Memorandum Prepared in the Office of National Estimates, CIA, May 1, 1951, 24. Telegram from the Station in Iran to the CIA, May 6, 1951, 25. Minutes of Director of Central Intelligence Smith's Meeting, May 9, 1951, 26. Memorandum for the Record, May 10, 1951, FRUS, Iran, 1951–1954.

303 **their oil:** 35. Note by the Acting Executive Secretary of the NSC (Gleason), June 27, 1951, FRUS, Iran, 1951–1954; Kinzer, pp. 97–98; Koch, p. 10.

303 **from office:** Kinzer, pp. 99–110.

303 **British diplomats:** Kinzer, pp. 3, 111–17.

304 **on Islam:** 40. Project Outline Prepared in the CIA, July 26, 1951, 41. Project Outline Prepared in the CIA, undated, 48. Memorandum for the Record, Oct. 9, 1951, FRUS, Iran, 1951–1954.

304 **"the Russians.":** Kinzer, p. 117.

305 **"of 8,000.":** Kinzer, pp. 118–32; 55. Despatch from the Embassy in Iran to the Department of State, Nov. 23, 1953, FRUS, Iran, 1951–1954.

305 **legislative coup:** Takeyh, p. 80; Kinzer, pp. 136–38; 62. Memorandum from the Assistant Director (Kent) to the Director of Central Intelligence, Jan. 30, 1952, 66. Memorandum from the Acting Chief of the Near East and Africa Division, Director of Plans, to the Deputy Director for Plans, Central Intelligence Agency, Feb. 20, 1952, FRUS, Iran, 1951–1954.

306 **out-then-in maneuver:** Kinzer, 134–41; Takeyh, p. 85.

306 **Iranian government:** 102. Minutes of Director of Central Intelligence Smith's Meeting, July 29, 1952, 106. Memorandum of Telephone Conversation, July 31, 1952, FRUS, Iran, 1951–1954.

306 **Smith speculated:** 104. Minutes of Director of Central Intelligence Smith's Meeting, July 30, 1952, FRUS, Iran, 1951–1954.

307 **official advised:** 109. Memorandum for the Record, July 31, 1952, FRUS, Iran, 1951–1954.

307 **oil back:** 110. Memorandum from FGW to the Director of the Policy Planning Staff (Joyce), undated, FRUS, Iran, 1951–1954; Halberstam, *The Fifties*, p. 366; Memo from FGW to Robert Joyce, Washington, on Joint U.S.-U.K. Planning on Emergency Operations in Iran, undated, WFC.

308 **six years:** Kinzer, pp. 142–44, 152; 55. Despatch from the Embassy in Iran to the Department of State, Nov. 23, 1951, FRUS, Iran, 1951–1954; Koch, pp. 18–19; Takeyh, p. 96; Clandestine Services History: Overthrow of Premier Mossadegh of Iran, November 1952–August 1953, CSH Paper No. 208, appendix E, pp. 5–6, NSA Electronic Briefing Book No. 435 on CIA role in 1953 Iran coup.

308 **back it up:** Kinzer, pp. 3, 144–48.

309 **that prize:** Takeyh, p. 93; FGWII, Jan. 13 and March 11, 2021; Kinzer, pp. 3–4, 148, 151–52.

309 **of Mossadegh:** 143. National Intelligence Estimate, Nov. 13, 1952, FRUS, Iran, 1951–1954; Official Diary (Acting DD/I), Nov. 26, 1952, CREST for FGW.

310 **that idea:** Clandestine Services History: Overthrow of Premier Mossadegh of Iran, November 1952—August 1953, CSH Paper No. 208, NSA Electronic Briefing Book No. 435 on CIA role in 1953 Iran coup; Roosevelt, pp. 119–20.

310 **"Dump him.":** Kinzer, p. 155; Stutesman, FAOH, p. 21; Roosevelt, pp. 115–16.

310 **mentally unstable:** Takeyh, pp. 94–99; Halberstam, *The Fifties*, p. 366; 155. Telegram from the Embassy in Iran to the Department of State, Feb. 20, 1953, FRUS, Iran, 1951–1954.

310 **for Mossadegh:** Takeyh, pp. 81, 85, 98–99.

311 **last name:** Roosevelt, pp. 120–22.

311 **"of power":** 169. Memorandum from Director of Central Intelligence Dulles to President Eisenhower, March 1, 1953, 170. Memorandum Prepared in the Directorate of Plans, Central Intelligence Agency, March 3, 1953, FRUS, Iran, 1951–1954.

311 **"right now.":** 171. Memorandum of Discussion at the 135th Meeting of the NSC, March 5, 1953, 176. Memorandum of Discussion at the 136th Meeting of the NSC, March 11, 1953, FRUS, Iran, 1951–1954.

312 **as $200,000:** Kinzer, p. 205; 177. Memorandum Prepared in the Office of National Estimates, CIA, March 11, 1953, 182. Information Reports Prepared in the CIA, March 31, 1953, FRUS, Iran, 1951–1954; Halberstam, *The Fifties*, p. 362; Roosevelt, p. 119.

312 **the CIA:** Kinzer, p. 164; Stutesman, FAOH, p. 22; Roosevelt, pp. 9, 16–17.

312 **a coup:** Ambrose, *Eisenhower*, p. 332; Kinzer, pp. 157–60; Dorril, p. 583; Clandestine Services History: Overthrow of Premier Mossadegh of Iran, November 1952–August 1953, CSH Paper No. 208, chapter I, pp. 3–4, NSA Electronic Briefing Book No. 435 on CIA role in 1953 Iran coup; Takeyh, p. 106.

313 **prime minister:** 188. Information Report Prepared in the CIA, April 8, 1953, 189. Telegram from the Station in Iran to the CIA, April 12, 1953, 190. Telegram from the Station in Iran to the CIA, April 14, 1953, 191. Information Report Prepared in the CIA, April 16, 1953, 193. Information Report Prepared in the CIA, April 17, 1953, 197. Information Report Prepared in the CIA, April 28, 1953, FRUS, Iran, 1951–1954.

316 **about Roosevelt:** 192. Memorandum from the Chief of the Iran Branch, Near East and Africa Division (Waller) to the Chief of the Near East and Africa Division, Directorate of Plans, CIA (Roosevelt), April 16, 1953, FRUS, Iran, 1951–1954.

316 **CIA history:** 202. Monthly Report Prepared in the Directorate of Plans, CIA, May 6, 1953, 203. Telegram from the Embassy in Iran to the Department of State, May 8, 1953, FRUS, Iran, 1951–1954; Clandestine Services History: Overthrow of Premier Mossadegh of Iran, November 1952–August 1953, CSH Paper No. 208, appendix B, pp. 18–19, 26, NSA Electronic Briefing Book No. 435 on CIA role in 1953 Iran coup.

317 **the opposition:** 209. Briefing Notes Prepared in the CIA for the Director of Central Intelligence Dulles, undated, 213. Monthly Report Prepared in the Directorate of Plans, CIA, undated, FRUS, Iran, 1951–1954.

317 **ambassador maintained:** 209. Briefing Notes Prepared in the CIA for the Director of Central Intelligence Dulles, undated, 213. Monthly Report Prepared in the Directorate of Plans, CIA, undated, FRUS, Iran, 1951–1954.

319   **"100 percent."**: Clandestine Services History: Overthrow of Premier Mossa-
       degh of Iran, November 1952–August 1953, CSH Paper No. 208, summary, p.
       vi, chapter II, pp. 5–6, 9, chapter v, p. 26, appendix A, pp. 1, 4, appendix B, pp.
       12, 15, appendix E, p. 22, NSA Electronic Briefing Book No. 435 on CIA role
       in 1953 Iran coup; Kinzer, pp. 162–63; 255. Memorandum from the Chief of the
       Iran Branch, Near East and Africa Division, Directorate of Plans (Waller) to
       FGW, July 30, 1953, FRUS, Iran, 1951–1954; Takeyh, p. 105.

319   **was true:** 216. Memorandum of Conversation, June 6, 1953, 233. Despatch from
       the Embassy in Iran to the Department of State, July 1, 1953, FRUS, Iran,
       1951–1954; Kinzer, p. 161.

320   **with Eisenhower:** Ambrose, *Eisenhower*, pp. 161, 333; Roosevelt, p. 135; 251.
       Editorial Note, FRUS, Iran, 1951–1954.

320   **90 percent illiterate:** Takeyh, pp. 106–7; Clandestine Services History: Over-
       throw of Premier Mossadegh of Iran, November 1952–August 1953, CSH Paper
       No. 208, summary, pp. vi–vii, x–xi, chapter II, pp. 9–10, chapter IV, p. 20, NSA
       Electronic Briefing Book No. 435 on CIA role in 1953 Iran coup.

320   **in mid-August:** Takeyh, p. 101; Clandestine Services History: Overthrow of
       Premier Mossadegh of Iran, November 1952–August 1953, CSH Paper No. 208,
       summary, p. vi, NSA Electronic Briefing Book No. 435 on CIA role in 1953
       Iran coup.

Chapter 19: Operation Ajax
322   **kidney stone:** Roosevelt, pp. 21, 23, 50, 68, 82, 137–43; 228. Letter from the
       Chief of the Near East and Africa Division, Directorate of Plans, CIA (Roo-
       sevelt) to the Chief of Station in Iran, June 29, 1953, FRUS, Iran, 1951–1954.

322   **was plunging:** Kinzer, p. 165; Roosevelt, pp. 141–42, 151.

322   **street mobs:** Roosevelt, pp. 140, 144–45, 165–66; Takeyh, p. 107.

322   **plans for him:** 240. Memorandum from the Chief of the Near East and Africa
       Division, Directorate of Plans, CIA (Roosevelt) to Mitchell, July 16, 1953, 249.
       Memorandum from the Acting Chief of the Near East and Africa Division,
       CIA, to Mitchell, July 23, 1953, FRUS, Iran, 1951–1954; Clandestine Services
       History: Overthrow of Premier Mossadegh of Iran, November 1952–August
       1953, CSH Paper No. 208, chapter V, p. 27, NSA Electronic Briefing Book No.
       435 on CIA role in 1953 Iran coup.

323   **the operation:** Roosevelt, p. 22; Clandestine Services History: Overthrow of
       Premier Mossadegh of Iran, November 1952–August 1953, CSH Paper No. 208,
       chapter V, p. 28, NSA Electronic Briefing Book No. 435 on CIA role in 1953
       Iran coup; 243. Memorandum from the Chief of the Near East and Africa Di-
       vision, Directorate of Plans (Roosevelt) to AWD, July 17, 1953, 253. Memoran-
       dum from FGW to the Chief of the Near East and Africa Division, Directorate
       of Plans, CIA (Roosevelt), July 28, 1953, FRUS, Iran, 1951–1954.

323   **memo warned:** 247. Paper Prepared in the CIA, July 22, 1953, FRUS, Iran,
       1951–1954.

323   **was tolerating:** Kinzer, p. 5; 252. Memorandum from the Chief of the Iran
       Branch, Near East and Africa Division (Waller) to AWD, July 27, 1953, 249.
       Memorandum from the Acting Chief of the Near East and Africa Division,
       Directorate of Plans, CIA, to Mitchell, July 23, 1953, FRUS, Iran, 1951–1954.

324   **of influence:** 255. Memorandum from the Chief of the Iran Branch, Near East
       and Africa Division, Directorate of Plans (Waller) to FGW, July 30, 1953, 168.
       Monthly Report, Prepared in the Directorate of Plans, CIA, undated, FRUS,
       Iran, 1951–1954.

324   **momentous step:** Kinzer, pp. 5–7; Takeyh, pp. 56–57, 93, 109.

325 **was unsuccessful:** Kinzer, pp. 7–8; Takeyh, pp. 107–8; Roosevelt, pp. 145–46.

325 **Roosevelt's team:** Kinzer, p. 64; Ambrose, *Ike's Spies*, p. 193; Clandestine Services History: Overthrow of Premier Mossadegh of Iran, November 1952–August 1953, CSH Paper No. 208, chapter V, p. 25, NSA Electronic Briefing Book No. 435 on CIA role in 1953 Iran coup; 227. Memorandum of Conversation, June 26, 1953, 228. Letter from the Chief of the Near East and Africa Division, Directorate of Plans, CIA (Roosevelt) to the Chief of Station in Iran, June 29, 1953, FRUS, Iran, 1951–1954; Roosevelt, pp. 146–47.

325 **nervous breakdown:** Kinzer, p. 8; Clandestine Services History: Overthrow of Premier Mossadegh of Iran, November 1952–August 1953, CSH Paper No. 208, chapter V, pp. 25–26, 29–30, NSA Electronic Briefing Book No. 435 on CIA role in 1953 Iran coup; Takeyh, p. 98; K. Roosevelt Notes on the Life of Allen Dulles, B: 10, RSP, HA.

326 **the meeting:** Kinzer, pp. 8–9.

326 **the palace:** Roosevelt, pp. 155–56; Clandestine Services History: Overthrow of Premier Mossadegh of Iran, November 1952–August 1953, CSH Paper No. 208, chapter V, pp. 33–34, NSA Electronic Briefing Book No. 435 on CIA role in 1953 Iran coup; Kinzer, pp. 9–10.

327 **to Baghdad:** Roosevelt, pp. 158–61; Kinzer, pp. 10–11.

327 **legislative body:** Takeyh, p. 100.

328 **"of battle":** Roosevelt, pp. 166–67; Koch, p. 64; Clandestine Services History: Overthrow of Premier Mossadegh of Iran, November 1952–August 1953, CSH Paper No. 208, appendix E, pp. 2–3, 7–8, 12, NSA Electronic Briefing Book No. 435 on CIA role in 1953 Iran coup; 1. Despatch from the Embassy in Iran to the Department of State, Feb. 23, 1951, FRUS, Iran, 1951–1954.

328 **Caspian coast:** Roosevelt, pp. 167–68.

329 **assumed power:** Kinzer, pp. 11–13; Roosevelt, p. 169; 259. Draft Intelligence Estimate, Aug. 12, 1953, 263. Telegram from the Station in Iran to the CIA, Aug. 14, 1953, FRUS, Iran, 1951–1954.

330 **had collapsed:** Kinzer, pp. 13–16; Clandestine Services History: Overthrow of Premier Mossadegh of Iran, November 1952–August 1953, CSH Paper No. 208, chapter VI, p. 39, chapter VII, p. 44–45, 47, NSA Electronic Briefing Book No. 435 on CIA role in 1953 Iran coup; 267. Telegram from the Embassy in Iran to the Department of State, Aug. 16, 1953, 307. Record of Meeting in the CIA, Aug. 28, 1953, FRUS, Iran, 1951–1954; Roosevelt, pp. 171–78.

330 **on Ajax:** Clandestine Services History: Overthrow of Premier Mossadegh of Iran, November 1952–August 1953, CSH Paper No. 208, chapter VII, pp. 47, 58, 64, NSA Electronic Briefing Book No. 435 on CIA role in 1953 Iran coup; 265. Telegram from the CIA, Aug. 16, 1953, FRUS, Iran, 1951–1954.

331 **the Russians:** Kinzer, p. 172; Clandestine Services History: Overthrow of Premier Mossadegh of Iran, November 1952–August 1953, CSH Paper No. 208, chapter VII, p. 59, NSA Electronic Briefing Book No. 435 on CIA role in 1953 Iran coup; 270. Telegram from the Station in Iran to the CIA, Aug. 17, 1953, 264. Telegram from the Station in Iran to the CIA, Aug. 16, 1953, 274. Memorandum Prepared in the Directorate of Plans, CIA, Aug. 17, 1953, 278. Telegram from the CIA to the Station in Iran, Aug. 18, 1953, FRUS, Iran, 1951–1954.

332 **his own coup:** Clandestine Services History: Overthrow of Premier Mossadegh of Iran, November 1952–August 1953, CSH Paper No. 208, chapter IX, pp. 78–79, Chapter X, pp. 85–86, NSA Electronic Briefing Book No. 435 on CIA role in 1953 Iran coup; Takeyh, pp. 109–10; Kinzer, pp. 167–69; Roosevelt, pp. 178–79; Koch, p. 55; 266. Telegram from the Embassy in Iran to the

Department of State, Aug. 16, 1953, 307. Record of Meeting in the CIA, Aug. 28, 1953, FRUS, Iran, 1951–1954.

332 **was doing:** Kinzer, pp. 169–70, 174; 307. Record of Meeting in the CIA, Aug. 28, 1953, FRUS, Iran, 1951–1954.

332 **remained silent:** Kinzer, p. 170; Clandestine Services History: Overthrow of Premier Mossadegh of Iran, November 1952–August 1953, CSH Paper No. 208, summary, p. xi, NSA Electronic Briefing Book No. 435 on CIA role in 1953 Iran coup; 269. Telegram from the Station in Iran, Aug. 16, 1953, 271. Telegram from the Embassy in Iraq to the Department of State, Aug. 17, 1953, 307. Record of Meeting in the CIA, Aug. 28, 1953, FRUS, Iran, 1951–1954.

333 **in Tehran:** Kinzer, pp. 170–75.

333 **a savior:** Clandestine Services History: Overthrow of Premier Mossadegh of Iran, November 1952–August 1953, CSH Paper No. 208, chapter VII, p. 52, NSA Electronic Briefing Book No. 435 on CIA role in 1953 Iran coup; Roosevelt, p. 179; Kinzer, pp. 172–73.

334 **had experienced:** Kinzer, pp. 171–77; 285. Telegram from the Station in Iran to the CIA, Aug. 19, 1953, FRUS, Iran, 1951–1954; Roosevelt, pp. 184–85; Takeyh, p. 111.

335 **chance encounter:** Koch, p. 60; Kinzer, p. 177.

335 **the country:** 307. Record of Meeting in the CIA, Aug. 28, 1953, FRUS, Iran, 1951–1954; Kinzer, pp. 177–78; Koch, p. 63; Clandestine Services History: Overthrow of Premier Mossadegh of Iran, November 1952–August 1953, CSH Paper No. 208, chapter VIII, p. 65, NSA Electronic Briefing Book No. 435 on CIA role in 1953 Iran coup.

336 **seen so far:** 307. Record of Meeting in the CIA, Aug. 28, 1953, FRUS, Iran, 1951–1954; Kinzer, pp. 180–82; Takeyh, p. 115.

336 **"love me!":** 307. Record of Meeting in the CIA, Aug. 28, 1953, FRUS, Iran, 1951–1954; Takeyh, pp. 113–14; Bayandor, p. 6; Clandestine Services History: Overthrow of Premier Mossadegh of Iran, November 1952–August 1953, CSH Paper No. 208, summary, p. xii, chapter VIII, p. 74, NSA Electronic Briefing Book No. 435 on CIA role in 1953 Iran coup; Kinzer, pp. 182–86.

337 **it to end:** 307. Record of Meeting in the CIA, Aug. 28, 1953, FRUS, Iran, 1951–1954; Clandestine Services History: Overthrow of Premier Mossadegh of Iran, November 1952–August 1953, CSH Paper No. 208, chapter VIII, p. 77, NSA Electronic Briefing Book No. 435 on CIA role in 1953 Iran coup.

338 **"the country.":** FGW memo to acting DCI on Proposed Commendation, Aug. 20, 1953, WFC; 292. Telegram from the CIA to the Station in Iran, Aug. 20, 1953, 283. Telegram from the Embassy in Tehran to the Department of State, Aug. 20, 1953, 328. Editorial Note, 304. Memorandum of Discussion at the 160th Meeting of the NSC, Aug. 27, 1953, FRUS, Iran, 1951–1954; Mosley, pp. 325–27; Halberstam, *The Fifties*, p. 368; Kinzer, p. 212; Snider, pp. 261–63, 306; Clandestine Services History: Overthrow of Premier Mossadegh of Iran, November 1952–August 1953, CSH Paper No. 208, chapter X, pp. 94–95, FGW Letters of Commendation, Aug. 20 and 26, 1953, NSA Electronic Briefing Book No. 435 on CIA role in 1953 Iran coup; Joseph Alsop, p. 443; Evan Thomas, p. 106.

338 **he said:** Kinzer, pp. 189–92; Roosevelt, pp. 198–200.

338 **"great adventure.":** Kinzer, p. 192; Roosevelt, pp. 206–7.

339 **not listening:** Roosevelt, pp. 208–10; Evan Thomas, p. 110; 328. Editorial Note, FRUS, Iran, 1951–1954.

339 **the country:** Kinzer, pp. 188–89; 317. Information Report Prepared in the Central Intelligence Agency, Sept. 14, 1953, 296. Telegram from the Station in

Iran to the CIA, Aug. 21, 1953, 297. Memorandum from FGW to Mitchell, Aug. 21, 1953, FRUS, Iran, 1951–1954.

340 **Iranian government:** 282. Memorandum for the Record by FGW, Aug. 19, 1953, 294. Memorandum Prepared by the Deputy Director for Plans, CIA, Aug. 20, 1953, 300. Telegram from the Embassy in the United Kingdom to the Department of State, Aug. 24, 1953, 298. Memorandum from the Chief of the Iran Branch, Near East and Africa Division, Directorate of Plans (Waller) to FGW, Aug. 24, 1953, 338. Memorandum from FGW for AWD, Oct. 27, 1953, FRUS, Iran, 1951–1954; Clandestine Services History: Overthrow of Premier Mossadegh of Iran, November 1952–August 1953, CSH Paper No. 208, summary, p. xiii, NSA Electronic Briefing Book No. 435 on CIA role in 1953 Iran coup.

340 **was permitted:** 307. Record of Meeting in the CIA, Aug. 28, 1953, 327. Memorandum by the Chief of the Near East and Africa Division, Directorate of Plans, CIA (Roosevelt), Oct. 2, 1953, FRUS, Iran, 1951–1954; Kinzer, pp. 193–95; Biographic Sketches, Mohammad Mossadegh, NSA Electronic Briefing Book No. 435 on CIA role in 1953 Iran coup.

340 **international consortium:** Ambrose, *Ike's Spies*, pp. 213–14; Kinzer, pp. 195–96; 305. Memorandum from FGW to AWD, Aug. 27, 1953, FRUS, Iran, 1951–1954; FGWII, March 11, 2021.

340 **he did:** 307. Record of Meeting in the CIA, Aug. 28, 1953, FRUS, Iran, 1951–1954.

341 **were ignored:** Clandestine Services History: Overthrow of Premier Mossadegh of Iran, November 1952–August 1953, CSH Paper No. 208, chapter X, pp. 88–94, NSA Electronic Briefing Book No. 435 on CIA role in 1953 Iran coup; Evan Thomas, p. 107.

341 **good luck:** Bayandor, pp. 8–9, Koch, pp. 87–88; Helms (Foundation for Iranian Studies), COH, pp. 1-4–1-5; Ambrose, *Ike's Spies*, pp. 241–42; Kinzer, p. 210.

342 **own momentum:** Takeyh, pp. 114–16; Koch, p. 86; Rountree, FAOH, pp. 12–13.

342 **in Guatemala:** Roosevelt, p. 210; Halberstam, *The Fifties*, p. 371; Koch, pp. 80–81.

343 **them out:** 347. National Intelligence Estimate, Nov. 16, 1953, 342. Monthly Status Project Report Prepared in the Directorate of Plans, CIA, undated, 371. Quarterly Report Prepared in the Directorate of Plans, CIA, July 8, 1954, 367. Information Report Prepared in the CIA, June 14, 1954, FRUS, Iran, 1951–1954; Minutes for Deputies' Meeting, July 16, 1956, CREST for FGW.

343 **not control:** Takeyh, pp. 4, 117–18, 125–26; Kinzer, p. 196; Prados, *Safe for Democracy*, p. 107; Corson, p. 353.

343 **terrorism abroad:** Kinzer, pp. 202–3; Takeyh, pp. 204, 238, 243.

344 **the world:** Ambrose, *Eisenhower*, p. 333; Grose, p. 368; Halberstam, *The Fifties*, p. 369.

Chapter 20: Guatemala

345 **Clover Dulles:** Gleijeses, pp. 10, 86–87, 368–83; Immerman, pp. 29–31; FGW memo to G. B Erskine, Oct. 22, 1953, CIAGC; Schlesinger and Kinzer, pp. 28, 38.

346 **the octopus:** Schlesinger and Kinzer, pp. 12, 65–67; Immerman, pp. 69–75; Gleijeses, pp. 88–92.

346 **1946 primary:** Schlesinger and Kinzer, pp. 106–7; Immerman, pp. 116, 124.

346 **striking workers:** Gleijeses, pp. 32–39, 42–48, 93; Immerman, pp. 76–77.

347 **"Communist activity.":** Gleijeses, pp. 85, 120–21; Cullather, pp. 8–9, 17.

348 **and irritability:** Immernman, pp. 57, 61–62; Gleijeses, pp. 3, 83, 134; Schlesinger and Kinzer, p. 46; Report on State of Arbenz's Health and Clinical Report on Arbenz's Mental Health, Jan. 25, 1962, CIAGC.

348 **reform policies:** Gleijeses, pp. 81, 142, 226–27; Cullather, p. 17.

348 **in Guatemala:** Immerman, pp. 63–64; Gleijeses, pp. 143–47, 150–52, 155–56, 161, 164–65; Schlesinger and Kinzer, p. 55.

349 **Communist "dupe.":** Gleijeses, pp. 140–42, 147–48; Immerman, p. 183; Cullather, p. 22; Schlesinger and Kinzer, pp. 58–61.

349 **wanted spread:** Immerman, pp. 79–80, 111; Schlesinger and Kinzer, pp. 86–90; FGWII, Jan. 13, 2021; Cullather, p. 19; Minutes of Director's Meeting, Dec. 5, 1951, CREST for FGW.

350 **the warning:** Memos to AWD, Aug. 3 and 5, 1953, on President of Panocean Company Inc., Panocean Company Inc. letters, July 21, July 29, and Aug. 3, 1953, CIAGC.

350 **American security:** Gleijeses, pp. 101–2, 134; Interview with E. Howard Hunt, Episode 18, Backyard, NSA; Cullather, pp. 20, 24–26.

351 **with him:** Report by Merle G. Ruffner, Jan. 13, 1950, Report on Colonel Carlos Castillo Armas, Jan. 19, 1950, CIAGC; Cullather, pp. 12–13; Cables to DCI, Oct. 13 and Oct. 27, 1952, Vincent B. Ogden memo to Chief, WHD, Oct. 15, 1952, CIAGC.

352 **weak leader:** Immerman, pp. 3, 142; Cullather, pp. 50–51, 72–73; Carlos Castillo Armas CIA bio, 1952, Memorandum for the Record to C/P, DC/P, May 14, 1954, Memorandum for Playdon, June 3, 1954, Plans of Colonel Carlos Castillo Armas for Armed Revolt Against the Government, Aug. 24, 1950, CIAGC; Gleijeses, p. 250.

352 **U.S. government:** Project Outline, Guatemala, No. LA-3, Aug. 23, 1950, CIAGC.

353 **to Colombia:** Gleijeses, pp. 81–83.

353 **the Pentagon:** Memo to Deputy Director, Plans from Assistant to the Director, Nov. 5, 1951, Memo to James Lay, Executive Secretary NSC, Nov. 14, 1951, CIA cable on attempt against Guatemalan government, Jan. 19, 1952, Cable from OPC/OSO, Jan. 22, 1952, CIA cable to State, Army, Navy, AIR, JCS, SECDEF, AFSA, Jan. 24, 1952, Cable to OPC/OSO, Jan. 23, 1952, CIAGC; Cullather, p. 27.

353 **was arrogant:** Phillips, p. 75; Cullather, pp. 27–28, Prados, *Safe for Democracy,* p. 100.

354 **to Truman:** Warner, *The CIA Under Harry Truman,* pp. xxv–xxvi, 51–53; Cullather, pp. 27–28; Operations Priority cable, March 22, 1952, CIAGC.

354 **it a try:** Cullather, p. 28; Gleijeses, pp. 228–30; Cable to DCI from SRYBER, Sept. 12, 1952, CIAGC.

354 **of $225,000:** Memo on FGW, AWD, Stuart Hedden, Tom Corcoran, and Major Burkett meeting, Oct. 8, 1952, Priority cable to Washington, June 25, 1952, Memorandum of Conversation on Meeting at the Westbury Hotel, May 2, 1952, ACWH memo to DDCI on Guatemalan Situation, July 9, 1952, CIAGC; Schlesinger and Kinzer, p. 92.

355 **his susceptibility:** Cable to Operations for WH (1-2-3), April 8, 1952, Message to Chief Western Hemisphere Division on Political Matters, Guatemala, with attachments, April 1, 1952, Cable from Operations WH (1-2), June 23, 1952, List of Members of the Guatemalan Congress (as of Dec. 1, 1953), CIAGC; Evan Thomas, p. 182.

355 **Guatemala station:** Chronology of Meetings Leading to Approval of Project A, Memo to Deputy Director (Plans) on Packaging and Transportation of

Material, July 28, 1952, Memo for DCI from J. C. King, Aug. 19, 1952, Message
to Operations from WH (1-2-3), July 10, 1952, CIAGC.

355 **was convinced:** Message to DCI from SR. REP., Guatemala, Sept. 9, 1952, CIA
memo on Calligeris plans, July 7, 1952, Message to Operations from WH (1-2-
3), July 10, 1952, Memo for DDCI on Conference with Seekford, Aug. 4, 1952,
CIAGC.

356 **been trounced:** Hunt, p. 71; Gleijeses, pp. 230–31; Schlesinger and Kinzer, p.
102; J. C. King memorandums for the record on Central American Situation,
Oct. 9 and 10, 1952, CIAGC; Cullather, pp. 28–30.

356 **it out:** Memorandum for the Record on Central American Situation, Oct. 9,
1952, CIAGC.

356 **CIA man:** Seekford memo to Chief WHD on New Plans of Calligeris, Oct. 28,
1952, CIAGC.

357 **arms export:** Cable to DCI from C/WH (1), Oct. 31, 1952, Program Schedule
for September 1952, Memorandum for the Record on PW Conference, Nov. 5,
1952, Memorandum for the Record on Central America Situation, Oct. 8, 1952,
CIAGC.

357 **governing coalition:** Gleijeses, p. 231.

357 **new administration:** Cullather, pp. 31–32.

357 **its dictators:** Gleijeses, pp. 235–36, 243, 268–70.

358 **unbiased intelligence:** Crosswell, p. 54.

358 **the operatives:** Crosswell, pp. 54–55; Cullather, pp. 39–40; Schlesinger
and Kinzer, pp. 92–93; Interview with E. Howard Hunt, Episode 18, Backyard, NSA.

358 **their mole:** Cullather, pp. 21–22, 37; Gleijeses, pp. 122–23, 195; Immerman, pp.
101, 183; Schlesinger and Kinzer, pp. xii–xiii; List of confirmed Communists
Supplied to JURANT Feb. 9, Nomina de Communistas, Individual with contacts in the Communist Party, Feb. 17, 1954, CIAGC.

359 **the trip:** Immerman, pp. 10, 103, 185; Schlesinger and Kinzer, p. 107; Gleijeses,
pp. 186–88; Cable to Director from WH (1-2), March 5, 1954, Memo on Bloc
Officials' travel to and from Guatemala, June 8, 1954, CIAGC.

359 **as tribute:** Immerman, p. 133; Cable to DCI from WH 4, April 14, 1953,
CIAGC.

359 **the president:** Halberstam, *The Fifties*, pp. 375–76; FGWII, Jan. 13, 2021; Gleijeses, p. 243.

360 **role in it:** 44. Memorandum for the Chief of the Western Hemisphere
Division, Central Intelligence Agency (King) to FGW, Aug. 27, 1953, FRUS,
Guatemala, 1952–1954; J. C. King memo to Deputy Director (Plans), Aug. 27,
1953, Memorandum for the Record on Meeting with DD/P Regarding Project
PBFortune, Sept. 3, 1953, CIAGC.

360 **carry it out:** 40. Memorandum for the Record, Aug. 12, 1953, FRUS, Guatemala, 1952–1954; Gleijeses, pp. 243–45; J. C. King to Chief, RI, memo on Request for Waiver of Procedure, Sept. 17, 1953; Immerman, pp. 138–39.

360 **be easy:** 51. Memorandum for the Record, Sept. 11, 1953, 54. Memorandum for
the Record, Sept. 18, 1953, FRUS, Guatemala, 1952–1954; Cullather, p. 43;
Gleijeses, p. 246.

360 **intelligence service:** Gleijeses, p. 198; Annex A, Part II, A. Guatemala, Enemy
Intelligence Assets in Guatemala, Total Strength of *Guardia Civil*, Jan. 7, 1954,
Listing of Guatemala military bases and their strength, Draft/LFW, April
29, 1953, Thumbnail sketches of key Guatemalan military officers as of Jan. 30,
1952, Annex A, Part IV, A. The Guatemalan Army, CIAGC.

361 **Guatemalan colleagues:** Gleijeses, p. 205; FGW memo to Chief, Western

Hemisphere Division, March 11, 1954, J. C. King memo to DDCI, April 29, 1953, CIAGC.

361 **had to go:** 51. Memorandum for the Record, Sept. 11, 1953, FRUS, Guatemala, 1952–1954; Schlesinger and Kinzer, p. 131; Memorandum for the Record on PBSuccess—Meeting of First Team, Sept. 18, 1953, Briefing of Ambassador John E. Peurifoy re Guatemala, Sept. 8, 1953, CIAGC; Evan Thomas, p. 116; Cullather, p. 45; Gleijeses, pp. 253–54; FGWII, Jan. 13, 2021; Interview with E. Howard Hunt, Episode 18, Backyard, NSA.

361 **"comes along.":** Gleijeses, pp. 252–56; Schlesinger and Kinzer, p. 135; Lincoln cable to Director, Jan. 25, 1954, CIAGC.

362 **and malleable:** Hunt, p. 73; Schlesinger and Kinzer, pp. 119–25; Immerman, pp. 141–42.

362 **be baked:** 56. Memorandum for the Record, Oct. 3, 1953, FRUS, Guatemala, 1952–1954; Gleijeses, p. 251; Immediate tasks for Rufus, Sept. 2, 1953, A Suggested Plan for Psychological Warfare Operations in Connection with Over-All Guatemalan Operations, Revised Psychological Warfare Plan for Operation PBSuccess, CIAGC; Cullather, p. 40.

363 **fully informed:** 57. Memorandum of Conversation, Oct. 8, 1953, FRUS, Guatemala, 1952–1954; Chief of Station, Guatemala, Kugown Priority Assignments, Nov. 16, 1953, CIA Station Guatemala City cable to Director, Jan. 7, 1954, CIAGC.

363 **he wrote:** Cullather, p. 43.

363 **agency history:** 51. Memorandum for the Record, Sept. 11, 1953, FRUS, Guatemala, 1952–1954.

364 **government accounts:** Jerome Dunbar memo on Financial Position of Guatemalan Government, May 28, 1954, FGW message to Senior Rep., Lincoln, May 29, 1954, FGW memo to Chief, Western Hemisphere Division, Dec. 30, 1953, Memorandum for Mr. Tofte, Sept. 16, 1953, Economic File—PBSuccess, Possibility of Controlling Newsprint Supply to Guatemala, Dec. 16, 1953, Memorandum for Chief, WH, on the Coffee Industry in Guatemala, July 31, 1953, Guatemala Coffee Project, March 12, 1953, Governmental Efforts to Acquire South American and European Markets for Agriculture Products, Guatemala, July 20, 1953, Memo for Chief, WH, on Guatemalan Cloaked Financial Transactions, with attachments, June 18, 1954, WH Div. cable to New York blocking bank transactions, June 27, 1954, CIAGC; Cullather, p. 41.

364 **American States:** Memo to DCI Through Deputy Director (Plans) on Guatemala—General Plan of Action, Sept. 11, 1953, CIAGC.

365 **and "Sequin.":** 51. Memorandum for the Record, Sept. 11, 1953, 61. Memorandum for the Record, Oct. 29, 1953, FRUS, Guatemala, 1952–1954; Memorandum for the Record on Status of PBSuccess, Oct. 29, 1953, Memorandum for Chief, WHD, on K-Program Plan, March 26, 1954, Report on Project PBSuccess, Stage Three, Buildup Period, p. 17, Nov. 16, 1954, CIAGC.

365 **a walk:** Memorandum on Location of Embassy, Guatemala, and Occupancy if Space Therein, Dec. 1, 1953, Security Information, Cover, and Personnel for U.S. embassy Guatemala City, Memorandum for the Record on Security Information, Profram for PBSuccess, Nov. 12, 1953, CIAGC.

366 **team players:** J. C. King memorandum of conversation on PBSuccess, Sept. 15, 1953, Memorandum for the Record PBSuccess—Conversation in New York, Nov. 3, 1953, FGW memo for DCI on Conversation with General Smith, Sept. 17, 1953, CIAGC; Cullather, p. 45.

366 **his operatives:** Memorandum for the Record on Meeting with DD/P, Sept. 15, 1953, Memorandum for the Record on PBSuccess, Sept. 24, 1953, PBSuccess Budget Summary for $3 million, CIAGC.

Chapter 21: Operation Success

368 **them any:** Contact Report at Pentagon with Director, ONI, Nov. 20, 1953, Contact Report for meeting at the Pentagon with ONI, Nov. 27, 1953, Secret /Rybat, Lincoln Regulation No. 4, Jan. 9, 1954, De-Briefing Reports for PBSuccess, pp. 1–2, Memorandum for the Record, "Tasks for RUFUS," Sept. 4, 1953, AWD memo to JEH, Dec. 22, 1953, Hans Tofte memorandum for the record, Dec. 1, 1953, CIAGC; Prados, *Safe for Democracy*, p. 113; Cullather, p. 45.

368 **Guatemala coup:** Bissell interview, B: 1, S: 1, PGP, PU; Bissell interview, B: 9, RSP, HA; Cullather, p. 44; WH Division cable to SLIEC PBSuccess/ Rybat, Dec. 31, 1953, WH Division cable to Chief of Station, Lincoln, Jan. 1, 1954, CIAGC; Gleijeses, p. 244; Grose, p. 378.

369 **or Wisner:** Bissell interview B: 9, RSP, HA; Gleijeses, pp. 288–89; Schlesinger and Kinzer, pp. 109–12, 116–17; Prados, *Safe for Democracy*, pp. 110–11; Evan Thomas, pp. 115, 117; Cullather, p. 46; Grose, p. 377; Bissell, p. 77.

369 **"lying acquaintance.":** Biographic Sketches of Guatemalan Communists, Nov. 23, 1953, Jerome Dunbar memo on Operational Matters, KUFIRE, PBSUC-CESS, Jan. 27, 1954, J. C. King memo to Deputy Director (Plans) on Equipment for PBSuccess, Feb. 10, 1954, Lincoln cable to Director, Feb. 14, 1954, Lincoln cable to Director, March 23, 1954, CIAGC.

370 **spy work:** FGW memo to DDCI on Status of U.S. Military Mission in Guatemala, Nov. 19, 1953, FGW memo to DCI, Nov. 20, 1953, WFC; J. D. Balmer memo to Mr. Jacobs, Oct. 15, 1953, Memorandum for the Record on PBSuccess, Oct. 5, 1953, Memorandum for the Record on meeting in FGW's office, Oct. 15, 1953, Memorandum for the Record on Guatemala, Dec. 29, 1953, FGW memo to SR. REP, for Skillet from Whiting, April 6, 1954, CIAGC; Memorandum for the Record on meeting in FGW's office, Oct. 15, 1953, CREST for FGW.

370 **scolded Wisner:** FGW letter to William Deakin, Jan. 29, 1954, B: 3, FWP, UVA; Minutes for Deputies' Meeting, May 17, 1954, CREST for FGW; Contact Report, DCI's Office, Nov. 16, 1953, To C/P from C/SEC on Director's Visit, March 31, 1954, CIAGC.

370 **was happening:** Hans Tofte Memorandum for the Record on Conference with DD/P, Dec. 1, 1953, Hans Tofte Memorandum for the Record on Operational Security (PBSuccess), Nov. 24, 1953, CIAGC.

371 **the pessimists:** Memo to J. C. King on PBSuccess, Jan. 20, 1954, CIAGC.

371 **"ever heard.":** Memorandum for the Record on Conference with DD/P, Dec. 1, 1953, J. D. Easterline memo to Chief, WH, Jan. 23, 1954, CIAGC.

372 **steal documents:** Gleijeses, pp. 287–89, 292; Immerman, p. 162–63; Annex B, Part IV, Kuhook Assets, Annex B, Part II, Honduras, d. Cover-f. Physical Security, Hans Tofte memo to CWH, Dec. 1, 1953, J. C. King memo on Activation of Staff Radio Station, Feb. 25, 1954, Weekly PBSuccess meeting with DD/P, March 2, 1954, CIAGC.

372 **capital Managua:** Gleijeses, p. 292; Schlesinger and Kinzer, p. 114.

373 **an execution:** Letter of Instructions, Dec. 23, 1953, Contact Report C/R #49, Central America was scene of meetings discussed herein, Week March 4–11, 1954, Memorandum C/P Basic Document #1, Feb. 10, 1954, A Study of Assassination, Training File, CIAGC.

373 **like terrorists:** FGW cable to Senior Rep., Lincoln, June 16, 1954, WFC; Cullather, pp. 141–42; OPC/OSO cables, WHD (1-2), Jan. 26 and 29, 1952, Priority cables, PBSuccess Budget Summary, William F. Donnelly memo to DCI, Report of Questionable Activity in Connection with Project PBSuccess, Oct. 11, 1979, Chief of Station memo to Chief, WHD, with attachment, June 25, 1952,

602 SOURCE NOTES

Guatemalan Communist Personnel to be disposed of during Military Operations of Calligeris, Sept. 18, 1952, Weekly PBSuccess Meeting, March 9,
1954, Liaison Between Calligeris and General Trujillo of Santo Domingo, Sept.
18, 1952, Selection of Individuals for disposal by Junta Group, March 31, 1954,
CIAGC.
374 **rebels attacked:** Plan to Assassinate Colonel Castillo Armas, June 15, 1954,
Cable to Senior Rep., Lincoln, from DCI, June 5, 1954, CIAGC; Gleijeses, pp.
17–18, 316; Hunt, p. 78–79.
374 **were killed:** Chief, Western Hemisphere Division, memo for All Latin
American Field Stations, April 22, 1953, CIAGC; Cullather, p. 137; CIA and
Guatemala Assassination Proposals, 1952–1954, CIA History Staff Analysis,
Gerald K. Haines, June 1995, https://www.cia.gov/readingroom/docs/DOC
_0005256960.pdf1.
374 **Guatemalan targets:** 15 February Conference on Black Flight, Feb. 15, 1954,
Sterile Pilots for Phase Four Operations, May 13, 1954, Lincoln cable to Director, April 26, 1954, Annex B, Part IV, Kuhook Assets, Assignments to date
concerning Black Flight, Dec. 30, 1953, CIAGC; Immerman, p. 138; Evan
Thomas, p. 113; Schlesinger and Kinzer, pp. 115–16.
375 **"expectant mother.":** Table I, Summary of Aircraft Strengths Total, Feb. 3,
1954, Memorandum for Chief, EW; Chief, FI, Request for Information, Feb.
24, 1954, Lincoln cable to Director, March 23, 1954, Clara M. Heagey memo to
Lincoln, March 30, 1954, Vernon J. Ingram memo on Railroad vulnerability,
March 29, 1954, Earl Bannister memo Operational, Lincoln, March 30, 1954,
Memorandum for Chief of Project, Paramilitary Activities, July 7, 1954, Cable
from Playdon to Goodbourne, CIAGC; Gleijeses, pp. 103, 339.
375 **Communist controlled:** Letter to General Manager, United Fruit Company,
Jan. 7, 1954, Lincoln cable to Director, March 15, 1954, Chief of Station, Guatemala, Memo to Chief, Lincoln, Feb. 2, 1954, Weekly PBSuccess Meeting with
DD/P, March 2, 1954, CIAGC.
376 **in the country:** Lincoln memo to Chief of Station, Guatemala City, March 17,
1954, Letter of Instruction #1, Jan. 7, 1954, Contact Report C/R #49, Week
4–11 March 1954, Lincoln cable to Director, March 4, 1954, CIAGC.
376 **they appreciated:** David M. Barrett, Sterilizing a "Red Infection," Congress,
the CIA, and Guatemala, 1954, CIA Library, https://www.cia.gov/resources
/csi/static/congress-cia-guatemala.pdf; AWD Memorandum for the Record,
Project PBSuccess, April 26, 1954, CIAGC; Snider, p. 264.
377 **were involved:** Halberstam, *The Fifties*, pp. 381–84; Evan Thomas, p. 117; Gleijeses, p. 232; Immerman, p. 112–14; David M. Barrett, Sterilizing a "Red Infection," Congress, the CIA, and Guatemala, 1954, CIA Library, https://www.cia
.gov/resources/csi/static/congress-cia-guatemala.pdf; FGW cable to SR. REP.,
Guatemala City, May 21, 1954, Routing and Record Sheet, June 25, 1954, William D. Playdon memo on Kugown Documentary Film on Guatemala with
newsclip, May 9, 1954, J. C. King memo to DCI on Walter Winchell Broadcast,
Jan. 7, 1954, CIAGC.
377 **"fellow wanderer.":** FGW memo to Henry Holland, June 18, 1954, Memorandum on Contact with Minor Rene Keilhauer and Jorge Toriello, May 31, 1954,
Guatemala City cables to Director, May 28, 1954, Director cable, May 27, 1954,
FGW memo to DCI on Sydney Gruson, June 2, 1954, FGW on conversation
with Stewart Alsop, note to AWD, June 2, 1954, CIAGC; Evan Thomas, p. 117;
Gleijeses, pp. 260–61; Immerman, pp. 113–14.
378 **Guatemala beat:** 182. Memorandum from FGW to AWD, June 14, 1954,
FRUS, Guatemala, 1952–1954; AWD letter to Arthur Hays Sulzberger, June 13,

1954, WFC; Herken, p. 219; FGW memo on Guatemala Friendship Societies to DCI, June 14, 1954, FGW memo to Henry Holland on Sydney Gruson, May 27, 1954, Jerome Dunbar memo to PBSuccess, Headquarters, June 2, 1954, Stanley Grogan memo to Director, May 28, 1954, Arthur Hays Sulzberger letter to AWD, June 8, 1954, AWD letter to Arthur Hays Sulzberger, June 13, 1954, FGW cable to Senior Rep., Guatemala City, June 1954 CIAGC; Schlesinger and Kinzer, pp. 154–55.

378 **nation's newspapers:** PBSuccess—Preliminary Analysis of RUFUS's Intelligence Assets, Nov. 16, 1953, Lincoln cable to Director, Jan. 30, 1954, Director cables to Lincoln, Feb. 1 and 3, 1954, CIAGC; Schlesinger and Kinzer, pp. 128–29.

378 **giving him:** Jerome Dunbar memo with attachment on Kufire—Operations, March 17, 1954, Progress Reports—PBSuccess for Period 9–15 March 1954, 23–29 March 1954, and 4–10 May 1954, The L C Flutter Excursion, April 2, 1954, Part One, Outlining Events Affecting Security of PBSuccess, April 22, 1954, Lincoln cables to Director, March 23, 1954, Résumé of the Current Situation in RE: Juvia, Juvia-I, and FT/11, May 12, 1954, CIAGC.

379 **Guatemalan government:** Cullather, p. 59; Evan Thomas, p. 114; Memorandum for the Record on PBSuccess papers left in hotel room, March 2, 1954, Memo on Compromise of Cable Traffic—PBSuccess, Feb. 20, 1954, CIAGC.

379 **"technical surveillance.":** Part One, Outlining Events Affecting Security of PBSuccess, April 22, 1954, Lincoln cable to Director, Feb. 27, 1954, Earl Bannister memo to Lincoln on Security Matters, Telephone in Station Office, April 23, 1954, Minutes of Weekly PBSuccess Meeting—Deputy Director, Plans, April 20, 1954, CIAGC.

379 **much pressure:** FGW cable to Senior Representative, April 10, 1954, WFC; Part One, Outlining Events Affecting Security of PBSuccess, April 22, 1954, Cable to Director, Lincoln, April 13, 1954, FGW cable to Senior Representative, April 10, 1954, Cable on Skillet messages being reviewed by Whiting, April 9, 1954, Cable to Director, Lincoln, from Skillet, April 8, 1954, CIAGC.

380 **"in the act.":** Memo to DCI, Position Paper on PBSuccess, April 24, 1954, WFC; Part One, Outlining Events Affecting Security of PBSuccess, April 22, 1954, Jerome C. Dunbar memo to COS, May 16, 1954, FGW's Memo of 28 April 1954 Regarding Cover and Deception, CIAGC.

381 **in the CIA:** FGW Notes on Conversation with Gillray, April 2, 1954, Earl N. Bannister memo, May 3, 1954, Earl N. Bannister memo to Chief, Lincoln, April 6, 1954, FGW memo to Chief of Station, Lincoln, May 13, 1954, Cable to Ser. Rep., Lincoln, May 3, 1954, CIAGC.

382 **garrison towns:** 135. Contact Report, April 28, 1954, FRUS, Guatemala, 1952–1954; Action Items taken up at PBSuccess meeting of 29 April 1954, CIAGC.

382 **up at night:** Evan Thomas, pp. 118–19, 122, 371; Jacob D. Easterline memo to Deputy Chief, WHD, Request for Technical Counter-sabotage guidance, April 19, 1954, RE: Cable IN: 14562, FGW had written a note to Colonel King, April 13, 1953, CIAGC.

383 **in the event:** Sherwood script on "Another Signal of Our Advancing Movement," Guatemala station to Lincoln, April 26, 1954, Cable to Lincoln, April 24, 1954, CIAGC; Hunt, p. 76.

383 **the homes:** Kugown Priority Assignments, "Psychological Barometer," Oct. 23, 1954, Telephone Team for Rumor Propagation, March 2, 1954, CIAGC; Gleijeses, pp. 208, 304–5.

383 **cranked up:** Memorandum for the Record on PBSuccess—Meeting of First Team, Sept. 18, 1953, CIAGC.

383 **at night:** Schlesinger and Kinzer, pp. 114–15; Progress Report—PBSuccess for the Period 23–29 March 1954, Notes re Interim Progress Report for DCI Meeting, 18 September 1953, Lincoln cable to Director, April 27, 1954, CIAGC; Gleijeses, pp. 289, 294–95; Interview with E. Howard Hunt, Episode 18, Backyard, NSA; Hunt, p. 74; Cullather, p. 76.

384 **in the coup:** Contact Report C/R #48, in the War Room, March 12, 1954, FGW memo on PBSuccess, Selection of clandestine radio site, March 12, 1954, CIAGC.

384 **the Communists:** Cullather, p. 75; FGW cable to SR. REP., Lincoln, June 5, 1954, Guatemala station cable to Lincoln, May 8, 1954, Lincoln cable to Director, June 16, 1954, Jerome C. Dunbar memo to Lincoln, March 31, 1954, CIAGC; Immerman, pp. 164, 167; Interview with E. Howard Hunt, Episode 18, Backyard, NSA; Hunt, p. 79.

384 **destroy it:** Cullather, pp. xv, 66–67; Material Plan for Radio Program, Notes on Radio Broadcasting—Guatemala, Prepared in RQM/OIS, Jan. 25, 1954, Lincoln Director cable to Guatemala station, May 6, 1954, CIAGC.

385 **eastern coast:** Cullather, pp. 52–53, 57; Schlesinger and Kinzer, pp. 148–50; Cable to Director on Royal Netherlands steamship, March 27, 1954, Lincoln cable to Director, May 16, 1954, FGW cable to Lincoln and Guatemala stations, May 16, 1954, CIAGC; Gleijeses, p. 294; Prados, *Safe for Democracy*, p. 117.

385 **of that:** Cable from DCI for Skillet, May 21, 1954, Memorandum For J. D. Easterline on Report on Transfer of Guatemalan Funds to Credit Czech, June 8, 1954, FGW memo to AWD on Indications of Soviet Involvement in ALF-HEM Shipment, Possibility of Further Shipments, May 20, 1954, Memorandum for C/P on Alfhem Arms Shipment, June 10, 1954, FGW memo to Henry F. Holland, June 21, 1954, with copy of report on Guatemalan Procurement of Arms from the Soviet Orbit, J. C. King memo on Quality and future disposition of Arms Received by Guatemala from the ship ALFHEM, Sept. 16, 1954, FGW cable to SR. REP., Lincoln, May 20, 1954, CIAGC; Cullather, pp. 79, 81–82; Immerman, p. 156; David M. Barrett, Sterilizing a "Red Infection," Congress, the CIA, and Guatemala, 1954, CIA Library, https://www.cia.gov/resources/csi/static/congress-cia-guatemala.pdf.

385 **the truth:** Cullather, pp. 80–81; Script for Sherwood: "Foreign Agents are Assisting in Distributing Soviet Arms to Communist Shock Troops!," Memo for Deputy Director (Plans) on Reported Contents of the ALFHEM Cargo, May 26, 1954, CIAGC; Gleijeses, p. 279.

386 **of insurrectionists:** Cullather, p. 74; Immerman, p. 162.

386 **mental condition:** Hunt, p. 78; Lincoln memo to ACOS, Guatemala City, on Intelligence Matters, April 28, 1954, Alan N. Reelfoot memo, May 11, 1954, CIAGC.

387 **the bait:** PBSuccess Developments timeline April–June, Memo for Chief of Project on Kuhook Assessment, April 19, 1954, Memo from Chief of Station, Guatemala, to Lincoln on Government Structure, Guatemala, April 6, 1954, Operational Plan, Guatemala City-A, Lincoln cable to Director on PBSuccess Rybat, April 6, 1954, Lincoln cable to PBSuccess, Headquarters, Kugown, Sherwood Policy Directive, May 9, 1954, CIAGC.

387 **of mess:** FGW cable to Senior Representative, Guatemala City, May 12, 1954, WFC; FGW cable to JMBLUG in Guatemala, May 13, 1954, Memorandum for Deputy Director, Plans, Something to Think About No. 3, April 23, 1954, Lincoln cable to Director, for Lugton, March 3, 1954, CIAGC.

387 **Armas's forces:** C. Tracy Barnes memo on Notes in Response to Questions in DIR 49887, May 12, 1954, FGW memo to DCI, May 25, 1954, Cable from Guatemala City to Director, May 27, 1954, FGW cable to Attn: Karmany, May 26, 1954, FGW cable to SR. REP., Lincoln, May 12, 1954, Thoughts and Possible Courses of Action concerning latest Developments in PBSuccess—Arrival of ALFHELM, May 18, 1954, Progress Report—PBSuccess for the Period 4–10 May 1954, Guatemala City cable to Director, Report form Razmara and Essence, May 13, 1954, Jerome Dunbar message on Operational Matters Need for Current Information, May 12, 1954, CIAGC.

388 **the airman:** Lincoln cable to Director, May 18, 1954, Jerome C. Dunbar memo on Character Assassination of Rogelio CRUZ Wer, April 7, 1954, Jerome Dunbar memo with KUGOWN News Item, March 24, 1954, CIAGC.

388 **compromise security:** Memo on Command Posts, Tracy Barnes cable to Lincoln, June 12, 1954, Guatemala City cable to Director, June 12, 1954, Guatemala City cable to Director, June 7, 1954, CIAGC.

388 **Barnes wondered:** Schlesinger and Kinzer, p. 9; Notes on Discussion with Mr. Barnes, May 30, 1954, FGW cable to Senior Rep., Lincoln, CIAGC.

389 **as well:** FGW cables to Senior Rep., Lincoln, June 1 and 14, 1954, Decisions taken at PBSuccess Meeting of 9 June 1954, CIAGC.

389 **telegraph lines:** Schlesinger and Kinzer, pp. 170–71; Cullather, pp. 87–88; Hunt, p. 81.

390 **to him:** J. D. Easterline cable to Senior Rep., Lincoln, June 14, 1954, To DIR, RYBAT/PBSuccess, for Whiting, June 15, 1954, Memo to FGW RE: Control of Guatemala, July 1, 1954, FGW cable to Senior Rep., Lincoln, June 14, 1954, CIAGC.

390 **"maximum results.":** FGW cables to SER. REP., Lincoln, June 5 and 16, 1954, WFC; DCI cable to SER. REP., Lincoln, June 15, 1954, Cable from Directorate, CIA, to Guatemala City station, June 16, 1954, Summary of DDP/PBSuccess Meeting of 16 June 1954, CIAGC.

391 **his own ranks:** Cullather, pp. 88, 95–96; Lincoln cable to Director, June 17, 1954, Gleijeses, p. 320; FGW cable to Senior Rep., Lincoln, June 18, 1954, CIAGC; Schlesinger and Kinzer, pp. 187–88.

392 **and children:** Schlesinger and Kinzer, pp. 13–17, 171–72; Immerman, p. 4; Cullather, p. 89; Lincoln cable to Director, June 18, 1954, CIAGC.

392 **Honduran border:** Prados, *Safe for Democracy*, p. 122; FGWII, Jan. 13, 2021; Gleijeses, pp. 323–25; Cullather, pp. 89, 96; Lincoln cable to Director, June 20, 1954, CIAGC.

393 **"constantly shifting.":** Memorandum by AWD to DDE, with attachment, June 20, 1954, FRUS, Guatemala, 1952–1954; Cullather, pp. 89–90; Gleijeses, pp. 326–27, 336–37; Schlesinger and Kinzer, pp. 22, 173–76; Cable for Director, to OPIM SLINC, June 22, 1954, Lincoln cable to Director, June 19, 1954, FGW cable to Senior Rep., Lincoln, June 19, 1954, Lincoln cable to Director on Daily OP Sitrep NBR 06, June 20, 1954, CIAGC.

394 **more Thunderbolts:** Cullather, p. 90; Lincoln cable to Director with attached note, June 21, 1954, FGW cables to Senior Rep., Lincoln, June 22 and 23, 1954, Lincoln cable to Director, June 22, 1954, R. M. Bissell cable to Senior Rep., Lincoln, June 22, 1954, CIAGC; Gleijeses, p. 337.

394 **his estimate:** Cullather, p. 98.

394 **officer corps:** Gleijeses, p. 332; Cullather, p. 97; Rumors of anti-Communist forces increasing, The wife of Arbenz is in El Salvador, June 22, 1954, FGW cable to SR. REP., Guatemala City, June 23, 1954, CIAGC.

395 **in restitution:** FGW cable on Venezuela cover for planes, June 23, 1954,

Richard Bissell cable to Lincoln, June 24, 1954, FGW cable to SR. REP., Lincoln, June 25, 1954, CIAGC; Schlesinger and Kinzer, p. 182.

395 **to serve:** Richard Bissell cable to Senior Rep., Lincoln, June 24, 1954, Lincoln cable to Director June 24, 1954, CIAGC; Schlesinger and Kinzer, p. 189.

396 **them any:** Cable from Ontrich to Director, June 25, 1954, CIAGC; Schlesinger and Kinzer, pp. 182–83; Gleijeses, pp. 332–33; Cullather, pp. 100–1.

396 **massive army:** Gleijeses, pp. 321, 341; Immerman, p. 167; Schlesinger and Kinzer, pp. 185–86.

396 **by Arbenz:** Lincoln cables to Director, June 26, 1954, WH/PW cable on positive reports from the field, June 26, 1954, FGW cables to Senior Rep., Lincoln, June 26, 1954, RE: LINC-4024, June 26, 1954, CIAGC.

397 **in judgment:** Gleijeses, pp. 343–44; FGW cable to Senior Rep., Lincoln, June 28, 1954.

397 **supported him:** Schlesinger and Kinzer, pp. 191, 198; Lincoln cable to Director, June 27, 1954, WH DIV cable to Senior Rep., Lincoln, June 27, 1954, CIAGC; Sherwood cassettes Nos. 137 and 298, pp. 232–34, PBSuccess, The Sherwood Tapes, foia.cia.gov.

398 **Arbenz's reforms:** Cullather, p. 101; Guatemala station to Director, June 28, 1954, CIAGC; Schlesinger and Kinzer, p. 197; Gleijeses, pp. 347–50.

398 **for that job:** Arbenz's Speech delivered at 0310–0320 EST, Rec'd DD/P office, June 27, 1954, Guatemala station cable to Director, June 28, 1954, Charles Cabell cable to Lincoln, June 28, 1954, Lincoln cable to Director, June 28, 1954, CIAGC; Gleijeses, pp. 346–47, 351–52; Cullather, pp. 101–2.

398 **his legs:** Gleijeses, pp. 353–54; Schlesinger and Kinzer, pp. 206–8.

399 **on July 2:** Cullather, p. 103.

399 **Washington's control:** Cullather, pp. 105–7; Report on Activity in Guatemala City, 4–16 July 1954, Memo for Deputy Director, Plans, Mechanics for Exploitation of Guatemala Documents, July 28, 1954, Guatemala station cable to Director, July 3, 1954, William D. Playdon memo to PBSuccess, Headquarters, June 29, 1954, CIAGC.

399 **of overwork:** FGW letter to his mother, July 27, 1954, B: 4, FWP, UVA; Schlesinger and Kinzer, pp. 214–15; Anderson, p. 401.

399 **September 1:** Schlesinger and Kinzer, pp. 215–16; Gleijeses, p. 357.

400 **the guests:** FGW cable to Senior Rep., Guatemala City, July 8, 1954, FGW cable to Senior Rep., Lincoln, June 30, 1954, WFC; Cullather, 103–4; FGW cable for Skillet and PRINCEP, June 30, 1954, Lincoln message to Director, June 30, 1954, J. D. Easterline cable to SER. REP., Guatemala, July 1, 1954, CIAGC.

400 **had encountered:** Cullather, pp. 109–10; Phillips, pp. 61–64.

401 **to Italy:** FGW letter to his mother, Aug. 18, 1954, B: 4, FWP, UVA; Memorandum for Chief of Project on PM Operation, July 8, 1954; Hunt, p. 83; Immerman, p. 5; Hughes, FAOH, p. 30.

401 **New York City:** Hunt, p. 84; Guatemala City cable to Director, July 30, 1954, CIAGC; Immerman, p. 179.

402 **explaining to do:** FGW cable to Senior Representative, Guatemala City, Aug. 16, 1954, DCI cable to Senior Representative, Guatemala City, Sept. 2, 1954, FGW memo to DCI on British "White Paper" on Guatemala, Oct. 21, 1954, Director cable on paperback book, July 8, 1954, FGW cable on MGM crew, July 1, 1954, Arthur Hays Sulzberger letters to AWD, June 30 and July 6, 1954, AWD letters to Arthur Hays Sulzberger, July 3 and 10, 1954, CIAGC; Halberstam, *The Fifties*, p. 387.

402 **or higher:** Gleijeses, pp. 367–68; Evan Thomas, p. 125; Halberstam, *The Fifties*, p. 386–87; Schlesinger and Kinzer, pp. 224–25; Ambrose, *Eisenhower*, p. 379.

402 **United States:** Cullather, pp. 111–13; Gleijeses, pp. 371–72.
403 **a bathtub:** Cullather, p. 109; Gleijeses, pp. 319–20, 389–92; March 26–May 1957, reports on Arbenz mail and movements, Memo on Current Activities Concerning Arbenz—for possible discussion with State, June 4, 1957, CIAGC.
403 **in 1972:** Immerman, p. 198; Schlesinger and Kinzer, pp. 92–93, 218; Cullather, p. 118; J. C. King memo on conversation with Mr. Joe Montgomery and Mr. Thomas Corcoran of the United Fruit Company, July 22, 1954, CIAGC.
404 **those operations:** Ambrose, *Ike's Spies*, p. 226; Gleijeses, p. 371; Evan Thomas, pp. 124–25; Corson, p. 358; Cullather, p. 105.
404 **with PBSuccess:** FGW memo to DCI on Proposal for the Organization of an Action Operations Unit, April 14, 1955, WFC.
404 **Communist plot:** Cullather, pp. 105–6, 113–17.
405 **of criticism:** Richard Bissell cable to Senior Representative, Guatemala City, July 4, 1954, RQM/OIS Support of PBSuccess, CIAGC.
405 **American history:** Schlesinger and Kinzer, pp. xxxii, 262; Gleijeses, pp. 383–87; Immerman, pp. 200–1.

Chapter 22: Investigations
406 **"Romanian gossip.":** Memo to A. H. Belmont from V. P. Keay, Jan. 11, 1954, R. R. Roach memo to A. H. Belmont, Oct. 13, 1955, Memo to Director, FBI, on FGW, SAC, WFO (65-6640), Oct. 14, 1955, Memo to Director, FBI, July 3, 1956, A. H. Belmont memo to L. V. Boardman, June 3, 1955, Sheffield Edwards letter to JEH with investigation report on FGW, May 24, 1955, FBIW.
407 **"with him.":** Minutes for Deputies' Meeting, July 28, 1954, FGW memo to AWD, July 1, 1955, JEH memo to the Attorney General, May 25, 1955, JEH letter to AWD, April 29, 1954, CREST for FGW; 175. Draft Memorandum from Director of Central Intelligence Dulles to Director of the Bureau of the Budget, March 30, 1954, FRUS, The Intelligence Community, 1950–1955; Memo to Director, FBI, Oct. 14, 1955, FBIW.
407 **aggressive oversight:** OLC Daily Log, April 1, 1954, CREST for FGW; Halberstam, *The Fifties*, pp. 250, 252; Snider, p. 8; Grose, p. 416.
407 **done right:** Weiner, pp. 108–9; Ambrose, *Ike's Spies*, pp. 187–88.
408 **a problem:** Report on the Covert Activities of the Central Intelligence Agency, by James Doolittle et al., Report #15b, HR70-14(N), released by the CIA Aug. 6, 1976; 185. Letter from DDE to General James H. Doolittle, July 26, 1954, FRUS, The Intelligence Community, 1950–1955; Lt. Gen. James H. Doolittle profile, Minutes for Deputies' Meeting, Nov. 8, 1954, CREST for FGW; Jackson, vol. 4, p. 113.
408 **Their department:** DD/A Diary Notes, July 12–14, 1954, Minutes for Deputies' Meeting, Sept. 12, 1956, Minutes of the Meeting of the Special Study Group, July 29, 1954, CREST for FGW; 188. Memorandum from the Deputy Operations Coordinator in the Office of the Under Secretary of State (Hulick) to the Under Secretary of State (Hoover), Aug. 23, 1954, FRUS, The Intelligence Community, 1950–1955.
409 **trimmed back:** Report on the Covert Activities of the Central Intelligence Agency, by James Doolittle et al., Report #15b, HR70-14(N), released by the CIA Aug. 6, 1976.
409 **good administrators:** 193. Memorandum of Conversation, Oct. 19, 1954, FRUS, The Intelligence Community, 1950–1955.
410 **panel's reforms:** 205. Memorandum from the NSC Representative on Internal Security (Coyne) to the President's Special Assistant for National Security

Affairs (Cutler) and the Executive Secretary of the NSC (Lay), Feb. 8, 1955, FRUS, The Intelligence Community, 1950–1955; Security Program of the Central Intelligence Agency, 1941–1968, pp. 70–71, Memo for DCI on Survey of the Office of Training, April 21, 1954, CREST for FGW.

410 **of property:** Staff Study, Permanent Select Committee on Intelligence, House of Representatives, Appendix C, CRS Report, Proposal for Intelligence Reorganization, 1949–1996, Feb. 28, 1996; 220. Report by the Task Force on Intelligence Activities of the Commission on Organization of the Executive Branch of the Government, May 1955, FRUS, The Intelligence Community, 1950–1955; Summary of the Nov. 4, 1955, Briefing of the Clark Task Force and Staff, Staff Conference meeting minutes, July 18, 1955, FGW memo to Director of Training, July 19, 1955, CREST for FGW; FGW letter to David K. E. Bruce, Aug. 28, 1957, B: 1, FWP, UVA.

411 **auditor review:** The DCI Historical Series, Internal Audit of the Central Intelligence Agency, 1947 Through 1967, December 1972, pp. 25–26, 32; Leary, p. 58.

411 **his shop:** Hersh, pp. 365–66; Memos among FGW, AWD, and Lyman Kirkpatrick over Duties of the Inspector General, January–February 1955, Inspector General's Survey of the Soviet Russia Division, DD/P, June 1956, CREST for FGW.

412 **was doing:** DD/S Diary Notes, Sept. 30, 1955, CREST for FGW; Anderson, COH, pp. 110–12; Staff Study, Permanent Select Committee on Intelligence, House of Representatives, Appendix C, CRS Report, Proposal for Intelligence Reorganization, 1949–1996, Feb. 28, 1996; Hersh, 406–7.

412 **foreign policy:** Jackson, vol. 3, pp. 24–25, 30, 34, 38, 43–44, 96, 107, vol. 4, p. 89.

413 **out of them:** Laurie, "A New President," p. 6; Hersh, pp. 407–8.

413 **told Gray:** Grose, p. 409; Killian, COH, p. 40; Jackson, vol. 4, pp. 83–84.

413 **Southeast Asia:** Harvey Overesch letter to FGW, Aug. 30, 1954, B: 8, FGW letter to Donald R. Heath, Nov. 15, 1954, Julian Harrington letter to FGW, Nov. 18, 1954, B: 6, FGW letter to Joe Alsop, March 20, 1956, B: 1, FWP, UVA; Project DTPillar, Amendment #1 Increase FY1955 Authorization, FGW memo to Secretary of the Project Review Committee on DTPillar with attachment, April 14, 1955, CREST for FGW.

414 **stamped "SECRET.":** Interview with Joseph C. King, B: 10, RSP, HA; FGW letter to Charles Empson, Nov. 29, 1955, B: 4, FWP, UVA; L. K. White Certificate, Jan. 31, 1956, Security Programs of the Central Intelligence Agency, 1941–1968, vol. II, Personnel Security, pp. 85, 99, Minutes for Deputies' Meeting, Sept. 30, 1955, CREST for FGW.

414 **a hole:** Herken, p. 221; DD/S Diary Notes, Nov. 15, 1955, FGW memo to DCI on Business Machine Facilities for DD/P, June 30, 1955, CREST for FGW.

415 **cables carried:** Evan Thomas, pp. 128–29; Murphy et al., pp. 214–37; Ranelagh, p. 290; Richard Helms, pp. 136–37; Clandestine Services History: The Berlin Tunnel Operation, 1952–1956, CSH Paper No. 150.

415 **intelligence collection:** Clandestine Services History: The Berlin Tunnel Operation, 1952–1956, CSH Paper No. 150; Richard Helms, pp. 134, 136; FGWII, Jan. 13, 2021.

415 **were located:** Clandestine Services History: The Berlin Tunnel Operation, 1952–1956, CSH Paper No. 150; On the Front Line of the Cold War: Documents on the Intelligence War in Berlin, 1946 to 1961, Part V: The Berlin Tunnel, https://www.cia.gov/resources/csi/static/920ab2fdc9608c580e053b51583dad71/On-the-Front-Lines-of-the-Cold-War-5-5-web.pdf.

416 **kept secret:** Clandestine Services History: The Berlin Tunnel Operation, 1952–1956, CSH Paper No. 150; On the Front Line of the Cold War: Documents on the Intelligence War in Berlin, 1946 to 1961, Part V: The Berlin Tunnel, https://www.cia.gov/resources/csi/static/920ab2fdc9608c580e053b51583dad71/On-the-Front-Lines-of-the-Cold-War-5-5-web.pdf.

416 **"Yankee ingenuity.":** Clandestine Services History: The Berlin Tunnel Operation, 1952–1956, CSH Paper No. 150.

416 **Kremlin leaders:** Ranelagh, p. 294; On the Front Line of the Cold War: Documents on the Intelligence War in Berlin, 1946 to 1961, Part V: The Berlin Tunnel, https://www.cia.gov/resources/csi/static/920ab2fdc9608c580e053b51583dad71/On-the-Front-Lines-of-the-Cold-War-5-5-web.pdf; Clandestine Services History: The Berlin Tunnel Operation, 1952–1956, CSH Paper No. 150; Murphy et al., pp. 424–25.

417 **a mandate:** Halberstam, *The Fifties*, p. 712; Ambrose, *Eisenhower*, pp. 394, 401, 420.

417 **the programs:** Meyer, pp. 114, 118, 120; An Estimate of the Effectiveness of Radio Liberation, by Wilbur Schramm, Sept. 1, 1955, WCA; Holmes memo to Merchant, Jan. 4, 1955, CREST for FGW; Rositzke, p. 38; Hazard, p. 234; Richard Helms, pp. 125–26; Fiscal Year 1955 Operational Program for Albania, CIA FOIA, cia.gov.

417 **propaganda tool:** DD/S Diary Notes, Feb. 17, 1955, CREST for FGW.

418 **feeler on it:** FGW memo to DCI on meeting with Nelson Rockefeller, April 1, 1955, CREST for FGW; Nelson Rockefeller memo to FGW, April 12, 1955, Nelson Rockefeller memo to C. D. Jackson, April 12, 1955, B: 89, Special Assistant to the President for Foreign Affairs (SAP), Subseries 7, NRP, RAC.

418 **Ku Klux Klan:** Secretary to FGW letter to Edward Plohne at the National Theatre, July 17, 1952, B: 8, FWP, UVA; Elisabeth Wisner Chisholm interview, Jan. 13, 1973, pp. 5–6, B: 37, S: 446, JGCL, CFA; Lindsey, July 14, 2020, and Oct. 12, 2021.

418 **of 1955:** C. V. Hulick memo to Nelson Rockefeller, July 6, 1955, and Rockefeller reply, July 11, 1955, Robert Breen letters to Nelson Rockefeller, July 20 and 21, 1955, Stacy May memo to Nelson Rockefeller, B: 80, Special Assistant to the President for Foreign Affairs (SAP), Subseries 7, NRP, RAC.

419 **of himself:** General Parker memo to Nelson Rockefeller, Sept. 12, 1955, "Red Ballet to U.S.—if U.S. Agrees," *New York Herald Tribune*, Sept. 30, 1955, Don memo to Nancy, Sept. 6, 1955, FGW memo to Nelson Rockefeller, Sept. 14, 1955, Nelson Rockefeller letter to FGW, Sept. 30, 1955, B: 80, Assistant to the President for Foreign Affairs (SAP), Subseries 7, NRP, RAC.

419 **to UVA:** FGW letter to Isaiah Berlin, Aug. 17, 1954, B: 1, FWP, UVA; Entries in Wisner Betting Book, WFC.

420 **the column:** Joseph Alsop interview, B: 9, RSP, HA; Herken, p. 201; Joseph Alsop, pp. 391–92; Stewart Alsop, pp. 195–96.

420 **thirty-ninth birthday:** "Whirlaway," *The Washington Post*, May 1954, news item on the Wisners at a dance party, CREST for FGW; Herken, p. 188; Katharine Graham interview with Polly Fritchey, Oct. 10, 1989, KGP; Graham, p. 213; Herken, p. 212; FGW letter to Phil Graham, May 15, 1956, B: 5, FWP, UVA.

420 **their families:** Minutes for Deputies' Meeting, Oct. 6, 1952, CREST for FGW; Thomas Marshall letter to FGW, July 6, 1955, B: 3, John Knowles letter to PKW, Sept. 29 and Oct. 13, 1954, Alexander Chisholm letter, Jan. 4, 1955, to "Col," FGW secretary letter to A. F. Chisholm, Sept. 10, 1954, B: 4, FWP, UVA; EW, Sept. 22, 2020; EW interview with William L. "Billy" Sigman, Feb. 8, 2013, WFC.

421 **handling secrets:** FGW Personnel Evaluation, July 7, 1955, FGW Fitness Report for Sept. 4, 1954, to Sept. 5, 1956, BHP; Notification of Personnel Action, FGW salary increase, Aug. 20, 1956, WFC; Evan Thomas, p. 139.

421 **the Russians:** Hersh, pp. 376, 383–84; Powers, p. 83.

422 **their friend:** Anderson, pp. 401, 403, 423–25; Powers, p. 83; FGW letter to Phil Graham, Dec. 20, 1954, B: 5, FWP, UVA.

422 **Eastern Shore:** Maior, p. 234; Evan Thomas, p. 317; GW, Aug. 3 and Sept. 16, 2020; EW, Oct. 20, 2020; FGW letter to The Right Honorable Viscount Harcourt, April 14, 1956, B: 6, FWP, UVA.

422 **alcohol abuse:** Gotlib and Hammen, p. 5; Davidson et al., pp. 47–51.

423 **manic state:** Goodwin and Jamison, vol. 1, pp. 39–40, 184; Mondimore, pp. 9, 12–13, 174; Jamison, p. 74.

423 **over time:** Mondimore, p. 240; Gotlib and Hammen, p. 143; Goodwin and Jamison, vol. 2, p. 470.

Chapter 23: Hungary and the Canal

424 **traumatized viewers:** Halberstam, *The Fifties*, pp. 475–76, 508–12, 522, 526, 565–70, 576–83, 596–98, 645–63, 664; Joseph Smith letter to FGW, Sept. 28, 1956, B: 9, J. Cowan letter to FGW, Sept. 5, B: 1, FWP, UVA.

425 **months earlier:** Minutes for Deputies' Meeting, Aug. 8, 1956, CREST for FGW; Wilford, pp. 119–20.

425 **"real life.":** FGW letter to Julius Fleischmann, March 10, 1956, Leona Reinzan letter to PKW, April 26, 1956, B: 4, FGW letter to B. Boursicot, Jan. 28, 1956, B: 1, FWP, UVA.

426 **prolonged applause:** Transcript of Special Report to the 20th Congress of the Communist Party of the Soviet Union, Feb. 24–25, 1956, https://www.marxists.org/archive/khrushchev/1956/02/24.htm; Ranelagh, p. 285.

426 **America's downfall:** Khrushchev and Stalin: Leaders of the Cult of Personality, March 1959, CIA report released Aug. 8, 1999; FGWII, Jan. 13, 2021; George Kennan letter to FGW, May 2, 1956, and FGW reply, May 3, 1956, vB: 7, FWP, UVA.

426 **the prize:** "Almost Successful Recipe," p. 76; Mosley, p. 375.

427 **were genuine:** Anderson, p. 429; Prados, *Safe for Democracy*, p. 154; Powers, p. 91; "Almost Successful Recipe," pp. 74–75; Evan Thomas, p. 137; Minutes for Deputies' Meeting, May 16, 1956, CREST for FGW; FGW letter to Arthur Mallet, Aug. 28, 1956, B: 8, FWP, UVA.

427 **on June 5:** Grose, pp. 425–26; Anderson, p. 415.

427 **the pun:** Minutes for Deputies' Meeting, June 11, 1956, CREST for FGW; O'Toole, p. 470; Grose, p. 427; FGWII, Jan. 13, 2021; EW, Dec. 9, 2020.

427 **easily endure:** "Almost Successful Recipe," p. 76–78; Swartz, p. 277.

428 **food aid:** "Almost Successful Recipe," pp. 77, 80–83, 88.

428 **egg breaking:** "Almost Successful Recipe," pp. 80–85, 92–94; FGWII, Dec. 11, 2020; Minutes for Deputies' Meeting, July 6, 1956, CREST for FGW.

429 **crisis passed:** "The 1956 Hungarian Revolution," pp. 4, 10; Ranelagh, p. 304; Sebestyen, pp. 99–100.

429 **"to [support]?":** "Almost Successful Recipe," pp. 53–54.

430 **that dilemma:** "Almost Successful Recipe," pp. 53–54; Tracy Barnes memo to Special Assistant to the Director, Nov. 18, 1953, NSA; Anderson, pp. 235–36; Ranelagh, p. 305; Swartz, p. 280.

430 **its hands:** 167. Draft Memorandum for FGW to AWD, Jan. 8, 1954, FRUS, The Intelligence Community, 1950–1955; Powers, p. 47.

430 **was "BGWoeful.":** "Almost Successful Recipe," pp. 59–60; Anderson, pp. 298–300; CIA cryptonyms list, catalog.archives.gov.

432 **Suez Canal:** FGWII, Jan. 13, 2021; Richard Helms, pp. 161–62; Evan Thomas, p. 141; Hersh, pp. 382–84; Bronson Tweedy interview, B: 10, RSP, HA; FGW memo on his attack of hepatitis, Jan. 4, 1957, WFC.

432 **political purges:** Sebestyen, pp. 9–19, 28–32, 41–42, 47.

432 **message stated:** Sebestyen, pp. 58–59; Clandestine Services History: Hungary, External Operations, 1946–1965, May 1972, vol. 2, p. 36.

432 **on the job:** Clandestine Services History: Hungary, vol. 2, p. 67; Sebestyen, pp. 56–57; Study Prepared for U.S. Army Intelligence, "Hungary: Resistance Activities and Potentials," Project No. 9570, January 1956, NSA.

433 **such heresies:** Sebestyen, pp. 63–68, 73–80, 84–87.

433 **and stationery:** Sebestyen, pp. 9, 89–90; Swartz, pp. 532, 582; Anderson, p. 432; Clandestine Services History: Hungary, vol. 1, p. 66.

434 **terrible choice:** Sebestyen, pp. 89–90, 94–95, 101–2.

434 **before him:** Sebestyen, pp. 96–99.

434 **was set:** Minutes for Deputies' Meeting, Oct. 22, 1956, CREST for FGW; Sebestyen, pp. 102–3.

435 **the Israelis:** "A Look Back . . . U-2 Monitors Suez Crisis," CIA News and & Information, cia.gov; Ranelagh, p. 296; Hugh Thomas, p. 32; Ricky-Dale Calhoun, The Art of Counterintelligence: The Musketeer's Cloak: Strategic Deception During the Suez Crisis of 1956, CIA Library, www.cia.gov/resources /csi/static/the-musketeers-cloak.pdf.

435 **"his senses.":** Alfred Ulmer interview, B: 10, RSP, HA; Hugh Thomas, pp. 13, 16–17, 21, 24–26, 31–37.

436 **did not:** Ricky-Dale Calhoun, The Art of Counterintelligence: The Musketeer's Cloak: Strategic Deception During the Suez Crisis of 1956, CIA Library, www.cia.gov/resources/csi/static/the-musketeers-cloak.pdf; Ambrose, *Eisenhower*, p. 416; Hugh Thomas, pp. 28, 48–49.

436 **September 1956:** Jackson, vol. 5, pp. 16, 23; Hugh Thomas, pp. 52–59, 69, 72.

436 **did so:** Ricky-Dale Calhoun, The Art of Counterintelligence: The Musketeer's Cloak: Strategic Deception During the Suez Crisis of 1956, CIA Library, www .cia.gov/resources/csi/static/the-musketeers-cloak.pdf; Jackson, vol. 5, pp. 14–17; Minutes for Deputies' Meeting, Aug. 13, 1956, CREST for FGW.

436 **at that point:** Hugh Thomas, pp. 70, 82.

437 **and French:** Soviet Staff Study: The Suez Crisis—A Test for the U.S.S.R.'s Middle Eastern Policy (Reference title: CAESAR V-A-56), Office of Current Intelligence, CIA, Jan. 3, 1957; Hugh Thomas, p. 81.

437 **was "Kadesh.":** Hugh Thomas, pp. 48, 83–85, 88–89, 94–99, 112.

437 **saying later:** Hugh Thomas, p. 105; Jackson, vol. 5, p. 24; FGWII, Jan. 13, 2021; Robert Amory interview, B: 9, RSP, HA.

438 **by surprise:** Sebestyen, pp. 107–11, 135; Swartz, pp. 282, 289; Press release, on Soviet documents previously published by NSA, Oct. 31, 2006, NSA; FGW memo to DCI on CIA Awareness of Pre–Hungarian Revolution Developments, March 1957, release June 22, 2012, CIA.

438 **"go home!":** Evan Thomas, p. 143.

438 **They refused:** Sebestyen, pp. 112–19.

439 **the airwaves:** Sebestyen, pp. 122–24.

439 **not be made:** Meyer, p. 127; Grose, p. 437.

440 **was "lunacy.":** FGW memo to DCI on CIA Awareness of Pre–Hungarian Revolution Developments, March 1957, release June 22, 2012, CIA; Document No. 40, Working Notes from the CPSU CC Presidium Session, Oct. 28, 1956, Press release on Hungarian revolution, Oct. 31, 2006, NSA; Swartz, pp. 311–12; "The 1956 Hungarian Revolution," pp. 71, 84.

440   **was tepid:** "The 1956 Hungarian Revolution," p. 81; Press release, May 10, 2017, NSA.

440   **under control:** Sebestyen, pp. 125–28.

441   **unleash it:** Sebestyen, pp. 128, 132–33, 136–37, 154.

441   **the revolt:** Sebestyen, pp. 138, 143–47, 150–51.

442   **questions yet:** Sebestyen, p. 146; Memorandum for the Record, Hungarian Conflict and FEC Action, Oct. 25, 1956, WCA.

442   **was marginalized:** Sebestyen, pp. 141–43, 152–53.

442   **the waterway:** Hugh Thomas, pp. 113–16.

443   **so grim:** 116. Memorandum of Discussion at the 301st Meeting of the NSC, Oct. 26, 1956, FRUS, Eastern Europe, vol. 25, 1955–1957; Grose, p. 437; Sebestyen, p. 157.

443   **to revolution:** "The 1956 Hungarian Revolution," pp. 31–32, 44; Grose, p. 437.

443   **air assets:** "A Look Back . . . U-2 Monitors Suez Crisis," CIA News & Information; Jackson, vol. 5, pp. 20–21; Ricky-Dale Calhoun, The Art of Counterintelligence: The Musketeer's Cloak: Strategic Deception During the Suez Crisis of 1956, CIA Library, www.cia.gov/resources/csi/static/the-musketeers-cloak .pdf.

444   **"undue caution.":** Sebestyen, pp. 161–68; "The 1956 Hungarian Revolution," p. 40.

444   **had triumphed:** Sebestyen, pp. 171, 178, 184; "The 1956 Hungarian Revolution," p. 48.

444   **stabilizing Hungary:** Hersh, p. 397; FGW letter to Charles Thayer, Oct. 16, 1956, B: 10, FWP, UVA.

445   **either side:** Ranelagh, p. 300; Hugh Thomas, pp. 120, 137, 141; Ambrose, *Eisenhower*, p. 430.

445   **imperial appetites:** Ambrose, *Ike's Spies*, p. 240; Hersh, p. 405; Swartz, p. 488; EW, Dec. 6, 2020; Ranelagh, p. 305; FGWII, Jan. 13, 2021.

445   **hurt deeply:** Powers, p. 85; EW, Dec. 6, 2020.

446   **done him in:** Evan Thomas, pp. 12, 144; Simpson, p. 288; Katharine Graham interview with Polly Fritchey, Oct. 10, 1989, p. 10, KGP; Interviews with Gerald Miller, Alfred Ulmer, Kermit Roosevelt, Bronson Tweedy, Lyman Kirkpatrick, B: 10, RSP, HA; In Memoriam: Frank Gardiner Wisner, 1909–1965, Langley, Virginia, Jan. 29, 1971, WFC.

447   **felled him:** Mondimore, pp. 71, 218; Goodwin and Jamison, vol. 1, p. 135; Gotlib and Hammen, p. 321.

447   **many words:** Goodwin and Jamison, vol. 1, pp. 31, 43, 133; Mondimore, pp. 1–3, 9–10; Sackeim, Jan. 27, 2022.

447   **of his life:** Sackeim, Jan. 27, 2022; Goodwin and Jamison, vol. 1, p. xxi.

448   **to be true:** The 1956 Hungarian Revolution: A History in Documents, Document No. 6, Working Notes and Attached Extract from the Minutes of the CPSU CC Presidium Meeting, Oct. 31, 1956, NSA Briefing Book, Nov. 4, 2002; Ambrose, *Eisenhower*, p. 426.

448   **would succeed:** Sebestyen, pp. 200–7, 210, 214–18; The 1956 Hungarian Revolution: A History in Documents, Document No. 6, Working Notes and Attached Extract from the Minutes of the CPSU CC Presidium Meeting, Oct. 31, 1956, NSA Briefing Book, Nov. 4, 2002; Ranelagh, p. 305.

449   **a defense:** Sebestyen, pp. 218–20.

449   **his cooperation:** Sebestyen, pp. 228–29, 233, 241–42.

449   **Joe McCarthy:** Heymann, p. 148.

450   **"same company.":** The Suez Crisis: A Brief Comint History, U.S. Cryptologic

History, Office of Archives and History, National Security Agency / Central
Security Service, 1988, vol. 2, pp. 1, 23; Document No. 40, Working Notes
from the CPSU CC Presidium Session, Oct. 28, 1956, NSA; 455. Memorandum
of Discussion at the 302nd Meeting of the NSC, Nov. 1, 1956, FRUS, Suez Crisis, 1955–1957.

450 **the Soviets:** Ranelagh, p. 305; Phone Conversation Guidance for Radio Free
Europe Broadcasts, Nov. 2, 1956, Suggested Guidance for Radio Free Europe,
Nov. 3, 1956, WCA.

450 **new government:** Sebestyen, pp. 248, 254–56, 263–65, 268; Ambrose, *Eisenhower*, p. 430.

451 **bipolar disorder:** Hersh, p. 399; Evan Thomas, p. 144; Grose, p. 443; Powers,
p. 85; Mondimore, p. 202; FGW letter to Sidney Stein, Jan 7, 1957, B: 9, FGW
letter to Janet Barnes, Jan. 17, 1957, B: 1, FGW letter to Charles Thayer, Oct.
16, 1956, B: 10, FWP, UVA.

451 **from Egypt:** Wisner Betting Book, p. 35, WFC; Hugh Thomas, pp. 143, 148;
Ambrose, *Eisenhower*, p. 432.

452 **frustrated him:** Hugh Thomas, pp. 14, 162, 166; Richard Helms, p. 162; FGW
memo to Richard Nixon, Dec. 8, 1956, B: 8, FWP, UVA.

452 **prison camps:** Sebestyen, pp. 275–76, 282–83, 286, 290–92; "The 1956 Hun-
garian Revolution," p. 2; Document No. 8, Report by Soviet Deputy Interior
Minister M. N. Holodkov to Interior Minister N. P. Dudorov, Nov. 15, 1956,
Thayer cable to Secretary of State, Nov. 13, 1956, NSA.

452 **report concluded:** Press release "CIA Had Single Officer in Hungary 1956,"
Oct. 31, 2006, NSA; Swartz, pp. 363–64; Clandestine Services History: The
Hungarian Revolution and Planning for the Future, Oct. 23–Nov. 4, 1956, vol.
1, pp. 76–77, 80–81, MN.

453 **in Budapest:** Swartz, p. 294; Clandestine Services History: The Hungarian
Revolution and Planning for the Future, Oct. 23–Nov. 4, 1956, vol. 1, pp. 77–78,
106, MN.

453 **operations—going:** FGW letter to Llewellyn Thompson, Jan. 8, 1957, B: 10,
FWP, UVA; FGW memo on his attack of hepatitis, Jan. 4, 1957, WFC; Swartz,
pp. 356, 557, 559; Evan Thomas, pp. 145–46.

454 **it anyway:** Evan Thomas, p. 146; "The 1956 Hungarian Revolution," pp. 53–55;
Swartz, p. 63.

454 **in the capital:** Clandestine Services History: The Hungarian Revolution
and Planning for the Future, Oct. 23–Nov. 4, 1956, vol. 1, pp. 81–91, MN; FGW
memo on his attack of hepatitis, Jan. 4, 1957, WFC; Fritz Molden interview, B:
10, RSP, HA; Swartz, p. 369–70, 594–95; Prados, *Safe for Democracy*, p. 124.

454 **to Washington:** Hersh, p. 400; Swartz, p. 594; Evan Thomas, p. 147; FGW
memo on his attack of hepatitis, Jan. 4, 1957, WFC; Clandestine Services History: The Hungarian Revolution and Planning for the Future, Oct. 23–Nov. 4,
1956, vol. 1, p. 92, MN; Georgetown Archive Notes, B: 17, GHP, HA; Letter to
Susan Mary, Dec. 3, 1956, B: 13, AP, LOC.

455 **addled mind:** Mondimore, p. 11; Evan Thomas, p. 375; Hersh, p. 400; FGW
memo on U.S. Policy Toward the Satellites and Western European Reactions
to Radio Free Europe, Nov. 9, 1956, WCA.

455 **somewhat intimidating:** Ridder, Sept. 7, 2021; Marie Ridder letter to PKW, B:
16, Walter Ridder copy, Nov. 18, 1956, B: 8, FWP, UVA.

456 **the residence:** Ridder, Sept. 7, 2021.

456 **turned him on:** Lyman B. Kirkpatrick diary entry, Dec. 6, 1956, Vol. 3,
CREST for FGW; Colby, p. 123; "Shots from a Luce Cannon": Combatting
Communism in Italy, 1953–1956, Defense Department historical study, pp.

2–5, 38, 61, NSA; Gerald Miller interview, B: 10, RSP, HA; FGW letter to Llewellyn Thompson, Jan. 8, 1957, B: 10, Letter to FGW, Oct. 6, 1956, B: 7, FWP, UVA.

456 **Communist Party:** Waller, *Disciples*, p. 429.

457 **the ambassador:** Colby, p. 135; Evan Thomas, pp. 147–48; "The 1956 Hungarian Revolution," pp. 85–86; Prados, *Safe for Democracy*, p. 158; Gerald Miller interview, B: 10, RSP, HA.

457 **reviewed it:** Prados, *Lost Crusader*, p. 61; FGW letter to Llewellyn Thompson, Jan. 8, 1957, B: 10, Clare Boothe Luce letter to FGW, Dec. 7, 1956, B: 7, FWP, UVA; Clare Boothe Luce draft letter to Eisenhower Dec. 7, 1956, B: 16, GHP, HA.

457 **the revolt:** FGW memo to Richard Nixon, Dec. 8, 1956, B: 8, FWP, UVA; FGW memo on his attack of hepatitis, Jan. 4, 1957, WFC.

458 **the effects:** GW, Dec. 1, 2020; FGWII, Jan. 13, 2021; FGW memo on his attack of hepatitis, Jan. 4, 1957, WFC; FGW letter to John Pierrepont, Jan. 4, 1957, B: 8, FGW letter to D. von Bothmer Jan. 4, 1957, B: 1, FGW letter to John Richardson, Dec. 19, 1956, B: 8, FGW letter to Jim, Jan. 3, 1957, B: 6, FWP, UVA; EW, Jan. 12, 2021; Evan Thomas, p. 148.

Chapter 24: Breakdown

461 **U.S. officials:** Hersh, p. 402; Jackson, vol. 1, p. 76; Minutes for Deputies' Meeting, Nov. 28, 1956, DD/S Diary Notes, Dec. 6, 1956, CREST for FGW.

461 **the prize:** FGW memo to Chief, International Organizations Division, Jan. 7, 1957, WCA; EW, Dec. 6, 2020; Wisner Betting Book, pp. 45–46, WFC; Nancy Cassella letter to FGW, Feb. 26, 1957, B: 2, Secretary to FGW letter to Nancy Payne, Dec. 13, 1956, B: 8, FWP, UVA.

462 **military intelligence:** Minutes for Deputies' Meeting, May 1, 1957, Lyman B. Kirkpatrick diary entry, vol. 3, Nov. 20, 1956, CREST for FGW; Grose, p. 450; Ambrose, *Eisenhower*, pp. 455–57; Ambrose, *Ike's Spies*, p. 243; FGW letter to Alexander Chisholm, March 1, 1957, B: 4, FWP, UVA.

462 **Hungarians on:** Meyer, pp. 125–26; Wilford, p. 49; Ranelagh, p. 308; Hersh, p. 409; Ambrose, *Ike's Spies*, p. 239.

463 **to lose:** Cord Meyer memo to DCI, Nov. 14, 1956, with attachment on RFE, Nov. 13, 1956, WCA; Loomis, FAOH, pp. 21–22; "The 1956 Hungarian Revolution," p. 14; FGW to William Deakin, Dec. 28, 1956, B; 3, FWP, UVA; Jim Greenleaf memo on Radio Free Europe and the 1956 Hungarian Uprising, April 20, 1990, declassified CIA document; Georgetown Archive Notes, B: 17, GHP, HA; The 1956 Hungarian Revolution: A History in Documents, Document No. 10, Policy Review of Voice for Free Hungary Programming, Oct. 23–Nov. 23, 1956, December 5, 1956, NSA Briefing Book, Nov. 4, 2002; Meyer, pp. 126–27; Horace Nickels letter to L. Randolph Higgs, Dec. 19, 1956, WCA.

463 **their homelands:** Corson, pp. 370–71; Wilford, p. 50.

464 **attending to him:** FGW memo on his attack of hepatitis, Jan. 4, 1957, WFC.

464 **mentally unwell:** FGW memo on his attack of hepatitis, Jan. 4, 1957, WFC; Mayo Clinic Overview of Hepatitis A; Evan Thomas, pp. 150, 376; Sackeim, Jan. 18, 2022; FGWII, Sept. 9, 2020; EW, Jan. 12, 2021; Secretary to FGW letter to CB, FGW letter to Tracy Barnes, Jan. 14, 1957, B: 1, FWP, UVA.

465 **with hepatitis:** Herken, p. 226; Letter dictated by FGW to Mr. and Mrs. Bruce, Jan. 18, 1957, Secretary to FGW letter to Philip Graham, July 5, 1958, CB letter to FGW, Jan. 9, 1957, Letter to C. T. Barnes, Dec. 21, 1956, B: 1, FGW letter

to Clare Boothe Luce, Dec. 21, 1956, B: 7, William Jackson letter to FGW, Jan. 4, 1957, B: 6, FWP, UVA.

465 **odd behavior:** FGW memo on his attack of hepatitis, Jan. 4, 1957, Office of Personnel letter to Wilfred Harren on FGW claim, Aug. 22, 1957, Employee's Notice of Injury or Occupational Disease for FGW, Dec. 16, 1956, WFC; FGW letter to Colonel and Mrs. J. C. King, Jan. 17, 1957, FGW letter to Mr. and Mrs. E. Allan Lightner, Jan. 17, 1957, B: 7, FGW letter to Mr. and Mrs. James Gibson, Jan. 14, 1957, B: 5, Chief, Benefits and Casualty Division memo to RMH on FGW Compensation Claim, B: 18, FWP, UVA.

465 **long convalescence:** FGW letter to Tracy Barnes, Jan. 14, 1957, B. J. Morrone letter to Tracy Barnes, Jan. 3, 1957, FGW letter to Joseph Alsop, Jan. 12, 1957, B: 1, FGW letter to Viscount Harcourt, Jan. 7, 1957, B: 6, FGW letter to Llewellyn Thompson, Jan. 8, 1957, B: 10, FWP, UVA; Dean Acheson letter to FGW, Dec. 28, 1956, DAP, YU.

466 **family property:** FGW to John S. Graham, Jan. 17, 1957, B: 5, FGW letter to James Vardaman, Jan. 10, 1957, Rough notes based on FGW's telephone conversation with Paul Nitze, Jan. 18, 1957, FGW letter to Henry Sears, Jan. 10, 1957, B: 9, FGW letter to Joseph Bryan, Jan. 12, 1957, B: 1, FGW letters to Ellis Knowles, March 28 and May 10, 1957, B: 4, FWP, UVA.

466 **a year off:** A Biographical Sketch of FGW by Arthur Jacobs, WFC; Katharine Graham interview with Polly Fritchey, Oct. 10, 1989, p. 11, KGP; Secretary to FGW letter to J. Lawn Thompson, Feb. 27, 1957, B: 10, Letter to FGW, Aug. 8, 1962, B: 2, FGW letter to Chis, Feb. 25, 1957, B: 4, FWP, UVA.

466 **offices' time:** Herken, p. 226; Powers, pp. 86–87; FGW medical form listing 17 hospital visits from Dec. 17, 1956, to Sept. 13, 1957, WFC; Minutes for Deputies' Meetings, March 29, April 3, Aug. 2, and Sept. 27, 1957, DD/S Diary Notes, Oct. 31, 1957, Staff Conference Minutes of Meeting Held in Director's Conference Room, Sept. 4, 1957, CREST for FGW; AWD letter to Gordon Gray, Feb. 27, 1958, AWD letter to Committee on Admissions, Metropolitan Club, Feb. 27, 1956, B: 59, AWD, PU.

467 **atop it:** J. H. Morse letter to FGW, June 15, 1957, B: 1, Itinerary for FGW trip to Nevada test site, June 25, 1957, B: 11, FWP, UVA; Ambrose, *Eisenhower*, pp. 458–59; Halberstam, *The Fifties*, pp. 624–26.

467 **his life:** Cynthia Helms, p. 177; Richard Helms, pp. 150–51; AWD letter to JEH with memo on Joseph Alsop incident, April 1, 1957, FBI file on Joseph Alsop; EW, Nov. 11, 2020; GW, Dec. 1, 2020.

467 **outside investigator:** Director of Personnel's Meeting with General John F. Cassidy, April 4, 1957, memorandum of conversation, CREST for FGW.

467 **"then down.":** Mondimore, pp. 33–37; EW, Dec. 6, 2020.

468 **important subjects:** Hersh, pp. 421–22; Gotlib and Hammen, p. 128; Powers, pp. 85–87; Mosley, p. 421; FGWII, Dec. 11, 2020.

468 **returned inside:** FGWII, Jan. 13, 2021; Hersh, p. 404; Powers, pp. 84, 87; Herken, p. 227; Reeder, Aug. 20, 2020; FGW letter to Edward Lansdale, June 30, 1958, WFC; Letter to Avis Bohlen, June 26, 1958, B: 1, FGW letter to Arthur Krock, July 3, 1958, and Krock letter to FGW, July 7, 1958, FGW letter to Clare Boothe Luce, June 25, 1958, B: 7, FWP, UVA; Interview with William Bundy, B: 9, RSP, HA.

469 **UVA's president:** Katharine Graham interview with Polly Fritchey, Oct. 10, 1989, pp. 9, 11, KGP; Graham, p. 280; EW, Oct. 6 and Dec. 6, 2020; EW letter to Donald Graham, March 22, 2005, Phil Graham letter to FGW, Aug. 7, 1958, WFC; FGW résumé for UVA, Frederick Deane letter to FGW, Aug. 8, 1958, B: 10, Norborne Berkeley letter to FGW, Sept. 8, 1958, B: 1, FWP, UVA.

469   **social standing:** FGWII, Aug. 19, 2020; GW, Aug. 3, 2020; EW, July 15, 2020.
469   **almost inexcusable:** GW, Dec. 10, 2020; Katharine Graham interview with
      Polly Fritchey, Oct. 10, 1989, p. 9, KGP; FGWII, Jan. 13, 2021.
469   **family crisis:** GW, Dec. 10, 2020; EW, Jan. 12, 2021; FGWII, Aug. 19, 2020;
      Ray Baine letter to FGW, April 22, 1957, B: 1, FGW letter to Jane Jantzen, July
      3, 1958, B: 6, FGW letter to Richard Orr, Sept. 5, 1958, B: 8, FGW letters to
      Peter Sichel, July 3 and Aug. 25, 1958, B: 9, FWP, UVA.
470   **he temporized:** RMH memo to DCI, Jan. 24, 1957, WCA; Richard Helms, p.
      163; Evan Thomas, pp. 150–51; Weiner, p. 11; FGWII, Sept. 9, 2020; Crypto-
      nym list, E: ZZ19, RG263, NA; Alfred Ulmer interview, Gerald Miller inter-
      view, B: 10, RSP, HA.
470   **a break:** Gerald Miller interview, B: 10, RSP, HA.
470   **wrote a friend:** Secretary to FGW letter to W. H. Petree, Feb. 11, 1959, B: 5,
      CB letter to PKW, undated, Billie Morrone letter, Aug. 25, 1958, FGW letter
      to Thomas Bell, Aug. 25, B: 1, FWP, UVA.
471   **he hated:** FGWII, Dec. 11, 2020, and Jan. 13, 2021; EW, Jan. 12, 2021; GW,
      Dec. 10, 2020; FGW letter to Mother, Dec. 7, 1957, B: 4, FWP, UVA.
472   **of the year:** Herken, p. 330; FGW papers, B: 16, GHP, HA; Psychological
      Summary—Case No. 25835, WFC.

Chapter 25: Sheppard Pratt

473   **to work:** DD/S Diary Notes, June 4, 1957, CREST for FGW; Sheppard Pratt
      receipts for FGW clothing PKW brought, Nov. 21, Dec. 1, and Dec. 3, 1958, B:
      5, FWP, UVA; Director of Personnel announcement on FGW assignment,
      Dec. 9, 1958, BHP.
473   **for now:** R. R. Roach memo to A. H. Belmont, Dec. 31, 1958, FBIW.
474   **a blessing:** Grose, pp. 454, 463–64; Srodes, p. 497.
474   **clandestine service:** Jackson, vol. 4, pp. 68, 71–74; James S. Lay memos to
      DDE, draft, and Dec. 29, 1958, OSNSA, NSC Series, Subject Subseries, Presi-
      dent's Board of Consultants on Foreign Intelligence Activities, DEL.
474   **oversight of it:** Memorandum of Conference with the President, Dec. 22, 1958,
      John E. Hull memo to DDE, Oct. 30, 1958, Third Report to the President by
      the President's Board of Consultants on Foreign Intelligence Activities, Oct.
      30, 1958, OSNSA, NSC Series, Subject Subseries, President's Board of Consul-
      tants on Foreign Intelligence Activities, DEL.
475   **told aides:** Memorandum for the Record, Director's Senior Staff Meeting on 8
      December 1958, Senior Staff Meeting Agenda, Jan. 12, 1959, CREST for FGW;
      AWD memo to Executive Secretary, NSC, Oct. 17, 1959, OSNSA, NSC Series,
      Subject Subseries, President's Board of Consultants on Foreign Intelligence
      Activities, DEL.
475   **that move:** Request for Personnel Action for FGW, Dec. 4, 1958, BHP; Letter
      to William Jackson, Dec. 7, 1958, CREST for FGW; Memo assigning FGW to
      Office of the DCI on Jan. 1, 1959, WFC.
476   **get along:** Ranelagh, p. 328; Notice N. 20-190-173, Personnel, Dec. 5, 1958,
      Announcement of Assignments to Key Positions, Office of the Deputy Director
      (Plans), CREST for FGW; Powers, pp. 88–91, 110–13; Richard Helms, pp. 163–
      65; The Central Intelligence Agency and Overhead Reconnaissance, The U-2
      and Oxcart Programs, 1954–1974, cia.gov, p. 39; Mrs. Wisner interview, B: 10,
      RSP, HA.
476   **his back:** John Hull memo to James Lay, Nov. 27, 1959, AWD memo to Exec-
      utive Secretary, NSC, July 28, 1959, OSNSA, NSC Series, Subject Subseries,
      President's Board of Consultants on Foreign Intelligence Activities, DEL.

476 **to wear:** Sheppard and Enoch Pratt Hospital cards for FGW, SPA; Sheppard and Enoch Pratt clothing and effects forms for FGW, Sept. 12 and 13, 1958, B: 5, FWP, UVA.

476 **the facility:** Forbush, pp. 130, 167; Forbush and Forbush, pp. 78–79; Sackeim, Jan. 18, 2022; H. M. Murdock letter to the Board of Directors, Sept. 23, 1958, B: 8, Sheppard Pratt Hospital brochure, B: 19, "Sheppard Pratt . . . Today, More Like a Campus," *Baltimore*, Sept. 1969, p. 21, B: 21, SP, NLM.

476 **husband's case:** H. M. Murdock letter to the Board of Directors, Jan. 29, 1958, B: 8, SP, NLM; Sheppard and Enoch Pratt Hospital cards for FGW, SPA; Agreement for FGW commitment to Sheppard Pratt, B: 5, FWP, UVA.

477 **out of control:** EW, Jan. 12 and March 26, 2021; GW, Dec. 10, 2020; Hill and Worden, pp. 228–43.

477 **disarmed Wisner:** Commentary of an Introduction to the Psychiatric Patient, Taken from Dr. Lewis Hill's Informal Lecture to the Residents of Sheppard–Enoch Pratt Hospital, B: 17, SP, NLM.

478 **sleep pattern:** Special Instructions for Sleep Therapy with Sodium Amytal, B: 14, SP, NLM; Forbush and Forbush, pp. 35, 39–40, 54, 90; Forbush, pp. 159–60; Hill and Worden, pp. 228–43, B: 17, SP, NLM; Sackeim, Jan. 18, 2022; EW, Dec. 6, 2020.

478 **schizophrenic patients:** Sackeim, Jan. 27, 2022; Forbush, p. 123; Forbush and Forbush, pp. 68–69.

479 **the treatment:** Issue 14: Does Electroshock Therapy Cure Depression? Essays by Max Fink and Leonard R. Frank, pp. 292–309, bmhs.norwalk.org; Forbush, pp. 123–24, 170; Sackeim, Jan. 27, 2022.

479 **the procedure:** Jonathan Sadowsky, "Electroconvulsive Therapy: A History of Controversy, but Also of Help," *Scientific American*, Jan. 13, 2017, www .scientificamerican.com/article/electroconvulsive-therapy-a-history-of -controversy-but-also-of-help/; Fink, p. 7; Abrams, p. 227; GW, Dec. 10, 2020; FGWII, Dec. 11, 2020; EW, Jan. 12, 2021; Katharine Graham interview with Polly Fritchey, Oct. 10, 1989, p. 11, KGP; Evan Thomas, p. 162; Powers, p. 87.

479 **bipolar disorder:** Abrams, pp. 3, 5; Payne, pp. 346–68; Edward Shorter, "The History of ECT: Unsolved Mysteries," *Psychiatric Times*, Feb. 1, 2004, www .psychiatrictimes.com/view/history-ect-unsolved-mysteries; "Convulsive Therapy: a review of the first 55 years," by Max Fink, *Journal of Affective Disorders* 63, nos. 1–2 (March 2001): p. 4; Sackeim, Jan. 18, 2022; Elias et al., "Electroconvulsive Therapy in Mania: A Review of 80 Years of Clinical Experience," by Alby Elias et. al., Nov. 10, 2021, pp. 2291, 2345, ajp.psychiatry online.org; Mondimore, pp. 125, 129.

479 **the medication:** Mondimore, pp. 28, 64–68; Sackeim, Jan. 18, 2022; Goodwin and Jamison, vol. 2, pp. 699, 715; López-Muñoz et al., p. 2143.

480 **shock therapy:** Sackeim, Jan. 18 and 27, 2022; Fink, p. 8; Mondimore, pp. 125–26; Issue 14: Does Electroshock Therapy Cure Depression? bmhs.norwalk.org; Forbush, pp. 161, 205.

480 **institute's treatments:** Sackeim, Jan. 18, 2022; Abrams, pp. 105–6, 151–52, 167, 169, 192, 194–54, 200–1, 230; Fink, pp. 6–8; EW, March 17, 2022.

480 **mental health:** Hill and Worden, pp. 228–43; Felix Stump letter to FGW, Oct. 20, 1958, B: 9, Etem Menderes letter to FGW, Nov. 10, 1958, B: 7, Sheppard Pratt receipt for clothing PKW sent to FGW, Sept. 22, 1958, B: 5, FWP, UVA.

481 **the sessions:** Forbush, p. 171; Sackeim, Jan. 18, 2022.

481 **the shops:** Forbush, pp. 144–45, 157, 165; Hill and Worden, pp. 228–43, B: 17, SP, NLM; Sackeim, Jan. 18, 2022; H. M. Murdock bill for PKW, Nov. 6, 1958, A file with Billie Morrone correspondence on FGW family finances, $20 bill

for W. Richard Ferguson services for FGW, Nov. 1, 1958, Itemized list of cigarettes, cookies, and other goods FGW buys, December 1958 and January 1959, B: 5, FWP, UVA.

481　**good carpenter:** Forbush and Forbush, pp. 43, 74–75, 84–85; Forbush, pp. 34, 44, 196, 210; EW, Sept. 22, 2020; Sheppard Pratt receipts for tennis rackets, tennis balls, and art supplies sent by PKW, Nov. 18, 20, 28, and Dec. 29, 1958, PKW letter to H. M. Murdock, Dec. 22, 1958, B: 5, FWP, UVA.

482　**East Bloc:** Sheppard-Pratt Hospital Library Department Report, Dec. 1956 through Nov. 1957, B: 8, SP, NLM; Sheppard-Pratt receipt for books PKW sent to FGW, which included *Doctor Zhivago*, Nov. 28, 1958, B: 5, FWP, UVA; Finn and Couvée, pp. 10–17, 131, 136–38, 214–18, 264.

482　**to Graham:** Katharine Graham interview with Polly Fritchey, Oct. 10, 1989, p. 9, KGP; Forbush, p. 167; A. S. Mike Moroney letter to FGW, Dec. 27, 1958, B: 8, Sheppard-Pratt receipts for Christmas gifts sent to FGW, December 1958, B: 5, Billie Morrone letter to R. H. Macy & Company, Dec. 15, 1958, B: 7, FWP, UVA.

482　**"to civilization.":** EW, Jan. 12, 2021; GW, Aug. 10 and Dec. 10, 2020; Forbush, pp. 135–36; FGWII, April 1, 2021; FGW letter to Cyrus Sulzberger, Feb. 22, 1959, B: 10, FGW letter to Henry Cabot Lodge, Feb. 22, 1959, B: 7, FWP, UVA.

483　**"for me.":** Sheppard Pratt Monthly Register for March 1959, entry for FGW, SPA; FGW letter to Ambler Moss, March 11, 1959, B: 7, FWP, UVA; FGWII, March 15, 2021.

483　**"greater activity."** Chief, Benefits and Services Division memo for Administrative Officer, Office of the Director on FGW 30-day sick leave, March 15, 1959, WFC; EW, Jan. 12, 2021; FGW letter to Bob Joyce, March 10, 1959, B: 6, Billie Morrone letter to Miss K. L. Osborne, B: 4, FGW letter to Archibald Alexander, March 11, 1959, B: 1, FGW letter to Roger Gorian, May 4, 1959, B: 5, FWP, UVA.

483　**his father:** R. R. Roach to A. H. Belmont, memo on FGW, June 17, 1959, memo on FGW recovery, June 18, 1959, FBIW; Wendell Little letter to FGW, May 19, 1959, B: 7, FWP, UVA; FGWII, Jan. 13, 2021.

484　**with a psychiatrist:** Forbush, pp. 59, 82; Sackeim, Jan. 18, 2022; Mondimore, p. 198.

484　**on a couch:** Lawrence S. Kubie Statement for the Hospital Committee of the Board of Trustees of the Sheppard and Enoch Pratt Hospital, Nov. 15, 1963, B: 17, SP, NLM; Goodwin and Jamison, vol. 2, pp. 797–98; Fink, p. 5; Mondimore, pp. 34, 129.

Chapter 26: London

485　**brother-in-law, Chis:** FGW letter to Sister and Chis, May 18, 1959, B: 4, FWP, UVA.

485　**in London:** Request for Personnel Action for FGW, June 1, 1959, B: 18, FWP, UVA; Interview with Mrs. Wisner, B: 10, RSP, HA.

486　**CIA network:** Request for Personnel Action for FGW, June 1, 1959, B: 18, FWP, UVA; Deputy Director (Support) letter to Director of Personnel, June 16, 1959, BHP; A Biographic Sketch of FGW by Arthur Jacobs, WFC; EW, Feb. 18, 2021; Ranelagh, p. 254; Hersh, p. 423; Hughes, FAOH, p. 96.

486　**the directorship:** FGW letter to David Bruce, May 27, 1959, B: 1, FGW letter to Sister and Chis, May 18, 1959, B: 4, FWP, UVA.

486　**chief's job:** FGWII, Oct. 19, 2020; FGW letters to Billie Morrone, Dec. 20, 1960, and June 27, 1961, B: 7, Joseph Cowen letter to FGW, June 5, 1959, and FGW letter to Dr. Cowen, June 9, 1959, FGW letter to William Petree, March

20, 1963, B: 5, FGW letter to Henry Tasca, Oct. 21, 1960, B: 10, FGW letter to David Bruce, June 15, 1959, B: 1, FWP, UVA.

487 **September 21:** FGW letter to David Bruce, June 15, 1959, B: 1, Surgeon SS *America* letter, Aug. 8, 1959, B: 7, FGW letter to John Richardson, June 12, 1959, FGW letters to Dimitri Papaefstration, May 20 and June 16, 1959, B: 10, FWP, UVA; Richard Bissell letter to Director of Personnel on FGW fitness report, March 31, 1960, BHP.

487 **Polly planned:** Reed, p. 46; EW, Aug. 19, 2020; FGW letter to Joseph A. Frank, Sept. 25, 1961, FGW letter to FGWII, March 19, 1962, B: 4, Change of address for FGW, April 26, 1962, B: 5, FGW correspondence with Bronson Tweedy, May 8 and 15 and July 13, 1959, B: 10, FWP, UVA.

487 **enjoyed reading:** GW, Aug. 8, 2020; Reeder, Aug. 20, 2020; Transcript of Kay Graham interview with Polly Fritchey, KGP; C. H. Graves letter to FGW, Aug. 23, 1961, B: 3, FGW correspondence on buying a Jaguar, Nov. 9–24, 1961, B: 7, FGW letters to Brooks's Club, St. James's Club, and New Zealand Golf Club, May 14, 1962, B: 2, FGW letters to Frank II, Oct. 25 and Dec. 7, 1960, B: 4, Eric Sevareid letter to FGW, Nov. 1, 1960, FGW letter to Eric Sevareid, July 14, 1961, B: 9, FGW letter to Christian Herter, July 9, 1958, B: 6, FWP, UVA; FGW horse racing chits, March 30, 1961, KCL; Ian Fleming letter to FGW, Sept. 14, 1961, WFC.

487 **returned to him:** Evan Thomas, pp. 315–16; Reed, p. 47.

488 **Morrone was:** FGWII, Dec. 11, 2020; Reed, pp. 1–13, 22–28, 40–41, 44–50, 58–59.

488 **Wisner found:** Evan Thomas, p. 316; EW, Jan. 27, 2021; Transcript of Kay Graham interview with Polly Fritchey, KGP.

489 **Polly did:** FGWII, Jan. 13, 2021; Robert Amory interview, B: 9, RSP, HA; Evan Thomas, p. 317; Bohlen, Nov. 17, 2020.

489 **his mother:** FGWII, July 8, 2020; FGW to John Bull, Oct. 15, 1959, B: 5, FGW letter to Mother, Sept. 9, 1955, B: 4, FWP, UVA; "Mrs. Frank Wisner Dies; Funeral Rites Thursday," *The Laurel Leader-Call*, Oct. 4, 1959, B: 3, S: 336, JGCL, CFA.

489 **his office:** Powers, p. 88; Reeder, Aug. 20, 2020; Reed, p. 47; FGW letter to Earl Mountbatten, Dec. 19, 1960, B: 7, RMH letter to FGW, Oct. 29, 1959, B: 6, FGW letter to John Baker, Jan. 30, 1961, B: 1, FWP, UVA; Broadcasting, FGW meeting with Mr. Murray, FCO 168/254/RC5011349, NAUK.

490 **West Germany:** Hersh, p. 436; Prados, *Safe for Democracy*, pp. 3–8; Evan Thomas, p. 316; Ranelagh, p. 392; 242. Special National Intelligence Estimate March 21, 1961, 255. Memorandum from the President's Special Assistant (Schlesinger) to the Deputy Under Secretary of State for Political Affairs (Johnson), Sept. 7, 1961, FRUS, American Republics, vol. XII, 1961–1963.

490 **its plots:** Weiner, p. 171; Ranelagh, pp. 336–39, 344–45; Waller, *Disciples*, p. 430; Ambrose, *Ike's Spies*, pp. 293–95, 304.

490 **invasion, resigned:** FGWII, Oct. 19, 2020; Transcript of Kay Graham interview with Polly Fritchey, KGP; Evan Thomas, pp. 237–38; Robarge, Part 2, p. 229; Srodes, pp. 509–10, Waller, *Disciples*, pp. 430–31; Ranelagh, p. 375; Michael Warner, "Lessons Unlearned: The CIA's Internal Probe of the Bay of Pigs Affair," CIA Library, https://www.cia.gov/resources/csi/static/Internal-Probe -Bay-Pigs.pdf.

491 **clandestine service:** EW, Oct. 20, 2020; Herken, p. 267; FGW letter to RMH, Feb. 16, 1962, B: 6, FGW letters to Michael and Pamela Berry, Aug. 24, 1962, and to AWD, March 19, 1962, FGW letter to Richard Bissell, Feb. 16, 1962, B: 1, FWP, UVA.

491　**of power:** Waller, *Disciples*, p. 431; FGWII, Oct. 19, 2020; EW, Oct. 20, 2020.
491　**CIA directorship:** Richard Bissell memo to Director of Personnel on FGW, March 31, 1960, WFC; Hersh, p. 436; EW, Aug. 19, 2020; Career Service Panel (Section A) to Deputy Director (Plans), memo on FGW, July 17, 1961, BHP.
491　**Polly thought:** Transcript of Kay Graham interview with Polly Fritchey, KGP.
492　**old days:** Minutes for Deputies' Meeting, June 7, 1961, CREST for FGW; Evan Thomas, p. 316; FGWII letter to mother and father, January 1961, B: 2, RMH letter to FGW, April 26, 1961, B: 6, FGW letters to Avis and Chip Bohlen, April 22, 1961, B: 1, FGW letter to John Ellis Knowles, May 17, 1961, FGW letters to FGWII, March 17, 1961, and Feb. 20, 1962, B: 4, FWP, UVA; FGW letter to RMH, May 1, 1961, RMH letter to FGW, May 8, 1961, B: 4, RHP, GU.
492　**manic state:** Evan Thomas, p. 317.
492　**to release:** Evan Thomas, p. 317; Hersh, pp. 436–37; FGW letter to Stewart Alsop, Oct. 4, 1961, B: 1, FGW letter to Diana Hood, Oct. 4, 1961, B: 6, FWP, UVA.
492　**once more:** Hersh, p. 437; GW, Dec. 10, 2020; Transcript of Kay Graham interview with Polly Fritchey, KGP.
493　**British physicians:** FGWII, Jan. 13, 2021; EW, March 17, 2022; Katharine Graham interview with Polly Fritchey, Oct. 10, 1989, p. 11, KGP; Sackeim, Jan. 18, 2022; Abrams, p. 157; FGW letter to H. M. Murdock, Nov. 14, 1961, Notification and Conditions of Employment, Nurses Act 1957, for FGW, B: 1, FWP, UVA; Hersh, p. 437; Bob Joyce letters to FGW, May 3 and 22, 1962, B: 6, Lyman Kirkpatrick letter to FGW, April 3, 1962, B: 7, FWP, UVA; Memo to Chief, Finance Division on Advance Sick and Annual Leave for FGW, May 31, 1962, BHP.
493　**he said:** Robarge, Part 1, pp. 6, 9–20, 29–33; Ranelagh, pp. 379, 409–15; FGW letter to RMH, Sept. 29, 1961, B: 6, FGW letter to the City Tavern Association, April 25, 1963, B: 7, FGW letter to C. L. Sulzberger, March 2, 1964, B: 2, FWP, UVA.
493　**to travel:** Robarge, Part 1, pp. 32, 34, Part 2, p. 277; Hersh, p. 437.
494　**"interesting tour.":** FGW letter to Mary Silver, Oct. 12, 1961, FGW letter to Bob Joyce, May 9, 1962, FGW letter to C. D. Jackson, Jan. 16, 1962, B: 6, FWP, UVA.
494　**his advantage:** CIA press release March 9, 1962, on FGW, CREST for FGW; FGW letter to Michael and Pamela Berry, March 19, 1962, FWP, UVA.
494　**of London:** Heymann, pp. 149–50; Reed, pp. 59–60; FGWII, Jan. 13, 2021; PKW and FGW notes for Archibald and Lucky Roosevelt, B: 8, FWP, UVA.
494　**emotionally drained:** Reed, pp. 56–58; Tish Freeman letter to FGW, June 13, 1962, B: 5, FWP, UVA.

Chapter 27: Outside
495　**a year:** Notification of Personnel Action for FGW, Aug. 31, 1962, WFC; FGW letters to Tish, July 18, 1962, B: 5, FGW to FGWII, July 16, 1962, B: 2, FGW letter to Mr. and Mrs. A. F. Chisholm, July 1, 1092, B: 4, FWP, UVA.
495　**the award:** Executive Committee Meeting No. 10, July 30, 1962, CREST for FGW; Robarge, Part 2, p. 283; Hersh, pp. 437–38; Memo on FGW change of status to consultant, Aug. 31, 1962, Presentation of Distinguished Intelligence Medal to FGW on Aug. 22, 1962, WFC; CIA Contracting Officer memo to FGW, June 22, 1962, BHP; Photo of FGW receiving the Distinguished Intelligence Medal and its citation, B: 20, FWP, UVA.
496　**Caribbean island:** Wisner consulting contracts, which run until June 30, 1966, Memo to Director of Security on FGW security clearance, Jan. 4, 1964, Memo to Chief, Contract Personnel Division, Office of Personnel on FGW consulting contract, Nov. 19, 1963, WFC; FGWII, Jan. 27, 2021; Ranelagh, pp. 396–98.

496 **her oversight:** Betty Beale, "Exclusively Yours," and Marie McNair, "George-towners Dine a la 1800," *The Washington Post,* CREST for FGW; FGWII, July 8, 2020; FGW letter to Julian Fay, Aug. 8, 1962, B: 4, FWP, UVA.

496 **breakdown there:** FGWII, Oct. 19, 2020, and Jan. 27, 2021; Gotlib and Hammen, p. 417; EW, Dec. 6, 2020.

497 **Street Northwest:** GW, Aug. 10, 2020; FGWII, Jan. 27, 2021; Evan Thomas, p. 315; "Frank G. Wisner Dies; Former Official of CIA," AP story, WFC.

497 **in Italy:** EW, Aug. 5, 2020, and Jan. 27, 2021; FGW letter to A. S. Alexander, Dec. 13, 1962, FGW letters to Charles Adams, May 14, 1963, and Sept. 4, 1964, B: 1, John Graham letter to Roswell Gilpatric, Jan. 17, 1964, FGW letter to Joseph Bryan, Nov. 14, 1963, B: 5, FGW letter to Peter Paine, June 24, 1963, FGW 1964 reports on trip to Italy, FGW letter to Charles Adams, Nov. 27, 1963, B: 6, FGW letter to Mrs. Henry Luce, June 15, 1964, B: 7, FGW letter to Michael Forrestal, April 24, 1964, B: 4, FWP, UVA.

497 **reconnaissance equipment:** FGW memo for the record on Reynolds Tobacco Company, Feb. 10, 1965, B: 5, FGW letters to Franklin Lindsay, Jan. 10 and May 12, 1964, B: 7, FGW memo for the record on Itek Corporation, Jan. 31, 1964, B: 6, FWP, UVA.

498 **on Wisner:** Memo for the Record on FGW, Feb. 19, 1965, BHP; FGW letter to JEH, June 2, 1964, and JEH response, June 8, 1964, B: 6, FWP, UVA; EW, Nov. 11 and Dec. 12, 2020; W. C. Sullivan memo to A. H. Belmont, May 6, 1965, FBIW.

498 **were American:** Christian Herter letter to FGW, July 3, 1963, Francis Wilcox letter to FGW, Dec. 8, 1963, B: 7, John McCone letter to FGW, March 20, 1965, FGW letter to John Bross and Lawrence White, April 19, 1965, FGW correspondence with William Deakin on St. Antony's College fundraising 1962–1963, B: 3, FWP, UVA.

498 **too widely:** FGW correspondence with the Conservation Foundation, 1963–1965, B: 3, FWP, UVA; EW, July 15, 2020.

499 **espionage movie:** FGW note to Gilpatric, Jan. 28, 1965, B: 5, FGW letter to Eric Sevareid, June 3, 1964, FGW letter to AWD, Dec. 30, 1964, B: 9, FGW correspondence with J. N. Henderson on *Prince Eugen of Savoy,* 1964–1965, B: 6, FGW letter to Charles Murphy, Dec. 10, 1963, B: 7, FGW letter to Tish, Dec. 4, 1963, B: 2, FGW letter to Burke Wilkinson, April 19, 1965, B: 1, FWP, UVA; FGW review of *The Craft of Intelligence, Studies in Intelligence,* CIA.

499 **"brilliant mind.":** EW, July 15, 2020; FGW letter to C. L. Sulzberger, Jan. 9, 1964, B: 10, FGW letter to Julian Muller, May 28, 1964, B: 8, FGW letter to Mrs. Gilbert Highet, June 3, 1964, B: 6, Helen letter to Doris, May 28, 1964, B: 7, FWP, UVA; FGW letter to Julian Muller, April 6, 1965, FGW letter to Mrs. Gilbert Highet with enclosures, Feb. 11, 1965, WFC.

499 **had become:** Photo of FGW with hunting party in Scotland, Alexander Lindsey photo provided to author; GW, Aug. 10, 2020; Lindsey, Oct. 12, 2021; EW, Oct. 6, 2020; FGWII, March 15, 2021.

500 **the trigger:** Graham, pp. 226, 232, 240–48, 260–65, 290, 292–93, 298–313, 325, 329–31.

500 **enjoy reading:** EW, Jan. 27, 2021; GW, Dec. 1, 2020; "Zigmond Lebensohn Dies," *The Washington Post,* Sept. 24, 2003; Zigmond Lebehsohn bill for FGW, April 1963, B: 7, Barbara Southcott letter to Zigmond Lebensohn, Jan. 11, 1965, B:7, FWP, UVA.

500 **with Russia:** EW, Oct. 20, 2020; FGW letter to Charles Adams, Nov. 27, 1963, B: 6, FWP, UVA; FGW letter to Frank, Ellis, Wendy, and Graham, Nov. 27, 1963, B: 2, FWP, UVA.

501 **proven wrong:** Katharine Graham interview with Polly Fritchey, Oct. 10, 1989, p. 25, KGP; FGW letter to Mrs. Philip Graham, Feb. 11, 1964, B: 5, FWP, UVA.

501 **he thought:** Katharine Graham interview with Polly Fritchey, Oct. 10, 1989, pp. 25, 38–39, 51, KGP; FGW letter to Frank, Ellis, Wendy, and Graham, Nov. 27, 1963, B: 2, FWP, UVA.

501 **"public mind":** FGWII, Nov. 10, 2020; Alexander Lindsey, Oct. 12, 2021; Frank G. Wisner, "How I Got Here," *Foreign Affairs*, May 29, 2020; FGW Report of Conversation with "Brigadier" Robert Thompson, B: 21, FGW letter to Charles Murphy, April 9, 1965, FWP, UVA.

501 **"on this.":** FGW memo to Deputy Director of Central Intelligence, Oct. 11, 1963, WFC.

502 **Ellis's help:** EW, Dec. 6, 2020 and Jan. 27 and Feb. 18, 2021.

502 **had expected:** Reed, p. 85; FGW "Personal and Confidential" letter, March 24, 1965, CREST for FGW; Talley letter to Polly, Nov. 11, B: 13, George Brown letter to FGW, Feb. 24, 1964, B: 1, FGW letter to Roy Melbourne, March 29, 1964, FWP, UVA.

502 **on it:** FGW letter to Russell Forgan, April 9, 1965, B: 100, WCP, HA; FGW notes to JA, March 30, 1965, JA response, April 1, 1965, B: 131, AP, LOC; FGW letter to Stewart Alsop with note to Dean Acheson, April 13 and 23, 1965, Dean Acheson letter to FGW, April 19, 1965, DAP, YU; FGW's "Box Score" B: 1, FWP, UVA.

503 **ignored him:** FGW letter to Howard Hunt, Jan. 9, 1965, FGW letter to Elizabeth, Oct. 1, 1964, FGW memos to Desmond FitzGerald and Rafford Herbert, Sept. 24, 1964, and Jan. 8, 1965, B: 11, FWP, UVA; EW, Jan. 27, 2021.

503 **into depression:** EW, March 17, 2022; Locust Hill guest book, WFC; FGW letter to John Gross, June 23, 1964, B: 5, FWP, UVA.

503 **anyone else:** FGW letter to Zigmond Lebensohn, April 19, 1965, B: 7, FWP, UVA; Ted Alt letter to PKW, Nov. 1, 1965, Kathleen Kennedy letter to PKW, Nov. 1, 1965, B: 15, FWP, UVA; EW, Jan. 12 and Feb. 18, 2021.

504 **to erode:** FGWII, Dec. 12, 2020, Jan. 27, 2021, and March 15, 2021.

504 **the CIA:** Barbara Southcott letter to Mrs. Gilbert Highet, June 28, 1965, B: 7, FGW letter to T. Ault, June 30, 1965, FGW letter to George Garrett, Aug. 5, 1965, B: 5, FWP, UVA; RMH memo for the record on lunch with FGW, Sept. 22, 1965, WFC.

Chapter 28: A Life Cut Short

505 **loaded weapon:** Heymann, pp. 140–41; FGW letter to George Green, Nov. 6, 1964, B: 5, FGW letter to Peggy Chisholm, Sept. 8, 1964, B: 4, FGW letter to Norman Clark, July 31, 1964, FGW letter to Francisco Mengotti Jan. 9, 1965, B: 2, FGW letter to Enrique Mengotti, Nov. 6, 1964, B: 3, FGW letter to Henry Morgan, Nov. 6, 1964, B: 7, FGW letter to Ronald Bassett, Jan. 5, 1965, B: 1, FWP, UVA.

505 **a guide:** EW, Feb. 18, 2021; FGW letter to Douglas Dillon, March 12, 1965, B: 3, FGW letter to Francisco Mengotti, Jan. 9, 1965, FGW letter to Jaime de Ojeda, and Jaime de Ojeda reply, Sept. 14, 1965, FGW letter to the Ritz Hotel, Jan. 9, 1965, B: 10, FWP, UVA.

506 **on edge:** Avis Bohlen interview, B: 16, GHP, HA; FGW itinerary for European trip, Oct. 11–Nov. 12, 1965, B: 21, FWP, UVA; FGW Personal and Confidential memo, March 24, 1965, CREST for FGW; Hersh, p. 440; GW, Dec. 10, 2020; Bohlen, Nov. 17, 2020.

506 **October 22:** FGW letter to Alfred Ulmer, Sept. 15, 1965, B: 10, FWP, UVA; EW, Dec. 6, 2020, and Jan. 27, 2021; Hersh, p. 441; Mondimore, p. 24.

507 **to them:** EW, Aug. 5 and Sept. 22, 2020 and March 18, 2021; EW interview with Richard Rhodes, WFC; Letter from de Virel Paris to PKW, B: 13, FWP, UVA.

507 **never knew:** FGW memo to John Bross, Sept. 16, 1953, B: 1, FGW letters to Carl Graybeal, Jan. 28 and May 13, 1954, B: 5, FWP, UVA.

507 **Locust Hill:** Hersh, p. 441; EW, March 17, 2022; EW interview with Richard Rhodes, WFC.

508 **had died:** EW interview with Richard Rhodes, WFC; EW, Feb. 18, 2021; FG-WII, July 8 and 30, 2020; "Frank G. Wisner Dead; U.S. Intelligence Figure," *The Washington Post*, Oct. 30, 1965; Frank Gardiner Wisner Dead; Former Top Official of C.I.A.," *New York Times*, Oct. 30, 1965; Maryland State Department of Health, Medical Examiner's Certificate of Death for FGW, Oct. 29, 1965.

508 **remain closed:** FGWII, Jan. 27, 2021; Maryland State Department of Health, Medical Examiner's Certificate of Death for FGW, Oct. 29, 1965; Joseph Gawler's Sons, Inc., invoice for PKW, Oct. 30, 1965, B: 18, FWP, UVA.

508 **"public service":** "Frank G. Wisner Dead; U.S. Intelligence Figure," *The Washington Post*, Oct. 30, 1965.

508 **he knew:** "One Head Less in the CIA," *The Worker*, Nov. 2, 1965, CREST for FGW; "Death in the CIA," WO No. 39 story, May 15, 1967, CREST for FGW; GW, Dec. 10, 2020; EW, Feb. 19, 2021; "A Silent Battle to the Death in the Dark World of Espionage," *Always*, Mexico City, Dec. 18, 1965; FGWII, Sept. 9, 2020.

509 **"done it.":** FGWII, Jan. 27, 2021; Reed, p. 85.

509 **black walls:** Katharine Graham interview with Polly Fritchey, Oct. 10, 1989, pp. 10–11, KGP; GW, Aug. 10 and Dec. 10, 2020.

509 **Ellis said:** FGWII, April 1, 2021; EW, March 17 and 26, 2021.

509 **final act:** Goodwin and Jamison, vol. 1, pp. xix, 66, 264; Sackeim, Jan. 27, 2022.

510 **the fact:** Goodwin and Jamison, vol. 1, pp. 247, 249 and vol. 2, p. 953.

510 **and affection:** FGWII, July 8, 2020; GW, Sept. 16, 2020, and April 14, 2021.

510 **not have:** Ridder, Sept. 7, 2021; FGWII, April 1, 2021; Goodwin and Jamison, vol. 1, pp. 344–46; EW, Jan. 13, 2021.

510 **could book:** Katharine Graham interview with Polly Fritchey, Oct. 10, 1989, p. 5, KGP; EW, March 26, 2021.

510 **killing him:** GW, Sept. 16, 2020; Reeder, Aug. 20, 2020; FGWII, Sept. 9, 2020; letter to PKW May 13, 1965, B: 59, ADP, PU.

511 **saved him:** Wisner, FAOH, pp. 11–12; FGWII, Nov. 10, 2020, and March 15, 2021; FGWII letter to Uncle Joe, Oct. 11, 1965, B: 73, AP, LOC.

511 **shot himself:** GW, Sept. 16 and Dec. 10, 2020, and April 14, 2021.

511 **"determined strength.":** EW, Aug. 18, 2020, and Feb. 18, 2021; FGWII, Jan. 27, 2021; GW, April 14, 2021; Evan Thomas, p. 320; FGW letter to Washington Cathedral Fund, Sept. 25, 1964, Senator Mike Monroney letter to FGW, Sept. 21, 1964, B: 7, FGW In Memoriam prayer, B: 20, FWP, UVA.

512 **suspicious activity:** Washington Home for Incurables note to PKW, Nov. 6, 1965, B: 18, FWP, UVA; Acting Director of Security memo on FGW funeral, Nov. 1, 1965, Memo # 9 291 on FBI agent report on surveillance at FGW funeral, Nov. 17, 1965, WFC.

512 **U.S. Navy:** EW, Aug. 19, 2020; Lindsey, Oct. 12, 2021; Department of the Army Office of the Chief of Support Services letter on FGW grave inscription, July 13, 1966, B: 18, FWP, UVA.

512 **to sit:** FitzGerald, Dec. 2, 2020.

513 **been answered:** EW, Oct. 6, 2020; Condolence letters sent to PKW, B: 13, 15,16, and 21, FWP, UVA; Arthur Krock letter to PKW, Oct. 31, 1965, B: 61, AKP, PU.

513 **on operations:** FGWII, Jan. 27, 2021; Hersh, pp. 441–46.
513 **country's affairs:** EW, Oct. 6, 2020; Katharine Graham interview with Polly Fritchey, Oct. 10, 1989, p. 11, KGP; Graham, p. 391.
513 **his children:** EW, Feb. 18, 2021; Third and Final Executors Account in the estate of FGW, B: 18, FWP, UVA.
514 **Cemetery grave site:** Memorandum on Exposure of CIA Personnel, such as FGW, Oct. 20, 1983, BHP; *Virginia Law Review* item on FGW, Jan. 1966, CFA; Herken, p. 71.

Epilogue
515 **so loved:** EW, Aug. 18, 2020, and Feb. 18, 2021; FGWII, Oct. 19, 2020, and Jan. 27, 2021; GW, Sept. 16, 2020; FitzGerald, Dec. 2, 2020; Wisner Betting Book, pp. 103, 106, 113, WFC.
515 **garden tours:** Cynthia Helms, p. 107; EW, Oct. 20, 2020; Eugenia Sheppard, the *Washington Post*, April 8, 1966, CREST for FGW; "Cool and Green Retreat," article on of PKW garden, April 1970, B: 1, CFC, UVA.
516 **the discussion:** Cynthia Helms, p. 107; "Party Favors for 1,000," *The Washington Post*, Nov. 1, 1985, p. B1; "Polly Fritchey Dies," *The Washington Post*, July 11, 2002.
516 **Georgetown set:** FGWII, Sept. 9, 2020; Cynthia Helms, pp. 14, 107; PKW letter to Paul Nitze, Jan. 10, 1969, B:1:42, PNP, LOC.
516 **second trauma:** FGWII, July 8, 2020, and Jan. 27, 2021; Herken, pp. 329–30; Maxine Chesire, "Very Interesting People," *The Washington Post*, Oct. 26, 1967, CREST for FGW.
517 **"to start?":** Transcript of Kay Graham interview with Polly Fritchey, KGP; FitzGerald, Dec. 2, 2020; EW, Oct. 6, 2020; Graham, pp. 391, 617–18.
517 **was pro-war:** EW, Aug. 5, 2020, and March 26, 2021; Heymann, p. 148; FGWII, July 8, 2020, Sept. 9, 2020, and March 13, 2021; Christine Wisner letter, June 22, 1981, B: 227, AP, LOC; "Fritchey, Wisner to Wed," *The Washington Post*, Jan. 25, 1975, p. E2; "Polly Fritchey Dies," *The Washington Post*, July 11, 2002.
517 **Architectural Digest:** Herken, p. 387; "Social Graces in Georgetown," p. 188.
517 **August 28, 1989:** Heymann, pp. 191–92; Cynthia Helms, p. 178; JA letter to PKW, Oct. 16, 1979, WFC; PKW letter to JA, undated, B: 227, AP, LOC.
518 **"nation's capital.":** "Polly Fritchey Dies," *The Washington Post*, July 11, 2002; Herken, p. 386; Heymann, pp. 291, 321–22; Lindsey, July 14, 2020; GW, April 14, 2021.
518 **Alzheimer's disease:** FGWII, Jan. 27, 2021; "Obituary: Elizabeth 'Wendy' Wisner Hazard," *Portland Press Herald*, https://www.pressherald.com/2020/06/05/obituarywisner-hazard/.
518 **environmental causes:** GW, Aug. 5, Sept. 22, and Oct. 20, 2020.
519 **no answer:** EW, March 26, 2021.
519 **Frank II says:** Wisner, FAOH, pp. 1–6; Frank G. Wisner, "How I Got Here" *Foreign Affairs*, May 29, 2020; FGWII, Jan. 27, 2021.
519 **"full life.":** In Memoriam: Frank Gardiner Wisner, 1909–1965, Langley, Virginia, Jan. 29, 1971, WFC.
520 **citation read:** Herken, p. 348; FGWII, April 1, 2021; Headquarters: Employee Bulletin, Jan. 8, 1973, CREST for FGW; Memorandum for the Record of Morning Meeting of March 20, 1969, for DDI, CREST for FGW; Photo of FGW display case at CIA, B: 2, CFC, UVA; Letter to William Hobbs, May 15, 1968, B: 21, FGW citation for CIA Trailblazers, B: 18, FWP, UVA.
520 **CIA ruled:** David Ginsberg correspondence with CIA on PKW benefits claim, Feb. 25 and June 14–15, 1988.

520 **security system:** William Bundy letter to PKW, May 10, 1967, B: 18, FWP, UVA; "Frank G. Wisner," editorial, Oceanside, California, Nov. 3, 1965, CREST for FGW; April 1, 2021.

521 **unacceptable acts:** Evan Thomas, p. 10; Church Committee, *Final Report*, book 1, p. 16; Rositzke, p. xvi.

521 **American ruthlessness:** John Bross letter to EW, May 12, 1986, B: 21, FWP, UVA.

521 **Soviet Union:** Rositzke, p. xxvi; Hersh, p. 454.

522 **any more:** Church Committee, *Final Report*, book 1, p. 11.

522 **wasting money:** Rositzke, pp. xxix, 1.

523 **the superpowers:** Ruffner, "Eagle and Swastika," pp. 288–89; Ranelagh, p. 138.

523 **intelligence organizations:** Wilford, pp. 252–54; Warner, "Hearts & Minds," p. xix; Rositzke, pp. 164–65; Church Committee, *Final Report*, book 1, p. 142.

524 **have survived:** Wilford, pp. 237, 240–41, 244; Leary, pp. 6–8; Church Committee, *Final Report*, book 1, pp. 10, 12, 148–49; Evan Thomas, p. 11.

524 **"was not lost.":** Waller, *Disciples*, pp. 448–50; Stewart Alsop, p. 215; RMH letter to PKW, Dec. 11, 1989, WFC.

525 **fatally flawed:** Hyland, p. 200.

525 **on others:** Members of the Intelligence Community, U.S. Intelligence Community Budget, Office of the Director of National Intelligence, www.dni.gov.

INDEX

ABOUT THE AUTHOR

Douglas Waller is a veteran journalist, author, and lecturer. In almost two decades as a Washington correspondent for *Newsweek* and *Time*, he covered the Pentagon, Congress, the State Department, the White House, and the CIA.